CW01654573

LL
ANNUAL 1986-87

EDITED BY PETER DUNK AND LIONEL FRANCIS

Macdonald
Queen Anne Press

A *Queen Anne Press* BOOK

© Queen Anne Press 1986

First published in Great Britain in 1986 by
Queen Anne Press, a division of
Macdonald & Co (Publishers) Ltd
3rd Floor
Greater London House
Hampstead Road
London NW1 7QX

A BPCC plc Company

Jacket photographs: All-Sport

All rights reserved. No part of this publication may be reproduced, stored in a retrieval system, or transmitted, in any form or by any means, without the prior permission in writing of the publisher, nor be otherwise circulated in any form of binding or cover other than that in which it is published and without a similar condition including this condition being imposed on the subsequent publisher.

British Library Cataloguing in Publication Data

Playfair football annual——1986/87
1. Soccer——Periodicals
796.334'05 GV942

ISBN 0-356-12332-4

Reproduced, printed and bound in Great Britain by
Hazell Watson & Viney Limited,
Member of the BPCC Group,
Aylesbury, Bucks.

CONTENTS

LIONEL FRANCIS

Lionel Francis, co-editor of the Playfair Football Annual since 1974, died suddenly at his home near Torquay on July 9 1986. He held senior rank in the Home Office prior to his retirement in 1981, but his abiding passion was always football. A keen supporter of Arsenal for more than fifty years, he was also an expert in non-League football, and was the author of *Seventy Five Years of Southern League Football,* published by Pelham in 1969. He leaves a widow, Winnie, to whom we extend our deepest sympathies. He will be greatly missed.

EDITORIAL

The baleful glare of Joao Havelange has dominated world football since the retirement of Sir Stanley Rous in 1974. The Brazilian was elected largely on the strength of his appeal to the more obscure footballing nations, who form the majority, and he has made it his business to keep them happy at all times, thus ensuring his continued supremacy.

Sometimes, his policies have been sensible. I am not one of those who criticised the expansion of the World Cup from 16 to 24 finalists, for example. FIFA's insistence on having some representatives from football's third world in the final tournament was difficult to justify when only 16 teams were present and it was so obvious that we were not watching the best 16 teams in the world, as we should have been. Their inclusion became easier to bear after the expansion, and some of those little countries have given us such memorable moments over the years. It has often been argued that a tournament with 24 finalists is unwieldy, but even the Mexicans, struggling in the aftermath of a dreadful earthquake only months before the competition was due to start, proved that 24 candidates can be handled reasonably efficiently.

Neither do I take issue with the decision to go straight to a knock-out format after the first round. Sudden-death matches are the essence of cup football. Few would argue with a league system for the first round, giving everybody a chance to play at least three games before catching the plane home, but thereafter knock-out matches are surely preferable.

The ubiquitous penalty shoot-out is another favourite target for the critics, but in fairness it is extremely difficult to devise an alternative – so difficult, indeed, that most of those who have condemned the practice as a travesty of football have been unwilling to grasp the nettle. The alternatives which have been suggested all have drawbacks of their own. They include playing on indefinitely until someone scores a goal *(drawback:* what happens after the last bus has gone and nobody is left in the stadium?); removing six players from each team and playing five-a-side until a goal is scored *(drawback:* this is as much a travesty of football as the penalty shoot-out); determining the result on the number of goals scored in the first round (*drawback:* it would be unfair on those teams who had qualified from the knock-out stages from a difficult group where goals were understandably hard to come by). So it goes on. Penalties are not ideal, but they do provide a result based on skill, which a toss of the coin certainly would not.

So much for those aspects of FIFA policy which I find acceptable. Now for those others, and where better to begin than the beginning? Originally, the 1986 World Cup final tournament was scheduled for Colombia. One would be hard pushed to think of a better example of a banana republic. It is a nasty little country, riddled with corruption, one of the world's main sources of cocaine, and quite obviously a thoroughly unsuitable choice. How FIFA could possibly have selected such a place at all is beyond comprehension, but they then proceeded to compound their folly by announcing that, on reflection, Colombia would be unable to organise a tournament with 24 finalists, and handed the competition to Mexico. Why was Colombia's unsuitability not apparent *before* the selection was made? What happened between FIFA's original announcement and their change of mind? We shall probably never know, but we will always have our suspicions.

Mexico was in many respects a less than satisfactory second choice. The well-publicised drawbacks of heat, humidity and altitude, coupled with the preposterous kick-off times (commercial considerations to the fore, as you would expect from FIFA) make life unnecessarily difficult for most of the finalists, especially the Europeans. But at least Mexico had the track record of having staged, in 1970, one of the most memorable tournaments in recent times. The Mexicans are football-crazy and have, in the Aztec stadium, one of the most breathtakingly beautiful sporting arenas in the world. So, given that we seem to be stuck with the idea that the World Cup must alternate between South/Central America and Europe, and giving FIFA the benifit of the doubt on the question of them being strapped for a venue at short notice, we move on to the 1986 finals themselves.

It became apparent very early in the tournament that the standard of refereeing was woefully inadequate. FIFA decided to invite referees from all over the world. A laudable sentiment, this, but it doesn't take account of the fact that few if any referees from outside Europe and South/Central America have the necessary experience to handle a competition of this stature. The players had enough to put up with from the climate – surely they were entitled to the best referees, chosen on merit rather than nationality? Clearly not.

The policy of choosing referees to run the line is also open to question. Lining is an art in itself, requiring the sort of fine judgement which can only come with experience. Although most referees started their careers as linesmen, by the time they get onto the FIFA referee's list they have left their line careers far behind them. George Courtney, the only English referee in Mexico, realised this and spent some weeks prior to his departure for the finals running the line in minor matches in order to refresh himself. Judging by the dubious nature of so much of the flag-waving in the tournament, not many of his colleagues took the trouble.

The FIFA public relations people went to great lengths to tell us that referees were under strict instructions to ensure fair play. Defensive walls would have to retreat the regulation distance under threat of caution, for example, and of course players would have to tuck their shirts in and pull their socks up. But what ever happened to injury time? We learned that if players went down injured, they would have to be removed from the pitch for treatment so that the game could proceed with the minimum of interruption. For this reason, stretcher-bearers were on standby ready to scramble whenever anybody bit the dust. Those players who like to waste time when their team is in front weren't fazed, however. They simply rolled around in agony until the stretcher arrived, wasted a few more moments arguing about it, and then struggled painfully to their feet, determined to carry on manfully for the sake of their team. A few more moments would be wasted while the hapless stretcher-bearers beat a retreat, and then the player concerned would effect a miraculous recovery and carry on as if nothing had happened. Maybe I'm wrong, but I can't remember a single one of these cynics being booked for ungentlemanly conduct.

All very well, provided that the referee is prepared to add time on at the end of each half to negate time-wasting tactics. Clearly, the referees in Mexico, with only one or two exceptions, were not, and so the cheats, thus encouraged, prospered. Cheating was not, of course, restricted to time-wasting. Diego Maradona, for all his brilliance, is a cheat and stands condemned as such out of his own mouth. It is understood that the decision of the referee is final, and it is also understood that if a player commits a foul which the referee does not see, there's nothing to be done about it. Such things happen in virtually every match, and everybody, even though they may get excited about it at the time, accepts the situation. However, Maradona stepped way out of line by admitting, on the following day, that he had scored Argentina's first goal against England with his hand. In these circumstances, given FIFA's apparent preoccupation with the concept of fair play, was it too much to expect them to take action, such as suspension for bringing the game into disrepute? Clearly it was, and so long as FIFA is controlled by Joao Havelange, who has as much relevance to principles of sensible, fair and perceptive management as Mickey Mouse has to Darwin's theory of evolution, it will continue to be so.

Finally, on the domestic front, there's good news and bad. First the good news. At last the First Division is to be reduced to 20 teams, a process that will take place over the next two seasons. This is good news for a number of reasons, not the least of which is that the job of the international managers will be made that little bit easier. Now for the bad news. New League President Phil Carter has already announced that he is exploring ideas for a new competition, perhaps along the lines of the Full Member's Cup, to fill the gap. Well, what did you expect?

FINAL HONOURS 1985-86

World Cup
Winners: Argentina
Runners-up: West Germany

European Cup
Winners: Steaua Bucharest
Runners-up: Barcelona

European Cup-Winners' Cup
Winners: Dynamo Kiev
Runners-up: Atletico Madrid

UEFA Cup
Winners: Real Madrid
Runners-up: Cologne

Canon League Division One
Champions: Liverpool
Runners-up: Everton
Division Two
Champions: Norwich City
Also promoted: Charlton Athletic, Wimbledon
Division Three
Champions: Reading
Also promoted: Plymouth Argyle, Derby County
Division Four
Champions: Swindon Town
Also promoted: Chester City, Mansfield Town, Port Vale

FA Cup
Winners: Liverpool
Runners-up: Everton

Milk Cup
Winners: Oxford United
Runners-up: Queen's Park Rangers

Full Members' Cup
Winners: Chelsea
Runners-up: Manchester City

Scottish League Premier Division
Champions: Celtic
Runners-up: Heart of Midlothian
Division One
Champions: Hamilton Academical
Also promoted: Falkirk
Division Two
Champions: Dunfermline Athletic
Also promoted: Queen of the South

Scottish Cup
Winners: Aberdeen
Runners-up: Heart of Midlothian

Scottish League (Skol) Cup
Winners: Aberdeen
Runners-up: Hibernian

FA Charity Shield
Winners: Everton
Runners-up: Manchester United

Welsh Cup
Winners: Wrexham
Runners-up: Kidderminster Harriers

Northern Irish Cup
Winners: Glentoran
Runners-up: Coleraine

Freight Rover Trophy
Winners: Bristol City
Runners-up: Bolton Wanderers

FA Challenge Trophy
Winners: Altrincham
Runners-up: Runcorn

FA Challenge Vase
Winners: Halesowen Town
Runners-up: Southall

Gola League
Champions: Enfield
Runners-up: Frickley

Multipart League
Champions: Gateshead
Runners-up: Marine

Southern League Premier Division
Champions: Welling United
Runners-up: Chelmsford City

Southern League Midland Division
Champions: Bromsgrove Rovers
Runners-up: Redditch United

Southern League Southern Division
Champions: Cambridge City
Runners-up: Salisbury

FA Youth Cup
Winners: Manchester City
Runners-up: Manchester United

FA Sunday Cup
Winners: Avenue
Runners-up: Glenn Sports

FOOTBALL LEAGUE CLUBS AND THEIR PLAYERS

ALDERSHOT DIV. 4

Barnes, David O.	Foyle, Martin J.	Rigby, Jonathan K.
Blankley, Barry S.	Johnson, Garry	Shrubb, Paul J.
Coles, David A.	McDonald, Ian C.	Smith, Colin R.
Fielder, Colin	Mazzon, Giorgio	

League Appearances: Barnes, David O. 14; Blankley, Barry S. 38; Butler, Martin 2; Coleman, Philip 24; Coles, David A. 29; Cox, Graham 1; Duncan, Colin J. 15; Fadida, Aharon 4(5); Ferns, Philip D. 24; Fielder, Colin 28(2); Foyle, Martin J. 20; Gillard, Ian T. 6; Johnson, Garry 43; Lange, Anthony S. 7; Lunn, Grant 9; McDonald, Ian C. 46; McMenemy, Paul C. 10; McNeil, Mark J. 5(1); Massey, Andrew T. 38(1); Mazzon, Giorgio 44; Morris, Mark J. 14; Rigby, Jonathan K. 1; Shrubb, Paul J. 36(2); Smith, Colin R. 34; Staff, Paul 12(9); Stein, Mark E.S. 2.
Goals – League (66): Johnson 15, Foyle 9, Barnes 8 (3 pens), Fielder 8, Staff 6, McMenemy 5, Fadida 4, Ferns 2 (1 pen), Massey 2 (1 pen), McDonald 2, Butler 1, Coleman 1, Shrubb 1, Smith 1, Stein 1.
Milk Cup (3): Foyle 2, Massey 1.
FA Cup (0).
Ground: Recreation Ground, High St., Aldershot GU11 1TW (0252 20211)
Nearest station: Aldershot
Manager: Len Walker **Secretary:** R. T. F. Bentley
Colours: Red and blue striped shirts with blue trim; blue shorts
Record home gate: 19,138 v Carlisle, January 1970 (FA Cup)
Honours: Nil

ARSENAL DIV. 1

Adams, Tony A.	Keown, Martin R.	Rocastle, David
Allen, Gregory F.	Lukic, Jovan	Sansom, Kenneth G.
Allinson, Ian J.R.	Merson, Paul C.	Smith, Paul S.
Anderson, Vivian A.	Nicholas, Charles	Thomas, Michael L.
Caesar, Gus C.	O'Leary, David A.	Williams, Stephen C.
Caton, Thomas	Osborne, Lawrence W.	Wilmot, Rhys J.
Davis, Paul V.	Quinn, Niall J.	Woodcock, Anthony S.
Hammond, Nicholas D.	Rix, Graham	
Hayes, Martin	Robson, Stewart T.	

League Appearances: Adams, Tony A. 10; Allinson, Ian J.R. 28(5); Anderson, Vivian A. 39; Caesar, Gus C. 2; Caton, Thomas 20; Davis, Paul V. 28(1); Hayes, Martin 11; Keown, Martin R. 22; Lukic, Jovan 40; Mariner, Paul 3(6); Nicholas, Charles 41; O'Leary, David A. 35; Quinn, Niall J. 10(2); Rix, Graham 38; Robson, Stewart T. 26(1); Rocastle, David 13(3); Sansom, Kenneth G. 42; Whyte, Christopher A. 4(3); Williams, Stephen C. 17; Wilmot, Rhys J. 2; Woodcock, Anthony S. 31(2).
Goals – League (49): Woodcock 11, Nicholas 10, Allinson 6 (5 pens), Davis 4, Robson 4, Rix 3, Anderson 2, Hayes 2, Caton 1, Quinn 1, Rocastle 1, Whyte 1, own goals 3.
Milk Cup (9): Nicholas 4, Allinson 1, Anderson 1, Hayes 1, Mariner 1, Robson 1.
FA Cup (11): Nicholas 4, Allinson 3 (1 pen), Rix 2, Robson 1, Rocastle 1.
Ground: Arsenal Stadium, Avenell Road, N5 1BU (01-226 0304)

Nearest stations: Arsenal (Piccadilly Line), Drayton Park (British Rail) or Finsbury Park (BR, Piccadilly Line or Victoria Line)
Manager: George Graham **Secretary:** Ken Friar
Colours: Red shirts, with white sleeves; white shorts
Record home gate: 73,295 v Sunderland, March 1935 (League)
Honours – Champions: Division 1: 1930-31, 1932-33, 1933-34, 1934-35, 1937-38, 1947-48, 1952-53,1970-71
FA Cup winners: 1929-30, 1935-36, 1949-50, 1970-71, 1978-79
Fairs Cup winners: 1969-70

ASTON VILLA DIV. 1

Birch, Paul
Blair, Andrew
Daley, Mark A.
Deacy, Eamonn S.
Dorigo, Anthony R.
Elliott, Paul M.
Evans, Allan
Gallacher, Bernard
Glover, Dean V.
Gray, Andrew M.
Hodge, Stephen B.
Howell, Peter J.
Hunt, Stephen K.
Kerr, Paul A.
Norton, David W.
Poole, Kevin
Robinson, Philip
Shaw, Gary R.
Spink, Nigel P.
Stainrod, Simon A.
Walker, Raymond
Walters, Mark
Williams, Gary

League Appearances: Birch, Paul 25(2); Blair, Andrew 12; Bradley, Darren M. 15(3); Daley, Mark A. 16(7); Dorigo, Anthony R. 38; Elliott, Paul M. 23; Evans, Allan 35; Gibson, Colin J. 7; Glover, Dean V. 15(3); Gray, Andrew M. 35; Hodge, Stephen B. 36; Hunt, Stephen K. 12; Kerr, Paul A. 5(1); McMahon, Stephen 3; Norton, David W. 20; Ormsby, Brendan T. 14; Poole, Kevin 11; Shaw, Gary R. 10(2); Spink, Nigel P. 31; Stainrod, Simon A. 29(1); Walker, Raymond 5(2); Walters, Mark 40; Williams, Gary 25.
Goals – League (51): Stainrod 10, Walters 10, Hodge 8, Gray 5, Evans 3 (pens), Birch 2, Daley 2, Elliott 2, Gibson 2, Hunt 2, Norton 2, Dorigo 1, Kerr 1, Shaw 1.
Milk Cup (25): Stainrod 9, Birch 3, Walters 3, Evans 2 (1 pen), Gray 2, Ormsby 2, Williams 2, Glover 1, Hodge 1.
FA Cup (6): Stainrod 2, Birch 1, Evans 1 (pen), Hodge 1, Kerr 1.
Ground: Villa Park, Birmingham B6 6HE (021-327 6604)
Nearest station: Witton and Aston
Manager: Graham Turner **Secretary:** Steven Stride
Colours: Claret shirts with blue trim; white shorts
Record home gate: 76,588 v Derby, March 1946 (FA Cup)
Honours – Champions: Division 1: 1893-94, 1895-96, 1896-97, 1898-99, 1899-1900, 1909-10, 1980-81; Division 2: 1937-38, 1959-60; Division 3: 1971-72
FA Cup winners: 1886-87, 1894-95, 1896-97, 1904-05, 1912-13, 1919-20, 1956-57. (Seven wins - joint record with Spurs)
League Cup winners: 1960-61, 1974-75, 1976-77
European Cup winners: 1981-82

BARNSLEY DIV. 2

Baker, Clive E.
Campbell, Winston R.
Cross, Paul
Futcher, Paul
Goodison, Christopher W.
Gray, Stuart
Hirst, David E.
Jeffels, Simon
Joyce, Joseph P.
Kiwomya, Andrew D.
May, Lawrence C.
Ogley, Mark A.
Owen, Gordon
Plummer, Calvin A.
Semley, Alan
Thomas, David G.
Walsh, Ian P.
Wylde, Roger J.

League Appearances: Agnew, Stephen M. 2; Aylott, Trevor K.C. 9; Baker, Clive E. 42; Burns, Kenneth 19(3); Campbell, Winston R. 28(1); Cross, Paul 20; Futcher, Paul 37; Glavin, Ronald M. 5(1); Goodison, Christopher W. 19(2); Gray, Stuart 36; Hirst, David E. 26(2); Jeffels, Simon 10(1); Jonsson, Sigurdur

5; Joyce, Joseph P. 40; Kiwemya, Andrew D. 1; Law, Nicholas 1; McKenzie, Ian E. 1; May, Lawrence C. 36; Ogley, Mark A. 2; Owen, Gordon 32; Plummer, Calvin A. 18(5); Ronson, William 1(1); Thomas, David G. 39; Walsh, Ian P. 33.
Goals – League (47): Walsh 15, Owen 11 (6 pens), Hirst 9, Thomas 5, Plummer 3, Gray 2 (1 pen), Campbell 1, own goals 1.
Milk Cup (1): Gray 1 (pen).
FA Cup (0).
Ground: Oakwell, Grove Street, Barnsley S71 1ET (0226-295353)
Nearest station: Barnsley
Manager: Allan Clarke **Secretary:** Michael Spinks
Colours: Red shirts; white shorts
Record home gate: 40,255 v Stoke 1936 (FA Cup)
Honours – Champions: Division 3 North: 1933-34, 1938-39, 1954-55
FA Cup winners: 1911-12

BIRMINGHAM CITY — DIV. 2

Bremner, Desmond G.
Clarke, Wayne
Dicks, Julian A.
Geddis, David
Gore, Ian G.
Hagan, James
Handysides, Ian R.
Hansbury, Roger R.
Hopkins, Robert
Jones, Mark A.W.
Kennedy, Andrew J.
Kuhl, Martin
Platnauer, Nicholas R.
Ranson, Raymond
Rees, Anthony A.
Roberts, Brian L.F.
Russell, Guy R.
Seaman, David A.
Storer, Stuart J.

League Appearances: Armstrong, Kenneth C. 22; Bremner, Desmond G. 32; Clarke, Wayne 28; Daly, Gerald A. 2; Dicks, Julian A. 18(5); Frain, John W. 1(2); Garton, William F. 5; Geddis, David 25(1); Hagan, James 31; Handysides, Ian R. 6; Hopkins, Robert 38; Jenkins, Lee R. 1; Jones, Mark A.W. 19; Kennedy, Andrew J. 27(5); Kuhl, Martin 33(4); Platnauer, Nicholas R. 12(5); Ranson, Raymond 37; Rees, Anthony A. 4(4); Roberts, Brian L.F. 31(2); Ronson, William 2; Russell, Guy R. (1); Seaman, David A. 42; Smalley, Mark A. 7; Storer, Stuart J. 2; Whitton, Stephen P. 8; Wright, William 29.
Goals – League (30): Geddis 6, Kennedy 2, Clarke 5 (1 pen), Hopkins 4, Whitton 3, Armstrong 1, Handysides 1, Kuhl 1, Platnauer 1, Wright 2 (1 pen).
Milk Cup (6): Kennedy 2, Wright 2 (1 pen), Geddis 1, own goals 1.
FA Cup (1): Hopkins 1.
Ground: St Andrews, Birmingham B9 4NH (021-772 0101 and 2689)
Nearest station: Birmingham, New Street
Manager: John Bond **Secretary:** A.R. Waterhouse
Colours: Blue shirts with white trim; white shorts
Record home gate: 66,844 v Everton, February 1939 (FA Cup)
Honours – Champions: Division 2: 1892-93, 1920-21, 1947-48, 1954-55; League South: 1945-46
League Cup winners: 1962-63

BLACKBURN ROVERS — DIV. 2

Barker, Simon
Branagan, James P.S.
Brotherston, Noel
Fazackerley, Derek W.
Garner, Simon
Hamilton, David
Keeley, Glenn M.
Mail, David
Miller, Ian
O'Keefe, James V.
Patterson, Mark A.
Quinn, James M.
Rathbone, Michael J.

League Appearances: Ainscow, Alan 5; Barker, Simon 41; Brannagan, James P.S. 32(1); Brotherston, Noel 18(1); Fazackerley, Derek W. 36(1); Garner, Simon 36(2); Gennoe, Terence W. 32; Hamilton, David 31(2); Keeley, Glenn M. 31; Lowey, John A. 23; Mail, David 17(1); Miller, Ian 38; O'Keefe, James V. 10; Patterson, Mark A. 24(2); Quinn, James M. 29(2); Rathbone, Michael J. 42; Thompson, Christopher D. 17.

Goals – League (53): Garner 12, Barker 10 (4 pens), Patterson 10, Keeley 4, Quinn 4, Hamilton 3, Lowey 3, Ainscow 2, Brotherston 1, Fazackerley 1 (pen), Mail 1, Miller 1, Thompson 1.
Milk Cup (2): Patterson 1, Quinn 1.
FA Cup (5): Thompson 2, Brotherston 1, Lowey 1, own goals 1.
Ground: Ewood Park, Nuttall Street, Blackburn BB2 4JF (0254 55432)
Nearest station: Blackburn
Manager: Bobby Saxton **Secretary:** John W. Howarth F.A.A.I.
Colours: Shirts: blue and white halves; white shorts
Record home gate: 61,783 v Bolton Wanderers, March 1929 (FA Cup)
Honours – Champions: Division 1: 1911 -12, 1913-14; Division 2: 1938-39; Division 3: 1974-75
FA Cup winners: 1883-84, 1884-85, 1885-86, 1889-90, 1890-91, 1927-28

BLACKPOOL DIV. 3

Britton, Ian
Butler, Brian F.
Conroy, Michael
Davies, Michael J.
Deary, John S.
Dyer, Alexander C.
Greenall, Colin A.
Law, Nicholas
Matthews, Neil P.
Moore, David
O'Keefe, Eamonn
O'Rourke, William J.
Sendall, Richard A.
Stewart, Paul A.
Thomson, Robert
Walsh, Michael C.
Windridge, David

League Appearances: Britton, Ian 25(5); Butler, Brian F. 18(1); Conroy, Michael 25; Davies, Michael J. 30(6); Deary, John S. 40; Dyer, Alexander C. 39; Greenall, Colin A. 43; Hetzke, Stephen E.R. 23; Law, Nicholas 37(2); Matthews, Neil P. 1; Moore, David 41; Morgan, Stephen A. 3(2); O'Keefe, Eamonn 19(3); O'Rourke, William J. 46; Ronson, William 3; Sendall, Richard A. 4(4); Stewart, Paul A. 42; Stonehouse, Kevin 14(2); Thomson, Robert 14(2); Walsh, Michael C. (25); Windridge, David 14(2).
Goals – League (66): O'Keefe 17 (6 pens), Dyer 8, Stewart 8 (2 pens), Deary 7 (2 pens), Davies 5, Hetzke 4, Stonehouse 3 (1 pen), Windridge 3, Britton 1, Butler 1, Greenall 1, Law 1, Thomson 2, Walsh 1, own goals 4.
Milk Cup (2): Davies 1, Greenall 1.
FA Cup (2): Stewart 1, own goal 1.
Ground: Bloomfield Road, Blackpool FY1 6JJ (0253 404331)
Nearest station: Blackpool North
Manager: Sam Ellis **Secretary:** D. Johnson
Colours: Tangerine shirts with white collar and cuffs; white shorts with tangerine stripe
Record home gate: 38,098 v Wolves, April 1952 (League)
Honours – Champions: Division 2: 1929-30
FA Cup winners: 1952-53
Anglo-Italian Cup winners: 1971

BOLTON WANDERERS DIV. 3

Allardyce, Samuel
Caldwell, Anthony
Came, Mark R.
Entwistle, Wayne P.
Farnworth, Simon
Gavin, Mark W.
Hartford, Richard A.
Joyce, Warren G.
Neal, Philip G.
Oghani, George W.
Phillips, James N.
Scott, Derek E.
Sutton, David W.
Thompson, Stephen J.

League Appearances: Allardyce, Samuel 14; Bell, Graham T.A. 30(6); Caldwell, Anthony 38(2); Came, Mark R. 35; Cross, David 19(1); Darby, Julian T. 2; Entwistle, Wayne P. 5(3); Farnworth, Simon 31; Felgate, David W. 15; Fitzpatrick, Paul J. 10(1); Gavin, Mark W. 8; Hartford, Richard A. 46; Joyce, Warren G. 31; Neal, Philip G. 20; Oghani, George W. 31(5); Phillips, James N. 33; Ring, Michael P. 1(2); Ripley, Stuart E. 5; Rudge, Simon J. 13(3); Scott, Derek E. 43;

Sutton, David 32; Thompson, Stephen J. 35; Walker, Roger A. 6(5); Winstanley, Mark A. 3.
Goals – League (54): Caldwell 10 (2 pens), Cross 8, Oghani 7, Thompson 8 (3 pens), Hartford 5, Joyce 4, Bell 2, Neal 2, Rudge 2, Sutton 2, Came 1, Gavin 1, Phillips 1, Ripley 1.
Milk Cup (5): Cross 2, Bell 1, Caldwell 1, Hartford 1.
FA Cup (1): Thompson 1 (pen).
Ground: Burnden Park, Manchester Rd., Bolton BL3 2QR (0204-389200)
Player/Manager: Phil Neal **Secretary:** Des McBain, FAAI
Nearest station: Bolton
Colours: Shirts: white, shorts: navy blue
Record home gate: 69,912 v Manchester City, February 1933 (FA Cup)
Honours – Champions: Division 2: 1908-09, 9177-78; Division 3: 1972-3
FA Cup winners: 1922-23, 1925-26, 1928-29, 1957-58

AFC BOURNEMOUTH DIV. 3

Brown, Roger W.
Clarke, Colin J.
Heffernan, Thomas P.
Howlett, Gary P.
Lewis, Morgan R.
Morrell Paul D.
Newson, Mark J.
O'Connor, Mark A.
O'Driscoll, Sean M.
Russell, Colin
Savage, Robert J.
Sulley, Christopher S.
Thompson, Ian P.
Williams, Keith D.

League Appearances: Beck, John A. 37(4); Brown, Roger W. 34; Claridge, Steve E. (1); Clark, William R. 1; Clarke, Colin J. 46; Coleman, David 1; Heffernan, Thomas P. 37; Howlett, Gary P. 17(3); Keane, Thomas J. (1); Leigh, Ian R. 12; Lewis, Morgan R. 4; Morrell, Paul D. 37(1); Newson, Mark J. 46; Nightingale, Mark B.D. 28(4); O'Connor, Mark A. 9; O'Driscoll, Sean M. 46; Randall, Adrian J. 2; Russell, Colin 29(3); Shaw, Christopher J. 6(2); Smeulders, John 34; Sulley, Christopher S. 37; Thompson, Ian P. 33; White, Anthony J. 1; Williams, Keith D. 9.
Goals – League (65): Clarke 26 (1 pen), Russell 8 (2 pens), Beck 5, O'Driscoll 5, Thompson 5, Newson 5, Heffernan 4, Howlett 2, Shaw 2, Brown 1, Morrell 1, O'Connor 1.
Milk Cup (7): Clarke 3, Thompson 2, Russell 2 (1 pen).
FA Cup (6): Clarke 2, Brown 1, Newson 1, O'Driscoll 1, Thompson 1.
Ground: Dean Court, Bournemouth, Dorset BH7 7AF (0202-35381)
Nearest station: Bournemouth
Manager: Harry Redknapp **Secretary:** B. Tiler
Colours: Red shirts with white pinstripe; red shorts with white stripe down side
Record home gate: 28, 799 v Manchester United, March 1957 (FA Cup)
Honours: Associate Member's Cup winners 1983-84

BRADFORD CITY DIV. 2

Abbott, Gregory S.
Beaumont, Nigel
Campbell, Robert M.
Clegg, Anthony
Ellis, Mark E.
Evans, David G.
Goodman, Donald
Graham, Arthur
Hendrie, John G.
Jackson, Peter A.
Litchfield, Peter
McCall, Stuart M.
Oliver, Gavin R.
Ormondroyd, Ian
O'Shaughnessy, Stephen
Singleton, Martin D.
Thorpe, Adrian
Withe, Christopher

League Appearances: Abbott, Gregory S. 38(1); Beaumont, Nigel 2; Campbell, Robert M. 41; Chalmers, Paul 2; Clegg, Anthony 16(5); Ellis, Mark E. 13(12); Evans, David G. 35; Goodman, Donald 19(1); Graham Arthur 23(2); Hendrie, John G. 42; Jackson, Peter A. 42; Litchfield, Peter 42; McCall, Stuart M. 38; Oliver, Gavin R. 27: Ormondroyd, Ian 8(4); Singleton, Martin D. 35(1); Thorpe, Adrian 6(4); Withe, Christopher 33.
Goals – League (51): Abbott 10 (7 pens), Campbell 10 (1 pen), Hendrie 10, Goodman 4, McCall 4, Ellis 3, Ormondroyd 3, Graham 2, Singleton 2, Clegg 1,

Oliver 1, Thorpe 1.
Milk Cup (8): Campbell 2, Hendrie 2, McCall 2, Abbott 1 (pen), Jackson 1.
FA Cup (4): Abbott 2 (1 pen), Goodman 1, Hendrie 1.
Club Address: Valley Parade, Bradford BD8 7DY (0274-306062); Ground: Odsal Stadium, Odsal Top, Bradford
Nearest station: Bradford Exchange
Manager: Trevor Cherry **Secretary:** T.F. Newman
Colours: Shirts: claret and amber stripes; claret shorts
Record home gate: 39,146 v Burnley, March 1911 (FA Cup)
Honours – Champions: Division 2: 1907-08, 1984-85; Division 3 North: 1928-29
FA Cup winners: 1910-11 (first holders of present trophy)

BRENTFORD DIV. 3

Booker, Robert
Cooke, Robert L.
Evans, Terence W.
Joseph, Francis
Joseph, Roger
Millen, Keith
Murray, James G.
Phillips, Gary C.
Salman, Danis M.M.
Sinton, Andrew
Wignall, Steven L.

League Appearances: Alexander, Rowan S. 24(4); Booker, Robert 44; Bullivant, Terence 7(1); Burke, Steven J. 10; Butler, Steven 15(3); Cooke, Robert L. 43(1); Cooper, Gary 9(1); Evans, Terrence W. 18(1); Holloway, Ian S. 13; Hurlock, Terence A. 27; Joseph, Francis 5(3); Joseph, Roger 27(1); Key, Richard M. 3; Lynch, Anthony J. 28(5); Millen, Keith 30(2); Murray, James G. 45; Phillips, Gary C. 43; Roberts, Gary P.M. 3; Salman, Danis M.M. 40; Sinton, Andrew 26; Torrance, George 18(3); Wignall, Steven L. 28.
Brentford
Goals – League (58): Cooke 17, Booker 8, Lynch 6, Alexander 4, Murray 3, Sinton 3 (1 pen), Butler 2, Holloway 2, Hurlock 2, Millen 2, Wignall 2, Bullivant 1, Burke 1, Evans 1, F. Joseph 1, R. Joseph 1, Roberts 1, own goals 1.
Milk Cup (5): Alexander 2, Cook 1 (pen), Evans 1, Hurlock 1.
FA Cup (1): Evans 1.
Ground: Griffin Park, Braemar Road, Brentford TW8 0NT (01-847 2511/3)
Nearest stations: Brentford (BR) or South Ealing (Piccadilly line)
Manager: Frank McLintock **Secretary:** Miss C. Mathews
Colours: Shirts: Red and white stripes; shorts: black with red stripe down side.
Record home gate: 39,626 v Preston North End, March 1968 (FA Cup)
Honours – Champions: Division 2: 1934-35; Division 3 South: 1932-33; Division 4: 1962-63.

BRIGHTON & HOVE ALBION DIV. 2

Biley, Alan P.
Connor, Terence F.
Digweed, Perry M.
Edwards, Sean W.
Fashanu, Justinus S.
Gatting, Stephen P.
Hutchings, Christopher
Mortimer, Dennis G.
Moseley, Graham
O'Regan, Kieran
O'Reilly, Gary M.
Penney, Steven A.
Saunders, Dean N.
Wilson, Daniel J.
Young, Eric

League Appearances: Biley, Alan P. 22; Connor, Terence F. 33; Digweed, Perry M. 33; Fashanu, Justinus S. 16; Ferguson, Michael J. 9; Gatting, Stephen P. 14(3); Hutchings, Christopher 29; Jacobs, Steve D. 29(1); Keown, Martin 5(2); Massimo, Franco (1); Mortimer, Dennis G. 40; Moseley, Graham 9; Newman, Darrel L. 1; Oliver, Gavin R. 15(1); O'Regan, Kieran 6(9); O'Reilly, Gary M. 35; Pearce, Graham 32; Penney, Steven A. 30(7); Saunders, Dean N. 39(3); Wilson, Daniel 33; Young, Eric 32.
Goals – League (64): Connor 14, Saunders 14, Wilson 11 (5 pens), Ferguson 5, Biley 4, Penney 3, Fashanu 2, Mortimer 2, Young 2, Hutchings 1, Jacobs 1, Keown 1, O'Regan 1, Pearce 1, own goals 2.

Milk Cup (7): Wilson 3 (1 pen), Biley 1, Ferguson 1, Keown 1, Penney 1.
FA Cup (8): Saunders 5, Connor 1, Jacobs 1, Young 1.
Ground: Goldstone Ground, Old Shoreham Road, Hove, Sussex BN3 7DE (0273-739535)
Nearest station: Hove
Manager: Alan Mullery **Secretary:** Kenneth J. Calver
Colours: Royal blue shirts with three horizontal white stripes on shoulders, white shorts
Record home gate: 36,747 v Fulham, December 1958 (League)
Honours – Champions: Division 3 South: 1957-58; Division 3: 1971-72; Division 4: 1964-65
FA Cup winners: Nil

BRISTOL CITY DIV. 3

Curle, Keith
Hutchinson, Robert
Johnson, Stephen
Llewellyn, Andrew
Marshall, Gary
Moyes, David W.
Neville, Steven F.
Newman, Robert N.
Pritchard, Howard K.
Riley, Glyn
Rogers, Lee M.
Tanner, Michael W.
Underhill, Graham S.
Walsh, Alan
Waugh, Keith
Williams, Brian

League Appearances: Bryant, Richard J. 2; Curle, Keith 44; Emmanuel, John G. 2; Harle, David 8; Hirst, Martyn P. 1; Honor, Christian R. 1; Hughes, Mark 2; Hutchinson, Robert 42; Johnson, Stephen 8(5); Llewellyn, Andrew D. 38; Marshall, Gary 14(5); Moore, Gordon (1); Moyes, David W. 27; Neville, Steven F. 46; Newman, Robert N. 37(2); Pritchard, Howard K. 32(2); Riley, Glyn 33(8); Rogers, Lee M. 21; Tanner, Michael W. 2; Tong, David J. 19; Underhill, Graeme S. 1; Vaughan, John 2; Walsh, Alan 44; Waugh, Keith 44; Williams, Brian 36.
Goals – League (68): Neville 19, Walsh 18 (7 pens), Riley 10, Pritchard 6, Hutchinson 4, Newman 3, Marshall 2, Moyes 2, Bryant 1, Curle 1, Llewellyn 1, Williams 1.
Milk Cup (3): Johnson 2, Hutchinson 1.
FA Cup (5): Neville 3, Riley 1, Walsh 1 (pen).
Ground: Ashton Gate, Bristol BS3 2EJ (0272-632812)
Nearest station: Bristol Temple Meads
Manager: Terry Cooper **Secretary** Miss J. Harrison
Colours: Shirts: red, with white trim, shorts white
Record home gate: 43,335 v Preston, February 1935 (FA Cup)
Honours – Champions: Division 2: 1905-06; Division 3 South: 1922-23, 1926-27, 1954-55. **Freight Rover Trophy winners:** 1985-86

BRISTOL ROVERS DIV. 3

Bater, Philip T.
England, Michael
Green, Ronald R.
Jones, Vaughan
Mehew, David S.
Morgan, Trevor J.
Parkin, Timothy J.
Penrice, Gary K.
Portch, Lee G.
Scales, John R.
Smart, Gary M.
Tanner, Nicholas
Weston, Ian R.

League Appearances: Badock, Stephen W. 14(3); Bater, Philip T. 26(1); Carr, Darren J. 1; Carter, Timothy D. 2; Cockram, Allan C. 1; Davies, Ian C. 13(1); England, Michael 17; Francis, Gerald C.J. 27; Green, Ronald R. 38; Iles, Richard 1; Jones, Vaughan 32; Mehew, David S. (4); Morgan, Trevor J. 35(1); Noble, Wayne I. 3(4); Obi, Anthony L. 1; O'Connor, Mark A. 34; Parkin, Timothy J. 43; Penrice, Gary K. 39; Purnell, Philip 9(2); Randall, Paul 15(2); Scales, John R. 27(2); Smart, Gary M. 2(1); Spring, Andrew J. 18(1); Stevenson, William B. 30(1); Tanner, Nicholas 35(2); Vaughan, John 6; White, Stephen J. 37(3).

Goals – League (51): Morgan 16 (1 pen), White 12, Penrice 5, Badock 3, Stevenson 3 (1 pen), O'Connor 2, Parkin 2, Purnell 2, Randall 2, Tanner 2, Davies 1, Scales 1.
Milk Cup (5): Randall 3, Badock 1, O'Connor 1.
FA Cup (8): Morgan 3 (1 pen), White 2, Francis 1, Penrice 1, Stevenson 1.
Ground: Twerton Park, Bath, Avon BA2 1DB (0225 230 87)
Nearest station: Bath Spa
Manager: Bobby Gould **Secretary:** L. T. Bell
Colours: Shirts: blue and white quarters, shorts: blue
Record home gate: 38,472 v Preston, January 1960 (FA Cup)
Honours – Champions: Division 3 South: 1952-53

BURNLEY DIV. 4

Deakin, Raymond J.
Devine, Peter
Gallagher, Joseph A.
Grewcock, Neil
Hampton, Peter J.
Heesom, Darren L.
Heggarty, James P.
Hoskin, James A.
Kennedy, Stephen
Lawrence, Leslie O.
Malley, Philip
Neenan, Joseph P.
Overson, Vincent D.
Parker, Derrick
Woodworth, Anthony D.

League Appearances: Biggins, Wayne 12; Chippendale, Brian A. 6(2); Deakin, Raymond J. 46; Devine, Peter 31(6); Edwards, Neil A. (1); Grewcock, Neil 36(2); Haddock, Peter M. 7; Hampton, Peter J. 39(1); Harrington, Philip 2; Heesom, Darren L. 23(2); Heggarty, James P. 33(3); Hird, Kevin 39; Holden, Richard (1); Hoskin, James A. 17(2); Kilner, Andrew W. 2(3); Lawrence, Leslie O. 16(5); Malley, Philip 43; Neenan, Joseph P. 36; Overson, Vincent D. 28; Palmer, Geoffrey 11; Parker, Derrick 19; Peacock, Dennis 8; Rhodes, Mark N. 3(1); Robinson, Andrew C. 5; Taylor, Alan D. 44(1).
Goals – League (60): Taylor 16, Grewcock 7, Hird 7 (4 pens), Lawrence 6, Parker 5, Biggins 3, Deakin 3, Devine 2, Hoskin 2, Malley 2, Hampton 1, Heesom 1, Heggarty 1, Robinson 1, own goals 3.
Milk Cup (5): Taylor 3, Biggins 1, Hird 1.
FA Cup (4): Devine 2, Malley 1, Parker 1.
Ground: Turf Moor, Brunshaw Road, Burnley BB10 4BX (0282 27777 and 38021)
Nearest station: Burnley Central
Manager: Martin Buchan **Secretary:** R. Bradshaw
Colours: Shirts: claret; shorts: white
Record home gate: 54,775 v Huddersfield, February 1924 (FA Cup)
Honours – Champions: Division 1: 1920-21, 1959-60; Division 2: 1897-98, 1972-73; Division 3: 1981-82
FA Cup winners: 1913-14

BURY DIV. 3

Dixon, Lee M.
Hill, Andrew
Hughes, Philip
Jakub, Yanek
Kerr, John
Pashley, Terence
Robinson, Andrew C.
Ross, Trevor
Valentine, Peter
White, Eric W.
Young, Kevin

League Appearances: Beckford, Darren R. 12; Bramhall, John 23(2); Buckley, Garry 1(2); Butcher, John M. 5; Cross, David 12(1); Dixon, Lee M. 45; Dobson, John M. 12(1); Grimshaw, Christopher 1(1); Harris, Carl S. 15(3); Hill, Andrew 35; Hughes, Philip 41; Jakub, Yenek 44; Kerr, John 19(4); Lee, David M. (1); Lowe, Gary 3(1); Madden, Craig 34; Pashley, Terence 36(3); Robinson, Andrew C. 5(5); Ross, Trevor 31; Valentine, Peter 46; Welsh, Andrew C. (1); White, Eric W. 43; Young, Kevin 43(1).
Goals – League (63): Madden 14, Dixon 6, Jakub 6, Young 6, Beckford 5, White 5, Dobson 4 (2 pens), Kerr 4, Harris 3, Ross 3 (1 pen), Valentine 3, Hill 2, Bramhall 1, Pashley 1.

Milk Cup (8): Madden 3, Jakub 2, Kerr 1, Ross 1 (pen), Young 1.
FA Cup (12): Madden 3, Young 2, Bramhall 1, Dixon 1, Jakub 1, Kerr 1, Ross 1 (pen), Valentine 1, own goals 1.
Ground: Gigg Lane, Bury BL9 9HR (061-764 4881/2)
Nearest station: Bury Metro Interchange
Manager: Martin Dobson Secretary: John Heap
Colours: Shirts: white; shorts: royal blue
Record home gate: 35,000 v Bolton, January 1960 (FA Cup)
Honours – Champions: Division 2: 1894-95; Division 3: 1960-61
FA Cup winners: 1899-1900, 1902-03

CAMBRIDGE UNITED — DIV. 4

Beattie, Andrew H.
Branagan, Keith G.
Crown, David I.
Dowman, Stephen J.
Fallon, Stephen P.
Massey, Stephen
Mundee, Brian G.
Rayment, Patrick J.
Spriggs, Stephen

League Appearances: Beattie, Andrew H. 22(1); Bennett, Michael 31; Branagan, Keith G. 9; Butler, Peter J. 14; Clark, Steven 25(3); Comfort, Alan 30: Conway, Patrick 1; Cooper, Mark D. 15(4); Crown, David I. 43; Dowman, Stephen J. 28; Fallon, Stephen P. 15; Finney, Tom 38; Galloway, Steven G. (1); Hansbury, Roger 37; Lee, Andrew G. 8(1); Littlejohns, Colin 1; Lockhart, Keith S. 9; McPherson, Keith A. 11; Massey, Kevin J. 1(2); Massey, Stephen 28(3); Moyes, David W. 9; Mundee, Brian G. 11; Osgood, Keith 2; Philliben, John 6; Pyle, Stephen 12(2); Rayment, Patrick J. 12(1); Richards, Gary V. 8; Richards, Sean C. 4; Scott, Geoffrey S. 19; Sinton, Andrew 19(1); Spriggs, Stephen 29; Towner, Antony J. 6; Walker, Colin 3.
Goals – League (65): Crown 24 (3 pens), Massey 12 (7 pens), Spriggs 5, Pyle 4, Comfort 3, Dowman 2, Finney 2, Lockhart 2, S. Richards 2, Butler 1, Cooper 1, Fallon 1, McPherson 1, Mundee 1, Rayment 1 (pen), Walker 1, own goals 2.
Milk Cup (1): Sinton 1 (pen).
FA Cup (1): Crown 1.
Ground: Abbey Stadium, Newmarket Road, Cambridge CB5 8LL (0223-241237)
Nearest station: Cambridge
Manager: Chris Turner **Secretary:** Paul Daw
Colours: Amber shirts with black stripes; black shorts.
Record home gate: 14,000 v Chelsea (friendly), May 1970
Honours – Champions: Division 4: 1976-77

CARDIFF CITY — DIV. 4

Brignull, Philip A.
Curtis, Mark W.
Ford, Michael P.
Giles, David C.
Gummer, Jason C.
Marustik, Christopher
Mullen, James
Rees, Melvyn J.
Turner, Robert P.
Vaughan, Nigel M.

League Appearances: Brignull, Philip A. 15; Carver, John W. 13; Christie, Derrick H.M. 18(1); Corner, David E. 6; Curtis, Wayne 24(3); Farrington, Mark A. 24(7); Flynn, Brian 10; Foley, William 5(2); Ford, Michael P. 44; Gibbins, Roger G. 11; Giles, David C. 34; Gummer, Jason C. 5; King, John 7; Leonard, Carleton C. 4; McLoughlin, Paul 26(6); Marustik, Christopher 26; Meacock, Kevin M. 2(2); Micallef, Constantinous 21(7); Mullen, James 44; Nardiello, Gerardo 7; O'Connor, Timothy D. 1(1); Price, Allen D. 2; Rees, Melvyn J. 9; Sander, Christopher A. 13; Smelt, Lee 24; Spring, Andrew J. 1; Stevenson, Nigel C. 14; Tong, David J. 1; Turner, Robert P. 31(3); Vaughan, Nigel M. 42(1); Wheeler, Paul 17(4); Withey, Graham A. 5.
Goals – League (53): Vaughan 12, Mullen 8 (pens), Turner 7, Ford 4, Nardiello 4, McLoughlin 4, Farrington 3, Christie 2, Curtis 2, Wheeler 2, Foley 1, Gummer 1, Marustik 1, Withey 1, own goals 1.

Milk Cup (3): Flynn 2, Farrington 1.
FA Cup (1): Stevenson 1.
Ground: Ninian Park, Sloper Road, Cardiff CF1 8SX (0222-398636)
Nearest stations: Cardiff Central and Queens Street
Manager: Frank Burrows **Secretary:** R. Jones
Colours: Blue shirts, white shorts
Record home gate: 61,655 Wales v England, October 1961 (Club record); 57,893 v Arsenal Division 1: 22 April, 1953
Honours – Champions: Division 3 South: 1946-47
FA Cup winners: 1926-27

CARLISLE UNITED DIV. 3

Ashurst, Jack
Baker, David P.
Bishop, Ian W.
Carr, Kevin
Cooke, John
Endersby, Scott A.G.
Gorman, Paul A.
Haigh, Paul
Halpin, John
Halsall, Michael
Hill, Andrew R.
Lomax, Geoffrey W.
Mayes, Alan K.
McCartney, Michael
Saunders, Wesley
Wakenshaw, Robert A.

League Appearances: Ashurst, Jack 35; Baker, David P. 33(2); Bishop, Ian W. 36; Carr, Kevin 15; Cooke, John 33; Endersby, Scott A.G. 27; Entwistle, Wayne P. 8(1); Gavin, Mark W. 12(1); Gorman, Paul A. 17(7); Haigh, Paul 27(1); Halpin, John 33; Halsall, Michael 41; Hill, Andrew R. 26(4); Lomax, Geoffrey W. 13; McCartney, Michael 40; McGarvey, Scott T. 10; Mayes, Alan K. 8(2); Robson, Bryan S. (2); Saunders, Wesley 35; Tolmie, James 7(1); Wakenshaw, Robert A. 6(2).
Goals – League (47): Hill 8, Bishop 6, Halpin 5, Cooke 4, Halsall 4, McGarvey 3 (1 pen), Saunders 3, Baker 2, Entwistle 2, Mayes 2, McCartney 2, Wakenshaw 2, Gavin 1, Tolmie 1 (pen), own goals 2.
Milk Cup (6): Halpin 2, Mayes 2, Bishop 1, Gavin 1.
FA Cup (1): Cooke 1.
Ground: Brunton Park, Warwick Road, Carlisle CA1 1LL (0228-26237)
Nearest station: Carlisle Citadel
Manager: Harry Gregg **Match Secretary:** N. Irving
Colours: Royal blue shirts with white pinstripe, white V neck with red and blue trim, royal blue shorts
Record home gate: 27,500 v Birmingham, January 1957 (FA Cup) and v Middlesbrough, February 1970 (FA Cup)
Honours – Champions: Division 3: 1964-65

CHARLTON ATHLETIC DIV. 1

Aizlewood, Mark
Berry, Leslie D.
Curbishley, Llewellyn C.
Flanagan, Michael A.
Gritt, Stephen J.
Humphrey, John
Johns, Nicholas P.
Lee, Robert M.
Melrose, James M.
Packyn, Roy D.
Pearson, John S.
Pender, John P.
Reid, Mark
Shipley, George M.
Stuart, Mark R.
Thompson, Steven P.

League Appearances: Aizlewood, Mark 35; Berry, Leslie D. 7; Curbishley, Llewellyn C. 30; Davies, Alan 1; Flanagan, Michael A. 33(4); Friar, John P. 4; Gritt, Stephen J. 11; Humphrey, John 39; Johns, Nicholas P. 38; Lange, Anthony S. 4; Lee, Robert M. 26(9); Loveridge, James C. 5(1); Melrose, James M. 11; Pearson, John S. 42; Pender, John P. 38; Reid, Mark 42; Shipley, George M. 37; Stuart, Mark R. 21(9); Thompson, Steven P. 38; Towner, Anthony J. (1).
Goals – League (78): Pearson 14, Stuart 12, Flanagan 11, Lee 8, Reid 8 (pens), Melrose 5, Curbishley 4, Shipley 4, Aizlewood 3, Gritt 2, Humphrey 2, own goals 5.

Milk Cup (2): Flanagan 1, Stuart 1.
FA Cup (0).
Ground: Selhurst Park, London SE25 6PH (01-771 6321)
Nearest station: Charlton (SR)
Manager: Lennie Lawrence **General Secretary:** G.I.S. Hortop
Colours: Red shirts with red and white trim; shorts; white
Record home gate: 75,031 v Aston Villa, February 1938 (FA Cup)
Honours – Champions: Division 3 South: 1928-29, 1934-35
FA Cup winners: 1946-47

CHELSEA DIV. 1

Bodley, Michael J.
Bumstead, John
Canoville, Paul K.
Dixon, Kerry M.
Dublin, Keith B.L.
Durie, Gordon S.
Francis, Stephen S.
Fridge, Leslie F.
Hall, Gareth D.
Hazard, Michael
Hollins, John W.
Howard, Terence
Isaac, Robert C.
Jones, Keith A.
Lee, Colin
McAllister, Kevin
McLaughlin, Joseph
McNaught, John
Millar, John
Murphy, Jeremiah M.
Nevin, Patrick K.F.
Niedzwiecki, Edward A.
Pates, Colin G.
Priest, Philip
Rougvie, Douglas
Spackman, Nigel J.
Speedie, David R.
Wood, Darren T.
West, Colin W.

League Appearances: Bumstead, John 32; Canoville, Paul K. 4(9); Davies, Gordon J. 1; Dixon, Kerry M.38; Dublin, Keith B.L. 11; Durie, Gordon 1; Francis, Stephen S. 3; Fridge, Leslie F. 1; Godden, Anthony L. 8; Hazard, Michael 17(1); Howard, Terence 1; Isaac, Robert C. 3; Jones, Keith A. 10(4); Lee, Colin 12(1); McAllister, Kevin 13(7); McLaughlin, Joseph 40; McNaught, John (1); Millar, John 7; Murphy, Jeremiah M. 21; Nevin, Patrick K.F. 39(1); Niedzwiecki, Edward A. 30; Pates, Colin G. 35; Rougvie, Douglas 34; Shearer, Duncan N. 2; Spackman, Nigel J. 37(2); Speedie, David R. 34; Wood, Darren T. 28.
Goals – League (57): Dixon 14, Speedie 14, Nevin 7, Spackman 7 (4 pens), Murphy 3, Jones 2, Rougvie 2, Bumstead 1, Canoville 1, Hazard 1 (pen), McLaughlin 1, Pates 1, Shearer 1, own goals 2.
Milk Cup (11): Dixon 5, Nevin 3, Hazard 1, McLaughlin 1, Speedie 1.
FA Cup (2): Speedie 2.
Ground: Stamford Bridge, Fulham Road, London SW6 1HS (01-385 5545)
Nearest station: Fulham Broadway (District Line)
Manager: John Hollins MBE **Secretary:** Miss S.F. Marson
Colours: Shirts: royal blue with two white stripes on trim: shorts royal blue
Record home gate: 82,905 v Arsenal, October 1935 (League)
Honours – Champions: Division 1: 1954-55; Division 2: 1983-84
FA Cup winners: 1969-70
League Cup winners: 1964-65
European Cup Winners Cup Winners: 1970-71 **Full Members Cup winners:** 1985-86

CHESTER CITY DIV. 3

Abel, Graham
Bennett, Gary M.
Butcher, John M.
Butler, Barry
Coy, Robert A.
Glenn, David A.
Graham, Milton M.
Holden, Andrew I.
Houghton, Peter
Kelly, John
Lane, Martin J.
Murray, David R.
Richardson, Ian P.
Rimmer, Stuart A.

League Appearances: Abel, Graham 23; Barrett, Earl D. 12; Bennett, Gary M. 40(3); Bramhall, John 4; Brett, David S. 5(2); Butcher, John M. 34; Butler, Barry, 10(4); Cashley, Alec R. 9; Coy, Robert A. 44; Croft, Brian G. (1); Fox, Stephen D. 1; Gage, Wakeley A.J. 17; Glenn, David A. 33; Graham, Milton M.

37(1); Greenough, Richard A. 28(5); Harley, Lee (1); Holden, Andrew I. 10; Houghton, Peter 34(3); Johnson, Stephen A. 10; Kaye, David N. 3; Kelly, John 43; Lane, Martin J. 44; Murray, David R. 3(3); Richardson, Ian P. 27: Rimmer, Stuart A. 18; Sconce, Mark A. 1(1); Speight, Michael 10; Wright, William 6.
Goals – League (83): Rimmer 16 (4 pens), Bennett 13 (1 pen), Houghton 10, Richardson 10 (5 pens), Kelly 8, Johnson 6 (3 pens), Greenough 5, Graham 3, Abel 2, Holden 2, Coy 1, Gage 1, Glenn 1, Lane 1, Murray 1, Wright 1, own goals 2.
Milk Cup (6): Rimmer 5 (3 pens), Murray 1.
FA Cup (0).
Ground: The Stadium, Sealand Road, Chester CH1 4LW (0244 371376 and 371809)
Nearest station: Chester
Manager: H. McNally **Secretary:** J.A. Eckersley
Colours: Royal blue shirts with white stripes; white shorts
Record home gate: 20,500 v Chelsea, January 1952 (FA Cup)
Honours: Nil

CHESTERFIELD DIV. 3

Baines, Stephen J.
Bellamy, Gary
Brown, Philip J.
Caldwell, David
Henderson, Michael R.
Hewitt, James R.
Marples, Christopher
Moss, Ernest
O'Neill, James J.
Reid, Anthony J.
Scrimgeour, Brian
Spooner, Stephen A.
Williamson, Charles H.

League Appearances: Armstrong, Gerard J. 12; Baines, Stephen J. 37(1); Batty, Paul W. 24(2); Bellamy, Gary 12; Bloomer, Robert 6; Brown, James G. 14; Brown, Philip J. 29(2); Caldwell, David 18(4); Henderson, Michael R. 43; Hewitt, James R. 16(1); Hunter, Leslie 32; Kendal, Stephen J. 8(1); Marples, Christopher 32; Moss, Ernest 39; O'Neill, James J. 43; Perry, David 1(1); Reid, Anthony J. 24(4); Scrimgeour, Brian 45; Spooner, Stephen A. 31(1); Walker, Philip A. 18(2); Williamson, Charles H. 22(5).
Goals – League (61): Moss 14, Scrimgeour 9 (5 pens), Henderson 5, Spooner 5, Walker 5, Hunter 4, Reid 4, Baines 3, Brown 3, Caldwell 3, Bellamy 2, Armstrong 1, Williamson 1, own goals 2.
Milk Cup (5): Moss 3, Brown 1 (pen), Henderson 1.
FA Cup (2): Batty 1, Henderson 1.
Ground: Recreation Ground, Chesterfield S40 4SX (0246 209765)
Nearest station: Chesterfield
Manager: John Duncan **Secretary:** R.F. Pepper
Colours: Royal blue shirts with white pinstripe, white shorts
Record home gate: 30,968 v Newcastle United, April 1939 (League)
Honours – Champions: Division 3 North: 1930-31, 1935-36; Division 4: 1969-70, 1984-85

COLCHESTER UNITED DIV. 4

Adcock, Anthony C.
Baker, Terence
Bowen, Keith B.
Burman, Simon J.
Chamberlain, Alec F.R.
Day, Keith
English, Anthony K.
English, Thomas S.
Farrell, Andrew J.
Ferguson, Michael J.
Game, Kirk M.
Groves, Perry
Hedman, Rudi
Norman, Sean
Phillips, Ian A.
Reeves, John C.
Turner, Robin D.

League Appearances: Adcock, Anthony 33; Baker, Terence 21; Bowen, Keith B. 15; Burman, Simon J. 10(1); Chamberlain, Alec F.A. 46; Day, Keith 30; English, Anthony K. 45; English, Thomas S. 16(7); Farrell, Andrew J. 24; Ferguson, Michael J. 9(1); Game, Kirk M. 3(1); Groves, Perry 42(1); Hedman,

Rudi 38(1); Houston, Stewart M. 36; Hull, Jeffrey 4(1); Irving, Russell 2(7); Osborne, Roger C. 28(6); Parkinson, Noel D. 35; Phillips, Ian A. 37; Reeves, John C. 24; Turner, Robin D. 6(5); Whymark, Trevor J. 2.
Goals – League (88): Adcock 15, A.English 13 (1 pen), Groves 12, T.English 8 (3 pens), Ferguson 7, Parkinson 7 (1 pen), Bowen 5, Day 5, Reeves 4, Hedman 3, Baker 2, Phillips 2, Burman 1, Farrell 1, Osborne 1, own goals 2.
Milk Cup (3): Bowen 3 (1 pen).
FA Cup (0).
Ground: Layer Road, Colchester CO2 7JJ (0206-574042)
Nearest station: Colchester North (2 miles)
Manager: Mike Walker **Secretary:** M.R. Bennet
Colours: Shirts: Royal blue with white pinstripe; shorts white
Record home gate: 19,072 v Reading, November 1948 (FA Cup)
Honours: Nil

COVENTRY CITY DIV. 1

Adams, Michael R.
Bennett, David A.
Borrows, Brian
Bowman, David
Brazil, Alan B.
Culpin, Paul
Downs, Gregory
Evans, Gareth J.
Gynn, Michael
Kilcline, Brian
McGrath, Lloyd A.
McInally, James E.
Ogrizovic, Steven
Peake, Trevor
Pickering, Nicholas
Regis, Cyrille
Rodger, Graham
Suckling, Perry J.
Turner, Wayne L.
Williams, Andrew

League Appearances: Adams, Michael R. 29(2); Bennett, David A. 33(5); Borrows, Brian 41; Bowman, David 29(1); Brazil, Alan B. 15; Culpin, Paul 4(3); Downs, Gregory 40(1); Evans, Gareth J. 5(1); Gibson, Terrance B. 24; Gynn, Michael 6(6); Hibbitt, Kenneth 11(3); Kilcline, Brian 32; McGrath, Lloyd A. 32; McInally, James E. 5; Ogrizovic, Steven 42; Peake, Trevor 37; Pickering, Nicholas 15; Regis, Cyrille 34; Rodger, Graham 10; Stephens, Kirk W. 1(1); Turner, Wayne L. 14(1); Williams, Andrew 3(5).
Goals – League (48): Gibson 11, Kilcline 7 (5 pens), Bennett 6, Regis 5, Pickering 4, Adams 3 (1 pen), Bowman 2, Brazil 2, Culpin 1, Gynn 1, Hibbitt 1, Peake 1, Turner 1, own goals 3.
Milk Cup (12): Regis 5, Bennett 2, Gibson 2, Bowman 1, Evans 1, Kilcline 1.
FA Cup (1): Kilcline 1.
Ground: Highfield Road Stadium, King Richard Street, Coventry CV2 4FW (0203-57171-6)
Nearest station: Coventry
Manager: G. W. Curtis **Secretary:** G.P. Hover
Colours: Sky blue shirts with navy pinstripe, navy and sky trim; shorts: sky blue with navy trim
Record home gate: 51,455 v Wolverhampton, April 1967 (League)
Honours – Champions: Division 2:1966-67; Division 3:1963-64; Division 3 South:1935-36

CREWE ALEXANDRA DIV. 4

Blissett, Gary P.
Cutler, Christopher P.
Davis, Steven P.
Hart, Nigel
Parkin, Brian
Pemberton, John M.
Platt, David A.
Power, Philip D.
Pullar, David H.
Thomas, Geoffrey R.
Waller, David A.

League Appearances: Allatt, Vernon 8(1); Anderson, Darren I. 5; Blissett, Gary P. 34(4); Booth, Paul 23(4); Callaghan, Aaron J. 8; Crabbe, Stephen 4; Cutler, Christopher P. 25(3); Davis, Stephen P. 45; Edwards, Levi W. 10(3); Farrell, Peter J. 19(1); Handford, Philip M. 9; Hart, Nigel 23; Holland, Robert J. 7; Johnson, Peter E. 8; Longley, Nicholas 3; McCarrick, Mark B. 10(1); McClure,

Douglas H. 3: Parkin, Brian 39; Pemberton, John M. 37(4); Platt, David 43; Power, Philip D. 7(4); Powner, Robert J. 4; Pullar, David H. 29(4); Saunders, Steven J. 15(7); Scott, Robert W. 1; Taylor, Peter M.R. 3; Thomas, Geoffrey R. 37; Waller, David H. 44; Watkiss, Stuart 3.
Goals – League (54): Waller 13, Blissett 11 (6 pens), Platt 9, Cutler 6, Thomas 6, Power 2, Allatt 1, Davis 1, Farrell 1, Saunders 1, own goals 3.
Milk Cup (10): Waller 3, Platt 2 (pens), Blissett 1, Cutler 1, Hart 1, Pemberton 1, Saunders 1.
FA Cup (1): own goals 1.
Ground: Gresty Road, Crewe CW2 6EB (0270 213014)
Nearest station: Crewe
Manager: Dario Grady **Secretary:** Mrs G.C. Palin
Colours: Red shirts; white shorts
Record home gate: 20,000 v Tottenham, January 1960 (FA Cup)
Honours: Nil

CRYSTAL PALACE DIV. 2

Aylott, Trevor C.K.	Gray, Andrew	Nebbeling, Gavin M.
Barber, Phillip A.	Higginbottom, Andrew J.	O' Doherty, Kenneth
Brush, Paul	Hone, Mark J.	Stebbing, Gary S.
Cannon, James A.	Irvine, James A.	Taylor, Kevin
Droy, Michael R.	Ketteridge, Stephen J.	Wood, George
Finnigan, Anthony	Lindsay, David J.	Wright, Ian E.

League Appearances: Aylott, Trevor C.K. 16(2); Barber, Phillip A. 38(1); Brush, Paul 26; Cannon, James A. 42; Droy, Michael R. 27; Finnigan, Anthony 34(2); Galloway, Steven G. 1; Gray, Andrew 29(1); Hardwick, Steven 3; Higginbottom, Andrew 12(4); Howard, Terrence 4; Hughton, Henry T. 10(1); Irvine, James A. 41; Ketteridge, Stephen J. 33; Lindsay, David J. 8(1); Lock, Gary R. 10; Nebbeling, Gavin M. 14; O'Doherty, Kenneth 13; Sparrow, Brian E. 12; Stebbing, Gary S. 3; Taylor, Kevin 31; Wood, George 39; Wright, Ian E. 16(16).
Goals – League (57): Gray 10 (2 pens), Barber 9, Wright 9, Taylor 6 (1 pen), Aylott 4, Droy 4, Ketteridge 4, Finnigan 3, Irvine 3, Brush 2, Higginbottom 2, Cannon 1.
Milk Cup (3): Barber 2, Gray 1.
FA Cup (1): Taylor 1.
Ground: Selhurst Park, SE25 6PU (01-653 4462)
Nearest stations: Selhurst, Norwood Junction or Thornton Heath
Manager: Steve Coppell **Secretary:** Alan J. Leather
Colours: Shirts: white with red and blue diagonal band over left shoulder, shorts white
Record home gate: 51,801 v Burnley, May 1979 (League)
Honours – Champions: Division 2: 1978-79; Division 3 South: 1920-21

DARLINGTON DIV. 3

Airey, Carl	Lloyd, Philip R.	Robinson, Peter
Astbury, Michael J.	MacDonald, Garry	Tupling, Stephen
Evans, Christopher B.	McLean, David J.	Ward, Paul T.
Green, John R.	Morgan, Gary	Woodcock, David K.
Haire, Garry	Roberts, Alan	

League Appearances: Airey, Carl 31(3); Aldred, Graeme 11(5); Astbury, Michael J. 14; Barber, Frederick 32; Carney, Stephen 10(2); Cook, Mitchel C. 3; Douglas, John S. 3; Evans, Christopher B. 33; Forster, Mark E. 1; Green, John R. 30; Haire, Garry 3(3); Huntley, John 5(1); Lloyd, Phillip R. 29; MacDonald, Garry 35(1); McLean, David J. 37(1); Morgan, Gary 41; Nattress,

Clive 1; Pallister, Garry A. 7; Poskett, Malcolm 18(3); Roberts, Alan 38; Robinson, Peter 29; Sanderson, Michael 1; Sbragia, Richard 6; Shute, Philip 2; Tupling, Stephen 38(2); Ward, Paul T. 35; Woodcock, David K. 13(10).
Goals – League (60): MacDonald 16, Airey 12, McLean 9 (7 pens), Poskett 4, Roberts 4, Tupling 4, Ward 2, Woodcock 2 (1 pen), Cook 1 (pen), Green 1, Morgan 1, Robinson 1, own goals 3.
Milk Cup (5): McLean 2 (1 pen), Forster 1, MacDonald 1, Poskett 1.
FA Cup (1): own goals 1.
Ground: Feethams Ground, Darlington DL1 5JB (0325-465097 and 467712)
Nearest station: Darlington
Manager: Cyril Knowles **Secretary:** Brian Anderson
Colours: White shirts, black collar and cuffs with black chevrons down sleeve; shorts white with black chevrons down side
Record home gate: 21,023 v Bolton, November 1960 (League Cup)
Honours – Champions: Division 3 North: 1924-25

DERBY COUNTY DIV. 2

Blades, Paul A.	Gee, Phillip J.	Micklewhite, Gary
Buckley, Steven	Gregory, John C.	Palmer, Charles A.
Chandler, Jeffrey G.	Harbey, Graham K.	Penney, David M.
Christie, Trevor	Hindmarch, Robert	Pratley, Richard G.
Davison, Robert	Lewis, Michael	Steele, Eric G.
Forsyth, Michael E.	McClaren, Stephen	Wallington, Francis M.
Garner, Andrew	MacLaren, Ross	Williams, David G.

League Appearances: Blades, Paul A. 24(6); Buckley, Steven 46; Chandler, Jeffrey G. 36(1); Christie, Trevor 45; Davison, Robert 41; Garner, Andrew 8(8); Gee, Phillip 2(2); Gregory, John C. 22; Harbey, Graham K. (3); Hindmarch, Robert 39; Lewis, Michael 5; McClaren, Stephen 22(1); MacLaren, Ross 46; Micklewhite, Gary 46; Palmer, Charles A. 18; Pratley, Richard G. 7; Steele, Eric G. 13; Streete, Floyd 5; Thomas, Michael R. 9; Wallington, Francis M. 33; Williams, David G. 39(1).
Goals – League (80): Davison 17, Christie 15 (2 pens), Micklewhite 11, Chandler 9 (1 pen), Hindmarch 6, Garner 5, Gregory 4, MacLaren 4 (2 pens), Williams 4, Gee 2, Buckley 1, Lewis 1, own goals 1.
Milk Cup (7): Davison 3, Chandler 2 (1 pen), MacLaren 1 (pen), McClaren 1.
FA Cup (17): Chandler 4 (1 pen), Christie 3, Davison 3, Micklewhite 3, Garner 2, Gregory 1, Hindmarch 1.
Ground: The Baseball Ground, Shaftesbury Crescent, Derby DE3 8NB (0332-40105)
Nearest station: Derby
Manager: Arthur Cox **Secretary:** M.J. Dunford
Colours: White shirts; blue shorts
Record home gate: 41,826 v Tottenham, September 1969 (League)
Honours – Champions: Division 1: 1971-72, 1974-75; Division 2: 1911-12, 1914-15, 1968-69; Division 3 North: 1956-57
FA Cup winners: 1945-46

DONCASTER ROVERS DIV. 3

Brown, Anthony J.	Douglas, Colin F.	Rhodes, Andrew C.
Buckley, John W.	Flynn, Brian	Rushbury, David
Cusack, David S.	Holmes, Paul	Stead, Michael J.
Deakin, John	Humphries, Glenn	Woods, Neil S.
Deane, Brian C.	Nesbitt, Michael D.	
Dobbin, James	Philliben, John	

League Appearances: Allen, Paul 3; Brown, Allan 2; Brown, Anthony J. 38;

Buckley, John W. 45; Butterworth, Andrew J. 12(9); Caswell, Brian L. 15; Cusack, David S. 43; Deakin, John 13(1); Deane, Brian C. 2(1); Deans, Raymond 4(1); Dobbin, James 25(6); Douglas, Colin F. 41(1); Flynn, Brian 27; Harle, David 15(2); Holmes, Paul 5; Humphries, Glenn 29; Joyce, Sean W. 15; Nesbitt, Michael D. 2(3); Peacock, Dennis 9; Peattie, Donald S. 3(1); Philliben, John 20(2); Rhodes, Andrew C. 30; Rushbury, David 45; Stead, Michael J. 19(1); Swinburne, Trevor 4; Travis, David A. (2); Wadsworth, Ian J. 1(1); Wakenshaw, Robert A. 8; Walker, Colin 3(2); Woods, Neil S. 28 (2).
Goals – League (45): Douglas 13, Woods 7, Dobbin 6, Buckley 5 (3 pens), Wakenshaw 3, Brown 2, Caswell 2, Cusack 2, Harle 2 (1 pen), Holmes 1, Joyce 1, Nesbitt 1.
Milk Cup (2): Dobbin 1, Douglas 1.
FA Cup (1): Douglas 1.
Ground: Belle Vue Ground, Doncaster DN4 5HT (0302 539441)
Nearest station: Doncaster
Manager: Dave Cusack **Secretary:** L.S. Holloway
Colours: Shirts: red and white; shorts: white
Record home gate: 37,149 v Hull City, October 1948 (League)
Honours – Champions: Division 3 North: 1934-35, 1946-47, 1949-50; Division 4: 1965-66, 1968-69

EVERTON — DIV. 1

Aspinall, Warren
Barber, Frederick
Billinge, Peter G.
Bracewell, Paul W.
Coyle, Robert D.
Danskin, Jason
Harper, Alan
Heath, Adrian P.
Lineker, Gary W.
Marshall, Ian P.
Mimms, Robert A.
Mountfield, Derek N.
Pointon, Neil G.
Ratcliffe, Kevin
Reid, Peter
Richardson, Kevin
Sharp, Graeme M.
Sheedy, Kevin M.
Southall, Neville
Steven, Trevor M.
Stevens, Michael G.
Stowell, Michael
Van Den Hauwe, Patrick W.R.
Walsh Derek
Wilkinson, Paul

League Appearances: Aspinall, Warren (1); Atkins, Ian (1); Bailey, John A. 1; Billinge, Peter G. 1; Bracewell, Paul W. 38; Harper, Alan 17(4); Heath, Adrian P. 24(12); Lineker, Gary W. 41; Marshall, Ian P. 8(1); Mimms, Robert A. 10; Mountfield, Derek N. 15; Pointon, Neil G. 14(1); Ratcliffe, Kevin 39; Reid, Peter 15; Richardson, Kevin 16(2); Sharp, Graeme M. 35(2); Sheedy, Kevin M. 31; Southall, Neville 32; Steven, Trevor M. 41; Stevens, Michael G. 41; Van Den Howe, Patrick W.R. 40; Wilkinson, Paul 3(1).
Goals – League (87): Lineker 30, Sharp 19 (2 pens), Heath 10, Steven 9 (4 pens), Sheedy 5, Bracewell 3, Mountfield 3, Richardson 3, Ratcliffe 1, Reid 1, Stevens 1, Van den Hauwe 1, Wilkinson 1.
Milk Cup (12): Lineker 3, Sheedy 2, Bracewell 1, Heath 1, Marshall 1, Richardson 1, Sharp 1, own goals 2.
FA Cup (12): Lineker 5, Heath 2, Harper 1, Sharp 1, Stevens 1, Van den Hauwe 1, own goals 1.
Ground: Goodison Park, Liverpool L4 4EL (051-521 2020)
Nearest station: Liverpool Lime Street
Manager: Howard Kendall **Secretary:** Jim Greenwood
Colours: Royal blue shirts with white trim on shoulder; white shorts with blue trim
Record home gate: 78,299 v Liverpool, September 1948 (League)
Honours – Champions: Division 1: 1890-91, 1914-1915, 1927-28, 1931-32, 1938-39, 1962-63, 1969-70, 1984-85; Division 2: 1930-31
FA Cup winners: 1905-06, 1932-33, 1965-66, 1983-84
European Cup Winners Cup Winners: 1984-85

EXETER CITY DIV. 4

Burgher, Symon G.
Crawford, Alan P.
Gale, Darren
Gwinnett, Melvyn L.
Harrower, Steven G.
Jackson, Gary A.
Keough, Daniel P.
King, Phillip G.
Ling, Martin
McCaffery, Aidan
McNichol, James A.
Marker, Nicholas R.T.
Shaw, John
Viney, Keith B.

League Appearances: Crawford, Alan P. 33; Gale, Darren 17(1); Gwinnett, Melvin L. 2; Harrower, Steven G. 36(2); Impey, John E. 26; Jackson, Gary A. 31(1); Johnson, Peter E. 5; Kellow, Tony 24(9); Keough, Daniel P. 31(1); Kimble, Alan F. 1; Kimble, Gary L. 1; King, Phillip G. 9(2); Kirkup, Graeme S. 8; Ling, Martin 45; McCaffery, Aidan 31(2); McNichol, James A. 45; Marker, Nicholas R.T. 40; Massey, Richard 2; Morgan, Trevor J. 4; Pratt, Raymond E. 10(8); Shaw, John 44; Viney, Keith B. 45; Walsh, Mark (1); Ward, Warren 14; Webber, Andrew 1; Williams, Paul S. 1(1).
Goals – League (47): Kellow 9 (6 pens), Ling 8, Harrower 6, Gale 5, McNichol 5, Crawford 3, Ward 3, Jackson 2, Pratt 2, Viney 2, own goals 2.
Milk Cup (5): Crawford 1, Kellow 1, G.Kimble 1, Marker 1, Pratt 1 (pen).
FA Cup (4): Gale 2, Crawford 1, Kellow 1.
Ground: St James' Park, Exeter, Devon EX4 6PX (0392 54073)
Nearest stations: Exeter Central or St David's
Manager: Colin Appleton **Secretary:** S. J. Brailey
Colours: Red and white vertical striped shirts; black shorts with white stripes
Record home gate: 20,984 v Sunderland, March 1931 (FA Cup)
Honours: Nil

FULHAM DIV. 3

Achampong, Kenneth
Barnett, Gary L.
Batty, Lawrence
Braithwaite, John R.
Carr, Clifford P.
Coney, Dean H.
Cottington, Brian A.
Donnellan, Leo J.
Elkins, Gary
Harlow, David S.
Hicks, James M.
Hoddy, Kevin R.
Hopkins, Jeffrey
Kerrins, Wayne M.
Marshall, John P.
Parker, Paul A.
Peyton, Gerald J.
Pike, Christopher
Scott, Peter R.
Thomas, Glen A.

League Appearances: Achampong, Kenneth 30(5); Barnett, Gary L. 34(2); Batty, Lawrence 2; Braithwaite, John R. (2); Burvill, Glenn 9; Carr, Clifford P. 35; Coney, Dean H. 37; Cottington, Brian A. 42; Donnellan, Leo J. 21(2); Dreyer, John B. 12; Elkins, Gary 12(1); Fishenden, Paul 3; Gore, Sean 5; Grew, Mark 4; Hicks, James M. 10; Hopkins, Jeffrey 23; Houghton, Raymond J. 5; Kerrins, Wayne M. 11(5); Marshall, John P. 42; Parker, Paul A. 30; Peyton, Gerald J. 36; Pike, Christopher 20(6); Scott, Peter R. 32; Sealy, Anthony J. 7; Smith, Gary N. (1).
Goals – League (45): Coney 12, Barnett 6 (2 pens), Scott 5, Carr 4 (1 pen), Pike 4, Achampong 3, Marshall 3, Sealy 3, Burvill 2, Dreyer 2 (1 pen), Braithwaite 1.
Milk Cup (6): Barnett 2, Carr 1 (pen), Coney 1, Marshall 1, Pike 1.
FA Cup (0).
Ground: Craven Cottage, Stevenage Road, Fulham SW6 6HH (01-736 6561)
Nearest stations: Putney Bridge (District) or Hammersmith (Metropolitan, District and Piccadilly)
Manager: Ray Lewington **Secretary** Mrs Y. Haines
Colours: White shirts with black trim; black shorts with white trim
Record home gate: 49,335 v Millwall, October 1938 (League)
Honours – Champions: Division 2: 1948-49; Division 3, South: 1931-32.
FA Cup winners: Nil

P.F.A.86.87.—2

GILLINGHAM DIV. 3

Byrne, David S.
Cascarino, Anthony G.
Cochrane, George T.
Collins, Paul
Elsey, Karl W.
Hillyard, Ronald W.
Hinnigan, Joseph P.
Mehmet, David
Oakes, Keith B.
Robinson, Martin J.
Sage, Melvyn
Shearer, David J.
Weatherly, Colin M.
Westley, Graham N.

League Appearances: Byrne, David S. 18(5); Cascarino, Anthony G. 34; Coch rane, George T. 37(1); Collins, Paul 20(3); Elsey, Karl W. 46; Hales, Derek D. 21(8); Hillyard, Ronald W. 46; Hinnigan, Joseph P. 37(2); Macowat, Ian S. 2(1); Mehmet, David 28(3); Musker, Russell 7(2); Oakes, Keith B. 39(1); Robinson, Martin J. 29(4); Sage, Melvyn 46; Shaw, Peter K. 23(1); Shearer, David J. 22(1); Tempest, Dale M. 9; Tong, David J. 5; Weatherby, Colin M. 36(2); Westley, Graham N.1.
Goals – League (81): Cascarino 14, Robinson 10, Shearer 9, Hales 7 (1 pen), Mehmet 7 (4 pens), Weatherly 7, Cochrane 5, Elsey 5, Tempest 4, Byrne 3, Hinnigan 2, Oakes 2, Sage 2, Collins 1, Musker 1, own goals 2.
Milk Cup (5): Cascarino 3, Shearer 1, own goals 1.
FA Cup (11): Robinson 3, Cascarino 2, Cochrane 2, Hales 1, Mehmet 1, Shearer 1, own goals 1.
Ground: Priestfield Stadium, Gillingham, Kent ME7 4DD (0634-51854)
Nearest station: Gillingham
Manager: Keith Peacock **Secretary:** R.J. Dennison
Colours: Blue shirts with white trim: white shorts with blue trim
Record home gate: 23,001 v Queen's Park Rangers, January 1948 (FA Cup)
Honours – Champions: Division 4: 1963-64

GRIMSBY TOWN DIV. 2

Agnew, Paul
Batch, Nigel A.
Bonnyman, Philip
Crombie, Dean M.
Cumming, Robert
Dixon, Andrew
Felgate, David W.
Ford, Tony
Gilligan, James M.
Henshaw, Gary
Hobson, Gordon
Lund, Gary J.
Lyons, Michael
Matthews, Neil
Moore, Andrew R.
Moore, Kevin T.
Peake, Andrew M.
Robinson, Neil

League Appearances: Agnew, Paul 14(2); Barratt, Anthony 20(2); Batch, Nigel A. 30; Bonnyman, Philip 29; Crombie, Dean M. 33(1); Cumming, Robert 22(2); Emson, Paul 21(2); Felgate, David W. 12; Ford, Tony 32(2); Gilligan, James M. 19(6); Grocock, Christopher R. (1); Henshaw, Gary 10; Hine, Mark 12(1); Hobson, Gordon 39(2); Lund, Gary J. 24(5); Lyons, Michael 24; Matthews, Neil 2(2); Moore, Andrew R. 31(2); Moore, Kevin T. 30(1); Peake, Andrew M. 36; Robinson, Neil 22.
Goals – League (58): Hobson 15, Lund 8, Emson 5, Gilligan 4, Henshaw 4 (1 pen), Lyons 4, Peake 4, Bonnyman 3 (1 pen), Ford 3, Cumming 2, K.Moore 2, Crombie 1, Hine 1, A.Moore 1, own goals 1.
Milk Cup (4): Gilligan 2, Hobson 2.
FA Cup (3): Lund 1, Lyons 1, Peake 1 (pen).
Ground: Blundell Park, Cleethorpes, DN35 7PY (0472-697111)
Nearest stations: Cleethorpes or Grimsby Town
Manager: Mike Lyons **Secretary:** B.J. Fleming
Colours: Black and white striped shirts with red line on collar and cuffs; black shorts with red and white stripes
Record home gate: 31,657 v Wolverhampton, February 1937 (FA Cup)
Honours – Champions: Division 2: 1900-01, 1933-34; Division 3 North: 1925-26, 1955-56; Division 3: 1979-80; Division 4: 1971-72

HALIFAX TOWN DIV. 4

Ayre, William	Knill, Alan R.	Roche, Patrick J.
Brown, Philip	Longhurst, David J.	Sanderson, Paul D.
Fleming, Paul	Martin, Dean	Shaw, Adrian
Galloway, Michael	Nicholson, Gary A.	Thornber, Stephen

League Appearances: Ayre, William 10; Brown, Philip 45; Diamond, Barry 12; Fleming, Paul 13; Gallagher, Barry 23(2); Galloway, Michael 19; Hotte, Timothy A. 2(2); Kellock, William 41(2); Kendall, Paul S. 18(3); Knill, Alan R. 33; Longhurst, David J. 44; Lowe, Simon J. 32(3); Nicholson, Gary A. 44: Podd, Cyril M. 11(5); Robinson, Peter 3(2); Roche, Patrick J. 46; Sanderson, Paul D. 27(1); Shaw, Adrian 34; Thornber, Stephen 17(1); Ward, Stephen C. 32(6).
Goals – League (60): Kellock 17 (4 pens), Longhurst 14, Lowe 7, Gallagher 5 (1 pen), Diamond 3, Nicholson 3, Brown 2, Kendall 2, Knill 2, Sanderson 2, Ward 1, own goals 2.
Milk Cup (1): Shaw 1.
FA Cup (1): Kendall 1.
Ground: The Shay, Halifax HX1 2YS (0422-53423)
Nearest station: Halifax
Manager: Mick Jones **Secretary:** Mrs C. Bell
Colours: Royal blue shirts with white trim; white shorts with blue trim
Record home gate: 36,885 v Tottenham, February 1953 (FA Cup)
Honours: Nil

HARTLEPOOL UNITED DIV. 4

Blackburn, Edwin H.	Honour, Brian	Shoulder, Alan
Borthwick, John	Linighan, David	Smith, Anthony
Dixon, Kevin L.	Newton, Robert	Walker, Nigel S.
Hogan, Roy D.	Nobbs, Alan K.	

League Appearances: Blackburn, Edwin H. 46; Borthwick, John 28(4); Carney, Stephen 7; Chilton, Anthony J.T. 3; Dixon, Kevin L. 21(1); Dobson, Paul 5(10); Gollogly, John 11(2); Hewitt, Martin D. (1); Hogan, Roy D. 36(2); Honour, Brian 46; Kelly, Thomas J. 14(1); Nobbs, Alan K. 38(1); Lester, Michael J. 11; Linighan, David 38(1); Little, Alan 12; Martin-Chambers, Philip 29, Newton, Robert 8(3); Poskett, Malcolm 4(1); Proudlock, Paul 1; Robinson, David A. 20(1); Shoulder, Alan 36; Smith, Anthony 46; Taylor, Peter M.R. 2(3); Walker, Nigel S. 44(1).
Goals – League (68): Shoulder 17 (6 pens), Borthwick 8, Hogan 8 (6 pens), Honour 8, Dixon 5, Walker 5, Smith 3, Dobson 2, Newton 2 (1 pen), Gollogly 1, Lester 1, Linighan 1, Little 1, Nobbs 1, Robinson 1, own goals 4.
Milk Cup (2): Hogan 1, Linighan 1.
FA Cup (2): Shoulder 2.
Ground: Victoria Ground, Clarence Road, Hartlepool TS24 8BZ (Ground 0429-272584)(Office 0429-222077)
Nearest station: Hartlepool
Manager: Billy Horner **Secretary:** M. Kirby
Colours: Shirts: blue and white stripes, shorts: blue
Record home gate: 17,426 v Manchester United, January 1957 (FA Cup)
Honours: Nil

HEREFORD UNITED DIV. 4

Butler, Paul J.	Halliday, Bruce	Phillips, Stewart G.
Carter, Michael	Harvey, James	Price, Christopher J.
Cegielski, Wayne	Kearns, Oliver A.	Rodgerson, Ian

Dalziel, Ian	Maddy, Paul M.	Rose, Kevin P.
Delve, John F.	Pejic, Melvyn	Wells, Ian M.

League Appearances: Beacock, Gary C. 9(4); Butler, Paul J. 19(2); Carter, Michael 30(1); Cegielski, Wayne 29(3); Dalziel, Ian 40(1); Davies, Kevin P. (1); Delve, John F. 38; Devine, Steven R. 8(3); Halliday, Bruce 30; Harvey, James 42; Kearns, Oliver A. 33; Maddy, Paul M. 32(1); Pejic, Melvyn 45; Phillips, Stewart G. 18(2); Price, Christopher J. 41; Rodgerson, Ian 14(5); Rose, Kevin P. 46; Wells, Ian M. 32(3).
Goals – League (74): Kearns 13, Carter 9, Harvey 9 (3 pens), Wells 9, Maddy 7, Delve 6, Phillips 5, Price 4, Dalziel 3, Cegielski 2, Beacock 1, Devine 1, Halliday 1, Pejic 1, Rodgerson 2, own goals 1.
Milk Cup (6): Phillips 2, Harvey 1 (pen), Kearns 1, Price 1, Wells 1.
FA Cup (4): Carter 3, Kearns 1.
Ground: Edgar Street, Hereford HR4 9JU (0432 276666)
Nearest station: Hereford
Manager: John Newman **Secretary:** D. H. Vaughan
Colours: Shirts: white with black pinstripes and trim; shorts: black with white side stripe
Record home gate: 18,114 v Sheffield Wednesday, 1958 (FA Cup)
Honours – Champions: Division 3: 1975-76

HUDDERSFIELD TOWN DIV. 2

Bray, Ian M.	Cowling, David R.	Robinson, Spencer L.
Brown, Malcolm	Cox, Brian R.	Shearer, Duncan N.
Burke, David I.	Doyle, Stephen C.	Tempest, Dale M.
Butler, Peter J. F.	Jones, Joseph P.	Webster, Simon P.
Cooper, Graham	Mason, Keith M.	Wilson, Phillip
Cork, David	Raynor, Paul J.	Winter, Julian

League Appearances: Bray, Ian M. 32; Brown, Malcolm 36(1); Butler Peter J. (1); Cork, David 37(1); Cowling, David R. 39; Cox, Brian R. 37; Curran, Edward 33(1); Doyle, Stephen C. 42; Jones, Joseph P. 38; Jones, Paul B. 14; Mason, Keith M. 5; Raynor, Paul J. 20(1); Robinson, Spencer L. (1); Shearer, Duncan N. 7(1); Stanton, Brian 7(6); Tempest, Dale M.29 (1); Webster, Simon P. 41; Wilson, Paul A. 7; Wilson, Philip 35; Winter, Julian 3(1).
Goals – League (51): Tempest 12 (1 pen), Cork 8, Curran 7, Shearer 7, Cowling 6, Raynor 5, Webster 2, Bray 1, Jones 1, Stanton 1, Wilson 1.
Milk Cup (3): Curran 1, Jones 1, Tempest 1.
FA Cup (1): Cowling 1.
Ground: Kirklees Stadium, Leeds Road, Huddersfield HD1 6PE (0484-20335/6)
Nearest station: Huddersfield
Manager: Mick Buxton **Secretary:** G.S. Binns
Colours: Blue and white striped shirts; white shorts
Record home gate: 67,037 v Arsenal, February 1932 (FA Cup)
Honours – Champions: Division 1: 1923-24, 1924-25, 1925-26; Division 2: 1969-70; Division 3: 1979-80
FA Cup winners: 1921-22

HULL CITY DIV. 2

Askew, William	Flounders, Andrew J.	Payton, Andrew P.
Booth, Dennis	Heard, Timothy P.	Pearson, Lawrence
Brentano, Stephen R.	Horton, Brian	Roberts, Garreth W.
Brown, Nicholas L.	Jobson, Richard I.	Saville, Andrew V.
Bunn, Frankie S.	McEwan, Stanley	Skipper, Peter D.
Corkain, Stephen	Norman, Anthony J.	Swann, Gary

Davies, John G.	Olsson, Paul	Williams, Neil J.F.
Doyle, Robert	Parker, Gary S.	

League Appearances: Askew, William 32(1); Brentano, Stephen R. 7(1); Brown, Nicholas L. (1); Bunn, Frankie, S. 42; Doyle, Robert 39; Flounders, Andrew J. 20(5); Heard, Timothy P. 7(1); Horton, Brian 10; Jobson, Richard I. 36; McEwan, Stanley 42; Norman, Anthony J. 42; Parker, Garry S. 12; Pearson, Lawrence 20; Ring, Michael P. 4(5); Roberts, Garreth W. 33; Saville, Andrew V. 4(5); Skipper, Peter D. 39(1); Swann, Gary 37(2); Whitehurst, William 18; Williams, Neil J.F. 18 (1);.
Goals – League (65): Bunn 14, Flounders 10, McEwan 10 (5 pens), Jobson 7, Whitehurst 7, Roberts 4, Williams 3, Askew 2, Doyle 2, Swann 2, Ring 1, Saville 1, Skipper 1, own goals 1.
Milk Cup (5): Bunn 2, Whitehurst 2 (1 pen), Flounders 1.
FA Cup (5): Flounders 2, Roberts 2, McEwan 1 (pen).
Ground: Boothferry Park, Hull HU4 6EU (0482-51119 and 563750)
Nearest stations: Hull or Boothferry Park Halt
Manager: Brian Horton **Secretary:** R. M. Linney
Colours: Shirts: amber with black and red trim; shorts: black and amber
Record home gate: 55,019 v Manchester United, February 1949 (FA Cup)
Honours – Champions: Division 3 North: 1932-33, 1948-49; Division 3: 1965-66

IPSWICH TOWN DIV. 2

Atkins, Ian L.	Forrest, Craig L.	Rimmer, Neill
Atkinson, Dalian R.	Gernon, Frederick A.J.	Steggles, Kevin P.
Brennan, Mark R.	Gleghorn, Nigel W.	Stockwell, Michael T.
Butcher, Terence I.	Gorman, Keith	Sunderland, Alan
Cole, Michael W.	Hallworth, Jonathan G.	Watson, George N.
Cooper, Paul D.	Humes, Anthony	Wilson, Kevin J.
Crane, Andrew D.	McCall, Stephen H.	Yallop, Frank W.
Cranson, Ian	O'Donnell, Christopher	Zondervan, Romeo
D'Avray, Jean M.	Parkin, Thomas A.	
Dozzell, Jason A.W.	Putney, Trevor A.	

League Appearances: Atkins, Ian L. 20(1); Atkinson, Dalian R. (1); Brennan, Mark R. 40; Burley, George E. 6; Butcher, Terence I. 27; Cole, Michael W. 12(6); Cooper, Paul D. 36; Cranson, Ian 42; D'avray, Jean M. 24(2); Dozzell, Jason A.W. 38(3); Gernon, Frederick A.J. 11; Gleghorn, Nigel W. 17(4); Hallworth, Jonathan G. 6; McCall, Stephen H. 33; Parkin, Thomas A. 13(1); Putney, Trevor A. 18(3); Rimmer, Neill 1(1); Steggles, Kevin P. 5(1); Stockwell, Michael T. 3(5); Sunderland, Alan 13(4); Wilson, Kevin J. 37(2); Yallop, Frank W. 32(2); Zondervan, Romeo 28.
Goals – League (32): Wilson 7, D'Avray 5, Butcher 4, Brennan 3 (1 pen), Dozzell 3, Atkins 2, Cleghorn 2, Zondervan 2, Cole 1, Cranson 1, Putney 1, Sunderland 1.
Milk Cup (15): Wilson 7, Cole 3, Butcher 2, Brennan 1, Dozzell 1, Yallop 1.
FA Cup (6): Brennan 2, D'Avray 1, Dozzell 1, Wilson 1, own goals 1.
Ground: Portman Road, Ipswich IP1 2DA (0473 219211)
Nearest station: Ipswich
Manager: Bobby Ferguson **Secretary:** D.C. Rose
Colours: Blue shirts with three white stripes down sleeves and white V-neck; white shorts with three blue stripes
Record home gate: 38,010 v Leeds United, March 1975 (FA Cup)
Honours – Champions: Division 1: 1961-62; Division 2: 1960-61, 1967-68; Division 3 South: 1953-54, 1956-57
FA Cup winners: 1977-78

LEEDS UNITED DIV. 2

Aspin, Neil
Baird, Ian J.
Caswell, Brian L.
Day, Mervyn R.
Harle, David
Ormsby, Brendan T. C.
Rennie, David
Ritchie, Andrew T.
Robinson, Ronald
Sellars, Scott
Sheridan, John J.
Simmonds, Robert L.
Snodin, Ian
Stiles, John C.
Swan, Peter H.
Taylor, Robert
Thompson, Nigel D.
Wright, Thomas

League Appearances: Aspin, Neil 38; Baird, Ian J. 34(1); Caswell, Brian L. 8; Day, Mervyn R. 40; Dickinson, Martin J. 17(2); Eli, Roger 1; Hamson, Gary 30; Harle, David 3; Irwin, Dennis J. 19; Linighan, Andrew 24; Lorimer, Peter P. 14; McClusky, George M.C. 20(2); McGregor, John R. 5; Ormsby, Brendan T.C. 12; Phelan, Terry 12(2); Rennie, David 16; Ritchie, Andrew T. 28(1); Robinson, Ronald 16; Sellars, Scott 13(4); Sheridan, John J. 31(1); Simmonds, Robert L. 6(2); Snodin, Ian 37; Stiles, John 11(1); Swan, Peter H. 16; Swinburne, Trevor 2; Taylor, Robert 2; Thompson, Nigel D. 1; Wright, Thomas 6(4).
Goals – League (56): Baird 12, Ritchie 11, Snodin 5, Lorimer 4 (2 pens), Sheridan 4, McCluskey 3, Simmonds 3 (1 pen), Swan 3, Aspin 2, Rennie 2, Sellars 2, Dickinson 1, Linighan 1, Ormsby 1, Stiles 1, Wright 1.
Milk Cup (3): Snodin 2, Linighan 1.
FA Cup (0).
Ground: Elland Road, Leeds LS11 0ES (0532-716037)
Nearest station: Leeds
Manager: Billy Bremner **Secretary:** D.J. Dowse
Colours: White shirts, white shorts
Record home gate: 57,892 v Sunderland, March 1967 (FA Cup)
Honours – Champions: Division 1: 1968-69, 1973-74; Division 2: 1923-24, 1963-64
FA Cup winners: 1971-72
League Cup winners: 1967-68
European Fairs Cup winners: 1967-68, 1970-71

LEICESTER CITY DIV. 1

Andrews, Ian E.
Banks, Ian F.
Bright, Mark A.
Bunce, Paul E.
Feeley, Andrew J.
Horner, Philip M.
Jobling, Kevin A.
Kelly, Robert A.
Lynex, Steven C.
McAllister, Gary
Mauchlen, Alister H.
Morgan, Simon C.
O' Neill, John P.
Osman, Russell C.
Ramsey, Paul
Reid, Paul R.
Roberts, Jeremy
Sealy, Anthony J.
Smith, Alan M.
Smith, Robert N.
Venus, Mark
Wilson, Ian W.

League Appearances: Andrews, Ian E. 39; Banks, Ian F. 24(7); Bright, Mark A. 22(2); Christenson, Tommy 1(1); Cunningham, Lawrence 13(2); Feeley, Andrew J. 26; Jones, Robert 2(1); Kelly, Robert A. 8(1); Lynex, Steven C. 28(1); McAllister, Gary 31; Mauchlen, Alister 35(2); Morgan, Simon C. 30; O'Neill, John P. 41; Osman, Russell C. 40; Ramsey, Paul 13; Rennie, David 3; Roberts, Jeremy 3; Sealy, Anthony J. 19(2); Smith, Alan M. 38(2); Smith, Robert N. 13(1); Venus, Mark 1; Williams, Thomas E. 8; Wilson, Ian W. 24(1).
Goals – League (54): A.Smith 19, Lynex 8 (7 pens), McAllister 7 (2 pens), Bright 6, Sealy 6, Banks 2 (1 pen), Mauchlen 2, Wilson 2, Ramsey 1, R. Smith 1.
Milk Cup (1): Wilson 1.
FA Cup (1): McAllister 1 (pen).
Ground City Stadium, Filbert Street, Leicester LE2 7FL (0533-555000)
Nearest station: London Road, Leicester
Manager: Bryan Hamilton **General Secretary:** A.K. Bennett
Colours: Blue shirts with white V-neck and double thin white pinstripes. Shorts:

white with double thin blue stripes
Record home gate: 47,298 v Tottenham Hotspur, February 1928 (FA Cup)
Honours – Champions: Division 2: 1924-25, 1936-37, 1953-54, 1956-57, 1970-71, 1979-1980
League Cup winners: 1963-64

LINCOLN CITY — DIV. 4

Cooper, Richard D.
Daniel, Peter W.
Gamble, Simon W.
Hodson, Simeon P.
Kilmore, Kevin
McGinley, John
McInnes, Ian
Mitchell, Robert
Redfearn, Neil D.
Strodder, Gary
Swinburne, Trevor
Turner, Philip
West, Gary
White, Devon W.

League Appearances: Burke, Steven J. 4(1); Collins, Stephen M. 11; Cooper, Richard D. 16(4); Daniel, Peter W. 16; Gamble, Simon W. 12(4); Greygoose, Dean 6; Harrison, Francis (1); Hodson, Simeon P. 15; Judge, Alan G. 2; Kilmore, Kevin 18; Latchford, Robert D. 14(1); McCarrick, Mark B. 13(1); McGinley, John 29; McInnes, Ian 21; McNeal, Robert M. 4; Mair, Gordon 26; Measham, Ian 6; Mitchell, Robert 14; Naylor, Stuart W. 20; Redfearn, Neil D. 43(2); Richards, Gary V. 2(5); Richards, Stephen C. 21; Strodder, Gary 41(2); Swinburne, Trevor 18; Toman, James A. 21(3); Turner, Philip 43; Ward, Warren 15(6); West, Gary 38; White, Devon W. 17(5).
Goals – League (55): Redfearn 8 (1 pen), Ward 8 (1 pen), McGinley 7, Gamble 5, Kilmore 4, Toman 4, Turner 4, Mair 3, White 3, Daniel 2, Latchford 2, McInnes 2, West 2, Strodder 1.
Milk Cup (2): Burke 1, Richards 1.
FA Cup (0).
Ground: Sincil Bank, Lincoln LN5 8LD (0522-22224)
Nearest stations: Lincoln Central and St Mark's
Manager: George Kerr **Secretary:** C.J.N. Rodman MSc
Colours: Red and white striped shirts; black shorts
Record home gate: 23,196 v Derby, November 1967 (League Cup)
Honours – Champions: Division 3 North: 1931-32, 1947-48, 1951-52; Division 4: 1975-76

LIVERPOOL — DIV. 1

Ablett, Gary I.
Beglin, James M.
Brown, John
Curry, Sean P.
Dalglish, Kenneth M.
de Mange, Kenneth J.P.P.
Durnin, John P.
Fairbrother, Ian A.
Gillespie, Gary T.
Grobbelaar, Bruce D.
Hansen, Alan D.
Harrison, Wayne
Hooper, Michael D.
Johnston, Craig P.
Lawrenson, Mark T.
Lee, Samuel
MacDonald, Kevin D.
McGregor, John R.
McMahon, Stephen
Magilton, James
Molby, Jan
Mooney, Brian J.
Mulvihill, James
Nicol, Stephen
Rush, Ian J.
Seagraves, Mark
Toale, Ian
Walsh, Paul A.
Wark, John
Watson, Alexander F.
Whelan, Ronald A.

League Appearances: Beglin, James M. 34; Dalglish, Kenneth M. 17(4); Gillespie, Gary T. 14; Grobbelaar, Bruce D. 42; Hansen, Alan D. 41; Johnston, Craig P. 38(3); Kennedy, Alan P. 8; Lawrenson, Mark T. 36(2); Lee, Samuel 13(2); McMahon, Stephen 23; MacDonald, Kevin D. 10(7); Molby, Jan 39; Neal, Philip G. 11(2); Nicol, Stephen 33(1); Rush, Ian J. 40; Walsh, Paul A. 17(3); Wark, John 7(2); Whelan, Ronald A. 39.
Goals – League (89): Rush 23, Molby 13 (6 pens), Walsh 11, Whelan 10, Johnston 7, McMahon 6, Nicol 4, Dalglish 3, Gillespie 3 (1 pen), Lawrenson 3, Wark 3, Beglin 1, MacDonald 1, Neal 1 (pen).

Milk Cup (19): Walsh 4, McMahon 3, Rush 3, Whelan 3, Molby 2 (1 pen), Dalglish 1, Johnston 1, MacDonald 1, Wark 1.
FA Cup (18): Rush 6, Molby 3 (2 pens), Wark 2, Dalglish 1, Johnston 1, Lawrenson 1, MacDonald 1, McMahon 1, Walsh 1, Whelan 1.
Ground: Anfield Road, Liverpool L4 0TH (051-263 2361)
Nearest station: All stations, Liverpool
Player/Manager: Kenny Dalglish MBE **Chief Executive/Secretary:** P.B. Robinson
Colours: Red shirts; red shorts
Record home gate: 61,905 v Wolverhampton, February 1952 (FA Cup)
Honours – Champions: Division 1: 1900-01, 1905-06, 1921-22, 1922-23, 1946-47, 1963-64, 1965-66, 1972-73, 1975-76, 1976-77, 1978-79, 1979-80, 1981-82, 1982-83, 1983-84, 1985-86; Division 2: 1893-94, 1895-96, 1904-05, 1961-62
FA Cup winners: 1964-65, 1973-74, 1985-86
League Cup winners: 1980-81, 1981-82
Milk Cup winners: 1981-82, 1982-83, 1983-84
European Champions Cup winners: 1976-77, 1977-78, 1980-81, 1983-84
UEFA Cup: 1972-73, 1975-76
Super Cup winners: 1977

LUTON TOWN — DIV. 1

Breacker, Timothy S.
Dibble, Andrew G.
Donaghy, Malachal
Foster, Stephen B.
Grimes, Agustine A.
Harford, Michael G.
Hill, Ricky A.
Johnson, Robert S.
King, Andrew E.
McEvoy, Richard P.
Newell, Michael C.
Nicholas, Peter
North, Mark V.
North, Stacey S.
Nwajiobi, Chukwuemeka
Oldfield, David C.
Preece, David W.
Sealey, Leslie J.
Stein, Brian
Stein, Earl M.S.
Thomas, Mitchell A.
Tuite, Marcus R.

League Appearances: Breacker, Timothy S. 34(2); Daniel, Raymond C. 2(3); Dibble, Andrew 7; Donaghy, Malachi 42; Elliott, Paul M. 3(3); Foster, Stephen B. 35; Grimes, Agustine A. 2(1); Harford, Michael G. 37; Hill, Ricky A. 38; Johnson, Robert S. 15; King, Andrew E. 3; Newell, Michael C. 16; Nicholas, Peter 41; North, Mark V. 9(4); North, Stacey S. 2; Nwajiobi, Chukwuemeka 20(1); Parker, Garry S. 4(4); Preece, David W. 40(1); Sealey, Leslie J. 35; Stein, Brian 33; Stein, Earl M.S. 3(3); Thomas, Mitchell A. 41.
Goals – League (61): Harford 22 (2 pens), B.Stein 14 (1 pen), Newell 6, Nwajiobi 5, Foster 3, Hill 3, M.North 3, Preece 2, Daniel 1, Thomas 1, own goals 1.
Milk Cup (5): Hill 1, North 1, Nwajiobi 1, Preece 1, B.Stein 1.
FA Cup (13): Harford 3, Hill 2, M.Stein 2, Foster 1, North 1, Preece 1, B.Stein 1, own goals 2.
Ground: 70-72 Kenilworth Road, Luton LU1 1DH (0582 411622)
Nearest station: Luton
Manager: John Moore **General Secretary:** G.H. Mackrell, FCCA
Colours: White shirts with navy and orange trim, navy shorts
Record home gate: 30,069 v Blackpool, March 1959 (FA Cup)
Honours – Champions: Division 2: 1981-82; Division 3 South: 1936-37; Division 4: 1967-68

MANCHESTER CITY — DIV. 1

Baker, Graham E.
Barrett, Earl D.
Beckford, Darren R.
Brightwell, Ian
Clarke, John T.
Kinsey, Stephen
Lillis, Mark A.
McCarthy, Michael
McMcIlroy, Samuel B.
McNab, Neil
Power, Paul C.
Redmond, Steven
Reid, Nicholas S.
Scott, Ian
Simpson, Paul D.

Clements, Kenneth H.
Crompton, Steven G.
Davies, Gordon J.
Johnson, Nigel M.
May, Andrew M.
Moulden, Paul A.
Nixon, Eric W.
Phillips, David O.
White, David
Williams, Alexander
Wilson, Clive

League Appearances: Baker, Graham E. 9(1); Barrett, Earl D. 1; Beckford, Darren R. 2(1); Clements, Kenneth H. 30; Davis, Gordon J. 26; Johnson, Nigel M. 4; Kinsey, Stephen 12(1); Lillis, Mark A. 39; McCarthy, Michael 38; McIlroy, Samuel B. 12; McNab, Neil 37; May, Andrew M. 36(1); Melrose, James M. 4(6); Moulden, Paul C. 1(1); Nixon, Eric W. 28; Phillips, David O. 39; Power, Paul C. 36; Redmond, Steven 9; Reid, Nicholas S. 30; Siddall, Barry 6; Simpson, Paul D. 30(7); Smith, Gordon D. (1); Tolmie, James 1(2); Williams, Alexander 8; Wilson, Clive 24(1).
Goals – League (43): Lillis 11 (3 pens), Davies 9, Simpson 8, Wilson 5, McNab 4, McIlroy 1, Melrose 1, Phillips 1, Power 1, own goals 2.
Milk Cup (5): Melrose 2, Davies 1, Lillis 1, Wilson 1.
FA Cup (5): Davies 2, Simpson 2, Kinsey 1.
Ground: Maine Road, Moss Side, Manchester M14 7WN (061-226 1191/3)
Nearest station: Manchester Piccadilly
Manager: Billy McNeill M.B.E. **Secretary:** J.B. Halford
Colours: Sky blue shirts with white trim; shorts white with blue trim
Record home gate: 84,569 v Stoke City, March 1934 (FA Cup)
Honours – Champions: Division 1: 1936-37, 1967-68; Division 2: 1898-99, 1902-03, 1909-10, 1927-28, 1946-47, 1965-66
FA Cup winners: 1903-04, 1933-34, 1955-56, 1968-69
League Cup winners: 1969-70, 1975-76
European Cup-Winner's Cup winners: 1969-70

MANCHESTER UNITED DIV. 1

Albiston, Arthur R.
Bailey, Gary R.
Barnes, Peter S.
Blackmore, Clayton G.
Brazil, Alan B.
Cronin, Denis
Davenport, Peter
Dempsey, Mark J.
Digby, Fraser C.
Duxbury, Michael
Garton, William F.
Gibson, Colin J.
Gibson, Terence B.
Gill, Anthony G.D.
Gidman, John
Hanrahan, Joseph G.
Higgins, Mark N.
Hogg, Graeme J.
Hughes, Leslie M.
McBride, Andrew
McGrath, Paul
Martin, Lee A.
Moran, Kevin B.
Moses, Remi M.
Murphy, Aidan J.
Olsen, Jesper
Ratcliffe, Simon
Robson, Bryan
Russell, Martin C.
Sivebaek, John
Stapleton, Francis A.
Strachan, Gordon D.
Todd, Mark K.
Turner, Christopher R.
Walsh, Gary
Whiteside, Norman
Wood, Nicholas A.

League Appearances: Albiston, Arthur R. 37; Barnes, Peter S. 12(1); Bailey, Gary R. 25; Blackmore, Clayton G. 12; Brazil, Alan B. 1(10); Davenport, Peter 11; Dempsey, Mark J. 1; Duxbury, Michael 21(2); Garton, William F. 10; Gibson, Colin J. 18; Gibson, Terence B. 2(5); Gidman, John 24; Hogg, Graeme, J. 17; Higgins, Mark N. 6; Hughes, Leslie M. 40; McGrath, Paul 40; Moran, Kevin B. 18(1); Moses, Remi M. 4; Olsen, Jesper 25(3); Robson, Bryan 21; Sivebaek, John 2(1); Stapleton, Francis A. 34(7); Strachan, Gordon D. 27(1); Turner, Christopher R. 17; Whiteside, Norman 37; Wood, Nicholas A. (1).
Goals – League (70): Hughes 17, Olsen 11 (4 pens), Robson 7 (2 pens), Stapleton 7, C.Gibson 5, Strachan 5 (1 pen), Whiteside 4, Blackmore 3, Brazil 3, McGrath 3, Barnes 2, Albiston 1, Davenport 1 (pen), Duxbury 1.
Milk Cup (4): Whiteside 2, Barnes 1, McGrath 1.
FA Cup (5): Olsen 2 (1 pen), Hughes 1, Stapleton 1, Whiteside 1.
Ground: Old Trafford, Manchester M16 0RA (061-872 1661/3)
Nearest station: All stations Manchester
Manager: Ron Atkinson **Secretary:** R.L. Olive

Colours: Red shirts with black and white trim, white shorts
Record home gate: 76,962 FA Cup semi-final (Wolverhampton v Grimsby Town) March 1939; **Club:** 70,504 v Aston Villa, December 1920 (League)
Honours – Champions: Division 1: 1907-08, 1910-11, 1951-52, 1955-56, 1956-57, 1964-65, 1966-67; Division 2: 1935-36, 1974-75
FA Cup winners: 1908-09, 1947-48, 1962-63, 1976-77, 1982-83, 1984-85
European Champions Cup Winners: 1967-68

MANSFIELD TOWN DIV. 3

Beasley, Andrew
Cassells, Keith B.
Chamberlain, Neville P.
Coleman, Simon
Collins, Roderick
Foster, George W.
Garner, Paul
Graham, Michael A.
Hitchcock, Kevin
Kearney, Mark J.
Kent, Kevin J.
Logan, David
Lowery, Anthony W.
McKernon, Craig A.
Pollard, Gary
Robinson, Leslie
Whatmore, Neil

League Appearances: Cassells, Keith B. 40; Chamberlain, Neville P. 39(1); Collins, Roderick 7(5); Foster, George W. 46; Galloway, Michael 4(2); Garner, Paul 28; Graham, Michael A. 45; Gunn, Brynley C. 5; Hitchcock, Kevin 46; Kearney, Mark J. 31; Kent, Kevin J. 31(1); Kenworthy, Anthony D. 13; Logan, David 24; Lowery, Anthony W. 40; Luke, Noel E. 8(6); McKernon, Craig A. 7(4); Pollard, Gary 35; Robinson, Leslie 6(1); Stringfellow, Ian R. (3); Vinter, Michael 21; Whatmore, Neil 30(1).
Goals – League (74): Chamberlain 16, Cassells 13, Whatmore 9, Kent 8, Kearney 7 (3 pens), Lowery 5, Garner 4, Vinter 4, Luke 3, Logan 1, Pollard 1, own goals 3.
Milk Cup (8): Chamberlain 2, Vinter 2, Cassells 1, Graham 1, Kearney 1, Pollard 1.
FA Cup (1): Chamberlain 1.
Ground: Field Mill, Quarry Lane, Mansfield Nottingham NG18 5DA (0623-23567)
Nearest station: Mansfield, Alfreton Parkway
Manager: Ian Greaves **Secretary:** J.D. Eaton
Colours: Amber shirts with blue trim, amber shorts with blue stripe down side
Record home gate: 24,657 v Nottingham Forest, January 1953 (FA Cup)
Honours – Champions: Division 3: 1976-77; Division 4: 1974-75

MIDDLESBROUGH DIV. 3

Beagrie, Peter S.
Cook, Mitchell C.
Cooper, Colin T.
Corden, Stephen
Gill, Gary
Hamilton, Gary J.
Kernaghan, Alan N.
Laws, Brian
Mowbray, Anthony M.
O'Riordan, Donald J.
Otto, Hendrikus M.
Pallister, Gary A.
Parkinson, Gary
Pears, Stephen
Ripley, Stuart E.
Rowell, Gary
Slaven, Bernard
Stephens, Arthur
Turnbull, Lee M.

League Appearances: Beagrie, Peter S. 21(5); Cook, Mitchell 3(3); Cooper, Colin T. 9(2); Corden, Stephen 1; Currie, David N. 21(5); Gill, Gary 9; Hamilton, Gary J. 33; Heard, Timothy P. 25; Kernaghan, Alan N. 2(4); Kite, Philip D. 2; Laws, Brian 42; McAndrew, Anthony 34; McManus, Charles E. 2; Mowbray, Anthony M. 35; Nattrass, Irving 19; O'Riordan, Donald J. 41; Pallister, Gary A. 28; Pears, Stephen 38; Ripley, Stuart E. 7(1); Roberts, Alan 1; Rowell, Gary 27; Slaven, Bernard 32; Stephens, Arthur 26(2); Turnbull, Lee M. 1(1); Ward, Paul T. 3.
Goals – League (44): Rowell 10 (2 pens), Slaven 8 (1 pen), Currie 4, Hamilton 4, Mowbray 4, Stevens 4, Heard 2, Laws 2, McAndrew 2, O'Riordan 2, Beagrie 1, own goals 1.

Milk Cup (4): Rowell 2 (1 pen), Currie 1, own goals 1.
FA Cup (1): O'Riordan 1.
Ground: Ayresome Park, Middlesbrough TS1 4PB (0642-819659)
Nearest station: Middlesbrough
Manager: Bruce Rioch **Secretary:** David A. Thorne
Colours: Red shirts with white chest band, red arrow on white piping across shoulders and down sleeves; white shorts with red arrow piping down sides
Record home gate: 53,596 v Newcastle United, December 1949 (League)
Honours – Champions: Division 2: 1926-27, 1928-29, 1973-74

MILLWALL DIV. 2

Briley, Leslie	Lovell, Stephen J.	Sansome, Paul E.
Chatterton, Nicholas J.	Lowndes, Stephen R.	Sheringham, Edward P.
Coleman, Nicholas	McLeary, Alan T.	Smith, Lindsay J.
Hinshelwood, Paul A.	Morgan, Darren J.	Stevens, Keith H.
Horne, Brian S.	Nutton, Michael W.	Walker, Alan
Leslie, John A.	Otulakowski, Antoni	Wilson, Robert J.

League Appearances: Briley, Leslie 39; Chatterton, Nicholas J. 15(2); Coleman, Nicholas 6; Fashanu, John 25; Granville, John 6; Hinshelwood, Paul A. 34(2); Kinsella, Anthony S. 13(1); Leslie, John A. 9(7); Lovell, Stephen J. 42; Lowndes, Stephen R. 39; McLeary, Alan T. 32(3); Nutton, Michael W. 22; Otulakowski, Antoni 23; Roffey, William R. 11(1); Sansome, Paul 36; Sheringham, Edward P. 9(9); Smith, Lindsay J. 14; Stevens, Keith H. 33; Walker, Alan 26; Wilson, Robert J. 28.
Goals – League (64): Lovell 14 (3 pens), Wilson 12 (3 pens), Fashanu 8, Lowndes 6, Chatterton 4 (2 pens), Sheringham 4, McLeary 3, Walker 3, Hinshelwood 2, Briley 1, Kinsella 1, Leslie 1, Nutton 1, Roffey 1, Stevens 1, own goals 2.
Milk Cup (7): Lovell 3 (2 pens), Fashanu 2, Leslie 1, Lowndes 1.
FA Cup (5): Fashanu 2, Lovell 1, McLeary 1, Walker 1.
Ground: The Den, Cold Blow Lane, London SE14 5RH (01-639 3143/4)
Nearest stations: New Cross or New Cross Gate (SR and Metropolitan line)
Manager: John Docherty **Secretary:** Mrs S. Shaw
Colours: Blue shirts with white trim; white shorts with blue trim
Record home gate: 48,672 v Derby County, February 1937 (FA Cup)
Honours – Champions: Division 3 South: 1927-28, 1937-38; Division 4: 1961-62

NEWCASTLE UNITED DIV. 1

Allon, Joseph B.	Gascoigne, Paul J.	Rutherford, Paul
Anderson, John	Haddock, Peter M.	Scott, Kevin W.
Bailey, John A.	Harbach, Peter C.	Stephenson, Paul
Beardsley, Peter A.	Kelly, Gary A.	Stewart, Ian E.
Bogie, Ian	McCreery, David	Thomas, Martin R.
Clarke, Jeffrey D.	McDonald, Neil R.	Tinnion, Brian
Cunningham, Anthony E.	Nesbit, Tony	Wharton, Kenneth
Davies, Alan	Roeder, Glenn V.	Whitehurst, William

League Appearances: Allon, Joseph B. 3; Anderson, John 38; Bailey, John A. 28; Beardsley, Peter A. 42; Clarke, Jeffrey D. 41; Cunningham, Anthony E. 10(7); Davies, Alan 14; Gascoigne, Paul J. 28(3); Haddock, Peter M. 6; Hedworth, Christopher 4; McCreery, David 39(2); McDonald, Neil R. 23(5); Mc Kellar, David 10; McKinnon, Robert 1; Megson, Gary J. 2(2); Reilly, George G. 17; Roeder, Glenn V. 42; Stephenson, Paul 22; Stewart, Ian 25(3); Thomas, Martin R. 32; Wharton, Kenneth 15; Whitehurst, William 20.
Goals – League (67): Beardsley 19 (1 pen), Gascoigne 9, Reilly 7, Whitehurst 7, Roeder 6, McDonald 4, Anderson 3, Clarke 3, Stewart 2, Wharton 2, Allon 1,

Cunningham 1, Davies 1, Stephenson 1, own goals 1.
Milk Cup (2): Cunningham 2.
FA Cup (0).
Ground: St James' Park, Newcastle-upon-Tyne NE1 4ST (0632 328361 information service 611571)
Nearest station: Newcastle Central
Manager: Willie McFaul **Secretary:** R. Cushing
Colours: Black and white vertical striped shirts; black shorts
Record home gate: 68,386 v Chelsea, September 1930 (League)
Honours – Champions: Division 1: 1904-05, 1906-07, 1908-09, 1926-27; Division 2: 1964-65
FA Cup winners: 1909-10, 1923-24, 1931-32, 1950-51, 1951-52, 1954-55
European Fairs' Cup winners: 1968-69
Anglo-Italian Cup winners: 1973

NEWPORT COUNTY DIV. 3

Berry, Stephen A.
Boyle, Terence D.J.
Carter, Roy W.
Freestone, Roger
James, Leighton
Jones, Linden
Jones, Peter
Kendall, Mark
Lewis, John
Mardenborough, Stephen A.
Peacock, Darren
Pulis, Anthony R.
Staniforth, Gordon

League Appearances: Berry, Stephen A. 26; Boyle, Terence D.J. 46; Carter, Roy W. 42; Dowman, Stephen J. 9; Gill, Kenneth J. 13(6); Hamer, Kevin (1); James, Leighton 21(7); Jones, Linden 31; Jones, Peter 36; Kendall, Mark 46; Latchford, Robert D. 20; Lewis, John 44; McManus, Stuart J. 4(1); Mardenborough, Stephen A. 30(9); Mayes, Alan K. 3; Miles, Andrew 3(1); Moore, John 2; Peacock, Darren 14(4); Pulis, Anthony R. 38(2); Reck, Sean M. 15; Relish, John D. 12(2); Rogers, Graham R. 6(1); Staniforth, Gordon 45; Tyler, Simon (2).
Goals – League (52): Staniforth 9 (3 pens), Boyle 7, Carter 7 (1 pen), Mardenborough 7, Latchford 6, Berry 3, James 2, Miles 2, Relish 2, Dowman 1, Gill 1, L. Jones 1, P. Jones 1, Lewis 1, Mayes 1, own goals 2.
Milk Cup (1): Beck 1.
FA Cup (5): Berry 1, Boyle 1, James 1, P. Jones 1, Mardenborough 1.
Ground: Somerton Park, Newport, Gwent NPT OHZ (0633 277543)
Nearest station: Newport
Player/Manager: John Relish **Secretary:** K. Saunders
Colours: Amber shirts with black collar, shorts black with amber stripe
Record home gate: 24,268 v Cardiff, October 1937 (League)
Honours – Champions: Division 3 South: 1938-39

NORTHAMPTON TOWN DIV. 4

Benjamin, Ian T.
Bushell, Mark
Chard, Phillip J.
Curtis, Paul A.E.
Donald, Warren R.
Gleasure, Peter
Hill, Richard W.
Lewis, Russell
McPherson, Keith A.
Mann, Adrian G.
Morley, Trevor W.
Reed, Graham
Schiavi, Mark A.
Sugrue, Paul A.

League Appearances: Benjamin, Ian T. 46; Cavener, Philip 13(4); Chard, Phillip J. 41; Curtis, Paul A.E. 27; Dawes, Ian M. 3(2); Donald, Warren A. 32; Friar, John P. 14; Garner, Timothy J. 2; Gleasure, Peter 44; Hamill, Stewart P. 3; Hill, Richard W. 41; Lewis, Russell 43; McPherson, Keith A. 20; Mann, Adrian G. 25(7); Morley, Trevor W. 43; Mundee, Brian G. 31; Nebbeling, Gavin M. 11; Reed, Graham 34(2); Schiavi, Mark A. 31(3); Sugrue, Paul A. 2(6).
Goals – League (79): Benjamin 22 (1 pen), Hill 17 (1 pen), Morley 13, Chard 7 (2 pens), Schiavi 5, Cavener 4 (3 pens), Donald 3, Mann 2, Sugrue 2, Curtis 1,

Hamill 1, Reed 1, own goals 1.
Milk Cup (3): Benjamin 1, Cavener 1 (pen), Chard 1.
FA Cup (0).
Ground: County Ground, Abington Avenue, Northampton NN1 4PS (0604 721103)
Nearest station: Northampton
Manager: Graham Carr **Secretary/General Manager:** Dave Bowen
Colours: White shirts, maroon sleeves and collar; white shorts
Record home gate: 24,523 v Fulham, April 1966 (League)
Honours – Champions: Division 3: 1962-63

NORWICH CITY DIV. 1

Barham, Mark F.
Benstead, Graham
Biggins, Wayne
Brooke, Garry J.
Brown, Kenneth J.
Bruce, Stephen R.
Chapple, Phillip R.
Clayton, Paul S.
Culverhouse, Ian B.
Deehan, John M.
Donowa, Brian J.
Drinkell, Kevin S.
Folkes, Paul A.
Fox, Ruel A.
Garwood, Richard J.
Gordon, Dale A.
Goss, Jeremy
Haylock, Paul
Lim, Harvey C.
Mendham, Peter S.
Metcalf, Mark
Phelan, Michael C.
Pritchard, Steven J.
Rosario, Robert M.
Spearing, Anthony
Watson, David
Williams, David M.
Woods, Christopher C.E.
Van Wyk, Dennis J.

League Appearances: Barham, Mark F. 35; Biggins, Wayne 28; Brooke, Garry J. 8(5); Bruce, Stephen R. 42; Clayton, Paul S. 1; Culverhouse, Ian B. 30; Deehan, John M. 22(4); Donowa, Brian L. (2); Drinkell, Kevin S. 41; Gordon, Dale A. 3(3); Haylock, Paul 12; Mendham, Peter S. 35; Phelan, Michael C. 42; Rosario, Robert M. 8; Spearing, Anthony 7(1); Van Wyjk, Dennis J. 27(2); Watson, David 42; Williams, David M. 37(2); Woods, Christopher C.E. 42.
Goals – League (84): Drinkell 22, Barham 9, Bruce 8, Mendham 8, Williams 8 (3 pens), Biggins 7, Deehan 4 (1 pen), Phelan 3, Watson 3, Brooke 2, Rosario 2, Gordon 1, Haylock 1, Van Wyk 1, own goals 5.
Milk Cup (6): Bruce 2, Brooke 1, Drinkell 1, Mendham 1, Rosario 1.
FA Cup (0).
Ground: Carrow Road Stadium, Norwich NR1 1JE (0603 612131)
Nearest station: Norwich Thorpe
Manager: Ken Brown **Secretary:** Nigel Pleasants
Colours: Yellow shirts; green shorts with yellow trim
Record home gate: 43,984 v Leicester, March 1963 (FA Cup)
Honours – Champions: Division 2: 1971-72, 1985-86; Division 3 South: 1933-34
FA Cup winners: Nil
League Cup winners: 1961-62
Milk Cup winners: 1984-1985

NOTTINGHAM FOREST DIV. 1

Andrews, Gary M.
Birtles, Garry
Butterworth, Ian S.
Campbell, David A.
Carr, Franz A.
Clough, Nigel H.
Fairclough, Courtney H.
Fleming, James G.
Heyes, Darren L.
Metgod, Johannes A.B.
Mills, Gary R.
Murphy, Colin C.
Murray, Steven
Palin, Leigh G.
Pearce, Stuart
Rice, Brian
Riley, David S.
Segers, Johannes C.A.
Sinclair, Ronald M.
Smalley, Mark A.
Sutton, Stephen J.
Walker, Desmond S.
Walsh, Colin D.
Webb, Neil J.
Williams, Brett
Wilson, Terry

League Appearances: Birtles, Garry 24(1); Bowyer, Ian 25(1); Butterworth, Ian S. 22(1); Campbell, David A. 14(4); Carr, Franz A. 23; Clough, Nigel H. 37(2); Davenport, Peter 27; Fleming, James G. 16; Hodge, Stephen B. 2; McInally, James E. 12; Metgod, Johannes A.B. 37(2); Mills, Gary R. 13(1); Pearce, Stuart 30; Rice, Brian 19; Robertson, John N. 10(1); Segers, Johannes A.B. 11; Sutton, Stephen J. 31; Walker, Desmond S. 36(3); Walsh, Colin D. 16(4); Webb, Neil J. 38; Wigley, Steven 8; Williams, Brett 11.
Goals – League (69): Clough 15 (2 pens), Webb 14, Davenport 13 (3 pens), Metgod 6, Walsh 6, Bowyer 3, Campbell 3, Carr 3, Rice 3, Pearce 1, own goals 2.
Milk Cup (10): Clough 3, Campbell 2, Rice 2, Carr 1, Davenport 1, Metgod 1.
FA Cup (3): Birtles 2, Walsh 1.
Ground: City Ground, Pavilion Road, Nottingham NG2 5FJ (0602 822202)
Nearest station: Nottingham Midland
Manager: Brian Clough **Secretary:** K. Smales
Colours: Red shirts; white shorts
Record home gate: 49,945 v Manchester United, October, 1967 (League)
Honours – Champions: Division 1: 1977-78; Division 2: 1906-07, 1921-22; Division 3 South: 1950-51
FA Cup winners: 1897-98, 1958-59
League Cup winners: 1977-78, 1978-79
European Champions Cup Winners: 1978-79, 1979-80

NOTTS COUNTY DIV. 3

Barnes, Paul L.
Benjamin, Tristan
Clarke, David A.
Davis, Darren J.
Downing, Keith G.
Edge, Declan J.
Fairclough, Wayne R.
Goodwin, Mark A.
Hunt, David
Leonard, Michael C.
McParland, Ian J.
Sims, Stephen F.
Smalley, Paul T.
Waitt, Michael H.
Yates, Dean R.
Young, Alexander F.

League Appearances: Barnes, Paul L. 11(3); Benjamin, Tristan 43; Clarke, David A. 41(1); Dalton, Richard T. 1; Davies, John G. 10; Davis, Darren J. 22; Daws, Anthony (1); Downing, Keith G. 3; Edge, Declan J. 7(3); Fairclough, Wayne R. 5; Goodwin, Mark A. 43; Harbottle, Mark S. 1(3); Harkouk, Rachid P. 19(1); Hesford, Iain 10; Hunt, David 34; Jackson, Craig (1); Kevan, David J. 2(1); Leonard, Michael C. 23; McParland, Ian J. 43(1); Mimms, Robert A. 2; Richards, Peter 19 (1); Robinson, Mark J. 3(9); Sims, Stephen F. 41; Smalley, Paul T. 24(2); Waitt, Michael H. 36(1); Yates, Dean R. 44; Young, Alexander F. 19.
Goals – League (71): McParland 15 (1 pen), Waitt 14, Hunt 8, Harkouk 7 (1 pen), Goowin 6 (2 pens), Young 6, Barnes 4, Yates 4, Edge 2, Clarke 1, Davis 1, Harbottle 1, Robinson 1, own goals 1.
Milk Cup (5): Clarke 1, Goodwin 1, Harkouk 1, McParland 1, Young 1.
FA Cup (13): McParland 4, Harkouk 3, Waitt 3, Hunt 2, Clarke 1, Young 1.
Ground: Meadow Lane, Nottingham NG2 3HJ (0602 861155)
Nearest station: Nottingham
Manager: Jimmy Sirrell **Secretary:** N.E. Hook, M.Inst.M.
Colours: Black and white striped shirts; black shorts with thin white stripes on side
Record home gate: 47,310 v York, March 1955 (FA Cup)
Honours – Champions: Division 2: 1896-97, 1913-14, 1922-23; Division 3 South: 1930-31, 1949-50; Division 4: 1970-71
FA Cup winners: 1893-94

OLDHAM ATHLETIC DIV. 2

Atkinson, Paul G.
Barlow, Andrew J.
Goram, Andrew L.
Gorton, Andrew W.
McGuire, Michael J.
Milligan, Michael J.

Bullock, Steven	Henry, Anthony	Palmer, Roger N.
Cecere, Michael J.	Hoolickin, Gary J.	Ryan, John B.
Colville, Robert J.	Jones, Paul B.	Williams, Gary A.
Donachie, William	Linigham, Andrew	
Futcher, Ronald	McDonough, Darron K.	

League Appearances: Atkinson, Paul G. 26; Barlow, Andrew J. 26; Bullock, Steven 4(4); Colville, Robert J. 13(4); Donachie, William 33; Fairclough, David 6(11); Futcher, Ronald 40; Goram, Andrew L. 41; Gorton, Andrew W. 1; Henry, Anthony 40; Hoolickin, Gary J. 32; Jones, Paul B. 18; Linighan, Andrew 15; McDonough, Darron K. 20; McGuire, Michael J. 40; Milligan, Michael J. 5; O'Callaghan, Brendan R. 1; Palmer, Roger N. 41; Quinn, Michael 24(2); Ryan, John B. 19(3); Smith, Gordon D. 14(1); Williams, Gary A. 3(6).
Goals – League (62): Futcher 17 (1 pen), Palmer 15, Quinn 11 (2 pens), Henry 7, Colville 2, McGuire 2, Atkinson 1, Fairclough 1, Jones 1, Linighan 1, M.Mill igan 1, Williams 1, own goals 2.
Milk Cup (2): Fairclough 2.
FA Cup (1): Palmer 1.
Ground: Boundary Park, Oldham OL1 2PA (061-624 8110 information service 4972)
Nearest station: Oldham, Werneth and Oldham Mumps
Manager: Joe Royle **Secretary:** T.M. Finn
Colours: Blue shirts, with white and red trim; white shorts with blue and red stripe on side
Record home gate: 47,671 v Sheffield Wednesday, January 1930 (FA Cup)
Honours – Champions: Division 3 North: 1952-53; Division 3: 1973-74

ORIENT DIV. 4

Brooks, Shaun	Godfrey, Kevin	Mountford, Peter
Castle, Stephen C.	Greygoose, Dean	Shinners, Paul
Comfort, Alan	Hales, Kevin P.	Sitton, John E.
Cornwell, John A.	Harvey, Lee D.	Sussex, Andrew R.
Cunningham, Thomas E.	John, Stephen P.	Wells, Peter A.
Dickenson, Kevin J.	Jones, Christopher H.	
Foster, Colin J.	Juryeff, Ian M.	

League Appearances: Brooks, Shaun 35(3); Castle, Stephen C. 19(4); Comfort, Alan 15; Corbett, Patrick A. 10; Cornwell, John A. 41(3); Cunningham, Thomas E. 13; Dickenson, Kevin J. 46; Foster, Colin J. 36; Godfrey, Kevin 13(3); Greygoose, Dean 1; Hales, Kevin P. 31; Harvey, Lee D. 11(1); John, Stephen P. 8; Jones, Christopher H. 40(1); Juryeff, Ian M. 25(2); Mountford, Peter 11(4); Shinners, Paul 32(2); Sitton, John E. 39; Sussex, Andrew R. 35(1); Wells, Peter A. 45.
Goals – League (79): Shinners 16, Juryeff 10, Jones 9, Cornwell 8, Brooks 7 (3 pens), Comfort 5, Castle 4, Godfrey 4, Sussex 4, Cunningham 2, Foster 2, Hales 2, Harvey 2, Dickenson 1, Mountford 1, own goals 2.
Milk Cup (7): Godfrey 3, Brooks 1, Jones 1, Shinners 1, Sussex 1.
FA Cup (13): Brooks 3 (1 pen), Juryeff 3, Shinners 2, Castle 1, Cornwell 1, Foster 1, Godfrey 1, Jones 1.
Ground: Leyton Stadium, Brisbane Road, Leyton, E10 5NE (01-539 2223/4)
Nearest station: Leyton (Central line)
Manager: Frank Clark **Secretary:** Miss C. Stokes
Colours: All red
Record home gate: 34,345 v West Ham United, January 1964 (FA Cup)
Honours – Champions: Division 3: 1969-70; Division 3 South: 1955-56

OXFORD UNITED DIV. 1

Aldridge, John W.
Briggs, Gary
Brock, Kevin S.
Charles, Jeremy M.
Dreyer, John B.
Fogg, David
Hamilton, William R.
Hardwick, Steven
Hebberd, Trevor N.
Houghton, Raymond J.
Jones, Mark
Judge, Alan G.
Langan, David
Leworthy, David J.
McDermott, Brian J.
McDonald, Robert W.
Obi, Anthony L.
Perryman, Stephen J.
Phillips, Leslie M.
Reck, Sean M.
Rhoades-Brown, Peter
Shotton, Malcolm
Slatter, Neil J.
Thomas, Andrew M.
Trewick, John

League Appearances: Aldridge, John W. 39; Barnet, Gary L. (2); Briggs, Gary 38; Brock, Kevin S. 18(5); Charles, Jeremy M. 23(5); Hamilton, William R. 8; Hardwick, Steven 23; Hebberd, Trevor N. 41; Houghton, Raymond J. 35; Jones, Mark 4(2); Judge, Alan G. 19; Langan, David 32(2); Leworthy, David J. 7; McDermott, Brian J. 2(2); McDonald, Robert W. 14; Perryman, Stephen J. 9; Phillips, Leslie M. 28; Rhoades-Brown, Peter 12(5); Shotton, Malcolm 42; Slatter, Neil J. 22; Thomas, Andrew M. 12(5); Trewick, John 34(1).
Goals – League (62): Aldridge 23 (5 pens), Charles 9, Houghton 4, Leworthy 4, Hamilton 3, Hebberd 3, McDonald 3, Rhoades-Brown 3, Trewick 3 (pens), Phillips 2, Slatter 2, Thomas 2, own goals 1.
Milk Cup (20): Aldridge 5 (1 pen), Phillips 3, Thomas 3, Charles 2, Hebberd 2, Houghton 2, Briggs 1, Rhoades-Brown 1, Slatter 1.
FA Cup (2): Aldridge 1, Slatter 1.
Ground: Manor Ground, Beech Road, Headington, Oxford OX3 7RS (0865-61503)
Nearest station: Oxford
Manager: Maurice Evans **Secretary:** Jim A. Hunt
Colours: Yellow shirts with navy blue trim; navy blue shorts
Record home gate: 22,730 v Preston, February 1964 (FA Cup)
Honours – Champions: Division 2: 1984-85; Division 3: 1967-68, 1983-84
Milk Cup Winners: 1985-86

PETERBOROUGH UNITED DIV. 4

Collins, Stephen M.
Gage, Wakely A.J.
Gallagher, Jackie C.
Paris, Alan
Pike, Martin R.
Quow, Trevor
Shepherd, Jamie G.
Slack, Trevor C.
Worrall, Gary G.

League Appearances: Astbury, Michael J. 4; Cassidy, Francis J. 13(2); Cavener, Philip 9(1); Collins, Stephen M. 21(1); Corder, Peter R. 2; Fuccillo, Pasquale 45; Gage, Wakeley A.J. 27; Gallagher, Jackie C. 40(2); Holmes, James 15; Johnson, David N. 2(3); Kelly, Errington E. 15(6); Kowalski, Andrew M. 35; McClure, Douglas H. 4; McManus, Charles E. 18; Nuttell, Michael J. 1(2); Paris, Alan 46; Pike, Martin R. 46; Quow, Trevor 29(1); Rees, Anthony A. 5: Shepherd, Jamie G. 23(2); Slack, Trevor C. 39(1); Turner, John G. 22; Whymark, Trevor J. 3; Wile, John D. 13(1); Worrall, Gary G. 29(1).
Goals – League (52): Gallagher 11, Shepherd 6, Slack 5, Worrall 5, Holmes 4 (3 pens), Kelly 4, Kowalski 4, Fuccillo 3, Quow 3, Cassidy 2, Pike 2, Rees 2, own goals 1.
Milk Cup (0).
FA Cup (10): Shepherd 3, Gallagher 2, Cassidy 1, Kelly 1, Kowalski 1, Worrall 1, own goals 1.
Ground: London Road Ground, Peterborough PE2 8AL (0733 63947)
Nearest station: Peterborough
Manager: John Wile **Secretary:** A.V. Blades
Colours: Blue shirts with white trim; blue shorts with white trim
Record home gate: 30,096 v Swansea, February 1965 (FA Cup)
Honours – Champions: Division 4: 1960-61, 1973-74

PLYMOUTH ARGYLE DIV. 2

Burrows, Adrian M.	Crudgington, Geoffrey	Nelson, Garry
Clayton, John	Goodyear, Clive	Nisbet, Gordon J.M.
Cooper, Leigh V.	Hodges, Kevin	Rowbotham, Darran
Cooper, Stephen B.	McElhinney, Gerrard	Summerfield, Kevin
Coughlin, Russell	Matthews, John M.	Uzzell, John E.

League Appearances: Brimacombe, John 1; Burrows, Adrian M. 7; Clayton, John 36; Cooper, Leigh V. 39(1); Cooper, Stephen B. 34(4); Coughlin, Russell 44(1); Crudgington, Geoffrey 46; Godfrey, Kevin 7; Goodyear, Clive 41; Hodges, Kevin 46; McElhinney, Gerrard 44; Matthews, John M. 29(2); Nelson, Garry 41(1); Nisbet, Gordon J.M. 46; Rowbotham, Darran 7(7); Summerfield, Kevin 21(5); Tynan, Thomas E. 9; Uzzell, John E. 8.
Goals – League (88): S.Hodges 16, Nelson 13, Clayton 12, Coughlin 10 (7 pens), Tynan 9, S.Cooper 8 (4 pens), Summerfield 7, Burrows 2, Goodyear 2, McElhinney 2 (pens), Brimacombe 1, L.Cooper 1, Godfrey 1, Holmes 1, Matthews 1, Rowbotham 1, own goals 2.
Milk Cup (2): McElhinney 1, Summerfield 1.
FA Cup (6): Cooper 2, Clayton 1, Coughlin 1, Nelson 1, Summerfield 1.
Ground: Home Park, Plymouth, Devon PL2 1BQ (0752 52561)
Nearest station: Plymouth North Road
Manager: Dave Smith **Secretary:** Graham Little
Colours: Green shirts; black shorts
Record home gate: 43,596 v Aston Villa, October 1936 (League)
Honours – Champions: Division 3 South: 1929-30, 1951-52; Division 3: 1958-59

PORTSMOUTH DIV. 2

Angell, Darren	Hilaire, Vincent	Russell, Kevin J.
Ball, Kevin	Kennedy, Michael F.	Sandford, Lee R.
Blake, Noel L.	Knight, Alan E.	Swain, Kenneth M.
Dillon, Kevin P.	McGarvey, Scott T.	Tait, Michael P.
Gilbert, William A.	Morgan, Nicholas	Waldron, Malcolm
Gosney, Andrew R.	O'Callaghan, Kevin	Wood, Paul A.
Hardyman, Paul G.	Quinn, Michael	

League Appearances: Ball, Kevin 9; Blake, Noel L. 42; Channon, Michael R. 34; Christensen, Tommy 3; Dillon, Kevin P. 30(1); Doyle, Robert 1; Gilbert, William A. 36; Gosney, Andrew R. 4; Hardyman, Paul G. 21; Hilaire, Vincent 41; Kennedy, Michael F. 39; Knight, Alan E. 38; McGarvey, Scott T. 2(3); Money, Richard 1; Morgan, Nicholas 28(2); O'Callaghan, Kevin 39; Quinn, Michael 11; Russell, Kevin J. (1); Sandford, Lee R. 6(1); Stanley, Gary E. 4(2); Sugrue, Paul 1(2); Swain, Kenneth M. 39; Tait, Michael P. 23(3); Wood, Paul A. 10(15).
Goals – League (69): Morgan 14, O'Callaghan 11, Hilaire 8, Channon 6, Quinn 6 (1 pen), Dillon 5 (4 pens), Blake 4, Wood 4, Christensen 2, Kennedy 2, Tait 2, Hardyman 1, McGarvey 1, own goals 3.
Milk Cup (9): Dillon 2 (pens), Blake 1, Morgan 1, O'Callaghan 1, Sandford 1, Stanley 1, Tait 1, Wood 1.
FA Cup (4): Stanley 2 (1 pen), Blake 1, Dillon 1 (pen).
Ground: Fratton Park, Frogmore Road, Portsmouth, PO4 8RA (0705 734129)
Nearest station: Fratton or Portsmouth and Southsea
Manager: Alan Ball **Secretary:** W.J.B. Davis
Colours: Blue shirts; white shorts
Record home gate: 51,385 v Derby County, February 1949 (FA Cup)
Honours – Champions: Division 1: 1948-49, 1949-50; Division 3 South; 1923-24; Division 3: 1961-62
FA Cup winners: 1938-39

PORT VALE — DIV. 3

Banks, Christopher
Bowden, John
Bromage, Russel
Earle, Robert
Ebanks, Michael W.A.
Hunter, Geoffrey
Jones, Andrew
McGuire, Paul B.
Sproson, Philip J.
Webb, Alan R.
Williams, Oshor J.
Williams, William J.

League Appearances: Arnold, James 41; Banks, Christopher 15(4); Biggins, Stephen J. 1(3); Bowden, John 35(1); Bromage, Russel 39(1); Brown, Alistair 22(5); Cammack, Stephen R. 1(2); Earle, Robert 46; Ebanks, Michael W.R. 9(3); Griffiths, Peter J. 2(3); Hunter, Geoffrey 45; Johnson, Jeffrey D. 10; Jones, Andrew 38(3); McGuire, Paul B. 45; Pearce, Christopher L. 5; Shankland, Andrew J. 2; Sproson, Philip J. 44; Webb, Alan R. 39; Williams, Oshor 31(1); Williams, William J. 36.
Goals – League (67): Earle 15, Jones 12 (4 pens), Maguire 10 (4 pens), Brown 5, Hunter 5, Sproson 4, Bowden 3, J.Williams 3, O.Williams 3, Banks 1, Bromage 1, Griffiths 1, Johnson 1, Shankland 1, Webb 1, own goals 1.
Milk Cup (5): Jones 2, Earle 1, Maguire 1, Sproson 1.
FA Cup (3): Brown 1, Earle 1, Maguire 1 (pen).
Ground: Vale Park, Hamil Road, Burslem, Stoke-on-Trent ST6 1AW (0782 814134)
Nearest station: Longport, and Stoke-on-Trent
Manager: John Rudge **Secretary:** R.J. Fairfax
Colours: White shirts with black stripes; black shorts
Record home gate: 50,000 v Aston Villa, February 1960 (FA Cup)
Honours – Champions: Division 3 North: 1929-30, 1953-54; Division 4: 1958-59

PRESTON NORTH END — DIV. 4

Allat, Vernon
Atkins, Robert G.
Brazil, Gary N.
Clark, Jonathan
Foster, Wayne P.
Gibson, Simon J.
Greenwood, Nigel P.
Kelly, Alan T.
McAteer, Andrew W.
McNeil, Robert M.
Thomas, John W.
Welsh, Paul W.

League Appearances: Allatt, Vernon 17(2); Atkins, Robert G. 34; Brazil, Gary N. 43; Chippendale, Brian A. 5(1); Clarke, Jonathan 6; Cooper, Robert C. 3(2); Foster, Wayne P. 25(6); Gibson, Simon J. 25; Gray, Terence I. 27; Greenwood, Nigel P. 25(5); Harrington, Philip 2; Ibbotson, Daniel 1; Jemson, Nigel R. (1); Jones, Mark T. 37; Keen, Nigel J. 24; Kelly, Alan T. 13; McAteer, Andrew W. 29; McNeil, Robert M. 19; Martin, Michael P. 35; Pilling, Andrew J. 1; Platt, John R. 31; Reid, Shaun 3; Rodgers, Mark 1; Rudge, Dale A. 23; Stevens, Ian D. 6(1); Thomas, John W. 34(6); Tottoh, Melvin D. (1); Twentyman, Geoffrey 26; Welsh, Paul W. 11(6).
Goals – League (54): Thomas 17, Brazil 14 (6 pens), Greenwood 9, Allatt 3 (1 pen), Foster 3, Atkins 2, Gibson 2, Gray 1, Jones 1, Stevens 1, Welsh 1.
Milk Cup (7): Brazil 3 (1 pen), Foster 1, Keen 1, Rudge 1, Twentyman 1.
FA Cup (3): Brazil 1, Martin 1, Thomas 1.
Ground: Deepdale, Preston PR1 6RU (0772 795919)
Nearest station: Preston
Manager: John McGrath **Secretary** D.J. Allan
Colours: White shirts with blue trim; blue shorts with white trim
Record home gate: 42,584 v Arsenal, April 1983 (League)
Honours – Champions: Division 1: 1888-89, 1889-90; Division 2: 1903-04, 1912-13, 1950-51; Division 3: 1970-71
FA Cup winners: 1888-89, 1937-38

QUEEN'S PARK RANGERS DIV. 1

Allen, Martin J.
Bannister, Gary
Barron, Paul G.
Byrne, John F.
Carter, James W.C.
Chivers, Gary P.S.
Davis, Paul E.
Dawes, Ian R.
Fenwick, Terence W.
Fereday, Wayne
Fillery, Michael C.
Hucker, Peter I.
James, Robert M.
Kerslake, David
Loram, Mark J.
McDonald, Alan
Maguire, Gavin T.
Neill, Warren A.
Peacock, Gavin K.
Robinson, Michael J.
Rosenior, Leroy D.
Waddock, Gary P.
Walker, Clive
Wicks, Stephen J.

League Appearances: Allen, Martin J. 26(5); Bakholt, Kurt (1); Bannister; Gary 36; Barron, Paul G. 31; Byrne, John F.30(6); Chiver, Gary P.S. 13(1); Dawes, Ian R. 42; De Graft Rosenior, Leroy 12(6); Fenwick, Terance W. 37; Fereday, Wayne 30(4); Fillery, Michael C. 17; Gregory, John C. 11; Hucker, Peter I. 11; James, Robert M. 25(3); Kerslake, David 9(5); McDonald, Alan 42; Neill, Warren A. 16; Robinson, Michael J. 25(1); Waddock, Gary P. 15; Walker, Clive 5; Wicks, Stephen J. 29.
Goals – League (53): Bannister 16, Byrne 12, Fenwick 7 (4 pens), Robinson 5, M.Allen 3, Rosenior 3, Fereday 2, Dawes 1, Kerslake 1, James 1, Walker 1, Wicks 1.
Milk Cup (18): Byrne 3, Kerslake 3, Bannister 2, Fenwick 2 (1 pen), Rosenior 2, Dawes 1, Fillery 1, McDonald 1, Robinson 1, own goals 2.
FA Cup (0).
Ground: Rangers Stadium, South Africa Road, Shepherds Bush, W12 7PA (01-743 0262)
Nearest stations: Shepherds Bush (Metropolitan and Central lines); White City (Central line)
Manager: Jim Smith **Secretary:** R.J. Phillips F.A.A.I.
Colours: Blue and white hooped shirts; white shorts
Record home gate: 35,353 v Leeds United, April 1974 (League)
Honours – Champions: Division 2: 1982-83; Division 3: 1966-67; Division 3 South: 1947-48
League Cup winners: 1966-67

READING DIV. 2

Bailie, Colin
Beavon, Michael S.
Bremner, Kevin J.
Burvill, Glen
Gilkes, Michael E.
Hicks, Martin
Horrix, Dean V.
Hurlock, Terence A.
Peters, Gary D.
Richardson, Steven E.
Roberts, Brian J.
Rogers, Andrew
Senior, Trevor
Westwood, Gary M.
White, Mark
Williams, Jeremy S.
Wood, Steven A.

League Appearances: Bailie, Colin 25(1); Beavon, Michael S. 44; Bremner, Kevin J. 18(4); Burvill, Glen 11(5); Gilkes, Michael E. 7(2); Hicks, Martin 34; Horrix, Dean V. 38(3); Hurlock, Terence A. 16; Peters, Gary D. 41; Platnauer, Nicholas R. 7; Reck, Sean M. 1; Richardson, Steven E. 32; Roberts, Brian J. (1); Rogers, Andrew 40; Senior, Trevor 46; Stevenson, Nigel C.A. 3; Westwood, Gary M. 46; White, Mark 25; Williams, Jeremy S. 26(5); Wood, Stephen A. 46.
Goals – League (67): Senior 27, Bremner 7, Horrix 6 (2 pens), Rogers 5, Williams 4, Wood 4, Beavon 3, White 3, Gilkes 2, Hicks 2, Peters 2, own goals 2.
Milk Cup (1): Rogers 1.
FA Cup (6): Senior 4, Horrix 2 (1 pen).
Ground: Elm Park, Norfolk Road, Reading RG3 2EF (0734 507878)
Nearest station: Reading
Manager: Ian Branfoot **Secretary:** Miss A. Meek
Colours: Sky blue shirts with white stripe and navy trim; shorts navy with amber stripes down side

Record home gate: 33,042 v Brentford, February 1927 (FA Cup)
Honours – Champions: Division 3: 1985-86; Division 3 South: 1925-26; Division 4: 1978-79

ROCHDALE DIV. 4

Cooke, Joseph
Grant, David
Hicks, Keith
Johnson, Ian
McMahon, Ian
Moore, Ronald D.
Redfern, David
Reid, Shaun
Seasman, John
Taylor, Steven J.
Thompson, David S.

League Appearances: Carney, Stephen 4; Cooke, Joseph 34; Diamond, Barry D. 7(2); Gamble, Francis 22(3); Grant, David 41; Haire, Garry 3; Heaton, Paul J. 43; Hicks, Keith 31; Hildersley, Ronald 12(4); Johnson, Ian 35(4); Johnson, Stephen A. 3(3); McCluskie, James A.J. 10(4); McMahon, Ian 32; Martin-Chambers, Philip 9(1); Measham, Ian 12; Moore, Ronald D. 43; Mossman, David J. 8; Redfern, David 46; Reid, Shaun 7(1); Seasman, John 30; Smart, Jason 1; Taylor, Steven J. 45; Thompson, David S. 24(3); Tong, David J. (2); Towner, Anthony 4(1).
Goals – League (57): Taylor 25 (8 pens), Moore 9 (1 pen), Gamble 4, Heaton 4, McMahon 3 (1 pen), Seasman 2, Thompson 2, Cooke 1, Diamond 1 pen, Grant 1, Hicks 1, S. Johnson 1, own goals 3.
Milk Cup (2): Cooke 1, Taylor 1.
FA Cup (6): Taylor 5 (1 pen), Moore 1.
Ground: Spotland, Sandy Lane, Rochdale OL11 5DS (0706 44648/9)
Nearest station: Rochdale
Manager: Vic Halom **Secretary:** W.H. Kenon
Colours: White shirts: blue shorts
Record home gate: 24,231 v Notts County, December 1949 (FA Cup)
Honours – Champions: Nil

ROTHERHAM UNITED DIV. 3

Ash, Mark C.
Barnsley, Andrew
Birch, Alan
Crosby, Philip A.
Dungworth, John H.
Eley, Kevin
Emerson, Dean
Gooding, Michael C.
Morris, Andrew D.
O'Hanlon, Kelham G.
Pepper, Nigel C.
Pickering, Michael J.
Pugh, Daral J.
Scott, Martin
Simmons, Anthony J.
Smith, Kevan
Trusson, Michael S.
Tynan, Thomas E.
Warburton, Raymond

League Appearances: Barnsley, Andrew 28; Birch, Alan 43(2); Cowdrill, Barry J. 2; Crosby, Philip A. 12; Dungworth, John H. 46; Eley, Kevin (5); Emerson, Dean 45; Forrest, Gerald 17; Gooding, Michael C. 35(5); Horner, Philip M. 3(1); Martin, Michael P. 5; O'Hanlon, Kelham G. 46; Pepper, Nigel C. 4(3); Pickering, Michael J. 46; Pugh, Daral J. 33(4); Simmons, Anthony J. 31(7); Smith, Kevan 43; Trusson, Michael G. 37; Tynan, Thomas E. 30.
Goals – League (61): Tynan 13 (1 pen), Birch 12 (5 pens), Gooding 8 (1 pen), Emerson 7, Simmons 7, Trusson 6, Smith 3, Dungworth 2, Pugh 2, own goals 1.
Milk Cup (2): Birch 1, Emerson 1.
FA Cup (14): Tynan 4, Birch 3, Gooding 2, Trusson 2, Pugh 1, Simmons 1, own goal 1.
Ground: Millmoor, Rotherham S60 1HR (0709 562434)
Nearest station: Rotherham
Manager: Norman Hunter **Secretary:** N. Darnhill
Colours: Red shirts with white sleeves; white shorts with red stripe
Record home gate: 25,000 v Sheffield United, December 1952 and Sheffield Wednesday, January 1952 (League)
Honours – Champions: Division 3: 1980-81; Division 3 North: 1950-51

SCUNTHORPE UNITED DIV. 4

Broddle, Julian R.	Hill, David M.	Longden, David P.
Cammack, Stephen R.	Houchen, Keith M.	Money, Richard
Ferry, William	Hunter, Leslie	Russell, William M.
Gregory, Paul G.	Lester, Michael J.	Stevenson, Andrew J.
Hawley, John E.	Lister, Stephen H.	Whitehead, Allan

League Appearances: Barnes, David O. 6; Broddle, Julian R. 36(5); Brolley, Michael J. 19(1); Cammack, Stephen R. 32(1); Dixon, Kevin L. 14; Ferry, William 2; Graham, Thomas 27(4); Green, John R. 9; Gregory, Paul G. 34; Hawley, John E. 18(3); Hill, David M. 42; Houchen, Keith M. 9; Hunter, Leslie 12; Johnson, Paul 12; Lester, Michael J. 18; Lister, Stephen H. 35(2); Longden, David P. 31; Matthews, Michael 9(2); Matthews, Neil 1; Money, Richard 25; Pointon, Neil G. 17; Russell, William M. 41(1); Smith, Mark C. (1); Stevenson, Andrew J. (2); Travis, David A. 12; Webster, Ian A. 4(1); Whitehead, Allan 41.
Goals – League (50): Cammack 12 (2 pens), Broddle 7, Hawley 7 (1 pen), Graham 5, Whitehead 3, Brolly 2, Dixon 2, Hill 2, Houchen 2, Lister 2, Green 1, Hunter 1, Matthews 1, Travis 1, own goals 2.
Milk Cup (2): Cammack 1, Lister 1.
FA Cup (6): Broddle 2, Hill 2, Graham 1, Lister 1.
Ground: Old Show Ground, Scunthorpe DN15 7RH (0724-848077)
Nearest station: Scunthorpe
Manager: Frank Barlow **Secretary:** A.D. Rowing
Colours: Claret and blue shirts; blue shorts with claret trim
Record home gate: 23,935 v Portsmouth, January 1954 (FA Cup)
Honours – Champions: Division 3 North: 1957-58

SHEFFIELD UNITED DIV. 2

Arnott, Kevin W.	Lewington, Raymond K.	Smith, Paul M.
Burridge, John	McGeeney, Patrick M.	Stancliffe, Paul I.
Eckhardt, Jeffrey	McNaught, Kenneth	Thompson, Philip B.
Edwards, Keith	Morris, Colin	Tomlinson, Paul
Foley, Steven	Peattie, Donald S.	Walshaw, Lee
Frain, David	Philliskirk, Anthony	Wigley, Steven
Geelan, Kenneth J.	Smith, Brian	Withe, Peter

League Appearances: Arnott, Kevin W. 17(1); Black, Russell P. 1(1); Bolton, Joseph 30; Burridge, John 42; Cockerill, Glenn 12; Eckhardt, Jeffrey 33; Edwards, Keith 32(3); Eves, Melvyn J. 8(1); Foley, Steven 22(6); Frain, David 7; Kenworthy, Anthony D. 13; Lewington, Raymond 36; McGeeney, Patrick M. 5(1); McNaught, Kenneth 34; Morris, Colin 40; Philliskirk, Anthony 4; Smith, Brian 7(1); Smith, Paul M. 13(5); Stancliffe, Paul I. 40; Thompson, Philip B. 26(1); Walshaw, Lee 3(1); Wigley, Steven 7(3); Withe, Peter 30.
Goals – League (64): Edwards 20 (1 pen), Withe 11, Morris 10 (5 pens), Foley 5, McNaught 5, Cockerill 2, Eckhardt 2, Arnott 1, Bolton 1, Eves 1, Frain 1, Stancliffe 1, Walshaw 1, Wigley 1, own goals 2.
Milk Cup (10): Bolton 3, Withe 2, Cockerill 1, Edwards 1, Foley 1, McNaught 1, Morris 1.
FA Cup (2): Morris 2.
Ground: Bramhall Lane, Sheffield S2 4SU (0742 738955)
Nearest station: Sheffield
Manager: Billy McEwan **Secretary:** G.E. Smith F.A.A.I., M.Inst.C.M.
Colours: Red and white striped shirts; black shorts
Record home gate: 68,287 v Leeds, February 1936 (FA Cup)
Honours – Champions: Division 1: 1897-98; Division 2: 1952-53; Division 3 North: 1945-46; Division 4: 1981-82
FA Cup winners: 1898-99, 1901-02, 1915-15, 1924-25

SHEFFIELD WEDNESDAY — DIV. 1

Chamberlain, Mark	Knight, Ian J.	Shutt, Carl S.
Chapman, Lee R.	Madden, Lawrence D.	Smith, Alan D.
Gregory, Anthony G.	Marwood, Brian	Smith, Mark C.
Hart, Paul A.	Megson, Gary J.	Snodin, Glynn
Hazel, Desmond L.	Morris, Christopher B.	Sterland, Melvyn
Hesford, Iain	Pressman, Kevin P.	Thompson, Gary L.
Hodge, Martin J.	Shelton, Gary	Worthington, Nigel
Jonsson, Sigurdur	Shirtliff, Peter A.	

League Appearances: Blair, Andrew 17; Chamberlain, Mark V. 3(18); Chapman, Lee R. 29(2); Gregory, Anthony G. 4(1); Hart, Paul A. 34; Hodge, Martin J. 42; Jonsson, Sigurdur 9 (1); Knight, Ian J. 4; Lyons, Michael 11; Madden, Lawrence D. 25; Marwood, Brian 37; Megson, Gary J. 20; Morris, Christopher B. 29(1); Shelton, Gary 30(1); Shirtliff, Peter A. 21; Shutt, Carl S. 17(2); Smith, Mark C. 13; Snodin, Glynn 27(1); Stainrod, Simon A. 3(3); Sterland, Melvyn 37(1); Thompson, Gary L. 35(1); Worthington, Nigel 15.
Goals – League (63): Marwood 13 (3 pens), Chapman 10, Shutt 9, Sterland 8 (2 pens), Thompson 6, Megson 3, Chamberlain 2, Jonsson 2, Hart 1, Lyons 1, Shelton 1, Snodin 1, Stainrod 1, own goals 5.
Milk Cup (4): Chapman 2, Sterland 1 (pen), Thompson 1.
FA Cup (16): Shutt 4, Chapman 2, Marwood 2 (1 pen), Sterland 2, Blair 1, Chamberlain 1, Smith 1, Thompson 1, Worthington 1, own goals 1.
Ground: Hillsborough, Sheffield S6 1SW (0742 343123, Box Office 343122)
Nearest station: Sheffield
Manager: Howard Wilkinson **Secretary:** R.H. Chester F.A.A.I.
Colours: Royal blue and white striped shirts; royal blue shorts with white stripes on sides
Record home gate: 72,841 v Manchester City, February 1934 (FA Cup)
Honours – Champions: Division 1: 1902-03, 1903-04, 1928-29, 1929-30; Division 2: 1899-1900, 1925-26, 1951-52, 1955-56, 1958-59
FA Cup winners: 1895-96, 1906-07, 1934-35

SHREWSBURY TOWN — DIV. 2

Bates, Philip D.	Johnson, Paul	Petts, Paul A.
Brown, Michael A.	Kelly, Mark D.	Robinson, Colin R.
Cross, Stephen C.	Leonard, Gary A.	Steele, Timothy W.
Daly, Gerald A.	McNally, Bernard A.	Tester, Paul L.
Griffin, Colin R.	Malcolm, Paul A.	Williams, Wayne
Hackett, Gary S.	Pearson, Nigel G.	
Hughes, Darren J.	Perks, Stephen J.	

League Appearances: Bates, Philip D. 1(4); Cross, Stephen C. 35; Daly, Gerald A. 27; Griffin, Colin R. 32; Gunn, Brynley C. 9; Hackett, Gary S. 42; Hughes, Darren J. 29(2); Johnson, Paul 13; Kerr, Andrew A. 9; Leonard, Gary A. 15(6); McNally, Bernard A. 34(1); Nardiello, Gerardo 19(3); Pearson, Nigel G. 35; Perks, Stephen J. 42; Rees, Anthony A. 1(1); Robinson, Colin R. 42; Steele, Timothy W. (2); Stevens, Gary M. 38; Tester, Paul L. 9; Williams, Wayne 30.
Goals – League (52): Robinson 10, Cross 8, Hackett 6, McNally 6 (2 pens), Nardiello 5, Daly 4, Stevens 4, Hughes 1, Leonard 1, Pearson 1, Tester 1, Williams 1, own goals 4.
Milk Cup (5): Robinson 2, Hackett 1, Stevens 1, own goals 1.
FA Cup (0).
Ground: Gay Meadow, Shrewsbury SY2 6AB (0743 60111)
Nearest station: Shrewsbury

Manager: Chic Bates **Secretary:** M.J. Starkey
Colours: Gold shirts with blue sleeves; shorts: blue with gold and white stripe down sides
Record home gate: 18,917 v Walsall, April 1961 (League)
Honours – Champions: Division 3: 1978-79

SOUTHAMPTON DIV. 1

Armstrong, David
Baker, Stephen
Blake, Mark C.
Bond, Kevin J.
Brown, Kevan
Case, James R.
Cockerill, Glenn
Dennis, Mark E.
Forrest, Gerald
Gittens, Jon
Hamilton, Ian R.
Holmes, Nicholas C.
Jordan, Joseph
Lawrence, George R.
Maskell, Craig D.
Moran, Stephen J.
Parkinson, Philip J.
Puckett, David C.
Shilton, Peter L.
Townsend, Andrew D.
Wallace, David L.
Whitlock, Mark
Wright, Mark

League Appearances: Armstrong, David 41; Baker, Stephen 13; Blake, Mark C. 1; Bond, Kevin J. 34; Case, James R. 36; Cockerill, Glenn 30; Curtis, Alan T. 10(1); Dennis, Mark E. 24; Forrest, Gerald 22; Gittens, Jon 4; Golac, Ivan 9; Granger, Keith W. 2; Holmes, Nicholas C. 26; Jordan, Joseph 12; Kite, Philip D. 3; Lawrence, George R. 12(9); McManus, Stuart 2; Maskell, Craig D. (2); Moran, Stephen 24(4); Puckett, David C. 13(2); Shilton, Peter L. 37; Tankard, Allen J. 3; Townsend, Andrew D. 25(2); Wallace, David L. 34(1); Whitlock, Mark 12(2); Wright, Mark 33.
Goals – League (51): Armstrong 10 (2 pens), Moran 8, Wallace 8, Cockerill 7 (1 pen), Puckett 4, Wright 3, Case 2, Lawrence 2, Bond 1, Curtis 1, Maskell 1, McManus 1, Townsend 1, own goals 2.
Milk Cup (5): Armstrong 3 (2 pens), Puckett 1, Wallace 1.
FA Cup (9): Wallace 4, Armstrong 2, Cockerill 2, Moran 1.
Ground: The Dell, Milton Road, Southampton SO9 4XX (0703 220505)
Nearest station: Southampton
Manager: Chris Nicholl **Secretary:** B. P. Truscott
Colours: Shirts: broad central white panel flanked by wide red stripe on either side with black piping; black shorts with white side seam
Record home gate: 31,044 v Manchester United, October 1969 (League)
Honours – Champions: Division 3 South: 1921-22; Division 3: 1959-60
FA Cup winners: 1975-76

SOUTHEND UNITED DIV. 4

Cadette, Richard R.
Clark, Paul P.
Engwell, Michael
Gymer, John P.
Lock, Kevin J.
McDonough, Roy
Neal, Dean J.
O'Shea, Daniel E.
Pennyfather, Glenn J.
Rogers, Alan J.
Seaden, John C.
Silkman, Barry
Stannard, James
Westley, Shane L.M.

League Appearances: Cadette, Richard R. 44; Clark, Paul P. 38(1); Engwell, Michael 1(1); Gymer, John P. 2(11); Hatter, Stephen J. 44; Lampard, Frank R.G. 34; Lock, Kevin J. 10; McDonough, Roy 32(6); May, Warren D. 23(2); Neal, Dean J. 10(1); O'Shea, Daniel E. 35; Pennyfather, Glenn J. 41; Phillips, Stephen E. 13; Pryer, Terence 2; Rogers, Alan J. 32; Seaden, John C. 4(1); Silkman, Barry 38(2); Stannard, James 46; Stead, Michael J. 17; Stebbing, Gary S. 5; Westley, Shane L.M. 35(1).
Goals – League (69): Cadette 25, O'Shea 9, McDonough 7, Pennyfather 7, Westley 5, Gymer 3, Neal 3, Hatter 2 (1 pen), Phillips 2, Clark 1, Engwell 1, Lampard 1, Rogers 1, Silkman 1, own goals 1.

Milk Cup (1): Clark 1.
FA Cup (0).
Ground: Roots Hall Ground, Victoria Avenue, Southend SS2 6NQ (0702 340707)
Nearest station: Prittlewell or Southend Central
Manager: David Webb **Secretary:** K. Hogg
Colours: Blue shirts with gold trim and chest band; shorts gold
Record home gate: 31,033 v Liverpool, January 1979 (FA Cup)
Honours – Champions: Division 4: 1980-81
Stockport County
Goals – League (63): Leonard 19, Sward 12 (8 pens), Hodkinson 6, Mossman 5, P.Smith 5, Coyle 4, Wroe 4, Chapman 3, Cammack 1, Evans 1, Hendrie 1, Newton 1, Posckett 1.
Milk Cup (2): Leonard 1, Smith 1.
FA Cup (0).
Stoke City
Goals – League (48): Bertschin 19 (3 pens), Heath 5, Shaw 5, Adams 4, Berry 3, Chamberlain 3, Maskery 3, Sanders 2, Devine 1, Donawa 1, Painter 1, Parkin 1.
Milk Cup (2): Bertschin 2.
FA Cup (0).

STOCKPORT COUNTY DIV. 4

Chapman, Leslie
Evans, Andrew C.
Hendrie, Paul
Hodkinson, Andrew J.
Leonard, Mark A.
Matthewson, Trevor
Mossman, David J.
Poskett, Malcolm
Salmon, Michael B.
Sword, Thomas W.
Walker, Gary
Williams, William R.

League Appearances: Cammack, Stephen R. 3(1); Chapman, Leslie 38; Coyle, Anthony 24(1); Devine, Stephen B. 2; Diamond, Barry 6; Evans, Andrew C. 33(2); Hendrie, Paul 36; Hodkinson, Andrew J. 41; Leonard, Mark A. 44; Lodge, Paul 1; Matthewson, Trevor 34(1); Mossman, David J. 17; Newton, Robert 6; Poskett, Malcolm 8; Power, Michael D. (1); Rutter, John T. 16(1); Salmon, Michael B. 26; Sherlock, Stephen E. 23(2); Smith, Nigel G. 3; Smith, Paul M. 7; Sword, Thomas W. 39(1); Thorpe, Andrew 30; Walker, Gary 20; Williams, William R. 22; Wroe, Mark 25(1); Yates, Stephen 2.
Goals – League (63): Leonard 19, Sword 12 (8 pens), Hodkinson 6, Mossman 5, P. Smith 5, Coyle 4, Wroe 4, Chapman 3, Cammack 1, Evans 1. Hendrie 1, Newton 1, Poskett 1.
Milk Cup (2): Leonard 1, Smith 1.
FA Cup (0).
Ground: Edgeley Park, Stockport SK3 9DD (061-480 8888)
Nearest station: Stockport
Player/Manager: Les Chapman **Secretary:** T.R. McCreery F.A.A.I.
Colours: Sky blue shirts with white stripes; shorts blue
Record home gate: 27,833 v Liverpool, February 1950 (FA Cup)
Honours – Champions: Division 3 North: 1921-22, 1936-37; Division 4: 1966-67

STOKE CITY DIV. 2

Adams, Neil J.
Beeston, Carl F.
Berry, George F.
Bertschin, Keith E.
Bould, Stephen A.
Callaghan, Aaron J.
Devine, John A.
Fox, Peter D.
Heath Philip A.
Hemming,Christopher A.J.
Hudson, Alan A.
Kelly, Anthony G.
Maskery, Christopher P.
Mills, Michael D.
Painter, Ian J.
Parkin, Stephen J.
Saunders, Carl S.
Shaw, Graham P.
Williams, Terence J.

League Appearances: Adams, Neil J. 31(1); Beeston, Carl F. 2(3); Berry, George F. 41; Bertschin, Keith E. 42; Bonnyman, Philip 7; Bould, Stephen A. 33; Callaghan, Aaron J. 6(2); Chamberlain, Mark V. 7; Curtis, Alan T. 3; Devine, John A. 15; Donowa, Brian L. 4; Dyson, Paul I. 31; Fox, Peter D. 37; Heath, Philip A. 38; Hemming, Christopher A.J. 23(1); Hudson, Alan A. 6; Kelly, Anthony G. 1; Maskery, Christopher P. 19; Mills, Michael D. 31; Painter, Ian J. 15(4); Parkin, Stephen J. 10(2); Saunders, Carl S. 33(4); Shaw, Graham P. 19(1); Siddall, Barry 5; Williams, Terence J. 3(3).
Goals – League (48): Bertschin 19 (3 pens), Heath 5, Shaw 5, Adams 4, Berry 3, Chamberlain 3, Maskery 3, Sanders 2, Devine 1, Donowa 1, Painter 1, Parkin 1.
Milk Cup (2): Bertschin 2.
FA Cup (0).
Ground: Victoria Ground, Stoke-on-Trent ST4 4EG (0782 413511)
Nearest station: Stoke-on-Trent
Player/Manager: Mick Mills **Secretary:** M. J. Potts
Colours: Shirts red and white stripes, red shorts
Record home gate: 51,380 v Arsenal, March 1937 (League)
Honours – Champions: Division 2: 1932-33, 1962-63; Division 3 North: 1926-27
League Cup winners: 1971-72

SUNDERLAND DIV. 2

Agboola, Reuben O.F.	Duncan, Cameron	Outterside, Mark J.
Armstrong, Gordon I.	Elliott, Shaun	Proctor, Mark G.
Atkinson, Paul	Gates, Eric L.	Saddington, Nigel J.
Bennett, Gary E.	Gray, Francis T.	Swindlehurst, David
Bolder, Robert J.	Hetze, Stephen E.R.	Venison, Barry
Burley, George E.	Kennedy, Alan P.	White, Dale
Corner, David E.	Lemon, Paul A.	
Cornforth, John M.	Moore, John	

League Appearances: Agboola, Reuben O.F. 12; Armstrong, Gordon I. 13(1); Atkinson, Paul 10(3); Bennett, Gary E. 28; Berry, Stephen A. 1; Bolder, Robert 22; Burley, George E. 27; Chisholm, Gordon W. 1; Corner, David E. 9; Daniel, Peter W. 8(1); Dibble, Andrew 12; Duncan, Cameron 1; Elliott, Shaun 32; Ford, Tony 8(1); Gates, Eric L. 38(1); Gayle, Howard 20(3); Gray, Francis T. 32(2); Hetzke, Stephen E.R. 8; Hodgson, David J. 9(6); Kennedy, Alan P. 32; Lemon, Paul A. 4(1); McDonagh, James M. 7; Pickering, Nicholas 22(2); Proctor, Mark G. 19; Swindlehurst, David 25; Venison, Barry 36; Walker, Clive 10(2); Wallace, Ian A. 14(5); White, Dale 2(2).
Goals – League (47): Gates 9 (2 pens), Proctor 7 (1 pen), Pickering 5 (1 pen), Swindlehurst 5, Gray 4, Bennett 3, Wallace 3, Armstrong 2, Elliott 2, Gayle 2, Kennedy 2, Ford 1, Hodgson 1 (pen), own goals 1.
Milk Cup (4): Walker 2, Bennett 1, Gates 1 (pen).
FA Cup (2): Burley 1, Corner 1.
Ground: Roker Park, Grantham Road, Sunderland SR6 9 SW (0783 40332)
Nearest station: Sunderland or Seaburn
Manager: Lawrie McMenemy **Secretary:** G. Davidson F.C.A.
Colours: Red shirts with white vertical stripes with white neckband and white sleeves; black shorts with red and white seams
Record home gate: 75,118 v Derby, March 1933 (FA Cup)
Honours – Champions: Division 1: 1891-92, 1892-93, 1894-95, 1901-02, 1912-13, 1935-36; Division 2: 1975-76
FA Cup winners: 1936-37, 1972-73

P.F.A.86.87.—3

SWANSEA CITY — DIV. 4

Andrews, Keri A.	Hughes, Michael R.	Price, Paul T.
Burrows, Paul S.	Hutchison, Thomas	Randell, Colin W.
French, Nigel P.	Lewis, Dudley K.	Rimmer, John J.
Harrison, Christopher C.	McCarthy, Sean C.	Stevenson, Nigel C.A.
Hough, David J	Pascoe, Colin J.	Williams, Philip D.

League Appearances: Andrews, Keri A. 1; Budd, Kevin J. 1; Burrows, Paul S. 1(2); Davis, Ian C. 11; Emmanuel, John G. 38(2); Foley, William 4(1); French, Nigel P. 11(3); Gibbins, Roger G. 35; Harrison, Christopher C. 34(2); Hough, David 30(1); Hughes, Michael R. 27; Hutchison, Thomas 38(3); Lewis, Dudley K. 22(2); McCarthy, Sean C. 16(6); McHale, Raymond 26(2); Marustik, Christopher 8; Melville, Andrew R. 2(3); Pascoe, Colin J. 18(1); Price, Neil (2); Price, Paul T. 41; Randell, Colin W. 18(1); Rimmer, John J. 19; Sharpe, John W.H. 5; Stevenson, Nigel C.A. 12; Sullivan, Colin J. 41; Turner, Robin D. 9; Waddle, Alan R. 27(1); Williams, Philip D. 11(1).
Goals – League (43): Gibbins 6, Harrison 5 (3 pens), Waddle 5, Emmanuel 3, Hough 3, Hutchison 3, McCarthy 3, Pascoe 3 (1 pen), Turner 3, Williams 3, Foley 2, French 1, McHale 1, Price 1, Randell 1.
Milk Cup (6): Randell 3, Marustik 1, Pascoe 1, Waddle 1.
FA Cup (3): Burrows 1, Waddle 1, Williams 1.
Ground: Vetch Field, Swansea SA1 3SU (0792 474114)
Nearest station: Swansea
Manager: Terry Yorath **Secretary:** George Taylor
Colours: White shirts with black trim; black shorts with white chevron down side
Record home gate: 32,796 v Arsenal, February 1968 (FA Cup)
Honours – Champions: Division 3 South: 1924-25, 1948-49

SWINDON TOWN — DIV. 3

Allen, Kenneth	Gardiner, Mark C.	Moss, David J.
Bamber, John D.	Gordon, Colin K.	Ramsey, Christopher L.
Barnard, Leigh K.	Henry, Charles A.	Reynolds, James A.
Calderwood, Colin	Hockaday, David	Rowland, Andrew A.
Cole, David A.	Hughes, Mark C.	Wade, Bryan A.
Coyne, Peter D.	Kamara, Christopher	

League Appearances: Allen, Kenneth 40; Bamber, John D. 23; Barnard, Leigh K. 37(1); Calderwood, Colin 46; Cole, David A. 44; Coleman, Nicholas 13; Coyne, Peter D. 30(1); Endersby, Scott A. 2; Evans, Anthony 8(2); Findley, John W. 4; Gardiner, Mark C. (1); Gordon, Colin K. 38(1); Hall, Derrick R. 9(1); Henry, Charles A. 37(1); Hockaday, David 34(3); Hughes, Nicholas S. 31(9); Kamara, Christopher 19(1); Macari, Luigi 7(2); Moss, David J. 4; Ramsey, Christopher L. 43; Roberts, Paul 25(2); Rowland, Andrew A. 12(6); Wade, Bryan A. 31(3).
Goals – League (82): Henry 18, Gordon 17 (3 pens), Coyne 10 (2 pens), Wade 10, Bamber 9, Coleman 4 (3 pens), Barnard 3, Cole 3, Ramsey 3, Calderwood 2, Hockaday 1, Kamara 1, own goals 1.
Milk Cup (11): Coyne 3 (1 pen), Rowlands 2, Wade 2, Hockaday 1, Moss 1, own goals 2.
FA Cup (2): Barnard 1, Ramsey 1.
Ground: County Ground, Swindon SN1 2ED (0793 22118 and 36170)
Nearest station: Swindon
Manager: Lou Macari **Secretary:** R.J. Jeffries
Colours: Red shirts with white pinstripe; white shorts with red trim
Record home gate: 32,000 v Arsenal, January 1972 (FA Cup)
Honours – Champions: Division 4: 1985-86; **League Cup winners:** 1968-69.
Anglo-Italian Cup winners: 1970

TORQUAY UNITED DIV. 4

Compton, Paul D.
Crowe, Mark A.
Phillips, Stephen E.
Pyle, Stephen
Walsh, Mario M.

League Appearances: Allen, Kenneth 4; Carpenter, Stephen 2; Compton, Paul D. 43; Crabbe, Steven 27(2); Crowe, Mark A. 45; Dawkins, Derek A. 34(5); Dreyer, John B. 5; Durham, Johnathan S. 8(4); Fowler, Derek W. 32)3); Fowler, Tony 8; Fry, David P. 30; Hirst, Martyn P. 4; Kelly, Edward P. 13; Lambert, Martin C. 4(2); Leigh, Ian R. 4; Loram, Mark 38; Perry, Michael A. 3; Phillips, Stephen E. 23; Pugh, Steven J. 45; Pyle, Stephen 14; Smith, Kevin J. 20(3); Walsh, Mario M. 37(4); Webber, Trevor 5; West, David C. 19(2); Wheeldon, Thomas E. 6(2); Wright, Stephen P. 33.
Goals – League (43): Phillips 8 (2 pens), Walsh 7, Loram 6, Dawkins 3, Pugh 3, Crabbe 2, Crowe 2, D.Fowler 2, Lambert 2, Pyle 2, West 2, Compton 1, Durham 1, Kelly 1, Smith 1 (pen).
Milk Cup (3): Kelly 1, Pugh 1, Smith 1.
FA Cup (7): Walsh 4, Loram 2, Durham 1.
Ground: Plainmoor, Torquay, Devon TQ1 3PS (0803 38666/7)
Nearest station: Torquay or Torre
Manager: Stuart Morgan **Secretary:** D.J. Easton
Colours: Blue shirts; blue shorts
Record home gate: 21,908 v Huddersfield, January 1955 (FA Cup)
Honours: Nil

TOTTENHAM HOTSPUR DIV. 1

Allen, Clive D.
Allen, Paul K.
Ardiles, Osvaldo C.
Bowen, Mark R.
Chiedozie, John O.
Clemence, Raymond N.
Close, Shaun C.
Cooke, Richard E.
Crook, Ian S.
Falco, Mark P.
Galvin, Anthony
Grenfell, Stephen J.
Hoddle, Glenn
Howells, David
Hughton,Christopher W.G.
Mabbutt, Gary V.
Maddix, Daniel S.
Miller, Paul R.
Moncur, John F.
Moran, Paul
O' Shea, Timothy J.
Parks, Anthony
Polston, John D.
Poole, Gary
Roberts, Graham P.
Ruddock, Neil
Samways, Vincent
Stevens, Gary A.
Stimson, Mark
Thomas, Daniel J.
Waddle, Christopher R.

League Appearances: Allen, Clive D. 16(3); Allen, Paul K. 29(4); Ardiles, Osvaldo C. 20(3); Bowen, Mark R. 1(1); Chiedozie, John O. 13(5); Clemence, Raymond N. 42; Cooke, Richard E. (2); Crook, Ian S. 1(3); Dick, Alistair J. 1; Falco, Mark P. 40; Galvin, Anthony 23; Hazard, Michael 3(1); Hoddle, Glenn 31; Howells, David 1; Hughton, Christopher W.G. 33; Leworthy, David J. 2(3); Mabbutt, Gary V. 29(3); Miller, Paul R. 29; Perryman, Stephen J. 22(1); Roberts, Graham P. 32; Stevens, Gary A. 28(1); Thomas, Daniel J. 27; Waddle, Christopher R. 39.
Goals – League (74): Falco 18, Waddle 11, C.Allen 9, Chiedozie 7, Hoddle 7 (1 pen), Galvin 4, Mabbutt 3, Miller 2, Stevens 2, P.Allen 1, Ardiles 1, Bowen 1, Cooke 1, Hazard 1, Howells 1, Hughton 1, Perryman 1, Roberts 1, Thomas 1, own goals 1.
Milk Cup (6): Roberts 2, Galvin 1, Leworthy 1, Mabbutt 1, Waddle 1.
FA Cup (10): C.Allen 3, Chiedozie 2, Falco 2, Waddle 2, Hoddle 1.
Ground: White Hart Lane, 748 High Road, Tottenham, N17 0AP (01-801 3411)
Nearest station: White Hart Lane (ER), Northumberland Park (ER), or Seven Sisters (Victoria Line) thence by bus
Manager: David Pleat **Secretary:** P. Day
Colours: White shirts, white shorts

Record home gate: 75,038 v Sunderland, March 1938 (FA Cup)
Honours – Champions: Division 1: 1950-51, 1960-61; Division 2: 1919-20, 1949-50
FA Cup winners: 1900-01, 1920-21, 1960-61, 1961-62, 1966-67, 1980-81, 1981-82
League Cup winners: 1970-71, 1972-73
European Cup-Winner's Cup winners: 1962-63
UEFA Cup winners: 1971-72, 1983-84

TRANMERE ROVERS DIV. 4

Adkins, Nigel H.	Hughes, Mark	Mungall, Stephen H.
Anderson, Douglas E.	Morrissey, John J.	Vickers, Stephen
Burgess, David J.	Muir, Ian J.	Williams, Gary

League Appearances: Adkins, Nigel H. 34; Anderson, Douglas E. 46; Ashcroft, William 16(7); Burgess, David J. 40(1); Clayton, John 3; Edwards, Stephen G. 34; Hilditch, Mark 5(2); Hollifield, Michael (1); Hughes, Mark 31(1); McVicar, Don 7; Miller, David B. 25(4); Morrissey, John 27(5); Muir, Ian J. 28(4); Mungall, Stephen H. 46; Robinson, Spencer L. 4; Rodaway, William V. 38(1); Siddall, Barry 12; Sinclair, Nicholas J.T. 6; Train, Raymond 36; Vickers, Stephen 3; Williams, Gary 25; Worthington, Frank S. 40(2).
Goals – League (74): Worthington 18 (7 pens), Muir 13, Anderson 11, Morrissey 5, Clayton 4, Rodaway 4, Williams 4, Hilditch 3, Robinson 3, Ashcroft 2, Edwards 2, Miller 1, Mungall 1, Sinclair 1, own goals 2.
Milk Cup (1): Worthington 1.
FA Cup (5): Anderson 1, Morrissey 1, Muir 1, Rodaway 1, Worthington 1.
Ground: Prenton Park, Birkenhead, L42 9PN (051-608 3677 and 4194)
Nearest station: Central Station Birkenhead and Rock Ferry
Manager: Frank Worthington **Secretary:** C. N. Wilson F.A.A.I.
Colours: Royal blue shirts with red pinstripe; royal blue shorts
Record home gate: 24,424 v Stoke, February 1972 (FA Cup)
Honours – Champions: Division 3 North: 1937-38

WALSALL DIV. 3

Armstrong, Kenneth C.	Hawker, Philip N.	Palgrave, Brian V.
Brazier, Colin J.	Jones, Mark	Prudhoe, Mark
Cherry, Steve R.	Jones, Paul A.	Rees, Mark
Childs, Gary P.C.	Kelly, David T.	Shakespeare, Craig
Cross, Nicholas J.H.	Mower, Kenneth M.	Taylor, Robert M.
Elliott, Stephen B.	Naughton, William B.S.	
Hart, Peter O.	O'Kelly, Richard F.	

League Appearances: Brazier, Colin J. 27; Cherry, Steve R. 30; Childs, Gary P.C. 30(3); Cross, Nicholas J.R. 44; Daley, Stephen 28; Elliott, Stephen B. 40(1); Gunn, Brynley C. 6; Handysides, Ian R. 8(2); Hart, Peter O. 44; Hawker, Philip N. 33; Jones, Paul A. 24(2); Kelly, David T. 7(21); Mower, Kenneth M. 43; Naughton, William B.S. 39; O'Kelly, Richard F. 25(3); Palgrave, Brian V. 1(1); Prudhoe, Mark 16; Rees, Mark 13(6); Shakespeare, Craig 31(1); Taylor, Robert M. 17(1).
Goals – League (90): Cross 21 (4 pens), Elliott 16, Kelly 10, O'Kelly 7 (4 pens), Childs 5, Naughton 5, Hawker 4, Shakespeare 4, Handysides 3, Brazier 2, Hart 2, Rees 2, Taylor 2, Daley 1, Jones 1, Mower 1, Palgrave 1, own goals 3.
Milk Cup (2): Cross 2.
FA Cup (10): Naughton 3, Childs 2, O'Kelly 2 (1 pen), Cross 1, Elliott 1, Hawker 1.

Ground: Fellows Park, Walsall WS2 9DB (0922-22791)
Nearest station: Walsall or Bescott (15 min walk-no public transport)
Manager: Alan Buckley **Secretary:** Mrs B. M. Westmancoat
Colours: White shirts with red trim, red shorts
Record home gate: 25,453 v Newcastle, August 1961 (League)
Honours – Champions: Division 4: 1959-60

WATFORD — DIV. 1

Allen, Malcolm
Bardsley, David J.
Barnes, John C.B.
Bishop, Darren C.
Blissett, Luther L.
Callaghan, Nigel
Coton, Anthony P.
Franklin, Paul L.
Gibbs, Nigel J.
Jackett, Kenneth F.
McClelland, John
Porter, Gary
Powell, Clifford G.
Rostron, John W.
Sherwood, Stephen
Sinnott, Lee
Smillie, Neil
Sterling, Worrell R.
Talbot, Brian E.
Taylor, Leslie
Terry, Steve G.
West, Colin

League Appearances: Allen, Malcolm 10(3); Bardsley, David J. 10(3); Barnes, John C.B. 39; Blissett, Luther L. 20(3); Callaghan, Nigel 21(2); Coton, Anthony P. 40; Franklin, Paul L. 4; Gibbs, Nigel J. 40; Jackett, Kenneth F. 41; Lohman, Johaanas H.P. (4); McClelland, John 31; Porter, Gary 7(1); Roberts, Iwan W. 1(3); Rostron, John W. 29(1); Sherwood, Stephen 2; Sinnott, Lee 18; Smillie, Neil 10(6); Sterling, Worrell R. 23(1); Talbot, Brian E. 41; Taylor, Leslie 1; Terry, Steve G. 41; West, Colin 33.
Goals – League (69): West 13, Barnes 9, Blissett 7, Talbot 7, Rostron 5, Callaghan 4, Jackett 4 (3 pens), Terry 4, Smillie 3, Sterling 3, Allen 2, Bardsley 2, Sinnott 2, Gibbs 1, Lohman 1, McClelland 1, Porter 1.
Milk Cup (6): Barnes 1, Blissett 1, Callaghan 1, Jackett 1, Rostron 1, Terry 1.
FA Cup (12): Barnes 3, West 3, Jackett 2 (1 pen), Sterling 2, Callaghan 1, Smillie 1.
Ground: Vicarage Road Stadium, Watford WD1 8ER (0923 30933)
Nearest station: Watford Junction, Watford High Street or Watford Stadium Halt
Manager: Graham Taylor **Secretary:** E. Plumley F.A.A.I.
Colours: Yellow shirts with black/red trim, red shorts
Record home gate: 34,099 v Manchester United, February 1969 (FA Cup)
Honours – Champions: Division 3: 1968-69; Division 4: 1977-78

WEST BROMWICH ALBION — DIV. 2

Anderson, Colin R.
Bennett, Martyn
Bradley, Darren M.
Bull, Stephen G.
Cowdrill, Barry L.
Crooks, Garth A.
Dearlove, Mark A.
Dennison, Robert
Dickenson, Martin J.
Dyson, Paul I.
Grenlish, Anthony P.
Mackenzie, Steven
Madden, Craig A.
Morley, William A.
Naylor, Stuart W.
Nicholl, James M.
Palmer, Carlton L.
Powell, David R.
Reilly, George G.
Robertson, Alistair
Robson, Gary
Statham, Derek
Thomas, Michael R.
Thompson, Andrew R.
Varadi, Imre
Whitehead, Clive R.

League Appearances: Anderson, Colin 7(4); Armstrong, Gerard J. 7(1); Bennett, Martyn 25; Bradley, Darren M. 10; Bradshaw, Paul W. 8; Bull, Stephen G. (1); Burrows, David 1; Cowdrill, Barry L. 9(1); Crooks, Garth A. 18(1); Dennison, Robert 7(5); Dickenson, Martin J. 7; Dyson, Paul I. 11; Forsyth, Michael E. 11; Godden, Anthony L. 21; Grealish, Anthony P. 14(2); Grew,

Mark 1; Hunt, Steven K. 19; Mackenzie, Steven 30(1); Madden, Craig 9; Naylor, Stuart W. 12; Nicholl, James M. 29; Owen, Gary A. 3(1); Palmer, Carlton L.16(4); Reilly, George G. 20; Robertson, Alistair 20; Robinson, Mark J. 1; Robson, Gary 9(5); Statham, Derek 37; Thomas, Michael R. 20; Thompson, Andrew R. 13(2); Valentine, Carl H. 15; Varadi, Imre 30(2); Whitehead, Clive R. 22(2).
Goals – League (35): Varadi 9, Crooks 5, Hunt 4 (1 pen), Mackenzie 4, Reilly 4 (1 pen), Bennett 2, Madden 2, Valentine 2, Dennison 1, Grealish 1, Thompson 1.
Milk Cup (10): Varadi 4, Crooks 2, Hunt 2, Armstrong 1, Bennett 1.
FA Cup (4): Hunt 1, Reilly 1, Statham 1, Thomas 1.
Ground: The Hawthorns, West Bromwich B71 4LF (021-525 8888)
Nearest station: Smethwick Rolfe Street or Birmingham New Street
Manager: Ron Saunders **Secretary:** G.H. Dimbleby, M.B.I.M.
Colours: Navy blue and white striped shirts; white shorts
Record home gate: 64,815 v Arsenal, March 1937 (FA Cup)
Honours – Champions: Division 1: 1919-20; Division 2: 1901-02, 1910-11
FA Cup winners: 1887-88, 1891-92, 1930-31, 1953-54, 1967-68
League Cup winners: 1965-66

WEST HAM UNITED DIV. 1

Bonds, William A.	Ince, Paul E.C.	Parkes, Philip B.F.
Campbell, Gregory R.	Keen, Kevin I.	Parris, George M.R.
Cottee, Antony R.	McAlister, Thomas G.	Pike, Geoffrey A.
Devonshire, Alan E.	McAvennie, Francis	Potts, Steven J.
Dickens, Alan W.	McGiven, Michael	Stewart, Raymond S.
Dolan, Eammon J.	McMenemy, Paul C.	Vaughan, John
Gale, Anthony P.	Martin, Alvin E.	Walford, Stephen J.
Goddard, Paul	Mayes, Robert G.	Ward, Mark W.
Hilton, Paul	Orr, Neil I.	Whitton, Stephen P.

League Appearances: Barnes, David O. (1); Campbell, Gregory R. 1(2); Cottee, Anthony R. 41(1); Devonshire, Alan E. 38; Dickens, Alan W. 40(1); Gale, Anthony P. 42; Goddard, Paul 1(5); Hilton, Paul 2; McAvennie, Francis 41; Martin, Alvin E. 40; Orr, Neil I. 33(3); Parkes, Philip B.F. 42; Parris, George 23(3); Pike, Geoffrey A. 10; Potts, Steven J. (1); Stewart, Raymond S. 39; Walford, Stephen J. 27; Ward, Mark 42.
Goals – League (74): McAvennie 26, Cottee 20, Stewart 6 (5 pens), Dickens 4, Martin 4 (1 pen), Devonshire 3, Ward 3, Orr 2, Goddard 1, Parris 1, own goals 4.
Milk Cup (6): Stewart 3 (pens), Cottee 2, McAvennie 1.
FA Cup (6): Cottee 3, McAvennie 1, Pike 1, Stewart 1 (pen).
Ground: Boleyn Ground, Green Street, Upton Park E13 9AZ (01-472 2740)
Nearest station: Upton Park (District line)
Manager: John Lyall **Chief Executive Secretary:** Eddie Chapman F.A.A.I.
Colours: Claret shirts with blue trim; white shorts with three claret stripes
Record home gate: 42,322 v Tottenham, October 1970 (League)
Honours – Champions: Division 2: 1957-58, 1980-81
FA Cup winners: 1963-64, 1974-75, 1979-80
European Cup Winner's cup winners: 1964-65

WIGAN ATHLETIC DIV. 3

Barrow, Graham	Jewell, Paul	Schofield, Mark A.
Beesley, Paul	Knowles, James B.	Stewart, William I.
Butler, John E.	Langley, Kevin J.	Tunks, Roy W.

Cook, Paul	Lowe, David A.	Walsh, Steven
Cribley, Alexander	Methven, Colin J.	
Griffiths, Ian J.	Mitchell, James B.	

League Appearances: Aspinall, Warren 33(8); Bailey, Neil 5(1); Barrow, Graham 26(4); Beesley, Paul 17; Butler, John E. 36; Cook, Paul 11(2); Cribley, Alexander 38; Griffiths, Ian J. 38; Jewell, Paul 14(15); Kelly, Anthony G. 32; Knowles, James B. 45; Langley, Kevin J. 42(1); Lowe, David A. 46; Methven, Colin J. 43; Newell, Michael C. 24; Stewart, William I. 8; Tunks, Roy W. 38; Walsh, Steven 10(3).
Goals – League (82): Aspinall 21 (6 pens), Newell 16, Kelly 9 (3 pens), Barrow 7, Methven 7, Jewell 6, Lowe 5, Griffiths 3, Cook 2, Cribley 2, Langley 2, Bailey 1, Walsh 1.
Milk Cup (2): Kelly 2 (1 pen).
FA Cup (12): Newell 3, Aspinall 2, Lowe 2, Methven 2, Kelly 1, Knowles 1, own goals 1.
Ground: Springfield Park, Wigan WN6 7BA (0942 44433)
Nearest stations: Wigan Wallgate and Wigan North West
Manager: Roy Mathias **Secretary:** J.A. Bennett
Colours: Blue and white shirts; blue shorts
Record home gate: 27,500 v Hereford United, December 1953 (FA Cup)
Honours – Champions: Northern Premier League 1970-71, 1974-75
Northern Premier League Cup: 1972 **Freight Rover Trophy winners:** 1984-85

WIMBLEDON — DIV. 1

Beasant, David	Gage, Kevin W.	Morris, Mark J.
Clement, Andrew D.	Galliers, Steven	Sanchez, Lawrence P.
Cork, Alan G.	Gannon, John S.	Sayer, Andrew C.
Downes, Walter J.	Gayle, Brian	Smith, Michael
Evans, Stewart	Hazel, Ian	Thorn, Andrew
Fairweather, Carlton	Hodges, Glyn P.	Tracey, Simon P.
Fashanu, John	Holloway, Ian S.	Winterburn, Nigel
Fiore, Garry D.	Kay, John	Wise, Dennis F.
Fishenden, Paul	Martin, David	

League Appearances: Beasant, David 42; Cork, Alan G. 36(2); Downes, Walter J. 5(4); Evans, Stewart 27(3); Fairweather, Carlton 18(2); Fashanu, John 8(1); Fishenden, Paul 16(2); Gage, Kevin W. 29; Galliers, Steven 32; Gannon, John S. 1; Gayle, Brian 13; Hodges, Glyn P. 18(12); Holloway, Ian S. 19; Kay, John 26; Martin, David 15; Morris, Mark J. 20; Sanchez, Lawrence P. 42; Sayer, Andrew C. 5(2); Smith, Michael 24; Thorn, Andrew 27(1); Winterburn, Nigel 38(1); Wise, Dennis F. 1(3).
Goals – League (58): Cork 11, Sanchez 9, Fairweather 7, Evans 6, Hodges 6 (1 pen), Fashanu 4, Smith 3, Fishenden 2, Holloway 2, Gage 1 (pen), Galliers 1, Gannon 1, Kay 1, Martin 1 (pen), Morris 1, Winterburn 1, own goals 1.
Milk Cup (6): Cork 4, Evans 1, Gayle 1.
FA Cup (1): Gage 1.
Ground: Plough Lane Ground, Durnsford Road, Wimbledon, SW19 (01-946 6311)
Nearest stations: Wimbledon or Haydons Road (BR) Wimbledon Park (District)
Manager: Dave Bassett **Secretary:** Adrian Cook
Colours: Shirts blue with yellow trim; shorts blue with yellow trim
Record home gate: 18,000 v HMS Victory, 1934-35 (FA Amateur Cup)
Honours – Champions: Division 4: 1982-83

WOLVERHAMPTON WANDERERS DIV. 4

Barnes, David	Edwards, Neil A.	Palmer, Geoffrey
Barrett, Scott	Eli, Roger	Purdie, Jon
Bartram, Vincent L.	Flowers, Timothy D.	Ryan, Derek A.
Cartwright, Ian J.	Heywood, David I.	Stoutt, Stephen P.
Clarke, Nicholas J.	Holmes, Michael A.	Streete, Floyd A.
Dougherty, Paul	Lockhart, Keith S.	Turley, Russell M.
Edwards, Dean S.	Mutch, Andrew	Zelem, Peter R.

League Appearances: Ainscow, Alan 16; Barnes, David 38; Barrett, Scott 21; Cartwright, Ian J. 13; Chapman, Campbell 29(4); Clarke, Nicholas J. 21(2); Coady, Michael L. 8; Crainie, Daniel 23; Dougherty, Paul 5(6); Edwards, Dean S. 20(3); Edwards, Neil A. 13; Eli, Roger 14; Flowers, Timothy D. 25; Hazell, Robert J. 1; Herbert, Ricki L. 19(1); Holmes, Michael A. 26; King, Andrew E. 20; Lockhart, Keith S. 12; Lomax, Geoffrey W. 5; Morrissey, John J. 5(5); Mutch, Andrew 15; North, Stacey S. 3; Palmer, Geoffrey 20(1); Purdie, Jon 41(1); Raynes, William 6(1); Rosario, Robert M. 2; Ryan, Derek A. 15(5); Smith, Richard F. (1); Stoutt, Stephen P. 26(2); Street, Floyd A. 25; Wassell, Kim D. 2; Whitehead, Clive R. 2; Wright, Darren J. 1; Zelem, Peter R. 14.
Goals – League (57): King 10 (3 pens), D.Edwards 7, N.Edwards 7, Mutch 7, Purdie 6, Ryan 4, Holmes 3, Chapman 2, Lockhart 2, Barnes 1, Cartwright 1, Clarke 1, Coady 1, Crainie 1, Dougherty 1, Morrissey 1, Rosario 1, Streete 1.
Milk Cup (1): Purdie 1.
FA Cup (0).
Ground: Molineux Grounds, Wolverhampton WV1 4QR (0902 712181)
Nearest station: Wolverhampton
Manager: Sammy Chapman **Secretary:** K. D. Pearson A.C.I.S.
Colours: Old gold shirts with black pinstripe, black shorts
Record home gate: 61,315 v Liverpool, February 1939 (FA Cup)
Honours – Champions: Division 1: 1953-54, 1957-58, 1958-59; Division 2: 1931-32, 1976-77; Division 3 North: 1923-24
FA Cup winners: 1892-93, 1907-08, 1948-49, 1959-60
League Cup winners: 1973-74, 1979-80

WREXHAM DIV. 4

Charles, Stephen	Emery, Stephen R.	Salathiel, David N.
Comstive, Paul T.	Horne, Barry	Steel, William J.
Cunnington, Shaun G.	Jones, Frank	Williams, Michael

League Appearances: Brignull, Philip A. 5; Buxton, Stephen C. 1(4); Chadwick, Simon L. 1(1); Charles, Stephen 39(1); Comstive, Paul T. 33(2); Cunnington, Shaun G. 42; Edwards, Andrew J. 25(9); Emery, Stephen R. 8(1); Ferguson, Donald S. 20; Gregory, David H. 35(3); Hencher, Nicholas H. 22(3); Hooper, Michael D. 14; Horne, Barry 46; Jones, Frank 27(1); Keay, John P. 40; Keen, Michael A.C. 5; Mooney, Brian J. 9; Morris, Mark 3; Muldoon, John P. 6(5); Salathiel, David N. 42; Scott, Robert W. 2(1); Stanton, Brian 8; Steel, William J. 43; Vaughan, John 4; Weetman, Darren G. 1; Williams, Michael 25(2).
Goals – League (68): Charles 20 (7 pens), Steel 14, Edwards 9, Hencher 4, Buxton 3, Comstive 3, Gregory 3, Horne 3, Cunnington 2, Mooney 2, Brignull 1, Salathiel 1, own goals 3.
Milk Cup (5): Gregory 3, Horne 1, Steel 1.
FA Cup (5): Cunnington 1, Gregory 1, Hencher 1, Horne 1, Keay 1.
Ground: The Racecourse, Mold Road, Wrexham LL1 2AN (0978 262129)
Nearest station: Wrexham General
Manager: Dixie McNeil **Secretary:** S. Gandy

Colours: Red shirts with white trim; white shorts with red trim
Record home gate: 34,445 v Manchester United, January 1957 (FA Cup)
Honours – Champions: Division 3: 1977-78

YORK CITY — DIV. 3

Banton, Dale C.
Butler, Martin
Canham, Anthony
Crosby, Malcolm
Ford, Gary
Gabbiadini, Marco
Haslegrave, Sean M.
Hay, Alan B.
Hood, Derek
Leaning, Andrew J.
MacPhail, John
McAughtrie, David
Mills, Simon A.
Pearce, Alan
Senior, Stephen
Sbragia, Richard
Smallwood, Neil
Walwyn, Keith I.

League Appearances: Astbury, Michael J. 16; Banton, Dale C. 33(2); Butler, Martin 8(6); Canham, Anthony 40(1); Evans, Christopher B. 7; Ford, Gary 40; Gabbiadini, Marco 10(12); Haslegrave, Sean M. 37(2); Hay, Alan B. 21; Hood, Derek 29(2); Houchen, Keith M. 20(5); Leaning, Andrew J. 30; McAughtrie, David 41; McKenzie, Stuart R. 4; MacPhail, John 42; Mills, Simon A. 35(1); Pearce, Alan 7; Sbragia, Richard 7; Senior, Stephen 33(1); Walwyn, Keith I. 46.
Goals – League (77): Walwyn 22, Canham 13 (1 pen), Banton 10 (1 pen), McPhail 7 (6 pens), Houchen 6 (2 pens), Gabbiadini 4, Ford 3, Senior 3, Mills 2, Evans 1, Hay 1, Hood 1, McAughtrie 1, own goals 3.
Milk Cup (7): Walwyn 3, Banton 1, Houchen 1 (pen), McAughtrie 1, McPhail 1 (pen).
FA Cup (11): Walwyn 4, Ford 3, Banton 1, Canham 1, Pearce 1, Sbragia 1.
Ground: Bootham Crescent, York YO3 7AQ (0904 24447)
Nearest station: York
Manager: Denis Smith **Secretary:** T.D. Hughes
Colours: Shirts red; shorts navy
Record home gate: 28,123 v Huddersfield, March 1938 (FA Cup)
Honours – Champions: Division 4: 1983-84

THE LEAGUE – DIVISION I

	Arsenal	Aston Villa	Birmingham	Chelsea	Coventry C.	Everton	Ipswich T.	Leicester C.	Liverpool
Arsenal	—	3–2	0–0	2–0	3–0	0–1	1–0	1–0	2–0
Aston Villa	1–4	—	0–3	3–1	1–1	0–0	1–0	1–0	2–2
Birmingham C.	0–1	0–0	—	1–2	0–1	0–2	0–1	2–1	0–2
Chelsea	2–1	2–1	2–0	—	1–0	2–1	1–1	2–2	0–1
Coventry C.	0–2	3–3	4–4	1–1	—	1–3	0–1	3–0	0–3
Everton	6–1	2–0	4–1	1–1	1–1	—	1–0	1–2	2–3
Ipswich T.	1–2	0–3	0–1	0–2	1–0	3–4	—	0–2	2–1
Leicester C.	2–2	3–1	4–2	0–0	2–1	3–1	1–0	—	0–2
Liverpool	2–0	3–0	5–0	1–1	5–0	0–2	5–0	1–0	—
Luton T.	2–2	2–0	2–0	1–1	0–1	2–1	1–0	3–1	0–1
Manchester C.	0–1	2–2	1–1	0–1	5–1	1–1	1–1	1–1	1–0
Manchester U.	0–1	4–0	1–0	1–2	2–0	0–0	1–0	4–0	1–1
Newcastle U.	1–0	2–2	4–1	1–3	3–2	2–2	3–1	2–1	1–0
Nottingham F.	3–2	1–1	3–0	0–0	5–2	0–0	3–1	4–3	1–1
Oxford U.	3–0	1–1	0–1	2–1	0–1	1–0	4–3	5–0	2–2
Q.P.R.	0–1	0–1	3–1	6–0	0–2	3–0	1–0	2–0	2–1
Sheffield W.	2–0	2–0	5–1	1–1	2–2	1–5	1–0	1–0	0–0
Southampton	3–0	0–0	1–0	0–1	1–1	2–3	1–0	0–0	1–2
Tottenham H.	1–0	4–2	2–0	4–1	0–1	0–1	2–0	1–3	1–2
Watford	3–0	1–1	3–0	3–1	3–0	0–2	0–0	2–1	2–3
W.B.A.	0–0	0–3	2–1	0–3	0–0	0–3	1–2	2–2	1–2
West Ham U.	0–0	4–1	2–0	1–2	1–0	2–1	2–1	3–0	2–2

1985-86 RESULTS

Luton T.	Manchester C.	Manchester U.	Newcastle U.	Nottingham F.	Oxford U.	Q.P.R.	Sheffield W.	Southampton	Tottenham H.	Watford	W.B.A.	West Ham U.
2–1	1–0	1–2	0–0	1–1	2–1	3–1	1–0	3–2	0–0	0–2	2–2	1–0
3–1	0–1	1–3	1–2	1–2	2–0	1–2	1–1	0–0	1–2	4–1	1–1	2–1
0–2	1–0	1–1	0–1	0–1	3–1	2–0	0–2	0–2	1–2	1–2	0–1	1–0
1–0	1–0	1–2	1–1	4–2	1–4	1–1	2–1	2–0	2–0	1–5	3–0	0–4
1–0	1–1	1–3	1–2	0–0	5–2	2–1	0–1	3–2	2–3	0–2	3–0	0–1
2–0	4–0	3–1	1–0	1–1	2–0	4–3	3–1	6–1	1–0	4–1	2–0	3–1
1–1	0–0	0–1	2–2	1–0	3–2	1–0	2–1	1–1	1–0	0–0	1–0	0–1
0–0	1–1	3–0	2–0	0–3	4–4	1–4	2–3	3–3	1–4	2–2	2–2	0–1
3–2	2–0	1–1	1–1	2–0	6–0	4–1	2–2	1–0	4–1	3–1	4–1	3–1
—	2–1	1–1	2–0	1–1	1–2	2–0	1–0	7–0	1–1	3–2	3–0	0–0
1–1	—	0–3	1–0	1–2	0–3	2–0	1–3	1–0	2–1	0–1	2–1	2–2
2–0	2–2	—	3–0	2–3	3–0	2–0	0–2	1–0	0–0	1–1	3–0	2–0
2–2	3–1	2–4	—	0–3	3–0	3–1	4–1	2–1	2–2	1–1	4–1	1–2
2–0	0–2	1–3	1–2	—	1–1	4–0	0–1	2–1	0–1	3–2	2–1	2–1
1–1	1–0	1–3	1–2	1–2	—	3–3	0–1	3–0	1–1	1–1	2–2	1–2
1–1	0–0	1–0	3–1	2–1	3–1	—	1–1	0–2	2–5	2–1	1–0	0–1
3–2	3–2	1–0	2–2	2–1	2–1	0–0	—	2–1	1–2	2–1	1–0	2–2
1–2	3–0	1–0	1–1	3–1	1–1	3–0	2–3	—	1–0	3–1	3–1	1–1
1–3	0–2	0–0	5–1	0–3	5–1	1–1	5–1	5–3	—	4–0	5–0	1–0
1–2	3–2	1–1	4–1	1–1	2–2	2–0	2–1	1–1	1–0	—	5–1	0–2
1–2	2–3	1–5	1–1	1–1	1–1	0–1	1–1	1–0	1–1	3–1	—	2–3
0–1	1–0	2–1	8–1	4–2	3–1	3–1	1–0	1–0	2–1	2–1	4–0	—

THE LEAGUE – DIVISION II

	Barnsley	Blackburn R.	Bradford C.	Brighton & HA	Carlisle U.	Charlton Ath.	Crystal Palace	Fulham	Grimsby T.
Barnsley	—	1–1	2–2	3–2	1–2	2–1	2–4	2–0	1–0
Blackburn R.	0–3	—	3–0	1–4	2–0	0–0	1–2	1–0	3–1
Bradford C.	2–0	3–2	—	3–2	1–0	1–2	1–0	3–1	0–1
Brighton & HA	0–1	3–1	2–1	—	6–1	3–5	2–0	2–3	2–2
Carlisle U.	1–1	2–1	1–2	2–0	—	2–3	2–2	2–1	1–2
Charlton Ath.	2–1	3–0	1–1	2–2	3–0	—	3–1	2–0	2–0
Crystal Palace	1–0	2–0	2–1	1–0	1–1	2–1	—	0–0	2–1
Fulham	2–0	3–3	4–1	1–0	0–1	0–3	2–3	—	2–1
Grimsby T.	1–2	5–2	2–0	0–2	1–0	2–2	3–0	1–0	—
Huddersfield T.	1–1	0–0	2–0	1–0	3–3	0–2	0–0	1–3	2–2
Hull C.	0–1	2–2	1–0	2–0	4–0	1–1	1–2	5–0	2–0
Leeds U.	0–2	1–1	2–1	2–3	2–0	1–2	1–3	1–0	1–1
Middlesbrough	0–0	0–0	1–1	0–1	1–3	1–3	0–2	1–0	3–1
Millwall	2–2	0–1	2–1	0–1	3–1	2–2	3–2	1–1	1–0
Norwich C.	1–1	3–0	0–0	3–0	2–1	3–1	4–3	2–1	3–2
Oldham Ath.	1–1	3–1	0–1	4–0	2–1	2–1	2–0	2–1	2–1
Portsmouth	1–1	3–0	4–0	1–2	4–0	1–0	1–0	1–1	3–1
Sheffield W.	3–1	3–3	3–1	3–0	1–0	1–1	0–0	2–1	1–1
Shrewsbury T.	3–0	2–0	2–0	2–1	0–0	2–1	0–2	2–1	0–2
Stoke C.	0–0	2–2	3–1	1–1	0–0	0–0	0–0	1–0	1–1
Sunderland	2–0	0–2	1–1	2–1	2–2	1–2	1–1	4–2	3–3
Wimbledon	1–0	1–1	1–0	0–0	4–1	3–1	1–1	1–0	3–0

1985-86 RESULTS

Huddersfield T.	Hull C.	Leeds U.	Middlesbrough	Millwall	Norwich C.	Oldham Ath.	Portsmouth	Sheffield W.	Shrewsbury T.	Stoke C.	Sunderland	Wimbledon
1–3	1–4	3–0	0–0	2–1	2–2	1–0	0–1	2–1	2–0	0–0	1–1	0–1
0–1	2–2	2–0	0–1	1–2	2–1	0–0	1–0	6–1	1–1	0–1	2–0	2–0
3–0	4–2	0–1	2–1	0–2	0–2	1–0	2–1	1–4	3–1	3–1	2–0	1–1
4–3	3–1	0–1	3–3	1–0	1–1	1–1	2–3	0–0	0–2	2–0	3–1	2–0
2–0	2–1	1–2	1–0	1–0	0–4	3–1	0–1	1–0	0–2	3–0	1–2	2–3
3–0	1–2	4–0	2–0	3–3	1–0	1–1	1–2	2–0	4–1	2–0	2–1	0–0
2–3	0–2	3–0	2–1	2–1	1–2	3–2	2–1	1–1	0–1	0–1	1–0	1–3
2–1	1–1	3–1	0–3	1–2	0–1	2–2	0–1	2–3	2–1	1–0	1–2	0–2
1–1	0–1	1–0	3–2	5–1	1–0	1–4	1–0	0–1	3–1	3–3	1–1	0–1
—	2–1	3–1	0–3	4–3	0–0	2–0	1–2	3–1	1–0	2–0	2–0	0–1
3–1	—	2–1	0–0	3–0	1–0	4–2	2–2	0–0	4–3	0–2	1–1	1–1
2–0	1–1	—	1–0	3–1	0–2	3–1	2–1	1–1	1–1	4–0	1–1	0–0
0–1	1–2	2–2	—	3–0	1–1	3–2	1–0	1–2	3–1	1–1	2–0	1–0
2–1	5–0	3–1	3–0	—	4–2	0–1	0–4	3–0	2–0	2–3	1–0	0–1
4–1	2–0	4–0	2–0	6–1	—	1–0	2–0	4–0	3–1	1–1	0–0	1–2
1–1	3–1	3–1	1–0	0–0	1–2	—	2–0	1–5	4–3	2–4	2–2	2–1
4–1	1–1	2–3	1–0	2–1	2–0	1–2	—	0–3	4–0	3–0	3–0	1–1
1–1	3–1	3–2	0–1	1–3	2–5	2–0	0–0	—	1–1	1–2	1–0	4–0
3–0	0–0	1–3	2–1	1–1	0–3	2–0	1–1	3–1	—	1–0	1–2	1–1
3–0	0–1	6–2	3–2	0–0	1–1	2–0	2–0	1–3	2–2	—	1–0	0–0
1–0	1–1	4–2	1–0	1–2	0–2	0–3	1–3	2–1	2–0	2–0	—	2–1
2–2	3–1	0–3	3–0	1–1	2–1	0–0	1–3	5–0	2–1	1–0	3–0	—

THE LEAGUE – DIVISION III

	Blackpool	Bolton W.	Bournemouth	Brentford	Bristol C.	Bristol R.	Bury	Cardiff C.	Chesterfield	Darlington
Blackpool	—	1–1	2–0	4–0	2–1	4–2	5–0	3–0	0–1	0–0
Bolton W.	1–3	—	1–0	1–2	0–4	0–2	1–4	5–0	2–1	0–3
Bournemouth	1–4	2–1	—	0–0	5–0	0–1	2–1	1–1	3–2	4–2
Brentford	1–1	1–1	1–0	—	1–2	1–0	1–0	3–0	1–0	2–1
Bristol C.	2–1	2–0	1–3	0–0	—	2–0	4–1	2–1	0–0	1–0
Bristol R.	1–0	2–1	2–3	0–1	1–1	—	2–1	2–1	1–1	3–1
Bury	4–1	2–1	3–0	0–0	6–3	1–1	—	3–0	1–1	0–1
Cardiff C.	1–0	0–1	0–1	1–0	1–3	2–0	0–0	—	0–2	0–1
Chesterfield	1–2	3–0	0–1	1–3	0–0	2–0	4–3	3–4	—	1–0
Darlington	2–1	0–1	0–0	3–5	1–1	3–3	1–1	4–1	2–1	—
Derby Co.	1–2	2–1	3–0	1–1	2–0	0–2	1–1	2–1	0–0	1–1
Doncaster R.	0–0	1–1	1–1	1–0	1–1	0–2	1–0	0–2	2–0	2–0
Gillingham	2–2	2–1	2–0	1–2	1–1	2–0	1–0	2–0	1–1	1–1
Lincoln C.	0–3	1–1	3–2	3–0	1–1	2–2	2–0	0–4	2–1	1–1
Newport Co.	1–1	0–1	2–1	1–2	1–1	3–0	1–0	1–2	3–3	3–0
Notts Co.	1–2	1–0	3–1	0–4	4–0	0–0	2–2	1–4	2–1	5–0
Plymouth Arg.	3–1	4–1	2–1	2–0	4–0	4–2	3–0	4–4	0–0	4–2
Reading	1–0	1–0	1–2	3–1	1–0	3–2	2–0	1–1	4–2	0–2
Rotherham U.	4–1	4–0	4–1	1–2	2–0	2–0	2–0	3–0	1–2	1–2
Swansea C.	2–0	3–1	1–1	2–0	1–3	0–1	1–0	2–0	1–1	2–2
Walsall	1–1	2–0	4–2	1–2	2–1	6–0	3–2	6–3	3–0	0–0
Wigan Ath.	1–1	1–3	3–0	4–0	1–1	4–0	1–0	2–0	2–0	5–1
Wolverhampton W.	2–1	0–2	0–3	1–4	2–1	3–4	1–1	3–1	1–0	2–1
York C.	3–0	3–0	2–1	1–0	1–1	4–0	0–0	1–1	2–0	7–0

1985-86 RESULTS

Derby Co.	Doncaster R.	Gillingham	Lincoln C.	Newport Co.	Notts Co.	Plymouth Arg.	Reading	Rotherham U.	Swansea C.	Walsall	Wigan Ath.	Wolverhampton W.	York C.
0–1	4–0	2–2	2–0	0–0	1–3	1–1	0–0	2–1	2–0	2–1	1–2	0–1	0–2
0–1	2–0	0–1	1–1	4–0	1–0	3–1	2–0	1–1	1–1	3–1	1–2	4–1	1–1
1–1	1–1	2–3	2–2	0–1	0–0	1–3	0–1	1–2	4–0	0–1	0–2	3–2	2–0
3–3	1–3	1–2	0–1	0–0	1–1	1–1	1–2	1–1	1–0	1–3	1–3	2–1	3–3
1–1	4–1	1–2	1–1	3–1	3–0	2–0	3–0	3–1	0–1	2–3	1–0	3–0	2–2
0–0	1–0	1–0	0–0	2–0	1–1	1–2	0–2	5–2	0–0	0–1	1–1	1–1	0–1
1–1	1–2	1–2	4–0	1–1	2–4	0–1	3–1	2–0	2–2	2–1	0–0	3–1	4–2
0–2	0–1	1–1	2–1	1–1	1–3	1–2	1–3	2–3	1–0	1–1	3–1	1–1	2–1
1–0	0–0	1–1	2–2	3–1	2–2	1–2	3–4	2–0	4–1	2–3	1–1	3–0	1–0
2–1	0–2	3–2	1–0	3–2	2–3	0–2	0–0	2–2	6–0	0–3	1–1	2–1	1–0
—	1–1	2–0	7–0	1–1	2–0	1–2	1–1	2–1	5–1	3–1	1–0	4–2	2–1
0–3	—	2–3	1–1	1–1	2–1	1–0	0–1	0–0	0–0	1–0	2–2	0–1	1–1
1–2	4–0	—	2–0	0–1	4–0	1–1	3–0	3–0	5–1	5–2	2–0	2–0	1–2
0–1	3–3	1–0	—	1–1	0–2	1–1	0–1	0–0	4–1	3–2	0–0	2–3	3–4
1–1	2–2	1–1	1–2	—	1–2	3–1	0–2	0–0	2–0	1–5	3–4	3–1	1–1
0–3	1–1	1–1	3–2	1–2	—	2–0	0–0	1–0	3–0	3–1	1–1	4–0	3–1
4–1	0–1	3–0	2–1	2–0	0–1	—	0–1	4–0	2–0	2–0	2–1	3–1	2–2
1–0	2–0	1–2	0–2	2–0	3–1	4–3	—	2–1	2–0	2–1	1–0	2–2	0–0
1–1	2–1	1–1	1–0	0–0	1–0	1–1	1–2	—	4–1	3–0	0–0	1–2	4–1
0–3	0–2	2–2	3–1	1–1	0–0	0–2	2–3	1–0	—	2–1	0–1	0–2	1–0
1–1	1–0	4–1	2–1	2–0	0–0	2–2	6–0	3–1	3–1	—	3–3	1–1	3–1
2–1	0–1	3–3	3–2	0–0	3–1	3–0	1–0	2–0	5–0	2–0	—	5–3	1–0
0–4	1–2	1–3	1–1	1–2	2–2	0–3	2–3	0–0	1–5	0–0	2–2	—	3–2
1–3	0–1	2–0	2–1	3–1	2–2	3–1	0–1	2–1	3–1	1–0	4–1	2–1	—

THE LEAGUE – DIVISION IV

	Aldershot	Burnley	Cambridge U.	Chester C.	Colchester U.	Crewe Alex.	Exeter C.	Halifax T.	Hartlepool U.	Hereford U.
Aldershot	—	0–2	2–1	1–1	1–1	3–2	4–0	1–2	0–1	2–0
Burnley	1–2	—	1–1	1–0	0–2	0–1	3–1	1–3	2–0	3–2
Cambridge U.	0–2	0–4	—	3–2	1–3	1–0	1–1	4–0	4–2	4–0
Chester C.	1–0	4–0	1–1	—	4–0	4–0	2–1	1–1	1–1	1–0
Colchester U.	4–0	2–2	4–1	2–3	—	1–2	1–1	3–1	3–1	4–1
Crewe Alex.	2–0	3–1	0–1	2–2	0–2	—	0–1	2–2	0–0	2–0
Exeter C.	2–0	0–2	0–0	1–3	2–2	1–2	—	1–0	1–2	3–2
Halifax T.	1–1	2–2	1–1	1–2	2–2	1–0	1–0	—	3–2	1–0
Hartlepool U.	2–1	3–1	2–1	1–1	4–1	4–1	0–0	3–0	—	2–1
Hereford U.	4–1	2–2	1–0	0–2	2–0	4–1	4–1	2–1	2–2	—
Mansfield T.	2–0	0–0	2–0	0–0	2–1	2–2	2–1	2–0	4–0	4–0
Northampton T.	2–3	2–0	0–2	2–2	1–0	0–1	2–2	4–0	3–0	1–3
Orient	1–1	3–0	3–1	0–0	1–2	0–1	2–2	1–0	1–1	2–2
Peterborough U.	3–0	0–0	0–0	3–0	1–2	0–0	1–1	1–1	3–1	0–0
Port Vale	3–1	1–1	4–1	1–1	1–1	3–0	0–0	3–2	4–0	1–0
Preston NE.	1–3	1–0	1–2	3–6	3–2	1–2	2–2	0–1	2–1	2–0
Rochdale	2–0	1–0	2–1	1–2	3–3	1–0	1–1	1–0	0–2	1–1
Scunthorpe U.	1–0	1–1	0–0	2–0	1–1	3–1	1–0	3–3	1–0	2–1
Southend U.	2–0	2–3	1–0	1–1	2–4	0–1	2–0	2–1	3–2	3–1
Stockport Co.	3–2	1–1	3–1	2–2	1–1	3–0	1–1	2–1	1–3	1–1
Swindon T.	4–1	3–1	1–0	4–2	2–1	1–0	2–1	3–2	3–1	1–0
Torquay U.	1–2	2–0	1–1	0–3	2–1	0–0	1–2	2–0	1–3	2–1
Tranmere R.	3–0	2–1	6–2	2–3	3–4	0–1	0–1	0–3	4–2	1–2
Wrexham	4–1	0–1	6–2	1–1	2–1	2–1	1–1	2–1	1–0	0–1

1985-86 RESULTS

Mansfield T.	Northampton T.	Orient	Peterborough U.	Port Vale	Preston NE.	Rochdale	Scunthorpe U.	Southend U.	Stockport Co.	Swindon T.	Torquay U.	Tranmere R.	Wrexham
1–2	1–0	1–1	1–0	0–0	4–0	2–1	2–1	1–3	6–1	2–4	1–1	3–1	6–0
2–1	3–2	1–0	1–1	1–2	1–1	1–0	1–2	1–3	0–1	0–2	3–0	3–1	5–2
4–2	2–5	1–2	3–1	1–3	2–0	1–0	0–1	1–2	1–2	1–1	3–0	3–2	4–3
1–0	2–3	3–0	2–1	4–1	2–0	1–1	1–1	2–0	1–2	0–1	3–1	1–0	2–1
0–0	0–2	4–0	5–0	1–0	4–0	0–1	1–1	2–0	3–1	1–1	0–0	1–2	5–2
2–1	0–1	1–3	1–1	0–1	3–3	4–2	4–0	1–1	0–1	2–0	1–0	2–1	3–2
0–1	1–2	1–1	1–0	1–0	3–0	2–0	2–0	0–2	1–0	0–3	2–2	1–0	0–1
1–2	2–0	2–1	1–1	2–0	2–1	1–1	2–1	2–3	0–0	1–3	0–0	1–2	5–2
1–1	2–1	1–2	2–1	1–1	1–0	2–0	0–1	3–2	1–1	1–0	1–0	1–0	3–3
4–2	3–0	3–2	2–1	1–1	1–1	2–2	1–1	2–1	3–2	4–1	4–1	1–4	3–1
—	1–0	1–1	0–1	2–1	2–3	3–2	1–1	3–0	4–2	1–1	4–0	0–0	1–1
1–0	—	2–3	2–2	2–2	6–0	1–0	2–2	0–0	3–1	0–1	5–1	2–2	1–2
0–1	0–1	—	2–2	1–0	2–0	5–0	3–0	3–0	0–1	1–0	4–2	3–1	1–3
4–2	0–5	2–2	—	1–0	1–1	1–1	1–0	1–1	2–0	3–0	2–0	0–1	1–1
0–0	0–0	2–0	2–0	—	0–1	1–1	3–1	4–0	1–1	3–0	1–0	0–0	4–0
0–2	1–1	1–3	2–4	0–1	—	1–1	0–1	3–2	1–2	0–3	4–0	2–2	1–0
1–1	3–2	1–4	2–1	3–3	1–1	—	1–0	2–1	4–1	1–2	5–0	1–1	3–2
0–3	1–0	2–2	2–0	0–0	1–3	3–1	—	2–0	2–3	0–2	4–0	0–1	1–1
3–1	0–4	5–1	0–1	2–1	2–1	5–0	2–1	—	0–0	0–0	1–2	2–2	3–0
0–2	1–0	2–3	2–2	1–2	2–1	3–0	0–0	2–1	—	0–2	1–1	1–1	2–0
2–1	3–2	4–1	3–0	0–0	4–1	4–0	1–1	2–1	1–0	—	2–1	2–1	0–1
1–2	1–1	2–2	2–0	0–1	1–0	1–2	1–0	2–2	4–3	0–1	—	1–2	1–3
1–2	1–3	0–3	7–0	1–2	2–3	2–0	2–1	1–1	2–3	3–1	2–0	—	1–3
1–2	1–0	1–3	0–1	1–3	1–1	2–0	1–0	0–0	3–0	0–1	3–2	1–1	—

FOOTBALL LEAGUE
FINAL TABLES 1985-86

First Division		Home			Goals		Away			Goals			
	P	*W*	*D*	*L*	*F*	*A*	*W*	*D*	*L*	*F*	*A*	*Pt*	*GD*
Liverpool	42	16	4	1	58	14	10	6	5	31	23	88	+52
Everton	42	16	3	2	54	18	10	5	6	33	23	85	+46
West Ham U.	42	17	2	2	48	16	9	4	8	26	24	84	+34
Manchester U.	42	12	5	4	35	12	10	5	6	35	24	76	+34
Sheffield W.	42	13	6	2	36	23	8	4	9	27	31	73	+9
Chelsea	42	12	4	5	32	27	8	7	6	25	29	71	+1
Arsenal	42	13	5	3	29	15	7	4	10	20	32	69	+2
Nottingham F.	42	11	5	5	38	25	8	6	7	31	28	68	+16
Luton T.	42	12	6	3	37	15	6	6	9	24	29	66	+17
Tottenham H.	42	12	2	7	47	25	7	6	8	27	27	65	+22
Newcastle U.	42	12	5	4	46	31	5	7	9	21	41	63	−5
Watford	42	11	6	4	40	22	5	5	11	29	40	59	+7
Q.P.R.	42	12	3	6	33	20	3	4	14	20	44	52	−11
Southampton	42	10	6	5	32	18	2	4	15	19	44	46	−11
Manchester C.	42	7	7	7	25	26	4	5	12	18	31	45	−14
Aston Villa	42	7	6	8	27	28	3	8	10	24	39	44	−16
Coventry C.	42	6	5	10	31	35	5	5	11	17	36	43	−23
Oxford U.	42	7	7	7	34	27	3	5	13	28	53	42	−18
Leicester C.	42	7	8	6	35	35	3	4	14	19	41	42	−22
Ipswich T.	42	8	5	8	20	24	3	3	15	12	31	41	−23
Birmingham C.	42	5	2	14	13	25	3	3	15	17	48	29	−43
W.B.A.	42	3	8	10	21	36	1	4	16	14	53	24	−54

Second Division		Home			Goals		Away			Goals			
	P	*W*	*D*	*L*	*F*	*A*	*W*	*D*	*L*	*F*	*A*	*Pt*	*GD*
Norwich C.	42	16	4	1	51	15	9	5	7	33	22	84	+47
Charlton Ath.	42	14	5	2	44	15	8	6	7	34	30	77	+33
Wimbledon	42	13	6	2	38	16	8	7	6	20	21	76	+21
Portsmouth	42	13	4	4	43	17	9	3	9	26	24	73	+28
Crystal Palace	42	12	3	6	29	22	7	6	8	28	30	66	+5
Hull C.	42	11	7	3	39	19	6	6	9	26	36	64	+10
Sheffield U.	42	10	7	4	36	24	7	4	10	28	39	62	+1
Oldham Ath.	42	13	4	4	40	28	4	5	12	22	33	60	+1
Millwall	42	12	3	6	39	24	5	5	11	25	41	59	−1
Stoke C.	42	8	11	2	29	16	6	4	11	19	34	57	−2
Brighton & HA	42	10	5	6	42	30	6	3	12	22	34	56	0
Barnsley	42	9	6	6	29	26	5	8	8	18	24	56	−3
Bradford C.	42	14	1	6	36	24	2	5	14	15	39	54	−12
Leeds U.	42	9	7	5	30	22	6	1	14	26	50	53	−16
Grimsby T.	42	11	4	6	35	24	3	6	12	23	38	52	−4
Huddersfield T.	42	10	6	5	30	23	4	4	13	21	44	52	−16
Shrewsbury T.	42	11	5	5	29	20	3	4	14	23	44	51	−12
Sunderland	42	10	5	6	33	29	3	6	12	14	32	50	−14
Blackburn R.	42	10	4	7	30	20	2	9	10	23	42	49	−9
Carlisle U.	42	10	2	9	30	28	3	5	13	17	43	46	−24
Middlesbrough	42	8	6	7	26	23	4	3	14	18	30	45	−9
Fulham	42	8	3	10	29	32	2	3	16	16	37	36	−24

Third Division		Home			Goals		Away			Goals			
	P	*W*	*D*	*L*	*F*	*A*	*W*	*D*	*L*	*F*	*A*	*Pt*	*GD*
Reading	46	16	3	4	39	22	13	4	6	28	29	94	+16
Plymouth Arg.	46	17	3	3	56	20	9	6	8	32	33	87	+35
Derby Co.	46	13	7	3	45	20	10	8	5	35	21	84	+39
Wigan Ath.	46	17	4	2	54	17	6	10	7	28	31	83	+34
Gillingham	46	14	5	4	48	17	8	8	7	33	37	79	+27
Walsall	46	15	7	1	59	23	7	2	14	31	41	75	+26
York C.	46	16	4	3	49	17	4	7	12	28	41	71	+19
Notts Co.	46	12	6	5	42	26	7	8	8	29	34	71	+11
Bristol C.	46	14	5	4	43	19	4	9	10	26	41	68	+9
Brentford	46	8	8	7	29	29	10	4	9	29	32	66	−3
Doncaster R.	46	7	10	6	20	21	9	6	8	25	31	64	−7
Blackpool	46	11	6	6	38	19	6	6	11	28	36	63	+11
Darlington	46	10	7	6	39	33	5	6	12	22	45	58	−17
Rotherham U.	46	13	5	5	44	18	2	7	14	17	41	57	+2
Bournemouth	46	9	6	8	41	31	6	3	14	24	41	54	−7
Bristol R.	46	9	8	6	27	21	5	4	14	24	54	54	−24
Chesterfield	46	10	6	7	41	30	3	8	12	20	34	53	−3
Bolton W.	46	10	4	9	35	30	5	4	14	19	38	53	−14
Newport Co.	46	7	8	8	35	33	4	10	9	17	32	51	−13
Bury	46	11	7	5	46	26	1	6	16	17	41	49	−4
Lincoln C.	46	7	9	7	33	34	3	7	13	22	43	46	−22
Cardiff C.	46	7	5	11	22	29	5	4	14	31	54	45	−30
Wolverhampton W.	46	6	6	11	29	47	5	4	14	28	51	43	−41
Swansea C.	46	9	6	8	27	27	2	4	17	16	60	43	−44

Fourth Division		Home			Goals		Away			Goals			
	P	*W*	*D*	*L*	*F*	*A*	*W*	*D*	*L*	*F*	*A*	*Pt*	*GD*
Swindon T.	46	20	2	1	52	19	12	4	7	30	24	102	+39
Chester C.	46	15	5	3	44	16	8	10	5	39	34	84	+33
Mansfield T.	46	13	8	2	43	17	10	4	9	31	30	81	+27
Port Vale	46	13	9	1	42	11	8	7	8	25	26	79	+30
Orient	46	11	6	6	39	21	9	6	8	40	43	72	+15
Colchester U.	46	12	6	5	51	22	7	7	9	37	41	70	+25
Hartlepool U.	46	15	6	2	41	20	5	4	14	27	47	70	+1
Northampton T.	46	9	7	7	44	29	9	3	11	35	29	64	+21
Southend U.	46	13	4	6	43	27	5	6	12	26	40	64	+2
Hereford U.	46	15	6	2	55	30	3	4	16	19	43	64	+1
Stockport Co.	46	9	9	5	35	28	8	4	11	28	43	64	−8
Crewe Alex.	46	10	6	7	35	26	8	3	12	19	35	63	−7
Wrexham	46	11	5	7	34	24	6	4	13	34	56	60	−12
Burnley	46	11	3	9	35	30	5	8	10	25	35	59	−5
Scunthorpe U.	46	11	7	5	33	23	4	7	12	17	32	59	−5
Aldershot	46	12	5	6	45	25	5	2	16	21	49	58	−8
Peterborough U.	46	9	11	3	31	19	4	6	13	21	45	56	−12
Rochdale	46	12	7	4	41	29	2	6	15	16	48	55	−20
Tranmere R.	46	9	1	13	46	41	6	8	9	28	32	54	+1
Halifax T.	46	10	8	5	35	27	4	4	15	25	44	54	−11
Exeter C.	46	10	4	9	26	25	3	11	9	21	34	54	−12
Cambridge U.	46	12	2	9	45	38	3	7	13	20	42	54	−15
Preston NE.	46	7	4	12	32	41	4	6	13	22	48	43	−35
Torquay U.	46	8	5	10	29	32	1	5	17	14	56	37	−45

DIVISION ONE

LEAGUE POSITIONS (1951-86)

	1985–86	1984–85	1983–84	1982–83	1981–82	1980–81	1979–80	1978–79	1977–78	1976–77	1975–76	1974–75	1973–74	1972–73	1971–72	1970–71	1969–70
Arsenal	7	7	6	10	5	3	4	7	5	8	17	16	10	2	5	1	12
Aston Villa	16	10	10	6	11	1	7	8	8	4	16	—	—	—	—	—	—
Birmingham City	21	—	20	17	16	13	—	21	11	13	19	17	19	10	—	—	—
Blackburn Rovers	—	—	—	—	—	—	—	—	—	—	—	—	—	—	—	—	—
Blackpool	—	—	—	—	—	—	—	—	—	—	—	—	—	—	—	22	—
Bolton Wanderers	—	—	—	—	—	—	22	17	—	—	—	—	—	—	—	—	—
Brighton & H.A.	—	—	—	22	13	19	16	—	—	—	—	—	—	—	—	—	—
Bristol City	—	—	—	—	—	—	20	13	17	18	—	—	—	—	—	—	—
Burnley	—	—	—	—	—	—	—	—	—	—	21	10	6	—	—	21	14
Cardiff City	—	—	—	—	—	—	—	—	—	—	—	—	—	—	—	—	—
Carlisle United	—	—	—	—	—	—	—	—	—	—	—	22	—	—	—	—	—
Charlton Athletic	—	—	—	—	—	—	—	—	—	—	—	—	—	—	—	—	—
Chelsea	6	6	—	—	—	—	—	22	16	—	—	21	17	12	7	6	3
Coventry City	17	18	19	19	14	16	15	10	7	19	14	14	16	19	18	10	6
Crystal Palace	—	—	—	—	—	22	13	—	—	—	—	—	—	21	20	18	20
Derby County	—	—	—	—	—	—	21	19	12	15	4	1	3	7	1	9	4
Everton	2	1	7	7	8	15	19	4	3	9	11	4	7	17	15	14	1
Fulham	—	—	—	—	—	—	—	—	—	—	—	—	—	—	—	—	—
Huddersfield Town	—	—	—	—	—	—	—	—	—	—	—	—	—	22	15	—	—
Ipswich Town	20	17	12	9	2	2	3	6	18	3	6	3	4	4	13	19	18
Leeds United	—	—	—	—	20	9	11	5	9	10	5	9	1	3	2	2	2
Leicester City	19	15	15	—	—	21	—	—	22	11	7	18	9	16	12	—	—
Liverpool	1	2	1	1	1	5	1	1	2	1	1	2	2	1	3	5	5
Luton Town	9	13	16	18	—	—	—	—	—	—	—	20	—	—	—	—	—
Manchester City	15	—	—	20	10	12	17	15	4	2	8	8	14	11	4	11	10
Manchester United	4	4	4	3	3	8	2	9	10	6	3	—	21	18	8	8	8
Middlesbrough	—	—	—	—	22	14	9	12	14	12	13	7	—	—	—	—	—
Newcastle United	11	14	—	—	—	—	—	—	21	5	15	15	15	9	11	12	7
Northampton Town	—	—	—	—	—	—	—	—	—	—	—	—	—	—	—	—	—
Norwich City	—	20	14	14	—	20	12	16	13	16	10	—	22	20	—	—	—
Nottingham F.	8	9	3	5	12	7	5	2	1	—	—	—	—	—	21	16	15
Notts Co.	—	—	21	15	15	—	—	—	—	—	—	—	—	—	—	—	—
Orient	—	—	—	—	—	—	—	—	—	—	—	—	—	—	—	—	—
Oxford United	18	—	—	—	—	—	—	—	—	—	—	—	—	—	—	—	—
Portsmouth	—	—	—	—	—	—	—	—	—	—	—	—	—	—	—	—	—
Preston North End	—	—	—	—	—	—	—	—	—	—	—	—	—	—	—	—	—
Queen's Park Rangers	13	19	5	—	—	—	—	20	19	14	2	11	8	—	—	—	—
Sheffield United	—	—	—	—	—	—	—	—	—	—	22	6	13	14	10	—	—
Sheffield Wednesday	5	8	—	—	—	—	—	—	—	—	—	—	—	—	—	—	22
Southampton	14	5	2	12	7	6	8	14	—	—	—	—	20	13	19	7	19
Stoke City	—	22	18	13	18	11	18	—	—	21	12	5	5	15	17	13	9
Sunderland	—	21	13	16	19	17	—	—	—	20	—	—	—	—	—	—	21
Swansea City	—	—	—	21	6	—	—	—	—	—	—	—	—	—	—	—	—
Tottenham Hotspur	10	3	8	4	4	10	14	11	—	22	9	19	11	8	6	3	11
Watford	12	11	11	2	—	—	—	—	—	—	—	—	—	—	—	—	—
West Bromwich A.	22	12	17	11	17	4	10	3	6	7	—	—	—	22	16	17	16
West Ham United	3	16	9	8	9	—	—	19	20	17	18	13	18	6	14	30	17
Wolverhampton W.	—	—	22	—	21	18	6	—	15	—	20	12	12	5	9	4	13

1968–69	1967–68	1966–67	1965–66	1964–65	1963–64	1962–63	1961–62	1960–61	1959–60	1958–59	1957–58	1956–57	1955–56	1954–55	1953–54	1952–53	1951–52	
4	9	7	14	13	8	7	10	11	13	3	12	5	5	9	12	1	3	Arsenal
—	—	21	16	16	19	15	7	9	—	21	14	10	20	6	13	11	6	Aston Villa
—	—	—	—	22	20	20	17	18	19	9	13	12	6	—	—	—	—	Birmingham City
—	—	—	22	10	7	11	16	8	17	10	—	—	—	—	—	—	—	Blackburn Rovers
—	—	22	13	17	18	13	13	20	11	8	7	4	2	19	6	7	9	Blackpool
—	—	—	—	—	21	18	11	18	6	4	15	9	8	18	5	14	5	Bolton Wanderers
—	—	—	—	—	—	—	—	—	—	—	—	—	—	—	—	—	—	Brighton & H.A.
—	—	—	—	—	—	—	—	—	—	—	—	—	—	—	—	—	—	Bristol City
14	13	14	3	12	9	3	2	4	1	7	6	7	7	10	7	6	14	Burnley
—	—	—	—	—	—	21	15	—	—	—	21	17	20	10	12	—	—	Cardiff City
—	—	—	—	—	—	—	—	—	—	—	—	—	—	—	—	—	—	Carlisle United
—	—	—	—	—	—	—	—	—	—	—	—	22	14	15	9	5	10	Charlton Athletic
5	6	9	5	3	5	—	22	12	18	14	11	13	16	1	8	19	19	Chelsea
20	20	—	—	—	—	—	—	—	—	—	—	—	—	—	—	—	—	Coventry City
—	—	—	—	—	—	—	—	—	—	—	—	—	—	—	—	—	—	Crystal Palace
—	—	—	—	—	—	—	—	—	—	—	—	—	—	—	—	22	17	Derby County
3	5	6	11	4	3	1	4	5	15	16	16	15	15	11	—	—	—	Everton
—	22	19	20	20	15	16	20	17	10	—	—	—	—	—	—	—	22	Fulham
—	—	—	—	—	—	—	—	—	—	—	—	—	21	12	3	—	21	Huddersfield Town
12	—	—	—	—	22	17	1	—	—	—	—	—	—	—	—	—	—	Ipswich Town
1	4	4	2	2	—	—	—	—	21	15	17	8	—	—	—	—	—	Leeds United
21	12	8	7	18	11	4	14	6	12	19	18	—	—	21	—	—	—	Leicester City
2	3	5	1	7	1	8	—	—	—	—	—	—	—	—	22	17	11	Liverpool
—	—	—	—	—	—	—	—	—	22	17	8	16	10	—	—	—	—	Luton Town
13	1	15	—	—	—	21	12	13	16	20	5	18	4	7	17	20	15	Manchester City
11	2	1	4	1	2	19	15	7	7	2	9	1	1	5	4	8	1	Manchester United
—	—	—	—	—	—	—	—	—	—	—	—	—	—	21	13	18		Middlesbrough
9	10	20	15	—	—	—	—	21	8	11	19	17	11	8	15	16	8	Newcastle United
—	—	—	21	—	—	—	—	—	—	—	—	—	—	—	—	—	—	Northampton Town
—	—	—	—	—	—	—	—	—	—	—	—	—	—	—	—	—	—	Norwich City
18	11	2	18	5	13	9	19	14	20	13	10	—	—	—	—	—	—	Nottingham Forest
—	—	—	—	—	—	—	—	—	—	—	—	—	—	—	—	—	—	Notts County
—	—	—	—	—	—	22	—	—	—	—	—	—	—	—	—	—	—	Orient
—	—	—	—	—	—	—	—	—	—	—	—	—	—	—	—	—	—	Oxford United
—	—	—	—	—	—	—	—	—	—	22	20	19	12	3	14	15	4	Portsmouth
—	—	—	—	—	—	—	—	22	9	12	2	3	19	14	11	2	7	Preston North End
22	—	—	—	—	—	—	—	—	—	—	—	—	—	—	—	—	—	Queen's Park R.
—	21	10	9	19	12	10	5	—	—	—	—	—	22	13	20	—	—	Sheffield United
15	19	11	17	8	6	6	6	2	5	—	22	14	—	22	19	18	—	Sheffield Wednesday
7	15	19	—	—	—	—	—	—	—	—	—	—	—	—	—	—	—	Southampton
19	18	12	10	11	17	—	—	—	—	—	—	—	—	—	—	21	20	Stoke City
17	16	17	19	15	—	—	—	—	—	—	21	20	9	4	18	9	12	Sunderland
—	—	—	—	—	—	—	—	—	—	—	—	—	—	—	—	—	—	Swansea City
6	7	3	8	6	4	2	3	1	3	18	3	2	18	16	16	10	2	Tottenham Hotspur
—	—	—	—	—	—	—	—	—	—	—	—	—	—	—	—	—	—	Watford
10	8	13	6	14	10	14	9	10	4	5	4	11	13	17	2	4	13	West Bromwich Albion
8	14	16	12	9	14	12	8	16	14	6	—	—	—	—	—	—	—	West Ham United
16	17	—	—	21	16	5	18	3	2	1	1	6	3	2	1	3	16	Wolverhampton W.

DIVISION TWO

LEAGUE POSITIONS (1951-86)

	1985–86	1984–85	1983–84	1982–83	1981–82	1980–81	1979–80	1978–79	1977–78	1976–77	1975–76	1974–75	1973–74	1972–73	1971–72	1970–71	1969–70	1968–69
Aston Villa	—	—	—	—	—	—	—	—	—	—	—	2	14	3	—	—	21	18
Barnsley	12	11	14	10	6	—	—	—	—	—	—	—	—	—	—	—	—	—
Birmingham City	—	2	—	—	—	—	3	—	—	—	—	—	—	—	2	9	18	7
Blackburn Rovers	19	5	6	11	10	4	—	22	5	12	15	—	—	—	—	21	8	19
Blackpool	—	—	—	—	—	—	—	—	20	5	10	7	5	7	6	—	2	8
Bolton Wanderers	—	—	—	22	19	18	—	—	1	4	4	10	11	—	—	22	16	17
Bradford City	13	—	—	—	—	—	—	—	—	—	—	—	—	—	—	—	—	—
Brentford	—	—	—	—	—	—	—	—	—	—	—	—	—	—	—	—	—	—
Brighton & H.A.	11	6	9	—	—	—	—	2	4	—	—	—	—	22	—	—	—	—
Bristol City	—	—	—	—	—	21	—	—	—	—	2	5	16	5	8	19	14	16
Bristol Rovers	—	—	—	—	—	22	19	16	18	15	18	19	—	—	—	—	—	—
Burnley	—	—	—	21	—	—	21	13	11	16	—	—	—	1	7	—	—	—
Bury	—	—	—	—	—	—	—	—	—	—	—	—	—	—	—	—	—	21
Cambridge United	—	—	22	12	14	13	8	12	—	—	—	—	—	—	—	—	—	—
Cardiff City	—	21	15	—	20	19	15	9	19	18	—	21	17	20	19	3	7	5
Carlisle United	20	16	7	14	—	—	15	—	—	20	19	—	3	18	10	4	12	12
Charlton Athletic	2	17	13	17	13	—	22	19	17	7	9	—	—	—	21	20	20	3
Chelsea	—	—	1	18	12	12	4	—	—	2	11	—	—	—	—	—	—	—
Chesterfield	—	—	—	—	—	—	—	—	—	—	—	—	—	—	—	—	—	—
Coventry City	—	—	—	—	—	—	—	—	—	—	—	—	—	—	—	—	—	—
Crystal Palace	5	15	18	15	15	—	—	1	9	—	—	—	20	—	—	—	—	2
Derby County	—	—	20	13	16	6	—	—	—	—	—	—	—	—	—	—	—	1
Doncaster Rovers	—	—	—	—	—	—	—	—	—	—	—	—	—	—	—	—	—	—
Everton	—	—	—	—	—	—	—	—	—	—	—	—	—	—	—	—	—	—
Fulham	22	9	11	4	—	—	20	10	10	17	12	9	13	9	20	—	—	22
Grimsby	15	10	5	19	17	7	—	—	—	—	—	—	—	—	—	—	—	—
Hereford United	—	—	—	—	—	—	—	—	—	22	—	—	—	—	—	—	—	—
Huddersfield Town	16	13	12	—	—	—	—	—	—	—	—	—	—	21	—	—	1	6
Hull	6	—	—	—	—	—	—	—	22	14	14	8	9	13	12	5	13	11
Ipswich Town	—	—	—	—	—	—	—	—	—	—	—	—	—	—	—	—	—	—
Leeds United	14	7	10	8	—	—	—	—	—	—	—	—	—	—	—	—	—	—
Leicester City	—	—	—	3	8	—	1	17	—	—	—	—	—	—	—	1	3	—
Lincoln City	—	—	—	—	—	—	—	—	—	—	—	—	—	—	—	—	—	—
Liverpool	—	—	—	—	—	—	—	—	—	—	—	—	—	—	—	—	—	—
Luton Town	—	—	—	—	1	5	6	18	13	6	7	—	2	12	13	6	—	—

1967–68	1966–67	1965–66	1964–65	1963–64	1962–63	1961–62	1960–61	1959–60	1958–59	1957–58	1956–57	1955–56	1954–55	1953–54	1952–53	1951–52	1950–51	
17	—	—	—	—	—	—	—	1	—	—	—	—	—	—	—	—	—	Aston Villa
—	—	—	—	—	—	—	—	—	22	14	19	18	—	—	22	20	15	Barnsley
4	10	10	—	—	—	—	—	—	—	—	—	—	1	7	6	3	4	Birmingham City
9	4	—	—	—	—	—	—	—	—	2	4	4	6	3	9	14	6	Blackburn Rovers
3	—	—	—	—	—	—	—	—	—	—	—	—	—	—	—	—	—	Blackpool
12	9	9	3	—	—	—	—	—	—	—	—	—	—	—	—	—	—	Bolton Wanderers
—	—	—	—	—	—	—	—	—	—	—	—	—	—	—	—	—	—	Bradford City
—	—	—	—	—	—	—	—	—	—	—	—	—	—	21	17	10	9	Brentford
—	—	—	—	—	—	22	16	14	12	—	—	—	—	—	—	—	—	Brighton & H. A.
19	15	5	—	—	—	—	—	22	10	17	13	11	—	—	—	—	—	Bristol City
—	—	—	—	—	—	21	17	9	6	10	9	6	9	9	—	—	—	Bristol Rovers
—	—	—	—	—	—	—	—	—	—	—	—	—	—	—	—	—	—	Burnley
—	22	19	16	18	8	18	—	—	—	—	21	16	13	17	20	17	20	Bury
—	—	—	—	—	—	—	—	—	—	—	—	—	—	—	—	—	—	Cambridge United
13	20	20	13	15	10	—	—	2	9	15	—	—	—	—	—	2	3	Cardiff City
10	3	14	—	—	—	—	—	—	—	—	—	—	—	—	—	—	—	Carlisle United
15	19	16	18	4	20	15	10	7	8	3	—	—	—	—	—	—	—	Charlton Athletic
—	—	—	—	—	2	—	—	—	—	—	—	—	—	—	—	—	—	Chelsea
—	—	—	—	—	—	—	—	—	—	—	—	—	—	—	—	—	21	Chesterfield
—	1	3	10	—	—	—	—	—	—	—	—	—	—	—	—	21	7	Coventry City
11	7	11	7	—	—	—	—	—	—	—	—	—	—	—	—	—	—	Crystal Palace
18	17	8	9	13	18	16	12	18	7	16	—	—	22	18	—	—	—	Derby County
—	—	—	—	—	—	—	—	—	—	22	14	17	18	12	13	16	11	Doncaster Rovers
—	—	—	—	—	—	—	—	—	—	—	—	—	—	2	16	7	—	Everton
—	—	—	—	—	—	—	—	—	2	5	11	9	14	8	8	—	—	Fulham
—	—	—	—	21	19	—	—	—	21	13	16	—	—	—	—	—	22	Grimsby
—	—	—	—	—	—	—	—	—	—	—	—	—	—	—	—	—	—	Hereford United
14	6	4	8	12	6	7	20	6	14	9	12	—	—	—	2	—	—	Huddersfield Town
16	12	—	—	—	—	—	—	21	—	—	—	22	19	15	18	18	10	Hull City
1	5	15	5	—	—	—	1	11	16	8	—	—	21	—	—	—	—	Ipswich Town
—	—	—	—	1	5	19	14	—	—	—	—	2	4	10	10	6	5	Leeds United
—	—	—	—	—	—	—	—	—	—	—	1	5	—	1	5	5	14	Leicester City
—	—	—	—	—	—	—	22	13	19	20	18	8	16	16	15	—	—	Lincoln City
—	—	—	—	—	—	1	3	3	4	4	3	3	11	—	—	—	—	Liverpool
—	—	—	—	—	22	3	13	—	—	—	—	—	2	6	3	8	19	Luton Town

DIVISION TWO
LEAGUE POSITIONS (1951-86)

	1985–86	1984–85	1983–84	1982–83	1981–82	1980–81	1979–80	1978–79	1977–78	1976–77	1975–76	1974–75	1973–74	1972–73	1971–72	1970–71	1969–70	1968–69
Manchester City	—	3	4	—	—	—	—	—	—	—	—	—	—	—	—	—	—	—
Manchester United	—	—	—	—	—	—	—	—	—	—	—	1	—	—	—	—	—	—
Mansfield Town	—	—	—	—	—	—	—	—	21	—	—	—	—	—	—	—	—	—
Middlesbrough	21	19	17	16	—	—	—	—	—	—	—	—	1	4	9	7	4	4
Millwall	9	—	—	—	—	—	—	21	16	10	—	20	12	11	3	8	10	10
Newcastle United	—	—	3	5	9	11	9	8	—	—	—	—	—	—	—	—	—	—
Northampton Town	—	—	—	—	—	—	—	—	—	—	—	—	—	—	—	—	—	—
Norwich City	1	—	—	—	3	—	—	—	—	—	—	3	—	—	1	10	11	13
Nottingham F.	—	—	—	—	—	—	—	—	—	8	16	7	14	—	—	—	—	—
Notts County	—	20	—	—	—	2	17	6	15	8	5	14	10	—	—	—	—	—
Oldham Athletic	8	14	19	7	11	15	11	14	8	13	17	18	—	—	—	—	—	—
Orient	—	—	—	—	22	17	14	11	14	19	13	12	4	15	17	17	—	—
Oxford United	—	1	—	—	—	—	—	—	—	—	20	11	18	8	15	14	15	20
Plymouth Argyle	—	—	—	—	—	—	—	—	—	21	16	—	—	—	—	—	—	—
Portsmouth	4	4	16	—	—	—	—	—	—	—	22	17	15	17	16	16	17	15
Port Vale	—	—	—	—	—	—	—	—	—	—	—	—	—	—	—	—	—	—
Preston North End	—	—	—	—	—	20	10	7	—	—	—	—	21	19	18	—	22	14
Queen's Park R.	—	—	—	1 1	5	8	5	—	—	—	—	—	—	2	4	11	9	—
Rotherham United	—	—	—	20	7	—	—	—	—	—	—	—	—	—	—	—	—	—
Scunthorpe	—	—	—	—	—	—	—	—	—	—	—	—	—	—	—	—	—	—
Sheffield United	7	18	—	—	—	—	—	20	12	11	—	—	—	—	—	2	6	9
Sheffield Wed.	—	—	2	6	4	10	—	—	—	—	—	22	19	10	14	15	—	—
Shrewsbury Town	17	8	8	9	18	14	13	—	—	—	—	—	—	—	—	—	—	—
Southampton	—	—	—	—	—	—	—	—	2	9	6	13	—	—	—	—	—	—
Stoke City	10	—	—	—	—	—	—	3	7	—	—	—	—	—	—	—	—	—
Sunderland	18	—	—	—	—	—	2	4	6	—	1	4	6	6	5	13	—	—
Swansea City	—	—	21	—	—	3	12	—	—	—	—	—	—	—	—	—	—	—
Swindon Town	—	—	—	—	—	—	—	—	—	—	—	—	22	16	11	12	5	—
Tottenham Hotspur	—	—	—	—	—	—	—	—	3	—	—	—	—	—	—	—	—	—
Walsall	—	—	—	—	—	—	—	—	—	—	—	—	—	—	—	—	—	—
Watford	—	—	—	—	2	9	18	—	—	—	—	—	—	—	22	18	19	—
West Bromwich Alb.	—	—	—	—	—	—	—	—	—	—	3	6	8	—	—	—	—	—
West Ham United	—	—	—	—	—	1	7	5	—	—	—	—	—	—	—	—	—	—
Wimbledon	3	12	—	—	—	—	—	—	—	—	—	—	—	—	—	—	—	—
Wolverhampton W.	—	22	—	2	—	—	—	—	—	1	—	—	—	—	—	—	—	—
Wrexham	—	—	—	—	21	16	16	15	—	—	—	—	—	—	—	—	—	—
York City	—	—	—	—	—	—	—	—	—	—	21	—	—	—	—	—	—	—

1967–68	1966–67	1965–66	1964–65	1963–64	1962–63	1961–62	1960–61	1959–60	1958–59	1957–58	1956–57	1955–56	1954–55	1953–54	1952–53	1951–52	1950–51	
—	—	1	11	6	—	—	—	—	—	—	—	—	—	—	—	—	2	Manchester City
—	—	—	—	—	—	—	—	—	—	—	—	—	—	—	—	—	—	Manchester United
—	—	—	—	—	—	—	—	—	—	—	—	—	—	—	—	—	—	Mansfield Town
6	—	21	17	10	4	12	5	5	13	7	6	14	12	—	—	—	—	Middlesbrough
7	8	—	—	—	—	—	—	—	—	—	—	—	—	—	—	—	—	Millwall
—	—	—	1	8	7	11	—	—	—	—	—	—	—	—	—	—	—	Newcastle United
—	21	—	2	11	—	—	—	—	—	—	—	—	—	—	—	—	—	Northampton Town
8	11	13	6	17	13	17	4	—	—	—	—	—	—	—	—	—	—	Norwich City
—	—	—	—	—	—	—	—	—	—	—	2	7	15	4	7	4	—	Nottingham Forest
—	—	—	—	—	—	—	—	—	—	21	20	20	7	14	19	15	17	Notts County
—	—	—	—	—	—	—	—	—	—	—	—	—	—	22	—	—	—	Oldham Athletic
—	—	22	19	16	—	2	19	10	17	12	15	—	—	—	—	—	—	Orient
—	—	—	—	—	—	—	—	—	—	—	—	—	—	—	—	—	—	Oxford United
22	16	18	15	20	12	5	11	19	—	—	—	21	20	19	4	—	—	Plymouth Argyle
5	14	12	20	9	17	—	21	20	—	—	—	—	—	—	—	—	—	Portsmouth
—	—	—	—	—	—	—	—	—	—	—	22	12	17	—	—	—	—	Port Vale
20	13	17	12	3	16	10	—	—	—	—	—	—	—	—	—	—	1	Preston North End
2	—	—	—	—	—	—	—	—	—	—	—	—	—	—	—	22	16	Queen's Park R.
21	18	7	14	7	14	9	15	8	20	18	17	19	3	5	12	9	—	Rotherham United
—	—	—	—	22	9	4	9	15	18	—	—	—	—	—	—	—	—	Scunthorpe
—	—	—	—	—	—	—	2	—	—	6	7	—	—	—	1	11	8	Sheffield United
—	—	—	—	—	—	—	—	—	1	—	—	1	—	—	—	1	—	Sheffield Wednesday
—	—	—	—	—	—	—	—	—	—	—	—	—	—	—	—	—	—	Shrewsbury Town
—	—	2	4	5	11	6	8	—	—	—	—	—	—	—	21	13	12	Southampton
—	—	—	—	—	1	8	18	17	5	11	5	13	5	11	—	—	—	Stoke City
—	—	—	—	2	3	3	6	16	15	—	—	—	—	—	—	—	—	Sunderland
—	—	—	22	19	15	20	7	12	11	19	10	10	10	20	11	19	18	Swansea City
—	—	—	21	14	—	—	—	—	—	—	—	—	—	—	—	—	—	Swindon Town
—	—	—	—	—	—	—	—	—	—	—	—	—	—	—	—	—	—	Tottenham Hotspur
—	—	—	—	—	21	14	—	—	—	—	—	—	—	—	—	—	—	Walsall
—	—	—	—	—	—	—	—	—	—	—	—	—	—	—	—	—	—	Watford
—	—	—	—	—	—	—	—	—	—	—	—	—	—	—	—	—	—	West Bromwich Albion
—	—	—	—	—	—	—	—	—	—	1	8	16	8	13	14	12	13	West Ham United
—	—	—	—	—	—	—	—	—	—	—	—	—	—	—	—	—	—	Wimbledon
—	2	6	—	—	—	—	—	—	—	—	—	—	—	—	—	—	—	Wolverhampton W.
—	—	—	—	—	—	—	—	—	—	—	—	—	—	—	—	—	—	Wrexham
—	—	—	—	—	—	—	—	—	—	—	—	—	—	—	—	—	—	York City

DIVISION THREE
LEAGUE POSITIONS (1962-86)

	1985–86	1984–85	1983–84	1982–83	1981–82	1980–81	1979–80	1978–79	1977–78	1976–77	1975–76	1974–75	1973–74	1972–73	1971–72	1970–71	1969–70	1968–69	1967–68	1966–67	1965–66	1964–65	1963–64	1962–63
Aldershot	—	—	—	—	—	—	—	—	—	—	21	20	8	—	—	—	—	—	—	—	—	—	—	—
Aston Villa	—	—	—	—	—	—	—	—	—	—	—	—	—	—	1	4	—	—	—	—	—	—	—	—
Barnsley	—	—	—	—	—	2	11	—	—	—	—	—	—	—	22	12	7	10	—	—	—	24	20	18
Barrow	—	—	—	—	—	—	—	—	—	—	—	—	—	—	—	—	23	19	8	—	—	—	—	—
Blackburn Rovers	—	—	—	—	—	—	2	—	—	—	—	1	13	3	10	—	—	—	—	—	—	—	—	—
Blackpool	12	—	—	—	—	23	18	12	—	—	—	—	—	—	—	—	—	—	—	—	—	—	—	—
Bolton Wanderers	18	17	10	—	—	—	—	—	—	—	—	—	—	1	7	—	—	—	—	—	—	—	—	—
AFC Bournemouth	15	10	17	14	—	—	—	—	—	—	—	21	11	7	3	—	21	4	13	20	18	11	4	5
Bradford PA	—	—	—	—	—	—	—	—	—	—	—	—	—	—	—	—	—	—	—	—	—	—	—	21
Bradford City	—	1	7	12	—	—	—	—	22	—	—	—	—	—	24	19	10	—	—	—	—	—	—	—
Brentford	10	13	20	9	8	9	19	10	—	—	—	—	—	22	—	—	—	—	—	—	23	5	16	—
Brighton & Hove Alb.	—	—	—	—	—	—	—	—	—	2	4	19	19	—	2	14	5	12	11	19	15	—	—	22
Bristol City	9	5	—	—	23	—	—	—	—	—	—	—	—	—	—	—	—	—	—	—	—	2	5	14
Bristol Rovers	16	6	—	7	15	—	—	—	—	—	—	—	2	5	6	6	3	16	16	5	16	6	12	19
Burnley	—	21	5	—	1	8	—	—	—	—	—	—	—	—	—	—	—	—	—	—	—	—	—	—
Bury	20	—	12	—	—	—	21	19	15	7	13	14	—	—	—	22	19	—	2	—	—	—	—	—
Cambridge United	—	24	—	—	—	—	—	—	2	—	—	—	21	—	—	—	—	—	—	—	—	—	—	—
Cardiff City	22	—	—	2	—	—	—	—	—	—	2	—	—	—	—	—	—	—	—	—	—	—	—	—
Carlisle United	—	—	—	—	2	19	6	6	13	—	—	—	—	—	—	—	—	—	—	—	—	—	—	23
Charlton Athletic	—	—	—	—	—	3	—	—	—	—	—	3	14	11	—	—	—	—	—	—	—	—	—	—
Chester	—	—	—	—	24	18	9	16	5	13	17	—	—	—	—	—	—	—	—	—	—	—	—	—
Chesterfield	17	—	—	24	11	5	4	20	9	18	14	15	5	16	13	5	—	—	—	—	—	—	—	—
Colchester United	—	—	—	—	—	22	5	7	8	—	22	11	—	—	—	—	—	—	23	13	—	23	17	12
Coventry City	—	—	—	—	—	—	—	—	—	—	—	—	—	—	—	—	—	—	—	—	—	—	1	4
Crewe Alexandra	—	—	—	—	—	—	—	—	—	—	—	—	—	—	—	—	—	23	—	—	—	—	22	—
Crystal Palace	—	—	—	—	—	—	—	—	—	3	5	5	—	—	—	—	—	—	—	—	—	—	2	11
Darlington	13	—	—	—	—	—	—	—	—	—	—	—	—	—	—	—	—	—	—	22	—	—	—	—
Derby County	3	7	—	—	—	—	—	—	—	—	—	—	—	—	—	—	—	—	—	—	—	—	—	—
Doncaster Rovers	11	14	—	23	19	—	8	—	—	—	—	—	—	—	—	23	11	—	—	23	—	—	—	—
Exeter City	—	—	24	19	18	11	8	8	17	—	—	—	—	—	—	—	—	—	—	—	22	17	—	—
Fulham	—	—	—	—	3	13	—	—	—	—	—	—	—	—	—	2	4	—	—	—	—	—	—	—
Gillingham	5	4	8	13	6	15	16	5	7	12	15	10	—	—	—	24	20	20	12	11	6	7	—	—
Grimsby Town	—	—	—	—	—	—	1	—	—	23	18	16	6	9	—	—	—	—	22	17	11	10	—	—
Halifax Town	—	—	—	—	—	—	—	—	—	—	24	17	9	20	17	3	18	—	—	—	—	—	—	24
Hartlepool United	—	—	—	—	—	—	—	—	—	—	—	—	—	—	—	—	—	22	—	—	—	—	—	—

Hereford United	—	—	—	—	—	—	—	—	23	—	1	12	18	—	—	—	—	—	—	—	—	—	—	—	Hereford United
Huddersfield Town	—	—	—	3	17	4	—	—	—	—	—	24	10	—	—	—	—	—	—	—	—	—	—	—	Huddersfield Town
Hull City	—	3	4	—	—	24	20	9	—	—	—	—	—	—	—	—	—	—	—	—	1	4	8	10	Hull City
Lincoln City	21	19	14	6	4	—	—	24	16	9	—	—	—	—	—	—	1	—	—	—	—	—	—	—	Lincoln City
Luton Town	—	—	—	—	—	—	—	—	—	—	—	—	—	—	—	—	2	3	—	—	—	21	18	—	Luton Town
Mansfield Town	—	—	—	—	—	—	23	18	—	1	11	—	—	—	21	7	6	15	21	9	19	3	7	—	Mansfield Town
Middlesbrough	—	—	—	—	—	—	—	—	—	—	—	—	—	—	—	—	—	—	1	2	—	—	—	—	Middlesbrough
Millwall	—	2	9	17	9	16	14	—	—	—	3	—	—	—	—	—	—	—	—	—	2	—	21	16	Millwall
Newport County	19	18	13	4	16	12	—	—	—	—	—	—	—	—	—	—	—	—	—	—	—	—	—	—	Newport County
Northampton Town	—	—	—	—	—	—	—	—	—	22	—	—	—	—	—	—	—	21	18	—	—	—	—	1	Northampton Town
Notts County	8	—	—	—	—	—	—	—	—	—	—	—	—	2	4	—	—	—	—	—	—	—	24	7	Notts County
Oldham Athletic	—	—	—	—	—	—	—	—	—	—	—	—	1	4	11	—	—	24	17	10	20	20	20	9	Oldham Athletic
Orient	—	22	11	20	—	—	—	—	—	—	—	—	—	—	—	—	1	18	19	14	—	—	—	—	Orient
Oxford United	—	—	1	5	5	14	17	11	18	17	—	—	—	—	—	—	—	—	1	15	14	—	—	—	Oxford United
Peterborough United	—	—	—	—	—	—	—	21	4	16	10	7	—	—	—	—	—	—	9*	15	13	8	10	6	Peterborough United
Plymouth Argyle	2	15	19	8	10	7	15	15	19	—	—	2	17	8	8	15	17	5	—	—	—	—	—	—	Plymouth Argyle
Portsmouth	—	—	—	1	13	6	—	—	24	20	—	—	—	—	—	—	—	—	—	—	—	—	—	—	Portsmouth
Port Vale	—	—	23	—	—	—	—	—	21	19	12	6	20	6	15	17	—	—	—	—	22	13	3	12	Port Vale
Preston North End	—	23	16	16	14	—	—	—	3	6	8	9	—	—	—	1	—	—	—	—	—	—	—	—	Preston North End
Queen's Park Rangers	—	—	—	—	—	—	—	—	—	—	—	—	—	—	—	—	—	—	—	1	3	14	15	13	Queen's Park Rangers
Reading	1	9	—	21	12	10	7	—	—	21	—	—	—	—	—	21	8	14	5	4	8	13	6	20	Reading
Rochdale	—	—	—	—	—	—	—	—	—	—	—	—	24	13	18	16	9	—	—	—	—	—	—	—	Rochdale
Rotherham United	14	12	18	—	—	1	13	17	20	4	16	—	—	21	5	8	14	11	—	—	—	—	—	—	Rotherham United
Scunthorpe United	—	—	21	—	—	—	—	—	—	—	—	—	—	24	—	—	—	—	24	18	4	18	—	—	Scunthorpe United
Sheffield United	—	—	3	11	—	21	12	—	—	—	—	—	—	—	—	—	—	—	—	—	—	—	—	—	Sheffield United
Sheffield Wednesday	—	—	—	—	—	—	3	14	14	8	20	—	—	—	—	—	—	—	—	—	—	—	—	—	Sheffield Wednesday
Shrewsbury Town	—	—	—	—	—	—	—	1	11	10	9	—	22	15	12	13	15	17	3	6	10	16	11	15	Shrewsbury Town
Southend United	—	—	22	15	7	—	22	13	—	—	23	18	12	14	—	—	—	—	—	—	21	12	14	8	Southend United
Southport	—	—	—	—	—	—	—	—	—	—	—	—	23	—	—	22	8	15	—	—	—	—	—	—	Southport
Stockport County	—	—	—	—	—	—	—	—	—	—	—	—	—	—	—	—	24	9	14	—	—	—	—	—	Stockport County
Swansea City	24	20	—	—	—	—	—	3	—	—	—	—	—	23	14	11	—	—	—	21	17	—	—	—	Swansea City
Swindon Town	—	—	—	—	22	17	10	4	10	11	19	4	—	—	—	—	—	2	10	8	7	—	—	2	Swindon Town
Torquay United	—	—	—	—	—	—	—	—	—	—	—	—	—	—	23	10	13	6	4	7	—	—	—	—	Torquay United
Tranmere Rovers	—	—	—	—	—	—	—	23	12	14	—	22	16	10	20	18	16	7	20	—	—	—	—	—	Tranmere Rovers
Walsall	6	11	6	10	20	20	—	22	6	15	7	8	15	17	9	20	12	13	7	12	9	19	19	—	Walsall
Watford	—	—	—	—	—	—	—	2	—	—	—	23	7	19	—	—	—	1	6	3	12	9	3	17	Watford
Wigan Athletic	4	16	15	18	—	—	—	—	—	—	—	—	—	—	—	—	—	—	—	—	—	—	—	—	Wigan Athletic
Wimbledon	—	—	2	—	21	—	24	—	—	—	—	—	—	—	—	—	—	—	—	—	—	—	—	—	Wimbledon
Wolverhampton W.	23	—	—	—	—	—	—	—	—	—	—	—	—	—	—	—	—	—	—	—	—	—	—	—	Wolverhampton W.
Workington	—	—	—	—	—	—	—	—	—	—	—	—	—	—	—	—	—	—	—	24	5	15	—	—	Workington
Wrexham	—	—	—	22	—	—	—	—	24	—	—	3	18	19	—	—	—	—	—	24	—	—	—	—	Wrexham
York City	7	8	—	—	—	—	—	—	5	6	13	4	12	16	9	—	—	—	—	—	—	23	9	—	York City

*Relegated by order of the Football League

DIVISION FOUR
LEAGUE POSITIONS (1962-86)

	1985–86	1984–85	1983–84	1982–83	1981–82	1980–81	1979–80	1978–79	1977–78	1976–77	1975–76	1974–75	1973–74	1972–73	1971–72	1970–71	1969–70	1968–69	1967–68	1966–67	1965–66	1964–65	1963–64	1962–63	
Aldershot	16	13	5	18	16	6	10	5	5	17	—	—	—	4	17	13	6	15	9	10	17	18	9	11	Aldershot
Barnsley	—	—	—	—	—	—	—	4	7	6	12	15	13	14	—	—	—	—	2	16	16	—	—	—	Barnsley
Barrow	—	—	—	—	—	—	—	—	—	—	—	—	—	—	22	24	—	—	—	3	12	21	24	9	Barrow
Blackpool	—	2	6	21	12	—	—	—	—	—	—	—	—	—	—	—	—	—	—	—	—	—	—	—	Blackpool
AFC Bournemouth	—	—	—	—	5	13	11	18	17	13	6	—	—	—	—	2	—	—	—	—	—	—	—	—	AFC Bournemouth
Bradford PA	—	—	—	—	—	—	—	—	—	—	—	—	—	—	—	—	24	24	24	23	11	7	13	—	Bradford PA
Bradford City	—	—	—	—	2	14	5	15	—	4	17	10	8	16	—	—	—	4	5	11	23	19	5	23	Bradford City
Brentford	—	—	—	—	—	—	—	—	4	15	18	8	19	—	3	14	5	11	14	9	—	—	—	1	Brentford
Brighton & Hove Alb.	—	—	—	—	—	—	—	—	—	—	—	—	—	—	—	—	—	—	—	—	—	1	8	—	Brighton & Hove Alb.
Bristol City	—	—	4	14	—	—	—	—	—	—	—	—	—	—	—	—	—	—	—	—	—	—	—	—	Bristol City
Burnley	14	—	—	—	—	—	—	—	—	—	—	—	—	—	—	—	—	—	—	—	—	—	—	—	Burnley
Bury	—	4	14	5	9	12	—	—	—	—	—	—	4	12	9	—	—	—	—	—	—	—	—	—	Bury
Cambridge United	22	—	—	—	—	—	—	—	—	1	13	6	—	3	10	20	—	—	—	—	—	—	—	—	Cambridge United
Carlisle United	—	—	—	—	—	—	—	—	—	—	—	—	—	—	—	—	—	—	—	—	—	—	2	—	Carlisle United
Chester City	2	16	24	13	—	—	—	—	—	—	—	4	7	15	20	5	11	14	22	19	7	8	12	21	Chester City
Chesterfield	—	1	13	—	—	—	—	—	—	—	—	—	—	—	—	—	1	20	7	15	20	12	16	15	Chesterfield
Colchester United	6	7	8	6	6	—	—	—	—	3	—	—	3	22	11	6	10	6	—	—	4	—	—	—	Colchester United
Crewe Alexandra	12	10	17	23	24	18	23	24	15	12	16	18	21	21	24	15	15	—	4	5	14	10	—	3	Crewe Alexandra
Darlington	—	3	16	17	13	8	22	21	19	11	20	21	20	24	19	12	22	5	16	—	2	17	19	12	Darlington
Doncaster Rovers	—	—	2	—	—	3	22	12	12	8	10	17	22	17	22	—	—	1	10	—	1	9	14	16	Doncaster Rovers
Exeter	21	18	—	—	—	—	—	—	—	2	7	9	10	8	15	9	18	17	20	14	—	—	4	17	Exeter
Gillingham	—	—	—	—	—	—	—	—	—	—	—	—	2	9	13	—	—	—	—	—	—	—	1	5	Gillingham
Grimsby Town	—	—	—	—	—	—	—	2	6	—	—	—	—	—	1	19	16	23	—	—	—	—	—	—	Grimsby Town
Halifax Town	20	21	21	11	19	23	18	23	20	21	—	—	—	—	—	—	—	2	11	12	15	23	10	—	Halifax Town
Hartlepool United	7	19	23	22	14	9	19	13	21	22	14	13	11	20	18	23	23	—	3	8	18	15	23	24	Hartlepool United
Hereford United	10	5	11	24	10	22	21	14	—	—	—	—	—	2	—	—	—	—	—	—	—	—	—	—	Hereford United
Huddersfield Town	—	—	—	—	—	—	1	10	11	9	5	—	—	—	—	—	—	—	—	—	—	—	—	—	Huddersfield Town
Hull City	—	—	—	2	8	—	—	—	—	—	—	—	—	—	—	—	—	—	—	—	—	—	—	—	Hull City

Lincoln City	—	—	—	—	—	2	7	—	—	—	1	5	12	10	5	21	8	8	13	24	22	22	11	22	Lincoln City
Luton Town	—	—	—	—	—	—	—	—	—	—	—	—	—	—	—	—	—	—	1	17	6	—	—	—	Luton Town
Mansfield Town	3	14	19	10	20	7	—	—	—	—	—	1	17	6	—	—	—	—	—	—	—	—	—	4	Mansfield Town
Millwall	—	—	—	—	—	—	—	—	—	—	—	—	—	—	—	—	—	—	—	—	2	—	—		Millwall
Newport County	—	—	—	—	—	—	3	8	16	19	22	12	9	5	14	22	21	22	12	18	9	16	15	20	Newport County
Northampton Town	8	23	18	15	22	10	13	19	10	—	2	16	5	23	21	7	14	—	—	—	—	—	—	—	Northampton Town
Notts County	—	—	—	—	—	—	—	—	—	—	—	—	—	—	—	1	7	19	17	20	8	13	—	—	Notts County
Oldham Athletic	—	—	—	—	—	—	—	—	—	—	—	—	—	—	—	3	19	—	—	—	—	—	—	2	Oldham Athletic
Orient	5	—	—	—	—	—	—	—	—	—	—	—	—	—	—	—	—	—	—	—	—	—	—	—	Orient
Oxford United	—	—	—	—	—	—	—	—	—	—	—	—	—	—	—	—	—	—	—	—	—	4	18	18	Oxford United
Peterborough United	17	11	7	9	4	5	8	—	—	—	—	—	1	19	8	16	9	18	—	—	—	—	—	—	Peterborough United
Portsmouth	—	—	—	—	—	—	4	7	—	—	—	—	—	—	—	—	—	—	—	—	—	—	—	—	Portsmouth
Port Vale	4	12	—	3	7	19	20	16	—	—	—	—	—	—	—	—	4	13	18	13	19	—	—	—	Port Vale
Preston NE	23	—	—	—	—	—	—	—	—	—	—	—	—	—	—	—	—	—	—	—	—	—	—	—	Preston NE
Reading	—	—	3	—	—	—	—	1	8	—	3	7	6	7	16	—	—	—	—	—	—	—	—	—	Reading
Rochdale	18	17	22	20	21	15	24	20	24	18	15	19	—	—	—	—	—	3	19	21	21	6	20	7	Rochdale
Rotherham United	—	—	—	—	—	—	—	—	—	—	—	3	15	—	—	—	—	—	—	—	—	—	—	—	Rotherham United
Scunthorpe United	15	9	—	4	23	16	14	12	14	20	19	24	18	—	4	17	12	16	—	—	—	—	—	—	Scunthorpe United
Sheffield United	—	—	—	—	1	—	—	—	—	—	—	—	—	—	—	—	—	—	—	—	—	—	—	—	Sheffield United
Shrewsbury Town	—	—	—	—	—	—	—	—	—	—	—	2	—	—	—	—	—	—	—	—	—	—	—	—	Shrewsbury Town
Southend United	9	20	—	—	—	1	—	—	2	10	—	—	—	—	2	18	17	7	6	6	—	—	—	—	Southend United
Southport	—	—	—	—	—	—	—	—	23	23	23	11	—	1	7	8	—	—	—	2	10	20	21	13	Southport
Stockport County	11	22	12	16	18	20	16	17	18	14	21	20	24	11	23	—	—	—	—	1	13	24	17	19	Stockport County
Swansea City	—	—	—	—	—	—	—	—	3	5	11	22	14	—	—	—	3	10	15	—	—	—	—	—	Swansea City
Swindon Town	1	8	15	8	—	—	—	—	—	—	—	—	—	—	—	—	—	—	—	—	—	—	—	—	Swindon Town
Torquay United	24	24	9	12	15	17	9	11	9	16	9	14	16	18	—	—	—	—	—	—	3	11	6	6	Torquay United
Tranmere Rovers	19	6	10	19	11	21	15	—	—	—	4	—	—	—	—	—	—	—	—	4	5	5	7	8	Tranmere Rovers
Walsall	—	—	—	—	—	—	2	—	—	—	—	—	—	—	—	—	—	—	—	—	—	—	—	—	Walsall
Watford	—	—	—	—	—	—	—	—	1	7	8	—	—	—	—	—	—	—	—	—	—	—	—	—	Watford
Wigan Athletic	—	—	—	—	3	11	6	6	—	—	—	—	—	—	—	—	—	—	—	—	—	—	—	—	Wigan Athletic
Wimbledon	—	—	—	1	—	4	—	3	13	—	—	—	—	—	—	—	—	—	—	—	—	—	—	—	Wimbledon
Workington	—	—	—	—	—	—	—	—	—	24	24	23	23	13	6	10	20	12	23	—	—	—	3	10	Workington
Wrexham	13	15	20	—	—	—	—	—	—	—	—	—	—	—	—	—	2	9	8	7	24	13	—	—	Wrexham
York City	—	—	1	7	17	24	17	9	22	—	—	—	—	—	—	4	13	21	21	22	—	3	22	14	York City

LEADING LEAGUE SCORERS 1985-86

Division One: 30 – Lineker (Everton); 26 – McAvennie (West Ham U.); 23 – Aldridge (Oxford U.); Rush (Liverpool); 22 – Harford (Luton T.); 20 – Cottee (West Ham U.); 19 – Beardsley (Newcastle U.); Sharp (Everton), A. Smith (Leicester C.); 18 – Falco (Tottenham H.); 17 – Hughes (Manchester U.); 16 – Bannister (Q.P.R.); 15 – Clough (Nottingham F.); 14 – Dixon (Chelsea), Speedie (Chelsea), B. Stein (Luton T.), Webb (Nottingham F.); 13 – Davenport (Nottingham F.), Marwood (Sheffield W.), Molby (Liverpool), West (Watford); 11 – Gibson (Coventry C.), Lillis (Manchester C.), Olsen (Manchester U.), Waddle (Tottenham H.), Walsh (Liverpool), Woodcock (Arsenal); 10 – Amrstrong (Southampton), Chapman (Sheffield W.), Heath (Everton), Nicholas (Arsenal), Stainrod (Aston Villa), Walters (Aston Villa), Whelan (Liverpool).

Division Two: 22 – Drinkell (Norwich C.); 20 – Edwards (Sheffield U.); 19 – Bertschin (Stoke C.); 17 – R. Futcher (Oldham Ath.); 15 – Hobson (Grimsby T.), Palmer (Oldham Ath.), Walsh (Barnsley); 14 – Bunn (Hull C.), Connor (Brighton & H.A.), Lovell (Millwall), Morgan (Portsmouth), Pearson (Charlton Ath)., Saunders (Brighton & H.A.); 12 – Baird (Leeds U.), Coney (Fulham), Garner (Blackburn R.), Stuart (Charlton Ath.), Tempest (Huddersfield T.), Wilson (Millwall); 11 – Cork (Wimbledon), Flanagan (Charlton Ath.), O'Callaghan (Portsmouth), Owen (Brighton & H.A.), Quinn (Oldham Ath.), Ritchie (Leeds U.), Wilson (Brighton & H.A.), Withe (Sheffield U.); 10 – Abbott (Bradford C.), Barker (Blackburn R.), Campbell (Bradford C.), Flounders (Hull C.), Gray (Crystal Palace), Hendrie (Bradford C.), McEwan (Hull C.), Morris (Sheffield W.), Patterson (Blackburn R.), Robinson (Shrewsbury T.), Rowell (Middlesbrough).

Division Three: 27 – Senior (Reading); 26 – Clarke (Bournemouth); 23 – Tynan (Rotherham U., inc. 10 for Plymouth Arg.); 22 – Walwyn (York C.); 21 – Aspinall (Wigan Ath.), Cross (Walsall); 19 – Neville (Bristol C.); 18 – Walsh (Bristol C.); 17 – Cooke (Brentford), Davison (Derby Co.), O'Keefe (Blackpool); 16 – Elliott (Walsall), Hodges (Plymouth Arg.), MacDonald (Darlington), Morgan (Bristol R.), Newell (Wigan Ath); 15 – Christie (Derby Co.), McParland (Notts Co.); 14 – Cascarino (Gillingham), Madden (Bury), Moss (Chesterfield), Waitt (Notts Co.); 13 – Canham (York C.), Douglas (Doncaster R.), Nelson (Plymouth Arg.); 12 – Airey (Darlington), Birch (Rotherham U.), Clayton (Plymouth Arg.), Vaughan (Cardiff C.), White (Bristol R.); 11 – Micklewhite (Derby Co.); 10 – Banton (York C.), Caldwell (Bolton W.), Coughlin (Plymouth Arg.), Kelly (Walsall), Riley (Bristol C.), Robinson (Gillingham).

Division Four: 25 – Cadette (Southend U.), Taylor (Rochdale); 24 – Crown (Cambridge U.); 22 – Benjamin (Northampton T.); 20 – Charles (Wrexham); 19 – Leonard (Stockport Co.); 18 – Henry (Swindon T.), Worthington (Tranmere R.); 17 – Gordon (Swindon T.), Hill (Northampton T.), Kellock (Halifax T.), Shoulder (Hartlepool U.), Thomas (Preston N.E.); 16 – Chamberlain (Mansfield T.), Rimmer (Chester C.), Shinners (Orient), Taylor (Burnley); 15 – Adcock (Colchester U.), Earle (Port Vale), Johnson (Aldershot); 14 – Brazil (Preston N.E.), Longhurst (Halifax T.), Steel (Wrexham); 13 – Bennett (Chester C.), Cassells (Mansfield T.), A. English (Colchester U.), Kearns (Hereford U.), Morley (Northampton T.), Muir (Tranmere R.), Waller (Crewe Alex.); 12 – Cammack (Scunthorpe U.), Groves (Colchester U.), Jones (Port Vale), Massey (Cambridge U.), Sword (Stockport Co.); 11 – Anderson (Tranmere R.), Blissett (Crewe Alex.), Gallagher (Peterborough U.); 10 – Coyne (Swindon T.), Houghton (Chester C.), Juryeff (Orient), Maguire (Port Vale), Richardson (Chester C.), Wade (Swindon T.).

TOP LEAGUE SCORERS SINCE 1946-47

1985-86	G. Lineker (Everton)	30
1984-85	J. Clayton (Tranmere R.) and T. Tynan (Plymouth Arg.)	31
1983-84	T. Senior (Reading)	36
1982-83	L. Blissett (Watford)	27
1981-82	K. Edwards (Sheffield U., inc. 1 for Hull C.)	36
1980-81	T. Kellow (Exeter C.) and D. Kemp (Plymouth Arg.)	24
1979-80	C. Allen (Queens Park Rangers)	28
1978-79	R. Jenkins (Watford)	29
1977-78	A. Curtis (Swansea City) and S. Phillips (Brentford)	32
1976-77	P. Ward (Brighton & Hove Albion)	32
1975-76	R. McNeil (Hereford United)	35
1974-75	R. McNeil (Hereford United)	31
1973-74	B. Yeo (Gillingham)	31
1972-73	B. Robson (West Ham United) and F. Binney (Exeter)	28
1971-72	E. MacDougall (Bournemouth) and A. Wood (Shrewsbury)	35
1970-71	E. MacDougall (Bournemouth)	42
1969-70	G. Jones (Bury) and A. Kinsey (Wrexham)	26
1968-69	J. Greaves (Tottenham Hotspur)	27
1967-68	G. Best (Manchester United) and R. Davies (Southampton)	28
1966-67	R. Davies (Southampton)	37
1965-66	K. Hector (Bradford)	44
1964-65	A. Jeffrey (Doncaster Rovers)	36
1963-64	H. MacIlmoyle (Carlisle United)	39
1962-63	J. Greaves (Tottenham Hotspur)	37
1961-62	R. Hunt (Liverpool) and B. Thomas (Scunthorpe and Newcastle United)	41
1960-61	T. Bly (Peterborough)	52
1959-60	C. Holton (Watford)	48
1958-59	B. Clough (Middlesbrough)	43
1957-58	T. Johnston (Blackburn Rovers and Leyton Orient)	44
1956-57	A. Rowley (Leicester City)	44
1955-56	R. Collins (Torquay United)	40
1954-55	T. Briggs (Blackburn Rovers)	33
1953-54	J. Charles (Leeds United)	42
1952-53	G. Rowley (Leicester City)	39
1951-52	D. Dooley (Sheffield W.)	46
1950-51	J. Shaw (Rotherham U.)	37
1949-50	T. Briggs (Grimsby T.)	35
1948-49	C. Wyman (Southampton)	32
1947-48	R. Rooke (Arsenal)	33
1946-47	C. Jordan (Doncaster R.)	42

LEAGUE CHAMPIONSHIP HONOURS

Division I

	First	Pt	Second	Pt	Third	Pt
1888–9	*a*Preston NE	40	Aston Villa	29	Wolverhampton W	28
1889–90	Preston NE	33	Everton	31	Blackburn R	27
1890–1	Everton	29	Preston NE	27	Wolverhampton W } Notts County }	26
1891–2	*b*Sunderland	42	Preston NE	37	Bolton W	36
1892–3	*c*Sunderland	48	Preston NE	37	Everton	36
1893–4	Aston Villa	44	Sunderland	38	Derby C	36
1894–5	Sunderland	47	Everton	42	Aston Villa	39
1895–6	Aston Villa	45	Derby C	41	Everton	39
1896–7	Aston Villa	47	Sheffield U	36	Derby C	36
1897–8	Sheffield U	42	Sunderland	37	Wolverhampton W	35
1898–9	*d*Aston Villa	45	Liverpool	43	Burnley	39
1899–1900	Aston Villa	50	Sheffield U	48	Sunderland	41
1900–1	Liverpool	45	Sunderland	43	Notts C	40
1901–2	Sunderland	44	Everton	41	Newcastle U	37
1902–3	Sheffield W	42	Aston Villa	41	Sunderland	41
1903–4	Sheffield W	47	Manchester C	44	Everton	43
1904–5	Newcastle U	48	Everton	47	Manchester C	46
1905–6	*e*Liverpool	51	Preston NE	47	Sheffield W	44
1906–7	Newcastle U	51	Bristol C	38	Everton	45
1907–8	Manchester U	52	Aston Villa	43	Manchester C	43
1908–9	Newcastle U	53	Everton	46	Sunderland	44
1909–10	Aston Villa	53	Liverpool	48	Blackburn R.	45
1910–11	Manchester U	52	Aston Villa	51	Sunderland	45
1911–12	Blackburn R	49	Everton	46	Newcastle U	44
1912–13	Sunderland	54	Aston Villa	50	Sheffield W	49
1913–14	Blackburn R	51	Aston Villa	44	Middlesbrough	43
1914–15	Everton	46	Oldham A	45	Blackburn R	43
1919–20	*f*WBA	60	Burnley	51	Chelsea	49
1920–21	Burnley	59	Manchester C	54	Bolton W	52
1921–22	Liverpool	57	Tottenham H	51	Burnley	49
1922–23	Liverpool	60	Sunderland	54	Huddersfield T	53
1923–24	*Huddersfield T	57	Cardiff C	57	Sunderland	43
1924–25	Huddersfield T	58	WBA	56	Bolton W	55
1925–26	Huddersfield T	57	Arsenal	52	Sunderland	48
1926–27	Newcastle U	56	Huddersfield T	51	Sunderland	49
1927–28	Everton	53	Huddersfield T	51	Leicester C	48
1928–29	Sheffield W	52	Leicester C	51	Aston Villa	50
1929–30	Sheffield W	60	Derby C	50	Manchester C	47
1930–31	Arsenal	66	Aston Villa	59	Sheffield W	52
1931–32	Everton	56	Arsenal	54	Sheffield W	50
1932–33	Arsenal	58	Aston Villa	54	Sheffield W	51
1933–34	Arsenal	59	Huddersfield T	56	Tottenham H	49
1934–35	Arsenal	58	Sunderland	54	Sheffield W	49
1935–36	Sunderland	56	Derby C	48	Huddersfield T	48
1936–37	Manchester C	57	Charlton A	54	Arsenal	52
1937–38	Arsenal	52	Wolverhampton W	51	Preston NE	49
1938–39	Everton	59	Wolverhampton W	55	Charlton A	50
1946–47	Liverpool	57	Manchester U	56	Wolverhampton W	56
1947–48	Arsenal	59	Manchester U	52	Burnley	52
1948–49	Portsmouth	58	Manchester U	53	Derby C	53

	First	Pt	Second	Pt	Third	Pt
1949–50	*Portsmouth	53	Wolverhampton W	53	Sunderland	52
1950–51	Tottenham H	60	Manchester U	56	Blackpool	50
1951–52	Manchester U	57	Tottenham H	53	Arsenal	53
1952–53	*Arsenal	54	Preston NE	54	Wolverhampton W	51
1953–54	Wolverhampton W	57	WBA	53	Huddersfield T	51
1954–55	Chelsea	52	Wolverhampton W	48	Portsmouth	48
1955–56	Manchester U	60	Blackpool	49	Wolverhampton W	49
1956–57	Manchester U	64	Tottenham H	56	Preston NE	56
1957–58	Wolverhampton W	64	Preston NE	59	Tottenham H	51
1958–59	Wolverhampton W	61	Manchester U	55	Arsenal	50
1959–60	Burnley	55	Wolverhampton W	54	Tottenham H	53
1960–61	Tottenham H	66	Sheffield W	58	Wolverhampton W	57
1961–62	Ipswich T	56	Burnley	53	Tottenham H	52
1962–63	Everton	61	Tottenham H	55	Burnley	54
1963–64	Liverpool	57	Manchester U	53	Everton	52
1964–65	Manchester U	61	Leeds U	61	Chelsea	56
1965–66	Liverpool	61	Leeds U	55	Burnley	55
1966–67	Manchester U	60	Nottingham F	56	Tottenham H	56
1967–68	Manchester C	58	Manchester U	56	Liverpool	55
1968–69	Leeds U	67	Liverpool	61	Everton	57
1969–70	Everton	66	Leeds U	57	Chelsea	55
1970–71	Arsenal	65	Leeds U	64	Tottenham H	52
1971–72	Derby C	58	Leeds U	57	Liverpool	57
1972–73	Liverpool	60	Arsenal	57	Leeds U	53
1973–74	Leeds U	62	Liverpool	57	Derby C	48
1974–75	Derby C	53	Liverpool	51	Ipswich T	51
1975–76	Liverpool	60	QPR	59	Manchester U	56
1976–77	Liverpool	57	Manchester C	56	Ipswich T	52
1977–78	Nottingham F	64	Liverpool	57	Everton	55
1978–79	Liverpool	68	Nottingham F	60	WBA	59
1979–80	Liverpool	60	Manchester U	58	Ipswich T	53
1980–81	Aston Villa	60	Ipswich T	56	Arsenal	53
1981–82*g*	Liverpool	87	Ipswich T	83	Manchester U	78
1982–83	Liverpool	82	Watford	71	Manchester U	70
1983–84	Liverpool	80	Southampton	77	Nottingham F	74
1983–84	Liverpool	80	Southampton	77	Nottingham F	74
1984–85	Everton	90	Liverpool	77	Tottenham H	77
1985–86	Liverpool	88	Everton	85	West Ham U.	84

*Won on goal average. Maximum points: *a*, 44; *b*, 56; *c*, 60; *d*, 58; *e*, 76; *f*, 84, *g*, 126.

Division II

1892–3	*a*Small Heath	36	Sheffield U	35	Darwen	30
1893–4	*b*Liverpool	50	Small Heath	42	Notts County	39
1894–5	*c*Bury	48	Notts C	39	Newton Heath	38
1895–6	*Liverpool	46	Manchester C	46	Grimsby T	42
1896–7	Notts C	42	Newton Heath	39	Grimsby T	38
1897–8	Burnley	48	Newcastle	45	Manchester C	39
1898–9	*d*Manchester C	51	Glossop NE	46	Leicester Fosse	45
1899–1900	Sheffield W	54	Bolton W	52	Small Heath	46
1900–1	Grimsby T	49	Small Heath	48	Burnley	44
1901–2	WBA	55	Middlesbrough	51	Preston NE	42
1902–3	Manchester C	54	Small Heath	51	W'lwich Arsenal	48
1903–4	Preston NE	50	W'lwich Arsenal	49	Manchester U	48
1904–5	Liverpool	58	Bolton W	56	Manchester U	53
1905–6	*e*Bristol C	66	Manchester U	62	Chelsea	53
1906–7	Nottingham F	60	Chelsea	57	Leicester Fosse	48
1907–8	Bradford C	54	Leicester Fosse	52	Oldham	50
1908–9	Bolton W	52	Tottenham H	51	WBA	51

	First	Pt	Second	Pt	Third	Pt
1909–10	Manchester C	54	Oldham A	53	Hull C	53
1910–11	WBA	53	Bolton W	51	Chelsea	49
1911–12	*Derby C	54	Chelsea	54	Burnley	52
1912–13	Preston NE	53	Burnley	50	Birmingham	46
1913–14	Notts County	53	Bradford	49	W'lwich Arsenal	49
1914–15	Derby C	53	Preston NE	50	Barnsley	47
1919–20	*f*Tottenham H	70	Huddersfield T	64	Birmingham C	56
1920–21	*Birmingham	58	Cardiff C	58	Bristol C	51
1921–22	Nottingham F	56	Stoke C	52	Barnsley	52
1922–23	Notts C	53	West Ham U	51	Leicester C	51
1923–24	Leeds U	54	Bury	51	Derby C	51
1924–25	Leicester C	59	Manchester U	57	Derby C	55
1925–26	Sheffield W	60	Derby C	57	Chelsea	52
1926–27	Middlesbrough	62	Portsmouth	54	Manchester C	54
1927–28	Manchester C	59	Leeds U	57	Chelsea	54
1928–29	Middlesbrough	55	Grimsby T	53	Bradford C	48
1929–30	Blackpool	58	Chelsea	55	Oldham A	53
1930–31	Everton	61	WBA	55	Tottenham H	51
1931–32	Wolverhampton W	56	Leeds U	54	Stoke C	52
1932–33	Stoke C	56	Tottenham H	55	Fulham	50
1933–34	Grimsby	59	Preston NE	52	Bolton W	51
1934–35	Brentford	61	Bolton W	56	West Ham U	56
1935–36	Manchester U	56	Charlton A	55	Sheffield U	52
1936–37	Leicester C	56	Blackpool	55	Bury	52
1937–38	Aston Villa	57	Manchester U	53	Sheffield U	53
1938–39	Blackburn R	55	Sheffield U	54	Sheffield W	53
1946–47	Manchester C	62	Burnley	58	Birmingham	55
1947–48	Birmingham	59	Newcastle U	56	Southampton	52
1948–49	Fulham	57	WBA	56	Southampton	55
1949–50	Tottenham H	61	Sheffield W	52	Sheffield U	52
1950–51	Preston NE	57	Manchester C	52	Cardiff C	50
1951–52	Sheffield W	53	Cardiff C	51	Birmingham C	51
1952–53	Sheffield U	60	Huddersfield T	58	Luton T	52
1953–54	Leicester C	56	Everton	56	Blackburn R	55
1954–55	*Birmingham C	54	Luton	54	Rotherham U	54
1955–56	Sheffield W	55	Leeds U	52	Liverpool	48
1956–57	Leicester C	61	Nottingham F	54	Liverpool	53
1957–58	West Ham U	57	Blackburn R	56	Charlton A	55
1958–59	Sheffield W	62	Fulham	60	Sheffield U	53
1959–60	Aston Villa	59	Cardiff C	58	Liverpool	50
1960–61	Ipswich T	59	Sheffield U	58	Liverpool	52
1961–62	Liverpool	62	Leyton O	54	Sunderland	53
1962–63	Stoke C	53	Chelsea	52	Sunderland	52
1963–64	Leeds U	63	Sunderland	61	Preston NE	56
1964–65	Newcastle U	57	Northampton T	56	Bolton W	50
1965–66	Manchester C	59	Southampton	54	Coventry C	53
1966–67	Coventry C	59	Wolverhampton W	58	Carlisle U	52
1967–68	Ipswich T	59	QPR	58	Blackpool	58
1968–69	Derby C	63	Crystal P	56	Charlton A	50
1969–70	Huddersfield T	60	Blackpool	53	Leicester C	51
1970–71	Leicester C	59	Sheffield U	56	Cardiff C	53
1971–72	Norwich C	57	Birmingham C	56	Millwall	55
1972–73	Burnley	62	QPR	61	Aston Villa	50
1973–74	Middlesbrough	65	Luton	50	Carlisle	49
1974–75	Manchester U	61	Aston Villa	58	Norwich C	53
1975–76	Sunderland	56	Bristol C	53	WBA	53
1976–77	Wolverhampton	57	Chelsea	55	Nottingham F	52

*Won on goal average.

	First	Pt	Second	Pt	Third	Pt
1977–78	Bolton W	58	Southampton	57	Tottenham H	56
1978–79	Crystal P	57	Brighton & HA	56	Stoke C	56
1979–80	Leicester C	55	Sunderland	54	Birmingham C	53
1980–81	West Ham U	66	Notts Co	53	Swansea C	50
1981–82	*g*Luton T	88	Watford	80	Norwich C	71
1982–83	Q.P.R.	85	Wolverhampton W	75	Leicester C	70
1983–84	Chelsea	88	Sheffield W	88	Newcastle U	80
1984–85	Oxford U	84	Birmingham C	82	Manchester C	74
1985–86	Norwich C	84	Charlton Ath	77	Wimbledon	76

Maximum points: *a*, 44; *b*, 56; *c*, 60; *d*, 58; *e*, 76; *f*, 84; *g*, 126
*Won on goal difference

Division III

	First	Pt	Second	Pt	Third	Pt
1958–59	*a*Plymouth A	62	Hull C	61	Brentford	57
1959–60	Southampton	61	Norwich C	59	Shrewsbury	52
1960–61	Bury	68	Walsall	62	QPR	60
1961–62	Portsmouth	65	Grimsby T	62	Bournemouth	59
1962–63	Northampton T	62	Swindon T	58	Port Vale	54
1963–64	*Coventry C	60	Crystal P	60	Watford	58
1964–65	Carlisle U	60	Bristol C	59	Mansfield T	59
1965–66	Hull C	69	Millwall	65	QPR	57
1966–67	QPR	67	Middlesbrough	55	Watford	54
1967–68	Oxford U	57	Bury	56	Shrewsbury T	55
1968–69	*Watford	64	Swindon T	64	Luton T	61
1969–70	Orient	62	Luton T	60	Bristol R	56
1970–71	Preston NE	61	Fulham	60	Halifax	56
1971–72	Aston Villa	70	Brighton & HA	65	Bournemouth	62
1972–73	Bolton W	61	Notts C	57	Blackburn R	55
1973–74	Oldham A	62	Bristol R	61	York C	61
1974–75	Blackburn R	60	Plymouth A	59	Charlton A	55
1975–76	Hereford U	63	Cardiff C	57	Millwall	56
1976–77	Mansfield T	64	Brighton & HA	61	Crystal P	59
1977–78	Wrexham	61	Cambridge U	58	Preston NE	56
1978–79	Shrewsbury T	61	Watford	60	Swansea C	60
1979–80	Grimsby T	62	Blackburn R	59	Sheffield W	58
1980–81	Rotherham U	61	Barnsley	59	Charlton Ath	59
1981–82	*b*Burnley	80	Carlisle U	80	Fulham	78
1982–83	Portsmouth	91	Cardiff C	86	Huddersfield T	82
1983–84	Oxford U	95	Wimbledon	87	Sheffield U	83
1984–85	Bradford C	94	Millwall	90	Hull C	87
1985–86	Reading	94	Plymouth Arg	87	Derby Co	84

*Won on goal average. Maximum points *a* 92; *b* 138

Division III (Southern Section)

	First	Pt	Second	Pt	Third	Pt
1920–21	*a*Crystal P	59	Southampton	54	QPR	53
1921–22	*Southampton	61	Plymouth A	61	Portsmouth	53
1922–23	Bristol C	59	Plymouth A	53	Swansea	53
1923–24	Portsmouth	59	Plymouth A	55	Millwall	54
1924–25	Swansea C	57	Plymouth A	56	Bristol C	53
1925–26	Reading	57	Plymouth A	56	Millwall	53
1926–27	Bristol C	62	Plymouth A	60	Millwall	56
1927–28	Millwall	65	Northampton T	55	Plymouth A	53
1928–29	*Charlton A	54	Crystal P	54	Northampton T	52
1929–30	Plymouth A	68	Brentford	61	QPR	51
1930–31	Notts C	59	Crystal P	51	Brentford	50
1931–32	Fulham	57	Reading	55	Southend U	53
1932–33	Brentford	62	Exeter	58	Norwich C	57
1933–34	Norwich C	61	Coventry C	54	Reading	54

*Won on goal average. Maximum points: *a*, 84; *b*, 92

	First	Pt	Second	Pt	Third	Pt
1934–35	Charlton A	61	Reading	53	Coventry C	51
1935–36	Coventry C	57	Luton T	56	Reading	54
1936–37	Luton T	58	Notts C	56	Brighton & HA	53
1937–38	Millwall	56	Bristol C	55	QPR	53
1938–39	Newport C	55	Crystal P	52	Brighton & HA	49
1946–47	Cardiff	66	QPR	57	Bristol C	51
1947–48	QPR	61	Bournemouth	57	Walsall	51
1949–49	Swansea	62	Reading	55	Bournemouth	52
1949–50	Notts C	58	Northampton T	51	Southend U	51
1950–51*b*	Nottingham F	70	Norwich C	64	Reading	57
1951–52	Plymouth A	66	Reading	61	Norwich C	61
1952–53	Bristol R	64	Northampton T	62	Millwall	62
1953–54	Ipswich T	64	Brighton & HA	61	Bristol C	56
1954–55	Bristol C	70	Leyton O	61	Southampton	59
1955–56	Leyton O	66	Brighton & HA	65	Ipswich T	64
1956–57	*Ipswich T	59	Torquay U	59	Colchester U	58
1957–58	Brighton & HA	60	Brentford	58	Plymouth A	58

Division III (Northern Section)

1921–22*a*	Stockport C	56	Darlington	50	Grimsby	50
1922–23	Nelson	51	Bradford	47	Walsall	46
1923–24*b*	Wolverhampton	63	Rochdale	62	Chesterfield	54
1924–25	Darlington	58	Nelson	53	New Brighton	53
1925–26	Grimsby T	61	Bradford	60	Rochdale	59
1926–27	Stoke C	63	Rochdale	58	Bradford	55
1927–28	Bradford	63	Lincoln C	55	Stockport C	54
1928–29	Bradford C	63	Stockport C	62	Wrexham	52
1929–30	Port Vale	67	Stockport C	63	Darlington	50
1930–31	Chesterfield	58	Lincoln C	57	Wrexham	54
1931–32*c*	*Lincoln C	57	Gateshead	57	Chester	50
1932–33*b*	Hull C	59	Wrexham	57	Stockport C	54
1933–34	Barnsley	62	Chesterfield	61	Stockport C	59
1934–35	Doncaster R	57	Halifax T	55	Chester	54
1935–36	Chesterfield	60	Chester	55	Tranmere R	55
1936–37	Stockport C	60	Lincoln C	57	Chester	53
1937–38	Tranmere R	56	Doncaster R	54	Hull C	53
1938–39	Barnsley	67	Doncaster R	56	Bradford C	52
1946–47	Doncaster R	72	Rotherham U	64	Chester	56
1947–48	Lincoln C	60	Rotherham U	59	Wrexham	50
1948–49	Hull C	65	Rotherham U	62	Doncaster R	50
1949–50	Doncaster R	55	Gateshead	53	Rochdale U	51
1950–51*d*	Rotherham U	71	Mansfield T	64	Carlisle U	62
1951–52	Lincoln C	69	Grimsby T	66	Stockport C	59
1952–53	Oldham A	59	Port Vale	58	Wrexham	56
1953–54	Port Vale	69	Barnsley	58	Scunthorpe	57
1954–55	Barnsley	65	Accrington S	61	Scunthorpe	58
1955–56	Grimsby T	68	Derby C	63	Accrington S	59
1956–57	Derby C	63	Hartlepool	59	Accrington S	58
1957–58	Scunthorpe U	66	Accrington S	59	Bradford C	57

*Won on goal average. Maximum points: *a*, 70; *b*, 84; *c*, 80; *d*, 90.
No championship during the World Wars.

Division IV

1958–59*a*	Port Vale	64	Coventry C	60	York C	60
1959–60	Walsall	65	Notts C	60	Torquay	60
1960–61	Peterborough	66	Crystal P	64	Northampton T	60

	First	Pt	Second	Pt	Third	Pt
1961–62	Millwall	56	Colchester U	55	Wrexham	53
1962–63	Brentford	62	Oldham A	59	Crewe A	59
1963–64	*Gillingham	60	Carlisle U	60	Workington T	59
1964–65	Brighton & HA	63	Millwall	62	York C	62
1965–66	*Doncaster R	59	Darlington	59	Torquay	58
1966–67	Stockport C	64	Southport C	59	Barrow	59
1967–68	Luton T	66	Barnsley	61	Hartlepool	60
1968–69	Doncaster R	59	Halifax T	57	Rochdale	56
1969–70	Chesterfield	64	Wrexham	61	Swansea T	60
1970–71	Notts C	69	Bournemouth	60	Oldham A	59
1971–72	Grimsby T	63	Southend U	60	Brentford	59
1972–73	Southport	62	Hereford U	58	Cambridge U	57
1973–74	Peterborough U	65	Gillingham	62	Colchester	60
1974–75	Mansfield T	68	Shrewsbury T	62	Rotherham U	59
1975–76	Lincoln C	74	Northampton T	68	Reading	60
1976–77	Cambridge U	65	Exeter C	62	Colchester	59
1977–78	Watford	71	Southend U	60	Swansea C	56
1978–79	Reading	65	Grimsby T	61	Wimbledon	61
1979–80	Huddersfield T	66	Walsall	64	Newport Co	61
1980–81	Southend U	67	Lincoln C	65	Doncaster R	56
1981–82	*b*Sheffield U	96	Bradford C	91	Wigan Ath	91
1982–83	Wimbledon	98	Hull C	90	Port Vale	88
1983–84	York C	101	Doncaster R	85	Reading	82
1984–85	Chesterfield	91	Blackpool	86	Darlington	85
1985–86	Swindon T	102	Chester C	84	Mansfield T	81

Maximum points *a*, 92; *b*, 138
*Won on goal average. 8

RELEGATED CLUBS

(Since inception of automatic promotion and relegation in 1898–99)

Season	Division I to Division II	Division II to Division III
1985–86	Ipswich T, Birmingham C, WBA	Carlisle U, Middlesbrough, Fulham
1984–85	Norwich C, Sunderland Stoke C.	Notts Co, Cardiff C, Wolverhampton W.
1983–84	Birmingham C., Notts Co., Wolverhampton W.	Derby Co., Swansea C., Cambridge U.
1982–83	Manchester C., Swansea C., Brighton & H.A.	Rotherham U., Burnley Bolton W.
1981–82	Leeds U., Middlesbrough, Wolverhampton W.	Cardiff, Wrexham, Orient.
1980–81	Norwich C., Leicester C., Crystal P.	Preston N.E., Bristol C., Bristol R.
1979–80	Bristol C., Derby Co., Bolton W.	Fulham, Burnley, Charlton Ath.
1978–79	QPR, Birmingham, Chelsea	Sheffield U., Millwall, B'burn
1977–78	West Ham, Newcastle, Leicester	Blackpool, Mansfield, Hull C.
1976–77	Sunderland, Stoke, Tottenham	Carlisle, Plymouth, Hereford
1975–76	Wolves, Burnley, Sheffield U.	Oxford, York, Portsmouth
1974–75	Luton, Chelsea, Carlisle	Millwall, Cardiff, Sheff. W.
1973–74	So'ton, Man. U., Norwich	C. Palace, Preston, Swindon
1972–73	Crystal P. and WBA	Huddersfield and Brighton
1971–72	Huddersfield and Nottingham F.	Charlton and Watford
1970–71	Burnley and Blackpool	Blackburn and Bolton
1969–70	Sunderland and Sheffield W.	Aston Villa and Preston
1968–69	Leicester and QPR	Bury and Fulham
1967–68	Sheffield U. and Fulham	Rotherham and Plymouth
1966–67	Aston Villa and Blackpool	Northampton and Bury
1965–66	Blackburn and Northampton	Leyton O. and Middlesbrough

1964–65	Birmingham and Wolverh'pton	Swindon and Swansea
1963–64	Bolton and Ipswich	Grimsby and Scunthorpe
1962–63	Manchester C. and Leyton O.	Walsall and Luton
1961–62	Cardiff and Chelsea	Bristol R. and Brighton
1960–61	Newcastle and Preston	Portsmouth and Lincoln
1959–60	Leeds and Luton	Hull and Bristol C.
1958–59	Aston V. and Portsmouth	Grimsby and Barnsley
1957–58	Sunderland and Sheffield W.	Notts Co. and Doncaster
1956–57	Cardiff and Charlton	Bury and Port Vale
1955–56	Huddersfield and Sheffield U.	Plymouth and Hull
1954–55	Leicester and Sheffield W.	Ipswich and Derby
1953–54	Middlesbrough and Liverpool	Brentford and Oldham
1952–53	Stoke and Derby	Southampton and Barnsley
1951–52	Fulham and Huddersfield	Coventry and QPR
1950–51	Sheffield W. and Everton	Chesterfield and Grimsby
1949–50	Manchester C. and Birmingham	Plymouth and Bradford
1948–49	Preston and Sheffield U.	Lincoln and Nottingham F.
1947–48	Blackburn and Grimsby	Doncaster and Millwall
1946–47	Brentford and Leeds	Swansea and Newport
1938–39	Birmingham and Leicester	Norwich and Tranmere
1937–38	Manchester C. and WBA	Barnsley and Stockport
1936–37	M'chester U. and Sheffield W.	Doncaster and Bradford C.
1935–36	Aston Villa and Blackburn	Port Vale and Hull
1934–35	Leicester and Tottenham	Oldham and Notts Co.
1933–34	Newcastle and Sheffield U.	Millwall and Lincoln
1932–33	Bolton and Blackpool	Chesterfield and Charlton
1931–32	Grimsby and West Ham	Barnsley and Bristol City
1930–31	Leeds and Manchester U.	Reading and Cardiff
1929–30	Burnley and Everton	Hull and Notts Co.
1928–29	Bury and Cardiff	Port Vale and Clapton O.
1927–28	Tottenham and Middlesbro'	Fulham and South Shields
1926–27	Leeds and WBA	Darlington and Bradford C.
1925–26	Manchester C. and Notts Co.	Stoke and Stockport
1924–25	Preston and Nottingham F.	Crystal Palace and Coventry
1923–24	Chelsea and Middlesbro'	Nelson and Bristol City
1922–23	Stoke and Oldham	Rotherham and W'ham'ton
1921–22	Bradford C. and Manchester U.	Bradford and Bristol City
1920–21	Derby and Bradford	Stockport
1919–20	Notts Co. and Sheffield W.	

1916–18 During the War the Football League competition was suspended. Previously the clubs relegated from Div. I to Div. II were:

1914–15 Tottenham and Chelsea
1913–14 Preston North End and Derby County
1912–13 Notts County and Woolwich Arsenal
1911–12 Preston North End and Bury
1910–11 Bristol City and Nottingham Forest
1909–10 Bolton Wanderers and Chelsea
1908–09 Manchester City and Leicester Fosse
1907–08 Bolton Wanderers and Birmingham
1906–07 Derby County and Stoke
1905–06 Nottingham Forest and Wolverhampton
1904–05 League extended. Bury and Notts County, two bottom clubs in First Division, re-elected.
1903–04 Liverpool and West Bromwich Albion
1902–03 Grimsby and Bolton
1901–02 Small Heath and Manchester City
1900–01 Preston North End and West Bromwich
1899–1900 Burnley and Glossop
1898–99 Bolton and Sheffield Wednesday

Season	Relegation from Division III to Division IV
1985–86	Lincoln C, Cardiff C, Wolverhampton W, Swansea C.
1984–85	Burnley, Orient, Preston NE, Cambridge U.
1983–84	Scunthorpe U., Southend U., Port Vale, Exeter C.
1982–83	Reading, Doncaster R., Wrexham, Chesterfield.
1981–82	Wimbledon, Swindon T., Bristol C., Chester
1980–81	Sheffield U., Colchester U., Hull C., Blackpool
1979–80	Bury, Southend U., Mansfield T. and Wimbledon
1978–79	Peterborough, Walsall, Tranmere and Lincoln
1977–78	Port Vale, Bradford, Hereford and Portsmouth
1976–77	Reading, Northampton, Grimsby and York
1975–76	Aldershot, Colchester, Southend U., and Halifax T.
1974–75	Bournemouth, Tranmere, Watford and Huddersfield
1973–74	Cambridge, Shrewsbury, Southport and Rochdale
1972–73	Rotherham, Brentford, Swansea and Scunthorpe
1971–72	Mansfield, Barnsley, Bradford C. and Torquay
1970–71	Reading, Bury, Doncaster and Gillingham
1969–70	Bournemouth, Southport, Barrow and Stockport
1968–69	Northampton, Hartlepool, Crewe and Oldham
1967–68	Grimsby, Colchester, Scunthorpe and Peterborough*
1966–67	Swansea, Darlington, Workington and Doncaster
1965–66	Southend, Exeter, Brentford, and York
1964–65	Luton, Port Vale, Colchester and Barnsley
1963–64	Millwall, Crewe, Wrexham and Notts County
1962–63	Bradford, Brighton, Carlisle and Halifax
1961–62	Torquay, Lincoln, Brentford and Newport
1960–61	Tranmere, Bradford C., Colchester and Chesterfield
1959–60	York, Mansfield, Wrexham and Accrington
1958–59	Stockport, Doncaster, Notts County and Rochdale

*Expelled to Fourth Division by League

APPLICATION FOR RE-ELECTION TO THIRD DIVISION UNTIL 1957-58

Seven times: Walsall.
Six: Exeter, Halifax, Newport.
Five: Accrington, Barrow, Gillingham, New Brighton, Southport.
Four: Norwich, Rochdale.
Three: Crewe, Crystal Palace, Darlington, Hartlepool, Merthyr Town, Swindon.
Two: Aberdare Athletic, Aldershot, Ashington, Bournemouth, Brentford, Chester, Colchester, Millwall, Durham City, Nelson, Queen's Park Rangers, Rotherham, Southend, Tranmere, Watford, Workington.
One: Bradford, Bradford City, Brighton, Bristol Rovers, Cardiff, Carlisle, Charlton, Gateshead, Grimsby, Mansfield, Shrewsbury, Thames, Torquay, York.

APPLICATION FOR RE-ELECTION TO FOURTH DIVISION

Eleven times: Hartlepool.
Seven: Crewe.
Six: Barrow, Halifax T., Rochdale, Southport and York.
Five: Chester C., Darlington, Lincoln, Stockport Co. and Workington.
Four: Bradford, Newport Co. and Northampton T.
Three: Doncaster R. and Hereford U.

Two: Bradford City, Exeter C., Oldham, Scunthorpe and Torquay U.
One: Aldershot, Blackpool, Cambridge United, Colchester, Gateshead, Grimsby, Port Vale, Preston NE., Swansea City, Tranmere R., and Wrexham.
Gateshead not re-elected, their place being taken by Peterborough in the 1960–61 season.
Accrington resigned March 1962, and Oxford United elected to replace them in 1962–63 season.
Bradford not re-elected, their place being taken by Cambridge United in the 1970–71 season.
Barrow not re-elected, their place being taken by Hereford United in the 1972–73 season.
Workington not re-elected, their place being taken by Wimbledon in the 1977–78 season.
Southport not re-elected, their place being taken by Wigan in the 1978–79 season.

LEAGUE TITLE WINS

League Division I–16–Liverpool; 8–Arsenal, Everton; 7–Aston Villa, Manchester U.; 6–Sunderland; 4–Newcastle, Sheffield Wed.; 3–Huddersfield, Wolves; 2–Blackburn, Burnley, Derby, Leeds, Manchester City, Portsmouth, Preston, Tottenham; 1–Chelsea, Ipswich, Nottingham Forest, Sheffield United, West Bromwich Albion.

League Division II–6–Manchester City, Leicester; 5–Sheffield Wed.; 4–*Birmingham, Liverpool; 3–Derby, Middlesbrough, Notts Co., Preston; 2–Aston Villa, Bolton, Burnley, Grimsby, Ipswich, Leeds, Manchester U., Norwich C., Nottingham Forest, Stoke, Tottenham, West Bromwich, West Ham, Wolverhampton; 1–Blackburn, Blackpool, Bradford City, Brentford, Bristol City, Bury, Chelsea, Coventry, Crystal Palace, Everton, Fulham, Huddersfield, Luton, Newcastle, Oxford U., Q.P.R., Sheffield United, Sunderland.
*Once as Small Heath.

League Division III–2–Oxford U., Portsmouth, 1–Aston Villa, Blackburn R., Bolton, Bradford C., Burnley, Bury, Carlisle, Coventry, Grimsby T., Hereford U., Hull, Mansfield, Northampton, Oldham Ath., Orient, Plymouth, Preston, Queen's Park Rangers, Reading, Rotherham U., Shrewsbury T., Southampton, Watford, Wrexham.

League Division IV–2–Chesterfield, Doncaster R., Peterborough U., 1–Brentford, Brighton, Cambridge, Gillingham, Grimsby, Huddersfield T., Lincoln C., Luton, Mansfield T., Millwall, Notts Co., Port Vale, Reading, Sheffield U., Southend U., Southport, Swindon T., Walsall, Watford, Wimbledon, York C.

To 1957-58
Division III (South): Bristol City, three times; Charlton, Ipswich, Millwall, Notts Co., Plymouth, Swansea, twice; Brentford, Brighton, Bristol R., Cardiff, Coventry, Crystal P., Fulham, Leyton Orient, Luton, Newport, Nottingham Forest, Norwich, Portsmouth, Queen's Park Rangers, Reading, Southampton, once.
Division III (North): Barnsley, Doncaster, Lincoln, three times; Chesterfield, Grimsby, Hull, Port Vale, Stockport, twice; Bradford, Bradford City, Darlington, Derby, Nelson, Oldham, Rotherham, Scunthorpe, Stoke, Tranmere, Wolverhampton, once.

TRANSFER TRAIL

(players with Football League Clubs)

First four-figure transaction
Alf Common: Sunderland to Middlesbrough £1,000 February 1905.
First five-figure transaction
David Jack: Bolton Wanderers to Arsenal £10,340 October 1928.
First six-figure transaction
Alan Ball: Blackpool to Everton £112,000, August 1966.
First £200,000 transaction
Martin Peters: West Ham United to Tottenham Hotspur £200,000, March 1970.
First seven-figure transaction
Trevor Francis: Birmingham City to Nottingham Forest £1,000,000, February 1979.
Bryan Robson: West Bromwich Albion to Manchester United £1,500,000, October 1981.
Andy Gray: Aston Villa to Wolverhampton W. £1,469,000, September 1979.
Steve Daley: Wolverhampton W. to Manchester City £1,450,000, September 1979.
Kenny Sansom: Crystal Palace to Arsenal £1,350,000, August 1980.
Clive Allen: Queen's Park Rangers to Arsenal £1,250,000, June 1980.
Clive Allen: Arsenal to Crystal Palace, £1,250,000, August 1980.
Garry Birtles: Nottingham Forest to Manchester United £1,250,000, October 1980.
Trevor Francis: Birmingham City to Nottingham Forest £1,000,000, February 1979.
Kevin Reeves: Norwich City to Manchester City £1,000,000, March 1980.
Justin Fashanu: Norwich City to Nottingham Forest £1,000,000, August 1981.
Trevor Francis: Nottingham Forest to Manchester City £1,000,000, September 1981.
Peter Barnes: West Bromwich Albion to Leeds United £930,000, August 1981.
Mark Lawrenson: Brighton & Hove Albion to Liverpool £900,000, August 1981.
Frank Stapleton: Arsenal to Manchester United £900,000, August 1981.
Steve Archibald: Aberdeen to Tottenham Hotspur £800,000, May 1980.
Paul Goddard: Queen's Park Rangers to West Ham United £800,000, August 1980.
Gary Linaker: Leicester City to Everton £800,000, July 1985.
Mick Robinson: Preston North End to Manchester City £756,000, July 1979.
Ray Wilkins: Chelsea to Manchester United £750,000, August 1979.
Charlie Nicholas: Celtic to Arsenal £750,000, July 1983.
Gordon Strachan: Aberdeen to Manchester United £750,000, May 1984.
Mike Flanagan: Charlton Athletic to Crystal Palace £722,000 August 1979.
Adrian Heath: Stoke City to Everton £700,000, January 1982.
Paul Walsh: Luton Town to Liverpool £700,000, May 1984.
Alan Brazil: Tottenham Hotspur to Manchester United £700,000, June 1984.
Clive Allen: Queen's Park Rangers to Tottenham Hotspur £700,000, August 1984.
Steve Wicks: Queen's Park Rangers to Crystal Palace £670,000, June 1981.
Peter Barnes: Manchester City to West Bromwich Albion £650,000, July 1979.
John Gidman: Aston Villa to Everton £650,000, October 1979.
Garth Crooks: Stoke City to Tottenham Hotspur £600,000, July 1980.
David Armstrong: Middlesbrough to Southampton £600,000, August 1981.
John Chiedozie: Orient to Notts County £600,000, August 1981.
Chris Waddle: Newcastle United to Tottenham Hotspur £590,000, July 1985.
Craig Johnston: Middlesbrough to Liverpool £575,000, April 1981.
Peter Davenport: Nottingham Forest to Manchester United £570,000, March 1986.
Phil Parkes: Queen's Park Rangers to West Ham United £565,000, February 1979.
Luther Blisset: A.C. Milan to Watford £550,000, August 1984.
David Mills: Middlesbrough to West Bromwich Albion £516,000, January 1979.
Asa Hartford: Manchester City to Nottingham Forest £500,000, July 1979.
Asa Hartford: Nottingham Forest to Everton £500,000, August 1979.
Peter Withe: Newcastle United to Aston Villa £500,000, May 1980.
Andrew Ritchie: Manchester U. to Brighton & Hove A. £500,000, October 1980.
Steve McKenzie: Manchester C. to West Bromwich A. £500,000, August 1981.
Remi Moses: West Bromwich A. to Manchester U. £500,000, September 1981.
Tony Woodcock: FC Cologne to Arsenal £500,000, July 1982.

P.F.A.86.87.—5

Lee Chapman: Stoke City to Arsenal £500,000, August 1982.
Gordan Strachan: Aberdeen to Manchester United £500,000, August 1984.
Steve Williams: Southampton to Arsenal £500,000, December 1984.
Gerry Francis: Queen's Park Rangers to Crystal Palace £465,000, July 1979.
Gordon McQueen: Leeds United to Manchester United £450,000, February 1978.
Brian Talbot: Ipswich Town to Arsenal £450,000, January 1979.
Garry Owen: Manchester City to West Bromwich Albion £450,000, June 1979.
David Hodgson: Middlesbrough to Liverpool £450,000, August 1982.
Vladimir Petrovic: Red Star Belgrade to Arsenal £450,000, December 1982.
Alan Brazil: Ipswich Town to Tottenham Hotspur £450,000, March 1983.
John Wark: Ipswich Town to Liverpool £450,000, March 1984.
Garry Thompson: West Bromwich Albion to Sheffield Wednesday £450,000, August 1985.
Garry Thompson: Sheffield Wednesday to Aston Villa £450,000, June 1986.
Kenny Dalglish: Celtic to Liverpool £440,000, August 1977.
Mick Baxter: Preston North End to Middlesbrough £425,000, August 1981.
Paul Proctor: Middlesbrough to Nottingham Forest £425,000, August 1981.
Osvaldo Ardiles: Huracan to Tottenham Hotspur £400,000, July 1978.
Charlie George: Derby County to Southampton £400,000, December 1978.
Tony Currie: Leeds United to Queen's Park Rangers £400,000, August 1979.
Frank Gray: Leeds United to Nottingham Forest £400,000, August 1979.
John Deehan: Aston Villa to West Bromwich Albion £400,000, September 1979.
Gordon Smith: Rangers to Brighton & Hove Albion £400,000, May 1980.
Ray Stewart: Dundee United to West Ham United £400,000, September 1979.
Dave Thomas: Everton to Wolverhampton Wanderers £400,000, October 1979.
Dave Swindlehurst: Crystal Palace to Derby County £400,000, April 1980.
Alex Sabella: Sheffield United to Leeds United £400,000, May 1980.
Kevin Keegan: Hamburg to Southampton £400,000, July 1980.
Michael Robinson: Manchester C. to Brighton & Hove Albion £400,000, July 1980.
Paul Barron: Arsenal to Crystal Palace £400,000, August 1980.
Thomas Langley: Chelsea to Queen's Park Rangers £400,000, August 1980.
Andrew King: Everton to Queen's Park Rangers £400,000, September 1980.
Peter Ward: Brighton & Hove A. to Nottingham Forest £400,000, October 1980.
Peter Nicholas: Crystal Palace to Arsenal £400,000, March 1981.
Clive Allen: Crystal Palace to Queen's Park Rangers £400,000, June 1981.
Jimmy Case: Liverpool to Brighton & Hove Albion £400,000, August 1981.
Andy King: Queen's Park Rangers to West Bromwich Albion £400,000 September 1981.
Kenny Burns: Nottingham Forest to Leeds United £400,000, October 1981.
Neil Orr: Greenock Morton to West Ham United £400,000, January 1982.
Paul Walsh: Charlton Athletic to Luton Town £400,000, July 1982.
Kevin MacDonald: Leicester City to Liverpool £400,000, November 1984.
Paul Allen: West Ham United to Tottenham Hotspur £400,000, June 1985.
Steve Hodge: Nottingham Forest to Aston Villa £400,000, July 1985.
Gordon Durie: Hibernian to Chelsea £400,000, May 1986.
Alan Curtis: Swansea City to Leeds United £375,000, May 1979.
Irving Nattrass: Newcastle United to Middlesbrough £375,000, August 1979.
John Chiedozie: Notts County to Tottenham Hotspur £375,000, August 1984.
Kevin Hird: Blackburn Rovers to Leeds United £360,000, March 1979.
Graeme Souness: Middlesbrough to Liverpool £352,000, January 1978.
Bob Latchford: Birmingham City to Everton £350,000, February 1974.
Joe Jordan: Leeds United to Manchester United £350,000, January 1978.
Paul Futcher: Luton Town to Manchester City £350,000, June 1978.
Richardo Villa: Racing Club to Tottenham Hotspur £350,000, July 1978.
Len Cantello: West Bromwich Albion to Bolton Wanderers £350,000, June 1979.
Garry Collier: Bristol City to Coventry City £350,000, July 1979.
Brian Greenhoff: Manchester United to Leeds United £350,000, August 1979.
Alan Biley: Cambridge United to Derby County £350,000, January 1980.
David Langan: Derby County to Birmingham City £350,000, July 1980.
Joe Gallagher: Birmingham City to Wolverhampton Wanderers £350,000, August 1981.
Colin Irwin: Liverpool to Swansea City £350,000, August 1981.
Kevin Bond: Seattle Sounders to Manchester City £350,000, September 1981.

Chris Kamara: Portsmouth to Brentford £350,000, October 1981.
Peter Shilton: Nottingham Forest to Southampton £350,000, August 1982
Tommy Caton: Manchester City to Arsenal £350,000, December 1983.
Jesper Olsen: Ajax, Amsterdam to Manchester United £350,000, July 1984.
Andy Gray: Everton to Aston Villa £350,000, July 1985.
Steve Mahon: Aston Villa to Liverpool £350,000, September 1985.
Frank McAvennie: St Mirren to West Ham United £340,000, June 1985.
Malcolm Macdonald: Newcastle United to Arsenal £333,333, August 1976.
Richard Money: Fulham to Liverpool £333,000, May 1980.
Paul Hart: Blackpool to Leeds United £330,000, March 1978.
Colin Todd: Derby County to Everton £330,000, September 1978.
Mick Walsh: Blackpool to Everton £325,000, August 1978.
John Gidman: Everton to Manchester United £325,000, August 1981.
Gary Gillespie: Coventry City to Liverpool £325,000, July 1983.
Claudio Marangoni: San Lorenzo (Arg.) to Sunderland £320,000, December 1979.
Allan Simonsen: Barcelona to Charlton Athletic £320,000, November 1982.
Alan Kennedy: Newcastle United to Liverpool £300,000, August 1978.
Mike Thomas: Wrexham to Manchester United £300,000, November 1978.
Frank McGarvey: St Mirren to Liverpool £300,000, May 1979.
John Gregory: Aston Villa to Brighton & Hove Albion £300,000, July 1979.
Bobby Shinton: Wrexham to Manchester City £300,000, July 1979.
Garry Stanley: Chelsea to Everton £300,000, August 1979.
Terry Yorath: Coventry City to Tottenham Hotspur £300,000, August 1979.
David Geddis: Ipswich Town to Aston Villa £300,000, September 1979.
Steve Wicks: Derby County to Queen's Park Rangers £300,000, September 1979.
Barry Powell: Coventry City to Derby County £300,000, October 1979.
Stan Cummins: Middlesbrough to Sunderland £300,000, November 1979.
Ian Rush: Chester to Liverpool £300,000, May 1980.
Gerrard Daly: Derby County to Coventry City £300,000, August 1980.
Drazen Muzinic: Hadjuk Split to Norwich City £300,000, September 1980.
Alexander Munro: St. Mirren to Stoke City £300,000, October 1980.
Frank Gray: Nottingham Forest to Leeds United £300,000, May 1981.
John Gregory: Brighton & Hove Albion to Queen's Park Rangers £300,000, June 1981.
Alan Biley: Derby Co. to Everton £300,000, July 1981.
Andy Blair: Coventry City to Aston Villa £300,000, August 1981.
Ray Clemence: Liverpool to Tottenham Hotspur £300,000, August 1981.
Ally McCoist: St Johnstone to Sunderland £300,000, August 1981.
Neil Whatmore: Bolton Wanderers to Birmingham City £300,000, August 1981.
Steve Nicol: Ayr United to Liverpool £300,000, October 1981.
Ray Hankin: Vancouver Whitecaps to Arsenal £300,000 November 1981.
Peter Beardsley: Vancouver Whitecaps to Newcastle United £300,000, September 1982.
Steve McMahon: Everton to Aston Villa £300,000, May 1983.
Gary Stevens: Brighton & Hove Albion to Tottenham Hotspur £300,000 June 1983.
Trevor Steven: Burnley to Everton £300,000, July 1983.
Tony Coton: Birmingham City to Watford, £300,000, September 1984.
Cyrille Regis: West Bromwich Albion to Coventry £300,000, October 1984.
Mark Chamberlain: Stoke City to Sheffield Wednesday £300,000, September 1985.
Mike Hazard: Tottenham Hotspur to Chelsea £300,000, September 1985.
Imre Varadi: Sheffield Wednesday to West Bromwich Albion £285,000, July 1985.
Peter Eastoe: Queen's Park Rangers to Everton £280,000, March 1979.
Mick Walsh: Everton to Queen's Park Rangers £280,000, March 1979.
Mick Ferguson: Coventry City to Everton £280,000, August 1981.
Steve Wicks: Chelsea to Derby County £275,000, January 1979.
Des Bremner: Hibernian to Aston Villa £275,000, September 1979.
Frank McGarvey: Liverpool to Celtic £275,000, March 1980.
Simon Stainrod: Oldham Athletic to Q.P.R. £275,000, November 1980.
Martin O'Neill: Norwich City to Manchester City £275,000, June 1981.
Micky Thomas: Manchester United to Everton, £275,000, August 1981.
Chris Turner: Sunderland to Manchester United £275,000, August 1985.
Colin Gibson: Aston Villa to Manchester United £275,000, November 1985.
Paul Maguire: Shrewsbury Town to Stoke City £262,000, September 1980.

FA CUP 1985-86

Dalglish goes one better

Taking over as manager of Liverpool in the footsteps of Shankly, Paisley and Fagan would be a task that few experienced men would relish. When Kenny Dalglish accepted the job days before the Brussels tragedy, therefore, many people wondered if he would be able to make a success of it. Not only was he taking over a club where at least one major success per season was the norm, but he also had to make the difficult transition from player to player-manager, exercising discipline over players who had so recently been his mates in the dressing room.

What an achievement, then, to crown his first season as manager with the League Championship and FA Cup Double. The FA Cup was the one trophy which had eluded both Paisley and Fagan (Liverpool last won the Cup in 1974 in Shankly's last season), and although the Anfield club were deprived of a chance to shine in the UEFA Cup in 1985-86 by the ridiculous ban on English clubs, Dalglish must have been extremely satisfied by his performance to date. This was underlined by the award of the Manager of the Year trophy.

The FA Cup tournament was plain sailing in the third and fourth rounds for Liverpool, but they hiccupped in the fifth round when they were held to a 1-1 draw by York before winning the replay at Anfield. They had to have two attempts in the quarter-finals as well, with Watford holding them up this time, and needed extra time in their semi-final against Southampton at White Hart Lane to reach the final for the first time since 1977.

Everton's progress appeared to be less difficult, beating Exeter and Blackburn before things started to hot up in the fifth round. Here they had to take Spurs out in an away tie, and were then held to a draw by Luton, winning the replay narrowly at Goodison. Their semi-final also needed extra time, but late goals by Harper and Sharp took them through to their third successive final. As with the last team to achieve this – Arsenal – they were doomed to get only one victory from the three matches.

The final was an entertaining one. Everton took the lead in the 27th minute when Lineker scored after Grobbelaar had only managed to parry the ball, and there was no further score in the first half. After the restart, Everton spent more than ten minutes battering the Liverpool defence and nearly scored on two or three occasions, but Rush equalised in the 57th minute after a brilliant through ball by Molby, and Everton never managed to regain the upper hand. Further goals by Rush and Johnston saw Liverpool through, and Kenny Dalglish became the first player-manager to win an FA Cup-winner's medal.

Liverpool: *Grobbelaar; Lawrenson, Beglin, Nicol, Whelan, Hansen, Dalglish, Johnston, Rush, Molby, MacDonald.*

Everton: *Mimms, Stevens, (Heath), Van den Hauwe, Ratcliffe, Mountfield, Reid, Steven, Lineker, Sharp, Bracewell, Sheedy.*

FA CUP 1985-86

First round

Bishop's Stortford	2	1	Peterborough U	2	3
Bournemouth	0	2	Dartford	0	0
Brentford	1		Bristol R	3	

Bury	2	Chester C	0
Chelmsford	1	Weymouth	0
Chorley	0	Altrincham	2
Dagenham	2	Cambridge U	1
Derby	5	Crewe Alex	1
Enfield	0	Bognor	2
Exeter	2	Cardiff C	1
Fareham	0	Maidstone	3
Farnborough	0	Bath	4
Frickley	1 3	Halesowen	1 1
Gillingham	3	Northampton T.	0
Halifax T	1	Scunthorpe U	3
Lincoln C	0	Blackpool	1
Macclesfield	1	Hartlepool U	2
Mansfield T	1 0	Port Vale	1 1
Notts Co	6	Scarborough	1
Nuneaton	2	Burnley	3
Plymouth Arg	1	Aldershot	0
Reading	1	Wealdstone	0
Rochdale	2	Darlington	1
Rotherham U	6	Wolverhampton W	0
Runcorn	2 1 4	Boston	2 1 1
Slough	2 5	Aylesbury	2 2
Southend U	0	Newport Co	1
Stockport Co	0	Telford	1
Swansea C	2	Leyton Wingate	0
Swindon T	0 2	Bristol C	0 4
Tranmere R	2 1	Chesterfield	2 0
VS Rugby	2 1	Orient	2 4
Walsall	7	Preston NE	3
Whitby	1	South Liverpool	0
Wigan Ath	4	Doncaster R	1
Windsor & Eton	1 0	Torquay U	1 3
Wrexham	3	Bolton W	1
Wycombe W	2	Colchester U	0
Yeovil	2	Hereford U	4
York C	0 2	Morecambe	0 0

Second round

Blackpool	1	Altrincham	2
Bournemouth	4	Dagenham	1
Bristol C	1	Exeter C	2
Derby Co	6	Telford	1
Gillingham	6	Bognor	1
Hartlepool U	0	Frickley	1
Newport Co	1 3	Torquay U	1 2
Notts Co	2 3	Wrexham	2 0
Orient	2 3	Slough	2 2
Peterborough U	1	Bath	0
Plymouth Arg	3	Maidstone	0
Port Vale	0 1	Walsall	0 2
Reading	2	Hereford U	0
Rotherham U	4	Burnley	1
Runcorn	1 0	Wigan Ath	1 4
Scunthorpe U	2 1	Rochdale	2 2
Swansea C	1	Bristol R	2
Tranmere R	1 1	Bury	1 2
Wycombe W	2	Chelmsford	0
York C	3	Whitby T	1

Third round	Fourth round	Fifth round	Quarter-finals	Semi-finals	Final
Sheffield U. 2	Sheffield U. 0	Derby Co. 1 0	Sheffield W. 2	Sheffield W. 1	**EVERTON (1) 1**
Fulham 0					*Scorer:* Lineker Wembley, att: 98,000
Gillingham 1 1	Derby Co. 1				
Derby Co. 1 3					
Sheffield W. 2 3	Sheffield W. 5	Sheffield W. 1 2			
W.B.A. 2 2					
Oldham Ath. 1	Orient 0				
Orient 2					
Charlton Ath. 0	West Ham U. 0 1 1	West Ham U. 1 2	West Ham U. 0		
West Ham U. 1					
Ipswich T. 4 1	Ipswich T. 0 1 0				
Bradford C. 4 0					
Sunderland 2	Sunderland 0 0	Manchester U. 1 0			
Newport Co. 0					
Manchester U. 2	Manchester U. 0 3				
Rochdale 0					
Crystal Palace 1	Luton T. 4	Luton T. 2 0 3	Luton T. 2 0	Everton 2	
Luton T. 2				(at Villa Park)	
Bristol R. 3	Bristol R. 0				
Leicester C. 1					
Grimsby T. 3	Arsenal 5	Arsenal 2 0 0			
Arsenal 4					
Frickley 1	Rotherham U. 1				
Rotherham U. 3					
Stoke C. 0	Notts Co. 1 0	Tottenham H. 1	Everton 2 1		
Notts Co. 2					
Oxford U. 1 1	Tottenham H. 1 5				
Tottenham H. 1 2					
Everton 1	Everton 3	Everton 2			
Exeter C. 0					
Nottingham F. 1 2	Blackburn R. 1				
Blackburn R. 1 3					

LIVERPOOL (0) 3

Scorers: Rush 2, Johnston Receipts: £1,100,000

Peterborough U. 1	Peterborough U. 1	Peterborough U. 2 0	Brighton & H.A. 0	Southampton 0
Leeds U. 0				
Carlisle U. 1	Carlisle U. 0			
Q.P.R. 0				
Hull C. 2 1	Hull C. 2	Brighton & H.A. 2 1		
Plymouth Arg. 2 0				
Newcastle U. 0	Brighton & H.A. 3			
Brighton & H.A. 2				
Middlesbrough 1	Southampton 3	Southampton 0 1	Southampton 2	
Southampton 3				
Wigan Ath. 3	Wigan Ath. 0			
Bournemouth 0				
Portsmouth 2 1	Aston Villa 1 0	Millwall 0 0		
Aston Villa 2 3				
Millwall 3	Millwall 1 1			
Wimbledon 0				
York C. 2	York C. 2	York C. 1 1	Liverpool 0 2	Liverpool 2 (at White Hart Lane)
Wycombe W. 0				
Birmingham C. 1	Altrincham 0			
Altrincham 2				
Shrewsbury T. 0	Chelsea 1	Liverpool 1 3		
Chelsea 1				
Liverpool 5	Liverpool 2			
Norwich C. 0				
Walsall 1	Manchester C. 1 1	Watford 1 3	Watford 0 1	
Manchester C. 3				
Coventry C. 1	Watford 1 3			
Watford 3				
Huddersfiled T. 0 1	Reading 1 0	Bury 1 0		
Reading 0 2				
Bury 2	Bury 1 3			
Barnsley 0				

PAST FA CUP FINALS

Some goalscorers are not available in the early years

1872	The Wanderers	1	Royal Engineers	0
	Betts			
1873	The Wanderers	2	Oxford University	0
	Kinnaird, Wollaston			
1874	Oxford University	2	Royal Engineers	0
	Mackarness, Patton			
1875	Royal Engineers	1	Old Etonians	1
	Unknown		*Bonsor*	
	Royal Engineers	2	Old Etonians	0
	Scorers in replay: Renny-Tailyour, Stafford			
1876	The Wanderers	1	Old Etonians	1
	Edwards		*Bonsor*	
	The Wanderers	3	Old Etonians	0
	Wollaston, Hughes 2			
1877	The Wanderers	2	Oxford University	1
	Kenrick, Heron		*Kinnaird (og) (After extra time)*	
1878	The Wanderers	3	Royal Engineers	1
	Kenrick 2, unknown		*Unknown*	
1879	Old Etonians	1	Clapham Rovers	0
	Clerke			
1880	Clapham Rovers	1	Oxford University	0
	Lloyd-Jones			
1881	Old Carthusians	3	Old Etonians	0
	Page, Wynard, Tod			
1882	Old Etonians	1	Blackburn Rovers	0
	Anderson			
1883	Blackburn Olympic	2	Old Etonians	1
	Costley, Matthews		*Goodhart (After extra time)*	
1884	Blackburn Rovers	2	Queen's Park	1
	Forrest, Brown		*Christie*	
1885	Blackburn Rovers	2	Queen's Park	0
	Forrest, Brown			
1886	Blackburn Rovers	0	West Bromwich Albion	0
	Blackburn Rovers	2	West Bromwich Albion	0
	Brown, Sowerbutts			
1887	Aston Villa	2	West Bromwich Albion	0
	Hunter, Hodgetts			
1888	West Bromwich Albion	2	Preston North End	1
	Woodall, Bayliss		*Goodall*	
1889	Preston North End	3	Wolverhampton W.	0
	Ross, Dewhurst, Thomson			
1890	Blackburn Rovers	6	Sheffield Wednesday	1
	Dewar, Lofthouse, John Southworth, Townley 3		*Bennett*	
1891	Blackburn Rovers	3	Notts County	1
	Dewar, John Southworth, Townley		*Oswald*	
1892	West Bromwich Albion	3	Aston Villa	0
	Reynolds, Nicholls, Geddes			
1893	Wolverhampton W.	1	Everton	0
	Allen			
1894	Notts County	4	Bolton Wanderers	1
	Watson, Logan 3		*Cassidy*	
1895	Aston Villa	1	West Bromwich Albion	0
	Chatt			
1896	Sheffield Wednesday	2	Wolverhampton W.	1
	Spiksley 2		*Black*	

1897	Aston Villa	3	Everton	2
	Crabtree, Campbell, Wheldon		*Boyle, Bell*	
1898	Nottingham Forest	3	Derby County	1
	McPherson, Capes 2		*Bloomer*	
1899	Sheffield United	4	Derby County	1
	Bennett, Beers, Almond, Priest		*Boag*	
1900	Bury	4	Southampton	0
	Wood, McLuckie 2, Plant			
1901	Tottenham Hotspur	2	Sheffield United	2
	Brown 2		*Bennett, Priest*	
	Tottenham Hotspur	3	Sheffield United	1
	Cameron, Smith, Brown		*Priest*	
1902	Sheffield United	1	Southampton	1
	Common		*Wood*	
	Sheffield United	2	Southampton	1
	Hedley, Barnes		*Brown*	
1903	Bury	6	Derby County	0
	Wood, Sagar, Ross, Plant, Leeming 2			
1904	Manchester City	1	Bolton Wanderers	0
	Meredith			
1905	Aston Villa	2	Newcastle United	0
	Hampton 2			
1906	Everton	1	Newcastle United	0
	Young			
1907	Sheffield Wednesday	2	Everton	1
	Stewart, Simpson		*Sharp*	
1908	Wolverhampton W.	3	Newcastle United	1
	Hunt, Harrison, Hedley		*Howie*	
1909	Manchester United	1	Bristol City	0
	A. Turnbull			
1910	Newcastle United	1	Barnsley	1
	Rutherford		*Tuffnell*	
	Newcastle United	2	Barnsley	0
	Shepherd 2 (1 pen)			
1911	Bradford City	0	Newcastle United	0
	Bradford City	1	Newcastle United	0
	Spiers			
1912	Barnsley	0	West Bromwich Albion	0
	Barnsley	2	West Bromwich Albion	0
	Tuffnell 2		*(After extra time)*	
1913	Aston Villa	1	Sunderland	0
	Barber			
1914	Burnley	1	Liverpool	0
	Freeman			
1915	Sheffield United	3	Chelsea	0
	Simmons, Fazackerley, Kitchen			
1920	Aston Villa	1	Huddersfield Town	0
	Kirton		*(After extra time)*	
1921	Tottenham Hotspur	1	Wolverhampton W.	0
	Dimmock			
1922	Huddersfield Town	1	Preston North End	0
	Smith (pen)			
1923	Bolton Wanderers	2	West Ham United	0
	Jack, J.R. Smith			
1924	Newcastle United	2	Aston Villa	0
	Harris, Seymour			
1925	Sheffield United	1	Cardiff City	0
	Tunstall			

1927	Cardiff City	1	Arsenal	0
	Ferguson			
1928	Blackburn Rovers	3	Huddersfield Town	1
	Roscamp 2, McLean		*A. Jackson*	
1929	Bolton Wanderers	2	Portsmouth	0
	Butler, Blackmore			
1930	Arsenal	2	Huddersfield Town	0
	Lambert, James			
1931	West Bromwich Albion	2	Birmingham City	1
	W.G Richardson 2		*Bradford*	
1932	Newcastle United	2	Arsenal	1
	Allen 2		*John*	
1933	Everton	3	Manchester City	0
	Dunn, Dean, Stein			
1934	Manchester City	2	Portsmouth	1
	Tilson 2		*Rutherford*	
1935	Sheffield Wednesday	4	West Bromwich Albion	2
	Hooper, Palethorpe, Rimmer 2		*Sandford, Boyes*	
1936	Arsenal	1	Sheffield United	0
	Drake			
1937	Sunderland	3	Preston North End	1
	Carter, Gurney, Burbanks		*F. O'Donnell*	
1938	Preston North End	1	Huddersfield Town	0
	Mutch (pen)			
1939	Portsmouth	4	Wolverhampton W	1
	Anderson, Barlow, Parker 2		*Dorsett*	
1946	Derby County	4	Charlton Athletic	1
	H. Turner (og), Stamps 2, Doherty		*H. Turner (After extra time)*	
1947	Charlton Athletic	1	Burnley	0
	Duffy		*(After extra time)*	
1948	Manchester United	4	Blackpool	2
	Anderson, Rowley 2, Pearson		*Shimwell (pen), Mortensen*	
1949	Wolverhampton W	3	Leicester City	1
	Smyth, Pye 2		*Griffiths*	
1950	Arsenal	2	Liverpool	0
	Lewis 2			
1951	Newcastle	2	Blackpool	0
	Milburn 2			
1952	Newcastle	1	Arsenal	0
	G. Robledo			
1953	Blackpool	4	Bolton Wanderers	3
	Mortensen 3, Perry		*Bell, Moir, Lofthouse*	
1954	West Bromwich Albion	3	Preston North End	2
	Griffin, Allen 2		*Wayman, Morrison*	
1955	Newcastle United	3	Manchester City	1
	Milburn, Hannah, Mitchell		*Johnstone*	
1956	Manchester City	3	Birmingham City	1
	Johnstone, Hayes, Dyson		*Kinsey*	
1957	Aston Villa	2	Manchester United	1
	McParland 2		*T. Taylor*	
1958	Bolton Wanderers	2	Manchester United	0
	Lofthouse 2			
1959	Nottingham Forest	2	Luton Town	1
	Dwight, Wilson		*Pacey*	
1960	Wolverhampton W	3	Blackburn Rovers	0
	Deeley 2, McGrath (og)			
1961	Tottenham Hotspur	2	Leicester City	0
	Smith, Dyson			

1962	Tottenham Hotspur ....3 *Blanchflower (p), Smith, Greaves*	Burnley ....1 *Robson*
1963	Manchester United ....3 *Herd 2, Law*	Leicester City ....1 *Keyworth*
1964	West Ham United ....3 *Boyce, Hurst, Sissons*	Preston North End ....2 *Dawson, Holden*
1965	Liverpool ....2 *Hunt, St John*	Leeds United ....1 *Bremner*
1966	Everton ....3 *Trebilcock 2, Temple*	Sheffield Wednesday ....2 *McCalliog, Ford*
1967	Tottenham Hotspur ....2 *Robertson, Saul*	Chelsea ....1 *Tambling*
1968	West Bromwich Albion ....1 *Astle*	Everton 0
1969	Manchester City ....1 *Young*	Leicester City 0
1970	Chelsea ....2 *Houseman, Hutchinson*	Leeds United ....2 *Charlton, Jones*
	Chelsea ....2 *Webb, Osgood*	Leeds United ....1 *Jones (After extra time)*
1971	Arsenal ....2 *Kelly, George*	Liverpool ....1 *Heighway (After extra time)*
1972	Leeds United ....1 *Clarke*	Arsenal 0
1973	Sunderland ....1 *Porterfield*	Leeds United 0
1974	Liverpool ....3 *Keegan 2, Heighway*	Newcastle United 0
1975	West Ham United ....2 *A. Taylor 2*	Fulham 0
1976	Southampton ....1 *Stokes*	Manchester United 0
1977	Manchester United ....2 *Pearson, J. Greenhoff*	Liverpool ....1 *Case*
1978	Ipswich Town ....1 *Osborne*	Arsenal 0
1979	Arsenal ....3 *Talbot, Stapleton, Sunderland*	Manchester United ....2 *McQueen, McIlroy*
1980	West Ham United ....1 *Brooking*	Arsenal 0
1981	Tottenham Hotspur ....1 *Hutchinson (og)*	Manchester City ....1 *Hutchinson*
	Tottenham Hotspur ....3 *Crooks, Villa 2*	Manchester City ....2 *Mackenzie, Reeves (pen)*
1982	Tottenham Hotspur ....1 *Hoddle*	Q.P.R. ....1 *Fenwick*
	Tottenham Hotspur ....1 *Hoddle (pen)*	Q.P.R. 0
1983	Manchester United ....2 *Stapleton, Wilkins*	Brighton & Hove Albion .....2 *Smith, Stevens*
	Manchester United ....4 *Robson 2, Whiteside, Muhren (pen)*	Brighton & Hove Albion 0
1984	Everton ....2 *Sharp, Gray*	Watford 0
1985	Manchester United ....1 *Whiteside*	Everton 0

FA CUP WINNERS SINCE 1871

Aston Villa	7
Tottenham Hotspur	7
Blackburn Rovers	6
Manchester United	6
Newcastle United	6
Arsenal	5
Wanderers	5
West Bromwich Albion	5
Bolton Wanderers	4
Everton	4
Manchester City	4
Sheffield United	4
Wolverhampton Wanderers	4
Liverpool	3
Sheffield Wednesday	3
West Ham United	3
Bury	2
Nottingham Forest	2
Old Etonians	2
Preston North End	2
Sunderland	2
Barnsley	1
Blackburn Olympic	1
Blackpool	1
Bradford City	1
Burnley	1
Cardiff City	1
Charlton Athletic	1
Chelsea	1
Clapham Rovers	1
Derby County	1
Huddersfield Town	1
Ipswich Town	1
Leeds United	1
Notts County	1
Old Carthusians	1
Oxford University	1
Portsmouth	1
Royal Engineers	1
Southampton	1

APPEARANCES IN FA CUP FINAL

Arsenal	11
Newcastle United	11
Everton	10
Manchester United	10
West Bromwich Albion	10
Aston Villa	9
Blackburn Rovers	8
Manchester City	8
Wolverhampton Wanderers	8
Bolton Wanderers	7
Liverpool	7
Preston North End	7
Tottenham Hotspur	7
Old Etonians	6
Sheffield United	6
Huddersfield Town	5
Sheffield Wednesday	5
Wanderers	5
Derby County	4
Leeds United	4
Leicester City	4
Oxford University	4
Royal Engineers	4
West Ham United	4
Blackpool	3
Burnley	3
Chelsea	3
Portsmouth	3
Southampton	3
Sunderland	3
Barnsley	2
Birmingham City	2
Bury	2
Cardiff City	2
Charlton Athletic	2
Clapham Rovers	2
Nottingham Forest	2
Notts County	2
Queen's Park (Glasgow)	2
Blackburn Olympic	1
Bradford City	1
Brighton & Hove Albion	1
Bristol City	1
Fulham	1
Ipswich Town	1
Luton Town	1
Old Carthusians	1
Queen's Park Rangers	1
Watford	1

MILK CUP 1985-86

First major trophy for Oxford

For the second successive year, a struggling First Division club won the Milk Cup, and for Oxford United it was a first major trophy to crown their debut season in the top flight.

There were no shocks in the early rounds of the competition, although Spurs went down 2-0 to Orient in the second round first leg and had to wait for five tense weeks before winning the second leg 4-0 at White Hart Lane, the police having delayed the match following riots on the Broadwater Farm estate. The third round also went according to form, except for a slight stutter by Chelsea, held to a 1-1 draw by Fulham at Stamford Bridge and scraping through 1-0 in the replay.

As the fourth round approached, all the leading First Division clubs were cruising, except Sheffield Wednesday, then in third position, who had gone down to Swindon Town. Inevitably, with the fourth round deciding the quarter-final line-ups, heads then began to roll. Spurs went out 1-0 to Alan Ball's Portsmouth after two goalless draws, and Forest succumbed to Queen's Park Rangers, but the two plum ties of the round were Liverpool v Manchester United and Chelsea v Everton.

At Anfield, United took a 1-0 lead with a rare goal from Paul McGrath, but two second-half goals from Jan Molby, one from the penalty spot, saw Liverpool through safely. On the same evening at Stamford Bridge, there were four goals in a furious first half, Dixon and Nevin scoring for the home side and Sheedy and Bracewell replying tor Everton. There were no further scores in a much tighter second half, and a fortnight later Chelsea became one of only three clubs to win at Goodison all season as Dixon and McLaughlin scored in reply to Gary Lineker's first-half effort.

In the quarter-finals, Aston Villa fought back well after a Charlie Nicholas goal had seen them trailing at Villa Park. A late reply by Glover forced the replay and Villa won 2-1 with a determind display at Highbury a couple of weeks later, much to the relief of manager Graham Turner, whose job was reportedly under pressure following a string of dismal League results. We didn't know it then, but the Arsenal manager was under even greater pressure!

Meanwhile, Chelsea were forced to another replay, this time against Queen's Park Rangers, but their luck ran out during extra time at Stamford Bridge, as MacDonald and Robinson scored the goals that took Rangers to a semi-final against Liverpool. In front of a disappointing crowd of only 15,000, Rangers' captain Terry Fenwick gave his side a 1-0 advantage to take to Anfield for the second leg, which turned out to be an astonishing affair. McMahon and Johnston scored for Liverpool, but their efforts were cancelled out by own goals from Whelan and Gillespie, and suddenly Rangers were at Wembley. In the other semi-final, Oxford went through 4-3 on aggregate against Villa to get there for the first time.

On the day of the final, Oxford were third from bottom in the First Division, with Rangers seven places above them, but they forgot their problems for the day and played uninhibited football, having been encouraged by publicity-shy manager Maurice Evans to enjoy thmselves. It was an attitude that paid dividends, as goals from Hebberd, Houghton and Charles sent them up those famous steps to collect the Milk Cup which, as the competition's sponsors will change next season, they will keep. Manager Evans, however, will have only his memories as a souvenir, because he declined his medal, sending the club's long-serving trainer, Ken Fish, up to the Royal Box in his place. It was a super gesture. We wondered what Jim Smith, Rangers' manager, was thinking at the time, having left Oxford a year earlier for the challenge of management in a more prestigious club.

PAST LEAGUE CUP FINALS

Played as two legs up to 1966

1961	Rotherham United	2	Aston Villa	0
	Webster, Kirkman			
	Aston Villa	3	Rotherham Utd	0*
	O'Neill, Burrows, McParland			
1962	Rochdale	0	Norwich City	3
			Lythgoe 2, Punton	
	Norwich City	1	Rochdale	0
	Hill			
1963	Birmingham City	3	Aston Villa	1
	Leek 2, Bloomfield		*Thomson*	
	Aston Villa	0	Birmingham City	0
1964	Stoke City	1	Leicester City	1
	Bebbington		*Gibson*	
	Leicester City	3	Stoke City	2
	Stringfellow, Gibson, Riley		*Viollet, Kinnell*	
1965	Chelsea	3	Leicester City	2
	Tambling, Venables (pen), McCreadie		*Appleton, Goodfellow*	
	Leicester City	0	Chelsea	0
1966	West Ham United	2	West Bromwich Albion	1
	Moore, Byrne		*Astle*	
	West Bromwich Albion	4	West Ham United	1
	Kaye, Brown, Clark, Williams		*Peters*	
1967	Queens Park Rangers	3	West Bromwich Albion	2
	Morgan R., Marsh, Lazarus		*Clark C. 2*	
1968	Leeds United	1	Arsenal	0
	Cooper			
1969	Swindon Town	3	Arsenal	1
	Smart, Rogers 2		*Gould*	
1970	Manchester City	2	West Bromwich Albion	1
	Doyle, Pardoe		*Astle*	
1971	Tottenham Hotspur	2	Aston Villa	0
	Chivers 2			
1972	Chelsea	1	Stoke City	2
	Osgood		*Conroy, Eastham*	
1973	Tottenham Hotspur	1	Norwich City	0
	Coates			
1974	Wolverhampton W.	2	Manchester City	1
	Hibbitt, Richards		*Bell*	
197	Aston Villa	1	Norwich City	0
	Graydon			
1976	Manchester City	2	Newcastle United	1
	Barnes, Tueart		*Gowling*	
1977	Aston Villa	0	Everton	0
Replay	Aston Villa	1	Everton	1*
	Kenyon (og)		*Latchford*	
Replay	Aston Villa	3	Everton	2*
	Little 2, Nicholl		*Latchford, Lyons*	
1978	Nottingham Forest	0	Liverpool	0*
Replay	Nottingham Forest	1	Liverpool	0
	Robertson (pen)			

1979	Nottingham Forest ....3 *Birtles 2, Woodcock*	Southampton ....2 *Peach, Holmes*
1980	Wolverhampton W ....1 *Gray*	Nottingham Forest 0
1981	Liverpool ....1 *Kennedy, A.*	West Ham U ....1* *Stewart (pen)*
Replay	Liverpool ....2 *Dalglish, Hansen*	West Ham U ....1 *Goddard*
1982	Liverpool ....3 *Whelan 2, Rush*	Tottenham ....1* *Archibald*
1983	Liverpool ....2 *Kennedy, Whelan*	Manchester U ....1* *Whiteside*
1984	Liverpool 0	Everton...0*
Replay	Liverpool...........................1 *Souness*	Everton 0
1985	Norwich C...........................1 *Chisholm (og)*	Sunderland 0

**After extra time*

LEAGUE MILK CUP 1985-86

First Round *(2 legs)*

Aldershot	1	2	Orient	3	2
Bolton W	4	1	Stockport Co	1	1
Bradford C	2	4	Chesterfield	2	3
Bristol R	2	0	Newport Co	0	1
Burnley	2	3	Bury	1	5
Cambridge U	1	0	Brentford	1	2
Cardiff C	2	1	Swansea C	1	3
Charlton Ath	1	1	Crystal Palace	2	1
Colchester U	2	1	Millwall	3	4
Crewe Alex	3	4	Carlisle U	3	3
Darlington	3	0	Scunthorpe U	2	0
Derby Co	3	0	Hartlepool U	0	2
Halifax T	1	0	Hull C	1	3
Hereford U	5	0	Bristol C	1	2
Mansfield T	2	4	Middlesbrough	0	4
Notts Co*	1	1	Doncaster R	0	2
Peterborough U	0	0	Northampton T	0	2
Plymouth Arg	2	0	Exeter C	1	2
Preston NE	2	3	Blackpool	1	1
Reading	1	0	Bournemouth	3	2
Rotherham U	1	1	Sheffield U	3	5
Southend U	1	0	Gillingham	1	2
Torquay U	1	2	Swindon T	2	2
Tranmere R	1	0	Chester C	3	0
Walsall	1	1	Wolverhampton W	1	0
Wigan Ath	2	0	Port Vale	1	2
Wrexham	4	1	Rochdale	0	2
York C	2	2	Lincoln C	1	1

**Won on away goals*

Second round *(2 legs)*

Team	1st leg	2nd leg
Leeds U.	0	3
Walsall	0	0
Exeter C.	1	1
Aston Villa.	4	8
Chester C..	1	2
Coventry C.	2	7
WBA	1	2
Port Vale	0	2
Bury	1	1
Manchester C.	2	2
Hereford U.	0	1
Arsenal	0	2
Bristol R.	2	1
Birmingham C.	3	2
Millwall	0	0
Southampton**	0	0
Oxford U.	2	2
Northampton T.	1	0
Newcastle U.*	0	1
Barnsley	0	1
Sheffield U.	1	1
Luton T.	2	3
Preston NE.	1	1
Norwich C.	1	2
Orient.	2	0
Tottenham H.	0	4
Wimbledon	5	1
Blackburn R.	0	2
Gillingham	1	1
Portsmouth	3	2
Wrexham	0	0
Stoke C.	1	1

Third round

Team	Score	Replay
Leeds U.	0	
Aston Villa	3	
Coventry C.	0	3
WBA	0	4
Manchester C.	1	
Arsenal	2	
Birmingham C.	1	0
Southampton	1	3
Oxford U.	3	
Newcastle U.	1	
Luton T.	0	
Norwich C.	2	
Tottenham H.	2	
Wimbledon	0	
Portsmouth	2	
Stoke C.	0	

Fourth round

Team	Score	Replay	2nd replay
Aston Villa	2	2	
WBA	2	1	
Arsenal	0	3	
Southampton	0	1	
Oxford U.	3		
Norwich C.	1		
Tottenham H.	0	0	0
Portsmouth	0	0	1

Fifth round

Team	Score	Replay
Aston Villa	1	2
Arsenal	1	1
Oxford U.	3	
Portsmouth	1	

Semi-finals *(2 legs)*

Team	1st leg	2nd leg
Aston Villa	2	1
Oxford U.	2	2

Final

OXFORD U (1) 3

Scorers: Hebberd, Houghton, Charles

Crewe Alex.	1	2
Watford.	3	3
Q.P.R.	3	5
Hull C.	0	1
Derby Co.	2	1
Leicester C.	0	1
Nottingham F.	4	3
Bolton W.	0	0
Mansfield T.	2	0
Chelsea.	2	2
Fulham	1	4
Notts Co.	1	2
Shrewsbury T.	2	2
Huddersfield T.	3	0
Everton	3	2
Bournemouth	2	0
Liverpool	3	5
Oldham Ath.	0	2
Brighton & H.A.	5	2
Bradford C.	2	0
Crystal Palace	0	0
Manchester U.	1	1
West Ham U.	3	3
Swansea C.	0	2
Grimsby T.	1	3
York C.	1	2
Ipswich T.	3	4
Darlington	1	1
Sunderland	3	1
Swindon T.	2	3
Brentford	2	0
Sheffield W.	2	2

*Won on away goals

**Won on penalties

Watford	0	
Q.P.R.	1	
Derby Co.	1	
Nottingham F.	2	
Chelsea	1	1
Fulham	1	0
Shrewsbury T.	1	
Everton	4	
Liverpool	4	
Brighton & H.A.	0	
Manchester U.	1	
West Ham U.	0	
Grimsby T.	0	
Ipswich T.	2	
Swindon T.	1	
Sheffield W.	0	

Q.P.R.	3	
Nottingham F.	1	
Chelsea	2	2
Everton	2	1
Liverpool	2	
Manchester U.	1	
Ipswich T.	6	
Swindon T.	1	

Q.P.R.	1	2
Chelsea	1	0
Liverpool	3	
Ipswich T.	0	

Q.P.R.	1	2
Liverpool	0	2

QPR (0) 0

Wembley, att: 90,396 Receipts: £897,646

FREIGHT ROVER TROPHY

In the first round, the teams in each section were divided into groups of three. The winner of each group went forward to the section quarter-finals.

NORTHERN SECTION
First round
Crewe Alex. 4, Stockport Co. 1
Stockport Co. 2, Bolton W. 2
Bolton W. 1, Crewe Alex. 0
Bolton W. qualify
Darlington 2, Chesterfield 0
Chesterfield 1, Burnley 2
Burnley 1, Darlington 1
Darlington qualify
York C. 0, Rotherham U. 0
Rotherham U. 3, Hartlepool U. 0
Hartlepool U. 3, York C. 2
Rotherham U. qualify
Lincoln C. 1, Scunthorpe U. 3
Scunthorpe U. 3, Halifax T. 2
Halifax T. 1, Lincoln C. 1
Scunthorpe U. qualify
Notts Co. 1, Doncaster R. 0
Doncaster R. 1, Mansfield T. 0
Mansfield T. 1, Notts Co. 0
Play-offs
Mansfield T. 4, Doncaster R. 2
Notts Co. 0, Mansfield T. 1
Mansfield T. qualify
Rochdale 1, Chester C. 0
Chester C. 0, Wigan Ath. 2
Wigan Ath. 6, Rochdale 0
Wigan Ath. qualify
Tranmere R. 2, Preston N.E. 0
Preston N.E. 2, Bury 0
Bury 1, Tranmere R. 2
Tranmere R. qualify
Wrexham 1, Port Vale 1
Blackpool 2, Wrexham 2
Port Vale 3 Blackpool 1
Port Vale qualify

Quarter – finals
Wigan Ath. 3, Rotherham U. 0
Scunthorpe U. 1, Port Vale 1
Port Vale won on penalties
Bolton W. 2, Tranmere R. 1
Darlington 3, Mansfield T. 0

Semi – finals
Port Vale 1, Wigan Ath. 2
Darlington 0, Bolton W. 3

Northern Final
Wigan Ath. 0,1, Bolton W. 1,3

SOUTHERN SECTION
First round
Aldershot 0, Cambridge U. 1
Cambridge U. 4, Peterborough U. 1
Peterborough U. 2, Aldershot 0
Cambridge U. qualify
Bristol C. 0, Plymouth Arg. 0
Plymouth Arg. 0, Walsall 1
Walsall 1, Bristol C. 2
Bristol C. qualify
Colchester U. 4, Southend U. 1
Northampton T. 2, Colchester U. 1
Southend U. 1, Northampton T. 3
Northampton T. qualify
Exeter C. 1, Wolverhampton W. 1
Wolverhampton W. 1, Torquay U. 1
Torquay U. 1, Exeter C. 0
Torquay U. qualify
Orient 3, Bournemouth 1
Bournemouth 5, Reading 0
Reading 0, Orient 3
Orient qualify
Brentford 0, Derby C. 0
Derby Co. 0, Gillingham 2
Gillingham 1, Brentford 1
Gillingham qualify
Hereford U. 2, Bristol R. 0
Bristol R. 2, Swindon T. 1
Swindon T. 1, Hereford U. 1
Hereford U. qualify
Swansea C. 1, Newport Co. 1
Newport Co. 1, Cardiff C.1
Cardiff C. 0, Swansea C. 2
Swansea C. qualify

Quarter – finals
Swansea C. 1, Torquay U. 0
Gillingham 2, Cambridge U. 0
Orient 1, Hereford U. 2
Bristol C. 3, Northampton T. 2

Semi – finals
Hereford U. 0, Swansea C. 0
Hereford U. won on penalties
Bristol C. 3, Gillingham 0

Southern Final
Hereford U. 2,0, Bristol C. 0,3

Final at Wembley, 24 May 1986, att.54,502, rec.£286,281
Bolton W. (0)0, Bristol C. (1)3
Bolton W.: Farnworth; Scott, Philips, Sutton, Came, Thompson, Neal, Oghani, Caldwell, Hartford, Gavin.
Bristol C.: Waugh; Newman, Williams, Curle, Moyes, Riley, Pritchard, Hutchinson, Harle, Walsh, Neville.
Scorers: Riley 2, Pritchard.

SCOTTISH CLUBS

ABERDEEN — PREM. DIV.

Ground: Pittodrie Stadium, Aberdeen (0224-632328)
Colours: All red with white trim.
Year formed: 1903.
Goals– League (62): McDougall 14 (1 pen), Black 8, Stark 8, Hewitt 6, Weir 5 (1 pen), Bett 3 (1 pen), McKimmie 3, McLeish 3, J. Miller 3, Angus 2, Wright 2, Gray 1, McMaster 1, McQueen 1 pen, W. Miller 1, Simpson 1.
Skol Cup (13): Black 4, McDougall 4, Stark 3, Hewitt 1, McQueen 1 pen.
Scottish Cup (15): Hewitt 4, Stark 3, Black 2, J. Miller 2, McDougall 1, McLeish 1, W. Miller 1, Weir 1.

AIRDRIEONIANS — DIV. 1

Ground: Broomfield Park, Gatlea Road, Airdrie ML6 9JL (Airdrie 62067)
Colours: White shirts with red diamond, white shorts.
Year formed: 1878.
Goals – League (51): Flood 11, Millar 10 (4 pens), MacCabe 9 (2 pens), Templeton 9, Ashwood 2, Fairlie 2, Gillies 2 pens, Christie 1, Docherty 1, Lawrie 1, McKeown 1, Rodger 1, own goal 1.
Skol Cup (0).
Scottish Cup (2): MacCabe 2.

ALBION ROVERS — DIV. 2

Ground: Clifton Hill Park, Coatbridge ML5 9XX (Coatbridge 32350)
Colours: Yellow shirts with white sleeves, white shorts with red trim.
Year formed: 1882.
Goals – League (38): Conn 6, Kasule 6, Rodgers 6 (4 pens), Nolan 5, McKay 4, Paisley 4, Cleland 3, Deakin 1, Gallagher 1, McAteer 1, Pacitti 1.
Skol Cup (0).
Scottish Cup (9): Paisley 3 (1 pen), Gallagher 2, Kasule 2, McAteer 1, Nolan 1.

ALLOA — DIV. 2

Ground: Recreation Park, Alloa (Alloa 722695)
Colours: Gold shirts with black trim, black shorts.
Year formed: 1883.
Goals – League (49): Jamieson 11, Sorbie 11, Murray 10, Cole 5, Barr 3, Donaldson 2 (2 pens), Smith 2, Thompson 2, Dall 1, Flaherty 1, Sullivan 1.
Skol Cup (0).
Scottish Cup (4): Murray 2, Sorbie 1, Sullivan 1 pen.

ARBROATH — DIV. 2

Ground: Gayfield Park, Arbroath DD11 12B (Arbroath 72157)
Colours: Maroon shirts, white shorts.
Year formed: 1878.
Goals– League (55): McWalter 14, Torrance 13 (2 pens), Brannigan 7, Curran 5 (2 pens), Fotheringham 3, Glass 2, Mackie 2, Bone 1, Cummings 1, Glover 1, Kirkcaldy 1, Lynch 1, O'Neill 1, Rodger 1, Taylor 1, own goal 1.
Skol Cup (0).
Scottish Cup (4): Torrance 3, Fotheringham 1.

AYR UNITED — DIV. 2

Ground: Somerset Park, Ayr KA8 9NB (Ayr 263435)
Colours: White shirts with black trim, black shorts.
Year formed: 1910.
Goals – League (41): Irons 6, Sludden 5 (1 pen), Ashwood 4, McDonald 4, McNiven 4, Murphy 4, Grant 3, Cowell 2, McAllister 2, McCracken 2, Adams 1, Collins 1, S. McIntyre 1 pen, Wilson 1, own goal 1.
Skol Cup (0).
Scottish Cup (1): McCracken 1.

BERWICK RANGERS — DIV. 2

Ground: Shiefield Park, Berwick-on-Tweed TD15 2EF (Berwick 307424)
Colours: Black and gold striped shirts, black shorts.
Year formed: 1881.
Goals – League (45): Sokoluk 12, Cavanagh 6, O'Connor 6, Blackie 3, Davidson 3, Conroy 2, McCann 2 pens, McGovern 2, Parker 2, Romaines 2, Fraser 1 pen, Gavine 1, Omond 1, Watson 1, own goal 1.
Skol Cup (1): Romaines 1.
Scottish Cup (6): Conroy 1, Davidson 1, Fraser 1 pen, O'Connor 1, Romaines 1, own goal 1.

BRECHIN CITY — DIV. 1

Ground: Glebe Park, Brechin DD9 6BJ (Brechin 2856)
Colours: All red.
Year formed: 1906.
Goals – League (58): Eadie 22, Perry 8 (4 pens), Powell 8, D. Lees 3, Brown 2, Kennedy 2, J. Kerr 2, Stewart 2, Anderson 1, Fleming 1, G. Lees 1, McKenzie 1, Park 1, Payne 1, Torrance 1, Wilson 1, own goal 1.
Skol Cup (3): Eadie 1, Park 1, Perry 1.
Scottish Cup (2): Eadie 1, Kennedy 1.

CELTIC — PREM. DIV.

Ground: Celtic Park, Glasgow G40 3RE (041-554 2710)
Colours: Green and white hooped shirts, white shorts.
Year formed: 1888.
Goals – League (67): McClair 22 (3 pens), Johnston 15, P. McStay 8 (2 pens), Burns 5, McGhee 4, Archdeacon 3, MacLeod 3, McGugan 2, Provan 2, Grant 1, McInally 1, own goal 1.
Skol Cup (15): Johnston 6, Aitken 2 (1 pen), McInally 2, Provan 2, Burns 1, McClair 1, McStay 1.
Scottish Cup (7): McClair 3 (1 pen), Aitken 1, Grant 1, Johnston 1, McGhee 1.

CLYDE — DIV. 1

Grounds: Shawfield Stadium, Glasgow G5 0AN (041-647 6329)
Colours: White shirts with red trim, black shorts.
Year formed: 1878.
Goals – League (49): Frye 12, Lloyd 7, Ahern 4 (3 pens), Ferguson 4, Flexney 4, Gillespie 4, Reilly 4, Willock 4, Doherty 2, McVeigh 2, Fleeting 1, own goal 1.
Skol Cup (0).
Scottish Cup (1): Gillespie 1.

CLYDEBANK PREM. DIV.

Ground: Kilbowie Park, Clydebank G81 2PB (041-952 2887)
Colours: Red shirts with broad white vertical stripe on front, black shorts.
Year formed: 1965.
Goals – League (29): Conroy 7, Lloyd 7, Larnach 3, Shanks 3, Hughes 2, Moore 2 (1 pen), Auld 1, Bain 1, Dickson 1, Gibson 1, own goal 1.
Skol Cup (7): Larnach 3, Lloyd 2, McCabe 1, Moore 1.
Scottish Cup (0).

COWDENBEATH DIV. 2

Ground: Central Park, Cowdenbeath (Cowdenbeath 511205)
Colours: Royal blue shirts with white stripes, white shorts.
Year formed: 1881.
Goals – League (52): McGlashen 15 (2 pens), Ward 8, Grant 6, Cochrane 3, McCulloch 3, Paterson 3, Quinn 3, Wilcox 3, Williamson 3 (2 pens), Blackie 1, Brown 1, Doig 1, Oliver 1, Wilson 1.
Skol Cup (3): Wilson 2, Quinn 1.
Scottish Cup (0).

DUMBARTON DIV. 1

Ground: Boghead Park, Dumbarton (Dumbarton 62569)
Colours: white shirts with gold and black trim, white shorts.
Year formed: 1872.
Goals – League (59): McCoy 13 (1 pen), MacIver 10, Bourke 8, T. Coyle 6 (1 pen), Craig 6, O. Coyle 5 (2 pens), Moore 4, Docherty (2 pens), P. McGowan 2, Ashwood 1, McCahill 1, McNeil 1.
Skol Cup (1): McCoy 1.
Scottish Cup (0).

DUNDEE PREM. DIV.

Ground: Dens Park, Dundee DD1 1RQ (Dundee 826104)
Colours: Dark blue shirts with red and white trim, white shorts.
Year formed: 1893.
Goals – League (45): Stephen 14 (1 pen), Brown 11 (4 pens), Harvey 5, Rafferty 3, Connor 2, Glennie 2, Kidd 2, McCormack 2, Black 1, Forsyth 1, McWilliams 1, Mennie 1.
Skol Cup (4): Stephen 2, Kidd 1, Smith 1.
Scottish Cup (12): Harvey 4, Shannon 2, Stephen 2, Brown 1, Hendry 1, Mennie 1, Rafferty 1.

DUNDEE UNITED PREM. DIV.

Ground: Tannadice Park, Dundee DD3 7JW (Dundee 826289)
Colours: Tangerine shirts with black trim, black shorts.
Year formed: 1909 as Dundee Hibernians, Dundee U. from 1923.
Goals – League (59): Dodds 12, Bannon 11 (5 pens), Sturrock 8, Gough 5, Hegarty 5, Redford 4, Beedie 3 (1 pen), Gallacher 3, Coyne 2, Malpas 2, Clark 1, Kirkwood 1, Milne 1, own goal 1.
Skol Cup (6): Gough 2, Milne 2, Bannon 1, Redford 1.
Scottish Cup (7): Coyne 2, Sturrock 2, Bannon 1 pen, Gough 1, Redford 1.

DUNFERMLINE ATHLETIC — DIV. 1

Ground: East End Park, Dunfermline KY12 7RB (Dunfermline 724295)
Colours: Black and white striped shirts, black shorts.
Year formed: 1885.
Goals – League (91): Watson 24, Campbell 15 (1 pen), Jenkins 14 (2 pens), McCathie 8, Hamilton 5, Morrison 5, Heddle 3, Smith 3, Young 3, Bowie 2, Forrest 2, Moyes 2, Thompson 2, own goals 3.
Skol Cup (6): Campbell 3, Watson 2, Jenkins 1.
Scottish Cup (7): Watson 5 (1 pen), Heddle 2.

EAST FIFE — DIV. 1

Ground: Bayview Park, Methil, Fife (Levin 26323)
Colours: Old gold shirts with black trim, black shorts.
Year formed: 1903.
Goals – League (54): Kirk 14, Burgess 10 (7 pens), Murray 9, Hunter 7, McCafferty 3, Porter 3, Hutt 2, Kirkwood 2, Halley 1, Jenkins 1, Mitchell 1, Stead 1.
Skol Cup (0).
Scottish Cup (2): Halley 1, own goal 1.

EAST STIRLINGSHIRE — DIV. 2

Ground: Firs Park, Falkirk FK2 7AY (Falkirk 23583)
Colours: White shirts with black pinstripe, black shorts, red stockings.
Year formed: 1881.
Goals – League (49): Maskrey 12 (5 pens), Gaffney 10, McGonigal 8 (1 pen), Doig 5, Rennie 3, Wylde 3, McLindon 2, Mason 2, Gilchrist 1, Mackay 1, Steel 1, Tollan 1.
Skol Cup (1): Maskrey 1.
Scottish Cup (2): Doig 1, Maskrey 1.

FALKIRK — PREM. DIV.

Ground: Brockville Park, Falkirk FK1 5AX (Falkirk 24121)
Colours: Navy blue shirts with white trim, white shorts.
Year formed: 1876.
Goals – League (57): Gilmour 15 (3 pens), A. Irvine 6, McGuire 6, Lytwyn 5, Clark 4 (1 pen), Houston 4, Hughes 4 (1 pen), Hetherston 3, Baptie 2, Paterson 2, Dempsey 1, McCormack 1, Martin 1, Purdie 1, own goals 2.
Skol Cup (1): A. Irvine 1 pen.
Scottish Cup (2): Gilmour 2 (1 pen).

FORFAR ATHLETIC — DIV. 1

Ground: Station Park, Forfar, Angus (Forfar 63576)
Colours: Sky blue shadow stripe, sky blue shorts and stockings.
Year formed: 1885.
Goals – League (51): Clark 10 (1 pen), Liddle 7, Murray 7, G. Scott 7, Brewster 3, McKillop 3, Farningham 2, Gallacher 2, Lyons 2, McPhee 2, Bell 1 pen, Brash 1, Lorimer 1, Ward 1, own goal 1.
Skol Cup (5): G. Scott 2, Brash 1 pen, Liddle 1, Lyons 1.
Scottish Cup (1): Clark 1 pen.

HAMILTON ACADEMICALS — PREM. DIV.

Ground: Douglas Park, Hamilton ML3 0DF (Hamilton 286103)
Colours: Red and white striped shirts, white shorts.
Year formed: 1875.
Goals – League (77): Brogan 23, McNaught 11, Reid 9 (1 pen), Mitchell 6, Clarke 5 (1 pen), Pelosi 5 (1 pen), O'Neill 4, Sprott 3, Watters 3, Jamieson 2, Collins 1, McGachie 1, Phillips 1, Wright 1, own goals 2.
Skol Cup (5): Brogan 3, Jamieson 1, Pelosi 1 pen.
Scottish Cup (3): Brogan 3.

HEART OF MIDLOTHIAN — PREM. DIV.

Ground: Tynecastle Park, Gorgie Road, Edinburgh EH11 2NL (031-337 6132)
Colours: White shirts with maroon centre panel at front, maroon trim, white shorts.
Year formed: 1874.
Goals– League (59): Robertson 20 (3 pens), Clark 12, Colquhoun 8, I. Jardine 7, G. Mackay 4, Berry 2, Black 2 pens, Levein 2, R. MacDonald 2.
Skol Cup (5): Cherry 1, Colquhoun 1, Kidd 1, McNaughton 1, Robertson 1.
Scottish Cup (10): Robertson 4 (1 pen), Colquhoun 2, G. Mackay 2, Black 1, McAdam 1.

HIBERNIAN — PREM. DIV.

Ground: Easter Road Park, Edinburgh EH7 5QG (031-661 2159)
Colours: Green shirts with white sleeves and collar, white shorts.
Year formed: 1875.
Goals – League (49): Cowan 19 (1 pen), Durie 6, Kane 5 (1 pen), Tortolano 3, Brazil 2, Chisholm 2, Harris 2, Rae 2, Sneddon 2, Callachan 1, Collins 1, McBraide 1, May 1, own goals 2.
Skol Cup (18): Durie 8, Cowan 6, Brazil 1, Chisholm 1, Harris 1, McBraide 1.
Scottish Cup (7): Cowan 3 (1 pen), May 3, Chisholm 1.

KILMARNOCK — DIV. 1

Ground: Rugby Park, Kilmarnock KA1 2DP (Kilmarnock 25184)
Colours: Royal blue shirts with white trim, royal blue shorts.
Year formed: 1869.
Goals – League (62): Bryson 14 (2 pens), McGivern 11, B. Millar 7, Clarke 6, Cuthbertson 6, McGuire 5, McLean 3 (2 pens), McNab 3, McKinna 2, Cockburn 1, McCafferty 1, Martin 1, Sarwar 1, own goal 1.
Skol Cup (1): B. Millar 1.
Scottish Cup (2): Bryson 1, McCafferty 1.

MEADOWBANK THISTLE — DIV. 2

Ground: Meadowbank Stadium, Edinburgh EH7 6AE (031-661 5351)
Colours: Amber with black trim.
Year formed: 1943 as Ferranti Thistle, Meadowbank Thistle from 1974.
Goals – League (68): Jackson 17, Lawrence 17 (1 pen), McGachie 12, Armstrong 6 (3 pens), Tierney 4, Scott 3, Sprott 3, I. Stewart 2, Campbell 1, Clark 1, Nisbet 1, Robertson 1.
Skol Cup (2): Jackson 1, Robertson 1.
Scottish Cup (5): Boyd 1, Jackson 1, Lawrence 1 pen, McGachie 1, Tierney 1.

MONTROSE DIV. 1

Ground: Links Park, Montrose DD10 8QD (Montrose 73200)
Colours: All royal blue.
Year formed: 1879.
Goals – League (43): Allan 6, Barr 5 (2 pens), Brown 5 (4 pens), Millar 5, Lennox 4 (1 pen), McManus 4, Bennett 3, Somner 3, Wright 3, Sheran 2, Caithness 1 pen, Forbes 1, own goal 1.
Skol Cup (1): Sheran 1.
Scottish Cup (1): Brown 1 pen.

MORTON DIV. 1

Ground: Cappielow Park, Greenock PA15 2TY (Greenock 23571)
Colours: Blue and white hooped shirts, white shorts.
Year formed: 1874.
Goals – League (57): McNeil 14 (4 pens), Robertson 8, Doak 7, T. Turner 7 (1 pen), Richardson 6 (1 pen), Clinging 4, O'Hara 4, Gillespie 3, Anderson 1, Diver 1, Holmes 1, Simpson 1.
Skol Cup (3): Anderson 1, Richardson 1, Robertson 1.
Scottish Cup (0).

MOTHERWELL PREM. DIV.

Ground: Fir Park, Motherwell (Motherwell 61437)
Colours: All amber with claret trim.
Year formed: 1886.
Goals– League (33): Reilly 9, Wright 6 (2 pens), Walker 4, Baptie 3, Gahagan 3, Blair 2, Harrow 2, Doyle 1, Kennedy 1, MacLeod 1, Stewart 1.
Skol Cup (2): Harrow 1, Kennedy 1.
Scottish Cup (6): Blair 1, Doyle 1, Harrow 1, Kennedy 1, Reilly 1, Wright 1 pen.

PARTICK THISTLE DIV. 1

Ground: Firhill Park, Glasgow G20 7Al (041-946 2673)
Colours: Yellow shirts with red trim, red shorts.
Year formed: 1876.
Goals – League (53): Smith 11, J. Donnelly 10 (4 pens), Watson 7 (3 pens), McDonald 5 (1 pen), Gallagher 4, Kelly 4, Law 3, Logan 3, Herd 2, McKenzie 1, Mackin 1, own goals 2.
Skol Cup (0).
Scottish Cup (1): J. Donnelly 1.

QUEEN OF THE SOUTH DIV. 1

Ground: Palmerston Park, Dumfries (Dumfries 54853)
Colours: Royal blue shirts with white trim, white shorts.
Year formed: 1919.
Goals– League (71): Bryce 15 (1 pen), Cochrane 15, McBride 8, Reid 8, Cloy 7 (5 pens), Dick 7, J. Robertson 5, Hetherington 3, Maskrey 2, G. Robertson 1.
Skol Cup (4): Bryce 3, Cloy 1.
Scottish Cup (0).

QUEEN'S PARK DIV. 2

Ground: Hampden Park, Glasgow G42 9BA (041-632 1275)
Colours: Black and white hooped shirts, white shorts.
Year formed: 1867.
Goals – League (61): Fraser 11 (2 pens), Walker 9 (1 pen), Caven 8, McCall 8, McKay 5, Crooks 4, Brannigan 3 pens, Smith 3, Cairns 2, McLean 2, Boyle 1 pen, McLaughlin 1, Shearer 1, own goals 3.
Skol Cup (1): Walker 1.
Scottish Cup (7): Crooks 3, Brannigan 2 (1 pen), Boyle 1 pen, Caven 1.

RAITH ROVERS DIV. 2

Ground: Stark's Park, Pratt Street, Kirkaldy KY1 15A (Kirkaldy 263514)
Colours: All royal blue.
Year formed: 1883.
Goals – League (67): Smith 21 (3 pens), Wright 21, McNeill 4, Marshall 4, Herd 3, Sweeney 3 (1 pen), Voy 3, Gavine 2, Robertson 2, Candlish 1, Elvin 1, Fairgrieve 1, own goal 1.
Skol Cup (5): Marshall 2, McNeill 1, Smith 1, Walker 1.
Scottish Cup (0).

RANGERS PREM. DIV.

Ground: Ibrox Stadium, Glasgow G51 2XD (041-427 5232)
Colours: Royal blue shirts, white shorts.
Year formed: 1873.
Goals – League (53): McCoist 24 (3 pens), Williamson 6, McPherson 5, Cooper 4 (1 pen), Burns 3, Fleck 3, Durrant 2, Fraser 2, McMinn 2, Dawson 1, Paterson 1.
Skol Cup (10): Williamson 6 (1 pen), Cooper 2 (1 pen), McCoist 1, Paterson 1.
Scottish Cup (2): Durrant 1, McCoist 1.

ST JOHNSTONE DIV. 2

Ground: Muirton Park, Perth PH1 5AP (Perth 26961)
Colours: Royal blue shirts, white shorts.
Year formed: 1884.
Goals – League (63): Brown 11, Morton 9 (5 pens), Adam 8, Ward 7, Evans 6, Thoms 6, McGonigle 3, McGurn 3, Barron 2, Johnston 2, Millen 2, Addison 1, Gibson 1, Mitchell 1, Winter 1 pen.
Skol Cup (1): Reid 1.
Scottish Cup (3): Morton 2, Evans 1.

ST MIRREN PREM. DIV.

Ground: St Mirren Park, Paisley PA3 2EJ (041-889 2558)
Colours: White shirts with black vertical stripes, black shorts.
Year formed: 1877.
Goals – League (42): Speirs 7 (3 pens), Gallagher 6, McGarvey 6, Rooney 6, Clarke 3, Fitzpatrick 3, Godfrey 3, Abercromby 2, Mackie 2, Jarvie 1, McDowall 1, Winnie 1, own goal 1.
Skol Cup (8): Gallagher 3, Fitzpatrick 2, McGarvey 1, Mackie 1, Speirs 1.
Scottish Cup (9): Gallagher 2, McGarvey 2, Rooney 2, Speirs 2 (1 pen), Clarke 1.

STENHOUSEMUIR DIV. 2

Ground: Ochilview Park, Stenhousemuir FK5 4QL (Larbert 562992)
Colours: Maroon shirts with white trim, white shorts.
Year formed: 1884.
Goals – League (55): Sinnet 11 (1 pen), Bateman 10, Erwin 8, McNaughton 6, Cairney 3 pens, McComb 3, Wilson 3, Buchanan 2, Gillen 2, Reid 2, Grant 1, McIntosh 1, Russell 1, Thomson 1, own goal 1.
Skol Cup (0).
Scottish Cup (3): Cairney 1 pen, Russell 1, Sinnet 1.

STIRLING ALBION DIV. 2

Ground: Annfield Stadium, Stirling FK8 2HE (Stirling 3584)
Colours: All red.
Year formed: 1945.
Goals – League (57): Irvine 17 (1 pen), Ormond 9, McTeague 5, Thompson 5, Walker 5, Hoggan 4, Spence 4 (3 pens), Maxwell 3, Gavin 2, Aitchison 1, Grant 1, McCulley 1.
Skol Cup (4): Hoggan 1, Irvine 1, Maxwell 1, Thompson 1.
Scottish Cup (6): Hoggan 2, Irvine 2, Dawson 1, Thompson 1.

STRANRAER DIV. 2

Ground: Stair Park, Stranraer (Stranraer 3271)
Colours: Royal blue shirts, white shorts.
Year formed: 1870.
Goals – League (41): McGuire 8 (1 pen), Mauchlen 8, McCurdy 4, Higgins 3, Knox 2, Logan 2, P. Quinn 2, Brown 1, Filson 1 pen, Irvine 1, McCabe 1, McGaig 1, McDaid 1, O'Donnell 1, Rose 1, Watt 1 pen, own goals 3.
Skol Cup (5): McGuire 3, Filson 1, Knox 1.
Scottish Cup (1): Knox 1.

SCOTTISH LEAGUE – PREMIER DIVISION RESULTS 1985-86

	Aberdeen	Celtic	Clydebank	Dundee	Dundee U	Hearts	Hibernian	Motherwell	Rangers	St. Mirren
Aberdeen	—	4–1 0–1	3–1 4–1	4–1 0–0	3–2 0–1	3–0 0–1	3–0 4–0	1–1 3–2	1–0 1–1	1–1 3–1
Celtic	2–1 1–1	—	2–0 2–0	2–1 2–0	0–3 1–1	0–1 1–1	1–1 2–0	2–1 3–2	1–1 2–0	2–0 1–1
Clydebank	2–1 0–6	0–2 0–5	—	4–0 0–0	1–2 1–1	1–0 1–1	2–4 1–3	1–1 1–1	0–1 2–1	1–1 0–2
Dundee	1–3 0–0	0–2 1–3	2–0 4–0	—	0–3 0–1	1–1 2–0	1–0 3–1	3–1 4–0	3–2 2–1	2–1 3–1
Dundee U	1–1 2–1	1–0 4–2	2–1 4–0	2–0 0–0	—	1–1 0–3	2–2 4–0	3–0 4–0	1–1 1–1	5–0 1–2
Hearts	1–0 1–1	1–1 1–1	4–1 1–0	1–1 3–1	2–0 1–1	—	2–1 3–1	3–0 2–0	3–0 3–1	3–0 3–0
Hibernian	1–1 0–1	0–5 2–2	5–0 2–3	2–1 1–0	0–1 1–2	0–0 1–2	—	1–0 4–0	1–3 1–1	2–3 3–0
Motherwell	1–1 0–1	1–2 0–2	0–0 3–0	1–3 2–2	0–1 2–0	2–1 1–3	2–0 3–1	—	0–3 1–0	3–1 1–2
Rangers	0–3 1–1	3–0 4–4	0–0 4–2	0–1 5–0	1–0 1–1	3–1 0–2	1–2 3–1	1–0 2–0	—	3–0 2–0
St. Mirren	1–0 1–1	1–2 0–5	0–2 3–0	1–0 1–2	1–0 1–1	6–2 0–1	1–3 0–2	4–1 1–0	2–1 2–1	—

SCOTTISH LEAGUE – DIVISION I RESULTS 1985-86

	Airdrieonians	Alloa	Ayr U.	Brechin C.	Clyde	Dumbarton	East Fife	Falkirk	Forfar Ath.	Hamilton A.	Kilmarnock	Montrose	Morton	Partick Th.
Airdrieonians	—	3–0 2–2	4–1 2–1	1–2 4–2	3–0	0–2 2–1	1–2	1–1	0–0	0–4 1–2	1–2 1–0	1–1	1–2	2–2 0–0
Alloa	0–0	—	1–1	2–3	1–1	2–4 1–3	1–1 1–2	0–2 0–2	1–2 2–2	4–5	1–4	1–1 1–3	3–0 2–0	1–1 2–2
Ayr U.	0–4	1–3 1–1	—	1–3	1–0 2–0	0–1	1–0	0–3 1–2	0–0 2–0	1–1 0–1	3–0	2–1	0–3	1–3 2–3
Brechin C.	0–2	1–1 3–1	4–1 1–1	—	1–2 2–2	3–1 1–1	4–0	1–1	1–0 0–3	1–3	2–4	3–1 4–2	1–1	2–0
Clyde	3–2 1–1	1–1 4–2	0–0	2–0	—	0–0	3–4 0–0	0–4 0–2	1–1	1–0 4–2	1–3 1–3	2–0	2–1	2–2
Dumbarton	3–0	4–0	1–1 2–0	4–1	1–1 0–0	—	2–1 2–3	2–0 2–1	1–1 0–2	2–2 1–4	1–0	2–2	1–2	1–2
East Fife	1–1 2–0	1–0	1–3 0–0	4–2 1–0	2–2	1–0	—	0–1	1–1 3–0	1–1 4–0	2–2	0–0 2–0	4–4	1–1
Falkirk	0–1 1–1	3–1	1–2	0–1 2–1	0–0	0–0	1–0 2–2	—	5–3 1–0	0–0	0–1 1–1	2–1	1–1 2–3	2–3 2–2
Forfar Ath.	2–0 1–1	0–4	1–0	2–0	2–1 2–1	4–0	0–2	2–1	—	2–2 2–0	0–0 1–0	1–2 1–2	2–0	1–1 2–1
Hamilton A.	3–1	1–2 1–1	2–0	0–0 1–0	3–0	6–1	2–1	2–0 0–3	1–0	—	4–1 3–2	4–2 1–0	5–0 2–1	2–2
Kilmarnock	0–2	3–0 2–0	1–2 3–2	3–1 1–2	1–1	1–4 3–0	2–2 2–0	1–0	1–0	1–0	—	0–0 3–0	3–0 1–1	5–0
Montrose	1–0 2–1	1–1	1–0 2–2	1–1	0–0 1–1	0–3 0–0	1–0	1–2 1–1	1–2	1–2	4–1	—	1–1 1–1	3–1 0–1
Morton	1–4 1–0	2–0	2–2 0–1	2–0 3–2	3–2 3–2	1–2 1–0	0–0 2–2	0–3	2–3 2–0	0–1	3–0	1–2	—	3–1
Partick Th.	1–0	1–2	2–2	2–1 1–1	1–3 2–2	1–2 2–2	1–0 0–1	1–2	0–3	1–2 0–2	1–1 2–0	2–0	1–1 3–3	—

Note: In the Scottish League Divisions I and II, each team plays each other twice and then after a draw made at the beginning of the season, half of the fixtures are repeated once.

SCOTTISH LEAGUE – DIVISION II RESULTS 1985-86

	Albion R.	Arbroath	Berwick R.	Cowdenbeath	Dunfermline At	East Stirling	Meadowbank Tl	Queen of the S.	Queen's Park	Raith R.	St. Johnstone	Stenhousemuir	Stirling A.	Stranraer
Albion R.	—	0–0	0–0	2–1	0–3	1–2 2–1	3–2 0–2	1–5 2–2	0–2 1–1	2–0	2–4	0–0 0–1	1–3 0–2	2–3
Arbroath	1–1 2–0	—	5–1	0–5 0–1	3–3	2–1	3–0 2–2	2–2 0–1	1–0 0–2	2–2 2–1	1–0	1–4	1–0	1–0
Berwick R.	0–0 1–2	0–2 0–4	—	1–1	4–4 0–4	1–1	0–0	0–1	0–5	4–3 1–0	3–1 1–1	1–1 1–1	1–0	2–2 4–0
Cowdenbeath	3–0 0–2	1–0	4–2 1–0	—	0–1 0–2	1–1 1–1	3–1 1–0	3–3	2–2	1–4	1–3 2–1	2–0	1–2 0–1	5–0
Dunfermline Ath.	6–0 4–0	0–0 2–0	4–2	3–2	—	2–1 4–0	1–1	2–1	3–2 0–0	3–3	4–0 4–0	3–2	2–3	1–0 4–1
East Stirling	5–1	1–2 1–1	0–2 4–2	2–1	0–4	—	1–3 2–3	0–0	2–1	0–2	1–3	0–2 2–0	0–2 1–0	3–1 1–2
Meadowbank Th.	1–1	2–1	0–3 3–1	1–1	2–2 4–0	2–1	—	0–0 1–0	2–1 1–1	6–0 0–3	4–1	3–1 1–0	1–1 4–1	1–1
Queen of the S.	5–2	2–0	2–0 2–1	6–1 3–0	0–0 3–1	2–1 3–1	1–0	—	0–1 0–3	2–0	2–1	2–0	3–1	1–1 1–2
Queen's Park	2–0	1–2	2–0 5–0	2–0 0–1	3–1	1–0 4–2	2–1	1–2	—	0–0	1–1 2–0	3–2 1–1	1–0 2–0	2–1 2–1
Raith R.	1–0 5–2	2–1	3–1	0–1 2–1	1–2 3–3	1–4 2–0	1–1	0–1 0–2	3–1 2–1	—	0–2	9–2	1–1	1–0 4–1
St. Johnstone	7–1 1–0	1–0 4–1	3–2	0–0	1–2	3–0 1–1	1–0 1–3	0–3 1–1	1–0	4–1 1–3	—	1–3	2–0 0–2	4–0
Stenhousemuir	4–2	1–1 2–1	3–1	1–0 2–1	1–1 0–0	4–3	1–5	1–5 1–0	4–0	2–0 1–0	3–2 0–0	—	2–5	1–2
Stirling A.	2–0	1–0 1–0	2–0 2–2	0–0	0–1 3–2	0–1	1–2	2–2 3–1	0–0	1–1 3–1	0–2	1–0 4–0	—	3–0 2–2
Stranraer	0–2 2–3	1–6 1–4	2–0	1–2 1–1	1–3	0–1	0–1 1–2	0–2	2–1	3–2	0–2 1–2	2–0 0–1	3–2	—

Note: In the Scottish League Divisions I and II, each team plays each other twice and then after a draw made at the beginning of the season, half of the fixtures are repeated once.

SCOTTISH FOOTBALL LEAGUE

FINAL TABLES 1985-86

Premier Division		Home			Goals		Away			Goals			
	P	*W*	*D*	*L*	*F*	*A*	*W*	*D*	*L*	*F*	*A*	*Pt*	*GD*
Celtic	36	10	6	2	27	15	10	4	4	40	23	50	+29
Hearts	36	13	5	0	38	10	7	5	6	21	23	50	+26
Dundee U.	36	10	6	2	38	15	8	5	5	21	16	47	+28
Aberdeen	36	11	4	3	38	15	5	8	5	24	16	44	+31
Rangers	36	10	4	4	43	18	3	5	10	19	27	35	+ 8
Dundee	36	11	2	5	32	20	3	5	10	13	31	35	− 6
St Mirren	36	9	2	7	26	24	4	3	11	16	39	31	−21
Hibernian	36	6	4	8	27	25	5	2	11	22	38	28	−14
Motherwell	36	7	3	8	23	23	0	3	15	10	43	20	−33
Clydebank	36	4	6	8	18	32	2	2	14	11	45	20	−48

First Division		Home			Goals		Away			Goals			
	P	*W*	*D*	*L*	*F*	*A*	*W*	*D*	*L*	*F*	*A*	*Pt*	*GD*
Hamilton A	39	14	3	2	43	17	10	5	5	34	27	56	+33
Falkirk	39	6	8	6	26	24	11	3	5	31	15	45	+18
Kilmarnock	39	12	4	4	37	17	6	4	9	25	32	44	+13
Forfar Ath	39	11	4	4	28	18	6	6	8	23	25	44	+ 8
East Fife	39	8	9	2	31	18	6	6	8	23	28	43	+ 8
Dumbarton	39	8	6	5	32	23	8	5	7	27	29	43	+ 7
Morton	39	10	3	7	32	27	4	8	7	25	36	39	− 6
Partick h	39	5	7	8	25	30	5	9	5	28	43	36	−11
Airdrieonians	39	7	6	7	30	27	5	5	9	21	23	35	+ 1
Brechin C.	39	8	6	5	35	27	5	3	12	23	37	35	− 6
Clyde	39	7	7	5	28	28	2	10	8	21	31	35	−10
Montrose	39	6	9	5	23	21	4	5	10	20	33	34	−11
Ayr U.	39	6	3	10	19	29	4	8	8	22	31	31	−19
Alloa	39	2	8	10	27	39	4	6	9	22	35	26	−25

Second Division		Home			Goals		Away			Goals			
	P	*W*	*D*	*L*	*F*	*A*	*W*	*D*	*L*	*F*	*A*	*Pt*	*GD*
Dunfermline Ath.	39	14	4	1	52	18	9	7	4	39	29	57	+44
Queen of the S.	39	14	2	3	40	16	9	7	4	31	20	55	+35
Meadowbank Th.	39	11	7	2	39	20	8	4	7	29	25	49	+23
Queen's Park	39	14	3	3	37	15	5	5	9	24	24	46	+22
Stirling A.	39	10	6	4	31	17	8	2	9	26	26	44	+14
St Johnstone	39	11	3	6	37	23	7	3	9	26	32	42	+ 8
Stenhousemuir	39	11	4	4	34	26	5	4	11	21	37	40	− 8
Arbroath	39	9	5	5	29	26	6	4	10	27	24	39	+ 6
Raith R.	39	11	3	6	41	27	4	4	11	26	38	37	+ 2
Cowdenbeath	39	9	4	7	32	26	5	5	9	20	27	37	− 1
East Stirling	39	7	2	10	26	32	4	4	12	23	37	28	−20
Berwick	39	5	9	6	25	33	2	2	15	20	47	25	−35
Albion R.	39	4	5	10	19	34	4	3	13	19	52	24	−48
Stranraer	39	5	1	13	21	38	4	4	12	20	45	23	−42

SCOTTISH LEAGUE HONOURS LIST

Premier Division (Maximum points: 72)

	First	Pt	Second	Pt	Third	Pt
1975–76	Rangers	54	Celtic	48	Hibernian	43
1976–77	Celtic	55	Rangers	46	Aberdeen	43
1977–78	Rangers	55	Aberdeen	53	Dundee United	40
1978–79	Celtic	48	Rangers	45	Dundee United	44
1979–80	Aberdeen	48	Celtic	47	St Mirren	42
1980–81	Celtic	56	Aberdeen	49	Rangers	44
1981–82	Celtic	55	Aberdeen	53	Rangers	43
1982–83	Dundee United	56	Celtic	55	Aberdeen	55
1983–84	Aberdeen	57	Celtic	50	Dundee United	47
1984–85	Aberdeen	59	Celtic	52	Dundee United	47
1985–86	Celtic	50	Hearts	50	Dundee United	47

First Division (Maximum points: 78)

	First	Pt	Second	Pt	Third	Pt
1975–76	Partick Thistle	41	Kilmarnock	35	Montrose	30
1976–77	St Mirren	62	Clydebank	58	Dundee	51
1977–78	*Morton	58	Hearts	58	Dundee	57
1978–79	Dundee	55	Kilmarnock	54	Clydebank	54
1979–80	Hearts	53	Airdrieonians	51	Ayr United	44
1980–81	Hibernian	57	Dundee	52	St Johnstone	51
1981–82	Motherwell	61	Kilmarnock	51	Hearts	50
1982–83	St Johnstone	55	Hearts	54	Clydebank	50
1983–84	Morton	54	Dumbarton	51	Partick Thistle	46
1984–85	Motherwell	50	Clydebank	48	Falkirk	45
1985–86	Hamilton Ath	56	Falkirk	45	Kilmarnock	44

Second Division (Maximum points: 78)

	First	Pt	Second	Pt	Third	Pt
1975–76	*Clydebank	40	Raith Rovers	40	Alloa	35
1976–77	Stirling Albion	55	Alloa	51	Dunfermline	50
1977–78	*Clyde	53	Raith Rovers	53	Dunfermline	48
1978–79	Berwick	54	Dunfermline	52	Falkirk	50
1979–80	Falkirk	50	East Stirlingshire	49	Forfar Athletic	46
1980–81	Queen's Park	50	Queen of the S	46	Cowdenbeath	45
1981–82	Clyde	59	Alloa	50	Arbroath	50
1982–83	Brechin	55	Meadowbank	54	Arbroath	49
1983–84	Forfar Athletic	63	East Fife	47	Berwick Rangers	43
1984–85	Montrose	53	Alloa	50	Dunfermline Ath	49
1985–86	Dunfermline Ath	57	Queen of the S	55	Meadowbank Th	49

First Division to 1974-75

	First	Pt	Second	Pt	Third	Pt
1890–1	*a*††Dumbarton	29	Rangers	29	Celtic	24
1891–2	*b*Dumbarton	37	Celtic	35	Hearts	30
1892–3	*a*Celtic	29	Rangers	28	St Mirren	23
1893–4	*a*Celtic	29	Hearts	26	St Bernards	22
1894–5	*a*Hearts	31	Celtic	26	Rangers	21
1895–6	*a*Celtic	30	Rangers	26	Hibernian	24
1896–7	*a*Hearts	28	Hibernian	26	Rangers	25
1897–8	*a*Celtic	33	Rangers	29	Hibernian	22
1898–9	*a*Rangers	36	Hearts	26	Celtic	24
1899–1900	*a*Rangers	32	Celtic	25	Hibernian	24
1900–1	*c*Rangers	35	Celtic	29	Hibernian	25

	First	Pt	Second	Pt	Third	Pt
1901–2	*a*Rangers	28	Celtic	26	Hearts	22
1902–3	*b*Hibernian	37	Dundee	31	Rangers	29
1903–4	*d*Third Lanark	43	Hearts	39	*Rangers	38
1904–5	*d*‡Celtic	41	Rangers	41	Third Lanark	35
1905–6	*e*Celtic	49	Hearts	43	Airdrieonians	38
1906–7	*f*Celtic	55	Dundee	48	Rangers	45
1907–8	*f*Celtic	55	Falkirk	51	Rangers	50
1908–9	*f*Celtic	51	Dundee	50	Clyde	48
1909–10	*f*Celtic	54	Falkirk	52	Rangers	46
1910–11	*f*Rangers	52	Aberdeen	48	Falkirk	44
1911–12	*f*Rangers	51	Celtic	45	Clyde	42
1912–13	*f*Rangers	53	Celtic	49	*Hearts	41
1913–14	*g*Celtic	65	Rangers	59	*Hearts	54
1914–15	*g*Celtic	65	Hearts	61	Rangers	50
1916–17	*g*Celtic	64	Morton	54	Rangers	53
1917–18	*f*Rangers	56	Celtic	55	Kilmarnock	43
1918–19	*f*Celtic	58	Rangers	57	Morton	47
1919–20	*h*Rangers	71	Celtic	68	Motherwell	57
1920–21	*h*Rangers	76	Celtic	66	Hearts	56
1921–22	*h*Celtic	67	Rangers	66	Raith Rovers	56
1922–23	*g*Rangers	55	Airdrieonians	50	Celtic	46
1923–24	*g*Rangers	59	Airdrieonians	50	Celtic	41
1924–25	*g*Rangers	60	Airdrieonians	57	Hibernian	52
1925–26	*g*Celtic	58	*Airdrieonians	50	Hearts	50
1926–27	*g*Rangers	56	Motherwell	51	Celtic	49
1927–28	*g*Rangers	60	*Celtic	55	Motherwell	55
1928–29	*g*Rangers	67	Celtic	51	Motherwell	50
1929–30	*g*Rangers	60	Motherwell	55	Aberdeen	53
1930–31	*g*Rangers	60	Celtic	58	Motherwell	56
1931–32	*g*Motherwell	66	Rangers	61	Celtic	48
1932–33	*g*Rangers	62	Motherwell	59	Hearts	50
1933–34	*g*Rangers	66	Motherwell	62	Celtic	47
1934–35	*g*Rangers	55	Celtic	52	Hearts	50
1935–36	*g*Celtic	66	*Rangers	61	Aberdeen	61
1936–37	*g*Rangers	61	Aberdeen	54	Celtic	52
1937–38	*g*Celtic	61	Hearts	58	Rangers	49
1938–39	*g*Rangers	59	Celtic	48	Aberdeen	46
1946–47	*f*Rangers	46	Hibernian	44	Aberdeen	39
1947–48	*j*Hibernian	48	Rangers	46	Partick Thistle	36
1948–49	*j*Rangers	46	Dundee	45	Hibernian	39
1949–50	*j*Rangers	50	Hibernian	49	Hearts	43
1950–51	*j*Hibernian	48	*Rangers	38	Dundee	38
1951–52	*j*Hibernian	45	Rangers	41	East Fife	37
1952–53	*j**Rangers	43	Hibernian	43	East Fife	39
1953–54	*j*Celtic	43	Hearts	38	Partick Thistle	35
1954–55	*j*Aberdeen	49	Celtic	46	Rangers	41
1955–56	*f*Rangers	52	Aberdeen	46	*Hearts	45
1956–57	*f*Rangers	55	Hearts	53	Kilmarnock	42
1957–58	*f*Hearts	62	Rangers	49	Celtic	46
1958–59	*g*Rangers	50	Hearts	48	Motherwell	44
1959–60	*f*Hearts	54	Kilmarnock	50	*Rangers	42
1960–61	*f*Rangers	51	Kilmarnock	50	Third Lanark	42
1961–62	*f*Dundee	54	Rangers	51	Celtic	46
1962–63	*f*Rangers	57	Kilmarnock	48	Partick Thistle	46
1963–64	*f*Rangers	55	Kilmarnock	49	*Celtic	47
1964–65	*f**Kilmarnock	50	Hearts	50	Dunfermline Ath.	49
1965–66	*f*Celtic	57	Rangers	55	Kilmarnock	45
1966–67	*f*Celtic	58	Rangers	55	Clyde	46

Maximum points: *a*, 36; *b*, 44; *c*, 40; *d*, 52; *e*, 60; *f*, 68; *g*, 76; *h*, 84; *j*, 60.

	First	Pt	Second	Pt	Third	Pt
1967–68	*f*Celtic	63	Rangers	61	Hibernian	45
1968–69	*f*Celtic	54	Rangers	49	Dunfermline Ath.	45
1969–70	*f*Celtic	57	Rangers	45	Hibernian	44
1970–71	*f*Celtic	56	Aberdeen	54	St Johnstone	44
1971–72	*f*Celtic	60	Aberdeen	50	Rangers	44
1972–73	*f*Celtic	57	Rangers	56	Hibernian	45
1973–74	*f*Celtic	53	Hibernian	49	Rangers	48

Second Division to 1974–75

	First	Pt	Second	Pt	Third	Pt
1921–22	*a*†Alloa	60	Cowdenbeath	47	Armadale	48
1922–23	*a*Queen's Park	57	Clydebank	**50	St Johnstone	**45
1923–24	*a*St Johnstone	56	Cowdenbeath	55	Bathgate	44
1924–25	*a*Dundee United	50	Clydebank	48	Clyde	47
1925–26	*a*Dunfermline A.	59	Clyde	53	Ayr United	52
1926–27	*a*Bo'ness	56	Raith Rovers	49	Clydebank	45
1927–28	*a*Ayr United	54	Third Lanark	45	King's Park	44
1928–29	*b*Dundee United	51	Morton	50	Arbroath	47
1929–30	*a**Leith Athletic	57	East Fife	57	Albion Rovers	54
1930–31	*a*Third Lanark	61	Dundee United	50	Dunfermline A.	47
1931–32	*a**East Stirling	55	St Johnstone	55	*Raith Rovers	46
1932–33	*c*Hibernian	54	Queen of the S.	49	Dunfermline A.	47
1933–34	*c*Albion Rovers	45	*Dunfermline A.	44	Arbroath	44
1934–35	*c*Third Lanark	52	Arbroath	50	St Bernard's	47
1935–36	*c*Falkirk	59	St Mirren	52	Morton	48
1936–37	*c*Ayr United	54	Morton	51	St Bernard's	48
1937–38	*c*Raith Rovers	59	Albion Rovers	48	Airdrieonians	47
1938–39	*c*Cowdenbeath	60	*Alloa	48	East Fife	48
1946–47	*d*Dundee	45	Airdrieonians	42	East Fife	31
1947–48	*e*East Fife	53	Albion Rovers	42	Hamilton A.	40
1948–49	*e**Raith Rovers	42	Stirling Albion	42	*Airdrieonians	41
1949–50	*e*Morton	47	Airdrieonians	44	*St Johnstone	36
1950–51	*e**Queen of the S.	45	Stirling Albion	45	*Ayr United	36
1951–52	*e*Clyde	43	Falkirk	33	Ayr United	39
1952–53	*e*Stirling Albion	44	Hamilton A.	43	Queen's Park	37
1953–54	*e*Motherwell	45	Kilmarnock	42	*Third Lanark	36
1954–55	*e*Airdrieonians	46	Dunfermline A.	42	Hamilton A.	39
1955–56	*b*Queen's Park	54	Ayr United	51	St Johnstone	49
1956–57	*b*Clyde	64	Third Lanark	51	Cowdenbeath	45
1957–58	*b*Stirling Albion	55	Dunfermline A.	53	Arbroath	47
1958–59	*b*Ayr United	60	Arbroath	51	Stenhousemuir	46
1959–60	*b*St Johnstone	53	Dundee United	50	Queen of the S.	49
1960–61	*b*Stirling Albion	55	Falkirk	54	Stenhousemuir	50
1961–62	*b*Clyde	54	Queen of the S.	53	Morton	44
1962–63	*b*St Johnstone	55	East Stirling	49	Morton	48
1963–64	*b*Morton	67	Clyde	53	Arbroath	46
1964–65	*b*Stirling Albion	59	Hamilton A.	50	Queen of the S.	45
1965–66	*b*Ayr United	53	Airdrieonians	50	Queen of the S.	49
1966–67	*b*Morton	69	Raith Rovers	58	Arbroath	57
1967–68	*b*St Mirren	62	Arbroath	53	East Fife	40
1968–69	*b*Motherwell	64	Ayr United	53	*East Fife	47
1969–70	*b*Falkirk	56	Cowdenbeath	55	Queen of the S.	58
1970–71	*b*Partick Thistle	56	East Fife	51	Arbroath	46
1971–72	*b*†Dumbarton	52	Arbroath	52	Stirling Albion	50
1972–73	*b*Clyde	56	Dunfermline A.	52	*Raith Rovers	47
1973–74	*b*Airdrieonians	60	Kilmarnock	59	Hamilton A.	55
1974–75	*b*Falkirk	54	*Queen of the S.	53	Montrose	53

Maximum points: *a*, 76; *b*, 72; *c*, 68; *d*, 52; *e*, 60.

*On goal average. †Held jointly after indecisive play-off. ‡Won on deciding match. ††Held jointly. **Two points deducted for fielding ineligible player. Competition suspended 1940–45.

RELEGATED CLUBS

From Premier Division

1975–76	Dundee, St Johnstone
1976–77	Hearts, Kilmarnock
1977–78	Ayr United, Clydebank
1978–79	Hearts, Motherwell
1979–80	Dundee, Hibernian
1980–81	Kilmarnock, Hearts
1981–82	Partick Th., Airdrieonians
1982–83	Morton, Kilmarnock
1983–84	St Johnstone, Motherwell
1984–85	Dumbarton, Morton
1985–86	*No relegation due to League reorganisation*

From Division 1

1975–76	Dunfermline A., Clyde
1976–77	Raith Rovers, Falkirk
1977–78	Alloa, East Fife
1978–79	Montrose, Queen of the S.
1979–80	Arbroath, Clyde
1980–81	Stirling A., Berwick R.
1981–82	East Stirling, Queen of the S.
1982–83	Dunfermline, Queen's Park
1983–84	Raith Rovers, Alloa
1984–85	Meadowbank Th, St Johnstone
1985–86	Ayr U, Alloa

Relegated from Division 1 to 1973-74

1921–22	*Queen's Park, Dumbarton, Clydebank
1922–23	Albion Rovers, Alloa
1923–24	Clyde, Clydebank
1924–25	Third Lanark, Ayr United
1925–26	Raith R., Clydebank
1926–27	Morton, Dundee United
1927–28	Dunfermline Athletic, Bo'ness
1928–29	Third Lanark, Raith R.
1929–30	St Johnstone, Dundee United
1930–31	Hibernian, East Fife
1931–32	Dundee United, Leith Athletic
1932–33	Morton, East Stirling
1933–34	Third Lanark, Cowdenbeath
1934–35	St Mirren, Falkirk
1935–36	Airdrieonians, Ayr United
1936–37	Dunfermline Athletic, Albion Rovers
1937–38	Dundee, Morton
1938–39	Queen's Park, Raith R.
1946–47	Kilmarnock, Hamilton Academicals
1947–48	Airdrieonians, Queen's Park
1948–49	Morton, Albion Rovers
1949–50	Queen of the South, Stirling Albion
1950–51	Clyde, Falkirk
1951–52	Morton, Stirling Albion
1952–53	Motherwell, Third Lanark
1953–54	Airdrieonians, Hamilton Academicals
1954–55	No clubs relegated
1955–56	Stirling Albion, Clyde
1956–57	Dunfermline Athletic, Ayr United
1957–58	East Fife, Queen's Park
1958–59	Queen of the S., Falkirk
1959–60	Arbroath, Stirling Albion
1960–61	Ayr United, Clyde
1961–62	St Johnstone, Stirling Albion
1962–63	Clyde, Raith Rovers
1963–64	Queen of the South, East Stirling
1964–65	Airdrieonians, Third Lanark
1965–66	Morton, Hamilton A.
1966–67	St Mirren, Ayr United
1967–68	Motherwell, Stirling Albion
1968–69	Falkirk, Arbroath
1969–70	Raith Rovers, Partick Thistle
1970–71	St Mirren, Cowdenbeath
1971–72	Clyde, Dunfermline Athletic
1972–73	Kilmarnock, Airdrieonians
1973–74	East Fife, Falkirk
1974–75	League reorganised at end of season

*Season 1921–22—only 1 club promoted, 3 clubs relegated.

SCOTTISH CUP 1985-86

Third round	Fourth round	Fifth round	Semi-finals	Final
Hibernian 2	Hibernian 1	Hibernian 4	Hibernian 0	**Aberdeen** 3
Dunfermline Ath. 0				*Hewitt 2, Stark*
Ayr U. 1	Ayr U. 0			
Stenhousemuir 0				
Celtic 2	Celtic 2	Celtic 3		
St Johnstone 0				
Queen's Park 1	Queen's Park 1			
Dumbarton 0				
Nairn 0	Dundee 2	Dundee 2 1	Aberdeen 3	
Dundee 7				
Airdrieonians 0 2	Airdrieonians 0			
Partick Th. 0 1				
Arbroath 0 2	Arbroath 0	Aberdeen 2 2		
Clyde 0 1				
Aberdeen 4	Aberdeen 1			
Montrose 1				
Berwick R. 2	Alloa 1	Motherwell 0	Dundee U. 0	**Hearts** 0
Alloa 3				*At Hampden Park*
Motherwell 1 1 2	Motherwell 2			*Attendance: 62,841*
Brechin C. 1 1 0				
Dundee U. 4	Dundee U. 1 1	Dundee U. 1		
Morton 0				
Kilmarnock 1	Kilmarnock 1 0			
Stirling A. 0				
Hamilton A. 2	Hamilton A. 1	Hearts 4	Hearts 1	
Forfar Ath. 1				
Hearts 3	Hearts 2			
Rangers 2				
East Fife 1 1	St Mirren 1 3	St Mirren 1		
St Mirren 1 3				
Clydebank 0 0	Falkirk 1 0			
Falkirk 0 1				

SCOTTISH CUP PAST FINALS

1874	Queens Park	2	Clydesdale	0
1875	Queens Park	3	Renton	0
1876	Queens Park	1 2	Third Lanark	1 0
1877	Vale of Leven	0 1 3	Rangers	0 1 2
1878	Vale of Leven	1	Third Lanark	0
1879	Vale of Leven	1	Rangers	1
	Vale of Leven awarded cup, Rangers did not appear for replay			
1880	Queens Park	3	Thornlibank	0
1881	Queens Park	2 3	Dumbarton	1 1
	Replayed because of protest			
1882	Queens Park	2 4	Dumbarton	2 1
1883	Dumbarton	2 2	Vale of Leven	2 1
1884	*Queens Park awarded cup when Vale of Leven did not appear for the final.*			
1885	Renton	0 3	Vale of Leven	0 1
1886	Queens Park	3	Renton	1
1887	Hibernian	2	Dumbarton	1
1888	Renton	6	Cambuslang	1
1889	Third Lanark	3 2	Celtic	0 1
	Replayed because of protest			
1890	Queens Park	1 2	Vale of Leven	1 1
1891	Hearts	1	Dumbarton	0
1892	Celtic	1 5	Queens Park	0 1
	Replayed because of protest			
1893	Queens Park	2	Celtic	1
1894	Rangers	3	Celtic	1
1895	St Bernards	2	Renton	1
1896	Hearts	3	Hibernian	1
1897	Rangers	5	Dumbarton	1
1898	Rangers	2	Kilmarnock	0
1899	Celtic	2	Rangers	0
1900	Celtic	4	Queens Park	3
1901	Hearts	4	Celtic	3
1902	Hibernian	1	Celtic	0
1903	Rangers	1 0 2	Hearts	1 0 0
1904	Celtic	3	Rangers	2
1905	Third Lanark	0 3	Rangers	0 1
1906	Hearts	1	Third Lanark	0
1907	Celtic	3	Hearts	0
1908	Celtic	5	St Mirren	1
1909	*After two drawn games between Celtic and Rangers, 2-2, 1-1, there was a riot and the cup was withheld.*			
1910	Dundee	2 0 2	Clyde	2 0 1
1911	Celtic	0 2	Hamilton	0 0
1912	Celtic	2	Clyde	0
1913	Falkirk	2	Raith Rovers	0
1914	Celtic	0 4	Hibernian	0 1
1920	Kilmarnock	3	Albion Rovers	2
1921	Partick Thistle	1	Rangers	0
1922	Morton	1	Rangers	0
1923	Celtic	1	Hibernian	0
1924	Airdrieonians	2	Hibernian	0
1925	Celtic	2	Dundee	1
1926	St Mirren	2	Celtic	0

1927	Celtic	3	East Fife	1
1928	Rangers	4	Celtic	0
1929	Kilmarnock	2	Rangers	0
1930	Rangers	0 2	Partick Thistle	0 1
1931	Celtic	2 4	Motherwell	2 2
1932	Rangers	1 3	Kilmarnock	1 0
1933	Celtic	1	Motherwell	0
1934	Rangers	5	St Mirren	0
1935	Rangers	2	Hamilton Academicals	1
1936	Rangers	1	Third Lanark	0
1937	Celtic	2	Aberdeen	1
1938	East Fife	1 4	Kilmarnock	1 2
1939	Clyde	4	Motherwell	0
1947	Aberdeen	2	Hibernian	1
1948	Rangers	1 1	Morton	1 0
1949	Rangers	4	Clyde	1
1950	Rangers	3	East Fife	0
1951	Celtic	1	Motherwell	0
1952	Motherwell	4	Dundee	0
1953	Rangers	1 1	Aberdeen	1 0
1954	Celtic	2	Aberdeen	1
1955	Clyde	1 1	Celtic	1 0
1956	Hearts	3	Celtic	1
1957	Falkirk	1 2	Kilmarnock	1 1
1958	Clyde	1	Hibernian	0
1959	St Mirren	3	Aberdeen	1
1960	Rangers	2	Kilmarnock	0
1961	Dunfermline Athletic	0 2	Celtic	0 0
1962	Rangers	2	St Mirren	0
1963	Rangers	1 3	Celtic	1 0
1964	Rangers	3	Dundee	1
1965	Celtic	3	Dunfermline Athletic	2
1966	Rangers	0 1	Celtic	0 0
1967	Celtic	2	Aberdeen	0
1968	Dunfermline Athletic	3	Hearts	1
1969	Celtic	4	Rangers	0
1970	Aberdeen	3	Celtic	1
1971	Celtic	1 2	Rangers	1 1
1972	Celtic	6	Hibernian	1
1973	Rangers	3	Celtic	2
1974	Celtic	3	Dundee United	0
1975	Celtic	3	Airdrieonians	1
1976	Rangers	3	Hearts	1
1977	Celtic	1	Rangers	0
1978	Rangers	2	Aberdeen	1
1979	Rangers	0 0 3	Hibernian	0 0 2
1980	Celtic	1	Rangers	0
1981	Rangers	0 4	Dundee United	0 1
1982	Aberdeen	4	Rangers	1
1983	Aberdeen	1	Rangers	0
1984	Aberdeen	2	Celtic	1
1985	Celtic	2	Dundee United	1

SKOL (SCOTTISH LEAGUE) CUP 1985-86

Quarter-finals		Semi-finals (2 legs)		Final	
Dundee U	2	Dundee U	0 0	Aberdeen	3
St Mirren	1			*Black 2, Stark*	
Aberdeen	1	Aberdeen	1 1		
Hearts	0				
Hibernian	4	Hibernian	2 0	Hibernian	0
Celtic	4*				
Hamilton A	1	Rangers	0 1		
Rangers	2				

**aet, Hibs won on penalties*

PAST SCOTTISH LEAGUE CUP FINALS

1946-47	Hampden Park	Rangers	4	Aberdeen	0
1947-48	Hampden Park	East Fife	0 4	Falkirk	0 1
1948-49	Hampden Park	Rangers	2	Raith Rovers	0
1949-50	Hampden Park	East Fife	3	Dunfermline	0
1950-51	Hampden Park	Motherwell	3	Hibernian	0
1951-52	Hampden Park	Dundee	3	Rangers	2
1952-53	Hampden Park	Dundee	2	Kilmarnock	0
1953-54	Hampden Park	East Fife	3	Partick Thistle	2
1954-55	Hampden Park	Hearts	4	Motherwell	2
1955-56	Hampden Park	Aberdeen	2	St Mirren	1
1956-57	Hampden Park	Celtic	0 3	Partick Thistle	0 0
1957-58	Hampden Park	Celtic	7	Rangers	1
1958-59	Hampden Park	Hearts	5	Partick Thistle	1
1959-60	Hampden Park	Hearts	2	Third Lanark	1
1960-61	Hampden Park	Rangers	2	Kilmarnock	0
1961-62	Hampden Park	Rangers	1 3	Hearts	1 1
1962-63	Hampden Park	Hearts	1	Kilmarnock	0
1963-64	Hampden Park	Rangers	5	Morton	0
1964-65	Hampden Park	Rangers	2	Celtic	1
1965-66	Hampden Park	Celtic	2	Rangers	1
1966-67	Hampden Park	Celtic	1	Rangers	0
1967-68	Hampden Park	Celtic	5	Dundee	3
1968-69	Hampden Park	Celtic	6	Hibernian	2
1969-70	Hampden Park	Celtic	1	St Johnstone	0
1970-71	Hampden Park	Rangers	1	Celtic	0
1971-72	Hampden Park	Partick Thistle	4	Celtic	1
1972-73	Hampden Park	Hibernian	2	Celtic	1
1973-74	Hampden Park	Dundee	1	Celtic	0
1974-75	Hampden Park	Celtic	6	Hibernian	3
1975-76	Hampden Park	Rangers	1	Celtic	0
1976-77	Hampden Park	Aberdeen	2	Celtic	1
1977-78	Hampden Park	Rangers	2	Celtic	1
1978-79	Hampden Park	Rangers	2	Aberdeen	1
1979-80	Hampden Park	Aberdeen	0 0	Dundee U.	0 3
1980-81	Hampden Park	Dundee	0	Dundee U.	3
1981-82	Hampden Park	Rangers	2	Dundee U.	1
1982-83	Hampden Park	Celtic	2	Rangers	1
1983-84	Hampden Park	Rangers	3	Celtic	2
1984-85	Hampden Park	Rangers	1	Dundee U	0

FOOTBALL LEAGUE ATTENDANCES 1985-86

Although there was a slight and curious rise in Fourth Division attendances during 1985-86, figures overall reflect another considerable slump. It is, of course, enormously difficult to pinpoint reasons other than the obvious ones (poor stadium facilities for spectators, high unemployment, dreadful weather) but it would be fair to assume that the disasters which hit British soccer at the end of the 1984-85 season, especially the Brussels tragedy, have had some effect. The exemplary behaviour of the British fans in Mexico may repair some of that damage – we shall see. As usual, top billing in the attendance stakes goes to Manchester United, and indeed, they were one of only six First Division clubs to see their gates rise compared with the season before. The club with the unhappy distinction of the biggest drop in attendance figures was Spurs – over 8,000 down – and spare a thought for Wolves, whose gates were virtually halved as they plummeted towards the Fourth Division. The divisional totals, with last year's figures in brackets and the percentage change, were:

Division One: 9,037,854 (9,865,023)−8.4%
Division Two: 3,551,968 (4,023,621)−11.7%
Division Three: 2,490,481 (2,638,721)− 5.6%
Division Four: 1,408,274 (1,379,080)+2.1%
Total: 16,488,577 (17,906,445)−7.9%

TOTAL LEAGUE ATTENDANCES SINCE 1946-47

Season	Matches	Total	Season	Matches	Total
1946-47	1848	35,604,606	1966-67	2028	28,902,596
1947-48	1848	40,259,130	1967-68	2028	30,107,298
1948-49	1848	41,271,414	1968-69	2028	29,382,172
1949-50	1848	40,517,865	1969-70	2028	29,600,972
1950-51	2028	39,584,967	1970-71	2028	28,194,146
1951-52	2028	39,015,866	1971-72	2028	28,700,729
1952-53	2028	37,149,966	1972-73	2028	25,448,642
1953-54	2028	36,174,590	1973-74	2027	24,982,203
1954-55	2028	34,133,103	1974-75	2028	25,577,977
1955-56	2028	33,150,809	1975-76	2028	24,896,053
1956-57	2028	32,744,405	1976-77	2028	26,182,800
1957-58	2028	33,562,208	1977-78	2028	25,392,872
1958-59	2028	33,610,985	1978-79	2028	24,540,627
1959-60	2028	32,538,611	1979-80	2028	24,623,975
1960-61	2028	28,619,754	1980-81	2028	21,907,569
1961-62	2015	27,979,902	1981-82	2028	20,006,961
1962-63	2028	28,885,852	1982-83	2028	18,766,158
1963-64	2028	28,535,022	1983-84	2028	18,358,631
1964-65	2028	27,641,168	1984-85	2028	17,849,835
1965-66	2028	27,206,980	1985-86	2028	16,488,577

DIVISION ONE

	League position	Home Average 1985-86	Home Average 1984-85	Difference
Arsenal	7	23,824	31,685	−7861
Aston Villa	16	15,237	18,289	−3052
Birmingham City*	21	10,899	12,522	−1623
Chelsea	6	21,984	23,062	−1078
Coventry City	17	11,589	12,791	−1202
Everton	2	32,226	32,725	−499
Ipswich Town	20	14,468	17,050	−2582
Leicester City	19	11,792	14,530	−2738
Liverpool	1	35,271	35,854	−583
Luton Town	9	11,062	10,816	+246
Manchester City*	15	24,229	24,206	+23
Manchester United	4	46,321	45,074	+1247
Newcastle United	11	23,433	26,046	−2613
Nottingham Forest	8	16,808	16,757	+51
Oxford United*	18	11,009	10,579	+430
Queen's Park Rangers	13	12,664	14,364	−1700
Sheffield Wednesday	5	23,110	27,762	−4652
Southampton	14	14,877	18,033	−3156
Tottenham Hotspur	10	20,859	28,932	−8073
Watford	12	15,359	18,375	−3016
West Bromwich Albion	22	12,163	14,121	−1958
West Ham United	3	21,179	18,435	+2744

**Promoted the previous season*

DIVISION TWO

	League position	Home Average 1985-86	Home Average 1984-85	Difference
Barnsley	12	6067	7225	−1158
Blackburn Rovers	19	5826	9641	−3815
Bradford City*	13	5815	6051	−236
Brighton & Hove Albion	11	9725	11,598	−1873
Carlisle United	20	4010	4081	−71
Charlton Athletic	2	6028	5039	+989
Crystal Palace	5	6787	6440	+347
Fulham	22	4623	6178	−1555
Grimsby Town	15	5157	6640	−1483
Huddersfield Town	16	6821	7238	−417
Hull City*	6	7671	8010	−339
Leeds United	14	13,258	14,662	−1404
Middlesbrough	21	6257	5127	+1130
Millwall*	9	5459	6442	−983
Norwich City+	1	13,722	16,058	−2336
Oldham Athletic	8	4651	4741	−90
Portsmouth	4	13,614	15,192	−1578
Sheffield United	7	10,798	12,415	−1617
Shrewsbury Town	17	3926	4710	−784
Stoke City+	10	8288	10,646	−2358
Sunderland+	18	16,052	18,358	−2306
Wimbledon	3	4578	4424	+154

**Promoted the previous season*
+Relegated the previous season

DIVISION THREE

	League position	Home Average 1985-86	Home Average 1984-85	Difference
Blackpool*	12	4535	4906	−371
Bolton Wanderers	18	4846	4951	−105
AFC Bournemouth	15	3423	3766	−343
Brentford	10	3956	4048	−92
Bristol City	9	6599	8471	−1872
Bristol Rovers	16	4195	4963	−768
Bury*	20	2888	3461	−573
Cardiff City+	22	3061	4369	−1308
Chesterfield*	17	3211	4071	−860
Darlington*	14	3026	3772	−746
Derby County	3	12,386	10,832	+1554
Doncaster Rovers	11	2803	4146	−1343
Gillingham	5	3690	4726	−1036
Lincoln City	21	2616	2550	+66
Newport County	19	2493	2431	+62
Notts County+	8	4403	6198	−1795
Plymouth Argyle	2	8297	5133	+3164
Reading	1	6892	3465	+3427
Rotherham United	13	3474	4441	−967
Swansea City	24	4305	4397	−92
Walsall	6	4890	4807	+83
Wigan Athletic	4	4148	3264	+884
Wolverhampton W.+	23	4019	8376	−4357
York City	7	4111	5526	−1415

**Promoted the previous season*
+Relegated the previous season

DIVISION FOUR

	League position	Home Average 1985-86	Home Average 1984-85	Difference
Aldershot	16	1479	2009	−530
Burnley+	14	3203	4220	−1017
Cambridge United+	22	2089	2102	−13
Chester City	2	2956	1879	+1077
Colchester United	6	2327	2076	+251
Crewe Alexandra	12	1817	2275	−458
Exeter City	21	1972	2348	−376
Halifax Town	20	1405	1381	+24
Hartlepool United	7	2593	2340	+253
Hereford United	10	2755	3881	−1126
Mansfield Town	3	3764	2316	+1448
Northampton Town	8	2384	1826	+558
Orient+	5	2628	2596	+32
Peterborough United	17	2590	3134	−544
Port Vale	4	3581	3242	+339
Preston North End+	23	3502	3749	−247
Rochdale	18	1789	1454	+335
Scunthorpe United	15	1777	2065	−288
Southend United	9	2784	1888	+896
Stockport County	11	2666	1895	+771
Swindon Town	1	6531	3020	+3511
Torquay United	24	1239	1437	−198
Tranmere Rovers	19	1566	1688	−122
Wrexham	13	1820	1596	+224

+Relegated the previous season

P.F.A.86.87.—7

SCREEN SPORT SUPER CUP

The six teams were divided into two groups of three, with the winner of each group going through to the semi-finals. The final of this competition will be held early in the 1986-87 season.

First round

Manchester U. (1)2 (Robson, pen, Stapleton)	18 September 1985
Everton (2)4 (Sheedy 2, Lineker, Sharp)	att. 33,859
Everton (0)1 (Lineker)	2 October 1985
Norwich C. (0)0	att. 10,329
Norwich C. (0)1 (Mendham)	23 October 1985
Everton (0)0	att. 12,196
Manchester U. (0)1 (Whiteside, pen)	6 November 1985
Norwich C. (1)1 (Biggins)	att. 20,130
Everton (0)1 (Stapleton, og)	4 December 1985
Manchester U. (0)0	att. 20,542
Norwich C. (1)1 (Williams)	11 December 1985
Manchester U. (0)1 (C. Gibson)	att. 15,449
Norwich City and Everton qualify for semi-finals	
Liverpool(2)2 (Molby, Dalglish)	17 September 1985
Southampton (1)1 (Wallace)	att. 16,189
Tottenham H. (2)2 (Falco 2)	2 October 1985
Southampton (0)1 (Morgan)	att. 11,549
Southampton (0)1 (Armstrong, pen)	22 October 1985
Liverpool (0)1 (Walsh)	att. 10,503
Liverpool (2)2 (Macdonald, Walsh)	3 December 1985
Tottenham H. (0)0	att.14,855
Southampton (0)1 (Wallace)	17 December 1985
Tottenham H. (2)3 (Falco, C. Allen, Leworthy)	att. 4680
Tottenham H. (0)0	14 January 1986
Liverpool (0)3 (Rush 2, Lawrenson)	att. 10,078
Liverpool and Tottenham Hotspur qualify for semi-finals	

Semi-finals, first leg

Norwich C. (0)1 (Drinkell)	5 February 1986
Liverpool (0)1 (Dalglish)	att. 15,313
Tottenham H. (0)0	5 February 1986
Everton (0)0	att. 7548

Semi-finals, second leg

Everton (0)3 (Heath, Mountfield, Sharp)	19 March 1986
Tottenham H. (0)1 (Falco)	att. 12,008
Liverpool (0)3 (MacDonald, Molby pen, Johnston)	6 May 1986
Norwich C. (1)1 (Brooke)	att. 26,696
Everton and Liverpool qualify for the final	

FULL MEMBERS' CUP

Originally consisting of eight groups of three teams each (four northern and four southern), this competition was disrupted by withdrawals, and three groups had only two teams. Only in the Grimsby Town/Sunderland Group did they play twice. Each group winner qualified for the sectional semi-finals.

NORTHERN SECTION
Grimsby 3,1, Sunderland 2,2
Sunderland qualify on penalties
Middlesbrough 2, Carlisle U. 0
Middlesbrough qualify
Manchester C. 6, Leeds U. 1
Leeds U. 1, Sheffield U. 1
Sheffield U. 1, Manchester C. 2
Manchester C. qualify
Hull C. 4, Bradford C. 1
Hull C. qualify

Northern semi-finals
Manchester C. 0, Sunderland 0
Manchester C. won on penalties
Hull C. 3, Middlesbrough 1

Northern final
Hull C. 2,0, Manchester C. 1,2

SOUTHERN SECTION
Oxford U. 3, Shrewsbury T. 0
Shrewsbury T. 0, Fulham 0
Fulham 0, Oxford U. 0
Oxford U. qualify
Stoke C. 3, Coventry C. 0
Millwall 2, Stoke C. 2
Coventry C. 1, Millwall 1
Stoke C. qualify
Portsmouth 4, Charlton Ath. 1
Chelsea 3, Portsmouth 0
Charlton Ath. 1, Chelsea 3
Chelsea qualify
Brighton & H.A. 1, W.B.A. 2
Crystal Palace 1, Brighton & H.A. 3
W.B.A. 2, Crystal Palace 1
W.B.A. qualify

Southern semi-finals
Stoke C. 0, Oxford U. 1
W.B.A. 2, Chelsea 2
Chelsea won on penalties

Southern final
Oxford U. 1,1, Chelsea 4,0

FINAL

Wembley, 23 March 1986, 68,000

Chelsea (2) 5,	Manchester C. (1) 4
Speedie 3	Kinsey
Lee 2	Lillis 2 (1 pen)
	Rougvie (og)

WELSH FA CUP WINNERS (Since 1901)

1900-1 Oswestry
1901-2 Wellington
1902-3 Wrexham
1903-4 Druids
1904-5 Wrexham
1905-6 Wellington
1906-7 Oswestry
1907-8 Chester
1908-9 Wrexham
1909-10 Wrexham
1910-11 Wrexham
1911-12 Cardiff
1912-13 Swansea
1913-14 Wrexham
1914-15 Wrexham
1915-16 Abandoned
1919-20 Cardiff
1920-21 Wrexham
1921-22 Cardiff
1922-23 Cardiff
1923-24 Wrexham
1924-25 Wrexham
1925-26 Ebbw Vale
1926-27 Cardiff
1927-28 Cardiff
1928-29 Connah's Quay
1929-30 Cardiff
1930-31 Wrexham
1931-32 Swansea
1932-33 Chester
1933-34 Bristol City
1934-35 Tranmere
1935-36 Crewe
1936-37 Crewe
1937-38 Shrewsbury
1938-39 S. Liverpool
1939-40 Wellington
1940-46 No contest
1946-47 Chester
1947-48 Lovell's Ath.
1948-49 Merthyr Tydfil
1949-50 Swansea
1950-51 Merthyr Tydfil
1951-52 Rhyl
1952-53 Rhyl
1953-54 Flint
1954-55 Bury
1955-56 Cardiff
1956-57 Wrexham
1957-58 Wrexham
1958-59 Cardiff
1959-60 Wrexham
1960-61 Swansea
1961-62 Bangor
1962-63 Borough Utd.
1963-64 Cardiff
1964-65 Cardiff
1965-66 Swansea
1966-67 Cardiff
1967-68 Cardiff
1968-69 Cardiff
1969-70 Cardiff
1970-71 Cardiff
1971-72 Wrexham
1972-73 Cardiff
1973-74 Cardiff
1974-75 Wrexham
1975-76 Cardiff
1976-77 Shrewsbury
1977-78 Wrexham
1978-79 Shrewsbury
1979-80 Newport County
1980-81 Swansea
1981-82 Swansea
1982-83 Swansea
1983-84 Shrewsbury
1984-85 Shrewsbury
1985-86 Wrexham

NORTHERN IRISH CUP FINALS 1881-1986

1880-81	Moyola Park	1	Cliftonville	0
1881-82	Queen's Island	2	Cliftonville	1
1882-83	Cliftonville	5	Ulster	0
1883-84	Distillery	5	Wellington Park	0
1884-85	Distillery	2	Limavady	0
1885-86	Distillery	1	Limavady	0
1886-87	Ulster	3	Cliftonville	0
1887-88	Cliftonville	2	Distillery	1
1888-89	Distillery	5	YMCA	4
1889-90	Gordon Highlanders	3	Cliftonville	1
1890-91	Linfield	4	Ulster	2
1891-92	Linfield	7	The Black Watch	0
1892-93	Linfield	5	Cliftonville	1
1893-94	Distillery	3	Linfield	2
1894-95	Linfield	10	Bohemians	1
1895-96	Distillery	3	Glentoran	1
1896-97	Cliftonville	3	Sherwood Foresters	1
1897-98	Linfield	2	St Columb's Hall Celtic	0
1898-99	Linfield	2	Glentoran	1
1899-1900	Cliftonville	2	Bohemians	1
1900-1	Cliftonville	1	Freebooters	0
1901-2	Linfield	5	Distillery	1
1902-3	Distillery	3	Bohemians	1
1903-4	Linfield	5	Derry Celtic	1
1904-5	Distillery	3	Shelbourne	0
1905-6	Shelbourne	2	Belfast Celtic	0
1906-7	Cliftonville	1	Shelbourne	0
1907-8	Bohemians	3	Shelbourne	1
1908-9	Cliftonville	2	Bohemians	1
1909-10	Distillery	1	Cliftonville	0
1910-11	Shelbourne	2	Bohemians	1
1911-12	Linfield were awarded Cup. Final not played.			
1912-13	Linfield	2	Glentoran	0
1913-14	Glentoran	3	Linfield	1
1914-15	Linfield	1	Belfast Celtic	0
1915-16	Linfield	1	Glentoran	0
1916-17	Glentoran	2	Belfast Celtic	0
1917-18	Belfast Celtic	2	Linfield	0
1918-19	Linfield	2	Glentoran	1
1919-20	Cup awarded to Shelbourne.			
1920-21	Glentoran	2	Glenavon	0
1921-22	Linfield	2	Glenavon	0
1922-23	Linfield	2	Glentoran	0
1923-24	Queen's Island	1	Willowfield	0
1924-25	Distillery	2	Glentoran	1
1925-26	Belfast Celtic	3	Linfield	2
1926-27	Ards	3	Cliftonville	2
1927-28	Willowfield	1	Larne	0
1928-29	Ballymena United	2	Belfast Celtic	1
1929-30	Linfield	4	Ballymena United	3

1930-31	Linfield	3	Ballymena United	0
1931-32	Glentoran	2	Linfield	1
1932-33	Glentoran	3	Distillery	1
1933-34	Linfield	5	Cliftonville	0
1934-35	Glentoran	1	Larne	0
1935-36	Linfield	2	Derry City	1
1936-37	Belfast Celtic	3	Linfield	0
1937-38	Belfast Celtic	2	Bangor	0
1938-39	Linfield	2	Ballymena United	0
1939-40	Ballymena United	2	Glenavon	0
1940-41	Belfast Celtic	1	Linfield	0
1941-42	Linfield	3	Glentoran	1
1942-43	Belfast Celtic	1	Glentoran	0
1943-44	Belfast Celtic	2	Linfield	1
1944-45	Linfield	4	Glentoran	2
1945-46	Linfield	3	Distillery	0
1946-47	Belfast Celtic	1	Glentoran	0
1947-48	Linfield	3	Coleraine	0
1948-49	Derry City	3	Glentoran	1
1949-50	Linfield	2	Distillery	1
1950-51	Glentoran	3	Ballymena United	1
1951-52	Ards	1	Glentoran	0
1952-53	Linfield	5	Coleraine	0
1953-54	Derry City	1	Glentoran	0
1954-55	Dundela	3	Glenavon	0
1955-56	Distillery	1	lentoran	0
1956-57	Glenavon	2	Derry City	0
1957-58	Ballymena United	2	Linfield	0
1958-59	Glenavon	2	Ballymena United	0
1959-60	Linfield	5	Ards	1
1960-61	Glenavon	5	Linfield	1
1961-62	Linfield	4	Portadown	0
1962-63	Linfield	2	Distillery	1
1963-64	Derry City	2	Glentoran	0
1964-65	Coleraine	2	Glenavon	1
1965-66	Glentoran	2	Linfield	0
1966-67	Crusaders	3	Glentoran	1
1967-68	Crusaders	2	Linfield	0
1968-69	Ards	4	Distillery	1
1969-70	Linfield	2	Ballymena United	1
1970-71	Distillery	3	Derry City	0
1971-72	Coleraine	2	Portadown	1
1972-73	Glentoran	3	Linfield	2
1973-74	Ards	2	Ballymena United	1
1974-75	Coleraine	1	Linfield	0
	(after 1-1 and 0-0 draws)			
1975-76	Carrick Rangers	2	Linfield	1
1976-77	Coleraine	4	Linfield	1
1977-78	Linfield	3	Ballymena United	1
1978-79	Cliftonville	3	Portadown	2
1979-80	Linfield	2	Crusaders	0
1980-81	Ballymena	1	Glenavon	0
1981-82	Linfield	2	Coleraine	1
1982-83	Glentoran	1 2	Linfield	1 1
1983-84	Ballymena	4	Carrick	1
1984-85	Glentoran	1 1	Linfield	1 0
1985-86	Glentoran	2	Coleraine	1

EUROPEAN FOOTBALL 1985-86

One out of three for Spain

It was a lively season in European club competitions, even though the field was weakened by the absence of the likes of Everton, Manchester United and Liverpool. Of the other British entrants, only Aberdeen (Champions' Cup) progressed beyond the last sixteen, and were perhaps a little unlucky not to go further, being beaten by the away goals rule in a tense quarter-final tie against IFK Gothenburg. The ever-improving Swedes, surprise winners of the UEFA Cup in 1982, were unlucky in their own turn when they saw a 3-0 first-leg advantage wiped out in the semi-final against Barcelona and then lost on penalties.

Barcelona's progress to the final had been full of tense moments. They had to rely on the away goals rule in the first two rounds, and then shaded their quarter-final against Juventus by the odd goal in three before having to go through the torture chamber of a penalty competition against IFK. Steaua of Bucharest, meanwhile, became only the second eastern bloc finalist in the history of the European Cup after a steady but unspectacular progress against moderate opposition, and few people gave them any chance of winning against Terry Venables' superstars.

The final itself was a most disappointing affair. Steaua seemed content to pack their defence, although one can hardly imagine that they were actually playing for a penalty shoot-out, and Barcelona failed to take the few good chances which they did manage to carve out, with Schuster and Archibald the main villains. There followed the most amazing series of penalties, with neither side seeming able to find the net. Eventually, the Rumanians did manage it twice, and Terry Venables was left to contemplate a season with no major trophies. Arch rivals Real Madrid had taken the championship and the UEFA Cup, just to make matters worse.

In the Cup-Winners' Cup, Celtic and Glentoran both fell at the first hurdle, leaving plucky Bangor City from the Welsh League as the sole British representatives in the second round, but there they were drawn against the relatively mighty Atletico Madrid, and duly came unstuck. Atletico went on to reach the final, where, like their compatriots from Barcelona, they faced eastern bloc opponents. This time it was Dynamo Kiev, who had trounced last year's losing finalists Rapid Vienna 9-2 on the way, and this time, too, the Spaniards failed at the final fence. Dynamo, the heart of the Soviet national side for many years now, won comfortably, with the evergreen Oleg Blokhin getting his name on the scoresheet, and so a second trophy went behind the iron curtain.

Yet a third final – the UEFA Cup – included a Spanish club, but this time there were to be no disappointments for them. Real Madrid, still one of the great names in European competition, virtually killed the match with a 5-1 first leg victory over Cologne, and although they made little attempt to add to their score in the second leg, their overall superiority was unquestioned.

KEY TO RESULTS GRIDS: A – Austria; AL – Albania; B – Bulgaria; BE – Belgium; CY – Cyprus; CZ – Czechoslovakia; D – Denmark; E – Eire; EG – East Germany; F – France; FI – Finland; G – Greece; H – Hungary; I – Italy; IC – Iceland; L – Luxembourg; M – Malta; N – Netherlands; NI – Northern Ireland; NO – Norway; P – Portugal; PO – Poland; R – Rumania; S – Switzerland; SP – Spain; SW – Sweden; T – Turkey; WG – West Germany; Y – Yugoslavia.

EUROPEAN CUP 1985-86

First round

Team	1st leg	2nd leg
Gornik Zabrze (PO)	1	1
Bayern Munich (WG)	2	4
Dynamo Berlin (EG)	0	1
FK Austria (A)	2	2
Anderlecht (BE) – bye		
Rabat Ajax (M)	0	0
Omonia Nicosia (CY)	5	5
Honved (H)	2	3
Shamrock Rovers (E)	0	1
Vejle (D)	1	1
Steaua Bucharest (R)	1	4
Zenit Leningrad (USSR)	2	2
Valerengen (NO)	0	0
Kuusysi Lahti (FI)	2	2
Sarajevo (Y)	1	1
Linfield (NI)	2	1
Servette Geneva (S)	2	2
Akranes (IC)	1	1
Aberdeen	3	4
IFK Gothenburg (SW)	3	2
Trakia Plovdiv (B)	2	1
Bordeaux (F)	2	0
Fenerbahce (T)	3	0
Sparta Prague (CZ)	1	1
Barcelona* (SP)	2	0
FC Porto (P)	2	0
Ajax Amsterdam (N)	0	0
Verona (I)	3	2
PAOK Salonika (G)	1	1
Jeunesse D' Esch (L)	0	1
Juventus (I)	5	4

**Won on away goals*

Second round

Team	1st leg	2nd leg
Bayern	4	3
FK Austria	2	3
Anderlecht	1	3
Omonia	0	1
Honved	1	1
Steaua	0	4
Zenit	2	1
Kuusysi Lahti	1	3
Servette	0	0
Aberdeen	0	1
IFK Gothenburg	4	1
Fenerbahce	0	2
Barcelona*	2	1
FC Porto	0	3
Verona	0	0
Juventus	0	2

Quarter-finals

Team	1st leg	2nd leg
Bayern	2	0
Anderlecht	1	2
Steaua	0	1
Kuusysi Lahti	0	0
Aberdeen	2	0
IFK Gothenburg*	2	0
Barcelona	1	1
Juventus	0	1

Semi-finals

Team	1st leg	2nd leg
Anderlecht	1	0
Steaua	0	3
IFK Gothenburg	3	0
Barcelona	0	3

Barcelona won 5-4 on penalties

Final

STEAUA BUCHAREST 0 — **BARCELONA 0**

Steaua won 2-0 on penalties

In Seville, 7 May 1986, 70,000

EUROPEAN CUP-WINNERS' CUP 1985-86

Final

ATLETICO MADRID 0 DYNAMO KIEV 3

In Lyons, 2 May 1986, 39,300

Scorers: Zavarov, Blokhin, Yevtushenko

First round

Lyngby (D)	1	3
Galway United (E)	0	2
Red Star Belgrade (Y)	2	2
Aarau (S)	0	2
Fredrikstad (NO)	1	0
Bangor City*	1	0
Atletico Madrid (SP)	1	2
Celtic	1	1
HJK Helsinki (FI)	3	2
Flamurtari (AL)	2	1
CS Bruges (BE)	3	1
Dynamo Dresden* (EG)	2	2
Zurrieq (M)	0	0
Bayer Uerdingen (WG)	3	9
Galatasaray* (T)	1	1
Widzew Lodz (PO)	0	2
Rapid Vienna (A)	5	1
Tatabanya (H)	0	1
Fram Reykjavik (IC)	3	0
Glentoran (NI)	1	1
Monaco (F)	2	0
Uni.Craiova (R)	0	3
Utrecht (N)	2	1
Dynamo Kiev (USSR)	1	4
AEL Limassol (CY)	2	0
Dukla Prague (CZ)	2	4
AIK Stockholm (SW)	8	5
Red Boys Differdange (L)	0	0
Benfica (P) – bye		
Larissa (G)	1	0
Sampdoria (I)	1	1

*Won on away golas

Second round

Lyngby	2	1
Red Star	2	3
Bangor C.	0	0
Atletico Madrid	2	1
HJK Helsinki	1	2
Dynamo Dresden	0	7
Bayer Uerdingen	2	1
Galatasaray	0	1
Rapid Vienna	3	1
Fram	0	2
Uni.Craiova	2	0
Dynamo Kiev	2	3
Dukla Prague	1	2
AIK Stockholm	0	2
Benfica	2	0
Sampdoria	0	1

Quarter-finals

Red Star	0	1
Atletico Madrid	2	1
Dynamo Dresden	2	3
Bayer Uerdingen	0	7
Rapid Vienna	1	1
Dynamo Kiev	4	5
Dukla Prague*	1	1
Benfica	0	2

Semi-finals

Atletico Madrid	1	3
Bayer Uerdingen	0	2
Dynamo Kiev	3	1
Dukla Prague	0	1

UEFA CUP 1985-86

Final

COLOGNE 1, 2 — REAL MADRID 5, 0

First leg in Madrid, 30 April 1986, 80,000
Scorers: Real Madrid – Sanchez, Gordillo, Valdano 2, Santillana; Cologne – K. Allofs.

Second leg in Berlin, 6 May 1986, 15,000
Scorers: Cologne – Bein, Geilenkirchen.

Second round

Team	1st leg	2nd leg
Liege (BE)	0	1
Athletic Bilbao (SP)	1	3
Dinamo Tirana (AL)	0	0
Sporting Lisbon (P)	0	1
Hammarby (SW)	3	2
St Mirren	3	1
Cologne (WG)	4	4
Bohemians Prague (CZ)	0	2
PSV Eindhoven (N)	2	0
Dnepr (USSR)	2	1
Torino (I)	1	1
Hajduk Split (Y)	1	3
Waregem (BE)	2	1
Osasuna (SP)	0	2
AC Milan* (I)	2	1
Lokomotiv Leipzig (EG)	0	3
Linzer ASK (A)	1	0
Inter Milan (I)	0	4
Videoton (H)	0	1
Legia Warsaw (PO)	1	1
Spartak Moscow (USSR)	1	3
Bruges (BE)	0	1
Partizan Belgrade (Y)	1	0
Nantes (F)	1	4
Sparta Rotterdam (N)	1	1
Bor. Moenchengladbach (WG)	1	5
Real Madrid (SP)	2	0
Chernomoretz Odessa (USSR)	1	0
Dundee U.	2	1
Vardar Skopje (Y)	0	1
Lokomotiv Sofia (B)	1	0
Xamax Neuchatel* (S)	1	0

Third round

Team	1st leg	2nd leg
Athletic Bilbao	2	0
Sporting Lisbon	1	3
Hammarby	2	1
Cologne	1	3
Dnepr	0	0
Hajduk Split	1	2
Waregem	1	2
AC Milan	1	1
Inter Milan	0	1
Legia Warsaw	0	0
Spartak Moscow	0	1
Nantes	1	1
Borussia	5	0
Real Madrid*	1	4
Dundee U.	2	1
Xamax Neuchatel	1	3

Quarter-finals

Team	1st leg	2nd leg
Sporting Lisbon	1	0
Cologne	1	2
Hajduk Split	1	0
Waregem†	0	1
Inter Milan	3	3
Nantes	0	3
Real Madrid	3	0
Xamax Neuchatel	0	2

Semi-finals

Team	1st leg	2nd leg
Cologne	4	3
Waregem	0	3
Inter Milan	3	1
Real Madrid	1	5

*Won on away goals
†Won on penalties

EUROPEAN CUP PAST FINALS

1956	Real Madrid	4	Stade de Rheims	3
1957	Real Madrid	2	Fiorentina	0
1958	Real Madrid	3	AC Milan	2**
1959	Real Madrid	2	Stade de Rheims	0
1960	Real Madrid	7	Eintracht Frankfurt	3
1961	SL Benfica	3	Barcelona	2
1962	SL Benfica	5	Real Madrid	3
1963	AC Milan	2	SL Benfica	1
1964	Inter Milan	3	Real Madrid	1
1965	Inter Milan	1	SL Benfica	0
1966	Real Madrid	2	Partizan Belgrade	1
1967	Celtic	2	Inter Milan	1
1968	Manchester United	4	SL Benfica	1
1969	AC Milan	4	Ajax Amsterdam	1
1970	Feyenoord	2	Celtic	1**
1971	Ajax Amsterdam	2	Panathinaikos	0
1972	Ajax Amsterdam	2	Inter Milan	0
1973	Ajax Amsterdam	1	Juventus	0
1974	Bayern Munich	1 4	Atlético Madrid	1 0
1975	Bayern Munich	2	Leeds United	0
1976	Bayern Munich	1	St Etienne (Fra)	0
1977	Liverpool	3	Borussia Munchengladbach	1
1978	Liverpool	1	FC Bruges	0
1979	Nottingham Forest	1	Malmoe	0
1980	Nottingham Forest	1	SV Hamburg	0
1981	Liverpool	1	Real Madrid	0
1982	Aston Villa	1	Bayern Munich	0
1983	SV Hamburg	1	Juventus	0
1984	Liverpool††	1	AS Roma	1
1985	Juventus	1	Liverpool	0

EUROPEAN CUP-WINNERS' CUP PAST FINALS

1961	Fiorentina	4	Rangers	1†
1962	Atlético Madrid *(After 1–1 draw)*	3	Fiorentina	0
1963	Tottenham Hotspur	5	Atlético Madrid	1
1964	Sporting Lisbon *(After 3–3 draw)*	1	MTK Budapest	0
1965	West Ham United	2	Munich 1860	0
1966	Borussia Dortmund	2	Liverpool	1**
1967	Bayern Munich	1	Rangers	0**
1968	AC Milan	2	SV Hamburg	0
1969	Slovan Bratislava	3	Barcelona	2
1970	Manchester City	2	Gornik Zabrze	1
1971	Chelsea *(After 1–1 draw)*	2	Real Madrid	1

1972	Rangers	3	Dynamo Moscow	2
1973	AC Milan	1	Leeds United	0
1974	FC Magdeburg	2	AC Milan	0
1975	Dynamo Kiev	3	Ferencvaros	0
1976	RSC Anderlecht	4	West Ham United	2
1977	SV Hamburg	2	Anderlecht	0
1978	RSC Anderlecht	4	Austria Wien	0
1979	Barcelona	4	Fortuna Dusseldorf	3
1980	Valencia ††	0	Arsenal	0
1981	Dinamo Tbilisi	2	Carl Zeiss Jena	1
1982	Barcelona	2	Standard Liege	1
1983	Aberdeen	2	Real Madrid	1
1984	Juventus	2	Porto	1
1985	Everton	3	Rapid Vienna	1

FAIRS CUP FINALS

1958	Barcelona	8	London	2†*
1960	Barcelona	4	Birmingham City	1†
1961	AS Roma	4	Birmingham City	2†
1962	Valencia	7	Barcelona	3†
1963	Valencia	4	Dynamo Zagreb	1†
1964	Real Zaragoza	2	Valencia	1
1965	Ferencvaros	1	Juventus	0
1966	Barcelona	4	Real Zaragoza	3†
1967	Dynamo Zagreb	2	Leeds United	0
1968	Leeds United	1	Ferencvaros	0†
1969	Newcastle United	6	Ujpest Dozsa	2†
1970	Arsenal	4	Anderlecht	3†
1971	Leeds United	3*	Juventus	3†

UEFA CUP PAST FINALS

1972	Tottenham Hotspur	2 1	Wolverhampton Wanderers	1 1
1973	Liverpool	3 0	Borussia Munchengladbach	0 2
1974	Feyenoord	2 2	Tottenham Hotspur	2 0
1975	Borussia Munchengladbach	0 5	Twente Enschede	0 1
1976	Liverpool	3 1	FC Bruges	2 1
1977	Juventus*	1 1	Athletico Bilbao	0 2
1978	PSV Eindhoven	0 3	SEC Bastia	0 0
1979	Borussia Munchengladbach	1 1	Red Star Belgrade	1 0
1980	Borussia Munchengladbach	3 0	Eintracht Frankfurt*	2 1
1981	Ipswich T.	3 2	AZ 67 Alkmaar	0 4
1982	IFK Gothenburg	1 3	SV Hamburg	0 0
1983	RSC Anderlecht	1 1	Benfica	0 1
1984	Tottenham Hotspur††	1 1	RSC Anderlecht	1 1
1985	Real Madrid	3 0	Videton	0 1

** Won on away goals*
*** After extra time*
† Aggregate score
†† Won on penalties

EUROPEAN SUPER CUP

1972	Ajax	3 3	Glasgow Rangers	1 2
1973	Ajax	0 6	AC Milan	1 0
1974	Not contested			
1975	Dynamo Kiev	1 2	Bayern Munich	0 0
1976	Anderlecht	4 1	Bayern Munich	1 2
1977	Liverpool	1 6	SV Hamburg	1 0
1978	Anderlecht	1 3	Liverpool	1 2
1979	Nottingham Forest	1 1	Barcelona	0 1
1980	Nottingham Forest	2 0	Valencia*	1 1
1981	Not contested			
1982	Not contested			
1983	Aston Villa	0 3	Barcelona	1 0
1984	Juventus	2	Liverpool	0
1985	Not contested			

**Won on away goals*

WORLD CLUB CHAMPIONSHIP

Played annually up to 1974 between the winners of the European Cup and the winners of the South American Champions Cup – known as the Copa Libertadores de America. Revived in February 1981 (for the calendar year 1980), but played on a single match basis on a neutral ground.

Year	*Winners*	*Runners-up*	*Score*
1960	Real Madrid	Penarol	0 – 0, 5 – 1
1961	Penarol (Uruguay)	Benfica	0 – 1, 5 – 0, 2 – 1
1962	Santos (Brazil)	Benfica	3 – 2, 5 – 2
1963	Santos	AC Milan	2 – 4, 4 – 2, 1 – 0
1964	Inter-Milan	Independiente	0 – 1, 2 – 0, 1 – 0
1965	Inter-Milan	Independiente	3 – 0, 0 – 0
1966	Penarol	Real Madrid	2 – 0, 2 – 0
1967	Racing Club (Argentina)	Celtic	0 – 1, 2 – 1, 1 – 0
1968	Estudiantes (Argentina)	Manchester Unted	1 – 0, 1 – 1
1969	AC Milan	Estudiantes	3 – 0, 1 – 2
1970	Feyenoord	Estudiantes	2 – 2, 1 – 0
1971	Nacional (Uruguay)	Panathinaikos	1 – 1, 2 – 1
1972	Ajax	Independiente	1 – 1, 3 – 0
1973	Independiente (Argentina)	Juventus	1 – 0
1974	Athletico Madrid	Independiente	0 – 1, 2 – 0
1980	Nacional	Nottingham Forest	1 – 0 (in Tokyo)
1981	Flamengo (Brazil)	Liverpool	3 – 0 (in Tokyo)
1982	Penarol	Aston Villa	2 – 0 (in Tokyo)
1983	Gremio Porto Alegre (Brazil)	SV Hamburg	2 – 1 (in Tokyo)
1984	Independiente	Liverpool	1 – 0 (in Tokyo)
1985	Juventus	Argentinos Juniors	2 – 2 (in Tokyo)
	Juventus won 4 – 2 on penalties		

EUROPEAN CHAMPIONSHIPS PAST FINALS

Paris, 10 July 1960
USSR 2, Yugoslavia 1 (*after extra time*)
USSR: Yachin; Tchekeli, Kroutikov, Voinov, Maslenkin, Netto, Metreveli, Ivanov, Ponedelnik, Bubukin, Meshki. **Scorers:** Metreveli, Ponedelnik.
Yugoslavia: Vidinic; Durkovic, Jusufi, Zanetic, Miladinovic, Perusic, Sekularac, Jerkovic, Galic, Matus, Kostic. **Scorer:** Netto og.

Madrid, 21 June 1964
SPAIN 2, USSR 1
Spain; Iribar; Rivilla, Calleja, Fuste, Olivella, Zoco, Amancio, Pereda, Marcellino, Suarez, Lapetra. **Scorers:** Pereda, Marcellino.
USSR: Yachin; Chustikov, Mudrik, Voronin, Shesternjev, Anitchkin, Chislenko, Ivanov, Ponedelnik, Kornaev, Khusainov. **Scorer:** Khusainov.

Rome, 8 June 1968
ITALY 1, YUGOSLAVIA 1
Italy: Zoff; Burgnich, Facchetti, Ferrini, Guarneri, Castano, Domenghini, Juliano, Anastasi, Lodetti, Prati. **Scorers:** Domenghini,
Yugoslavia: Pantelic; Fazlagic, Damjanovic, Pavlovic, Paunovic, Holcer, Petkovic, Acimovic, Musemic, Trivic, Dzajic. **Scorer:** Dzajic.

Replay: Rome, 10 June 1968
ITALY 2, YUGOSLAVIA 0
Italy: Zoff; Burgnich, Facchetti, Rosato, Guarneri, Salvadore, Domenghini, Mazzola, Anastasi, De Sisti, Riva. **Scorers:** Riva, Anastasi.
Yugoslavia: Pantelic; Fazlagic, Damjanovic, Pavlovic, Paunovic, Holcer, Hosic, Acimovic, Musemic, Trivic, Dzajic.

Brussels, 18 June 1972
WEST GERMANY 3, USSR 0
West Germany: Maier; Hottges, Schwarzenbeck, Beckenbauer, Breitner, Hoeness, Wimmer, Netzer, Heynckes, Muller, Kremers. **Scorers:** Muller 2, Wimmer.
USSR: Rudakov; Dzodzuashvili, Khurtislava, Kaplichny, Istomin, Troshkin, Kolotov, Baidachini, Konkov (Dolmatov), Banishevski (Konzinkievits), Onishenko.

Belgrade, 20 June 1976
CZECHOSLOVAKIA 2, WEST GERMANY 2 (*after extra time*)
Czechoslovakia: Viktor; Dobias (Vesely, F.), Pivarnik, Ondrus, Capkovic, Gogh, Moder, Panenka, Svehlik (Jurkemik), Masny, Nehoda. **Scorers:** Svehlik, Dobias;
West Germany: Maier; Vogts, Beckenbauer, Schwarzenbeck, Dietz, Bonhof, Wimmer, (Flohe), Muller, D., Beer (Bongartz), Hoeness, Holzenbein. **Scorers:** Muller, Holzenbein.
Czechoslovakia won 5-3 on penalties.

Rome, 22 June 1980
WEST GERMANY 2, BELGIUM 1
West Germany: Schumacher; Briegel, Foerster, Dietz, Schutz, Rummenigge, Hrubesch, Mueller, Allofs, Stielike, Kaltz. **Scorers:** Hrubesch 2.
Belgium: Pfaff; Gerets, Millecamps, Meeuws, Renquin, Cools, Van der Eycken, Van, Moer, Mommens, Van der Elst, Cuelemans. **Scorer:** Van der Eycken.

Paris, 27 June 1984
FRANCE 2, SPAIN 0
France: Bats; Battiston (Amoros), Le Roux, Bossis, Domergue, Giresse, Platini, Tigana, Fernandez, Lacombe (Genghini), Bellone. **Scorers:** Platini, Bellone
Spain: Arconada; Urquiaga, Salva (Roberto), Gallego, Camacho, Francisco, Julio, Alberto (Sarabia), Senor, Victor, Carrasco, Santillana.

EUROPEAN CHAMPIONSHIP 1986-88

DRAW AND FIXTURE LIST

West Germany qualify automatically as host nation

Group 1 (Spain, Rumania, Austria, Albania)
10.9.86 Rumania v Austria, 15.10.86 Austria v Albania, 12.11.86 Spain v Rumania, 3.12.86 Albania v Spain, 25.3.87 Rumania v Albania, 1.4.87 Austria v Spain, 29.4.87 Albania v Austria, 29.4.87 Rumania v Spain, 14.10.87 Spain v Austria, 28.10.87 Albania v Rumania, 18.11.87 Spain v Albania, 18.11.87 Austria v Rumania.

Group 2 *(Portugal, Sweden, Switzerland, Italy, Malta)*
24.9.86 Sweden v Switzerland, 12.10.86 Portugal v Sweden, 29.10.86 Switzerland v Portugal, 15.11.86 Italy v Switzerland, 16.11.86 Malta v Sweden, 6.12.86 Malta v Italy, 24.1.87 Italy v Malta, 14.2.87 Portugal v Italy, 29.3.87 Portugal v Malta, 15.4.87 Switzerland v Malta, 6.5.87 Sweden v Malta, 23.5.87 or 3.6.87 Sweden v Italy, 10 or 17.6.87 Switzerland v Sweden, 23.9.87 Sweden v Portugal, 17.10.87 Switzerland v Italy, 11.11.87 Portugal v Switzerland, 14.11.87 Italy v Sweden, 15.11.87 Malta v Switzerland, 5.12.87 Italy v Portugal, 20.12.87 Malta v Portugal.

Group 3 *(France, USSR, East Germany, Norway, Iceland)*
10.9.86 Iceland v France, 24.9.86 Iceland v USSR, 24.9.86 Norway v East Germany, 11.10.86 France v USSR, 29.10.86 USSR v Norway, 29.10.86 East Germany v Iceland, 19.11.86 East Germany v France, 29.4.87 France v Iceland, 29.4.87 USSR v East Germany, 3.6.87 Norway v USSR, 3.6.87 Iceland v East Germany, 16.6.87 Norway v France, 9.9.87 USSR v France, 9.9.87 Iceland v Norway, 23.9.87 Norway v Iceland, 10.10.87 East Germany v USSR, 14.10.87 France v Norway, 28.10.87 USSR v Iceland, 28.10.87 East Germany v Norway, 18.11.87 France v East Germany.

Group 4 *(England, Northern Ireland, Turkey, Yugoslavia)*
15.10.86 Northern Ireland v England, 15.10.86 Yugoslavia v Turkey, 12.11.86 England v Yugoslavia, 12.11.86 Turkey v Northern Ireland, 1.4.87 England v Northern Ireland, 29.4.87 Northern Ireland v Yugoslavia, 29.4.87 Turkey v England, 14.10.87 Yugoslavia v Northern Ireland, 14.10.87 England v Turkey, 11.11.87 Yugoslavia v England, 11.11.87 Northern Ireland v Turkey, 16.12.87 Turkey v Yugoslavia.

Group 5 *(Netherlands, Hungary, Poland, Greece, Cyprus)*
15.10.86 Hungary v Netherlands, 15.10.86 Poland v Greece, 12.11.86 Greece v Hungary, 19.11.86 Netherlands v Poland, 3.12.86 Cyprus v Greece, 21.12.86 Cyprus v Netherlands, 14.1.87 Greece v Cyprus, 8.2.87 Cyprus v Hungary, 25.3.87 Netherlands v Greece, 12.4.87 Poland v Cyprus, 29.4.87 Greece v Poland, 29.4.87 Netherlands v Hungary, 17.5.87 Hungary v Poland, 23.9.87 Poland v Hungary, 14.10.87 Hungary v Greece, 14.10.87 Poland v Netherlands, 28.10.87 Netherlands v Cyprus, 11.11.87 Cyprus v Poland, 2.12.87 Hungary v Cyprus, 16.12.87 Greece v Netherlands.

Group 6 *(Denmark, Wales, Czechoslovakia, Finland)*
10.9.86 Finland v Wales, 15.10.86 Czechoslovakia v Finland, 29.10.86 Denmark v Finland, 12.11.86 Czechoslovakia v Denmark, 1.4.87 Wales v Finland, 29.4.87 Finland v Denmark, 29.4.87 Wales v Czechoslovakia, 3.6.87 Denmark v Czechoslovakia, 9.9.87 Wales v Denmark, 9.9.87 Finland v Czechoslovakia, 14.10.87 Denmark v Wales, 11.11.87 Czechoslovakia v Wales.

Group 7 *(Belgium, Bulgaria, Eire, Scotland, Luxembourg)*
10.9.86 Scotland v Bulgaria, 10.9.86 Belgium v Eire, 15.10.86 Luxembourg v Belgium, 15.10.86 Eire v Scotland, 12.11.86 Scotland v Luxembourg, 19.11.86 Belgium v Bulgaria, 18.2.87 Scotland v Eire, 1.4.87 Belgium v Scotland, 29.4.87 Eire v Belgium, 30.4.87 Luxembourg v Bulgaria, 20.5.87 Bulgaria v Luxembourg, 28.5.87 Luxembourg v Eire, 9.9.87 Eire v Luxembourg, 23.9.87 Bulgaria v Belgium, 14.10.87 Scotland v Belgium, 14.10.87 Eire v Bulgaria, 11.11.87 Belgium v Luxembourg, 11.11.87 Bulgaria v Scotland, 2.12.87 Luxembourg v Scotland.

WORLD CUP 1986

FINAL TOURNAMENT

GROUP A

Bulgaria (0) 1 *(Sirakov),* Italy (1) 1 *(Altobelli)* 105,000

Bulgaria: Mikhailov; Arabov, Zdravkov, Dimitrov, Markov A, Sirakov, Isrenov (Kostadinov), Sadkov, Mladenov, Gospodinov (Jeliaskov), Getov

Italy: Galli; Bergomi, Cabrini, De Napoli, Vierchowod, Scirea, Conti (Vialli), Di Gennaro, Galderisi, Bagni, Altobelli

Referee: E. Fredriksson (Sweden) Azteca, Mexico City, 31 May

Argentina (2) 3 *(Valdano 2, Ruggeri),* S. Korea (0) 1 *(Park Chang-Sun)* 62,000

Argentina: Pumpido; Clausen, Brown, Ruggeri, Garre, Giusti, Batista (Olarticoechea), Burruchaga, Pasculli (Tapia), Maradona, Valdano

S. Korea: Oh Yun-Kyo; Park Kyung-Hoon, Jung Yong-Hwan, Cho Min-Kook, Kim Yong-See (Byun Byung-Joo), Huh Jung-Moo, Kim Pyung-Suk (Cho Kwang-Rae), Park Chang-Sun, Choi Soon-Ho, Kim Joo-Sung, Cha Bum-Kun

Referee: Sanchez Arminio (Spain) Irapuato, 2 June

Italy (1) 1, *(Altobelli pen),* Argentina (1) 1, *(Maradona)* 30,000

Italy: Galli; Bergomi, Cabrini, De Napoli (Baresi), Vierchowod, Scirea, Conti (Vialli), Di Gennaro, Galderisi, Bagni, Altobelli

Argentina: Pumpido; Cuciuffo, Brown, Ruggeri, Garre, Giusti, Batista (Olarticoechea), Burruchaga, Borghi (Enrique), Maradon, Valdano

Referee: J. Keizer (Holland) Cuauhtemoc, Puebla, 5 June

S. Korea (0)1 *(Kim Jong-Boo),* Bulgaria (1) 1*(Getov)* 20,000

S. Korea: Oh Yun-Kyo; Park Kyung-Hoon, Jung Yong-Hwan, Cho Young-Jeung, Cho Kwang-Rae (Choe Min-Kook), Huh Jung-Moo, Park Chang-Sun, No Soo-Jin (Kim Jong-Boo), Byun Byung-Joo, Kim Joo-Sung, Cha Bum-Kun

Bulgaria: Mikhailov; Arabov, Zdravkov, Dimitrov, Petrov, Sirakov, Iskrenov, Sadkov, Mladenov, Gospodinov (Jeliaskov), Getov (Kostadinov)

Referee: F. Al-Shanar (Suadi Arabia) Olimpico '68, Mexico City, 5 June

Argentina (1) 2 *(Valdano, Burruchaga),* Bulgaria (0) 0 63,000

Argentina: Pumpido; Cuciuffo, Brown, Ruggeri, Garre, Giusti, Batista, (Enrique), Burruchaga, Borghi (Olarticoechea), Maradona, Valdano

Bulgaria: Mikhailov; Sirakov, Markov A, Dimitrov, Jordanov, Markov, P. Petrov, Jeliaskov, Mladenov (Velitchkov), Sadkov, Getov

Referee: B. Ulloa (Costa Rica) Olimpico '68, Mexico City, 10 June

S. Korea (0) 2 *(Choi Soon-Ho, Huh Jung-Moo)* Italy (1) 3 *(Altobelli 2, Cho Kwang-Rae (og))* 10,000

S. Korea: On Yun-Kyo; Park Kyung-Hoon, Jung Yong-Hwan, Cho Young-Jeung, Cho Kwang-Rae, Huh Jung-Moo, Park Chang-Sun, Byun Byung-Joo (Kim Jong-Boo), Cho Soon-Ho, Kim Joo-Sung (Chung Jong-Soo), Cha Bum-Kun

Italy: Galli; Collovati, Cabrini, De Napoli, Vierchowod, Scirea, Conti, Di Gennaro, Galderisi (Vialli), Bagni (Baresi), Altobelli

Referee: D. Socha (USA) Cuauhtemoc, Puebla, 10 June

GROUP B

Belgium (1) 1 *(Vandenbergh)*, Mexico (2) 2 *(Quirarte, Sanchez)* 100,000

Belgium: Pfaff; Gerets, Van der Elst F, Broos, De Wolf, Scifo, Vandereycken, Vercauteren, Desmet (Classen), Vandenbergh (Demol), Ceulemans

Mexico: Larios; Trejo, Quirarte, Felix Cruz, Servin, Munoz, Aguirre, Negrete, Boy (Espana), Sanchez, Flores (Javier Cruz)

Referee: C. Esposito (Argentina) Azteca, Mexico City, 3 June

Paraguay (1) 1 *(Romero)* Iraq (0) 0 12,500

Paraguay: Fernandez; Torales, Zabala, Schettina, Delgado, Nunez, Ferreira, Romero, Cabanas, Canete, Mendoza (Guasch)

Iraq: Hammoudi; Allawi, Shaker N, Shaker B, Hussein, Mohammed (Hameed), Radi, Saeed, Gorgis (Quassem), Hashem, Uraibi

Referee: S. Picon (Mauritius) Toluca, 4 June

Mexico (1) 1 *(Flores)*, Paraguay (0) 1 *(Romero)* 114,000

Mexico: Larios; Trejo, Quirarte, Felix Cruz, Servin, Munoz, Aguirre, Negrete, Boy (Espana), Sanchez, Flores (Javier Cruz)

Paraguay: Fernandez; Torales (Hicks), Zabala, Schettina, Delgado, Nunez, Ferreira, Romero, Cabanas, Canete, Mendoza (Guasch)

Referee: G. Courtney (England) Azteca, Mexico City, 7 June

Iraq (0) 1 *(Radi)*, Belgium (2) 2 *(Scifo, Claesen pen)* 11,200

Iraq: Hammoudi; Allawi, Shaker N, Shaker B, Hussein, Mohammed, Radi, Saddam (Hameed), Gorgis, Hashem, Uraibi

Belgium: Pfaff; Gerets, Van der Elst F, Demol (Grun), De Wolf, Scifo (Clysters), Vandereycken, Vercauteren, Desmet, Claesen, Ceulemans

Referee: J. Diaz (Columbia) Toluca, 8 June

Paraguay (0) 2*(Cabanas 2)*, Belgium (1) 2 *(Vercauteren, Veyt) 10,000*

Paraguay: Fernandez; Torales, Zabala, Delgado, Guasch, Nunez, Ferreira, Romero, Cabanas, Canete, Mendoza (Hicks)

Belgium: Pfaff; Grun (Van der Elst L), Broos, Renquin, Vervoort, Scifo, Demol, Ceulemans, Vercauteren, Veyt, Claesen

Referee: B. Dochev (Bulgaria) Toluca, 11 June

Iraq (0) 0 , Mexico (0) 1*(Quirarte)* 108,000

Iraq: Jasim; Majeed, Allawi, Nadhum, Hussein, Ghanem, Hashem, Radi, Abid (Shaker N), Minshed, Kassim (Hameed)

Mexico: Larios; Amador (Dominguez), Quirarte, Felix Cruz, Servin, De los Cobos (Javier Cruz), Aguirre, Negrete, Boy, Espana, Flores

Referee: Z. Petrovic (Yugoslavia) Azteca, Mexico City, 11 June

GROUP C

Canada (0) 0, France (0) 1 *(Papin)* 35,748

Canada: Dolan; Lenarduzzi, Wilson, Bridge, Samuel, Ragan, Valentine, Norman, James (Segota), Sweeny (Lowery), Vrablic

France: Bats; Amoros, Tusseau, Battiston, Bossis, Fernandez, Giresse, Tigana, Papin, Platini, Rocheteau (Stopyra)

Referee: Silva Arce (Chile) Leon, 1 June

USSR (3) 6 *(Yakovenko, Aleinikov, Belanov pen), Yaremchuk 2, Rodionov),* Hungary (0) 0 16,500

USSR: Dasayev; Larionov, Bessonov, Kuznetsov, Demyanenko, Yaremchuk, Yakovenko (Yevtushenko), Rats, Belanov (Rodionov), Zavarov, Aleinikov

Hungary: Disztip; Sallai, Roth (Burcsa), Garaga, Kardos, Kiprich, Nagy, Detari, Peter (Dajka), Esterhazy, Bognar

Referee: L. Agnolin (Italy) Irapuato, 2 June

France (0) 1 *(Fernandez),* USSR (0) 1 *(Rats)* 36,540

France: Bats, Amoros, Ayache, Battison, Bossis, Fernandez, Giresse (Vercruysse), Tigana, Papin (Bellone), Platini, Stopyra

USSR: Dasayev; Larionov, Bessonov, Kuznetsov, Demyanenko, Yaremchuk, Yakovenko, Rats, Belanov, Zavarov (Blokhin), Aleinikov

Referee: Arrpi Filho (Brazil) Leon, 5 June

Hungary (1) 2 *(Esterhazy, Detari),* Canada (0) 0 13,800

Hungary: Szendrei; Sallai, Varga, Garaba, Kardos, Kiprich, Nagy (Dajka), Detari, Burcsa (Roth), Esterhazy, Bognar

Canada: Lettieri; Lenarduzzi, Wilson (Sweeney), Bridge, Samuel, Ragan, Valentine, Norman, James (Segota), Gray, Vrablic

Referee: J. Al-Sharif (Syria) Irapuato, 6 June

Hungary (0) 0, France (1) 3 *(Stopyra, Tigana, Rocheteau)* 31,420

Hungary: Disztl P; Sallai, Roth, Varga, Kardos, Garaba, Hannich (Nagy), Detari, Dajka, Esterhazy, Kovacs (Bognar)

France: Bats; Ayache, Amoros, Battiston, Bossis, Fernandez, Giresse, Tigana, Papin (Rocheteau), Platini, Stopyra (Ferreri)

Referee: C. Silva (Portugal) Leon, 9 June

USSR (0) 2 *(Blokhin, Zavarov),* Canada (0) 0 14,200

USSR: Chanov; Morozov, Bubnov, Kuznetsov, Bal, Litovchenko, Yevtushenko, Aleinikov, Rodionov, Protasov (Belanov), Blokhin (Zavarov)

Canada: Lettieri; Lenarduzzi, Wilson, Bridge, Samuel, Ragan, Valentine, Norman, James (Segota), Gray (Pakos), Mitchell

Referee: I. Traore (Mali) Irapuato, 9 June

GROUP D

Spain (0) 0, Brazil (0) 1 *(Socrates)* 62,500

Spain: Zubizarreta; Tomas, Camacho, Maceda, Giocoechea, Julio Alberto, Michel, Victor, Butragueno, Francisco (Senor), Julio Salinas

Brazil: Carlos; Branco, Edson, Edhino, Julio Cesar, Junior (Falcao), Alemao, Casagrande (Muller), Careca, Socrates, Elzo

Referee: C. Bambridge (Australia) Jalisco, Guadalajara, 1 June

Algeria (0) 1 *(Zidane),* N. Ireland (1) 1 *(Whiteside)* 22,000

Algeria: Larbi; Medjadi, Mansouri, Kourichi, Guendoz, Kaci Said, Assad, Benmabrouk, Zidane (Belloumi), Maroc, Madjer (Harkouk)

N. Ireland: Jennings; Nicholl, Donaghy, O'Neill, McDonald, Worthington, Penney (Stewart), McIlroy, McCreery, Hamilton, Whiteside (Clarke)

Referee: V. Butenko (USSR) 3 de Marzo, Guadalajara, 3 June

N. Ireland (0) 1 *(Clarke),* Spain (2) 2 *(Butragueno, Salinas)* 30,000

N. Ireland: Jennings; Nicholl, Donaghy, O'Neill, McDonald, Worthington (Hamilton), Penney (Stewart), McIlroy, McCreery, Clarke, Whiteside

Spain: Zubizarreta; Tomas, Camacho, Gallego, Goicoechea, Gordillo (Caldere), Michel, Victor, Butragueno, Francisco, Julio Salinas (Senor)
Referee: H. Brummener (Austria) 3 de Marzo, Guadalajara, 7 June

Brazil (0) 1 *(Careca),* Algeria (0) 0 30,000
Brazil: Carlos; Edson (Falcao), Branco, Edinho, Cesar, Junior, Alemao, Casagrande (Muller), Careca, Socrates, Elzo
Algeria: Drid; Medjadi, Mansouri, Megharia, Guendouz, Kaci Said, Assa (Bensaoula), Benmabrouk, Menad, Belloumi (Zidane), Madjer
Referee: R. Molina (Guatemala) Jalisco, Guadalajara, 6 June

Algeria (0) 0, Spain (1) 3 *(Caldere 2, Eloy)* 20,000
Algeria: Drid (Larbi); Megharia, Mansouri, Kourichi, Guendouz, Kaci Said, Madjier, Maroc, Harkouk, Belloumi, Zidane (Menad)
Spain: Zubizarreta; Tomas, Camacho, Gallego, Goicoechea, Caldere, Michel (Senor), Victor, Butragueno (Eloy), Francisco, Julio Salinas
Referee: S. Takada (Japan) Tecnologico, Monterrey, 12 June

N. Ireland (0) 0, Brazil (2) 3 *(Careca 2, Josimar)* 51,000
N. Ireland: Jennings; Nicholl, Donaghy, O'Neill, McDonald, McCreery, McIlroy, Stewart, Clarke, Whiteside (Hamilton), Campbell (Armstrong)
Brazil: Carlos; Josimar, Julio Cesar, Edinho, Branco, Elzo, Alemao, Junior, Socrates (Zico), Muller (Casagrande), Careca
Referee: A. Kirschen (E. Germany) Jalisco, Guadalajara, 12 June

GROUP E
Uruguay (1) 1 *(Alzamendi),* W. Germany (0) 1 *(Allofs)* 32,000
Uruguay: Alvez; Gutierrez, Acevedo, Diogo, Bossio, Batista, Alzamendi (Ramos), Barrios (Saralegui), Da Silva, Francescoli, Santin
W. Germany: Schumacher; Briegel, Berthold, Forster, Augenthaler, Eder, Matthaus (Rummenigge), Magath, Brehme (Littbarski), Voller, Allofs
Referee: V. Christov (Czechoslovakia) La Corregidora, Queretaro, 4 June

Scotland (0) 0, Denmark (0) 1 *(Elkjaer)* 17,000
Scotland: Leighton; Gough, Malpas, Souness, McLeish, Miller, Strachan (Bannon), Aitken, Nicol, Nicholas, Sturrock (McAvennie)
Denmark: Rasmussen; Busk, Olsen M, Nielson, Lerby, Olsen J (Molby), Berggreen, Elkjaer, Laudrup, Bertelsen, Arnesen (Sivebaek)
Referee: L. Nemeth (Hungary) Neza '86 Nezahualcoyotl, 4 June

Denmark (2) 6 *(Elkjaer 3, Olsen J, Laudrup, Lerby),* Uruguay (1) 1*(Francescoli)* 20,000
Denamrk: Rasmussen; Busk, Olsen M, Nielson, Lerby, Andersen, Berggreen, Elkjaer, Laudrup (Olsen J.), Bertelsen (Molsby), Arnsen
Uruguay: Alvez; Gutierrez, Acevedo, Diogo, Bossio, Batista, Alzamendi (Ramos), Saralegui, Da Silva, Francescoli, Santin (Salazar)
Referee: A. Marquez (Mexico) Neza '86, Nezahualcoyotl, 8 June

W. Germany (1) 2 *(Voller, Allofs),* Scotland (1) 1 *(Strachan)* 35,000
W. Germany: Schumacher; Briegel (Jakobs), Berthold, Forster, Augenthaler, Eder, Matthaus, Magath, Littbarski (Rummenigge), Voller, Allofs
Scotland: Leighton; Gough, Malpas, Souness, Narey, Miller, Strachan, Aitken, Nicol (McAvennie), Archibald, Bannon (Cooper)
Referee: I. Igna (Romania) Corregidora, Queretaro, 8 June

Scotland (0) 0, Uruguay (0) 0 20,000

Scotland: Leighton; Gough, Albiston, Aitken, Narey, Miller, Strachan, McStay, Sharp, Nicol (Cooper), Sturrock (Nicholas)

Uruguay: Alvez; Diogo, Acevedo, Gutierrez, Pereyra, Batista, Ramos (Saralegui), Barrios, Cabrera, Francescoli (Alzamendi), Santin

Referee: J. Quiniou (France) Neza '86, Nezahualcoyotl, 13 June

Denmark (1) 2 *(Olsen J. pen, Eriksen),* W. Germany (0) 0 36,000

Denmark: Hogh; Sivebaek, Busk, Olsen M, Andersen, Arnesen, Lerby, Molby, Laudrup, Olsen J. (Simonsen), Elkjaer (Eriksen)

W. Germany: Schumacher; Berthold, Jakobs, Forster (Rummenigge), Herget, Eder, Brehme, Matthaus, Voller, Rolff (Littbarski), Allofs

Referee: A. Ponnet (Belgium) Queretaro, 13 June

GROUP F

Morocco (0) 0, Poland (0) 0 19,900

Morocco: Zaki; Labd, Lemriss, El-Biyaz, Bouyahiaoui, Mustapha El-Haddaoui (Souleimani), Dolmy, Bouderbala, Krimau, Timoumi (Khairi), Merry

Poland: Mlynarczyk; Ostrowski, Wojcicki, Majewski, Matysik, Kubicki, Komornicki (Przybys), Buncol, Smolarek, Dziekanowski (Urban), Boniek

Referee: Martinez Bazan (Uruguay) Universitario, Monterrey, 2 June

Portugal (0) 1 *(Carlos Manuel),* England (0) 0 19,998

Portugal: Bento; Alvaro, Frederico, Oliveira, Inacio, Diamantino (Jose Antonio), Andre, Carlos Manuel, Pacheco, Sousa, Gomes, (Futre)

England: Shilton; Stevens, Sansom, Hoddle, Fenwick, Butcher, Robson (Hodge), Wilkins, Hateley, Lineker, Waddle (Beardsley)

Referee: V. Roth (West Germany) Technologico, Monterrey, 3 June

England (0) 0, Morocco (0) 0 22,600

England: Shilton; Stevens, Sansom, Hoddle, Fenwick, Butcher, Robson (Hodge), Wilkins, Hateley (Stevens GA), Lineker, Waddle

Morocco: Zaki; Labd, Lemriss (Heina), El-Biyaz, Bouyahiaoui, Khairi, Dolmy, Bouderbala, Krimau, Timoumi, Merry (Souleimani)

Referee: G. Gonzalez (Paraguay) Technologico, Monterrey, 6 June

Poland (0) 1, *(Smolarek)* Portugal (0) 0 19,915

Poland: Mlynarczyk; Ostrowski, Wojcicki, Majewski, Matysik, Urban, Komornicki (Karas), Pawlak, Smolarek (Zgutczynski), Dziekanowski, Boniek

Portugal: Damas; Alvaro, Frederico, Oliveira, Inacio, Diamantino, Andre (Magalhaes), Carlos Manuel, Pacheco, Sousa, Gomes (Futre)

Referee: Ali ben Nasser (Tunisia) Universitario, Monterrey, 7 June

England (3) 3 *(Lineker 3),* Poland (0) 0 22,600

England: Shilton; Stevens, Sansom, Hoddle, Fenwick, Butcher, Steven, Reid, Lineker (Dixon), Beardsley (Waddle), Hodge

Poland: Mlynarczyk; Ostrowski, Wojcicki, Matysik (Buncol), Urban, Majewski, Smolerek, Komonicki (Karas), Pawlak, Dziekanowski, Boniek

Referee: A.Daina (Switzerland) Universitario, Monterrey, 11 June

Portugal (0) 1 *(Diamantino),* Morocco (2) 3 *(Khairi 2, Krimau)* 28,000

Portugal: Damas; Alvaro (Aguas), Frederico, Oliveira, Inacio, Magalhaes, Carlos Manuel, Pacheco, Sousa (Diamantino), Gomes, Futre

Morocco: Zaki; Labd, Lemriss, El-Biyas, Bouyahiaoui, Dolmy, Mustapha El-Haddaoui (Souleimani), Bouderbala, Krimau, Timoumi, Khairi
Referee: A.Snoddy (N. Ireland) 3 de Marzo, Guadalajara, 11 June

SECOND ROUND

Mexico (1) 2 *(Negrete, Servin),* Bulgaria (0) 0 114,580
Mexico: Larios; Amador, Quirarte, Felix Cruz, Servin, Espana, Aguirre, Munoz, Boy (De los Cobos), Sanchez, Negrete
Bulgaria: Mikhailov; Arabov, Zdravkov, Dimitrov, Petrov, Jordanov, Sadkov, Kostadinov, Getov (Sirakov), Gospodinov, Paschev (Iskrenov)
Referee: Arppi Filho (Brazil) Azteca, Mexico City, 15 June

USSR (1) 3 *(Belanov 3, 1 pen),* Belgium (0) 4 *(Scifo, Ceulemans, Demol, Claesen)* 32,000
(aet; 90 mins 2-2)
USSR: Dasayev; Bessonov, Bal, Kuznetsov, Demyanenko, Yaremchuk, Yakovenko (Yevtushenko), Aleinikov, Rats, Belanov, Zavarov (Rodionov)
Belgium: Pfaff; Gerets, Grun (Clijsters), Vervoort, Demol, Renquin, Scifo, Vercauteren, Claesen, Veyt, Ceulemans
Referee: E.Fredriksson (Sweden) Leon, 15 June

Brazil (1) 4 *(Socrates pen, Josimar, Edinho, Careca pen),* Poland (0) 0 35,000
Brazil: Carlos; Josimar, Branco, Edinho, Julio Cesar, Alemao, Muller (Silas), Socrates (Zico), Careca, Junior, Elzo
Poland: Mlynarczyk; Ostrowski, Majewski, Wojcicki, Przybys (Furtok), Urban (Zmuda), Karas, Tarasiewicz, Dziekanowski, Boniek, Smolarek
Referee: V.Roth (West Germany) Jalisco, Guadalajara, 16 June

Argentina (1) 1 *(Pasculli),* Uruguay (0) 0 26,000
Argentina: Pumpido; Cuciuffo, Brown, Garre, Giusti, Ruggeri, Batista (Olaricoechea), Burruchaga, Pasculli, Maradona, Valdano
Uruguay: Alvez; Rivero, Bossio, Gutierrez, Acevedo (Paz), Pereyra, Ramos, Cabrera (Da Silva), Francescoli, Barrios, Santin
Referee: L.Agnolin (Italy) Cuauhtemoc, Puebla, 16 June

France (1) 2 *(Platini, Stopyra)* Italy (0) 0 71,449
France: Bats; Ayache, Amoros, Battiston, Bossis, Fernandez (Tusseau), Giresse, Tigana, Rocheteau, Platini (Ferreri), Stopyra
Italy: Galli; Bergomi, Cabrini, De Napoli, Vierchowod, Scirea, Conti, Bagni, Galderisi (Vialli), Baresi (Di Gennaro), Altobelli
Referee: C.Esposito (Argentina) Olimpico '68, Mexico City, 17 June

Morocco (0) 0, W. Germany (0) 1 *(Matthaus)* 21,000
Morocco: Zaki; Labd, Lemriss, Bouyahiaoui, Dolmy, Mustapha El-Haddaoui, Bouderbala, Krimau, Timoumi, Hcina, Khairi
W. Germany: Schumacher; Berthold, Briegel, Jakobs, Forster, Eder, Matthaus, Rummenigge, Voller (Littbarski), Magath, Allofs
Referee: Z.Petrovic (Yugoslavia) Universitario, Monterrey, 17 June

England (1) 3 *(Lineker 2, Beardsley),* Paraguay (0) 0 98,000
England: Shilton; Stevens, Sansom, Hoddle, Martin, Butcher, Steven, Reid (Stevens GA), Lineker, Beardsley (Hateley), Hodge
Paraguay: Fernandez; Torales (Guasch), Zabala, Schettina, Delgado, Nunez, Ferreira, Romero, Cabanas, Canete, Mendoza

Referee: J.Al-Sharif (Syria) Azteca, Mexico City, 18 June

Denmark (1) 1 *(Olsen J pen),* Spain (1) 5 *(Butragueno 4, 1 pen, Goicoechea pen)* 37,000
Denmark: Hogh; Andersen (Eriksen), Olsen M, Busk, Nielsen, Lerby, Olsen J (Molby), Bertelsen, Laudrup, Berggreen, Elkjaer
Spain: Zubizarreta; Tomas, Camacho, Gallego, Goicoechea, Julio Alberto, Victor, Michel (Francisco), Butragueno, Caldere, Julio Salinas (Eloy)
Referee: J.Keizer (Holland) Queretaro, 18 June

QUARTER-FINALS

France (1) 1 *(Platini),* Brazil (1) 1 *(Careca)* 66,000
France: Bats; Amoros, Bossis, Battiston, Tusseau, Tigana, Giresse (Ferreri), Platini, Fernandez, Stopyra, Rocheteau (Bellone)
Brazil: Carlos; Josimar, Julio Cesar, Edinho, Branco, Elzo, Alemao, Socrates, Junior (Silas), Muller (Zico), Careca
France won 4-3 on penalties
Referee: I. Igna (Rumania) Jalisco, Guadalajara, 21 June

West Germany (0), 0 Mexico (0) 0 44,386
West Germany: Schumacher; Jakobs, Eder (Littbarski), Berthold, Forster, Briegal, Matthaus, Magath, Brehme, Rummenigge (Hoeness), Allofs
Mexico: Larios; Servin, Cruz Barbosa, Quirarte, Amador, (Cruz), Munoz, Boy (De los Cobos), Espana, Aguirre, Negrete, Sanchez
West Germany won 4-1 on penalties
Referee: Jesus Diaz (Colombia) Universitario, Monterrey, 21 June

Argentina (0) 2 *(Maradona 2),* England (0) 1 *(Lineker)* 114,580
Argentina: Pumpido; Ruggeri, Brown, Cuciuffo, Giusti, Batista, Burruchaga (Tapia), Enrique, Olarticoechea, Valdan, Maradona
England: Shilton; Stevens, Sansom, Butcher, Fenwick, Steven (Barnes), Hoddle, Reid (Waddle), Hodge, Lineker, Beardsley
Referee: Ali ben Nasser (Tunisia) Azteca, Mexico City, 22 June

Belgium (1) 1 *(Ceulemans),* Spain (0) 1 *Senor)* 45,00
Belgium: Pfaff; Gerets, Renquin, De Mol, Vervoort, Scifo, Ceulemans, Grun, Vercauteren (L. Van der Elst), Veyt (Broos), Claesen
Spain: Zubizarreta; Tomas (Senor), Gallego, Camacho, Chendo, Victor, Caldere, Michel, Julio Alberto, Salinas (Eloy), Butragueno
Belgium won 5-4 on penalties
Referee: A. Kirschen (East Germany) Puebla, 22 June

SEMI-FINALS

Argentina (0) 2 *(Maradona 2),* Belgium (0) 0 110,420
Argentina: Pumpido; Ruggeri, Brown, Cuciuffo, Giusti, Enrique, Batista, Burruchaga (Bochini), Olarticoechea, Valdano, Maradona
Belgium: Pfaff; Gerets, Renquin (Desmet), De Mol, Vervoot, Scifo, Veyt, Broos, Ceulemans, Vercauterren, Claesen
Referee: A. Marquez (Mexico) Azteca, Mexico City, 25 June

P.F.A.86.87.—8

West Germany (1) 2 *(Brehme, Voller),* France (0) 0 45,000

West Germany: Schumacher; Jakobs, Brehme, Forster, Briegel, Eder, Matthaus, Magath, Rolff, Rummenigge (Voller), Allofs

France: Bats; Ayache, Bossis, Battiston, Amoros, Fernandez, Giresse (Vercruysse), Tigana, Platini, Bellone (Xuereb), Stopyra

Referee: L. Agnolin (Italy) Jalisco, Guadalajara, 25 June

THIRD PLACE MATCH

France (2) 4 *(Ferreri, Papin, Genghini, Amoros),* Belgium (1) 2 *(Ceulemans, Claesen)* 21,500

France: Rust; Ayache, Battiston, Le Roux (Bossis), Amoros, Bibard, Ferreri, Tigana (Tusseau), Genghini, Papin, Bellone

Belgium: Pfaff; Gerets, Renquin (F. Van der Elst), De Mol, Vervoort, Scifo (L. Van der Elst), Grun, Mommens, Ceulemans, Veyt, Claesen
After extra time, 90 mins 2-2

Referee: G. Courtney (England) Puebla, 28 June

FINAL

Argentina (1) 3 *(Brown, Valdano, Burruchaga),* West Germany (0) 2 *(Rummenigge, Voller)* 115,000

Argentina: Pumpido; Ruggeri, Brown, Cuciuffo, Giusti, Enrique, Batista, Burruchaga (Trobbiani), Olarticoechea, Valdano, Maradona

West Germany: Schumacher; Brehme, Jakobs, K. Forster, Berthold, Matthaus, Magath (Hoeness), Eder, Briegel, Rummenigge, Allofs (Voller).

Referee: Arripi Filho (Brazil) Azteca, Mexico City, 29 June

WORLD CUP LEADING GOAL SCORERS

6 – Lineker (England); 5 – Butragueno (Spain), Careca (Brazil), Maradona (Argentina); 4 – Altobelli (Italy), Belanov (USSR), Elkjaer (Denmark), Valdano (Argentina); 3 – Ceulemans (Belgium), Claesen (Belgium), Jesper Olsen (Denmark), Voller (West Germany).

WORLD CUP 1986
THE QUALIFYING COMPETITION

EUROPE

Group 1 (Albania, Belgium, Greece, Poland)

Belgium (0) 3, Albania (0) 1	17 October 1984
Poland (0) 3, Greece (1) 1	17 October 1984
Poland (1) 2, Albania (0) 2	31 October 1984
Greece (0) 0, Belgium (0) 0	19 December 1984
Albania (0) 2, Belgium (0) 0	22 December 1984
Greece (2) 2, Albania (0) 0	27 February 1985
Belgium (0) 2, Greece (0) 0	27 March 1985
Belgium (1) 2, Poland (0) 0	1 May 1985
Greece (0) 1, Poland (1) 4	19 May 1985
Albania (0) 0, Poland (1) 1	30 May 1985
Poland (0) 0, Belgium (0) 0	11 September 1985
Albania (1) 1, Greece (0) 1	30 October 1985

Final Table	P	W	D	L	F	A	Pts	GD
Poland	6	3	2	1	10	6	8	+4
Belgium	6	3	2	1	7	3	8	+4
Albania	6	1	2	3	6	9	4	–3
Greece	6	1	2	3	5	10	4	–5

Group 2 (Czechoslovakia, Malta, Portugal, Sweden, West Germany)

Sweden (2) 4, Malta (0) 0	23 May 1984
Sweden (0) 0, Portugal (0) 1	12 September 1984
Portugal (1) 2, Czechoslovakia (1) 1	14 October 1984
West Germany (0) 2, Sweden (0) 0	17 October 1984
Czechoslovakia (2) 4, Malta (0) 0	31 October 1984
Portugal (1) 1, Sweden (3) 3	14 November 1984
Malta (1) 2, West Germany (1) 3	16 December 1984
Malta (0) 1, Portugal (2) 3	11 February 1985
Portugal (0) 1, West Germany (2) 2	24 February 1985
West Germany (5) 6, Malta (0) 0	27 March 1985
Malta (0) 0, Czechoslovakia (0) 0	21 April 1985
Czechoslovakia (0) 1, West Germany (4) 5	1 May 1985
Sweden (0) 2, Czechoslovakia (0) 0	5 June 1985
Sweden (0) 2, West Germany (2) 2	25 September 1985
Czechoslovakia (1) 1, Portugal (0) 0	25 September 1985
Portugal (1) 3, Malta (0) 2	12 October 1985
Czechoslovakia (1) 2, Sweden (1) 1	16 October 1985
West Germany (0) 0, Portugal (0) 1	16 October 1985
West Germany (1) 2, Czechoslovakia (0) 2	17 November 1985
Malta (0) 1, Sweden (1) 2	17 November 1985

Final Table	P	W	D	L	F	A	Pts	GD
West Germany	8	5	2	1	22	9	12	+13
Portugal	8	5	0	3	12	10	10	+2
Sweden	8	4	1	3	14	9	9	+5
Czechoslovakia	8	3	2	3	11	12	8	–1
Malta	8	0	1	7	6	25	1	–19

Group 3 (England, Finland, Northern Ireland, Rumania, Turkey)

Finland (0) 1 (Valvee) — Pori, att. 8115
Northern Ireland (0) 0 — 27 May 1984

Northern Ireland (1) 3 (Iorgulescu og, Whiteside, O' Neill) — Belfast, att. 18,000
Rumania (1) 2 (Hagi, Geolgau) — 12 September 1984

England (2) 5 (Hateley 2, Woodcock, Robson, Sansom) — Wembley, att. 47,234
Finland (0) 0 — 17 October 1984

Turkey (0) 1, Finland (1) 2 — 31 October 1984

Northern Ireland (1) 2 (J. O' Neill, Armstrong) — Belfast, att. 25,000
Finland (1) 1 (Lipponen) — 14 November 1984

Turkey (0) 0 — Istanbul, att. 40,000
England (3) 8 (Robson 3, Woodcock 2, Barnes 2, Anderson) — 14 November 1984

Northern Ireland (0) 0 — Belfast, att. 28,000
England (0) 1 (Hateley) — 27 February 1985
Rumania (3) 3, Turkey (0) 0 — 3 April 1985

Northern Ireland (1) 2 (Whiteside 2) — Belfast, att 18,000
Turkey (0) 0 — 1 May 1985

Rumania (0) 0 — Bucharest, att. 70,000
England (0) 0 — 1 May 1985

Finland (1) 1 (Rantanen) — Helsinki, att. 30,000
England (0) 1 (Hateley) — 22 May 1985

Finland (1) 1, Rumania (1) 1 — 6 June 1985
Rumania (1) 2, Finland (0) 0 — 28 August 1985

Turkey (0) 0 — Izmir, att. 42,500
Northern Ireland (0) 0 — 11 September 1985
Turkey: Yasar; Ismail, Rasit, Sedat, Erdogan, Ilyas (Bahattin), Mujdat, Hasan, Metin, Senol, Erdal (Tanju).
Northern Ireland: Jennings; Nicholl J., McClelland, O'Neill, Donaghy, Ramsey, Quinn, McIlroy (McCreery), Penney, Armstrong, Worthington.

England (1) 1 (Hoddle) — Wembley, att. 59,500
Rumania (0) 1 (Camataru) — 11 September 1985
England: Shilton; Stevens, Wright, Fenwick, Sansom, Hoddle, Robson, Reid, Hateley, Lineker (Woodcock), Waddle (Barnes).
Rumania: Lung; Negrila, Stefanescu, Ungureanu, Rednic, Iovan, Coras (Gabor), Klein (Mateut), Camataru, Boloni, Hagi.

Finland (1) 1, Turkey (0) 0 — 25 September 1985

Rumania (0) 0 — Bucharest, att. 45,000
Northern Ireland (1) 1 (Quinn) — 16 October 1985
Rumania: Lung; Negrila (Geolgau), Iovan, Ungureanu, Mateut, Iorgulescu, Rednic, Klein, Coras (Piturca), Boloni, Hagi.
Northern Ireland: Jennings; Nicholl J., Donaghy, O'Neill J., McDonald, McCreery, Penney (Armstrong), McIlroy, Quinn, Whiteside, Stewart (Worthington).

England (4) 5 (Waddle, Lineker 3, Robson) — Wembley, att. 52,500
Turkey (0) 0 — 16 October 1985
England: Shilton; Stevens, Wright, Fenwick, Sansom, Hoddle, Wilkins, Robson (Steven), Lineker, Hateley (Woodcock), Waddle.
Turkey: Yasar; Ismail, Yusuf, Rasit, Sedat, Abdulkerim, Huseyin, Mujdat, Senol (Hasan Sengun), Hasan, Vezir, Selcuk.

England (0) 0 — Wembley, att. 70,500
Northern Ireland (0) 0 — 13 November 1985
England: Shilton; Stevens, Sansom, Hoddle, Wright, Fenwick, Bracewell, Wilkins, Dixon, Lineker, Waddle.
Northern Ireland: Jennings; Nicholl J., Donaghy, O'Neill, McDonald, McCreery, Penney (Armstrong), McIlroy, Quinn, Whiteside, Stewart (Worthington).

Turkey (0) 1, Rumania (2) 3 — 13 November 1985

Final Table	P	W	D	L	F	A	Pts	GD
England	8	4	4	0	21	2	12	+19
Northern Ireland	8	4	2	2	8	5	10	+3
Rumania	8	3	3	2	12	7	9	+5
Finland	8	3	2	3	7	12	8	−5
Turkey	8	0	1	7	2	24	1	−22

Group 4 (East Germany, France, Luxembourg, Yugoslavia)

Yugoslavia (0) 0, Bulgaria (0) 0	29 September 1984
Luxembourg (0) 0, France (4) 4	13 October 1984
East Germany (1) 2, Yugoslavia (1) 3	20 October 1984
Luxembourg (0) 0, East Germany (0) 5	17 November 1984
France (0) 1, Bulgaria (0) 0	21 November 1984
Bulgaria (2) 4, Luxembourg (0) 0	5 December 1984
France (1) 2, East Germany (0) 0	8 December 1984
Yugoslavia (1) 1, Luxembourg (0) 0	27 March 1985
Yugoslavia (0) 0, France (0) 0	3 April 1985
Bulgaria (0) 1, East Germany (0) 0	6 April 1985
Luxembourg (0) 0, Yugoslavia (0) 1	1 May 1985
Bulgaria (1) 2, France (0) 0	2 May 1985
East Germany (3) 3, Luxembourg (0) 1	18 May 1985
Bulgaria (1) 2, Yugoslavia (1) 1	1 June 1985
East Germany (0) 2, France (0) 0	11 September 1985
Luxembourg (0) 1, Bulgaria (3) 3	25 September 1985
Yugoslavia (0) 1, East Germany (0) 2	28 September 1985
France (4) 6, Luxembourg (0) 0	30 October 1985
France (1) 2, Yugoslavia (0) 0	16 November 1985
East Germany (2) 2, Bulgaria (1) 1	16 November 1985

Final Table	P	W	D	L	F	A	Pts	GD
France	8	5	1	2	15	4	11	+11
Bulgaria	8	5	1	2	13	5	11	+8
East Germany	8	5	0	3	16	9	10	+7
Yugoslavia	8	3	2	3	7	8	8	−1
Luxembourg	8	0	0	8	2	27	0	−25

Group 5 (Austria, Cyprus, Hungary, Netherlands)

Cyprus (0) 1, Austria (1) 2	2 May 1984
Hungary (0) 3, Austria (1) 1	26 September 1984
Netherlands (1) 1, Hungary (1) 2	17 October 1984
Austria (1) 1, Netherlands (0) 0	14 November 1984
Cyprus (1) 1, Hungary (0) 2	17 November 1984
Cyprus (0) 0, Netherlands (0) 1	23 December 1984
Netherlands (3) 7, Cyprus (1) 1	27 February 1985
Hungary (0) 2, Cyprus (0) 0	3 April 1985
Austria (0) 0, Hungary (2) 3	17 April 1985
Netherlands (0) 1, Austria (0) 1	1 May 1985
Austria (2) 4, Cyprus (0) 0	7 May 1985
Hungary (0) 0, Netherlands (0) 1	14 May 1985

Final Table	P	W	D	L	F	A	Pts	GD
Hungary	6	5	0	1	12	4	10	+8
Netherlands	6	3	1	2	11	5	7	+6
Austria	6	3	1	2	9	8	7	+1
Cyprus	6	0	0	6	3	18	0	−15

Group 6 (Denmark, Eire, Norway, Switzerland, USSR)

Eire (0) 1 (Walsh) — Dublin, att. 28,000
USSR (0) 0 — 12 September 1984

Norway (0) 0, Switzerland (1) 1 — 12 September 1984
Denmark (1) 1, Norway (0) 0 — 26 September 1984
Norway (0) 1, USSR (0) 1 — 10 October 1984
Switzerland (1) 1, Denmark (0) 0 — 17 October 1984

Norway (1) 1 (P. Jacobsen) — Oslo, att. 12,468
Eire (0) 0 — 17 October 1984

Denmark (1) 3 (Elkjaer 2, Lerby) — Copenhagen, att. 45,300
Eire (0) 0 — 14 November 1984

Switzerland (1) 2, USSR (1) 2 — 17 April 1985

Eire (0) 0 — Dublin, att. 16,000
Norway (0) 0 — 1 May 1985

USSR (4) 4, Switzerland (0) 0 — 2 May 1985

Eire (2) 3 (Sheedy, Stapleton, Grealish) — Dublin, att. 20,000
Switzerland (0) 0 — 2 June 1985

Denmark (2) 4, USSR (1) 2 — 5 June 1985

Switzerland (0) 0 — Berne, att. 24,000
Eire (0) 0 — 11 September 1985
Switzerland: Engel; Schallibaum (Brigger), In-Albon, Egli, Geiger, Hermann, Perret, Koller, Luthi, Bregy, Matthey.
Eire: McDonagh; Hughton, Beglin, McCarthy, O'Leary, Brady, Daly (McGrath), Lawrenson, Cascarino, Stapleton, Sheedy (O'Callaghan).

USSR (0) 1, Denmark (0) 0 — 25 September 1985
Denmark (0) 0, Switzerland (0) 0 — 9 October 1985
Norway (1) 1, Denmark (0) 5 — 16 October 1985

USSR (0) 2 (Cherenkov, Protasov) — Moscow, att. 100,000
Eire (0) 0 — 16 October 1985
USSR: Dasayev; Morozov, Chivadze, Demianenko, Bubnov, Zavarov (Bessonov), Gotsmanov, Cherenkov, Aleinikov, Protasov, Blohkin (Kondratiev).
Eire: McDonagh; Hughton, Beglin (O'Callaghan), McCarthy, O'Leary, Brady, Waddock, Lawrenson, Cascarino, Stapleton, Grealish (Whelan).

USSR (0) 1, Norway (0) 0 — 30 October 1985
Switzerland (0) 1, Norway (1) 1 — 13 November 1985

Eire (1) 1 (Stapleton) — Dublin, att. 12,000
Denmark (2) 4 (Elkjaer 2, Laudrup, Siveback) — 13 November 1985
Eire: McDonagh; Lawrenson, Beglin, Moran, O'Leary, Brady, McGrath, Grealish (Byrne P.), Cascarino, Stapleton, Sheedy (Robinson).
Denmark: Rasmussen; Siveback, Busk, Olsen M. (Arnesen), Nielsen, Lerby (Bertelsen), Molby, Olsen J., Berggren, Elkjaer, Laudrup.

Final Table	P	W	D	L	F	A	Pts	GD
Denmark	8	5	1	2	17	6	11	+11
USSR	8	4	2	2	13	8	10	+5
Switzerland	8	2	4	2	5	10	8	−5
Eire	8	2	2	4	5	10	6	−5
Norway	8	1	3	4	4	10	5	−6

Group 7 (Iceland, Scotland, Spain, Wales)

Iceland (0) 1 (Bergs) — Reykjavic, att. 14,500
Wales (0) 0 — 12 September 1984

Spain (1) 3 (Rincon, Carrasco, Butragueno) — Seville, att. 42,500
Wales (0) 0 — 17 October 1984

Scotland (2) 3 (McStay 2, Nicholas) — Glasgow, att. 52,829
Iceland (0) 0 — 17 October 1984

Scotland (2) 3 (Johnston 2, Dalglish) — Glasgow, att. 74,299
Spain (0) 1 (Goicoechea) — 14 November 1984

Wales (1) 2 (Thomas, Hughes) — Cardiff, att. 10,506
Iceland (0) 1 (Petursson) — 14 November 1984

Spain (0) 1 (Clos) — Seville, att. 70,000
Scotland (0) 0 — 27 February 1985

Scotland (0) 0 — Glasgow, att. 62,424
Wales (1) 1 (Rush) — 27 March 1985

Wales (1) 3 (Rush 2, Hughes) — Wrexham, att. 23,494
Spain (0) 0 — 30 April 1985

Iceland (0) 0 — Reykjavic, att. 16,000
Scotland (0) 1 (Bett) — 28 May 1985

Iceland (1) 1, Spain (0) 2 — 12 June 1985

Wales (1) 1 (Hughes) — Cardiff, att. 39,500
Scotland (0) 1 (Cooper, pen) — 10 September 1985
Wales: Southall; Jones J., Van den Hauwe, Ratcliffe, Jackett, James R. (Lovell), Phillips, Nicholas, Thomas (Blackmore), Rush, Hughes.
Scotland: Leighton (Rough); Gough, Malpas, Aitken, McLeish, Miller, Nicol, Strachan (Cooper), Sharp, Bett, Speedie.

Spain (1) 2, Iceland (1) 1 — 25 September 1985

Final Table	P	W	D	L	F	A	Pts	GD
Spain	6	4	0	2	9	8	8	+1
Scotland	6	3	1	2	8	4	7	+4
Wales	6	3	1	2	7	6	7	+1
Iceland	6	1	0	5	4	10	2	−6

EUROPEAN PLAY-OFF

Belgium (0) 1, Netherlands (0) 0	16 October 1985
Netherlands (0) 2, Belgium (0) 1	20 November 1985

Belgium qualify on away goals

SOUTH AMERICA

Group 1 (Argentina, Colombia, Peru, Venezuela)

Colombia (1) 1, Peru (0) 0	26 May 1985
Venezuela (1) 2, Argentina (2) 3	26 May 1985
Colombia (0) 1, Argentina (1) 3	2 June 1985
Venezuela (0) 0, Peru (0) 1	2 June 1985
Argentina (1) 3, Venezuela (0) 0	9 June 1985
Peru (0) 0, Colombia (0) 0	9 June 1985
Argentina (1) 1, Colombia (0) 0	16 June 1985
Peru (2) 4, Venezuela (1) 1	16 June 1985
Peru (1) 1, Argentina (0) 0	23 June 1985
Venezuela (1) 2, Colombia (1) 2	23 June 1985
Argentina (1) 2, Peru (2) 2	30 June 1985
Colombia (2) 2, Venezuela (0) 0	30 June 1985

	P	W	D	L	F	A	Pts
Argentina	6	4	1	1	12	6	9
Peru	6	3	2	1	8	4	8
Colombia	6	2	2	2	6	6	6
Venezuela	6	0	1	5	5	15	1

Group 2 (Chile, Ecuador, Uruguay)

Ecuador (1) 1, Chile (1) 1	3 March 1985
Uruguay (1) 2, Ecuador (0) 1	10 March 1985
Chile (4) 6, Ecuador (2) 2	17 March 1985
Chile (1) 2, Uruguay (0) 0	24 March 1985
Ecuador (0) 0, Uruguay (2) 2	31 March 1985
Uruguay (1) 2, Chile (1) 1	7 April 1985

	P	W	D	L	F	A	Pts
Uruguay	4	3	0	1	6	4	6
Chile	4	2	1	1	10	5	5
Ecuador	4	0	1	3	4	11	1

Group 3 (Bolivia, Brazil, Paraguay)

Bolivia (1) 1, Paraguay (0) 1	26 May 1985
Bolivia (0) 0, Brazil (0) 2	2 June 1985
Paraguay (2) 3, Bolivia (0) 0	9 June 1985
Paraguay (0) 0, Brazil (1) 2	16 June 1985
Brazil (1) 1, Paraguay (1) 1	23 June 1985
Brazil (1) 1, Bolivia (0) 1	30 June 1985

	P	W	D	L	F	A	Pts
Brazil	4	2	2	0	6	2	6
Paraguay	4	1	2	1	5	4	4
Bolivia	4	0	2	2	2	7	2

PLAY-OFF MATCHES

Paraguay (2) 3, Colombia (0) 0	27 October 1985
Chile (3) 4, Peru (1) 2	27 October 1985
Colombia (0) 2, Paraguay (0) 1	3 November 1985
Peru (0) 0, Chile (0) 1	3 November 1985

Play-Off Final

Paraguay (1) 3, Chile (0) 0	10 November 1985
Chile (1) 2, Paraguay (2) 2	17 November 1985

CONCACAF

First Round *(Cup System)*

Group 1

29.7.84	San Salvador	El Salvador (4) 5, Puerto Rico (0) 0
5.8.84	San Juan	Puerto Rico (0) 0, San Salvador (2) 3
	Canada v Jamaica – *Jamaica expelled 14.3.84*	
29.9.84	Curacao	Neth. Antilles (0) 0, USA (0) 0
6.10.84	St Louis	USA (0) 4, Neth. Antilles (0) 0

Group 2

Barbados v Costa Rica – *Barbados withdrew 7.3.84*

15.6.84	Colon	Panama (0) 0, Honduras (2) 3
24.6.84	Tegucigalpa	Honduras (0) 1, Panama (0) 0
	Guatemala – *walkover*	

Group 3

Trinidad/Tobago v Grenada – *Grenada withdrew 24.2.84*

4.8.84	Port-au-Prince	Antigua (0) 0, Haiti (2) 4
7.8.84	Port-au-Prince	Haiti (1) 1, Antigua (1) 2
15.8.84	Paramaribo	Surinam (1) 1, Guyana (0) 0
29.8.84	Georgetown	Guyana (1) 1, Surinam (0) 1

Second Round *(League System)*

Group 1

24.2 85	San Salvador	Surinam (0) 0, El Salvador (1) 3
27.2.85	San Salvador	El Salvador (0) 3, Surinam (0) 0
3.3.85	Tegucigalpa	Surinam (1) 1, Honduras (1) 1
6.3.85	Tegucigalpa	Honduras (1) 2, Surinam (0) 1
10.3.85	San Salvador	El Salvador (0) 1, Honduras (1) 2
14.3.85	Tegucigalpa	Honduras (0) 0, El Salvador (0) 0

Honduras qualified for third round

Group 2

13.4.85	Vancouver	Canada (2) 2, Haiti (0) 0
20.4.85	Vancouver	Canada (2) 2, Guatemala (0) 1
26.4.86	Port-au-Prince	Haiti (0) 0, Guatemala (0) 1
5.5.85	Guatemala	Guatemala (1) 1, Canada (1) 1
8.5.85	Port-au-Prince	Haiti (0) 0, Canada (1) 2
15.5.85	Guatemala	Guatemala (0) 4, Haiti (0) 0

Canada qualified for third round

Group 3

24.4.85	San Jose	Trinidad/Tobago (Q) 0, Costa Rica (1) 3
24.4.85	San Jose	Costa Rica (1) 1, Trinidad/Tobago (0) 1
15.5.85	St Louis	Trinidad/Tobago (1) 1, USA (1) 2
19.5.85	Los Angeles	USA (1) 1, Trinidad/Tobago (0) 0
26.5.85	San Jose	Costa Rica (1) 1, USA (1) 1
31.5.85	Los Angeles	USA (0) 0, Costa Rica (1) 1

Costa Rica qualified for third round

Third Round *(League System)*

11.8.85	San Jose	Costa Rica (1) 2, Honduras (2) 2
17.8.85	Toronto	Canada (0) 1, Costa Rica (1) 1
25.8.85	Tegucigalpa	Honduras (0) 0, Canada (0) 1
1.9.85	San Jose	Costa Rica (0) 0, Canada (0) 0
8.9.85	Tegucigalpa	Honduras (1) 3, Costa Rica (1) 1
14.9.85	St John's	Canada (1) 2, Honduras (0) 1

Canada qualified for the finals

ASIA

First Round *(League System)*

Group 1 Sub-Group 1A

12.4.85	Riyadh	Saudi Arabia (0) 0, UAE (0) 0
19.4.85	Dubai	UAE (1) 1, Saudi Arabia (0) 0

UAE qualified for second round

Sub-Group 1B

15.3.85	Amman	Jordan (0) 1, Qatar (0) 0
29.3.85	Amman	Jordan (0) 2, Iraq (1) 3
5.4.85	Doha	Qatar (1) 3, Iraq (0) 0
12.4.85	Doha	Qatar (0) 2, Jordan (0) 0
19.4.85	Kuwait	Iraq (0) 2, Jordan (0) 0
5.5.85	Calcutta	Iraq (1) 2, Qatar (1) 1

Iraq qualified for second round

Group 2 Sub-Group 2A

22.3.85	Damascus	Syria (1) 1, Kuwait (0) 0
29.3.85	Sana'a	Yemen AR (0) 0, Syria (0) 1
5.4.85	Kuwait	Kuwait (1) 5, Yemen AR (0) 0
12.4.85	Kuwait	Kuwait(0) 0, Syria (0) 0
19.4.85	Damascus	Syria (2) 3, Yemen AR (0) 0
26.4. 85	Sana'a	Yemen AR (0) 1, Kuwait (2) 3

Syria qualified for second round

Sub-Group 2B

29.3.85	Aden	Yemen PDR (0) 1, Bahrain (2) 4
12.4.85	Bahrain	Bahrain (0) 3, Yemen PDR (1) 3

Bahrain qualified for second round

Group 3 Sub-Group 3A

2.3.85	Kathmandu	Nepal (0) 0, South Korea (1) 2
10.3.85	Kuala Lumpur	Malaysia (0) 1, South Korea (0) 0
16.3.85	Kathmandu	Nepal (0) 0, Malaysia (0) 0
31.3.85	Kuala Lumpur	Malaysia (5) 5, Nepal (0) 0
6.4.85	Seoul	South Korea (3) 4, Nepal (0) 0
19.5.85	Seoul	South Korea (2) 2, Malaysia (0) 0

South Korea qualified for second round

Sub-Group 3B

15.3.85	Jakarta	Indonesia (0) 1, Thailand (0) 0
18.3.85	Jakarta	Indonesia (0) 2, Bangladesh (0) 0
21.3.85	Jakarta	Indonesia (1) 2, India (1) 1
23.3.85	Bangkok	Thailand (1) 3, Bangladesh (0) 0
26.3.85	Bangkok	Thailand (0) 0, India (0) 0
29.3.85	Bangkok	Thailand (0) 0, Indonesia (1) 1
30.3.85	Dhaka	Bangladesh (1) 1, India (1) 2
2.4.85	Dhaka	Bangladesh (0) 2, Indonesia (1) 1
5.4.85	Dhaka	Bangladesh (0) 1, Thailand (0) 0
6.4.85	Calcutta	India (0) 1, Indonesisa (1) 1
9.4.85	Calcutta	India (0) 1, Thailand (0) 1
12.4.85	Calcutta	India (1) 2, Bangladesh (1) 1

Indonesia qualified for second round

Group 4 Sub-Group 4A

17.2.85	Macao	Macao (0) 2, Brunei (0) 0
17.2.85	Hong Kong	Hong Kong (0) 0, China PR (0) 0
20.2.85	Macao	Macao (0) 0, China PR (1) 4
23.2.85	Hong Kong	Hong Kong (3) 8, Brunei (0) 0
26.2.85	Macao	China PR (4) 8, Brunei (0) 0
1.3.85	Hong Kong	Brunei (0) 0, China PR (2) 4
6.4.85	Band.S.B.	Brunei (1) 1, Hong Kong (3) 5
13.4.85	Band.S.B.	Brunei (0) 1, Macao (0) 2
28.4.85	Macao	Macao (0) 0, Hong Kong (0) 2
4.5.85	Hong Kong	Hong Kong (0) 2, Macao (0) 0
12.5.85	Beijing	China PR (3) 6, Macao (0) 0
19.5.85	Beijing	China PR (1) 1, Hong Kong (1) 2

Hong Kong qualified for second round

Sub-Group 4B

19.1.85	Singapore	Singapore (1) 1, North Korea (0) 1
23.2.85	Singapore	Singapore (1) 1, Japan (1) 3
21.3.85	Tokyo	Japan (1) 1, North Korea (0) 0
30.4.85	Pyongyang	North Korea (0) 0, Japan (0) 0
18.5.85	Tokyo	Japan (0) 5, Singapore (0) 0
25.5.85	Pyongyang	North Korea (2) 2, Singapore (0) 0

Japan qualified for second round

Second Round *(Cup System)*

20.9.85	Dubai	UAE (1) 2, Iraq (1) 3
27.9.85	Taif	Iraq (0) 1, UAE (1) 2
6.9.85	Bahrain	Bahrain (1) 1, Syria (0) 1
20.9.85	Damascus	Syria (1) 1, Bahrain (0) 0
21.7.85	Seoul	South Korea (0) 2, Indonesia (0) 0
30.7.85	Jakarta	Indonesia (0) 1, South Korea (3) 4
11.8.85	Kobe	Japan (2) 3, Hong Kong (0) 0
22.9.85	Hong Kong	Hong Kong (0) 1, Japan (1) 2

Third Round *(Cup System)*

15.11.85	Damascus	Syria (0) 0, Iraq (0) 0
29.11.85	Taif	Iraq (1) 3, Syria (0) 1
26.10.85	Tokyo	Japan (1) 1, South Korea (2) 2
3.11.85	Seoul	South Korea (0) 1, Japan (0) 0

Iraq and South Korea qualified for the finals

AFRICA

First Round *(Cup System)*

28.8.84	Cairo	Egypt (1) 1, Zimbabwe (0) 0
30.9.84	Harare	Zimbabwe (1) 1, Egypt (1) 1
13.10.84	Nairobi	Kenya (1) 2, Ethiopia (1) 1
28.10.84	Addis Ababa	Ethiopia (2) 3, Kenya (0) 3
15.7.84	Curecipe	Mauritius (0) 0, Malawi (1) 1
28.7.84	Lilongwe	Malawi (1) 4, Mauritius (0) 0
29.7.84	Ndola	Zambia (1) 3, Uganda (0) 0
25.8.84	Kampala	Uganda (0) 1, Zambia (0) 0
	Madagascar v Lesotho – *Lesotho refused to play and were excluded*	
13.10.84	Mwanza	Tanzania (1) 1, Sudan (0) 1
27.10.84	Khartoum	Sudan (0) 0, Tanzania (0) 0
30.6.84	Freetown	Sierra Leone (0) 0, Morocco (0) 1
15.7. 84	Rabat	Morocco (1) 4, Sierra Leone (0) 0
	Libya v Niger – *Niger withdrew 8.10.84*	
28.10.84	Cotonou	Benin (0) 0, Tunisia (0) 2
13.11 84	Tunis	Tunisia (2) 4, Benin (0) 0
	Togo v Guinea – *Togo withdrew 13.4.84*	
21.10.84	Abidjan	Ivory Coast (0) 4, Gambia (0) 0
4.11.84	Banjul	Gambia (1) 3, Ivory Coast (1) 2
20.10.84	Lagos	Nigeria (2) 3, Liberia (0) 0
4.11.84	Monrovia	Liberia (0) 0, Nigeria (1) 1
1.7.84	Luanda	Angola (0) 1, Senegal (0) 0
15.7.84	Dakar	Senegal (1) 1, Angola (0) 0
		Angola won 4-3 on penalties

Second Round *(Cup System)*

Algeria, Cameroon, Ghana qualified by walkover

7.4.85	Lusaka	Zambia (4) 4, Cameroon (0) 1
21.4.85	Yaounde	Cameroon (1) 1, Zambia (1) 1
7.4.85	Rabat	Morocco (1) 2, Malawi (0) 0
21.4.85	Lilongwe	Malawi (0) 0, Morocco (0) 0
31.3.85	Luanda	Angola (0) 0, Algeria (0) 0
19.4.85	Algiers	Algeria (2) 3, Angola (0) 2
6.4.85	Nairobi	Kenya (0) 0, Nigeria (2) 3
20.4.85	Lagos	Nigeria (2) 3, Kenya (1) 1
5.4.85	Cairo	Egypt (0) 1, Madagascar (0) 0
21.4.85	Antananarivo	Madagascar (0) 1, Egypt (0) 0
		Egypt won 4-2 on penalties
10.2.85	Conakry	Guinea (1) 1, Tunisia (0) 0
24.2.85	Tunis	Tunisia (1) 2, Guinea (0) 0
22.2.85	Khartoum	Sudan (0) 0, Libya (0) 0
8.3.85	Tripoli	Libya(0) 4, Sudan (0) 0
7.4.85	Abidjan	Ivory Coast (0) 0, Ghana (0) 0
21.4.85	Accra	Ghana (0) 2, Ivory Coast (0) 0

Third Round *(Cup System)*

13.7.85	Algiers	Algeria (1) 2, Zambia (0) 0
28.7.85	Lusaka	Zambia (0) 0, Algeria (0) 1
14.7.85	Accra	Ghana (0) 0, Libya (0) 0
26.7.85	Benghazi	Libya (1) 2, Ghana (0) 0
6.7.85	Lagos	Nigeria (0) 1, Tunisia (0) 0
20.7.85	Tunis	Tunisia (2) 2, Nigeria (0) 0
12.7.85	Cairo	Egypt (0) 0, Morocco (0) 0
28.7.85	Casablanca	Morocco (1) 2, Egypt (0) 0

Fourth Round *(Cup System)*

6.10.85	Tunis	Tunisia (1) 1, Algeria (2) 4
18.10.85	Algiers	Algeria (2) 3, Tunisia (0) 0
6.10.85	Rabat	Morocco (1) 3, Libya (0) 0
18.10.85	Benghazi	Libya (1) 1, Morocco (0) 0

Algeria and Morocco qualified for the finals

OCEANIA/ISRAEL

First Round *(League System)*

3.9.85	Tel Aviv	Israel (3) 6, Chinese Taipei (0) 0
8.9.85	Tel Aviv	Chinese Taipei (0) 0, Israel (2) 5
21.9.85	Auckland	New Zealand (0) 0, Australia (0) 0
5.10.85	Auckland	New Zealand (3) 5, Chinese Taipei (1) 1
8.10.85	Tel Aviv	Israel (0) 1, Australia (0) 2
12.10.85	Christchurch	Chinese Taipei (0) 0, New Zealand (2) 5
20.10.85	Melbourne	Australia (1) 1, Israel (0) 1
23.10.85	Adelaide	Australia (2) 7, Chinese Taipei (0) 0
26.10.85	Auckland	New Zealand (2) 3, Israel (1) 1
27.10.85	Sydney	Chinese Taipei (0) 0, Australia (1) 8
3.11.85	Sydney	Australia (1) 2, New Zealand (0) 0
10.11.85	Tel Aviv	Israel (0) 3, New Zealand (0) 0

Second Round
(Home and away play-off against the Runner-up of UEFA Group 7)
Glasgow, 20 November 1985, attendance 60,000
Scotland (0) 2 *(Cooper, McAvennie)*
Australia (0) 0
Scotland: Leighton; Nicol, Malpas, Souness, McLeish, Miller, Dalglish (Sharp), Strachan, McAvennie, Aitken, Cooper.
Australia: Greedy; Davidson, Jennings, Yankos, Ratcliffe, O'Connor, Watson, Mitchell, Kosmina, Murphy, Crino.

Melbourne, 4 December 1985, attendance 29.500
Australia (0) 0
Scotland (0) 0
Australia: Greedy; Davidson, Jennings, Yankos, Ratcliffe, Dunn (Farina), Murphy, Crino (Odzakov), Kosmina, Mitchell,Patikas.
Scotland: Leighton; Gough, Malpas, McLeish, Miller, Aitken, McAvennie, Souness, McStay, Speedie (Sharp), Cooper.

THE WORLD CUP FINALS

URUGUAY 1930

Uruguay 4, Argentina 2 (1–2)
Uruguay: Ballesteros; Nasazzi (capt), Mascheroni, Andrade, Fernandez, Gestido, Dorado, Scarone, Castro, Cea, Iriarte.
Argentina: Botasso; Della Torre, Paternoster, Evaristo, J., Monti, Suarez, Peucelle, Varallo, Stabile, Ferreira (capt), Evaristo, M.
Scorers: Dorado, Cea, Iriarte, Castro for Uruguay; Peucelle, Stabile for Argentina.
Leading scorers: Stabile (Argentina) 8.

ITALY 1934

Italy 2, Czechoslovakia 1 (0–0) (1–1) after extra time. *Rome*
Italy: Combi (capt), Monzeglio, Allemandi, Ferraris IV, Monti, Bertolini, Guaita, Meazza, Schiavio, Ferrari, Orsi.
Czechoslovakia: Planicka (capt), Zenisek, Ctyroky, Kostalek, Cambal, Krcil, Junek, Svoboda, Sobotka, Nejedly, Puc.
Scorers: Orsi, Schiavio for Italy, Puc for Czechoslovakia.
Leading scorers: Schiavio (Italy), Nejedly (Czechoslovakia), Conen (Germany) each 4.

FRANCE 1938

Italy 4, Hungary 2 (3–1). *Paris*
Italy: Olivieri; Foni, Rava, Serantoni, Andreolo, Locatelli, Biavati, Meazza (capt), Piola, Ferrari, Colaussi.
Hungary: Szabo; Polgar, Biro, Szalay, Szucs, Luzar, Sas, Vincze, Sarosi, (capt), Szengeller, Titkos.
Scorers: Colaussi (2), Piola (2) for Italy, Titkos, Sarosi for Hungary.
Leading scorer: Leonidas (Brazil) 8.

BRAZIL 1950

Final pool replaced knock-out system.
Final pool
Uruguay 2, Spain 2
Brazil 7, Sweden 1
Uruguay 3, Sweden 2
Brazil 6, Spain 1
Sweden 3, Spain 1
Uruguay 2, Brazil 1

Final positions	*P*	*W*	*D*	*L*	*F*	*A*	*Pts*
Uruguay	3	2	1	0	7	5	5
Brazil	3	2	0	1	14	4	4
Sweden	3	1	0	2	6	11	2
Spain	3	0	1	2	4	11	1

Leading scorers: Ademir (Brazil) 7, Schiaffino (Uruguay), Basora (Spain) 5.

SWITZERLAND 1954

West Germany 3, Hungary 2.
West Germany: Turek; Posipal, Kohlmeyer, Eckel, Liebrich, Mai, Rahn, Morlock, Walter, O., Walter, F. (capt), Schaefer.
Hungary: Grosics; Buzansky, Lantos, Boszik, Lorant, Zakarias, Czibor, Kocsis, Hidegkuti, Puskas (capt), Toth, J.
Scorers: Morlock, Rahn (2) for Germany, Puskas, Czibor for Hungary.
Leading scorer: Kocsis (Hungary) 11.

SWEDEN 1958

Brazil 5, Sweden 2 (2–1). *Stockholm.*
Brazil: Gilmar; Santos, D., Santos, N., Zito, Bellini, Orlando, Garrincha, Didi, Vava, Pele, Zagalo.
Sweden: Svensson; Bergmark, Axbom, Boerjesson, Gustavsson, Parling, Hamrin, Gren, Simonsson, Liedholm, Skoglund.
Scorers: Vava (2), Pele (2), Zagalo for Brazil, Liedholm, Simonsson for Sweden.
Leading scorer: Fontaine 13 (present record total).

CHILE 1962

Brazil 3, Czechoslovakia 1 (1–1). *Santiago.*
Brazil; Gilmar; Santos, D., Mauro, Zozimo, Santos, N., Zito, Didi, Garrincha, Vava, Amarildo, Zagalo.
Czechoslovakia: Schroiff; Tichy, Novak, Pluskal, Popluhar, Masopust, Pospichal, Scherer, Kvasniak, Kadraba, Jelinek.
Scorers: Amarildo, Zito, Vava for Brazil, Masopust for Czechoslovakia.
Leading scorers: Albert (Hungary), Ivanov (Russia), Sanchez, L. (Chile), Garrincha, Vava (Brazil), Jerkovic (Yugoslavia) each 4.

ENGLAND 1966

England 4, West Germany 2 (1–1) (2–2) after extra time. *Wembley.*
England: Banks; Cohen, Wilson, Stiles, Charlton, J., Moore, Ball, Hurst, Hunt, Charlton, R., Peters.
West Germany: Tilkowski; Hottges, Schulz, Weber, Schnellinger, Haller, Beckenbauer, Overath, Seller,Held, Emmerich.
Scorers: Hurst 3, Peters for England, Haller, Weber for Germany
Leading Scorer: Eusebio (Portugal)9.

MEXICO 1970

Brazil 4, Italy 1. *Mexico City.*
Brazil: Felix; Carlos Alberto, Brito, Piazza, Everaldo, Gerson, Clodoaldo, Jairzinho, Pele, Tostao, Rivelino. No subs.
Italy: Albertosi, Burgnich, Cera, Rosato, Facchetti, Bertini, Riva, Domenghini, Mazzola, De Sisti, Boninsegna. Subs: Juliano for Bertini, Rivera for Boninsegna.
Scorers: Pele, Gerson, Jairzinho, Carlos Alberto for Brazil, Boninsegna for Italy.
Leading Scorer: Müller (W. Germany) 10

WEST GERMANY 1974

West Germany 2, Netherlands 1 (2–1). *Munich.*
West Germany: Maier; Vogts, Schwarzenbeck, Beckenbauer, Breitner, Bonhof, Hoeness, Overath, Grabowski, Muller, Holzenbein.
Netherlands: Jongbloed; Suurbier, Rijsbergen (De Jong), Haan, Krol, Jansen, Van Hanegem, Neeskens, Rep, Cruyff, Rensenbrink (Van der Kerkhof, R.).
Scorers: Breitner *(pen),* Muller for West Germany, Neeskens *(pen)* for Netherlands.
Leading Scorer: Lato (Poland) 7

ARGENTINA 1978

Argentina 3, Netherlands 1 (after extra time). *Buenos Aires.*
Argentina: Fillol; Olguin, Passarella, Galvan, Tarantini (Larossa), Gallego, Ortiz (Houseman), Bertoni, Luque, Kempes.
Netherlands: Jongbloed; Poortvliet, Brandts, Krol, Jansen (Suurbier), Neeskens, W. Van der Kerkhof, R. Van der Kerkhof, Haan, Rep (Nanninga), Rensenbrink.
Scorers: Kempes 2,Bertoni for Argentina, Nanninga for Netherlands.
Leading Scorer: Kempes (Argentina) 6

SPAIN 1982

Italy 3, West Germany 1. *Madrid*
Italy: Zoff; Bergomi, Cabrini, Collovati, Scirea, Gentile, Oriali, Tardelli, Conti, Graziani (Altobelli) (Causio), Rossi.
West Germany: Schumacher; Kaltz, K-H. Forster, Stielike, B. Forster, Breitner, Dremmler (Hrubesch), Littbarski, Briegel, Fischer, Rummenigge (Muller).
Scorers: Rossi, Tardelli, Altobelli for Italy, Breitner for West Germany.
Leading Scorer: Rossi (Italy) 6

OTHER BRITISH INTERNATIONAL MATCHES 1985-86

Cardiff, 16 October 1985, 3505
Wales (0)0
Hungary (1)3 *(Esterhazy, Hajszan, Detari)*
Wales: Southall; J. Jones (Slatter), Van den Hauwe, Ratcliffe, Jackett, Phillips, Nicholas, A. Davies (Blackmore), M. Thomas, Hughes, Curtis (Lovell).
Hungary: P. Disztl; Sallai, Roth, Petr, L. Disztl, Garaba, Esterhazy (Kovacs), Nyilasi, Nagy(Gyimesi), Detari, Hajszan.

Glasgow, 16 October 1985, 41,114
Scotland (0)0
East Germany (0)0
Scotland: Leighton (Goram); Gough, Albiston, McLeish, Miller, Dalglish, Nicol, Johnston (Speedie), Aitken (McStay), Cooper.
East Germany: Muller (Weissflog); Kreer, Rohde, Sanger, Zotzsche, Pilz, Liebers, Stubner, Kirsten, Ernst (Bielau), Thom.

Tel Aviv, 28 January 1986, 7000
Israel (0)0
Scotland (0)1 *(McStay)*
Israel: Ran; Aharoni, Merili, Davidi, A.Cohen, Shimanov, Armeli, Malmilian, Ivanir (Bagleibter), Turk (E.Cohen), Eli Ohana (Rosenthal).
Scotland: Leighton; Gough, Malpas, Aitken, Narey, Miller, Bett, McStay, Sharp (Sturrock), Nicholas, Bannon.

Cairo, 29 January 1986, 20,000
Egypt (0)0
England (2)4 *(Steven, Omar og, Wallace, Cowans)*
Egypt: El Batal; Sidki, Yassin, Omar, Saleh, Ghani, Majhoub, Zeid (Hamid), Hazem (Tilissi), Abdou, Yehia.
England: Shilton (Woods); Stevens, Wright, Fenwick, Sansom, Steven (Hill), Wilkins, Cowans, Wallace, Hateley, Lineker (Beardsley).

Dhahran, 25 February 1986, 20,000
Saudi Arabia (0)1 *(Al-Thani, pen)*
Wales (0)2 *(Slatter, G. Davies)*
Saudi Arabia: Samir Suleiman; Nasser Al-Mansour, Ahmed Jamil, Samir Abdul Satter, Essam Sefian, Yousef Khamis (Abdul Gamad), Yousef Al-Thani, Ismail Hatemi, Jamal Mohammed (Abdullah Zaki), Abdullah Al-Harbi, Saeed Al-Nefisa.
Wales: Southall; Slatter, Ratcliffe, Jackett, Aizlewood, R. James (Lowndes), Nicholas, Phillips (D. Williams), Blackmore (M. Thomas), G. Davies (M. Allen), Rush.

Ramat Gan, 26 February 1986, 15,000
Israel (1)1 *(Ohana)*
England (0)2 *(Robson 2)*
Israel: Ran; Aharoni, Davidi (Aluf), Ivanir, A. Cohen, Shimonov, Sinai, Malmilian, Armeli, Turk (E. Cohen), Ohana (Rosenthal).
England: Shilton (Woods); Stevens, Martin, Butcher, Sansom, Hoddle, Robson, Wilkins, Beardsley, Dixon (Woodcock), Waddle (Barnes).

Paris, 26 February 1986, 25,000
France (0)0
Northern Ireland (0)0

France: Bats; Ayache (Le Roux), Bossis, Battiston, Amoros, Giresse, Fernandez, Tusseau (ferreri), Platini, Rocheteau, Papin.
Northern Ireland: Jennings; Nicholl, J. O'Neill, McDonald, Donaghy, Clarke, McCreery (McClelland), McIlroy, Whiteside, Penney (Caughey), Quinn (Armstrong).

Belfast, 26 March 1986, 20,000
Northern Ireland (1)1 *(McDonald)*
Denmark (0)1 *(Christensen)*
Northern Ireland: Jennings; Donaghy, Worthington, J. O'Neill, McDonald, McCreery (Armstrong), Penney, McIlroy, Clarke (Quinn), Whiteside, Stewart (Caughey),
Denmark: Rasmussen; Sivebaek, K. Nielsen, M. Olsen (Frimann), Bartram, Molby, Lauridsen, J. Olsen, Simonsen (Christensen), Berggren, Laudrup (H. Andersen).

Dublin, 26 March 1986, 16,500
Republic of Ireland (0)0
Wales (1)1 *(Rush)*
Republic of Ireland: Peyton; Langan, Beglin, Anderson (McCarthy), O'Leary, Brady, McGrath, Houghton, Aldridge, Robinson (P. Byrne), Whelan.
Wales: Southall (Norman); R. James, Jackett, Nicholas, Charles, J. Jones, Lowndes, Phillips, Rush, Blackmore, Davies (Saunders).

Tbilisi, 26 March 1986, 62,500
USSR (0)0
England (0)1 *(Waddle)*
USSR: Dassayev; Bessonov (Litovchenk), Chivadze, Demianenko, Bubnov, Kuznetsov, Gotsmanov, Zavarov (Dobrobolsky), Alienikov, Kondratiev, Rodionov (Blokhin).
England: Shilton; Anderson, Sansom, Hoddle, Wright, Butcher, Cowans (Hodge), Wilkins, Beardsley, Lineker, Waddle (Steven).

Glasgow, 26 March 1986, 53,589
Scotland (2)3 *(Strachan, Gough, Aitken)*
Rumania (0)0
Scotland: Goram; Gough, Malpas, Souness, Narey, Miller (Hansen), Dalglish, Strachan (Nevin), Sharp (Nicholas), Aitken, Bannon.
Rumania: Lung; Rednic, Movila, Ungureanu, Andone (Cireasa), Iorgulescu (Nicolae), Coras (Gabor), Klein, Camataru, Mateut, Hagi.

Cardiff, 21 April 1986, 11,154
Wales (0)0
Uruguay (0)0
Wales: Norman; R. James, Blackmore, Ratcliffe, J. Jones, D. Williams, Lowndes, Nicholas, Rush, Phillips, Hughes.
Uruguay: Rodriguez; Gutierrez, Acevedo, Diogo, Bossio (Saralegui), Batista, Alzamendi, Barrios, Da Silva, Francescoli, Santin.

Wembley, 23 April 1986, 68,357
England (2)2 *(Butcher, Hoddle)*
Scotland (0)1 *(Souness, pen)*
England: Shilton; Stevens (Everton) (Stevens, Tottenham), Sansom, Hoddle (Reid), Watson, Butcher, Wilkins, Francis, Hateley, Hodge, Waddle.
Scotland: Rough, Gough, Malpas, Souness, McLeish, Miller, Nicol, Speedie, Nicholas (Nevin), Aitken, Bannon.

Dublin, 23 April 1986, 14,000
Republic of Ireland (1)1 *(Daly, pen)*
Uruguay (1)1 *(Paz)*
Republic of Ireland: Bonner; Langan, Hughton (Eccles), Daly, McCarthy, Murphy, Houghton, O'Brien, Aldridge, Stapleton (Byrne), Galvin.
Uruguay: Alvez; Gutierrez, Diogo, Vega, Saralegui, Ramos, Barrios, Cabrera, Salazar, Rivero, Paz.

Belfast, 23 April 1986, 10,000
Northern Ireland (1)2 *(Clarke, Quinn)*
Morocco (0)1 *(Timoumi)*
Northern Ireland: Jennings (Platt); Ramsey, Donaghy, McNally, O'Neill, McDonald, Penney (Quinn), McIlroy, Clarke, Whiteside (Campbell), Stewart (Hamilton).
Morocco: Fetah; Khalifa, Badidi (Labied), Biyaz, Bouyahaqui, Dolmi, Merry (Otmani), Kahri, Mohammed, Timoumi (Dehani), Amanallah.

Eindhoven, 29 April 1986, 14,500
Netherlands (0)0
Scotland (0)0
Netherlands: Van Breukelen; Blind, Silloy, Koeman, Van Tiggelen, Wouters, Vanenburg, Valke, Bosman, van't Schip, De Wit.
Scotland: Goram; Malpas, Albiston, Narey, McLeish, Miller, Sturrock, Bett, McCoist, Connor, Cooper.

Toronto, 10 May1986, 13,142
Canada (2)2 *(Vrablic, Gray)*
Wales (0)0
Canada: Dolan; Miller, Wilson, Lowery, Ragan, Samuel, Ion, Gray, Vrablic, James, Mitchell (Pakos).
Wales: Norman (Dibble); R. James, Slatter (Bowen), Jackett, J. Jones, D. Williams, Lowndes, Nicholas, Saunders, Aizlewood, M. Allen (Lovell).

Los Angeles, 17 May 1986, 45,000
Mexico (0)0
England (3)3 *(Hateley 2, Beardsley)*
Mexico: Larios; Trejo, Felix Cruz, Manzo (Quirate), Servin, Munos, Espana (Alex Dominguez), Aguirre, Hermosillo (Francisco Cruz), Flores, Negrete.
England: Shilton; Anderson, Sansom, Hoddle, Fenwick, Butcher, Robson (Stevens, Spurs), Wilkins (Steven), Hateley (Dixon), Beardsley, Waddle (Barnes).

Vancouver, 20 May 1986, 9007
Canada (0)0
Wales (1)3 *(Saunders 2, M. Allen)*
Canada: Dolan; Lenarduzzi, Bridge (Samuel), Moore, Wilson, Gray, Ragan, Sweeney (Norman), Valentine, Vrablic (Segota), Mitchell (Pakos).
Wales: Dibble; R. James, J. Jones, Jackett, Slatter, Lowndes, Nicholas, D. Williams (Bowen), Aizlewood, Saunders, Lovell (M. Allen).

Burnaby, 24 May 1986, 10,000
Canada (0)0
England (0)1 *(Hateley)*
Canada: Dolan; Lenarduzzi, Samuel, Moore, Wilson, James, Gray (Lowery), Ragan, Sweeney, Valentine (Mitchell), Vrablic.
England: Shilton (Woods); Stevens, Sansom, Martin, Butcher, Hoddle, Wilkins (Reid), Hodge, Hateley, Lineker (Beardsley), Waddle (Barnes).

BRITISH INTERNATIONAL GOALSCORERS SINCE 1946

ENGLAND

A'Court, A. 1
Allen, R......................2
Anderson, V. 1
Astall, G. 1
Atyeo, P.J.W. 5

Baily, E.F. 5
Baker, J.H. 4
Ball, A.J. 8
Barnes, J. 3
Barnes, P.S. 4
Beardsley, P.A. 2
Beattie, T.K. 1
Bell, C. 9
Bentley, R.T.F. 9
Blissett, L. 3
Bowles, S. 1
Bradford, G.R.W. 1
Bradley, W. 2
Bridges, B.J. 1
Broadbent, P.F. 2
Broadis, I.A. 8
Brooking, T.D. 5
Brooks, J. 2
Butcher, T. 3
Byrne, J.J. 8

Carter, H.S. 7
(inc. 2 scored pre-war)
Chamberlain, M. 1
Channon, M.R. 21
Charlton, J. 6
Charlton, R. 49
Chivers, M. 13
Clarke, A.J. 10
Connelly, J.M. 7
Coppell, S.J. 7
Cowans, G. 2
Crawford, R. 1
Currie, A.W. 3

Dixon, K.M. 4
Douglas, B. 11

Eastham, G. 2
Edwards, D. 5
Elliot, W.H. 3

Finney, T. 30
Flowers, R. 10
Francis, G.C.J. 3
Francis, T. 12
Froggatt, J. 2
Froggatt, R. 2

Goddard, P. 1
Grainger, C. 3
Greaves, J. 44

Haines, J.T.W. 2
Hancocks, J. 2
Hassall, H.W. 4
Hateley, M. 9
Haynes, J.N. 17
Hinton, A.T. 1
Hitchens, G.A. 5
Hoddle, G. 8
Hughes, E.W. 1
Hunt, R. 18
Hunter, N. 2
Hurst, G.C. 24

Johnson, D.E. 5

Kay, A.H. 1
Keegan, J.K. 21
Kennedy, R. 3
Kevan, D.T. 8
Kidd, B. 1

Langton, R. 1
Latchford, R.D. 5
Lawler, C. 1
Lawler, T. 22
(inc. 6 scored pre-war)
Lee, F. 10
Lee, J. 1
Lee, S. 2
Lineker, G. 12
Lofthouse, N. 30

Macdonald, M. 6
Mannion, W.J. 11
Mariner, P. 14
Marsh, R.W. 1
Matthews, S. 11
(inc. 8 scored pre-war)
McDermott, T. 3
Medley, L.D. 1
Melia, J. 1
Milburn, J.E.T. 9
Moore, R.F. 2
Morris, J. 3
Mortensen, S.H. 24
Mullen, J. 6
Mullery, A.P. 1

Neal, P.G. 5
Nicholls, J. 1
Nicholson, W.E. 1

O'Grady, M. 3

Own goals 13

Paine, T.L. 7
Parry, R.A. 1
Peacock, A. 3
Pearson, J.S. 5
Pearson, S.C. 5
Perry, W. 2
Peters, M. 20
Pickering, F. 5
Pointer, R. 2

Ramsey, A.E. 3
Revie, D.G. 4
Robson, B. 21
Robson, R. 4
Rowley, J.F. 6
Royle, J. 2

Sansom, K. 1
Sewell, J. 3
Shackleton, L.F. 1
Smith, R. 13
Steven, T.M. 3
Stiles, N.P. 13
Summerbee, M.G. 1

Tambling, R.V. 1
Taylor, P.J. 2
Taylor, T. 16
Thompson, P.B. 1
Tueart, D. 2

Viollet, D.S. 1

Waddle, C.R. 2
Wallace, D.L. 1
Walsh, P. 1
Watson, D.V. 4

Weller, K. 1
Wignall, F. 2
Wilkins, R.G. 3
Wilshaw, D.J. 10
Withe, P. 1
Woodcock, T. 16
Worthington, F.S. 2
Wright, W.A. 3

SCOTLAND

Aitken, R. 1
Archibald, S. 4

Baird, S. 2
Bannon, E. 1
Bauld, W. 2
Baxter, J.C. 3
Bett, J. 1
Bone, J. 1
Brand, R. 8
Brazil, A. 1
Bremner, W.J. 3
Brown, A.D. 6
Buckley, P. 1
Burns, K. 1

Caldow, E. 4
Campbell, R. 1
Chalmers, S. 3
Collins, R.V. 10
Combe, J.R. 1
Conn, A. 1
Cooper, D. 4
Craig, J. 1
Curran, H.P. 1

Dalglish, K. 30
Davidson, J.A. 1
Docherty, T.H. 1
Dodds, D. 1
Duncan, D.M. 1

Fernie, W. 1
Flavell, R. 2
Fleming, C. 2

Gemmell, T. *(St Mirren)* 1
Gemmell, T. *(Celtic)* 1
Gemmill, A. 8
Gibson, D.W. 3
Gilzean, A.J. 10
Gough, C.R. 3
Graham, A. 2
Graham, G. 3

Gray, A. 7
Gray, E. 3
Gray, F. 1
Greig, J. 5

Hamilton, G. 4
Harper, J.M. 2
Hartford, R.A. 4
Henderson, J.G. 1
Henderson, W. 5
Herd, D.G. 4
Hewie, J.D. 2
Holton, J.A. 2
Houliston, W. 2
Howie, H. 1
Hughes, J. 1
Hunter, W. 1
Hutchison, T. 1

Jackson, C. 1
Jardine, A. 1
Johnston, L.H. 1
Johnston, M. 4
Johnstone, D. 2
Johnstone, J. 4
Johnstone, R. 9
Jordan, J. 11

Law, D. 30
Leggat, G. 8
Lennox, R. 3
Liddell, W. 6
Linwood, A.B. 1
Lorimer, P 4

Macari, L. 5
MacDougall, E.J. 3
MacKay, D.C. 4
MacKenzie, J.A. 1
Mason, J. 4
Masson, D.S. 5
McAvennie, F. 1
McCalliog, J. 1
McGhee, M. 2
McKinnon, R. 1
McLaren, A. 4
McLean, T. 1
McLintock, F. 1
McMillan, I.L. 2
McNeill, W. 3
McPhail, J. 3
McQueen, G. 5
McStay, P. 3
Miller, W. 1
Mitchell, R.C. 1
Morgan, W. 1
Morris, H. 3
Mudie, J.K. 9

Mulhall, G. 1
Murdoch, R. 5
Murray, J. 1

Narey, D. 1
Nicholas, C. 5

O'Hare, J. 5
Ormond, W.E. 1
Orr, T. 1

Own goals 7

Parlane, D. 1
Pettigrew, W. 2
Provan, D. 1

Quinn, P.

Reilly, L. 22
Ring, T. 2
Rioch, B.D. 6
Robertson, A. 2
Robertson, J. 8

Scott, A.S. 5
Smith, G. 4
Souness, G.J. 3
St John, I. 9
Steel, W. 12
Stein, C. 10
Stewart, R. 1
Strachan, G. 4
Sturrock, P. 3

Thornton, W. 1

Waddell, W. 6
Wallace, I.A. 1
Wark, J. 7
Weir, A 1
White, J.A. 3
Wilson, D. 9

Young, A. 5

WALES

Allchurch, I.J. 23
Allen, M. 1

Barnes, W. 1
Bowen, D.L. 1
Boyle, T. 1
Burgess, W.A.R. 1

Charles, J. 1
Charles, M. 6

P.F.A.86.87.—9

Charles, W.J. 15
Clarke, R.J. 5
Curtis, A. 6

Davies, G. 2
Davies, R.T. 7
Davies, R.W. 8
Deacy, N. 4
Durban, A. 2
Dwyer, P. 2

Edwards, G 2
Edwards, R.I. 4
England, H.M. 3
Evans, I. 1

Flynn, B. 7
Ford, T. 23
Foulkes, W.I. 1

Giles, D. 2
Godfrey, B.C. 2
Griffiths, A.T. 6
Griffiths, M.W. 2
Harris, C.S. 1
Hewitt, R. 1
Hockey, T. 1
Hughes, M. 5

James, L. 10
James, R. 7
Jones, B.S. 2
Jones, Cliff 15
Jones, D.E. 1
Jones, J.P. 1

Kryzwicki, R.L. 1

Leek, K. 5
Lovell, S. 1
Lowrie, G. 2

Mahoney, J.F. 1
Medwin, T.C. 6
Moore, G. 1

Nicholas, P. 2

O'Sullivan, P.A. 1

Own goals 3

Palmer, D 1
Paul R. 1
Powell, A. 1
Powell, D. 1
Price, P. 1
Reece, G.I 2
Rees, R.R. 3
Roberts, P.S. 1
Rush, I. 12

Saunders, D 2
Slatter, N. 1
Smallman, D.P. 1

Tapscott, D.R. 4
Thomas, M. 4
Toshack, J.B. 13

Vernon, T.R. 8

Walsh, I. 7
Williams, G.E. 2
Woosnam, A.P. 4

Yorath, T.C. 2

NORTHERN IRELAND

Anderson, T 4
Armstrong, G. 12

Barr, H.H. 1
Best, G. 9
Bingham, W.L. 10
Blanchflower, D. 2
Blanchflower, J. 1
Brennan, R.A. 1
Brotherston, N. 3

Campbell, W.G. 1
Casey, T. 2
Caskey, W. 1
Cassidy, T. 1
Clarke, C.J. 2
Clements, D. 2
Cochrane, T. 1
Crossan, E. 1
Crossan, J.A. 10
Cush, W.W. 5

D'Arcy, S.D. 1
Doherty, L. 1
Doherty, P.D. 3
(inc. 1 scored pre-war)
Dougan, A.D. 8
Elder, A.R. 1

Ferguson, W. 1
Ferris, R.O. 1
Finney, T. 2

Hamilton, B. 4
Hamilton, W. 5
Harkin, J.T. 2
Harvey, M. 3
Hughes, L.M. 1
Humphries, W. 1
Hunter, A. 1

Irvine, W.J. 8

Johnston, W.C. 1
Jones, J. 1

Lockhart, N. 3

McAdams, W.J. 7
McClelland, J. 1
McCrory, S. 1
McCurdy, C. 1
McDonald, A. 1
McGarry, J.K. 1
McGrath, R.C. 4
McIlroy, J. 10
McIlroy, S.B. 5
McLaughlin, J.C. 6
McMordie, A.S. 3
McMorran, E.J. 4
McParland, P.J. 10
Moreland, V. 1
Morgan, S. 3

Neill, W.J.T. 2
Nelson, S. 1
Nicholl, C.J. 3
Nicholl, J.M. 1
Nicholson, J.J. 6

O'Kane, W.J. 1
O'Neill, J. 1
O'Neill, M.H. 9

Own goals 4

Peacock, R. 2

Quinn, J.M. 3

Simpson, W.J. 5
Smyth, S. 5
Spence, D.W. 3
Stewart, I. 2

Tully, C.P. 3

Walker, J. 1
Walsh, D.J. 5
Welsh, E. 1
Whiteside, N. 8
Wilson, S.J. 7

POST-WAR INTERNATIONAL APPEARANCES

As at 30 June, 1986

Abbreviations *A*—Albania;*Alg*—Algeria; *Arg*—Argentina; *Aust*—Austria; *Au*—Australia; *Bel*—Belgium; *Braz*—Brazil; *Bulg*—Bulgaria; *Can*—Canada *Ch*—Chile; *Czecho*—Czechoslovakia; *Co*—Colombia; *C*—Cyprus; *D*—Denmark; *Ec*—Ecuador; *E*-England; *E/Germ*—East Germany; *Eg*—Egypt; *F*—France; *FIFA*—Federation of International Associations; *Fin*—Finland; *G*—West Germany; *Gr*—Greece; *H*—Hungary; *Holl*—Holland; *Hon*—Honduras; *I*—N Ireland; *Ic*—Iceland; *Ir*—Iran; *Isr*—Israel; *It*—Italy; *K*—Kuwait; *Lux*—Luxembourg; *M*—Malta; *Mex*—Mexico; *Mor*—Morocco; *N*—Norway; *NZ*—New Zealand; *P*—Paraguay; *Per*—Peru; *Pol*—Poland; *Port*—Portugal; *Ru*—Rumania; *Rus*—Russia; *S*—Scotland; *Sar*—Saudi Arabia; *Sp*—Spain; *Swdn*—Sweden; *Switz*—Switzerland; *T*—Turkey; *U*—Uruguay; *UK*—Rest of United Kingdom; *US*—United States of America; *W*—Wales; *Y*—Yugoslavia; *Z*—Zaire.

ENGLAND

A'court, A. (5) (Liverpool) 1957/8 *I, Braz, Aust, Rus;* 1958/9 *W.*

Allen, C. (3) (Q.P.R.) 1983/4 *Braz, U, Ch.*

Allen, R. (5) (West Bromwich Albion) 1951/2 *Switz*; 1953/4 *US, Y*; 1954/5 *W, G.*

Allen, T. (3) (Stoke City) 1959/60 *W, Swdn, I.*

Anderson, S. (2) (Sunderland) 1961/2 *Aust, S.*

Anderson, V. (21) (Nottingham Forest) 1978/9 *Czecho,Swdn;* 1979/80 *Bulg, Sp;* 1980/81 *N, Ru, W, S;* 1981/82 *I, Ic;* 1983/4 *I;* 1984/85 *T, I, Eire,Ru, Fin, S, Mex, US;* 1985/6 *USSR, Mex.*

Angus, J. (1) (Burnley) 1960/1 *Aust.*

Armfield, J. (43) (Blackpool) 1958/9 *Braz, Per, Mex, US*; 1959/60 *S, Y, Sp, H*; 1960/1 *Lux, Sp, W, S, Mex, Port, It, Aust*; 1961/2 *Lux, W, Port, I, Aust, S, Switz, Per, H, Arg, Bulg, Braz*; 1962/3 *F, I, W, F, S, Braz, E/Germ, Switz*; 1963/4 *W, FIFA, I, S*; 1965/6 *Y, Fin.*

Armstrong, D. (3) (Middlesbrough) 1979/80 *Au;* (Southampton) 1982/3 *G;* 1983/4 *W.*

Armstrong, K. (1) (Chelsea) 1954/5 *S.*

Astall, G. (2) (Birmingham) 1955/6 *Fin, G.*

Astle, J. (5) (West Bromwich Albion) 1968/9 *W;* 1969/70 *Port, S, Braz, Czecho.*

Aston, J. (17) (Manchester United) 1948/9 *W, S, D, Switz, Swdn, N, F;* 1949/50 *W, I, S, Eire, It, Port, Bel, Ch, US;* 1950/1 *I.*

Atyeo, J. (6) (Bristol City) 1955/6 *Sp, Braz, Swdn;* 1956/7 *Eire, D, Eire.*

Bailey, G.R. (2) (Manchester United) 1984/5 *Eire, Mex.*

Bailey, M. (2) (Charlton) 1963/4 *US*; 1964/5 *W.*

Baily, E. (9) (Tottenham Hotspur) 1949/50 *Sp*; 1950/1 *I, W, Y*; 1951/2 *W, Aust* (2), *Switz*; 1952/3 *I.*

Baker, J. (8) (Hibernian) 1959/60 *I, S, Y, Sp, H;* 1965/6 (Arsenal) *I, Sp, Pol.*

Ball, A. (72) (Blackpool) 1964/5 *Y, G, Swdn*; 1965/6 *Sp, Pol, G, S, Fin, D, Pol, U, Arg, Port, G*; 1966/7 (Everton) *I, Czecho, W, S, Sp, Aust*; 1967/8 *W, Rus, S, Sp* (2), *G, Y*; 1968/9 *Ru* (2), *I, W, S, Mex, U, Braz*; 1969/70 *Port, Bel, W, S, Co, Ec, Ru, Braz, Czecho, G*; 1970/1 *E/Germ, M, Gr, M, I, S*; 1971/2 *Switz, Gr* (Arsenal), *G* (2), *S*; 1972/3 *Y, W* (2), *S, I, W, S, Czecho, Pol*; 1973/4 *Port*; 1974/5 *G, C* (2), *I, W, S.*

Banks, G. (73) (Leicester) 1962/3 *S, Braz, Czecho, E/Germ*; 1963/4 *W, FIFA, I, S, U, Port, US, Port, Arg*; 1964/5 *I, S, H, Y, G, Swdn*; 1965/6 *I, Sp, Pol, G, S, Y, Fin, Pol, Y, Mex, F, Arg, Port, G;* 1966/7 *I, Czecho, W, S;* 1967/8 (Stoke) *W, I,*

Rus, S, Sp, G, Y, Rus; 1968/9 *Ru* (2), *F, I, S, U, Braz*; 1969/70 *Holl, Bel, W, I, S, Co, Ec, Ru, Braz, Czecho*; 1970/1 *M, Gr, M, I, S*; 1971/2 *Switz, Gr, G* (2), *W, S.*
Banks, T. (6) (Bolton Wanderers) 1957/8 *Rus* (2), *Braz, Aust, Rus*; 1958/9 *I.*
Barham, M. (2) (Norwich C.) 1982/83 *Au* (2).
Barlow, R. (1) (West Bromwich Albion) 1954/5 *I.*
Barnes, J. (28) (Watford) 1982/3 *I, Au* (3);1983/4 *D, Lux, F, S, Rus, Braz, U, Ch;* 1984/5 *E/Germ, Fin, T, I, Ru, Fin, S, It, Mex, G, US;* 1985/6 *Ru, Isr, Mex, Can, Arg.*
Barnes, P. (22) (Manchester City) 1977/8 *It, G, Braz, W, S, H*; 1978/9 *D, Eire, Czecho, I, I, S, Bulg, Aust*;1979/80 (West Bromwich Albion) *D, W;* 1980/81 *Sp, Braz, W, Switz;* 1981/2 (Leeds U.) *N, Holl.*
Barrass, M. (3) (Bolton Wanderers) 1951/2 *W, I*; 1952/3 *S.*
Baynham, R. (3) (Luton Town) 1955/6 *D, I, Sp.*
Beardsley, P.A. (9) (Newcastle United) 1985/6 *Eg, Isr, USSR, Mex, Can, Port, Pol, P, Arg.*
Beattie, T. K. (9) (Ipswich Town) 1974/5 *C* (2),*S*; 1975/6 *Switz, Port*; 1976/7 *Fin, It, Holl*; 1977/8 *Lux.*
Bell, C. (48) (Manchester City) 1967/8 *Swdn, G*; 1968/9 *Bulg, F, W, U, Braz*; 1969/70 *Holl, Port, Holl, I, Braz, Czecho, G*; 1971/2 *Gr, G* (2), *W, I, S*; 1972/3 *Y, W* (2), *S, I, W, S, Czecho, Pol*; 1973/4 *Pol, It, W, I, S, Arg, Aust, E/Germ, Bulg, Y*; 1974/5 *Czecho, Port, G, C* (2), *I, S*; 1975/6 *Switz, Czecho.*
Bentley, R. (12) (Chelsea) 1948/9 *Swdn*; 1949/50 *S, Port, Bel, Ch, US*; 1952/3 *W, Bel*; 1954/5 *W, G, Sp, Port.*
Berry, J. (4) (Manchester United) 1952/3 *Arg, Ch, U*; 1955/6 *Swdn.*
Birtles, G. (3) (Nottingham Forest) 1979/80 *Arg, It;* 1980/81 (Manchester U.) *Ru.*
Blisset, L. (14) (Watford) 1982/3 *G, Lux, W, Gr, H, I, S Au* (2); 1983/4 (AC Milan) D, *H, W, S, Rus.*
Blockley, J. (1) (Arsenal) 1972/3 *Y.*
Blunstone, F. (5) (Chelsea) 1954/5 *W, S, F, Port*; 1956/7 *Y.*
Bonetti, P. (7) (Chelsea) 1965/6 *D*; 1966/7 *Sp, Aust*; 1967/8 *Sp*; 1969/70 *Holl, Port, G.*
Bowles, S. (5) (Q.P.R.) 1973/4 *Port, W, I*; 1976/7 *It, Holl.*
Boyer, P. (1) (Norwich City) 1975/6 *W.*
Brabrook, P. (3) (Chelsea) 1957/8 *Rus*; 1959/60 *I, Sp.*
Bradford, G (1) (Bristol Rovers) 1955/6 *D.*
Bradley, W. (3) (Manchester United) 1958/9 *It, Mex, US.*
Bracewell, P.W. (3) (Everton) 1984/5 *G, US;* 1985/6 *I.*
Bridges, B. (4) (Chelsea) 1964/5 *S, H, Y*; 1965/6 *Aust.*
Broadbent, P. (7) (Wolverhampton Wanderers) 1957/8 *Rus*; 1958/9 *I, W, S, It, Braz*; 1959/60 *S.*
Broadis, I. (14) (Manchester City) 1951/2 *Aust, S, It*; 1952/3 *S, Arg, Ch, U, US* (Newcastle United); 1953/4 *S, Y, H, Bel, Switz, U.*
Brooking, T. (46) (West Ham United) 1973/4 *Port, Arg, E/Germ, Bulg, Y*; 1974/5 *Czecho, Port*; 1975/6 *W, Port, Braz, It, Fin*; 1976/7 *Eire, Fin, It, Hol, I, W*; 1977/8 *It, G, W, S, H*; 1978/9 *D, Eire, I, S, Bulg, Swdn, Aust*; 1979/80 *D, I, Arg, W, I, S, Bel, Sp;* 1980/81 *Switz, Sp, Ru, H;* 1981/2 *H, S, Fin, Sp.*
Brooks, J. (3) (Tottenham Hotspur) 1956/7 *W, Y, D.*
Brown, Tony (1) (West Bromwich Albion) 1970/1 *W.*
Brown, K. (1) (West Ham United) 1959/60 *I.*
Butcher, T. (45) (Ipswich T.) 1979/80 *Au;* 1980/81 *Sp;* 1981/2 *W, S, F, Czecho, G, Sp;* 1982/3 *D, G, Lux, W, Gr, H, I, S, Au* (3); 1983/4 *D, H, Lux, F, I;* 1984/5 *E$Germ, Fin, T, I, Eire, Ru, Fin, S, It, G, US;* 1985/6 *Isr, USSR, S, Mex, Can, Port, Mor, Pol, P, Arg.*
Byrne, G. (2) (Liverpool) 1962/3 *S*; 1965/6 *N.*
Byrne, J. (11) (Crystal Palace) 1961/2 *I*; 1962/3 (West Ham United) *Switz*; 1963/4 *S, U, Port, Eire, Braz, Arg*; 1964/5 *W, S.*

Byrne, R. (33) (Manchester United) 1953/4 *S, Y, H, Bel, Switz, U*; 1954/5 *I, W, G, S, F, Sp, Port*; 1955/6 *D, W, I, Sp, Braz, Swdn, Fin, G*; 1956/7 *I, W, Y, D, S, Eire*; 1957/8 *W, I, F.*
Callaghan, I. (4) (Liverpool) 1965/6 *Fin, F*; 1977/8 *Switz, Lux.*
Carter, H. (7) (Derby County) 1946/7 *I, W, S, Eire, Holl, F, Switz.*
Chamberlain, M. (8) (Stoke City) 1982/3 *Lux;* 1983/4 *D, S, Rus, Braz, U. Ch;* 1984/5 *Fin.*
Channon, M. (46) (Southampton) 1972/3 *Y, S, I, W, S, Czecho, Rus, It;* 1973/4 *Pol, It, Port, W, I, S, Arg, Aust, E/Germ, Bulg, Y*; 1974/5 *Czecho, Port, G, C* (2), *I, W, S*; 1975/6 *Switz, Czecho, Port, W, I, S, Braz, It, Fin*; 1976/7 *Fin, It, Lux, I, W, S, Braz, Arg, U*; 1977/8 *Switz.*
Charlton, J. (35) (Leeds United) 1964/5 *S, H, Y, G, Swdn*; 1965/6 *W, Aust, I, Sp, Pol, G, S, Y, Fin, D, Pol, U, Mex, F, Arg, Port, G*; 1966/7 *I, Czecho, W, S*; 1967/8 *W, Sp*; 1968/9 *Ru, F, W*; 1969/70 *Holl, Port, Holl, Czecho.*
Charlton, R. (106) (Manchester United) 1957/8 *S, Port, Y*; 1958/9 *I, Rus, W, S, It, Braz, Per, Mex, US*; 1959/60 *W, Swdn, S, Y, Sp, H*; 1960/1 *I, Lux, Sp, W, S, Mex, Port, It, Aust*; 1961/2 *Lux, W, Port, I, Aust, S, Switz, Per, H, Arg, Bulg, Braz*; 1962/3 *F, S, Braz, Czecho, E/Germ, Switz*; 1963/4 *W, FIFA, I, S, U, Port, Eire, US, Braz, Arg*; 1964/5 *I, Holl, S*; 1965/6 *W, Aust, I, G, S, Sp, Y, Fin, N, Pol, U, Mex, F, Arg, Port, G*; 1966/7 *I, Czecho, W, S*; 1967/8 *W, I, Rus, S, Sp* (2), *Swdn, Y, Rus*; 1968/9 *Ru, Bulg, Ru, I, W, S, Mex, Braz*; 1969/70 *Holl, Port, Holl, W, I, Co, Ec, Ru, Braz, Czecho, G.*
Charnley, R. (1) (Blackpool) 1961/2 *F.*
Cherry, T. (27) (Leeds United) 1975/6 *W, S, Braz, Fin*; 1976/7 *Eire, It, Lux, I, S, Braz, Arg, U*; 1977/8 *Switz, Lux, It, Braz, W*; 1978/9 *Czecho, W, Swdn*; 1979/80 *Eire, Arg, W, I, S, Au, Sp.*
Chilton, A. (2) (Manchester United) 1950/1 *I*; 1951/2 *F.*
Chivers, M. (24) (Tottenham Hotspur) 1970/1 *M, Gr, M, I, S*; 1971/2 *Switz* (2), *Gr, G* (2), *S*; 1972/3 *W* (2), *S, I, W, S, Czecho, Pol, Rus, It*; 1973/4 *Pol, Aust.*
Clamp, E. (4) (Wolverhampton Wanderers) 1957/8 *Rus* (2), *Braz, Aust.*
Clapton, D. (1) (Arsenal) 1958/9 *W.*
Clarke, A. (19) (Leeds United) 1969/70 *Czecho*; 1970/1 *E/Germ, M, I, W, S*; 1972/3 *S, W, S, Czecho, Pol, Rus, It*; 1973/4 *Pol, It, Aust*; 1974/5 *Port*; 1975/6 *Czecho, Port.*
Clarke, H. (1) (Tottenham Hotspur) 1953/4 *S.*
Clayton, R. (35) (Blackburn Rovers) 1955/6 *I, Sp, Braz, Swdn, Fin, G*; 1956/7 *I, W, Y, D, S, Eire*; 1957/8 *W, I, F, S, Port, Y, Rus*; 1958/9 *I, Rus, W, S, It, Braz, Per, Mex, US*; 1959/60 *W, Swdn, I, S, Y.*
Clemence, R. (61) (Liverpool) 1972/3 *W* (2); 1973/4 *E/Germ, Bulg, Y*; 1974/5 *Czecho, Port, G, C, I, W, S*; 1975/6 *Switz, Czecho, Port, U* (2), *I, S, Braz, Fin*; 1976/7 *Eire, Fin, It, Holl, Lux, S, Braz, Arg, U*; 1977/8 *Switz, Lux, It, G, I, S*; 1978/9 *D, Eire, I, I, S, Bulg, Aust*; 1979/80 *D, Bulg, Eire, Arg, W, S, Bel, Sp;* 1980/81 *Ru, Sp, Braz, Switz, H;* 1981/2 (Tottenham H.) *N, I, Fin;* 1982/3 *Lux;* 1983/4 *Lux.*
Clement, D. (5) (Queens Park Rangers) 1975/6 *W* (2), *It*; 1976/7 *It, Holl.*
Clough, B. (2) (Middlesbrough) 1959/60 *W, Swdn.*
Coates, R. (4) (Burnley) 1969/70 *I*; 1970/1 *Gr,* (Tottenham Hotspur) *M, W.*
Cockburn, H. (13) (Manchester United) 1946/7 *I, W, Eire*; 1947/8 *S, It*; 1948/9 *I, S, D, Switz*; 1950/1 *Arg, Port*; 1951/2 *F.*
Cohen, G. (37) (Fulham) 1963/4 *U, Port, Eire, US, Braz*; 1964/5 *I, Bel, W, Holl, S, H, Y, G, Swdn*; 1965/6 *W, Aust, I, Sp, Pol, G, S, N, D, Pol, U, Mex, F, Arg, Port, G*; 1966/7 *I, Czecho, W, S, Sp*; 1967/8 *W, I.*
Compton, L. (2) (Arsenal) 1950/1 *W, Y.*
Connelly J. (20) (Burnley) 1959/60 *W, Swdn, I, S*; 1961/2 *W, Port, Aust, Switz*; 1962/3 *W, F*; 1964/5 (Manchester United) *H, Y, Swdn*; 1965/6 *W, Aust, I, S, N, D, U.*

Cooper, T. (20) (Leeds United) 1968/9 *F, W, S, Mex*; 1969/70 *Holl, Bel, Co, Ec, Ru, Braz, Czecho, G*; 1970/1 *E/Germ, M, I, W, S*; 1971/2 *Switz* (2); 1974/5 *Port.*
Coppell, S. (41) (Manchester United) 1977/8 *It, G, Braz, W, I, S, H*; 1978/9 *D, Eire, Czecho, I, I, S, Bulg, Aust*; 1979/80 *D, I, Eire, Sp, Arg, W, S, Bel, It;* 1980/81 *Ru, Switz, Ru, Braz, W, S, Switz, H;* 1981/2 *H, S, Fin, F, Czecho, K, G*; 1982/3 *Lux, Gr.*
Corrigan J. (9) (Manchester City) 1975/6 *It;* 1977/8 *Braz;* 1978/9 *W*; 1979/80 *I, Au;* 1980/81 *W, S;* 1981/2 *W, Ic.*
Cowans, G. (9) (Aston Villa) 1982/3 *W, H, I, S, Au*(3); 1985/6 (Bari) *Eg, USSR.*
Crawford, R. (2) (Ipswich Town) 1961/2 *I, Aust.*
Crowe, C. (1) (Wolverhampton Wanderers) 1962/3 *F.*
Cunningham, L. (6) (West Bromwich Albion) 1978/9 *W, Swdn, Aust*; (Real Madrid) 1979/80 *Eire, Sp;* 1980/81 *Ru.*
Currie, A. (17) (Sheffield United) 1971/2 *I*; 1972/3 *Rus, It*; 1973/4 *Pol, It, Aust*; 1975/6 *Switz*; (Leeds United) 1977/8 *Braz, W, I, S, H*; 1978/9 *Czecho, I, I, W, Swdn.*

Davenport, P. (1) (Nottingham Forest) 1984/5*Eire.*
Deeley, N. (2) (Wolverhampton Wanderers) 1958/9 *Braz, Per.*
Devonshire, A. (8) (West Ham United) 1979/80 *I, Au;* 1981/2 *Holl, Ic;* 1982/3 *G, W, Gr;* 1983/ *Lux.*
Dickinson, J. (48) (Portsmouth) 1948/9 *N, F*; 1949/50 *W, S, Eire, Port, Bel, Ch, US, Sp*; 1950/1 *I, W, Y*; 1951/2 *W, I, Aust* (2), *S, It, Switz*; 1952/3 *I, W, Bel, S, Arg, Ch, U, US*; 1953/4 *W, FIFA, I, H* (2), *S, Y, Bel, Switz, U*; 1954/5 *Sp, Port*; 1955/6 *D, W, I, Sp, S*; 1956/7 *W, Y, D.*
Ditchburn, E. (6) (Tottenham Hotspur) 1948/9 *Switz, Swdn*; 1952/3 *US*; 1956/7 *W, Y, D.*
Dixon, K.M. (7) (Chelsea) 1984/5 *Mex, G, US;* 1985/6 *I, Isr, Mex, Pol.*
Dobson, M. (5) (Burnley) 1973/4 *Port, E/Germ, Bulg, Y*; 1974/5 (Everton) *Czecho.*
Douglas, B. (36) (Blackburn Rovers) 1957/8 *W, I, F, S, Port, Y, Rus* (2), *Braz, Aust*; 1958/9 *Rus, S*; 1958/9 *Rus, S*; 1959/60 *Y, H*; 1960/1 *I, Lux, Sp, W, S, Mex, Port, It, Aust*; 1961/2 *Lux, W, Port, I, S, Per, H, Arg, Bulg, Braz*; 1962/3 *S, Braz, Switz.*
Doyle, M. (5) (Manchester City) 1975/6 *W, S, Braz, It*; 1976/7 *Holl.*
Duxbury, M. (10) (Manchester U.) 1983/4 *Lux, F, W, S,Rus, Braz, U. Ch;* 1984/5 *E/Germ, Fin.*

Eastham, G. (19) (Arsenal) 1962/3 *Braz, Czecho, E/Germ*; 1963/4 *W, FIFA, I, S, U, Port, Eire, US, Braz, Arg*; 1964/5 *H, G, Swdn*; 1965/6 *Sp, Pol, D.*
Eckersley, W. (17) (Blackburn Rovers) 1949/50 *Sp*; 1950/1 *Y, S, Arg, Port*; 1951/2 *Aust* (2), *Switz*; 1952/3 *I, Arg, Ch, U, US*; 1953/4 *W, FIFA, I, H.*
Edwards, D. (18) (Manchester United) 1954/5 *S, F, Sp, Port*; 1955/6 *S, Braz, Swdn, Fin, G*; 1956/7 *I, D, S, Eire, D, Eire*; 1957/8 *W, I, F.*
Ellerington, W. (2) (Southampton) 1948/9 *N, F.*
Elliott, W. H. (5) (Burnley) 1951/2 *It, Aust*; 1952/3 *I, W, Bel.*

Fantham, J. (1) (Sheffield Wednesday) 1961/2 *Lux.*
Fenwick, T. (19) (Q.P.R.) 1983/4 *W, S, Rus, Braz, U,Ch;* 1984/5 *Fin, S, Mex, US;* 1985/6 *Ru, T, I, Eg,Mex, Port, Mor, Pol, Arg.*
Finney, T. (76) (Preston) 1946/7 *I, Eire, Holl, F, Port*; 1947/8 *W, I, S, Bel, Swdn, It*; 1948/9 *I, W, S, Swdn, N, F*; 1949/50 *W, I, S, Eire, It, Port, Bel, Ch, US, Sp*; 1950/1 *W, S, Arg, Port*; 1951/2 *F, W, I, S, It, Aust, Switz*; 1952/3 *I, W, Bel, S, Arg, Ch, U, US*; 1953/4 *D, S, Y, H, Bel, Switz, U*; 1954/5 *G;* 1955/6 *D, W, I, Sp, S*; 1956/7 *W, Y, D, S, Eire, D, Eire*; 1957/8 *W, F, S, Port, Y, Rus* (2); 1958/9 *I, Rus.*
Flowers, R. (49) (Wolverhampton Wanderers) 1954/5 *F*; 1958/9 *W, S, It, Braz, Per, Mex, US*; 1959/60 *W, S, Y, Sp, H, Swdn, I*; 1960/1 *Lux, Sp, W, S, Mex, Port,*

It, Aust; 1961/2 *Lux, W, Port, I, Aust, S, Switz, Per, H, Arg, Bulg, Braz*; 1962/3 *F, I, W, F, S, Switz*; 1963/4 *Eire, US, Port*; 1964/5 *W, Holl, G*; 1965/6 *N*.
Foster, S. (3) (Brighton) 1981/2 *I, Holl, K*.
Foulkes, W. (1) (Manchester United) 1954/5 *I*.
Francis, G. (12) (Q.P.R.) 1974/5 *Czecho, Port, W, S*; 1975/6 *Switz, Czecho, Port, W, I, S, Braz, Fin*.
Francis, T. (52) (Birmingham City) 1976/7 *Holl, Lux,S, Braz*; 1977/8 *Switz, Lux, It, G, Braz, W, S, H*;1978/9 *Bulg, Swdn, Aust*; (Nottingham Forest) 1979/80*I, Bulg, Sp;* 1980/81 *Sp, Ru, S, Switz;* 1981/2(Manchester C.) *N, I, W, S, Fin, F, Czecho, K, G, Sp;* 1982/3 (Sampdoria) *D, Gr, H, I, S, Au* (3); 1983/4*D, I, Rus;* 1984/5 *E/Germ, T, I, Ru, Fin, S, It,Mex;* 1985/6 *S*.
Franklin, N. (27) (Stoke City) 1946/7 *I, W, S, Eire, Holl, F, Switz, Port*; 1947/8 *W, I, S, Bel, Swdn, It*; 1948/9 *I, W, S, D, Switz, Swdn, N, F*; 1949/50 *W, I, S, Eire, It*.
Froggatt, J. (13) (Portsmouth) 1949/50 *I, It*; 1950/1 *S*; 1951/2 *Aust* (2), *S, It, Switz*; 1952/3 *I, W, Bel, S, US*.
Froggatt, R. (4) (Sheffield Wednesday) 1952/3 *W, Bel, S, US*.

Garrett, T. (3) (Blackpool) 1951/2 *S, It*; 1953/4 *W*.
Gates, E. (2) (Ipswich T.) 1980/81 *N, Ru*.
George, F. C. (1) (Derby County) 1976/7 *Eire*.
Gidman, J. (1) (Aston Villa) 1976/7 *Lux*.
Gillard, I. (3) (Queens Park Rangers) 1974/5 *G, W*; 1975/6 *Czecho*.
Goddard, P. (1) (West Ham U.) 1981/2 *Ic*.
Grainger, C. (7) (Sheffield United) 1955/6 *Braz, Swdn, Fin, G*; 1956/7 *I, W*, (Sunderland) *S*.
Greaves, J. (57) (Chelsea) 1958/9 *Per, Mex, US*; 1959/60 *W, Swdn, Y, Sp*; 1960/1 *I, Lux, Sp, W, S, Port, It, Aust*; 1961/2 (Tottenham Hotspur) *S, Switz, Per, H, Arg, Bulg, Braz*; 1962/3 *F, I, W, F, S, Braz, Czecho, Switz*; 1963/4 *W, FIFA, I, U, Port, Eire, Braz, Port, Arg*; 1964/5 *I, Bel, Holl, S, H, Y*; 1965/6 *W, Aust, Y, N, D, Pol, U, Mex, F*; 1966/7 *S, Sp, Aust*.
Greenhoff, B. (18) (Manchester United) 1975/6 *W, I*; 1976/7 *Eire, Fin, It, Holl, I, W, S, Braz, Arg, U*; 1977/8 *Braz, W, I, S, H*; 1979/80 *Au*.
Gregory, J. (6) (Q.P.R.) 1982/3 *Au* (3); 1983/4 *D, H, W*.

Hagan, J. (1) (Sheffield United) 1948/9 *D*.
Haines, J. (1) (West Bromwich Albion) 1948/9 *Switz*.
Hall, J. (17) (Birmingham City) 1955/6 *D, I, W, Sp, S, Braz, Swdn, Fin, G*; 1956/7 *I, W, Y, D, S, Eire, D, Eire*.
Hancocks, J. (3) (Wolverhampton Wanderers) 1948/9 *Switz*; 1949/50 *W*; 1950/1 *Y*.
Hardwick, G. (13) (Middlesbrough) 1946/7 *I, W, S, Eire, Holl, F, Switz, Port*; 1947/8 *W, I, S, Bel, Swdn*.
Harris, G. (1) (Burnley) 1965/6 *Pol*.
Harris, P. (2) (Portsmouth) 1949/50 *Eire*; 1953/4 *H*.
Harvey, C. (1) (Everton) 1970/1 *M*.
Hassall, H. (5) (Huddersfield Town) 1950/1 *S, Arg, Port*; 1951/2 *F* (Bolton Wanderers); 1953/4 *I*.
Hateley, M. (21) (Portsmouth) 1983/4 *Rus, Braz, U,Ch;* 1984/5 (AC Milan) *E/Germ, Fin, I, Eire, Fin, S, It,Mex;* 1985/6 *Ru, T, Eg, S, Mex, Can, Port, Mor, P*.
Haynes, J. (56) (Fulham) 1954/5 *I*; 1955/6 *I, Sp, S, Swdn, Fin, G*; 1956/7 *W, Y, Eire, D, Eire*; 1957/8 *W, I, F, S, Port, Y, Rus* (2), *Braz, Aust, Rus*; 1958/9 *I, Rus, S, It, Braz, Per, Mex, US*; 1959/60 *I, Y, Sp, H*; 1960/1 *I, Lux, Sp, W, S, Mex, Port, It, Aust*; 1961/2 *W, Port, I, Aust, S, Switz, H, Per, Arg, Bulg, Braz*.
Hector, K. (2) (Derby County) 1973/4 *Pol, It*.
Hellawell, M. (2) (Birmingham City) 1962/3 *F, I*.
Henry, R. (1) (Tottenham Hotspur) 1962/3 *F*.

Hill, F. (2) (Bolton Wanderers) 1962/3 *I, W.*
Hill, G. (6) (Manchester United) 1975/6 *It*; 1976/7 *Eire, Fin, Lux*; 1977/8 *Switz, Lux.*
Hill, R. (3) (Luton Town) 1982/3 *D, G;* 1985/6*Eg.*
Hinton, A. (3) (Wolverhampton W.) 1962/3 *F*; 1964/5 (Nottingham Forest) *Bel, W.*
Hitchens, G. (7) (Aston Villa) 1960/1 *Mex, It, Aust* (Inter Milan); 1961/2 *Switz, Per, H, Braz.*
Hoddle, G. (38) (Tottenham Hotspur) 1979/80 *Bulg, W,Au, Sp;* 1980/81 *Sp, W, S;* 1981/2 *N, I, W, Ic,Czecho, K;* 1982/3 *Lux, I, S;* 1983/4 *H, Lux, F;* 1984/5 *Eire, S, It, Mex, G, US;* 1985/6 *Ru, T, I,Isr, USSR, S, Mex, Can, Port, Mor, Pol, P, Arg.*
Hodge, S.B. (8)(Aston Villa) 1985/6 *USSR, S, Can,Port, Mor, Pol, P, Arg.*
Hodgkinson, A. (5) (Sheffield United) 1956/7 *S, Eire,D, Eire*; 1960/1 *W.*
Holden, D. (5) (Bolton Wanderers) 1958/9 *S, It, Braz, Per, Mex.*
Holliday, E. (3) (Middlesbrough) 1959/60 *W, Swdn, I.*
Hollins, J. (1) (Chelsea) 1966/7 *Sp.*
Hopkinson, E. (14) (Bolton Wanderers) 1957/8 *W, I, F, S, Port, Y*; 1958/9 *S, It, Braz, Per, Mex, US*; 1959/60 *W, Swdn.*
Howe, D. (23) (West Bromwich Albion) 1957/8 *W, I, E, F, S, Port, Y, Rus* (2), *Braz, Aust, Rus*; 1958/9 *I, Rus, W, S, It, Braz, Per, Mex, US*; 1959/60 *W, Swdn, I.*
Howe, J. (3) (Derby County) 1947/8 *It*; 1948/9 *I, S.*
Hudson, A. (2) (Stoke City) 1974/5 *G, C.*
Hughes, E. (61) (Liverpool) 1969/70 *Holl, Port, Bel, W, I, S*; 1970/1 *E/Germ, M, Gr, M, W*; 1971/2 *Switz, Gr, G* (2), *W, I, S*; 1972/3 *W* (2), *S, W, S, Pol, Rus, It*; 1973/4 *Pol, It, W, I, S, Arg, Aust, E/Germ, Bulg, Y*; 1974/5 *Czecho, Port, C, I*; 1976/7 *It, Lux, W, S, Braz, Arg, U*; 1977/8 *Switz, Lux, It, G, I, S, H*; 1978/9 *D, I, W, Swdn*; (Wolverhampton Wanderers) 1979/80 *Sp, I, S.*
Hughes, L. (3) (Liverpool) 1949/50 *Ch, US, Sp.*
Hunt, R. (34) (Liverpool) 1961/2 *Aust*; 1962/3 *E/Germ*; 1963/4 *S* (2), *US, Port*; 1964/5 *W*; 1965/6 *Sp, Pol, G, S, Fin, N, Pol, U, Mex, F, Arg, Port, G*; 1966/7 *I, Czecho, W, Sp, Aust*; 1967/8 *W, I, Rus, Sp* (2), *Swdn, Y, Rus*; 1968/9 *Ru* (2).
Hunt, S. (2) (W.B.A.) 1983/4 *S, USSR.*
Hunter, N. (28) (Leeds United) 1965/6 *Sp, G, Y, Fin*; 1966/7 *Aust*; 1967/8 *Sp, Swdn, G, Y, Rus*; 1968/9 *Ru, W*; 1969/70 *Holl, G*; 1970/1 *M*; 1971/2 *G* (2), *W, I, S*; 1972/3 *W* (2), *Rus*; 1973/4 *Pol, I, S, Aust*; 1974/5 *Czecho.*
Hurst, G. (49) (West Ham United) 1965/6 *G, S, Y, Fin, D, Arg, Port, G*; 1966/7 *I, Czecho, W, S, Sp, Aust*; 1967/8 *W, I, Rus, S, Swdn, G, Rus*; 1968/9 *Ru, Bulg, Ru, F, I, S, Mex, U, Braz*; 1969/70 *Holl* (2), *Bel, W, I, S, Co, Ec, Ru, Braz, G*; 1970/1 *E/Germ, Gr, W, S*; 1971/2 *Switz* (2), *Gr, G.*

Jezzard, B. (2) (Fulham) 1953/4 *H*; 1955/6 *I.*
Johnson, D. (8) (Ipswich Town) 1974/5 *W, S*; 1975/6 *Switz*; (Liverpool) 1979/80 *Eire, Arg, I, S, Bel.*
Johnston, H. (10) (Blackpool) 1946/7 *S, Holl*; 1950/1 *S*; 1952/3 *Arg, Ch, U, US*; 1953/4 *W, I, H.*
Jones, M. (3) (Sheffield United) 1964/5 *G, Swdn* (Leeds United); 1969/70 *Holl.*
Jones, W. H. (2) (Liverpool) 1949/50 *Port, Bel.*

Kay, A. (1) (Everton) 1962/3 *Switz.*
Keegan, K. (63) (Liverpool) 1972/3 *W* (2); 1973/4 *W, I, Arg, E/Germ, Bulg, Y*; 1974/5 *Czecho, G, C* (2), *I, S*; 1975/6 *Switz, Czecho, Port, W* (2), *I, S, Braz, Fin*; 1976/7 *Eire, Fin, It, Holl, Lux,* (SV Hamburg), *W, Braz, Arg, U*; 1977/8 *Switz, It, G, Braz, H*; 1978/9 *D, Eire, Czecho, I, W, S, Bulg, Swdn, Aust*; 1979/80 *D, I, Eire, Sp, Arg, Bel, It, Sp;* 1980/81 *Sp, Switz, H;* 1981/2 (Southampton) *N, H, I, S, Fin, Sp.*
Kennedy, A. (2) (Liverpool) 1983/4 *I, W.*

Kennedy, R. (17) (Liverpool) 1975/6 *W* (2), *I, S*; 1976/7 *Lux, W, S, Braz, Arg*; 1977/8 *Switz, Lux*; 1979/80 *Bulg, Sp, Arg, W, Bel, It.*
Kevan, D. (14) (West Bromwich Albion) 1956/7 *S;* 1957/8 *W, I, S, Port, Y, Rus* (2), *Braz, Aust, Rus*; 1958/9 *Mex, US*; 1960/1 *Mex.*
Kidd, B. (2) (Manchester United) 1969/70 *I, Ec.*
Knowles, C. (4) (Tottenham Hotspur) 1967/8 *Rus, Sp, Swdn, G.*

Labone, B. (26) (Everton) 1962/3 *I, W, F*; 1966/7 *Sp, Aust*; 1967/8 *S, Sp, Swdn, G, Y, Rus,* 1968/9 *Ru, Bulg, I, S, Mex, U, Braz*; 1969/70 *Bel, W, S, Co, Ec, Ru, Braz, G.*
Lampard, F. (2) (West Ham United) 1972/3 *Y*; 1979/80 *Au.*
Langley, J. (3) (Fulham) 1957/8 *S, Port, Y.*
Langton, R. (11) (Blackburn Rovers) 1946/7 *I, W, Eire, Holl, F, Switz*; 1947/8 *Swdn*; 1948/9 (Preston North End) *D, Swdn*; 1949/50 (Bolton Wanderers) *S*; 1950/1 *I.*
Latchford, R. (12) (Everton) 1977/8 *It, Braz, W*; 1978/9 *D, Eire, Czecho, I, I, W, S, Bulg, Aust.*
Lawler, C. (4) (Liverpool) 1970/1 *M, W, S*; 1971/2 *Switz.*
Lawton, T. (15) (Chelsea) 1946/7 *I, W, S, Eire, Holl, F, Switz, Port*; 1947/8 *W, I* (Notts County), *S, Bel, Swdn, It*; 1948/9 *D.*
Lee, F. (27) (Manchester City) 1968/9 *Bulg, F, I, W, S, Mex, U*; 1969/70 *Holl, Port, Holl, Bel, W, Co, Ec, Ru, Braz, G*; 1970/1 *E/Germ, Gr, M, I, W, S*; 1971/2 *Switz* (2), *Gr, G.*
Lee, J. (1) (Derby County) 1950/1 *I.*
Lee, S. (14) (Liverpool) 1982/3 *Gr, Lux, W, Gr, H, S, Au;* 1983/4 *D, H, Lux, F, I, W, Ch.*
Lindsay, A. (4) (Liverpool) 1973/4 *Arg, E/Germ, Bulg, Y.*
Lineker, G. (18) (Leicester C.) 1983/4 *S;* 1984/5*Eire, Ru, S, It, G, US;* (Everton) 1985/6 *Ru, T, I,Eg, USSR, Can, Port, Mor, Pol, P, Arg.*
Little, B. (1) (Aston Villa) 1974/5 *W.*
Lloyd, L. (4) (Liverpool) 1970/1 *W*; 1971/2 *Switz, I*; (Nottingham F.) 1979/80 *W.*
Lofthouse, N. (33) (Bolton Wanderers) 1950/1 *Y*; 1951/2 *W, I, Aust* (2), *It, Switz*; 1952/3 *I, W, Bel, S, Arg, Ch, U, US*; 1953/4 *W, FIFA, I, Bel, U*; 1954/5 *I, S, F, Sp, Port*; 1955/6 *D, W, Sp, S, Fin*; 1958/9 *Rus, W.*
Lowe, E. (3) (Aston Villa) 1946/7 *F, Switz, Port.*

Mabbutt, G. (9) (Tottenham Hotspur) 1982/3 *G, Gr, Lux, W, Gr, H, I, S;* 1983/4 *H.*
Macdonald, M. (14) (Newcastle United) 1971/2 *W, I, S*; 1972/3 *Rus;* 1973/4 *Port, S, Y*; 1974/5 *G, C* (2), *I,* (Arsenal) 1975/6 *Switz, Czecho, Port.*
Madeley, P. (24) (Leeds United) 1970/1 *I*; 1971/2 *Switz* (2), *Gr, G* (2), *W, S*; 1972/3 *S, Czecho, Pol, Rus, It*; 1973/4 *Pol, It, Aust*; 1974/5 *Czecho, Port, C*; 1975/6 *Czecho, Port, Fin*; 1976/7 *Eire, Holl.*
Mannion, W. (26) (Middlesbrough) 1946/7 *I, W, S, Eire, Holl, F, Switz, Port*; 1947/8 *W, I, Bel, Swdn, It*; 1948/9 *N, F*; 1949/50 *S, Eire, Port, Bel, Ch, US*; 1950/1 *I, W, Y, S*; 1951/2 *F.*
Mariner, P. (35) (Ipswich Town) 1976/7 *Lux, I*;1977/8 *Lux, W, S*; 1979/80 *W, I, S, Au, It, Sp;* 1980/81 *N, Switz, Sp, Switz, H;* 1981/2 *N, H,Holl, S, Fin, F, Czecho, K, G, Sp*; 1982/3 *D, G, Gr, W;* 1983/4 *D, H, Lux;* 1984/5 (Arsenal) *E/Germ, Ru.*
Marsh, R. (9) (Q.P.R.) 1971/2 *Switz,* (ManchesterCity), *G* (2), *W, I, S*; 1972/3 *Y, W*(2).
Martin, A. (16) (West Ham U.) 1980/81 *Braz, S;* 1981/2 *H, Fin*; 1982/3 *Gr, Lux, W, Gr, H;* 1983/4 *H, Lux, W;* 1984/5 *I;* 1985/6 *Isr,Can, P.*
Matthews, R. (5) (Coventry City) 1955/6 *S, Braz,Swdn, G*; 1956/7 *I,* (Chelsea).
Matthews, S. (37) (Stoke City) 1946/7 *S* (Blackpool), *Switz, Port*; 1947/8 *W, I, S, Bel, It*; 1948/9 *I, W, S, D, Switz*; 1949/50 *Sp*; 1950/1 *I, S*; 1953/4 *FIFA, I, H, Bel,*

U; 1954/5 *I, W, G, S, F, Sp, Port*; 1955/6 *W, Braz*; 1956/7 *I, W, Y, D, S, Eire, D.*

McDermott, T. (24) (Liverpool) 1977/8 *Switz, Lux*; 1978/9 *I, W, Swdn*; 1979/80 oll, S,Ic.

McDonald, C. (8) (Burnley) 1957/8 *Rus* (2), *Braz, Aust, Rus*; 1958/9 *I, Rus, W.*

McFarland, R. (28) (Derby County) 1970/1 *M, Gr, M, I, S*; 1971/2 *Switz, Gr, G, W, S*; 1972/3 *W* (2), *I, W, S, Czecho, Pol, Rus, It*; 1973/4 *Pol, It, W, I, Aust*; 1975/6 *Czecho, S*; 1976/7 *Eire, It.*

McGarry, W. (4) (Huddersfield Town) 1953/4 *Switz, U*; 1955/6 *D, W.*

McGuinness, W. (2) (Manchester United) 1958/9 *I, Mex.*

McNab, R. (4) (Arsenal) 1968/9 *Ru, Bulg, Ru, I.*

McNeil, M. (9) (Middlesbrough) 1960/1 *I, Lux, Sp, W, Mex, Port, It*; 1961/2 *Lux.*

Meadows, J. (1) (Manchester City) 1954/5 *S.*

Medley, L. (6) (Tottenham Hotspur) 1950/1 *W, Y*; 1951/2 *F, W, I, Aust.*

Melia, J. (2) (Liverpool) 1962/3 *S, Switz.*

Merrick, G. (23) (Birmingham City) 1951/2 *I, Aust* (2), *S, It, Switz*; 1952/3 *I, W, Bel, S, Arg, Ch, U*; 1953/4 *W, FIFA, I, H* (2), *S, Y, Bel, Switz, U.*

Metcalfe, V. (2) (Huddersfield Town) 1950/1 *Arg, Port.*

Milburn, J. (13) (Newcastle United) 1948/9 *I, W, S, Switz*; 1949/50 *W, Port, Bel, Sp*; 1950/1 *W, Arg, Port*; 1951/2 *F*; 1955/6 *D.*

Miller, B. (1) (Burnley) 1960/1 *Aust.*

Mills, M. (44) (Ipswich Town) 1972/3 *Y*; 1975/6 *W* (2), *I, S, Braz, It, Fin*; 1976/7 *Fin, It, I, W, S*; 1977/8 *G, Braz, W, I, S, H*; 1978/9 *D, Eire, I, I, S, Bulg, Aust*; 1979/80 *D, I, Sp, I, S, Sp*; 1980/81 *Switz, Switz, H*; 1981/2 *N, H, S, Fin, F, Czecho, K, G, Sp.*

Milne, G. (14) (Liverpool) 1962/3 *Braz, Czecho, E/Germ*; 1963/4 *W, FIFA, I, S, U, Port, Eire, Braz, Arg*; 1964/5 *I, Bel.*

Milton, C. A. (1) (Arsenal) 1951/2 *Aust.*

Moore, I. (1) (Nottingham Forest) 1969/70 *Holl.*

Moore, R. (108) (West Ham United) 1961/2 *Per, H, Arg, Bulg, Braz*; 1962/3 *F, I, W, F, S, Braz, Czecho, E/Germ, Switz*; 1963/4 *W, FIFA, I, S, U, Port, Eire, Braz, Port, Arg*; 1964/5 *I, Bel, S, H, Y, G, Swdn*; 1965/6 *W, Aust, I, Sp, Pol, G, S, N, D, Pol, U, Mex, F, Arg, Port, G*; 1966/7 *I, Czecho, W, S, Sp, Aust*; 1967/8 *W, I, Rus, S, Sp* (2), *Swdn, G, Y, Rus*; 1968/9 *Ru, Bulg, F, I, W, S, Mex, U, Braz*; 1969/70 *Holl, Port, Bel, W, I, S, Co, Ec, Ru, Braz, Czecho, G*; 1970/1 *E/Germ, Gr, M, I, S*; 1971/2 *Switz* (2), *Gr, G* (2), *W, S*; 1972/3 *Y, W* (3), *S* (2), *I, Czecho, Pol, Rus, It*; 1973/4 *It.*

Morley, A (6) (Aston Villa) 1981/2 *H, I, W, Ic*;1982/3 *D, Gr.*

Morris, J. (3) (Derby County) 1948/9 *N, F*; 1949/50 *Eire.*

Mortensen, S. (25) (Blackpool) 1946/7 *Port*; 1947/8 *W, I, S, Bel, Swdn, It*; 1948/9 *I, W, S, Swdn, N*; 1949/50 *W, I, S, It, Port, Bel, Ch, US, Sp*; 1950/1 *S, Arg*; 1953/4 *FIFA, H.*

Mozley, B. (3) (Derby County) 1949/50 *W, I, Eire.*

Mullen, J. (12) (Wolverhampton Wanderers) 1946/7 *S*; 1948/9 *N, F*; 1949/50 *Bel, Ch, US*; 1953/4 *W, FIFA, I, S, Y, Switz.*

Mullery, A. (35) (Tottenham Hotspur) 1964/5 *Holl*; 1966/7 *Sp, Aust*; 1967/8 *W, I, Rus, S, Sp* (2), *Swdn, Y*; 1968/9 *Ru, Bulg, F, I, S, Mex, U, Braz*; 1969/70 *Holl, Port, Holl, W, I, S, Co, Ec, Ru, Braz, Czecho, G*; 1970/1 *E/Germ, M, Gr*; 1971/2 *Switz.*

Neal, P. (50) (Liverpool) 1975/6 *W, It*; 1976/7 *W, S, Braz, Arg, U*; 1977/8 *Switz, It, G, I, S, H*; 1978/9 *D, Eire, I, I, S, Bulg, Aust*; 1979/80 *D, I, Sp, Arg, W, Bel, It*; 1980/81 *Ru, Switz, Sp, Braz, H*; 1981/2 *N, H, W, Holl, Ic, F, K*; 1982/3 *D, Gr, Lux, W, Gr, H, I, S, Au* (2); 1983/4 *D.*

Newton, K. (27) (Blackburn Rovers) 1965/6 *G, S*; 1966/7 *Sp, Aust*; 1967/8 *W, S, Sp, Swdn, G, Y*; 1968/9 *Ru, Bulg, F, I, W, S, Mex, U, Braz*; 1969/70 (Everton) *Holl, I, S, Co, Ec, Ru, Czecho, G.*

Nicholls, J. (2) (West Bromwich Albion) 1953/4 *S, Y.*
Nicholson, W. (1) (Tottenham Hotspur) 1950/1 *Port.*
Nish, D. (5) (Derby County) 1972/3 *I;* 1973/4 *Port, W, I, S.*
Norman, M. (23) (Tottenham Hotspur) 1961/2 *Per, H, Arg, Bulg, Braz*; 1962/3 *F, S, Braz, Czecho, E/Germ*; 1963/4 *W, FIFA, I, S, U, Port, US, Braz, Port, Arg*; 1964/5 *I, Bel, Holl.*

Owen, S. (3) (Luton Town) 1953/4 *H, Bel.*
O'Grady, M. (2) (Huddersfield Town) 1962/3 *I;* 1968/9 (Leeds United) *F.*
Osgood, P. (4) (Chelsea) 1969/70 *Bel, Ru, Czecho*; 1973/4 *It.*
Osman, R. (11) (Ipswich Town) 1979/80 *Au;* 1980/81 *Sp, Ru, Switz;* 1981/2 *N, Ic*; 1982/3 *D, Au* (3); 1983/4 *D.*

Paine, T. (19) (Southampton) 1962/3 *Czecho, E/Germ*; 1963/4 *W, FIFA, I, S, U, US, Port*; 1964/5 *I, H, Y, G, Swdn*; 1965/6 *W, Aust, Y, N, Mex.*
Parkes, P. (1) (Queens Park Rangers) 1973/4 *Port.*
Parry, R. (2) (Bolton Wanderers) 1959/60 *I, S.*
Peacock, A. (6) (Middlesbrough) 1961/2 *Arg, Bulg*; 1962/3 *I, W*; 1965/6 (Leeds United) *W, I.*
Pearson, Stan (8) (Manchester United) 1947/8 *S;* 1948/9 *I, S*; 1949/50 *I, It*; 1950/1 *Port*; 1951/2 *S, It.*
Pearson, Stuart (15) (Manchester United) 1975/6 *W, I, S, Braz, Fin*; 1976/7 *Eire, Holl, W, S, Braz, Arg, U*; 1977/8 *It, G, I.*
Pegg, D. (1) (Manchester United) 1956/7 *Eire.*
Pejic, M. (4) (Stoke City) 1973/4 *Port, W, I, S.*
Perry, W. (3) (Blackpool) 1955/6 *I, Sp, S.*
Perryman, S. (1) (Tottenham H.) 1981/2 *Ic.*
Peters, M. (67) (West Ham United) 1965/6 *Y, Fin, Pol, Mex, F, Arg, Port, G*; 1966/7 *I, Czecho, W, S*; 1967/8 *W, I, Rus, S, Sp* (2), *Swdn, Y, Rus*; 1968/9 *Ru, Bulg, F, I, S, Mex, U, Braz*; 1969/70 *Holl, Port, Holl, Bel,* (Tottenham Hotspur) *W, I, S, Co, Ec, Ru, Braz, Czecho, G*; 1970/1 *E/Germ, M, Gr, M, I, W, S*; 1971/2 *Switz, Gr, G* (2), *I;* 1972/3 *S, I, W, S, Czecho, Pol, Rus, It*; 1973/4 *Pol, It, Port, S, Aust.*
Phillips, L. (3) (Portsmouth) 1951/2 *I*; 1954/5 *W, G.*
Pickering, F. (3) (Everton) 1963/4 *US*; 1964/5 *I, Bel.*
Pickering, N. (1) (Sunderland) 1982/3 *Au.*
Pilkington, B. (1) (Burnley) 1954/5 *I.*
Pointer, R. (3) (Burnley) 1961/2 *Lux, W, Port.*
Pye, J. (1) (Wolverhampton Wanderers) 1949/50 *Eire.*

Quixall, A. (5) (Sheffield Wednesday) 1953/4 *W, FIFA, I*; 1954/5 *Sp, Port.*

Radford, J. (2) (Arsenal) 1968/9 *Ru*; 1971/2 *Switz.*
Ramsey, A. (32) (Southampton) 1948/9 *Switz*; 1949/50 (Tottenham Hotspur) *S, It, Port, Bel, Ch, US, Sp*; 1950/1 *I, W, Y, S, Arg, Port*; 1951/2 *F, W, I, Aust* (2), *S, It, Switz*; 1952/3 *I, W, Bel, S, Arg, Ch, U, US*; 1953/4 *FIFA, H.*
Reaney, P. (3) (Leeds United) 1968/9 *Bulg*; 1969/70 *Port*; 1970/1 *M.*
Reeves, K. (2) (Norwich City) 1979/80 *Bulg, I.*
Regis, C. (3) (W.B.A.) 1981/2 *I, Ic*; 1982/3 *G.*
Reid, P. (9) (Everton) 1984/5 *Mex, G, US;* 1985/6*Ru, S, Can, Pol, P, Arg.*
Revie, D. (6) (Manchester City) 1954/5 *I, S, F*; 1955/6 *D, W*; 1956/7 *I.*
Richards, J. (1) (Wolverhampton Wanderers) 1972/3 *I.*
Rickaby, S. (1) (West Bromwich Albion) 1953/4 *I.*
Rimmer, J. (1) (Arsenal) 1975/6 *It.*
Rix, G. (17) (Arsenal) 1980/81 *N, Ru, Switz, Braz, W, S;* 1981/2 *Holl, Fin, F, Czecho, K, G, Sp*; 1982/3 *D, G, Gr;* 1983/4 *I.*
Robb, G. (1) (Tottenham Hotspur) 1953/4 *H.*

Roberts, G. (6) (Tottenham Hotspur) 1982/3 *I, S;* 1983/4 *F, I, S, Rus.*
Robson, B. (53) (West Bromwich Albion) 1979/80 *Eire,Au;* 1980/81 *N, Ru, Switz, Sp, Ru, Braz, W, S, Switz, H;* 1981/2 *N,* (Manchester U.) *H, I, W, Holl, S, Fin,F, Czecho, G, Sp*; 1982/3 *D, Gr, Lux, S;* 1983/4 *H,Lux, F, I, S, Rus, Braz, U, Ch;* 1984/5 *E/Germ, Fin, T, Eire, Ru, Fin, S, Mex, It, G, US;* 1985/6 *Ru, T, Isr, Mex, Port, Mor.*
Robson, R. (20) (West Bromwich Albion) 1957/8 *F, Rus*(2), *Braz, Aust*; 1959/60 *Sp, H*; 1960/1 *I, Lux, Sp, W, S, Mex, Port, It*; 1961/2 *Lux, W, Port, I, Switz.*
Rowley, J. (6) (Manchester United) 1948/9 *Switz, Swdn, F*; 1949/50 *I, It*; 1951/2 *S.*
Royle, J. (6) (Everton) 1970/1 *M*; 1972/3 *Y;* (Manchester City) 1975/6 *I, It*; 1976/7 *Fin, Lux.*

Sadler, D. (4) (Manchester United) 1967/8 *I, Rus*; 1969/70 *Ec*; 1970/1 *E/Germ.*
Sansom, K. (70) (Crystal Palace) 1978/9 *W;* 1979/80 *Bulg, Eire, Arg, W, I, S, Bel, It;* 1980/81 (Arsenal) *N, Ru, Switz, Sp, Ru, Braz, W, S, Switz;* 1981/2 *I, W, Holl, S, Fin, F, Czecho, G, Sp*; 1982/3 *D, G,Gr, Lux, Gr, H, I, S;* 1983/4 *D, H, Lux, F, S, Rus, Braz,U, Ch;* 1984/5 *E/Germ, Fin, T, I, Eire, Ru, Fin, S, It,Mex, G, US;* 1985/6 *Ru, T, I, Eg, Isr, USSR, S, Mex, Can,Port, Mor, Pol, P, Arg.*
Scott, L. (17) (Arsenal) 1946/7 *I, W, S, Eire, Holl, F, Switz, Port*; 1947/8 *W, I, S, Bel, Swdn, It*; 1948/9 *I, W, D.*
Sewell, J. (6) (Sheffield Wednesday) 1951/2 *I, Aust, Switz*; 1952/3 *I;* 1953/4 *H* (2).
Shackleton, L. (5) (Sunderland) 1948/9 *W, D*; 1949/50 *W;* 1954/5 *W, G.*
Shaw, G. (5) (Sheffield United) 1958/9 *Rus, W, S, It*; 1962/3 *W.*
Shellito, K. (1) (Chelsea) 1962/3 *Czecho.*
Shilton, P. (86) (Leicester City) 1970/1 *E/Germ, W*; 1971/2 *Switz, I*; 1972/3 *Y,S, I, W, S, Czecho, Pol, Rus, It*; 1973/4 *Pol, It, W, I,S, Arg, Aust*; 1974/5 (Stoke City) *C;* 1976/7 *I,W*; (Nottingham Forest) 1977/8 *W, H*; 1978/9 *Czecho, Swdn, Aust*; 1979/80 *I, Sp, It;* 1980/81 *N, Switz, Ru;* 1981/2 *H, Holl, S, F, Czecho, K, G, Sp*; (Southampton) 1982/3 *D, G, Gr, W, Gr, H, I, S, Au* (3); 1983/4 *D, H, F, I, W, S, Rus, Braz, U, Ch;* 1984/5 *E/Germ, Fin, T, I,Ru, Fin, S, It, G;* 1985/6 *Ru, T, I,Eg, Isr, USSR, S, Mex, Can, Port, Mor, Pol, P, Arg.*
Shimwell, E. (1) (Blackpool) 1948/9 *Swdn.*
Sillett, P. (3) (Chelsea) 1954/5 *F, Sp, Port.*
Slater, W. (12) (Wolverhampton Wanderers) 1954/5 *W, G*; 1957/8 *S, Port, Y, Rus* (2), *Braz, Aust, Rus*; 1958/9 *Rus*; 1959/60 *S.*
Smith, L. (6) (Arsenal) 1950/1 *W*; 1951/2 *W, I*; 1952/3 *W, Bel, S.*
Smith, R. (15) (Tottenham Hotspur) 1960/1 *I, Lux, Sp, W, S, Port*; 1961/2 *S*; 1962/3 *F, S, Braz, Czecho, E/Germ*; 1963/4 *W, FIFA, I.*
Smith, Tom (1) (Liverpool) 1970/1 *W.*
Smith, Trevor (2) (Birmingham City) 1959/60 *W, Swdn.*
Spink, N. (1) (Aston Villa) 1982/3 *Au.*
Springett, R. (33) (Sheffield Wednesday) 1959/60 *I, S, Y, Sp, H*; 1960/1 *I, Lux, Sp, Mex, Port, It, Aust*; 1961/2 *Lux, W, Port, I, Aust, S, Switz, Per, H, Arg, Bulg, Braz*; 1962/3 *F, I, W, F, Switz*; 1965/6 *W, Aust, N.*
Staniforth, R. (8) (Huddersfield Town) 1953/4 *S, Y, H, Bel, Switz, U*; 1954/5 *W, G.*
Statham, D. (3) (West Bromwich Albion) 1982/3 *W, Au* (2).
Stein, B. (1) (Luton T.) 1983/4 *F.*
Stepney, A. (1) (Manchester United) 1967/8 *Swdn.*
Steven, T.M. (13) (Everton) 1984/5 *I, Eire, Ru, Fin, It, US;* 1985/6 *T, Eg, USSR, Mex, Pol, P, Arg.*
Stevens, G.A. (7) (Tottenham Hotspur) 1984/5 *Fin, T, I;* 1985/6 *S, Mex, Mor, P.*
Stevens, M.G. (14) (Everton) 1984/5 *It, G;* 1985/6 *Ru, T, I, Eg, Isr, S, Can, Port, Mor, Pol, P, Arg.*
Stiles, N. (28) (Manchester United) 1964/5 *S, H, Y, Swdn;* 1965/6 *W, Aust, I, Sp, Pol, G, S, N, D, Pol, U, Mex, F, Arg, Port, G;* 1966/7 *I, Czecho, W, S;* 1967/8

Rus; 1968/9 *Ru;* 1969/70 *I, S.*
Storey, P. (1) (Arsenal) 1970/1 *Gr, I, S;* 1971/2 *Switz, G, W, I, S;* 1972/3 *Y, W* (2) *S, I, W, S, Czecho, Pil, Rus, It.*
Streten B. (1) (Luton Town) 1949/50 *I.*
Summerbee, M. (8) (Man.C.) 1967/8 *S, Sp, G;* 1971/2 *Switz, G, W, I;* 1972/3 *Rus.*
Sunderland, A. (1) (Arsenal) 1979/80 *Au.*
Swan, P. (19) (Sheffield Wednesday) 1959/60 *Y, Sp;* 1960/1 *I, Lux, Sp, W, S, Mex, Port, It, Aust;* 1961/2 *Lux, W, Port, I, Aust, S, Switz.*
Swift, F. (19) (Manchester City) 1946/7 *I, W, S, Eire, Holl, F, Switz, Port;* 1947/8 *W, I, S, Bel, Swdn, It;* 1948/9 *I, W, S, D, N.*

Talbot, B. (6) (Ipswich Town) 1976/7 *I, S, Braz, Arg, U;* 1979/80 *Au.*
Tambling, R. (3) (Chelsea) 1962/3 *W, F;* 1965/6 *Y.*
Taylor, E. (1) (Blackpool) 1953/4 *H.*
Taylor, J. (2) (Fulham) 1950/51 *Arg, Port.*
Taylor, P. (3) (Liverpool) 1947/8 *W, I, Swdn.*
Taylor, P. (4) (Crystal Palace) 1975/6 *W* (2), *I, S.*
Taylor, T. (19) (Manchester United) 1952/3 *Arg, Ch, U;* 1953/4 *Bel, Switz;* 1955/6 *S, Braz, Swdn, Fin, G;* 1956/7 *I, Y, D, Eire, D, Eire;* 1958/9 *W, I, F.*
Temple, D. (1) (Everton) 1964/5 *G.*
Thomas, Dave (8) (Q.P.R.) 1974/5 *Czecho, Port, C* (2), *W, S;* 1975/6 *Czecho, Port.*
Thomas, Danny (2) (Coventry C.) 1982/3 *Au* (2).
Thomson, R. (8) (Wolverhampton W.) 1963/4 *I, US, Port, Arg;* 1964/5 *I, Bel, W, Holl.*
Thompson, P. (16) (Liverpool) 1963/4 *Port, Eire, US, Braz, Port, Arg;* 1964/5 *I, Bel, W, Holl, S;* 1965/6 *I;* 1967/8 *G;* 1969/70 *Holl.*
Thompson, P. (42) (Liverpool) 1975/6 *W* (2), *I, S, Braz, It, Fin;* 1976/7 *Fin;* 1978/9 *Eire, Czecho, I, S, Bulg, Swdn, Aust;* 1979/80 *D, I, Bulg, Eire, Sp, Arg, W, S, Bel, It, Sp;* 1980/1 *N, Ru, H;* 1981/2 *N, H, W, Holl, S, Fin, F, Czecho, K, G, Sp;* 1982/3 *G, Gr.*
Thompson, T. (2) (Aston Villa) 1951/2 *W* (Preston); 1956/7 *S.*
Todd, C. (27) (Derby County) 1971/2 *I;* 1973/4 *Port, W, I, S, Arg, E/Germ, Bulg, Y;* 1974/5 *Port, G, C* (2), *I, W, S;* 1975/6 *Switz, Czecho, Port, I, S, Braz, Fin;* 1976/7 *Eire, Fin, Holl, I.*
Towers, T. (2) (Sunderland) 1975/6 *W, It.*
Tueart, D. (6) (Manchester City) 1974/5 *C, I;* 1976/7 *Fin, I, W, S.*

Ufton, D. (1) (Charlton Athletic) 1953/4 *FIFA.*

Venables, T. (2) (Chelsea) 1964/5 *Bel, Holl.*
Viollet, D. (Manchester United) 1959/60 *H;* 1961/2 *Lux.*
Vitjoen, C. (2) (Ipswich Town) 1974/5 *I, W.*

Waddle, C.R. (20) (Newcastle United) 1984/5 *Eire, Ru, Fin, S, It, Mex, G, US;* (Tottenham Hotspur) 1985/6 *Ru, T, I, Isr, USSR, S, Mex, Can, Port, Mor, Pol, Arg.*
Waiters, A. (5) (Blackpool) 1963/4 *Eire, Braz;* 1964/5 *Bel, W, Holl.*
Wallace, D.L. (1) (Southampton) 1985/6 *Eg.*
Walsh, P. (5) (Luton T.) 1982/3 *Au* (2); 1983/4 *F, W.*
Ward, P. (1) (Brighton) 1979/80 *Au.*
Ward, T. (2) (Derby County) 1947/8 *Bel;* 1948/9 *W.*
Watson, D. (65) (Sunderland) 1973/4 *Port, S, Arg, E/Germ, Bulg, Y*; 1974/5 *Czecho, Port, G, C* (2), *I, W, S*; 1975/6 (Manchester City) *Switz, Czecho, Port*; 1976/7 *Holl, Lux, I, W, S, Braz, Arg, U*; 1977/8 *Switz, Lux, It, G, Braz, W, I, S, H*; (Southampton) 1978/9 *D, Eire, Czecho, I, I, W, S, Bulg, Swdn, Aust*; 1979/80

D, I, Bulg, Eire, Sp, Arg, I, S, Bel, It, Sp; 1980/81 *N, Ru, Switz, Ru, W, S, Switz, H;* 1981/2 (Stoke C.) *I, Ic.*
Watson, D. (6) (Norwich C.) 1983/4 *Braz, U, Ch;* 1984/5 *Mex, Us;* 1985/6 *S.*
Watson, W. (4) (Sunderland) 1949/50 *I, It*; 1950/1 *W, Y.*
Weller, K. (4) (Leicester City) 1973/4 *W, I, S, Arg.*
West, G. (3) (Everton) 1968/9 *Bulg, W, Mex.*
Wheeler, J. (1) (Bolton Wanderers) 1954/5 *I.*
Whitworth, S. (7) (Leicester City) 1974/5 *G, C, I, W, S*; 1975/6 *Switz, Port.*
Whymark, T. (1) (Ipswich Town) 1977/8 *Lux.*
Wignall, F. (2) (Nottingham Forest) 1964/5 *W, Holl.*
Wilkins, R. (82) (Chelsea) 1975/6 *It*; 1976/7*Eire, Fin, I, Braz, Arg, U*; 1977/8 *Switz, Lux, It, G,W, I, S, H*; 1978/9 *D, Eire, Czecho, I, W, S, Bulg, Swdn,Aust*; (Manchester United) 1979/80 *D, I, Bulg, Sp, Arg, W,I, S, Bel, It, Sp;* 1980/81 *Sp, Ru, Braz, W, S, Switz, H;* 1981/2 *I, W, Holl, S, Fin, F, Czecho, K, G, Sp*; 1982/3 *D, G;* 1983/4 *D, I, W, S, Rus, Braz, U, Ch;* 1984/5 (AC Milan) *E/Germ, Fin, T, I, Eire, Ru, Fin, S,It, Mex;* 1985/6 *T, I, Isr, Eg, USSR, S, Mex, Can, Port,Mor.*
Williams, B. (24) (Wolverhampton Wanderers) 1948/9 *F*; 1949/50 *W, S, Eire, It, Port, Bel, Ch, US, Sp*; 1950/1 *I, W, Y, S, Arg, Port*; 1951/2 *F, W*; 1954/5 *G, S, F, Sp, Port*; 1955/6 *W.*
Williams, S. (6) (Southampton) 1982/3 *Au* (2);1983/4 *F;* 1984/5 *E/Germ, Fin, T.*
Willis, A. (1) (Tottenham Hotspur) 1951/2 *F.*
Wilshaw, D. (12) (Wolverhampton Wanderers) 1953/4 *W, Switz, U*; 1954/5 *S, F, Sp, Port*; 1955/6 *W, I, Fin, G*; 1956/7 *I.*
Wilson, R. (63) (Huddersfield Town) 1959/60 *S, Y, Sp, H*; 1961/2 *W, Port, I, Aust, S, Switz, Per, H, Aust, Bulg, Braz*; 1962/3 *F, I, Braz, Czecho, E/Germ, Switz*; 1963/4 *W, FIFA, S, U, Port, Eire, Braz, Port, Arg*; 1964/5 (Everton) *S, H, Y, G, Swdn*; 1965/6 *W, Aust, I, Sp, Pol, G, Y, Fin, D, Pol, U, Mex, F, Arg, Port, G*; 1966/7 *I, Czecho, W, S, Aust*; 1967/8 *I, Rus, S, Sp* (2), *Y, Rus.*
Withe, P. (11) (Aston Villa) 1980/81 *Braz, W, S;* 1981/2 *N, W, Ic*; 1982/3 *H, I, S;* 1983/4*H;* 1984/5 *T.*
Wood, R. (3) (Manchester United) 1954/5 *I, W*;1955/6 *Fin.*
Woodcock, A. (42) (Nottingham Forest) 1977/8 *I;* 1978/9 *Eire, Czecho, Bulg, Swdn*; (FC Cologne) 1979/80*I, Bulg, Eire, Sp, Arg, Bel, It, Sp;* 1980/81 *N, Ru,Switz, Ru, W, S;* 1981/2 *I, Holl, Fin,* (Arsenal) *G, Sp*; 1982/3 *G, Gr, Lux, Gr;* 1983/4 *Lux, F,I, W, S, Braz, U;* 1984/5 *E/Germ, Fin, T, I;* 1985/6*Ru, T, Isr.*
Woods, C.C.E. (4) (Norwich City) 1984/5 *US;* 1985/6 *Eg, Isr, Can.*
Worthington, F. (8) (Leicester City) 1973/4 *I, S,Arg, E/Germ, Bulg, Y*; 1974/5 *Czecho, Port.*
Wright M. (13) (Southampton) 1983/4 *W;* 1984/5*E/Germ, Fin, T, Eire, Ru, It, G;* 1985/6 *Ru, T, I, Eg,USSR.*
Wright, T. (11) (Everton) 1967/8 *Rus*; 1968/9 *Ru* (2), *Mex, U, Braz*; 1969/70 *Holl, Bel, W, Ru, Braz.*
Wright, W. (105) (Wolverhampton Wanderers) 1946/7 *I, W, S, Eire, Holl, Switz, Port*; 1947/8 *W, I, S, Bel, Swdn, It*; 1948/9 *I, W, S, D, Switz, Swdn, N, F*; 1949/50 *W, I, S, Eire, It, Port, Bel, Ch, US, Sp*; 1950/1 *I, S, Arg*; 1951/2 *F, W, I, Aust* (2), *S, It, Switz*; 1952/3 *I, W, Bel, S, Arg, Ch, U, US*; 1953/4 *W, FIFA, I, H* (2), *S, Y, Bel, Switz, Y*; 1954/5 *I, W, G, S, F, Sp, Port*; 1955/6 *D, W, I, Sp, Braz, Swdn, Fin, G*; 1956/7 *I, W, Y, D, S, Eire, D, Eire*; 1957/8 *W, I, F, S, Port, Y, Rus* (2), *Braz, Aust, Rus*; 1958/9 *Rus, W, S, It, Braz, Per, Mex, US.*

Young, G. (1) (Sheffield Wednesday) 1964/5 *W.*

NORTHERN IRELAND

Aherne, T. (4) (Belfast Celtic) 1946/7 *E*; 1947/8 *S*; 1948/9 *W*; 1949/50 (Luton Town) *W*.
Anderson, T. (22) (Manchester United) 1972/3 *C, E, S, W*; 1973/4 *Bulg, Port*; 1974/5 (Swindon Town) *S*; 1975/6 *Isr*; 1976/7 *Holl, G, Bel, E, S, W, Ic*; 1977/8 *Ic, Holl, Bel, S, E, W*; 1978/9 *D*.
Armstrong, G. (63) (Tottenham Hotspur) 1976/7 *G, E,W, Ic*; 1977/8 *Bel, S, E, W*; 1978/9 *Eire, D, Bulg,E, Bulg, E, S, W, D*; 1979/80 *E, Eire, Isr, S, E, W, Au,Au, Au;* 1980/81 *Swdn* (Watford), *Port, S, Port, S,Swdn;* 1981/2 *S, Isr, F, E, W, Y, Hon, Sp, Aust, F*;1982/3 *Aust, T, A, S, E, W;* (Real Mallorca) 1983/4*Aust, G, E, W, Fin;* 1984/5 *Ru, Fin, E, Sp;* (WBA)1985/6 *T, Ru, E, F,* (Chesterfield) *D, Braz.*

Barr, H. (Linfield) 1961/2 *E*; 1962/3 (Coventry City) *Pol, E.*
Best, G. (37) (Manchester United) 1963/4 *W, U*; 1964/5 *E, Switz* (2), *S, Holl* (2), *A*; 1965/6 *S, E, A*; 1966/7 *E*; 1967/8 *S*; 1968/9 *T, E, S, W*; 1969/70 *Rus, S, E, W*; 1970/1 *Sp, C* (2), *E, S, W*; 1971/2 *Rus, Sp*; 1972/3 *Bulg*; 1973/4 *Port*; 1976/7 *Holl, G, Bel*; (Fulham) 1977/8 *Ic, Holl.*
Bingham, W. (56) (Sunderland) 1950/1 *F*; 1951/2 *S, E, W*; 1952/3 *E, S, F, W*; 1953/4 *S, E, W*; 1954/5 *E, S, W*; 1955/6 *S, E, W*; 1956/7 *E, S, W, It, Port* (2); 1957/8 *S, E, It, W, Czecho, Arg, G, It, Czecho, F*; 1958/9 (Luton Town) *E, S, W, Sp*; 1959/60 *S, E, W*; 1960/1 (Everton) *E, G, S, It, Gr, G*; 1961/2 *Gr, E*; 1962/3 *Pol, E, S, Pol, Sp*; 1963/4 (Port Vale) *S, Sp, E.*
Blair, R. (5) (Oldham Athletic) 1974/5 *Swdn, S, W*; 1975/6 *Swdn, Isr.*
Blanchflower, D. (54) (Barnsley) 1949/50 *S, W*; 1950/1 *E, S, F*; 1951/2 (Aston Villa) *W*; 1952/3 *E, S, F, W*; 1953/4 *S, E, W*; 1954/5 *E, S* (Tottenham Hotspur), *W;* 1955/6 *S, E, W*; 1956/7 *E, S, W, It, Port*; 1957/8 *S, E, It* (2); *W, Czecho, Arg, Czecho, F*; 1958/9 *E, S, W, Sp*; 1959/60 *S, E, W*; 1960/1 *F, G, S, W, G*; 1961/2 *S, Gr, E, W, Holl*; 1962/3 *Pol, E, S, Pol.*
Blanchflower, J. (11) (Manchester United) 1953/4 *W*; 1954/5 *E, S*; 1955/6 *S.W*; 1956/7 *E, S*; 1957/8 *S, E, It* (2).
Bowler, G. (4) (Hull City) 1949/50 *S, E, W, G.*
Braithwaite, R. (10) (Linfield) 1961/2 *W*; 1962/3 *Pol, Sp* (Middlesbrough) 1963/4 *W, U*; 1964/5 *E, Switz* (2), *S, Holl.*
Brennan, R. (5) (Luton Town) 1948/9 *W*; 1949/50 (Birmingham City) *S, E, W,* (Fulham); 1950/1 *E.*
Briggs, R. (2) (Manchester United) 1961/2 *W*; 1964/5 (Swansea) *Holl.*
Brotherston, N. (27) (Blackburn Rovers) 1979/80 *S, E,W, Au, Au, Au;* 1980/81 *Swdn, Port;* 1981/2 *S, Isr,F, E, S, W, Hon, Aust*; 1982/3 *Aust, G, A, T, A, S, E, W:* 1983/4 *T;* 1984/5 *Isr, T.*
Bruce, W. (2) (Glentoran) 1960/1 *S*; 1966/7 *W.*

Campbell, D.A. (2)(Nottingham Forest) 1985/6 *Mor, Braz.*
Campbell, J. (2) (Fulham) 1950/1 *E, S.*
Campbell, R. (2) (Crusaders) 1962/3 *W*; 1964/5 *Switz.*
Cambell, R.M. (2) (Bradford C) 1981/2 *S, W.*
Campbell, W. (6) (Dundee) 1967/8 *S, E*; 1968/9 *T*; 1969/70 *Rus, S, W.*
Carey, J. (7) (Manchester United) 1946/7 *E, S, W*; 1947/8 *E*; 1948/9 *E, S, W.*
Casey, T. (11) (Newcastle United) 1954/5 *W*; 1955/6 *W*; 1956/7 *E, S, W, It, Port*; 1957/8 *G, F*; 1958/9 (Portsmouth) *E, Sp.*
Caskey, A. (6) (Derby County) 1978/9 *Bulg, E, Bulg, E*; 1979/80 *E;* 1981/2 (Tulsa Roughnecks) F.
Cassidy, T. (25) (Newcastle United) 1970/1 *E*; 1971/2 *Rus*; 1973/4 *Bulg, S, E, W*; 1974/5 *N*; 1975/6 *S, E, W*; 1976/7 *G*; 1979/80 *E, Eire, Isr, S, E, W, Au, Au, Au;* 1980/81 *Swdn, Port;* 1981/2 (Burnley) *Isr, Sp.*
Caughey, M. (2)(Linfield) 1985/6 *F, D.*

Clarke, C.J. (6)(Bournemouth) 1985/6 *F, D, Mor, Alg,Sp, Braz.*
Cleary, J. (5) (Glentoran) 1981/2 *S, W*; 1982/3*W;* 1983/4 *T;* 1984/5 *Isr.*
Clements, D. (48) (Coventry City) 1964/5 *Holl, W*; 1965/6 *Mex*; 1966/7 *S, W*; 1967/8 *S, E;* 1968/9 *T* (2), *S, W;* 1969/70 *Rus* (2), *S, E, W;* 1970/1 *Sp, C, E, S, W;* 1971/2 (Sheffield Wednesday) *Rus* (2), *Sp, S, E, W*; 1972/3 *Bulg, C, Port, C, E, S, W*; (Everton) 1973/4 *Bulg, Port, S, E, W*; 1974/5 *N, Y, E, D, Bulg, E, Bulg,* (Middlesbrough) *E*; 1979/80 *Isr, E, W, Au, Au, Au;* 1980/81 *Swdn, Port, S, Port, S, Swdn;* 1981/2 *F, E:* *(Gillingham) 1983/4 *S, Fin.*
Cochrane, D. (10) (Leeds United) 1946/7 *E, S, W*; 1947/8 *S, E, W*; 1948/9 *S, W*; 1949/50 *S, E.*
Cowan, J. (1) (Newcastle United) 1969/70 *E.*
Coyle, F. (3) (Coleraine) 1955/6 *S, E*; 1957/8 (Nottingham Forest) *Arg.*
Coyle, R. (3) (Sheffield Wednesday) 1972/3 *Port, W*; 1973/4 *Bulg.*
Craig, D. (25) (Newcastle United) 1966/7 *W*; 1967/8 *W*; 1968/9 *T* (2), *E, S, W*; 1969/70 *Rus, S, E, W*; 1970/1 *Sp, C* (2), *S*; 1971/2 *Rus, S*; 1972/3 *C* (2), *E, S, W*; 1973/4 *Bulg, Port*; 1974/5 *N.*
Crossan, E. (3) (Blackburn Rovers) 1949/50 *S*; 1950/1 *E*; 1954/5 *W.*
Crossan, J. (23) (Rotterdam Sparta) 1959/60 *E*; 1962/3 (Sunderland) *Pol, W, Sp*; 1963/4 *S, Sp, E, W, U*; 1964/5 *E, Switz* (2), *S, Holl* (2), *W*; 1965/6 (Manchester City) *S, E, A, G*; 1966/7 *E, S*; 1967/8 (Middlesbrough) *S.*
Cunningham, W. (29) (St Mirren) 1950/1 *W*; 1952/3 *E*; 1953/4 *S*; 1954/5 *S*; 1955/6 *S, E, W*; 1956/7 (Leicester City) *E, S, W, It, Port*; 1957/8 *S, It, W, Czecho, Arg, G, Czecho, F*; 1958/9 *E, S, W*; 1959/60 *S, E, W*; 1960/1 (Dunfermline Athletic) *W, Holl.*
Cush, W. (25) (Glentoran) 1950/1 *E, S*; 1953/4 *S, E*; 1956/7 *W, It, Port*; 1957/8 *It* (Leeds United), *W, Czecho, Arg, F, Czecho, It, F*; 1958/9 *E, S, W, Sp*; 1959/60 *S, E, W*; 1960/1 (Portadown) *Gr, G*; 1961/2 *Gr.*

D'Arcy, S. (5) (Chelsea) 1951/2 *W*; 1952/3 *E,* (Brentford), *S, F, W.*
Dickson, D. (2) (Coleraine) 1972/3 *C, Port.*
Dickson, T. (1) (Linfield) 1956/7 *S.*
Dickson, W. (12) (Chelsea) 1950/1 *W, F*; 1951/2 *S, E, W*; 1952/3 *E, S, F, W*; (Arsenal) 1953/4 *E, W*; 1954/5 *E.*
Dixon, D. (2) (Coleraine) 1969/70 *S, W.*
Doherty, L. (1) (Linfield) 1984/5 *Isr.*
Doherty, P. (6) (Derby County) 1946/7 *E* (Huddersfield Town), *W*; 1947/8 *E, W*; 1948/9 *S*; 1950/1 *S.*
Donaghy, M. (45) (Luton Town) 1979/80 *S, E, W;* 1980/81 *Swdn, Port, S;* 1981/2 *S, Isr, F, E, S, W, Y, Hon, Sp, F*; 1982/3 *Aust, G, A, T, A, S, E, W;* 1983/4 *Aust, T, G, S, E, W, Fin;* 1984/5 *Ru, Fin, E, Sp, T;* 1985/6 *T, Ru, E, F, D, Mor, Alg, Sp, Braz.*
Dougan, D. (41) (Portsmouth) 1957/8 *Czecho*; 1959/60 (Blackburn Rovers) *S*; 1960/1 *W, It, Gr*; 1962/3 (Aston Villa) *Pol, S, Pol*; 1965/6 (Leicester City) *S, E, A, W, G, Mex*; 1966/7 *E* (Wolverhampton Wanderers), *W*; 1967/8 *S, W*; 1968/9 *Isr, T, T, E, S, W*; 1969/70 *Rus* (2), *S, E*; 1970/1 *Sp, C* (2), *E, S, W*; 1971/2 *Rus* (2), *S, E, W*; 1972/3 *Bulg, C.*
Douglas, S. (1) (Belfast Celtic) 1946/7 *E.*
Dowd, D. (3) (Glentoran) 1972/3 *W*; 1974/5 (Sheffield Wednesday) *N, Swdn.*
Dunlop, G. (1) (Linfield) 1984/5 *Isr.*

Eglington, T. (6) (Everton) 1946/7 *S, W*; 1947/8 *S, E, W*; 1948/9 *E.*
Elder, A. (39) (Burnley) 1959/60 *W*; 1960/1 *E, G, S, W, Gr*; 1961/2 *S, Gr, E*; 1962/3 *Pol, E, S, Pol, W, Sp*; 1963/4 *W, U*; 1964/5 *W, Switz* (2), *S, Holl* (2), *W*; 1965/6 *S, E, A, W, Mex*; 1966/7 *E, S, W*; (Stoke City) 1967/8 *E, W*; 1968/9 *E, S, W*; 1969/70 *Rus.*

Farrell, P. (7) (Everton) 1946/7 *S, W*; 1947/8 *S, E, W*; 1948/9 *E, W.*

Feeney, A. (1) (Glentoran) 1975/6 *Isr.*
Feeney, J. (2) (Linfield) 1946/7 *S* (Swansea City); 1949/50 *E.*
Ferguson, W. (2) (Linfield) 1965/6 *Mex*; 1966/7 *E.*
Ferris, R. (3) (Birmingham City) 1949/50 *S*; 1950/1 *F*; 1951/2 *S.*
Finney, T. (14) (Sunderland) 1974/5 *N, E, S, W*; 1975/6 *N, Y, S*; (Cambridge United) 1979/80 *E, Isr, S, E, W, Au, Au.*
Forde, T. (4) (Ards) 1958/9 *Sp*; 1960/1 *E, G, S.*

Gaston, R. (1) (Coleraine) 1968/9 *Isr.*
Gallogly, C. (2) (Huddersfield Town) 1950/1 *E, S.*
Gorman, W. (4) (Brentford) 1946/7 *E, S, W*; 1947/8 *W.*
Graham, R. (13) (Doncaster Rovers) 1950/1 *W, F*; 1951/2 *S, E, W*; 1952/3 *S, F*; 1953/4 *E, W*; 1954/5 *S, W*; 1955/6 *E*; 1958/9 *E.*
Gregg, H. (24) (Doncaster Rovers) 1953/4 *W*; 1956/7 *E, S, W, It, Port*; 1957/8 *E* (Manchester United) *W, Czecho, Arg, G, F, It*; 1958/9 *E, W*; 1959/60 *S, E, W*; 1960/1 *E, S*; 1961/2 *S, Gr*; 1963/4 *S, E.*

Hamilton, B. (50) (Linfield) 1968/9 *T*; 1970/1 *C* (2), *E, S, W*; 1971/2 (Ipswich Town) *Rus* (2), *Sp*; 1972/3 *Bulg, C, Port, C, E, S, W*; 1973/4 *Bulg, S, E, W*; 1974/5 *N, Swdn, Y, E*; 1975/6 *Swdn, N, Y,* (Everton) *Isr, S, E, W*; 1976/7 *Holl, G, Bel, E, S, W, Ic*; 1977/8 *S, E, W*; (Millwall) 1978/9 *Eire, Bulg, Bulg,* (Swindon) *S, E, W, D, Au, Au.*
Hamilton, W. (41) (Q.P.R.) 1977/8 *S*; 1979/80(Burnley) *S, E, W, Au, Au;* 1980/81 *Swdn, Port, S,Port, S, Swdn;* 1981/2 *S, Isr, E, W, Y, Hon, Sp, Aust,F*; 1982/3 *Aust, G, A, A, S, E, W;* 1983/4 *Aust, T,G, S, E, W, Fin;* 1984/5 (Oxford United) *Ru, Sp;* 1985/6 *Mor, Alg, Sp, Braz.*
Harkin, T. (5) (Southport) 1967/8 *W*; 1968/9 *T, W*; 1969/70 *Rus*; 1970/1 *Sp.*
Harvey, M. (34) (Sunderland) 1960/1 *It*; 1961/2 *Holl*; 1962/3 *W, Sp*; 1963/4 *S, Sp, E, W, U*; 1964/5 *W, Switz* (2), *E, S, Holl* (2), *A*; 1965/6 *S, E, A, W, G, Mex*; 1966/7 *E, S*; 1967/8 *E, W*; 1968/9 *Isr, T, T, E*; 1969/70 *Rus*; 1970/1 *C, W.*
Hatton, S. (2) (Linfield) 1962/3 *Pol, S.*
Healy, P. (3) (Coleraine) 1981/2 *S, W, Hon*; 1982/3 *Aust.*
Hegan, D. (7) (West Bromwich Albion) 1969/70 *Rus*; 1971/2 (Wolverhampton Wanderers) *Rus, S, E, W*; 1972/3 *Bulg, C.*
Hill, J. (6) (Norwich C.) 1958/9 *W*; 1959/60 *W*; 1960/1 *G* (Everton); 1963/4 *S, Sp, E.*
Hinton, E. (7) (Fulham) 1946/7 *S, W*; 1947/8 *S, E, W* (Millwall); 1950/1 *W, F.*
Hughes, W. (1) (Bolton Wanderers) 1950/1 *W.*
Humphries, W. (13) (Ards) 1961/2 *W* (Coventry City) *Holl*; 1962/3 *Pol, E, S, W, Sp*; 1963/4 *S, Sp, E*; 1964/5 *S, Holl, W.*
Hunter, A. (53) (Blackburn Rovers) 1969/70 *Rus*; 1970/1 *C* (2), *E, S, W*; 1971/2 (Ipswich Town) *Rus* (2), *Sp, S, E, W*; 1972/3 *Bulg, C, Port, C, E, S, W*; 1973/4 *Bulg, S, E, W*; 1974/5 *N, Swdn, Y, E, S, W*; 1975/6 *Swdn, N, Y, Isr, S, E, W*; 1976/7 *Holl, G, Bel, E, S, W, Ic*; 1977/8 *Ic, Holl, Bel*; 1978/9 *Eire, D, S, W, D*; 1979/80 *E, Eire.*

Irvine, R. (8) (Linfield) 1961/2 *Holl*; 1962/3 *Pol, E, S, Pol, W, Sp*; (Stoke City) 1964/5 *W.*
Irvine, W. (22) (Burnley) 1962/3 *W, Sp*; 1964/5 *Switz, S, Holl* (2), *W*; 1965/6 *S, E, A, W, Mex*; 1966/7 *E, S*; 1967/8 *E, W*; 1968/9 (Preston North End) *Isr, T, E*; (Brighton & Hove Albion) 1971/2 *S, E, W.*

Jackson, T. (35) (Everton) 1968/9 *Isr, E, S, W;* 1969/70 *Rus* (2); 1970/1 (Nottingham Forest) *Sp;* 1971/2 *S, E, W;* 1972/3 *C, E, S, W;* 1973/4 *Bulg, Port, S, E, W;* 1974/5 *N, Swdn, Y, E, S, W*; 1975/6 *Swdn, N, Y*; 1976/7 *Holl, G, Bel, E, S, W, Ic.*
Jamison, A. (1) (Glentoran) 1975/6 *N.*

Jennings, P. (119) (Watford) 1963/4 *W, U*; 1964/5(Tottenham Hotspur) *E, Switz* (2), *S, Holl, A*; 1965/6 *S, E, A, W, G*; 1966/7 *E, S*; 1967/8 *S,E, W*; 1968/9 *Isr, T* (2), *E, S, W*; 1969/70*Rus* (2), *S, E*; 1970/1 *C* (2), *E, S,W*; 1971/2 *Rus, Sp, S, E, W*; 1972/3 *Bulg, C, Port,E, S, W*; 1973/4 *Port, S, E, W*; 1974/5 *N, Swdn, Y,E, S, W*; 1975/6 *Swdn, N, Y, Isr, S, E, W*; 1976/7*Holl, G, Bel, E, S, W, Ic*; (Arsenal) 1977/8 *Ic, Holl,Bel*; 1978/9 *Eire, D, Bulg, E, Bulg, E, S, W, D*;1979/80 *E, Eire, Isr;* 1980/81 *S, Port, S, Swdn;* 1981/2 *S, Isr, E, W, Y, Hon, Sp, F*; 1982/3 *A, S,E, W;* 1983/4 Aust, T, G, S, W, Fin; 1984/5 *Ru, Fin,E, Spo, T;* (Tottenham Hotspur) 1985/6 *T, Ru, E, F, D,Mor, Alg, Sp, Braz.*
Johnston, W. (1) (Glentoran) 1961/2 *W.*
Johnston, W. (1) (Oldham Athletic) 1965/6 *Mex.*
Jones, J. (4) (Glenavon) 1955/6 *W*; 1956/7 *E, S, W.*

Keane, T. (1) (Swansea City) 1948/9 *S.*
Keith, R. (23) (Newcastle United) 1957/8 *E, W, Czecho, Arg, G, Czecho, F*; 1958/9 *It, E, S, W, Sp*; 1959/60 *S, E*; 1960/1 *E, G, S, W, It, Gr, G*; 1961/2 *W, Holl.*
Kelly, H. (4) (Fulham) 1949/50 *E, W* (Southampton); 1950/1 *E, S.*
Kelly, P. (1) (Barnsley) 1949/50 *S.*

Lawther, I. (4) (Sunderland) 1959/60 *W*; 1960/1 *It*; 1961/2 (Blackburn Rovers) *S, Holl.*
Lockhart, N. (8) (Linfield) 1946/7 *E*; 1949/50 (Coventry City) *W*; 1950/1 *W*; 1951/2 *W*; 1953/4 (Aston Villa) *S, E*; 1954/5 *W*; 1955/6 *W.*
Lutton, B. (5) (Wolverhampton Wanderers) 1969/70 *S, E*; 1972/3 (West Ham United) *S, W*; 1973/4 *Port.*

Magill, E. (25) (Arsenal) 1961/2 *S, Gr, E*; 1962/3 *Pol, E, S, Pol, W, Sp*; 1963/4 *S, Sp, E, W, U*; 1964/5 *E, Switz* (2), *S, Holl*; 1965/6 *S, E,* (Brighton & Hove Albion) *A, W, G, Mex.*
Martin, C. (6) (Glentoran) 1946/7 *S*; 1947/8 (Leeds United) *S, E, W*; 1948/9 (Aston Villa) *E*; 1949/50 *W.*
McAdams, W. (16) (Manchester City) 1953/4 *W*; 1954/5 *S*; 1956/7 *E, S*; 1957/8 *S, It*; 1960/1 (Bolton Wanderers) *E, G, S, W, It, Gr, G*; 1961/2 (Leeds United) *Gr, E, Holl.*
McAlinden, J. (2) (Portsmouth) 1946/7 *E*; 1948/9 (Southend United) *E.*
McCabe, J. (6) (Leeds United) 1948/9 *S, W*; 1949/50 *E*; 1950/1 *W*; 1952/3 *W*; 1953/4 *S.*
McCavana, T. (3) (Coleraine) 1954/5 *S*; 1955/6 *S, E.*
McCleary, J. W. (1) (Cliftonville) 1954/5 *W.*
McClelland, J. (6) (Arsenal) 1960/1 *G, W, It, Gr, G*; 1965/6 (Fulham) *Mex.*
McClelland, J. (38) (Mansfield Town) 1979/80 *S, Au,Au, Au;* 1980/81 *Swdn, S, S, Swdn;* 1981/2 (Rangers)*S, W, Y, Hon, Sp, Aust, F*; 1982/3 *Aust, G, A, T, A,S, E, W;* 1983/4 *Aust, T, G, S, E, W, Fin;* 1984/5*Ru,* (Watford) *Fin, Isr, E, Sp, T;* 1985/6 *T,F.*
McCourt, F. (6) (Manchester City) 1951/2 *E, W*;1952/3 *E, S, F, W.*
McCreery, D. (56) (Manchester United) 1975/6 *S, E,W*; 1976/7 *Holl, G, Bel, E, S, W, Ic*; 1977/8 *Ic,Holl, Bel, S, E, W*; 1978/9 *Eire, D, Bulg, E, Bulg, W,D*; 1979/80 (Q.P.R.) *E, Eire, S, E, W, Au, Au;* 1980/81 *Swdn, Port, S, Port* (Tulsa Roughnecks),*Swdn;* 1981/2 *S, Isr, F, E, Y, Hon, Sp, Aust, F*;1982/3 (Newcastle United) *Aust;* 1983/4 *T;* 1984/5*Ru, Sp;* 1985/6 *T, Ru, E, F, D, Alg, Sp, Braz.*
McCrory, S. (1) (Southend United) 1957/8 *E.*
McCullough, W. (10) (Arsenal) 1960/1 *It*; 1962/3 *Sp*; 1963/4 *S, Sp, E, W, U*; 1964/5 *E, Switz*; 1966/7 (Millwall) *E.*
McCurdy, C. (1) (Linfield) 1979/80 *Au.*
McDonald, A. (8) (QPR) 1985/6 *Ru, E, F, D, Mor, Alg,Sp, Braz.*
McElhinney, G. (6) (Bolton W.) 1983/4 *G, S, E, W,Fin;* 1984/5 *Ru.*

McFaul, I. (6) (Linfield) 1966/7 *E*; 1969/70(Newcastle United) *W*; 1970/1 *Sp*; 1971/2 *Rus*; 1972/3 *C*; 1973/4 *Bulg*.
McGarry, J. K. (3) (Cliftonville) 1950/1 *S, W, E*.
McGaughey, M. (1) (Linfield) 1984/5 *Isr*.
McGrath, R. (21) (Tottenham Hotspur) 1973/4 *S, E, W*; 1974/5 *N*; 1975/6 *Isr;* (Manchester United) 1976/7 *Holl, G, Bel, E, S, W, Ic*; 1977/8 *Ic, Holl, Bel, S, E, W*; 1978/9 *Bulg, E, E*.
McIlroy, J. (53) (Burnley) 1951/2 *S, E, W*; 1952/3 *E, S, W*; 1953/4 *S, E, W*; 1954/5 *E, S, W*; 1955/6 *S, E, W*; 1956/7 *E, S, W, It, Port*; 1957/8 *S, E, It, W, Czecho, Arg, Czecho, F, It*; 1958/9 *E, S, W, Sp*; 1959/60 *S, W, E*; 1960/1 *E, G, W, Gr, G*; 1961/2 *S, Gr, E, Holl*; 1962/3 *Pol, E, S, Pol, W*; 1965/6 (Stoke City) *S, E, A*.
McIlroy, S. (87) (Manchester United) 1971/2 *Sp,S*; 1973/4 *S, E, W*; 1974/5 *N, Swdn, Y, E, S,W*; 1975/6 *Swdn, N, Y, S, E, W*; 1976/7 *Holl, Bel,E, S, W, Ic*; 1977/8 *Ic, Holl, Bel, S, E, W*; 1978/9*Eire, D, Bulg, E, Bulg, E, S, W, D*; 1979/80 *E, Eire,Isr, S, E, W;* 1980/81 *Swdn, Port, S, Port, S, Swdn;* 1981/2 (Stoke C.) *F, E, S, W, Y, Hon, Sp, Aust, F*;1982/3 *Aust, G, A, T, A, S, E, W;* 1983/4 *Aust, T, S,E, W, Fin;* 1984/5 *Fin, E, T;* (Manchester City) 1985/6*T, Ru, E, F, D, Mor, Alg, Sp, Braz*.
McKeag, W. (2) (Glentoran) 1967/8 *S, W*.
McKenna, J. (7) (Huddersfield Town) 1949/50 *S, E, W*; 1950/1 *E, S, F*; 1951/2 *E*.
McKenzie, R. (1) (Airdrieonians) 1966/7 *W*.
McKinney, W. (1) (Falkirk) 1965/6 *G*.
McLaughlin, J. (12) (Shrewsbury Town) 1961/2 *S, Gr, E, W*; 1962/3 *W*, (Swansea City); 1963/4 *W, U*; 1964/5 *E, Switz* (2); 1965/6 *W*.
McMichael, A. (39) (Newcastle United) 1949/50 *S, E*; 1950/1 *E, S, F*; 1951/2 *S, E, W*; 1952/3 *E, S, F, W*; 1953/4 *S, E, W*; 1954/5 *E, W*; 1955/6 *W*; 1956/7 *E, S, W, It, Port*; 1957/8 *E, S, It, W, Czecho, Arg, G, Czecho, F, It*; 1958/9 *S, W, Sp*; 1959/60 *S, E, W*.
McMillan, S. (2) (Manchester United) 1962/3 *E, S*.
McMordie, E. (21) (Middlesbrough) 1968/9 *Isr, T, T, E, S, W*; 1969/70 *Rus, S, E, W*; 1970/1 *C* (2) *E, S, W*; 1971/2 *Rus, Sp, S, E, W*; 1972/3 *Bulg*.
McMorran, E. (15) (Belfast Celtic) 1946/7 *E* (Barnsley); 1950/1 *E, S, W*; 1951/2 *E, S, W*; 1952/3 *E, S, F* (Doncaster Rovers), *W*; 1953/4 *E*; 1955/6 *W*; 1956/7*It, Port*.
McNally, B.A. (1) (Shrewsbury Town) 1985/6 *Mor*.
McParland, P. (34) (Aston Villa) 1953/4 *W*; 1954/5*E, S*; 1955/6*S, E*; 1956/7 *E, S, W, Port*; 1957/8*S, E, It, W, Czecho, Arg, G, Czecho, F, It*; 1958/9 *E, S, W, Sp*; 1959/60 *S, F, W*; 1960/1 *E, G, S, W, It, Gr, G*; 1961/2 (Wolverhampton W.) *Holl*.
Montgomery, F.) (Coleraine) 1954/5 *E*.
Moore, C. (1) (Glentoran) 1948/9 *W*.
Moreland, A. (5) (Derby County) 1978/9 *Bulg, E, S*; 1979/80 *E, Eire*.
Morgan, S. (18) (Port Vale) 1971/2 *Sp*; 1972/3 *Bulg, Port, C, E, S, W*; 1973/4 (Aston Villa) *Bulg, Port, S, E*; 1974/5 *Swdn*; 1975/6 *Swdn, N, Y* (Brighton & Hove Albion), *S, W*; 1978/9 *D*.
Mullen, G. (3) (Glentoran) 1982/3 *S, E, W*.

Napier, R. (1) (Bolton Wanderers) 1965/6 *G*.
Neill, T. (58) (Arsenal) 1960/1 *It, Gr, G*; 1961/2 *S, Gr, E, W*; 1962/3 *E, Pol, W, Sp*; 1963/4 *S, Sp, E, W, U*; 1964/5 *E, Switz, S, Holl* (2), *W*; 1965/6 *S, E, A, W, G, Mex*; 1966/7 *S, W*; 1967/8 *S, E*; 1968/9 *Isr, T, T, E, S, W*; 1969/70 *Rus* (2), *S, E, W*; 1970/1 *Sp, C*; 1971/2 (Hull City) *Rus* (2), *Sp, S, E, W*; 1972/3 *Bulg, C, Port, C, E, S, W*.
Nelson, S. (51) (Arsenal), 1969/70 *E, W*; 1970/1 *Sp, C, E, S, W*; 1971/2 *Rus* (2), *Sp, S, E, W*; 1972/3 *Bulg, C, Port*; 1973/4 *S, E*; 1974/5 *Swdn, Y*; 1975/6 *Swdn, N,*

Isr, E; 1976/7 *G, Bel, W, Ic*; 1977/8 *Ic, Holl, Bel*; 1978/9 *Eire, D, Bulg, E, Bulg, E, S, W, D*; 1979/80 *E, Eire, Isr;* 1980/81 *S, Port, S, Swdn;* 1981/2 (Brighton) *E, S, Sp, Aust.*

Nicholl, C. (52) (Aston Villa) 1974/5 *Swdn, Y, E, S, W*; 1975/6 *Swdn, N, Y, S, E, W*; 1976/7 *W*; 1977/8 *Bel, S, E, W* (Southampton); 1978/9 *Eire, Bulg, E, Bulg, E, W*; 1979/80 *E, Eire, Isr, S, E, W, Au, Au, Au* 1980/81 *Swdn, Port, S, Port, S, Swdn;* 1981/2 *S, Isr, F, E, W, Y, Hon, Sp, Aust, F*; 1982/3 *S, E, W;* (Grimsby T.) 1983/4 *Aust, T.*

Nicholl, J.M. (73) (Manchester United) 1975/6 *Isr, W*; 1976/7 *Holl, Bel, E, S, W, Ic*; 1977/8 *Ic, Holl, Bel, S, E, W*; 1978/9 *Eire, D, Bulg, E, Bulg, E, S, W, D*; 1979/80 *E, Eire, Isr, S, E, W, Au, Au, Au;* 1980/81 *Swdn, Port, S, Port, S, Swdn;* 1981/2 *S, Isr, F, E,* (Toronto Blizzards) *W, Y, Hon, Sp, Aust, F*; 1982/3 (Sunderland) *Aust, G, A, T,* (Toronto Blizzards) *A, S, E, W;* (Rangers) 1983/4 *T, G, S, E;* (Toronto Blizzards) *Fin;* 1984/5 *Ru,* (West Bromwich Albion) *Fin, E, Sp, T;* 1985/6 *T, Ru, E, F, Alg, Sp, Braz.*

Nicholson, J. (40) (Manchester United) 1960/1 *S, W*; 1961/2 *Gr, E, W, Holl*; 1962/3 *Pol, E, S, Pol*; 1964/5 (Huddersfield Town) *Holl* (2), *W*; 1965/6 *S, E, A, W, Mex*; 1966/7 *S, W*; 1967/8 *S, E, W*; 1968/9 *T, T, E, S, W*; 1969/70 *Rus* (2), *S, E, W*; 1970/1 *C* (2), *E, S, W*; 1971/2 *Rus* (2).

O'Doherty, A. (3) (Coleraine) 1969/70 *S, E, W.*

O'Driscoll, J. (3) (Swansea City) 1948/9 *E, S, W.*

O'Kane, L. (20) (Nottingham Forest) 1969/70 *E, W, S*; 1970/1 *Sp, E, S, W*; 1971/2 *Rus* (2); 1972/3 *Port, C*; 1973/4 *Bulg, Port, S, E, W*; 1974/5 *N, Swdn, E, S.*

O'Neill, J. (1) (Sunderland) 1961/2 *W.*

O'Neill, J. (39) (Leicester City) 1979/80 *Isr, S, E, W, Au, Au, Au;* 1980/81 *Port, S, Port, S, Swdn;* 1981/2 *S, Isr, F, E, S, F*; 1982/3 *Aust, G, A, T, A, S;* 1983/4 *S;* 1984/5 *Isr, Fin, E, Sp, T;* 1985/6 *T, Ru, E, F, D, Mor, Alg, Sp, Braz.*

O'Neill, M. (64) (Distillery) 1971/2 *Rus,* (Nottingham Forest), *Sp, W*; 1972/3 *Port, C, E, S, W*; 1973/4 *Bulg, Port, E, W*; 1974/5 *Swdn, Y, E, S*; 1975/6 *Y*; 1976/7 *E, S*; 1977/8 *Ic, Holl, S, E, W*; 1978/9 *Eire, D, Bulg, E, Bulg, D*; 1979/80 *Eire, Isr, Au, Au, Au;* 1980/81 *Swdn, Port,* (Norwich C.) *Port, S, Swdn;* 1981/2 (Manchester C.) *S,* (Norwich C.) *F, E, S, Y, Hon, Sp, Aust, F*; 1982/3 *Aust, G, A, T, A, S, E;* (Notts Co.) 1983/4 *Aust, T, G, E, W, Fin;* 1984/5 *Ru, Fin.*

Parke, J. (13) (Hibernian) 1963/4 *S, Sp, E*; 1964/5 (Sunderland) *Switz, S, Holl* (2), *W*; 1965/6 *G*; 1966/7 *E, S*; 1967/8 *S, E.*

Peacock, R. (31) (Glasgow Celtic) 1951/2 *S*; 1952/3 *F*; 1953/4 *W*; 1954/5 *E, S*; 1955/6 *S, E*; 1956/7 *W, It, Port*; 1957/8 *S, E, It, W, Czecho, Arg, G, Czecho, It*; 1958/9 *E, S, W*; 1959/60 *S, E*; 1960/1 *E, G, S, It, Gr, G*; 1961/2 *S.*

Penney, S. (9) (Brighton & Hove Albion) 1984/5 *Isr;* 1985/6 *T, Ru, E, F, D, Mor, Alg, Sp.*

Platt, J.A. (23) (Middlesbrough) 1975/6 *Isr*; 1977/8 *S, E, W*; 1979/80 *S, E, W, Au (3);* 1980/81 *Swdn, Port;* 1981/2 *F, S, W, Aust;* 1982/3 *Aust, G, A, T;* (Ballymena United) 1983/4 *E, W;* (Coleraine) 1985/6 *Mor.*

Quinn, J.M. (11) (Blackburn Rovers) 1984/5 *Isr, Fin, E, Sp, T;* 1985/6 *T, Ru, E, F, D, Mor.*

Rafferty, W. (1) (Wolverhampton Wanderers) 1979/80 *E.*

Ramsey, P. (9) (Leicester C.) 1983/4 *Aust, G, S*; 1984/5 *Isr, E, Sp, T;* 1985/6 *T, Mor.*

Rice, P. (49) (Arsenal) 1968/9 *Isr*; 1969/70 *Rus*; 1970/1 *E, S, W*; 1971/2 *Rus, Sp, S, E, W*; 1972/3 *Bulg, C, E, S, W*; 1973/4 *Bulg, Port, S, E, W*; 1974/5 *N, Y, E, S, W*; 1975/6 *Swdn, N, Y, Isr, S, E, W*; 1976/7 *Holl, G, Bel, E, S, Ic*; 1977/8 *Ic, Holl, Bel*; 1978/9 *Eire, D, E, E, S, W, D*; 1979/80 *E.*

Ross, E. (1) (Newcastle United) 1968/9 *Isr.*

Russell, A. (1) (Linfield) 1946/7 *E.*
Ryan, R. (1) (West Bromwich Albion) 1949/50 *W.*

Scott, J. (2) (Grimsby Town) 1957/8 *Czecho, F.*
Scott, P. (8) (Everton) 1974/5 *W*; 1975/6 (York City) *Y, Isr, S, W*; 1977/8 *S, E, W.*
Sharkey, P. (1) (Ipswich Town) 1975/6 *S.*
Shields, J. (1) (Southampton) 1956/7 *S.*
Simpson, W. (12) (Glasgow Rangers) 1950/1 *W, F*; 1953/4 *S, E*; 1954/5 *E*; 1956/7 *It, Port*; 1957/8 *S, E, It, W*; 1958/9 *S.*
Sloan, A. (1) (Manchester United) 1978/9 *S.*
Sloan, D. (2) (Oxford) 1968/9 *Isr*; 1970/1 *Sp.*
Sloan, W. (1) (Arsenal) 1946/7 *W.*
Smyth, S. (9) (Wolverhampton Wanderers) 1947/8 *S, E, W*; 1948/9 *S, W*; 1949/50 *S, E, W* (Stoke City); 1951/2 *E.*
Smyth, W. (4) (Distillery) 1948/9 *E, S*; 1953/4 *S, E.*
Spence, D. (27) (Bury) 1974/5 *Y, E, S, W*; 1975/6 *Swdn, Isr, E, W, S*; (Blackpool) 1976/7 *Holl, G, E, S, W, Ic*; 1978/9 *Eire, D, E, E, S, W, D*; 1979/80 *Eire, Isr, Au;* 1980/81 (Southend U.) *Swdn;* 1981/82 *F.*
Stevenson, A. (3) (Everton) 1946/7 *S, W*; 1947/8 *S.*
Stewart, A. (6) (Glentoran) 1966/7 *W*; 1967/8 *S, E,* (Derby) *W*; 1968/9 *Isr. T.*
Stewart, I. (29) (Q.P.R.) 1981/2 *F*; 1982/3*Aust, G, A, T, A, S, E, W*; 1983/4 *Aust, T, G, S, E,W, Fin;* 1984/5 *Ru, Fin, Isr, E, Sp, T;* (NewcastleUnited) 1985/6 *Ru, E, D, Mor, Alg, Sp, Braz.*
Stewart, P. (1) (Linfield) 1960/1 *W.*
Stewart, D. (1) (Hull City) 1977/8 *Bel.*

Todd, S. (9) (Burnley) 1966/7 *E*; 1967/8 *W*; 1968/9 *E, S, W*; 1969/70 *Rus, S*; 1970/1 *Sp* (Sheffield Wednesday), *C* (2).
Trainor, D. (1) (Crusaders) 1966/7 *W.*
Tulley, C. (10) (Glasgow Celtic) 1948/9 *E*; 1949/50 *E*; 1951/2 *S*; 1952/3 *E, S, F, W*; 1953/4 *S*; 1955/6 *E*; 1958/9 *Sp.*

Uprichard, N. (18) (Swindon Town) 1951/2 *S, E, W*; 1952/3 *E, S,* (Portsmouth) *F, W*; 1954/5 *E, S, W*; 1955/6 *S, E, W*; 1957/8 *S, It, Czecho*; 1958/9 *S, Sp.*
Whiteside, N. (29) (Manchester U.) 1981/2 *Y, Hon, Sp,Aust, F*; 1982/3 *G, A, T*; 1983/4 *Aust, T, G, S, E,W, Fin;* 1984/5 *Ru, Fin, Isr, E, Sp, T;* 1985/6 *Ru,E, F, D, Mor, Alg, Sp, Braz.*
Worthington, N. (10) (Sheffield W.) 1983/4 *W, Fin;*1984/5 *Isr, Sp;* 1985/6 *T, Ru, E, D, Alg, Sp.*

SCOTLAND

Aird, J. (4) (Burnley) 1953/4 *N* (2), *Aust, U.*
Aitken, G.G. (8) (East Fife) 1948/9 *E, F;* 1949/50*I, W, Switz;* 1952/3 (Sunderland) *W, I;* 1953/4*E.*
Aitken, R. (23) (Celtic) 1979/80 *Per, Bel, W, E,Pol*; 1982/3 *Bel, Can* (2); 1983/4 *Bel, I, W;* 1984/5 *E, Ic;* 1985/6 *W, E/Germ, Au(2),Isr, Ru, E, D, G, U.*
Albiston, A. (14) (Manchester U.) 1981/2 *I;* 1983/4*U, Bel, E/Germ, W, E;* 1984/5 *Y, Ic, Sp, Sp, W;* 1985/6 *E/Germ, Holl, U.*
Allan, T. (2) (Dundee) 1973/4 *G, N.*
Anderson, J. (1) (Leicester City) 1953/4 *Fin.*
Archibald, S. (27) (Aberdeen) 1979/80 *Port, I, Pol,H;* 1980/81 (Tottenham H.) *Swdn, Isr, I, Isr, I, E;* 1981/2 *I, Port, Holl, Sp, NZ, Braz, Rus*; 1982/3*E/Germ, Switz, Bel*; 1983/4*E/Germ, E, F;* 1984/5 (Barcelona) *Sp, E,Ic;* 1985/6 *G.*
Auld, B. (3) (Celtic) 1958/9 *Holl, Port;* 1959/60 *W.*

Baird, H. (1) (Airdrieonians) 1955/6 *Aust.*
Baird, S. (7) (Rangers) 1956/7 *Y, Sp, Switz, G, Sp;* 1957/8 *I, F.*
Bannon, E. (11) (Heart of Midlothian) 1979/80*Bel*; 1982/3 (Dundee U.) *I, W, E, Can*; 1983/4*E/Germ;* 1985/6 *Isr, Ru, E, D, G.*
Bauld, W. (3) (Heart of Midlothian) 1949/50 *E, Switz, Port.*
Baxter, J. (34) (Rangers) 1960/1 *I, Eire* (2), *Czecho;* 1961/2 *Czecho, I, W, Czecho, E, U;* 1962/3 *W, I, E, Aust, N, Eire, Sp;* 1963/4 *N, W, E, G;* 1964/5 *W, Fin, I* (Sunderland); 1965/6*I, It, W, E, Port, Braz;* 1966/7 *W, E, Rus;* 1967/8 *W.*
Bell, W. (2) (Leeds United) 1965/6 *Port, Braz.*
Bett, J. (16) (Rangers) 1981/2 *Holl*; 1982/3*Bel*(Lokeren); 1983/4 *Bel, W, E, F;* 1984/5 *Y,Ic, Sp, Sp, W, E, Ic;* (Aberdeen) 1985/6 *W, Isr, Holl.*
Black, I. (1) (Southampton) 1947/8 *E.*
Blacklaw, A. (3) (Burnley) 1962/3 *N, Sp;* 1965/6 *It.*
Blackley, J. (7) (Hibernian) 1973/4 *Czecho, E, Bel, Z;* 1975/6 *Switz;* 1976/7 *W, Swdn.*
Blair, J. (1) (Blackpool) 1946/7 *W.*
Blyth, J. (2) (Coventry City) 1977/8 *Bulg, W.*
Bone, J. (1) (Norwich City) 1972/3 *D.*
Brand, R. (8) (Rangers) 1960/1 *I, Eire* (2), *Czecho;* 1961/2 *I, W, Czecho, U.*
Brazil, A. (13) (Ipswich Town) 1979/80 *Pol, H;* 1981/2 *Holl, Sp, I, W, E, NZ, Rus*; 1982/3 *E/Germ, Switz,* (Tottenham Hotspur) *W, E.*
Bremner, D. (1) (Hibernian) 1975/6 *Switz.*
Bremner, W. (54) (Leeds United) 1964/5 *Sp;* 1965/6 *Pol, It* (2), *E, Port, Braz;* 1966/7 *W, I, E;* 1967/8 *W, E;* 1968/9 *D, C, Aust, G, W, I, E, C;* 1969/70 *Eire, G, Aust;* 1970/1 *W, E;* 1971/2 *Port, Bel, Holl, I, W, E, Y, Czecho, Braz;* 1972/3 *D* (2), *E, I, E, Switz, Braz;* 1973/4 *Czecho, G, I, W, E, Bel, N, Z, Braz, Y;* 1974/5 *Sp* (2); 1975/6 *D.*
Brennan, F. (7) (Newcastle United) 1946/7 *W, I;* 1952/3 *W, I, E;* 1963/4 *I, E.*
Brogan, J. (4) (Celtic) 1970/1 *Port, W, I, E.*
Brown, A. (14) (East Fife) 1949/50 *Switz, Port, F;* (Blackpool) 1951/2 *US, D, Swdn;* 1952/3 *W;* 1953/4 *W, E, N* (2), *Fin, Aust, U.*
Brown, H. (3) (Partick Thistle) 1946/7 *W, Bel, Lux.*
Brown, J. (1) (Sheffield United) 1974/5 *Rus.*
Brown, R. (3) (Rangers) 1946/7 *I;* 1948/9 *I;* 1951/2 *E.*
Brown, W. (28) (Dundee) 1957/8 *F;* 1958/9 *W, I, E;* 1959/60 (Tottenham Hotspur) *I, N, Pol, Aust, H, T;* 1961/2 *Czecho, I, W, E;* 1962/3 *W, I, E, Aust;* 1963/4 *I, N, W;* 1964/5 *E, Sp, Pol, Fin;* 1965/6 *I, Pol, It.*
Brownlie, J. (7) (Hibernian) 1970/1 *Rus;* 1971/2 *Per, I, E;* 1972/3 *D* (2); 1975/6 *Ru.*
Buchan, M. (34) (Aberdeen) 1971/2 *Bel* (Manchester United) *W, Y, Port, Czecho, Braz;* 1972/3 *D (2), E;* 1973/4 *G, I, W, N, Braz, Y;* 1974/5 *E/Germ, Sp,*

Port; 1975/6 *D, Ru;* 1976/7 *Fin, Czecho, Ch, Arg, Braz;* 1977/8 *E/Germ, W, I;* 1978/9 *Per, Ir, Holl, Aust, N, Port.*
Buckley, P. (3) (Aberdeen) 1953/4 *N;* 1954/5 *W, I.*
Burley, G. (11) (Ipswich Town) 1978/9 *W, I, E, N, Arg;* 1979/80 *Port, I, E, Pol;* 1981/2 *W, E.*
Burns, F. (1) (Manchester United) 1969/70 *Aust.*
Burns, K. (20) (Birmingham City) 1973/4 *G;* 1974/5 *E/Germ, Sp* (2); 1976/7 *Czecho, W, Swdn, W;* (Nottingham Forest) 1977/8 *I, W, E;* 1978/9 *Per, Ir, N;* 1979/80 *Per, Aust, Bel;* 1980/81 *Isr, I, W.*
Burns, T. (5) (Celtic) 1980/81 *I;* 1981/2 *Holl, W*; 1982/3 *Bel, I.*

Caldow, E. (40) (Rangers) 1956/7 *E, Sp, Switz, G, Sp;* 1957/8 *I, Switz, W, H, Pol, Y, Per, F;* 1958/9 *W, I, E, G, Holl, Port;* 1959/60 *I, W, E, Aust, H, T;* 1960/1 *W, I, E, Eire* (2), *Czecho;* 1961/2 *Czecho, I, W, Czecho, E, U;* 1962/3 *W, I, E.*
Callaghan, T. (2) (Dunfermline) 1969/70 *Eire, W.*
Campbell, R. (3) (Chelsea) 1949/50 *Switz, Port, F.*
Campbell, W. (7) (Morton) 1946/7 *I, Bel, Lux;* 1947/8 *E, Bel, Switz, F.*
Carr, W. (6) (Coventry City) 1969/70 *I, W, E;* 1970/1 *D;* 1971/2 *Per;* 1972/3 *D.*
Chalmers, S. (5) (Celtic) 1964/5 *W, Fin;* 1965/6 *Port, Braz;* 1966/7 *I.*
Clark, J. (4) (Celtic) 1965/6 *Braz;* 1966/7 *W, I, Rus.*
Clark, R. (16) (Aberdeen), 1967/8 *W, Holl;* 1969/70 *I;* 1970/1 *Port, W, I, E, D, Rus;* 1971/2 *Bel, I, W, E, Czecho, Braz;* 1972/3 *D, E.*
Collins, R. (31) (Celtic) 1950/1 *W, I, Aust;* 1954/5 *Y, Aust, H;* 1955/6 *I, W;* 1956/7 *W, E, Sp, Switz, G, Sp;* 1957/8 *I, Switz, W, H, Pol, Y, Par, F;* 1958/9 (Everton) *W, I, E, G, Holl, Port;* 1964/5 (Leeds United) *E, Sp, Pol.*
Colquhoun, E. (9) (Sheffield United) 1971/2 *Port, Holl, Per, Y, Czecho, Braz;* 1972/3 *d)2), E.*
Combe, R. (3) (Hibernian) 1947/8 *E, Bel, Switz.*
Conn, A. (1) (Heart of Midlothian) 1955/6 *Aust.*
Conn, A. (2) (Tottenham Hotspur) 1974/5 *I, E.*
Connachan, E. (2) (Dunfermline Athletic) 1961/2 *Czecho, U.*
Connelly, G. (2) (Celtic) 1973/4 *Czecho, G.*
Connolly, J. (1) (Everton) 1972/3 *Switz.*
Connor, R. (1) (Dundee) 1985/6 *Holl.*
Cooke, C. (16) (Dundee) 1965/6 *W, It, Port, Braz*(Chelsea); 1967/8 *E, Holl;* 1968/9 *C, Aust, G, W,I, C;* 1969/70 *Aust;* 1970/1 *Bel;* 1974/5*Sp, Port.*
Cooper, D. (16) (Rangers) 1979/80 *Per, Aust*;1983/4 *W, E;* 1984/5 *Y, Ic, Sp, Sp, W;* 1985/6*W, E/Germ, Au(2), Holl, G, U.*
Cormack, P. (9) (Hibernian) 1965/6 *Braz;* 1969/70 *Eire, G, Aust;* (Nottingham Forest) 1970/1 *D, Port, W, E;* 1971/2 *Holl.*
Cowan, J. (25) (Morton) 1947/8 *Bel, Switz, F;* 1948/9 *W, E, F;* 1949/50 *I, W, E, Switz, Port, F;* 1950/1 *W, I, Aust* (2), *E, D, F, Bel;* 1951/2 *I, W, US, D, Swdn.*
Cowie, D. (20) (Dundee) 1952/3 *E, Swdn;* 1953/4 *I, W, N, Fin, Aust, U;* 1954/5 *W, I, Aust, H;* 1955/6 *W, Aust;* 1956/7 *I, W;* 1957/8 *H, Pol, Y, Par.*
Cox, S. (25) (Rangers) 1947/8 *F;* 1948/9 *E, F;* 1949/50 *I, W, E, Switz, Port, F;* 1950/1 *e* (2), *F, Bel, Aust;* 1951/2 *I, W, US, D, Swdn;* 1952/3 *W, I, E;* 1953/4 *I, W, E.*
Craig, J. (1) (Celtic) 1967/8 *W.*
Craig, J. (1) (Celtic) 1976/7 *Swdn.*
Craig, T. (1) (Newcastle United) 1975/6 *Switz.*
Crerand, P. (16) (Celtic) 1960/1 *Eire* (2), *Czecho;* 1961/2 *Czecho, I, W, Czecho, E, W;* 1962/3 *W, I;* 1963/4 *I;* 1964/5 (Manchester United) *E, Pol, Fin;* 1965/6 *Pol.*
Cropley, A. (2) (Hibernian) 1971/2 *Port, Bel.*
Cruickshank, J. (6) (Heart of Midlothian) 1963/4 *G;* 1969/70 *W, E;* 1970/1 *D, Bel;* 1975/6 *Ru.*
Cullen, M. (1) (Luton Town) 1955/6 *Aust.*

Cumming, J. (9) (Heart of Midlothian) 1954/5 *H, E, Port, Y;* 1959/60 *E, Pol, Aust, H, T.*
Cunningham, W. (8) (Preston North End) 1953/4 *N (2), Fin, Aust, U;* 1954/5 *W, H, E.*
Curran, H. (5) (Wolverhampton Wanderers) 1969/70 *Aust;* 1970/1 *I, E, D, Rus.*

Dalglish, K. (100) (Celtic) 1971/2 *Bel, Holl;* 1972/3 *D* (2), *E, W, I, E, Switz, Braz;* 1973/4 *Czecho* (2), *G* (2), *I, W, E, Bel, N, Z, Braz, Y;* 1974/5 *E/Germ, Sp* (2), *Swdn, Port, W, I, E, Ru;* 1975/6 *D* (2), *Ru, Switz, I, E;* 1976/7 *Fin, Czecho, W, Swdn, W I, E, Ch, Arg, Braz;* (Liverpool) 1977/8 *E/Germ, Czecho, W* (2), *Bulg, I, W, E;* 1978/9 *Per, Ir, Holl, Aust, N, Port, W, I, E, N, Arg;* 1979/80 *Per, Aust, Bel, Bel, Port, I, W, E, Pol, H;* 1980/81 *Swdn, Port, Isr;* 1981/2 *Swdn, I, Holl, Sp, I, W, E, NZ, Braz;* 1982/3 *Bel, Switz;* 1983/4 *U, Bel, E/Germ;* 1984/5 *Y, Ic, Sp, W;* 1985/6 *e/Germ, Au, Ru.*
Davidson, J. (8) (Partick Thistle) 1953/4 *N (2), Aust, U;* 1954/5 *W, I, H, E.*
Dawson, A. (5) (Rangers) 1979/80 *Pol, H;* 1982/3 *I, Can* (2).
Deans, D. (2) (Celtic) 1974/5 *E/Germ, Sp.*
Delaney, J. (4) (Manchester United) 1946/7 *E;* 1947/8 *I, W, E.*
Dick, J. (1) (West Ham United) 1958/9 *E.*
Dickson, A. (5) (Kilmarnock) 1969/70 *I, W, E;* 1970/1 *D, Rus.*
Docherty, T. (25) (Preston North End) 1951/2 *W;* 1952/3 *E, Swdn;* 1953/4 *N (2), Aust, U;* 1954/5 *W, H (2), F, Aust;* 1956/7 *E, Sp, Switz, G, Sp;* 1957/8 *I, Switz, W, E;* 1958/9 (Arsenal) *W, I, E.*
Dodds, D. (2) (Dundee U.) 1983/4 *U, I.*
Donachie, W. (35) (Manchester City) 1971/2 *Per, I, E, Y, Czecho, Braz;* 1972/3 *D, E, W, I;* 1973/4 *I;* 1975/6 *Ru, I, W, E;* 1976/7 *Fin, Czecho, W, Swdn, W, I, E, Ch, Arg, Braz;* 1977/8 *E/Germ, W* (2), *Bulg, E;* 1978/9 *Ir, Holl, Aust, N, Port.*
Dougall, C. (1) (Birmingham City) 1946/7 *W.*
Dougan, R. (1) (Heart of Midlothian) 1949/50 *Switz.*
Doyle, J. (1) (Ayr United) 1975/6 *Ru.*
Duncan, A. (6) (Hibernian) 1974/5 *Port, W, I, E, Ru;* 1975/6 *D.*
Duncan, D. (3) (East Fife) 1947/8 *Bel, Switz, F.*
Duncanson, J. (1) (Rangers) 1946/7 *I.*

Evans, A. (4) (Aston Villa) 1981/2 *Holl, I, E, NZ.*
Evans, R. (48) (Celtic) 1948/9 *W, I, E, F;* 1949/50 *I, W, Switz, Port;* 1950/1 *Aust, E;* 1951/2 *I;* 1952/3 *Swdn;* 1953/4 *I, W, E, N, Fin;* 1954/5 *I, Port, Y, Aust, H;* 1955/6 *I, W, E, Aust;* 1956/7 *G, Sp;* 1957/8 *I, Switz, W, E, H, Pol, Y, Par, F;* 1958/9 *e, g, holl, Port;* 1959/60 *I, W, E,* (Chelsea) *Pol, Aust, H, T.*
Ewing, T. (2) (Partick Thistle) 1957/8 *W, E.*

Farm, G. (10) (Blackpool) 1952/3 *W, I, E, Swdn;* 1953/4 *I, W, E;* 1958/9 *G, Holl, Port.*
Ferguson, R. (7) (Kilmarnock) 1965/6 *W, E, Holl, Port, Braz;* 1966/7 *W, I.*
Fernie, W. (11) (Celtic) 1953/4 *Fin, Aust, U;* 1954/5 *W, I;* 1956/7 *Y, W, E;* 1957/8 *Switz, W, Per.*
Flavell, R. (2) (Airdrieonians) 1946/7 *Bel, Lux.*
Fleming, C. (1) (East Fife) 1953/4 *I.*
Forbes, A. (14) (Sheffield United) 1946/7 *E, Bel, Lux;* 1947/8 *I, W,* (Arsenal); 1949/50 *E, Port, F;* 1950/51 *W, I, Aust;* 1951/52 *W, D, Swdn.*
Ford, D. (3) (Heart of Midlothian) 1973/4 *Czecho, G, W.*
Forrest, J. (1) (Motherwell) 1957/8 *E.*
Forrest, J. (2) (Rangers) 1965/6 *W, It.*
Forrest, J. (3) (Aberdeen) 1970/1 *Bel, D, Rus.*
Forsyth, A. (18) (Partick Thistle) 1971/2 *Y, Czecho, Braz;* 1972/3 *D,* (Manchester United), *E;* 1974/5 *E/Germ, Sp, I, Ru;* 1975/6 *D;* 1977/8 *Czecho, W* (2), *I, E;* 1978/9 *Per, Ir, Holl.*

Forsyth, C. (3) (Kilmarnock) 1963/4 *E;* 1964/5 *W, Fin.*
Forsyth, T. (14) (Motherwell) 1970/1 *D* (Rangers); 1973/4 *Czecho;* 1975/6 *Switz, I, W, E;* 1976/7 *Fin, Swdn, W, I, E, Ch, Arg, Braz.*
Fraser, D. (2) (West Bromwich Albion) 1967/8 *Holl;* 1968/9 *C.*
Fraser, W. (2) (Sunderland) 1954/5 *D, I.*

Gabriel, J. (1) (Everton) 1960/1 *W.*
Gardiner, W. (1) (Motherwell) 1957/8 *W.*
Gemmell, T. (2) (St Mirren) 1954/5 *Port, Y.*
Gemmell, T. (18) (Celtic) 1965/6 *E;* 1966/7 *W, I, E, Rus;* 1967/8 *I, E;* 1968/9 *Aust, D, G, W, I, E, C;* 1969/70 *Eire, G, E;* 1970/1 *Bel.*
Gemmill, A. (43) (Derby County) 1970/1 *Bel;* 1971/2 *Port, Holl, Per, I, W, E;* 1975/6 *D, Ru, I, W, E,* 1976/7 *Fin, Czecho, W* (2), *I, E, Ch, Arg, Braz;* (Nottingham Forest) 1977/8 *E/Germ, Bulg, I, W, E;* 1978/9 *Per, Ir, Holl, Aust, N, Port, N;* (Birmingham City) 1979/80 *Aust, Port, I, W, E;* 1980/81 *Swdn, Port, Isr, I.*
Gibson, D. (7) (Leicester City) 1962/3 *Aust, N, Eire, Sp;* 1963/4 *I;* 1964/5 *W, Fin, H.*
Gilzean, A. (22) (Dundee) 1963/4 *N, W, E, G;* 1964/5 *I* (Tottenham Hotspur), *Sp;* 1965/6 *I, Pol, It, W;* 1967/8 *W;* 1968/9 *C, Aust, G, W, E, C;* 1969/70 *G, Aust, I, E;* 1970/1 *Port.*
Glavin, R. (1) (Celtic) 1976/7 *Swdn.*
Glen, A. (2) (Aberdeen) 1955/6 *I, E.*
Goram, A.L. (3) (Oldham Athletic) 1985/6*E/Germ, Ru, Holl.*
Gough, R. (26) (Dundee United) 1982/3 *Switz, I, W, E,Can* (3); 1983/4 *U, Bel, E/Germ, I, W, E, F;* 1984/5 *Sp, E, Ic;* 1985/6 *W, E/Germ, Au,Isr, Ru, E, D, G, U.*
Govan, J. (6) (Hibernian) 1947/8 *W, E, Bel, Switz, F;* 1948/9 *I.*
Graham, G. (11) (Arsenal) 1971/2 *Port, Holl, I, Y, Czecho, Braz;* 1972/3 *D* (2), (Manchester United) *E, W, I.*
Graham, A. (10) (Leeds United) 1977/8 *E/Germ;* 1978/9 *Aust, N, W, I, E, N, Arg;* 1979/80 *Aust;* 1980/81 *W.*
Gray, A. (20) (Aston Villa) 1975/6 *Ru, Switz;* 1976/7 *Fin, Czecho;* 1978/9 *Aust, N, Arg;* (Wolverhampton Wanderers) 1979/80 *Port, E;* 1980/1 *Swdn, Port, Isr, I;* 1981/2 *Swdn*; 1982/3 *I, W,E, Can* (2); 1984/5 (Everton) *Ic.*
Gray, E. (12) (Leeds United) 1968/9 *E, C;* 1969/70 *G, Aust;* 1970/1 *W, I;* 1971/2 *Bel, Holl;* 1975/6 *W, E;* 1976/7 *Fin, W.*
Gray, F. (31) (Leeds United) 1975/6 *Switz;* 1978/9 *N, Port, W, I, E;* 1979/80 (Nottingham F.) *Bel;* 1980/81 *Swdn, Port, Isr, I, Isr* (Leeds U.) *W, I, E;* 1981/2 *Swdn, I, Port, Holl, Sp, W, NZ, Braz, Rus*; 1982/3 *E/Germ, Switz, Bel, Switz, W, E, Can.*
Grant, J. (2) (Hibernian) 1958/9 *W, I.*
Green, A. (16) (Blackpool) 1970/1 *Bel, Port, I, E;* (Newcastle United) 1971/2 *W, E.*
Greig, J. (44) (Rangers) 1963/4 *E, G;* 1964/5 *W, Fin, I, E, Sp, Pol, Fin;* 1965/6 *I, Pol, It, W, It, E, Holl, Port, Braz;* 1966/7 *W, I, E;* 1967/8 *I, W, E, Holl;* 1968/9 *D, C, Aust, G, W, I, E, C;* 1969/70 *Eire, G, Aust, W, E;* 1970/1 *D, Bel, W, I, E;* 1975/6 *D.*

Haddock, H. (6) (Clydebank) 1954/5 *H* (2), *E, Port, Y;* 1957/8 *E.*
Haffey, H. (2) (Celtic) 1959/60 *E;* 1960/1 *E.*
Hamilton, A. (24) (Dundee) 1961/2 *W, Czecho, E, U;* 1962/3 *W, I, E, Aust, N, I, Eire;* 1963/4 *I, N, W, E, G;* 1964/5 *W, Fin, I, E, Sp, Pol, Fin;* 1965/6 *I, Pol.*
Hamilton, G. (5) (Aberdeen) 1946/7 *I;* 1950/1 *Bel, Aust;* 1953/4 *N* (2).
Hamilton, W. (1) (Hibernian) 1964/5 *Fin.*
Hansen, A. (23) (Liverpool) 1978/9 *W, Arg;* 1979/80 *Bel, Port;* 1980/81 *Swdn, Port, Isr;* 1981/2 *Swdn, I, Port, Sp, I, W, E, NZ, Braz, Rus*; 1982/3 *E/Germ, Switz, Bel, Switz;* 1984/5 *W;* 1985/6 *R.*

Hansen, J. (1) (Partick Thistle) 1971/2 *Bel.*
Harper, J. (4) (Aberdeen) 1972/3 *D* (2); 1975/6 *D;* 1978/9 *Ir.*
Hartford, A. (49) (West Bromwich Albion) 1971/2 *Per, W, E, Y, Czecho, Braz;* 1975/6 (Manchester City) *D, Ru, I;* 1976/7 *Czecho, W, Swdn, W, I, E, Ch, Arg, Braz;* 1977/8 *E/Germ, Czecho, W* (2), *Bulg, E;* 1978/9 *Per, Ir, Holl, Aust, N, Port, W, I, E, N, Arg;* 1979/80 (Everton) *Per, Bel;* 1980/81 *Isr, W, I, E;* 1981/2 *Swdn,* (Manchester C.) *I, Port, Sp, I, W, E, Braz.*
Harvey, D. (16) (Leeds United) 1972/3 *D;* 1973/4 *Czecho, G, I, W, E, Bel, Z, Braz, Y;* 1974/5 *E/Germ, Sp* (2); 1975/6 *D* (2); 1976/7 *Fin.*
Haughney, M. (1) (Celtic) 1953/4 *E.*
Hay, D. (27) (Celtic) 1969/70 *I, W, E;* 1970/1 *D, Bel, Port, W;* 1971/2 *Port, Bel, Holl;* 1972/3 *W, I, E, Switz, Braz;* 1973/4 *Czecho* (2), *G, I, W, E, Bel, N, Z, Braz, Y.*
Hegarty, P. (7) (Dundee United) 1978/9 *W, I, E, Arg;* 1979/80 *W, E*; 1982/3 *I.*
Henderson, J. (7) (Portsmouth) 1952/3 *Swdn;* 1953/4 *I, E, N;* 1955/6 *W;* 1958/9 (Arsenal) *W, I.*
Henderson, W. (29) (Rangers) 1962/3 *W, I, E, Aust, N, Eire, Sp;* 1963/4 *I, N, W, E, G;* 1964/5 *E, Sp, Pol, Fin;* 1965/6 *I, Pol, It, W, Holl;* 1966/7 *W, I;* 1967/8 *Holl;* 1968/9 *I, E, C;* 1969/70 *Eire, Czecho.*
Herd, D. (5) (Arsenal) 1958/9 *W, I, E;* 1960/1 *Eire*; 1970/1 *Port.*
Herd, G. (5) (Clydebank) 1957/8 *E;* 1959/60 *H, T;* 1960/1 *W, I.*
Herriot, J. (8) (Birmingham City) 1968/9 *D, C, W, I, E, C;* 1969/70 *Eire, G.*
Hewie, J. (19) (Charlton Athletic) 1955/6 *E, Aust;* 1956/7 *Y, I, W, E, Sp, Switz, G, Sp;* 1957/8 *W, Pol, Y, F;* 1958/9 *Holl, Port;* 1959/60 *I, W, Pol.*
holt, D. (4) (Heart of Midlothian) 1962/3 *Aust, N, Eire, Sp.*
Holton, J. (15) (Manchester United) 1972/3 *W, I, E, Switz, Braz;* 1973/4 *Czecho, G, I, W, E, N, Z, Braz, Y;* 1974/5 *E/Germ.*
Hope, R. (2) (West Bromwich Albion) 1967/8 *Hol;* 1968/9 *D.*
Houliston, W. (3) (Queen of the South) 1948/9 *I, E, F.*
Houston, S. (1) (Manchester United) 1975/6 *D.*
Howie, H. (1) (Hibernian) 1948/9 *W.*
Hughes, J. (8) (Celtic) 1964/5 *Sp, Pol;* 1965/6 *I, It* (2); 1967/8 *E;* 1968/9 *Aust;* 1969/70 *Eire.*
Hughes, W. (1) (Sunderland) 1974/5 *Swdn.*
Humphries, W. (1) (Motherwell) 1951/2 *Swdn.*
Hunter, A. (3) (Kilmarnock) 1971/2 *Per;* 1972/3 (Celtic) *E;* 1973/4 *Czecho.*
Hunter, N. (3) (Motherwell) 1959/60 *H, T;* 1960/1 *W.*
Husband, J. (1) (Partick Thistle) 1946/7 *W.*
Hutchison, T. (17) (Coventry City) 1973/4 *Czecho* (2), *G* (2), *I, W, Bel, N, Z, Y;* 1974/5 *E/Germ, Sp* (2), *Port, E, Ru;* 1975/6 *D.*

Imlach, S. (4) (Nottingham Forest) 1957/8 *H, Pol, Y, F.*

Jackson, C. (8) (Rangers) 1974/5 *Swdn, Port, W;* 1975/6 *D, Ru, I, W, E.*
Jardine, A. (37) (Rangers) 1970/1 *D;* 1971/2 *Port, Bel, Holl;* 1972/3 *E, Switz, Braz;* 1973/4 *Czecho* (2), *G* (2), *I, W, E, Bel, N, Z, Braz, Y;* 1974/5 *E/Germ, Sp* (2), *Swdn, Port, W, I, E;* 1976/7 *Swdn, Ch;* 1977/8 *Czecho, W, I;* 1978/9 *Ir;* 1979/80 *Per, Aust, Bel* (2).
Jarvie, A. (3) (Airdrieonians) 1970/1 *Port, I, E.*
Johnston, M. (9) (Watford) 1983/4 *W, E, F; 1984$5(Celtic) Y, Ic, Sp, Sp, W;* 1985/6 *E/Germ.*
Johnston, W. (21) (Rangers) 1965/6 *Pol, W, E, Holl;* 1967/8 *W, E;* 1968/9 *I;* 1969/70 *I;* 1970/1 *D;* (West Bromwich Albion) 1976/7 *Swdn, W, I, Ch, Arg, Braz;* 1977/8 *E/Germ, Czecho, W* (2), *E.*
Johnstone, D. (15) (Rangers) 1972/3 *W, I, E, Switz, Braz;* 1974/5 *E/Germ, Swdn;* 1975/6 *Switz, I, E;* 1977/8 *Bulg, I, W;* 1978/9 *Per;* 1979/80 *Bel.*
Johnstone, J. (23) (Celtic) 1964/5 *W, Fin;* 1965/6 *E;* 1966/7 *W, Rus;* 1967/8 *W;*

1968/9 *Aust, G;* 1969/70 *G, E;* 1970/1 *D, E;* 1971/2 *Port, Bel, Holl, I, E;* 1973/4 *W, E, Bel, N;* 1974/5 *E/Germ, Sp.*
Johnstone, L. (2) (Clydebank) 1947/8 *Bel, Switz.*
Johnstone, R. (17) (Hibernian) 1950/1 *E, D, F;* 1951/2 *I, E;* 1952/3 *E, Swdn;* 1953/4 *W, E, N, Fin;* 1954/5 *I, H,* (Manchester City), *E;* 1955/6 *I, W, E.*
Jordan, J. (52) (Leeds United) 1972/3 *E, Switz, Braz;* 1973/4 *Czecho* (2), *G, I, W, E, Bel, N, Z, Braz, Y;* 1974/5 *E/Germ, Sp* (2); 1975/6 *I, W, E;* 1976/7 *Czecho, W, I, E;* (Manchester United) 1977/8 *E/Germ, Czecho, W, Bulg, I, E;* 1978/9 *Per, Ir, Holl, Aust, Port, W, I, E, N;* 1979/80 *Bel, I, W, E, Pol;* 1980/81 *Isr, W, E;* 1981/2 (AC Milan) *Swdn, Holl, W, E, Rus.*

Kelly, H. (1) (Blackpool) 1951/2 *US.*
Kelly, J. (2) (Barnsley) 1948/9 *W, I.*
Kennedy, J. (6) (Celtic) 1963/4 *W, E, G;* 1964/5 *W, Fin, I.*
Kennedy, S. (12) (Rangers) 1974/5 *Swdn, Port, W, I, E;* 1977/8 *Bulg, W, E;* 1978/9 *Per, Holl, Aust, Port.*
Kerr, A. (2) (Partick Thistle) 1954/5 *Aust, H.*

Law, D. (55) (Huddersfield Town) 1958/9 *W, I, Holl, Port;* 1959/60 *I, W,* (Manchester City) *E, Pol, Aust;* 1960/1 *I, E;* 1961/2 (Torino) *Czecho* (2), *E;* 1962/3 (Manchester United) *W, I, E, Aust, N, Eire, Sp;* 1963/4 *N, W, E, G;* 1964/5 *W, Fin, I, E, Sp, Pol, Fin;* 1965/6 *I, Pol, E;* 1966/7 *W, E, Rus;* 1967/8 *I;* 1968/9 *Aust, G, I;* 1971/2 *Per, I, W, E, Y, Czecho, Braz;* 1973/4 (Manchester City) *Czecho* (2), *G* (2), *I, Z.*
Lawrence, T. (3) (Liverpool) 1962/3 *Eire;* 1968/9 *G, W.*
Leggat, G. (18) (Aberdeen) 1955/6 *E;* 1956/7 *W;* 1957/8 *I, H, Pol, Y, Par;* 1958/9 (Fulham) *W, I, E, G, Holl;* 1959/60 *I, W, E, Pol, Aust, H.*
Leighton, J. (29) (Aberdeen) 1982/3 *E/Germ,Switz, Bel, Switz, W, E, Can* (2); 1983/4 *U, Bel, I, W, E,F;* 1984/5 *Y, Ic, Sp, Sp, W, E, Ic;* 1985/6 *W,E/Germ, Au(2),Isr, D, G, U.*
Lennox, R. (10) (Celtic) 1966/7 *I, E, Rus;* 1967/8*W, E;* 1968/9 *D, W, Aust, G, C.*
Leslie, L. (5) (Airdrieonians) 1960/1 *W, I, Eire* (2), *Czecho.*
Liddell, W. (28) (Liverpool) 1946/7 *W, I;* 1947/8 *I, W, E;* 1949/50 *W, E, Port, F;* 1950/1 *W, I, Aust, E;* 1951/2 *I, W, E, US, D, Swdn;* 1952/3 *W, I, E;* 1953/4 *W;* 1954/5 *Port, Y, Aust, H;* 1955/6 *I.*
Linwood, A. (1) (Clydebank) 1949/50 *W.*
Little, A. (1) (Rangers) 1952/3 *Swdn.*
Logie, J. (1) (Arsenal) 1952/3 *I.*
Long, H. (1) (Clyde) 1946/7 *I.*
Lorimer, P. (21) (Leeds United) 1969/70 *Aust;* 1970/1 *W, I;* 1971/2 *I, W, E;* 1972/3 *D* (2), *E* (2); 1973/4 *G, E, Bel, N, Z, Braz, Y;* 1974/5 *Sp;* 1975/6 *D* (2), *Ru.*

Macari, L. (24) (Celtic) 1971/2 *W, E, Y, Czecho, Braz;* 1972/3 *D,* (Manchester United) *F, W, I, E;* 1974/5 *Swdn, Port, W, E, Ru;* 1976/7 *I, E, Ch, Arg;* 1977/8 *E/Germ, W, Bulg;* 1978/9 *Per, Ir.*
Macaulay, A. (7) (Brentford) 1946/7 *E* (Arsenal); 1947/8 *I, W, E, Bel, Switz, F.*
Macdougall, E. (7) (Norwich City) 1974/5 *Swdn, Port, W, I, E;* 1975/6 *D, Ru.*
Mackay, D. (22) (Heart of Midlothian) 1956/7 *Sp;* 1957/8 *F;* 1958/9 *W, I,* (Tottenham Hotspur) *E, G;* 1959/60 *I, W, Pol, Aust, H, T;* 1960/1 *W, I, E;* 1962/3 *E, Aust, N;* 1963/4 *I, N, W;* 1965/6 *I.*
Malpas, M. (12) (Dundee U.) 1983/4 *F;* 1984/5*E, Ic;* 1985/6 *W, Au(2), Isr, Ru, E, Holl, D, G.*
Martin, F. (7) (Aberdeen) 1953/4 *N* (2), *Aust, U;* 1954/5 *N, E, N.*
Martin, N. (3) (Hibernian) 1964/5 *Pol, Fin;* 1965/6 (Sunderland) *It.*
Martis, J. (1) (Motherwell) 1960/1 *W.*
Mason, J. (7) (Third Lanark) 1948/9 *W, I, E;* 1949/50 *I;* 1950/1 *I, Bel, Aust.*

Masson, D. (17) (Queens Park Rangers) 1975/6 *I, W, E;* 1976/7 *Fin, Czecho, W, I, E, Ch, Arg, Braz;* (Derby County) 1977/8 *E/Germ, Czecho, W, I, E;* 1978/9 *Per.*
Mathers, D. (1) (Partick Thistle) 1953/4 *Fin.*
McAvennie, F. (4) (West Ham United) 1985/6 *Au(2), D,G.*
McBride, J. (2) (Celtic) 1966/7 *W, I.*
McCalliog, J. (5) (Sheffield Wednesday) 1966/7 *E,Rus;* 1967/8 *I;* 1968/9 *D;* 1970/1 (Wolverhampton Wanderers) *Port.*
McCann, A. (5) (Motherwell) 1958/9 *G;* 1959/60 *I, W, E;* 1960/1 *E.*
McCloy, P. (4) (Rangers) 1972/3 *Switz, Braz, W,I.*
McCoist, A. (1) (Rangers) 1985/6 *Holl.*
McColl, I. (14) (Rangers) 1949/50 *E, F;* 1950/1*W, I, Bel;* 1956/7 *Y, I, W, E, Sp, Switz, G;* 1957/8 *I,E.*
McCreadie, E. (23) (Chelsea) 1964/5 *E, Sp, Pol, Fin;* 1965/6 *I, Pol, W, It, Port;* 1966/7 *E, Rus;* 1967/8 *I, W, E, Holl;* 1968/9 *D, C, Aust, G, W, I, E, C.*
MacDonald, A. (1) (Rangers) 1975/6 *Switz.*
MacDonald, J. (2) (Sunderland) 1955/6 *I, W.*
McFarlane, W. (1) (Heart of Midlothian) 1946/7 *Lux.*
McGarr, E. (2) (Aberdeen) 1969/70 *Eire, Aust.*
McGarvey, A. (1) (St Mirren) 1978/9 *Arg.*
McGarvey, F. (5) (Celtic) 1983/4 *U, Bel, E/Germ, I,W.*
McGhee, M. (4) (Aberdeen) 1982/3 *Can* (2); 1983/4 *I, E.*
McGrain, D. (62) (Celtic) 1972/3 *W, I, E, Switz, Braz;* 1973/4 *Czecho* (2); *G, W, E, Bel, N, Z, Braz, Y;* 1974/5 *Sp, Swdn, Port, W, I, E, Ru;* 1975/6 *D* (2), *Switz, I, W, E;* 1976/7 *Fin, Czecho, W, Swdn, W, I, E, Ch, Arg, Braz;* 1977/8 *E/Germ, Czecho;* 1979/80 *Bel, Port, I, W, E, Pol, H;* 1980/81 *Swdn, Port, Isr, I, Isr, W, I, E;* 1981/2 *Swdn, Holl, Sp, I, E, NZ, Rus.*
McGrory, J. (3) (Kilmarnock) 1964/5 *Fin, I;* 1965/6 *Port, Pol, H.*
McKay, D. (13) (Celtic) 1958/9 *E, G, Holl, Port;* 1959/60 *E, Pol, Aust, H, T;* 1960/1 *W, I;* 1961/2 *Czecho, I.*
McKean, R. (1) (Rangers) 1975/6 *Switz.*
McKenzie, J. (9) (Partick Thistle) 1953/4 *W, E, N, Fin, Aust, U;* 1954/5 *H, E;* 1955/6 *Aust.*
McKinnon, R. (28) (Rangers) 1965/6 *It, W, It, E, Holl, Braz;* 1966/7 *W, I, E;* 1967/8 *I, W, E, Holl;* 1968/9 *D, C, Aust, G;* 1969/70 *Eire, G, Aust, I, W, E;* 1970/1 *D, Bel, Port, D, Rus.*
McLaren, A. (4) (Preston North End) 1946/7 *E, Bel, Lux;* 1947/8 *W.*
McLean, G. (1) (Dundee) 1967/8 *Holl.*
McLean, T. (5) (Kilmarnock) 1968/9 *D, W;* 1969/70 *I, W;* 1970/1 (Rangers) *D.*
McLeish, A. (44) (Aberdeen) 1979/80 *F, I, W, E, Pol,H;* 1980/1 *Swdn, Isr, I, Isr, I, E;* 1981/2 *Swdn,Sp, I, Braz;* 1982/3 *Bel, Switz, W, E, Can, Can, Can;* 1983/4 *U, Bel, E/Germ, I, W, E, F;* 1984/5 *Y, Ic,Sp, Sp, W, E, Ic;* 1985/6 *W, E/Germ, Au(2), E,Holl, D.*
McLeod, J. (4) (Hibernian) 1960/1 *E, Eire* (2),*Czecho.*
McLeod, M. (1) (Celtic) 1984/5 *E.*
McLintock, F. (8) (Leicester City) 1962/3 *Eire, Sp;* 1964/5 (Arsenal) *I;* 1966/7 *Rus;* 1969/70 *I;* 1970/1 *W, I, E.*
McMillan, I. (6) (Airdrieonians and Rangers) 1951/2 *E, US, D;* 1954/5 *E;* 1955/6 *E;* 1960/1 *Czecho.*
McNaught, W. (5) (Raith Rovers) 1950/1 *W, I, Aust;* 1951/2 *E;* 1954/5 *I.*
McNeill, W. (28) (Celtic) 1960/1 *E, Eire* (2), *Czecho;* 1961/2 *Czecho, I, E, U;* 1962/3 *Eire, Sp;* 1963/4 *W, E, G;* 1964/5 *E, Sp, Pol, Fin;* 1965/6 *I, Pol;* 1966/7 *Rus;* 1967/8 *E;* 1968/9 *W, E, C;* 1969/70 *G;* 1971/2 *I, W, E.*
McPhail, J. (5) (Celtic) 1949/50 *W;* 1950/1 *W, I, Aust;* 1953/4 *I.*
McQueen, G. (30) (Leeds United) 1973/4 *Bel;* 1974/5 *Sp* (2), *Port, W, I, E, Ru;* 1975/6 *D;* 1976/7 *Czecho, W* (2), *I, E;* (Manchester U.) 1977/8 *E/Germ, Czecho, W* (2), *Bulg, I;* 1978/9 *Aust, N, Port, I, E, N;* 1979/80 *Per, Aust, Bel;* 1980/81 *W.*
McStay, P. (14) (Celtic) 1983/4 *U, Bel,E/Germ, I, W, E;* 1984/5 *Ic, Sp, Sp, W;* 1985/6*E/Germ, Au, Isr, U.*
Millar, W. (6) (Celtic) 1946/7 *W, E, Bel, Lux;* 1947/8 *I, W.*
Miller, J. (2) (Rangers) 1962/3 *Aust, Eire.*

Miller, W. (51) (Aberdeen) 1974/5 *Ru;* 1977/8*Bulg;* 1979/80 *Bel, W, E, Pol, H;* 1980/81*Swdn, Port, Isr, I, W, I, E;* 1981/2 *I, Port, Holl,Braz, Rus*; 1982/3 *E/Germ, Switz, Switz, W, E, Can*(3); 1983/4 *U, Bel, E/Germ, W, E, F;* 1984/5*Y, Ic, Sp, Sp, W, E, Ic;* 1985/6 *W, E/Germ,Au(2), Isr, Ru, E, Holl, D, G, U.*
Mitchell, R. (2) (Newcastle United) 1950/1 *F, D.*
Mochan, H. (3) (Celtic) 1953/4 *N, Aust, U.*
Moir, W. (1) (Bolton Wanderers) 1949/50 *E.*
Moncur, R. (16) (Newcastle United) 1967/8 *Hol;* 1969/70 *Eire, I, W, E;* 1970/1 *D, Bel, Port, W, I, E, D;* 1971/2 *Per, I, W, E.*
Morgan, W. (21) (Burnley) 1967/8 *I;* (Manchester United) 1971/2 *Per, Y, Czecho, Braz;* 1972/3 *D* (2), *E, W, I, E, Switz, Braz;* 1973/4 *Czecho* (2), *G* (2), *I, Bel, Braz, Y.*
Morris, H. (1) (East Fife) 1949/50 *I.*
Mudie, J. (17) (Blackpool) 1956/7 *Y, I, W, E, Sp, Switz, G, Sp*; 1957/8 *I, Switz, W, E, H, Pol, Y, Par, F.*
Mulhall, G. (3) (Aberdeen) 1959/60 *I*; 1962/3 (Sunderland) *I*; 1963/4 *I.*
Munro, F. (9) (Wolverhampton Wanderers) 1970/1 *I, E, D, Rus*; 1974/5 *Swdn, W, I, E, Ru.*
Munro, J. (7) (St Mirren) 1978/9 *N, Arg*; 1979/80 *Per, Aust, Bel, W, E.*
Murdoch, R. (12) (Celtic) 1965/6 *It, W, It, E*; 1966/7 *I*; 1967/8 *I*; 1968/9 *C, G, W, I, E*; 1969/70 *Aust.*
Murray, J. (5) (Heart of Midlothian) 1957/8 *E, H, Pol, Y, F.*
Murray, S. (1) (Aberdeen) 1971/2 *Bel.*

Narey, D. (30) (Dundee United) 1976/7 *Swdn*;1978/9 *Port, I, Arg*; 1979/80 *Port, I, Pol, H;* 1980/81 *W, E;* 1981/2 *Holl, W, E, NZ, Braz,Rus*; 1982/3 *E/Germ, Switz, Bel, I, W, E, Can*(3); 1985/6 *Isr, Ru, Holl, G, U.*
Nevin, P.K.F. (2) (Chelsea) 1985/6 *Ru, E.*
Nicholas, C. (17) (Celtic) 1982/3 *Switz, I, E, Can*(3); (Arsenal) 1983/4 *Bel, F;* 1984/5 *Y, Ic, Sp,W*; 1985/6 *Isr, Ru, E, D, U.*
Nicol, S. (11) (Liverpool) 1984/5 *Y, Ic, Sp, W*;1985/6 *W, E/Germ, Au, E, D, G, U.*
O'Hare, J. (13) (Derby County) 1969/70 *I, W, E*; 1970/1 *D, Bel, W, I*; 1971/2 *Port, Bel, Holl, Per, I, W.*
Ormond, W. (6) (Hibernian) 1953/4 *E, N, Fin, Aust, U*; 1958/9 *E.*
Orr, T. (2) (Morton) 1951/2 *I, W.*

Parker, A. (15) (Falkirk) 1954/5 *Port, Y, Aust*; 1955/6 *I, W, E, Aust*; 1956/7 *Y, I, W*; 1957/8 *I, Switz, W, E, Par.*
Parlane, D. (13) (Rangers) 1972/3 *W, Switz, Braz*; 1974/5 *Sp, Swdn, Port, W, I, E, Ru*; 1975/6 *D*; 1976/7 *W, Braz.*
Paton, A. (2) (Motherwell) 1951/2 *D, Swdn.*
Pearson, T. (2) (Newcastle United) 1946/7 *E, Bel.*
Penman, A. (1) (Dundee) 1965/6 *Holl.*
Pettigrew, W. (5) (Motherwell) 1975/6 *Switz, I, W*; 1976/7 *W, Swdn.*
Plenderleith, J. (1) (Manchester City) 1960/1 *I.*
Provan, D. (5) (Rangers) 1963/4 *I, N*; 1965/6 *It* (2), *Holl.*
Provan, D. (10) (Celtic) 1979/80 *Bel, Bel, Port, I;* 1980/81 *Isr, W, E;* 1981/2 *Swdn, Port, I.*

Quinn, P. (4) (Motherwell) 1960/1 *E, Eire* (2); 1961/2 *U.*

Redpath, W. (9) (Motherwell) 1948/9 *W, I*; 1950/1 *E, D, F, Bel, Aust*; 1951/2 *I, E.*
Reilly, L. (38) (Hibernian) 1948/9 *W, E, F*; 1949/50 *I, W, Switz, F*; 1950/1 *W, E, D, F, Bel, Aust*; 1951/2 *I, W, E, US, D, Swdn*; 1952/3 *W, I, E, Swdn*; 1953/4 *W*; 1954/5 *H* (2), *E, Port, Y, Aust*; 1955/6 *I, W, E, Aust*; 1956/7 *Y, I, W, E.*
Ring, T. (12) (Clydebank) 1952/3 *Swdn*; 1954/5 *W, I, H, E*; 1956/7 *E, Sp, Switz, G, Sp*; 1957/8 *I, Switz.*

Rioch, B. (24) (Derby County) 1974/5 *Port, W, I, E, Ru*; 1975/6 *D* (2), *Ru, I, W, E*; 1976/7 *Fin, Czecho, W,* (Everton) *W, I, E, Ch, Braz*; (Derby County) 1977/8 *Czecho, I, E*; 1978/9 *Per, Holl.*
Robb, D. (5) (Aberdeen) 1970/1 *Port, W, E, D, Rus.*
Robertson, A. (5) (Clydebank) 1954/5 *Port, Aust, H*; 1957/8 *Switz, Par.*
Robertson, H. (1) (Dundee) 1961/2 *Czecho.*
Robertson, J. (1) (Tottenham Hotspur) 1964/5 *W.*
Robertson, J. (26) (Nottingham Forest) 1977/8 *I*; 1978/9 *Ir, Port, N*; 1979/80 *Per, Aust, Bel, Bel, Port;* 1980/81 *Swdn, Port, Isr, I, Isr, I, E;* 1981/2 *Swdn, I, I, E, NZ, Braz, Rus*; 1982/3 *E/Germ, Switz;* (Derby Co.) 1983/4 *U, Bel.*
Robinson, B. (4) (Dundee) 1973/4 *G*; 1974/5 *Swdn, I, Ru.*
Rough, A. (53) (Partick Thistle) 1975/6 *Switz, I, W, E*; 1976/7 *Fin, Czecho, W, Swdn, W, I, E, Ch, Arg, Braz*; 1977/8 *Czecho, W, I, E*; 1978/9 *Per, Ir, Holl, Aust, Port, W, N, Arg*; 1979/80 *Per, Aust, Bel, Bel, Port, W, E, Pol, H;* 1980/81 *Swdn, Port, Isr, I, Isr, W, E;* 1981/2 *Swdn, I, Holl, Sp, W, E, NZ, Braz, Rus*; (Hibernian) 1985/6 *W, E.*
Rougvie, D. (1) (Aberdeen) 1983/4 *I.*

Rutherford, E. (1) (Rangers) 1947/8 *F.*

Schaedler, E. (1) (Hibernian) 1973/4 *G.*
Scott, A. (16) (Rangers) 1956/7 *Y, I, G*; 1957/8 *Switz, W*; 1958/9 *Port*; 1961/2 *Czecho, I, W, E, W* (Everton); 1963/4 *N, W*; 1964/5 *Fin*; 1965/6 *Port, Braz.*
Scott, A. (1) (Hibernian) 1965/6 *Holl.*
Stanton, P. (16) (Hibernian) 1965/6 *Holl*; 1968/9 *I*; 1969/70 *Eire, Aust*; 1970/1 *D, Bel, Port, D, Rus*; 1971/2 *Port, Bel, Holl, W*; 1972/3 *W, I*; 1973/4 *G.*
Steel, W. (30) (Morton) 1946/7 *E, Bel, Lux*; 1947/8 (Derby County) *I, W, E, F*; 1948/9 *W, I, E, F*; 1949/50 *I, W, E, Switz, Port, F* (Dundee); 1950/1 *W, I, Aust* (2), *E, D, F, Bel*; 1951/2 *W*; 1952/3 *W, I, E, Swdn.*
Stein, C. (20) (Rangers) 1968/9 *D, C, W, I, E, C*; 1969/70 *Eire, G, I, W, E*; 1970/1 *D, Bel, D, Rus*; 1971/2 *Czecho*; (Coventry City), *E, W, I, E.*
Stephen, J. (2) (Bradford City) 1946/7 *W*; 1947/8 *W.*
Stewart, D. (2) (Leeds United) 1977/8 *E/Germ*; 1978/9 *N.*
Stewart, J. (1) (Kilmarnock) 1976/7 *Ch.*
Stewart, R. (7) (West Ham U.) 1980/81 *W, I, E;* 1981/2 *I, Port, W*; 1983/4 *F.*
St John, I. (31) (Motherwell) 1958/9 *G*; 1959/60 *I, W, E, Pol, Aust*; 1960/1 *E*; 1961/2 (Liverpool) *Czecho, I, W, Czecho, E, W*; 1962/3 *W, I, E, N, Eire, Sp*; 1963/4 *I*; 1964/5 *E.*
Strachan, G. (31) (Aberdeen) 1979/80 *I, W, E, Pol, H;* 1980/81 *Swdn, Port;* 1981/2 *I, Port, Holl, Sp, NZ, Braz, Rus*; 1982/3 *E/Germ, Switz, Bel, Switz, I, W, E; Can* (3); 1983/4 *E/Germ, I, E, F;* (Manchester United) 1984/5 *Sp, E, Ic.*
Sturrock, P. (15) (Dundee United) 1980/81 *W, I, E*; 1981/2 *Port, I, W, E*; 1982/3 *E/Germ, Switz, Bel*, Can (3); 1983/4 *W;* 1984/5 *Y.*

Telfer, W. (1) (St Mirren) 1953/4 *W.*
Thomson, W. (8) (St Mirren) 1979/80 *I;* 1980/81 *I;* 1981/2 *Port*; 1982/3 *I, Can* (3); 1983/4 *E/Germ.*
Thornton, W. (7) (Rangers) 1946/7 *W*; 1947/8 *I, E*; 1948/9 *F*; 1951/2 *D, Swdn.*
Toner, W. (2) (Kilmarnock) 1958/9 *W, I.*
Turnbull, E. (8) (Hibernian) 1957/8 *Bel, Switz*; 1950/1 *Aust*; 1957/8 *H, Pol, Y, Par, F.*

Ure, I. (11) (Dundee) 1961/2 *W, Czecho*; 1962/3 *W, I, E, Aust, N, Sp,* (Arsenal); 1963/4 *I, N*; 1967/8 *I.*

Waddell, W. (17) (Rangers) 1946/7 *W*; 1948/9 *W, I, E, F*; 1949/50 *I, E*; 1950/1 *E, D, F, Bel, Aust*; 1951/2 *I, W*; 1953/4 *I*; 1954/5 *W, I.*
Wallace, I. (3) (Coventry City) 1977/8 *Bulg*; 1978/9 *Port, W.*
Wallace, W. (7) (Heart of Midlothian) 1964/5 *I*; 1965/6 *E, Holl*; 1966/7 (Celtic) *E, Rus*; 1967/8 *I*; 1968/9 *E.*

WALES

Aizlewood, M. (3) (Charlton Athletic) 1985/6*Sar, Can(2).*

Allchurch, I. (68) (Swansea City) 1950/1 *E, I, Port, Switz*; 1951/2 *E, S, UK, I*; 1952/3 *S, E, I, F, Y*; 1953/4 *E, S, I, Aust*; 1954/5 *Y, S, E, I*; 1955/6 *E, S, Aust, I*; 1956/7 *S, E*; 1957/8 *Isr* (2), *I, H, Mex, Swdn, H, Braz*; 1958/9 (Newcastle United) *S, E, I*; 1959/60 *E, S*; 1960/1 *T, Sp* (2), *H*; 1961/2 *E, S, Braz* (2), *Mex*; 1962/3 (Cardiff City) *S, H, E, H, I*; 1963/4 *E*; 1964/5 *S, E, Gr, I, It, Rus*; 1965/6 (Swansea City) *E, Rus, S, D, Braz, Braz 'B', Ch.*

Allchurch, L. (11) (Swansea City) 1954/5 *I*; 1955/6 *Aust*; 1957/8 *E/Germ, S, Isr, I*; 1958/9 *S*; 1961/2 (Sheffield United) *S, I, Braz*; 1963/4 *E.*

Allen, B. (2) (Coventry City) 1950/1 *S, E.*

Allen, M. (3) (Watford) 1985/6 *Sar, Can(2).*

Baker, C. (7) (Cardiff City) 1957/8 *Mex*; 1959/60*S, I*; 1960/1 *Eire, S, E*; 1961/2 *S.*

Baker, W. (1) (Cardiff City) 1947/8 *I.*

Barnes, W. (22) (Arsenal) 1947/8 *E, S, I*; 1948/9 *S, E, I*; 1949/50 *E, S, Bel, I*; 1950/1 *S, E, I, Port*; 1951/2 *E, S, UK, I*; 1953/4 *E, S*; 1954/5 *Y. S.*

Berry, G. (5) (Wolverhampton Wanderers) 1978/9 *G*; 1979/80 *Eire, G, T*; 1982/3 (Stoke City) *E.*

Blackmore, C.G. (6) (Manchester United) 1984/5 *N*;1985/6 *S, H, Sar, Eire, U.*

Bowen, D. (19) (Arsenal) 1954/5 *Y, S*; 1956/7 *I, Czecho, E/Germ*; 1957/8 *E/Germ, E, S, Isr* (2), *I, H, Mex, Swdn, H, Braz*; 1958/9 *S, E, I.*

Bowen, M.R. (2) (Tottenham Hotspur) 1985/6*Can(2).*

Boyle, T. (2) (Crystal Palace) 1980/81 *Eire, S.*

Burgess, R. (32) (Tottenham Hotspur) 1946/7 *S, E,I*; 1947/8 *E, S*; 1948/9 *S, E, I, Port, Bel, Switz*; 1949/50 *E, S, Bel, I*; 1950/1 *S, I, Port, Switz*; 1951/2 *E, S, UK, I*; 1952/3 *S, E, I, F, Y*; 1953/4 *E, S, I, Aust.*

Burton, O. (9) (Norwich City) 1962/3 *H, I,* (Newcastle United); 1963/4 *E*; 1968/9 *It, E/Germ, S, E, I*; 1971/2 *Czecho.*

Cartwright, L. (6) (Coventry City) 1973/4 *E, S, I*; 1975/6 *S*; 1976/7 *G*; (Wrexham) 1978/9 *M.*

Charles, J. (38) (Leeds United) 1949/50 *I*; 1950/1 *Switz*; 1952/3 *I, F, Y*; 1953/4 *E, S, I, Aust*; 1954/5 *Y, S, E, I*; 1955/6 *E, S, Aust, I*; 1956/7 *S, E, I,* (Juventus Turin) *Czecho, E/Germ, Czecho*; 1957/8 *Isr* (2), *H, Mex, Swdn, H*; 1959/60 *S*; 1961/2 *E, Braz* (2), *Mex*; 1962/3 (Leeds United) *S,* (Cardiff City); 1963/4 *S*; 1964/5 *S, Rus.*

Charles, J.M. (18) (Swansea C.) 1980/81 *Czecho, T, S,Rus;* 1981/2 *Ic*; 1982/3 *N, Y, Bulg, S, I,Braz*; 1983/4 *Bulg, Y,* (Q.P.R.) *S;* (Oxford United) 1984/5 *Ic, Sp,Ic*; 1985/6 *Eire.*

Charles, M. (31) (Swansea City) 1954/5 *I*; 1955/6 *E, S, Aust*; 1956/7 *E, I, Czecho, E/Germ, Czecho*; 1957/8 *E/Germ, E, S, Isr (2), H, Mex, Swdn, H, Braz*; 1958/9 *S, E,* (Arsenal) 1960/1 *I, Sp* (2), *H*; 1961/2 *E, S,* (Cardiff City) *I, Braz*; 1962/3 *S, H.*

Clarke, R. (22) (Manchester City) 1948/9 *E*; 1949/50 *S, Bel, I*; 1950/1 *S, E, I, Port, Switz*; 1951/2 *E, S, UK, I*; 1952/3 *S, E*; 1953/4 *E, S, I*; 1954/5 *Y, S, E*; 1955/6 *I.*

Crowe, V. (16) (Aston Villa) 1958/9 *E*; 1959/60 *E, I*; 1960/1 *Eire, S, E, I, Sp* (2), *H*; 1961/2 *E, S, Braz, Mex*; 1962/3 *H.*

Curtis, A. (34) (Swansea City) 1975/6 *E* (2),*S, I, Y* (2); 1976/7 *G, S, I*; 1977/8 *G, E,S*; 1978/9 *G, S, E, I, M*; 1979/80 *Eire, G, T;* 1981/2 *Czecho, Ic, Rus, Sp, E, S, I*; 1982/3*N*; 1983/4 *Ru,* (Southampton) *S;* 1984/5*Sp, N, N*; 1985/6 *H.*

Daniel, R. (21) (Arsenal) 1950/1 *E, I, Port*; 1951/2 *E, S, UK, I*; 1952/3 *S, E, I, F, Y*; 1953/4 (Sunderland) *E, S, I*; 1954/5 *E, I*; 1956/7 *S, E, I, Czecho.*

Davies, A. (6) (Manchester United) 1982/3 *I, Braz;*1983/4 *E, I;* 1984/5 *Ic*; (NewcastleUnited)1985/6 *H*.
Davies, D. (52) (Everton) 1974/5 *H, Lux, S, E, I*;1975/6 *Y* (2), *E, I*; 1976/7 *G, S*,(2) *Czecho, E, I*; 1977/8 *K, S* (2), *Czecho, G, Ir, E, I*; (Wrexham) 1978/9 *M, T, G, S, E, I, M*; 1979/80 *Eire, G, T, E, S, I, Ic;* 1980/81 *T, Czecho, Eire, T, S, E, Rus;* 1981/2 *Czecho, Ic, Rus*, (Swansea C.) *Czecho, Ic, Rus, Sp, E, S, F*; 1982/3 *Y*.
Davies, G. (18) (Fulham) 1979/80 *T, Ic;* 1981/2 *Sp, F*; 1982/3 *E, Bulg, S, I, Braz*;1983/4 *Ru, S, E, I;* 1984/5 *Ic, Ic*, (Chelsea)*N*; (Manchester City) 1985/6 *Sar, Eire*.
Davies, Reg (6) (Newcastle United) 1952/3 *S, E*; 1953/4 *E, S*; 1957/8 *E/Germ, E*.
Davies, Ron (29) (Norwich City) 1963/4 *I*; 1964/5 *E*; 1965/6 *Braz, Braz 'B', Ch*; 1966/7 (Southampton) *S, E, I*; 1967/8 *I, G*; 1968/9 *It, G, S, E, I*; 1969/70 *UK, E, S, I*; 1970/1 *Czecho, S, E, I*; 1971/2 *Ru, E, S, I*; 1973/4 (Portsmouth) *E*.
Davies, R. Wyn (34) (Bolton Wanderers) 1963/4 *E*; 1964/5 *S, D, E, Gr, I, Rus*; 1965/6 *E, Rus, S, D, I, Braz, Braz 'B', Ch*; 1966/7 *S* (Newcastle United) *E*; 1967/8 *S, I, G*; 1968/9 *It, S, E, I*; 1969/70 *E/Germ*; 1970/1 *Ru, Czecho*; 1971/2 (Manchester City) *E, S, I*; 1972/3 (Manchester United) *E, S, I*; 1973/4 *Pol*.
Davis, G. (4) (Wrexham) 1977/8 *I, E*; 1979/80 *T, Ic*.
Deacy, T. (11) (PSV Eindhoven) 1976/7 *Czecho, S, E, I*; 1977/8 *K, S* (2), *Czecho, G, I*; 1978/9 *T*.
Derrett, S. (4) (Cardiff City) 1968/9 *G, S*; 1969/70 *It*; 1970/1 *Fin*.
Dibble, A. (2) (Luton Town) 1985/6 *Can(2)*.
Durban, A. (26) (Derby County) 1966/7 *I*; 1967/8*E, S, I, G*; 1968/9 *G, E/Germ, S, E, I*; 1969/70*E/Germ, It, E, S, I*; 1970/1 *Ru, Czecho, S, E, I, Fin*; 1971/2 *Fin, Czecho, E, S, I*.
Dwyer, A. (8) (Wrexham) 1977/8 *E, S, I*; 1978/9 *T, S, E, I*; 1979/80 *G*.

Edwards, I. (4) (Chester) 1977/8 *K*; 1978/9 *M, G*; 1979/80 *T*.
Edwards, G. (12) (Birmingham City) 1946/7 *S, E, I*; 1947/8 *E, S, I*(Cardiff City); 1948/9 *I, Port, Bel, Switz*; 1949/50 *E, S*.
Edwards, T. (2) (Charlton Athletic) 1956/7 *I, E/Germ*.
Emanuel, J. (2) (Bristol City) 1972/3 *E, I*.
England, M. (44) (Blackburn Rovers) 1961/2 *I, Braz, Mex*; 1962/3 *H, I*; 1963/4 *E, S, I*; 1964/5 *D, E, Gr* (2), *I, It, Rus*; 1965/6 *E, Rus, S, D, I*; 1966/7 (Tottenham Hotspur) *S, E*; 1967/8 *E, I, G*; 1968/9 *E/Germ*; 1969/70 *UK, E/Germ, It, E, S, I*; 1970/1 *Ru*; 1971/2 *Fin, E, S, I*; 1972/3 *E* (2), *S, E*; 1973/4 *Pol*; 1974/5 *H, Lux*.
Evans, I. (13) (Crystal Palace) 1975/6 *Aust, E, Y* (2), *E, I*; 1976/7 *G, S* (2), *Czecho, E, I*; 1977/8 *K*.
Evans, R. (1) (Swansea City) 1963/4 *I*.

Felgate D. (1) (Lincoln C.) 1983/4 *Ru*.
Flynn, B. (65) (Burnley) 1974/5 *Lux* (2), *H, S, E, I*; 1975/6 *Aust, E* (2), *Y* (2), *I*; 1976/7 *G, S, Czecho, S, E, I*; 1977/8 *K* (2), *S* (2), *Czecho, G, E, I*; (Leeds United) 1978/9 *M, T, S, E, I, M*; 1979/80 *Eire, G, E, S, I, Ic;* 1980/81 *T, Czecho, Eire, T, S, E, Rus;* 1981/2 *Czecho, Rus, E, S, I, F*; 1982/3 *N*, (Burnley) *Y, E, Bulg, S, I, Braz*; 1983/4 *N, Ru, Bulg, Y, S, N, Isr*.
Ford, T. (38) (Swansea City) 1946/7 *S*, (Aston Villa) *I*; 1947/8 *S, I*; 1948/9 *S, E, I, Port, Bel, Switz;* 1949/50 *E, S, Bel, I*; 1950/1 *S*, (Sunderland), *E, I, Port, Switz*; 1951/2 *E, S, UK, I*; 1952/3 *S, E, I, F, Y* (Cardiff City); 1953/4 *Aust*; 1954/5 *Y, S, E, I*; 1955/6 *E, S, Aust, I, I*; 1956/7 *S*.
Foulkes, W. (11) (Newcastle United) 1951/2 *E, S, UK, I*; 1952/3 *S, E, F, Y*; 1953/4 *E, S, I*.

Giles, D. (12) (Wrexham) 1979/80 *E, S, I, Ic;* 1980/81 (Swansea City) *T, Czecho, T, E, Rus;* 1981/2 (Crystal Palace) *Sp*; 1982/3 *I, Braz*.
Godfrey, B. (3) (Preston North End) 1963/4 *I*; 1964/5 *D, It*.

Green, C. (15) (Birmingham City) 1964/5 *It, Rus*; 1965/6 *E, Rus, S, Braz, Braz 'B'*; 1966/7 *E*; 1967/8 *E, S, I, G*; 1968/9 *It, S, I.*
Griffiths, A. (17) (Wrexham) 1970/1 *Czecho;* 1974/5 *Aust, H* (2), *Lux* (2), *E, I;* 1975/6 *Aust, E* (2), *Y* (2), *S, I;* 1976/7 *G, S.*
Griffiths, H. (1) (Swansea City) 1952/3 *I.*
Griffiths, M. (11) (Leicester City) 1946/7 *I;* 1948/9 *Port, Bel;* 1949/50 *E, S, Bel;* 1950/1 *E, I, Port, Switz;* 1953/4 *Aust.*
Harrington, A. (11) (Cardiff City) 1955/6 *I;* 1956/7 *S, E;* 1957/8 *S, Isr* (2), *I;* 1960/1 *S, E;* 1961/2 *E, S.*
Harris, C. (19) (Leeds United) 1975/6 *S, E;* 1977/8 *G, E, S, I;* 1978/9 *M, T, G, M;* 1979/80 *I;* 1980/1 *T, Czecho, Eire, T, S, E, Rus;* 1981/2 *Czecho, Ic.*
Harris, W. (6) (Middlesbrough) 1953/4 *Aust;* 1956/7 *E/Germ, Czecho;* 1957/8 *E/Germ, E, S.*
Hennessey, T. (39) (Birmingham City) 1961//2 *I, Braz* (2); 1962/3 *S, H, E, H;* 1963/4 *E, S;* 1964/5 *S, D, E, Gr, Rus;* 1965/6 *E, Rus,* (Nottingham Forest), *S, D, I, Braz, Braz 'B', Ch;* 1966/7 *S, E;* 1967/8 *E, S, I;* 1968/9 *G, E/Germ;* 1969/70 *UK, E/Germ,* (Derby County), *E, S, I;* 1971/2 *Fin, Czecho, E, S;* 1972/3 *E.*
Hewitt, R. (5) (Cardiff City) 1957/8 *Isr, I, Swdn, H, Braz.*
Hill, M. (2) (Ipswich Town) 1971/2 *Czecho, Ru.*
Hockey, T. (9) (Sheffield United) 1971/2 *Fin, Ru;* 1972/3 *E* (1), (Norwich City), *Pol, S, E, I;* 1973/4 (Aston Villa) *Pol.*
Hodges, G. (2) (Wimbledon) 1983/4 *N, Isr.*
Holden, A. (1) (Chester C.) 1983/4 *Isr.*
Hole, B. (30) (Cardiff City) 1962/3 *I;* 1963/4 *I;* 1964/5 *S, D, E, Gr* (2), *I, It, Rus;* 1965/6 *E, Rus, S, D, I, Braz 'B', Ch;* 1966/7 (Blackburn Rovers) *S, E, I;* 1967/8 *E, S, I, G;* 1968/9 (Aston Villa) *It, G, E/Germ;* 1969/70 *It; (Swansea City) 1970$71 Ru.*
Hollins, D. (11) (Newcastle United) 1961/2 *Braz, Mex;* 1962/3 *H, I;* 1963/4 *E;* 1964/5 *Gr, I, It;* 1965/6 *S, D, Braz.*
Hopkins, J. (14) (Fulham) 1982/3 *I, Braz;* 1983/4 *N, Ru, Bulg, Y, S, E, I, N, Isr;* 1984/5 *Ic, Ic, N.*
Hopkins, M. (34) (Tottenham Hotspur) 1955/6 *I;* 1956/7 *S, E, I, Czecho, E/Germ, Czecho;* 1957/8 *E/Germ, E, S, Isr* (2), *I, H, Mex, Swdn, H, Braz;* 1958/9 *S, E, I;* 1959/60 *E, S;* 1960/1 *I, Sp* (2), *H;* 1961/2 *I, Braz* (2), *Mex;* 1962/3 *S, H, I.*
Howells, R. (2) (Cardiff City) 1953/4 *E, S.*
Hughes, I. (4) (Luton Town) 1950/1 *E, I, Port, Switz.*
Hughes, L.M. (12) (Manchester U.) 1983/4 *E, I;* 1984/5 *Ic, Sp, Ic, N, S, Sp, N;* 1985/6 *S, H, U.*
Hughes, W. (3) (Birmingham City) 1946/7 *S, E, I.*
Hughes, W.A. (5) (Blackburn Rovers) 1948/9 *E, I, Port, Bel, Switz.*
Humphreys, J. (1) (Everton) 1946/7 *I.*

Jackett, K. (25) (Watford) 1982/3 *N, Y, E, Bulg, S;* 1983/4 *N, Ru, Y, S, I, N, Isr;* 1984/5 *Ic, Sp, Ic, N, S, Sp, N;* 1985/6 *S, H, Sar, Eire, Can* (2).
James, G. (9) (Blackpool) 1965/6 *Braz, Braz 'B', Ch;* 1966/7 *I;* 1967/8 *S;* 1970/1 *Czecho, S, E, I.*
James, L. (60) (Burnley) 1971/2 *Czecho, Rus, S;* 1972/3 *E* (2), *Pol, S, E, I;* 1973/4 *Pol, E, S, I;* 1974/5 *Aust, H* (2), *Lux* (2), *S, E, I;* 1975/6 *Aust, E, S, Y* (2), *I;* (Derby County) 1976/7 *G, S, Czecho, S, E, I;* 1977/8 *K* (2), *G* (Swansea City); 1978/9 *M, T, S, E, I, M;* 1979/80 *G, E, S, I, Ic;* 1980/81 *T, Eire, T, S, E;* 1981/2 *Czecho, Ic, Rus, E, S, I, F;* 1982/3 (Sunderland) *E.*
James, R. (40) (Swansea C.) 1981/2 *Czecho, Ic, Sp, E, S, I, F;* 1982/3 *N, Y, E, Bulg;* (Stoke C.) 1983/4 *N, Ru, Bulg, Y, S, E, I, N, Isr;* 1984/5 *Ic, Sp, Ic,* (Q.P.R.) *N, S, Sp, N;* 1985/6 *S, Sar, Eire, U, Can* (2).
Jarvis, A. (3) (Hull City) 1966/7 *S, E, I.*
Johnson, M. (1) (Swansea City) 1963/4 *I.*
Jones, Barrie. (14) (Swansea City) 1962/3 *S, H, E, I;* 1963/4 *S, I;* 1964/5

(Plymouth Argyle) *D;* 1968/9 (Cardiff City) *G, E/Germ, S, E, I;* 1969/70 *UK.*

Jones, Bryn. (4) (Arsenal) 1946/7 *S, I;* 1947/8 *E;* 1948/9 *S.*

Jones, C. (59) (Swansea City) 1953/4 *Aust;* 1955/6 *E, S, Aust, I;* 1956/7 *S, E, J, Czecho, E/Germ, Czecho;* 1957/8 *E/Germ, E, S, Isr* (2), (Tottenham Hotspur), *I, H,* *Czecho, E/Germ, Czecho*; 1957/8 *E/Germ, E, S, Isr* (2), (Tottenham Hotspur), *I, H,* *Mex, Swdn, H, Braz*; 1958/9 *I*; 1959/60 *E, S, I*; 1960/1 *Eire, S, E, I, Sp, H*; 1961/2 *E, S, I, Braz* (2), *Mex*; 1962/3 *S, H, I*; 1963/4 *E, S, I*; 1964/5 *S, D, E, Gr* (2), *I, It, Rus*; 1966/7 *S, E*; 1967/8 *E, S, G*; 1968/9 (Fulham) *It*; 1969/70 *UK.*

Jones, D. (11) (Norwich City) 1975/6 *E, S*; 1977/8 *S, Czecho, G, E*; 1979/80 *Eire, G, T, E, I, Ic.*

Jones, E. (4) (Swansea City) 1947/8 *S, E* (Tottenham Hotspur); 1948/9 *S, E.*

Jones, J. (66) (Liverpool) 1975/6 *Aust, E, S*;1976/7 *G, S* (2), *Czecho, E, I*; 1977/8 *K*(2), *S* (2), *Czecho, G, Ir, E, I*; (Wrexham) 1978/9*M, T, G, S, E, I, M*; 1979/80 *Eire, G, T, E, S, I, Ic;*1980/81 *T, Eire, T, S, E, Rus;* 1981/2 *Czecho, Ic,Rus, Sp, E, S, I, F*; 1982/3 *N,* (Chelsea) *Y, E,Bulg, S, I, Braz*; 1983/4 *N, Ru, Bulg, Y, S, E, I, N, Isr;*1984/5 *Ic, S, N, S.*

Jones, K. (1) (Aston Villa) 1949/50 *S.*

Jones, T. G. (13) (Everton) 1946/7 *S, E*; 1947/8 *E, S, I*; 1948/9 *E, I, Port, Bel, Switz*; 1949/50 *E, S, Bel.*

Jones, W. (1) (Bristol Rovers) 1970/1 *Fin.*

Kelsey, J. (41) (Arsenal) 1953/4 *I, Aust*; 1954/5 *Y, S, I*; 1955/6 *E, S, Aust, I*; 1956/7 *S, E, I, Czecho, E/Germ, Czecho*; 1957/8 *E, S, Isr* (2), *I, H, Mex, Swdn, H, Braz*; 1958/9 *S, E*; 1959/60 *E, S, I*; 1960/1 *S, E, I, Sp* (2), *H*; 1961/2 *E, S, I, Braz* (2).

King, J. (1) (Swansea City) 1954/5 *E.*

Kinsey, N. (7) (Norwich City) 1950/1 *I, Port, Switz*; 1951/2 *E*; 1953/4 (Birmingham City) *I*; 1955/6 *E, S.*

Krzywicki, R. (8) (West Bromwich Albion) 1969/70 *E/Germ, It,* (Huddersfield Town) *E, S, I*; 1970/1 *Ru, Fin*; 1971/2 *Czecho.*

Lambert, R. (5) (Liverpool) 1946/7 *S*; 1947/8 *E*; 1948/9 *Port, Bel, Switz.*

Lea, C. (2) (Ipswich Town) 1964/5 *I, It.*

Leek, L. (13) (Leicester City) 1960/1 *S, E, I, Sp* (2), *H*; 1961/2 (Newcastle United) *S,* (Birmingham City) *Braz, Mex*; 1962/3 *E*; 1964/5 *S, Gr* (2).

Lever, A. (1) (Leicester City) 1952/3 *S.*

Lewis, D. (1) (Swansea C.) 1982/3 *Braz.*

Lloyd, B. (3) (Wrexham) 1975/6 *Aust, S, E.*

Lovell, S. (2) (Crystal Palace) 1981/2 *Rus;* (Millwall) 1984/5 *N.*

Lowndes, S. (3) (Newport Co.) 1982/3 *S, Braz;* (Millwall) 1984/5 *N.*

Lowrie, G. (4) (Coventry City) 1947/8 *E, S, I*; 1948/9 (Newcastle United) *Port.*

Lucas, M. (4) (Leyton Orient) 1961/2 *I, Mex*; 1962/3 *S, E.*

Lucas, W. (7) (Swansea City) 1948/9 *S, I, Port, Bel, Switz*; 1949/50 *E*; 1950/1 *E.*

Mahoney, J. (50) (Stoke City) 1967/8 *E*; 1968/9 *E/Germ*; 1970/1 *Czecho*; 1972/3 *E* (2), *Pol, S, E, I*; 1973/4 *Pol, E, S, I*; 1974/5 *Aust, H* (2), *Lux* (2), *S, E, I*; 1975/6 *Aust, Y* (2), *E, I*; 1976/7 *G, Czecho, S, E, I*; 1977/8 *K* (2), *S*(2), *Czecho, E, I*; (Middlesbrough) 1978/9 *G, S, E, I, M*; 1979/80 *Eire, G, T;* 1981/2 (Swansea C.) *Ic Rus*; 1982/3 *Y, E.*

Marustik, C. (6) (Swansea C.) 1981/2 *Sp, E, S, I, F*; 1982/3 *N.*

Medwin, T. (30) (Swansea City) 1952/3 *I, F, Y*; 1956/7 (Tottenham Hotspur) *S, E, I, Czecho, E/Germ, Czecho*; 1957/8 *E, S, Isr* (2), *I, H, Mex, H, Braz*; 1958/9 *S, E, I*; 1959/60 *E, S, I*; 1960/1 *Eire, S, E, Sp*; 1962/3 *H, E.*

Mielczarek, R. (1) (Rotherham United) 1970/1 *Fin.*

Millington, A. (21) (West Bromwich Albion) 1962/3 *S, H, E*; 1964/5 (Crystal Palace) *E, Rus*; 1965/6 (Peterborough United) *Braz 'B', Ch*; 1966/7 *E, I*; 1967/8

I, G; 1968/9 *It, E/Germ*; 1969/70 (Swansea City) *E, S, I*; 1970/1 *Czecho, Fin*; 1971/2 *Fin, Czecho, Ru.*

Moore, G. (21) (Cardiff City) 1959/60 *E, S, I*; 1960/1 *Eire, Sp*; 1961/2 (Chelsea) *Braz*; 1962/3 *H, I*; (Manchester United) 1963/4 *S, I*; (Northampton Town) 1965/6 *I, Ch*; 1968/9 (Charlton Athletic) *S, E, I*; 1969/70 *UK, It, E, S, I*; 1970/1 *Ru.*
Morris, W. (5) (Burnley) 1946/7 *I*; 1948/9 *E*; 1951/2 *S, UK, I.*

Nardiello, D. (2) (Coventry City) 1977/8 *Czecho, G.*
Nicholas, P. (45) (Crystal Palace) 1978/9 *S, I, M*; 1979/80 *Eire, G, T, E, S, I, Ic;* 1980/8 *T, Czecho, Eire,* (Arsenal) *T, S, E, Rus;* 1981/2 *Czecho, Ic, Rus, Sp, E, S, I, F*; 1982/3 *Y, Bulg, S,I; (Crystal Palace) 1983$4 N, Bulg, N, Isr;* 1984/5 *Sp,* (Luton Town) *N, S, Sp, N*; 1985/6 *S, H,Sar, Eire, U, Can(2).*
Niedzwiecki, E. A. (1) (Chelsea) 1984/5 *N.*
Norman, A.J. (3) (Hull City) 1985/6 *Eire, U,Can.*
Nurse, M. (12) (Swansea City) 1959/60 *E, I*;1960/1 *Eire, S, E, I, Sp* (2), *H*; 1962/3 (Middlesbrough) *H,E*; 1963/4 *S.*

O'Sullivan, P. (3) (Brighton & Hove Albion) 1972/3 *S*; 1975/6 *S*; 1978/9 *M.*

Page, M. (27) (Birmingham City) 1970/1 *Fin*; 1971/2 *S, I*; 1972/3 *E* (2), *I*; 1973/4 *S, I*; 1974/5 *H, Lux, S, E, I*; 1975/6 *E* (2), *Y* (2), *I*; 1976/7 *G, S*; 1977/8 *K* (2), *G, E, S*; 1978/9 *M, G.*
Palmer, D. (3) (Swansea City) 1956/7 *Czecho*; 1957/8 *E/Germ, E.*
Parry, J. (1) (Swansea City) 1950/1 *S.*
Pascoe, C. (2) (Swansea C.) 1983/4 *N, Isr.*
Paul, R. (33) (Swansea City) 1948/9 *S, E, I, Port, Switz*; 1949/50 *E, S, Bel, I*; (Manchester City) 1950/1 *S, E, I, Port, Switz*; 1951/2 *E, S, UK, I*; 1952/3 *S, E, I, F, Y*; 1953/4 *E, S, I*; 1954/5 *Y, S, E*; 1955/6 *E, S, Aust, I.*
Phillips, D. (13) (Plymouth Argyle) 1983/4 *E, I, N;* (Manchester City) 1984/5 *Sp, Ic, S, Sp, N*; 1985/6 *S, H, Sar, Eire, U.*
Phillips, J. (4) (Chelsea) 1972/3 *E*; 1973/4 *E*; 1974/5 *H*; 1977/8 *K.*
Phillips, L. (58) (Cardiff City) 1970/1 *Czecho, S, E, I*; 1971/2 *Czecho, Ru, S, I*; 1972/3 *E*; 1973/4 *Pol, I*; 1974/5 *Aust,* (Aston Villa) *H* (2), *Lux* (2), *S, E, I*; 1975/6 *Aust, E* (2), *Y* (2), *I*; 1976/7 *G, S, Czecho, S, E*; 1977/8 *K* (2), *S* (2), *Czecho, G, E*; 1978/9 *M, T, G,* (Swansea City) *S, E, I, M*; 1979/80 *Eire, G, T, S, I, Ic;* 1980/81 *T, Czecho, T, S, E, Rus;* 1981/2 (Charlton Ath.) *Czecho, Rus.*
Pontin, K. (2) (Cardiff City) 1979/80 *E, S.*
Powell, A. (8) (Leeds United) 1946/7 *S, E*; 1947/8 *E, S, I*; 1948/9 (Everton) *E*; 1949/50 *Bel*; 1950/1 (Birmingham City) *S.*
Powell, D. (11) (Wrexham) 1967/8 *G*; 1968/9 (Sheffield United) *It, G, S, E, I*; 1969/70 *E/Germ, E, S, I*; 1970/1 *Ru.*
Powell, J. (8) (Queen's Park Rangers) 1946/7 *E*; 1947/8 *E, S*; 1948/9 (Aston Villa) *Bel*; 1949/50 *S, Bel*; 1950/1 *S.*
Price, P. (25) (Luton Town) 1979/80 *E, S, I, Ic;* 1980/81 *T, Czecho, Eire, T, S, E, Rus;* 1981/2 (Tottenham H.) *Rus, Sp, F*; 1982/3 *N, Y, E, Bulg, S, I*;* 1983/4 *N, Ru, Bulg, Y, S.*
Pring, K. (3) (Rotherham United) 1965/6 *D, Ch*; 1966/7 *I.*
Pritchard, H. K. (1) (Bristol City) 1984/5 *N.*

Rankmore, F. (1) (Peterborough United) 1965/6 *Ch.*
Ratcliffe, K. (36) (Everton) 1980/81 *Czecho, Eire, T,S, E, Rus;* 1981/2 *Czecho, Ic, Rus, Sp, E*; 1982/3 *Y, E, Bulg, S, I, Braz*; 1983/4 *N, Ru, Bulg, Y, S, E,I, N, Isr;* 1984/5 *ic, Sp, Ic, N, S, Sp*; 1985/6 *S,H, Sar, U.*
Reece, G. (29) (Sheffield United) 1965/6 *E, Rus, S, I*; 1966/7 *S*; 1969/70 *UK, It*; 1970/1 *S, E, I, Fin*; 1971/2 *Fin, Ru, E, S, I*; (Cardiff City) 1972/3 *E, I*; 1973/4 *Pol, E, S, I*; 1974/5 *Aust, H* (2), *Lux* (2), *S, I.*
Reed, W. (2) (Ipswich Town) 1954/5 *Y, S.*
Rees, A. (1) (Birmingham C.) 1983/4 *N.*

Rees, R. (37) (Coventry City) 1964/5 *S, D, E, Gr* (2), *I, It, Rus*; 1965/6 *E, Rus, S, D, I, Braz, Braz 'B', Ch*; 1966/7 *E, I*; 1967/8 *E, S, I* (West Bromwich Albion), *G*; 1968/9 *It,* (Nottingham Forest) *G, E/Germ, S*; 1969/70 *UK, E/Germ, It, E, S, I*; 1970/1 *Ru,*
Rees, W. (4) (Cardiff City) 1948/9 *I, Bel, Switz,* (Tottenham Hotspur); 1949/50 *I.*
Richards, S. (1) (Cardiff City) 1946/7 *E.*
Roberts, D. (17) (Oxford United) 1972/3 *Pol, E, I*; 1973/4 *E, S*; 1974/5 *Aust,* (Hull City) *Lux, I*; 1975/6 *Y, S, I*; 1976/7 *E, I*; 1977/8 *K* (2), *S, I.*
Roberts, J. (21) (Arsenal) 1970/1 *S, E, I, Fin*; 1971/2 *Fin, E, I*; 1972/3 (Birmingham City) *E, Pol, S, E, I*; 1973/4 *Pol, E, S, I*; 1974/5 *Aust, H, S, E*; 1975/6 *S.*
Roberts, J. (1) (Bolton Wanderers) 1948/9 *Bel.*
Roberts, P. (4) (Portsmouth) 1973/4 *E*; 1974/5 *Aust, H, Lux.*
Rodrigues, P. (40) (Cardiff City) 1964/5 *Gr* (2), *I*; 1965/6 *E, Rus, S, D,* (Leicester City), *I, Braz, Braz 'B', Ch*; 1966/7 *S*; 1967/8 *E, S, I*; 1968/9 *E/Germ, E, I*; 1969/70 *UK, E/Germ, E, S, I*; (Sheffield Wednesday) 1970/1 *Ru, Czecho, S, E, I*; 1971/2 *Fin, Czecho, Ru, E, I*; 1972/3 *E* (2), *Pol, S, E, I*; 1973/4 *Pol.*
Rouse, V. (1) (Crystal Palace) 1958/9 *I.*
Rowley, T. (1) (Tranmere Rovers) 1958/9 *I.*
Rush, I. (28) (Liverpool) 1979/80 *S, I;* 1980/81 *E;* 1981/2 *Rus, E, S, I, F*; 1982/3 *N, Y, E, Bulg*; 1983/4 *N, Ru, Bulg, Y, S, E, I;* 1984/5 *Ic, N, S, Sp;* 1985/6 *S, Sar, Eire, U.*

Saunders, D. (3) (Brighton & Hove Albion) 1985/6 *Eire, Can*(2);.
Sayer, P. (7) (Cardiff City) 1976/7 *Czecho, S, E, I*; 1977/8 *K* (2), *S.*
Scrine, F. (2) (Swansea City) 1949/50 *E, I.*
Sear, C. (1) (Manchester City) 1962/3 *E.*
Sherwood, A. (41) (Cardiff City) 1946/7 *E*; 1947/8 *S, I*; 1948/9 *S, E, I, Port, Switz*; 1949/50 *E, S, Bel, I*; 1950/1 *S, E, I, Port, Switz*; 1951/2 *E, S, UK, I*; 1952/3 *S, E, I, F, Y*; 1953/4 *E, S, I, Aust*; 1954/5 *Y, S, E, I*; 1955/6 *S, E, Aust, I*; 1955/6 *S, E, Aust, I*; 1956/7 (Newport County) *S, E.*
Shortt, W. (12) (Plymouth Argyle) 1946/7 *I*; 1949/50 *Bel, I*; 1951/2 *E, S, UK, I*; 1952/3 *S, E, I, F, Y.*
Showers, D. (2) (Cardiff City) 1974/5 *E, I.*
Sidlow, C. (7) (Liverpool) 1946/7 *S, E*; 1947/8 *E, S, I*; 1948/9 *S*; 1949/50 *E.*
Slatter, N. (14) (Bristol Rovers) 1982/3 *S**; 1983/4 *N, Isr;* 1984/5 *Ic, Sp, Ic, N, S, Sp, N;* (Oxford United) 1985/6 *H, Sar, Ca*(2).
Smallman, D. (7) (Wrexham) 1973/4 *E, S, I*; 1974/5 *H, E, I*; 1975/6 (Everton) *Aust.*
Southall, N. (27) (Everton) 1981/2 *I*; 1982/3 *N, E, Bulg, S, I, Braz*; 1983/4 *N, Ru, Bulg, Y, S, E, I, N, Isr;* 1984/5 *Ic, Sp, Ic, N, S, Sp, N;* 1985/6 *S, H, Sar, Eire.*
Sprake, G. (37) (Leeds United) 1963/4 *S, I*; 1964/5 *S, D, Gr*; 1965/6 *E, Rus, I*; 1966/7 *S*; 1967/8 *E, S*; 1968/9 *G, S, E, I*; 1969/70 *UK, E/Germ, It*; 1970/1 *Ru, S, E, I*; 1971/2 *Fin, E, S, I*; 1972/3 *E* (2), *Pol, S, I*; 1973/4 (Birmingham City) *Pol, S, I*; 1974/5 *Aust, H, Lux.*
Stansfield, G. (1) (Cardiff City) 1948/9 *S.*
Stevenson, B. (15) (Leeds United) 1977/8 *I*; 1978/9 *M, T, S, E, I, M*; 1979/80 *G, T, Ic;* 1981/2 *Czecho,* (Birmingham C.) *Sp, S, I, F.*
Stevenson, N. (4) (Swansea C.) 1981/2 *E, S, I*; 1982/3 *N.*
Stitfall, R. (2) (Cardiff City) 1952/3 *E*; 1956/7 *Czecho.*
Sullivan, D. (17) (Cardiff City) 1952/3 *I, F, Y*; 1953/4 *I*; 1954/5 *E, S*; 1956/7 *S, E*; 1957/8 *I, H, Swdn, H, Braz*; 1958/9 *S, I*; 1959/60 *E, I.*

Tapscott, D. (14) (Arsenal) 1953/4 *Aust*; 1954/5 *Y, S, E, I*; 1955/6 *E, S, Aust, I*; 1956/7 *I, Czecho, E/Germ*; 1958/9 (Cardiff City) *E, I.*
Thomas, D. (2) (Swansea City) 1956/7 *Czecho*; 1957/8 *E/Germ.*

Thomas, M. (51) (Wrexham) 1976/7 *G, S* (2), *I*; 1977/8 *K, S, Czecho, E*; 1978/9 *M, T, G*; (Manchester United) 1979/80 *Eire, G, T, E, S, I;* 1980/81 *Czecho, S, E, USSR;* 981/2 (Everton) *Czecho,* (Brighton) *Rus, Sp, E, S, I*; 1982/3 (Stoke City) *N, Y, E, Bulg, S, I, Braz*; 1983/4 *Ru, Bulg, Y,* (Chelsea) *S, E;* 1984/5 *Ic, Sp, Ic, S, Sp, N;* 1985/6 *S,* (WBA) *H, Sar.*
Thomas, R. (50) (Swindon Town) 1966/7 *I*; 1967/8 *G*; 1968/9 *It, G, E, I*; 1969/70 *UK, E/Germ, It, E, S, I*; 1970/1 *Ru, Czecho, S, E, I*; 1971/2 *Fin, Czecho, Ru, E, S, I*; 1972/3 *E* (2), *Pol, S, E, I*; 1973/4 (Derby County) *Pol, E, S, I*; 1974/5 *H* (2), *Lux* (2), *S, E, I*; 1975/6 *Aust, Y, E*; 1976/7 *S, Czecho, E, I*; 1977/8 *K, S, Czecho.*
Thomas, S. (4) (Fulham) 1947/8 *E, S, I*; 1948/9 *S.*
Toshack, J. (39) (Cardiff City) 1968/9 *G, E/Germ, S, E, I*; 1969/70 *UK, E/Germ, It*; 1970/1 *S, E, I, Fin*; 1971/2 (Liverpool) *Fin, E*; 1972/3 *E* (2), *Pol, S, E*; 1974/5 *Aust, H* (2), *Lux* (2), *S, E*; 1975/6 *Y* (2), *E*; 1976/7 *S*; 1977/8 *K* (2), *S, Czecho*; (Swansea City) 1978/9 *S, E, I, M*; 1979/80 *G.*

Van den Hauwe, P.W.R. (3) (Everton) 1984/5 *Sp;* 1985/6 *S, H.*
Vaughan, N. (10) (Newport County) 1982/3 *Y, Braz*; 1983/4 *N Ru Bulg, Y,* (Cardiff C.) *I N, Isr;* 1984/5 *Sp.*
Vearncombe, G. (2) (Cardiff City) 1957/8 *E/Germ*; 1960/1 *Eire.*
Vernon, R. (32) (Blackburn Rovers) 1956/7 *I, Czecho, E/Germ, Czecho;* 1957/8 *E/Germ, E, S, Swdn*; 1958/9 *S*; 1959/60 (Everton) *I*; 1960/1 *Eire, S, E*; 1961/2 *I, Braz* (2), *Mex*; 1962/3 *S, H, E*; 1963/4 *E, S*; 1964/5 (Stoke City) *Gr, I, It*; 1965/6 *E, Rus, S, D, I*; 1966/7 *I*; 1967/8 *E.*
Villars, A. (2) (Cardiff City) 1973/4 *E, S.*

Walley, T. (1) (Watford) 1970/1 *Czecho.*
Walsh, I. (18) (Crystal Palace) 1979/80 *Eire, T, E, S, Ic;* 1980/81 *T, Czecho, Eire, T, S, E, USSR;* 1981/2 *Czecho, Ic,* (Swansea C.) *Sp, S, I, F.*
Ward, D. (2) (Bristol Rovers) 1958/9 *E*; 1961/2 (Cardiff City) *E.*
Webster, C. (4) (Manchester United) 1956/7 *Czecho*; 1957/8 *H, Mex, Braz.*
Williams, D.M. (4) (Norwich City) 1985/6 *Sar, U, Can* (2).
Williams, G. (1) (Cardiff City) 1950/1 *Switz.*
Williams, G. E. (26) (West Bromwich Albion) 1959/60 *I*; 1960/1 *Eire, S, E*; 1962/3 *I*; 1963/4 *H, E, S, I*; 1964/5 *S, D, E, Gr* (2), *I, It, Rus*; 1965/6 *I, Braz, Braz 'B', Ch*; 1966/7 *S, E, I*; 1967/8 *I*; 1968/9 *It.*
Williams, G. G. (5) (Swansea City) 1960/1 *I, Sp* (2), *H*; 1961/2 *E.*
Williams, H. (4) (Newport County) 1948/9 *I, Switz* (Leeds United); 1949/50 *I*; 1950/1 *S.*
Williams, Herbert (3) (Swansea City) 1964/5 *Gr* (2); 1970/1 *Ru.*
Williams, S. (43) (West Bromwich Albion) 1953/4 *Aust*; 1954/5 *E, I*; 1955/6 *E, S, Aust*; 1957/8 *E, S, Isr* (2), *I, H, Mex, Swdn, H, Braz*; 1958/9 *S, E, I*; 1959/60 *E, S, I*; 1960/1 *Eire, I, Sp* (2), *H*; 1961/2 *E, S, I, Braz* (2), *Mex*; 1962/3 (Southampton) *S, H, E, H*; 1963/4 *E, S*; 1964/5 *S, D, E*; 1965/6 *D.*
Witcombe, D. (3) (West Bromwich Albion) 1946/7 *S, E,* Sheffield Wednesday) *I.*
Woosnam, P. (17) (Leyton Orient) 1958/9 *S,* (West Ham United), *E*; 1959/60 *E, S, I*; 1960/1 *Eire, S, E, I, Sp, H*; 1961/2 *E, S, I, Braz*; 1962/3 (Aston Villa) *H, I.*

Yorath, T. (58) (Leeds United) 1969/70 *It*; 1970/1 *S, E, I*; 1971/2 *Czecho, E, S, I*; 1972/3 *E, Pol, S*; 1973/4 *Pol, E, S, I*; 1974/5 *Aust, H* (2), *Lux* (2), *S*; 1975/6 *Aust, E* (2), *Y* (2), *S, I*; (Coventry City) 1976/7 *G, S, Czecho, S, E, I*; 1977/8 *K* (2), *S* (2), *Czecho, G, E, I*; 1978/9 *T, G, S, E, I*; (Tottenham Hotspur) 1979/80 *Eire, T, E, S, I, Ic;* 1980/81 *T, Czecho, Eire, T, USSR.*

UEFA UNDER-21 TOURNAMENT 1984-86

Group 1 (Albania, Greece, Poland)

Poland (4) 5, Greece (0) 1 — Krakow, 16 October 1984
Poland (0) 2, Albania (0) 0 — Zamosc, 30 October 1984
Greece (0) 2, Albania (0) 0 — Halkida, 26 February 1985
Greece (1) 2, Poland (1) 1 — Athens, 18 May 1985
Albania (0) 1, Poland (0) 2 — Beret, 29 May 1985

Poland qualify for quarter-finals – Albania v Greece not played

	P	W	D	L	F	A	Pt
Poland	4	3	0	1	10	4	6
Greece	3	2	0	1	5	6	4
Albania	3	0	0	3	1	6	0

Group 2 (Czechoslovakia, Portugal, Sweden, West Germany)

Sweden (0) 1, Portugal (0) 1 — Sødertaelje, 11 September 1984
Portugal (0) 0, Czechoslovakia (0) 1 — Pacos Ferreira, 13 October 1984
West Germany (1) 1, Sweden (0) 0 — Münster, 16 October 1984
Portugal (0) 0, Sweden (0) 1 — Montijo, 13 November 1984
Portugal (1) 2, West Germany (0) 1 — Lisbon, 23 February 1985
Czechoslovakia (1) 1, West Germany (1) 1 — Mlada Boleslav, 30 April 1985
Sweden (0) 1, Czechoslovakia (0) 0 — Enkoeping, 4 June 1985
Sweden (1) 2, West Germany (0) 1 — Eskilstuna, 24 September 1985
Czechoslovakia (1) 3, Portugal (1) 1 — Vlasim, 24 September 1985
West Germany (0) 2, Portugal (1) 1 — Karlsruhe, 15 October 1985
Czechoslovakia (0) 0, Sweden (0) 2 — Teplice, 15 October 1985
West Germany (1) 3, Czechoslovakia (0) 1 — Regensburg, 16 November 1985

	P	W	D	L	F	A	Pt
Sweden	6	4	1	1	7	3	9
West Germany	6	3	1	2	9	6	7
Czechoslovakia	6	2	1	3	6	8	5
Portugal	6	1	1	4	4	9	3

Sweden qualify for quarter-finals

Group 3 (England, Finland, Rumania, Turkey)

England (1) 2, Finland (0) 0 — Southampton, 16 October 1984
Turkey (1) 1, Finland (0) 1 — Isparta, 30 October 1984
Turkey (0) 0, England (0) 0 — Bursa, 13 November 1984
Rumania (0) 1, Turkey (0) 0 — Slatina, 2 April 1985
Rumania (0) 0, England (0) 0 — Brasov, 30 April 1985
Finland (2) 3, England (0) 1 — Mikkeli, 21 May 1985
Finland (0) 2, Rumania (1) 2 — Varkaus, 5 June 1985
Rumania (0) 0, Finland (0) 0 — Constanta, 27 August 1985
England (1) 3, Rumania (0) 0 — Ipswich, 10 September 1985
Finland (0) 0, Turkey (0) 0 — Kokkola, 24 September 1985
England (1) 3, Turkey (0) 0 — Bristol, 14 October 1985
Turkey (1) 2, Rumania (1) 2 — Izmir, 12 November 1985

	P	W	D	L	F	A	Pt
England	6	3	2	1	9	3	8
Finland	6	1	4	1	6	6	6
Rumania	6	1	4	1	5	7	6
Turkey	6	0	4	2	3	7	4

England qualify for quarter-finals

Group 4 (Bulgaria, East Germany, France, Yugoslavia)

Yugoslavia (1) 1, Bulgaria (0) 2	Zrenjanin, 28 September 1984
East Germany (1) 1, Yugoslavia (0) 1	Halle, 19 October 1984
France (0) 2, Bulgaria (0) 1	Auxerre, 20 November 1984
France (0) 1, East Germany (1) 1	Lorient, 7 December 1984
Yugoslavia (0) 0, France (0) 0	Sarajevo, 2 April 1985
Bulgaria (2) 3, East Germany (0) 2	Plovdiv, 5 April 1985
Bulgaria (1) 4, France (0) 0	Plovdiv, 1 May 1985
Bulgaria (2) 3, Yugoslavia (3) 6	Plovdiv, 2 June 1985
East Germany (1) 1, France (0) 1	Karl-Marx-Stadt, 11 September 1985
Yugoslavia (0) 2, East Germany (2) 3	Subotica, 27 September 1985
East Germany (0) 1, Bulgaria (0) 1	Halle, 15 November 1985
France (3) 7, Yugoslavia (0) 0	Reims, 16 November 1985

	P	*W*	*D*	*L*	*F*	*A*	*Pt*
France	6	2	3	1	11	7	7
Bulgaria	6	3	1	2	14	12	7
East Germany	6	1	4	1	9	9	6
Yugoslavia	6	1	2	3	10	16	4

France qualify for quarter-finals

Group 5 (Austria, Cyprus, Hungary, Netherlands)

Cyprus (1) 1, Austria (1) 1	Limassol, 1 May 1984
Hungary (1) 2, Austria (0) 0	Szombathely, 25 September 1984
Netherlands (0) 1, Hungary (0) 0	Breda, 16 October 1984
Austria (0) 0, Netherlands (0) 0	Krems, 13 November 1984
Cyprus (0) 1, Hungary (1) 3	Paphos, 17 November 1984
Cyprus (0) 1, Netherlands (1) 3	Paralimni, 22 December 1984
Netherlands (1) 5, Cyprus (0) 0	Leeuwarden, 26 February 1985
Hungary (1) 1, Cyprus (0) 0	Vac, 2 April 1985
Austria (1) 1, Hungary (1) 2	Fürstenfeld, 16 April 1985
Netherlands (2) 2, Austria (0) 1	Roosendaal, 30 April 1985
Hungary (0) 1, Netherlands (0) 0	Budapest, 13 May 1985
Austria (0) 0, Cyprus (0) 0	Graz, 7 May 1985

	P	*W*	*D*	*L*	*F*	*A*	*Pt*
Hungary	6	5	0	1	9	3	10
Netherlands	6	4	1	1	11	3	9
Austria	6	0	3	3	3	7	3
Cyprus	6	0	2	4	3	13	2

Hungary qualify for quarter-finals

Group 6 (Denmark, Norway, Switzerland, USSR)

Norway (1) 3, Switzerland (0) 0	Sandefjord, 11 September 1984
Denmark (2) 2, Norway (0) 2	Broendby, 25 September 1984
Norway (1) 2, USSR (1) 1	Fredrikstad, 10 October 1984
Switzerland (0) 1, Denmark (0) 1	Berne, 17 October 1984
Switzerland (3) 4, USSR (0) 2	Grenchen, 16 April 1985
USSR (0) 1, Switzerland (0) 0	Moscow, 30 April 1985
Denmark (0) 1, USSR (0) 0	Naestved, 4 June 1985
USSR (1) 2, Denmark (0) 0	Moscow, 24 September 1985
Denmark (2) 4, Switzerland (0) 1	Copenhagen, 8 October 1985
Norway (1) 1, Denmark (2) 3	Oslo, 16 October 1985
USSR (1) 2, Norway (0) 1	Moscow, 29 October 1985
Switzerland (1) 1, Norway (0) 1	Freiburg, 12 November 1985

	P	W	D	L	F	A	Pt
Denmark	6	3	2	1	11	7	8
Norway	6	2	2	2	10	9	6
USSR	6	3	0	3	8	8	6
Switzerland	6	1	2	3	8	13	4

Denmark qualify for quarter-finals

Group 7 (Iceland, Scotland, Spain)

Scotland (0) 1, Iceland (0) 0 — Motherwell, 16 October 1984
Scotland (0) 0, Spain (1) 2 — Dundee, 13 November 1984
Spain (0) 0, Scotland (0) 0 — Cadiz, 26 February 1985
Iceland (1) 2, Scotland (0) 0 — Kopavogsvoellur, 27 May 1985
Iceland (0) 0, Spain (0) 1 — Kopavogsvoellur, 11 June 1985
Spain (0) 1, Iceland (0) 0 — Huelva, 24 September 1985

	P	W	D	L	F	A	Pt
Spain	4	3	1	0	4	0	7
Scotland	4	1	1	2	1	4	3
Iceland	4	1	0	3	2	3	2

Spain qualify for quarter-finals

Group 8 (Belgium, Italy, Luxembourg)

Belgium (3) 5, Luxembourg (0) 1 — Brussels, 17 October 1984
Belgium (0) 1, Italy (0) 1 — Brussels, 27 March 1985
Italy (1) 5, Luxembourg (0) 1 — Benevento, 17 April 1985
Luxembourg (0) 0, Italy (4) 6 — Luxembourg, 16 October 1985
Luxembourg (2) 3, Belgium (0) 1 — Luxembourg, 20 November 1985
Italy (2) 3, Belgium (0) 0 — San Benedetto, 18 December 1985

	P	W	D	L	F	A	Pt
Italy	4	3	1	0	14	1	7
Belgium	4	1	1	2	6	7	3
Luxembourg	4	1	0	3	5	17	2

Italy qualify for quarter-finals

Quarter-finals, first leg

Sweden (0) 1, Italy (0) 1 — Gothenburg, 12 March 1986
France (0) 1, Spain (1) 3 — Auxerre, 12 March 1986
Denmark (0) 0, England (0) 1 — Copenhagen, 12 March 1986
Poland (0) 1, Hungary (0) 0 — Opole, 19 March 1986

Quarter-finals, second leg

Hungary (0) 5, Poland (0) 0 — Budapest, 26 March 1986
Spain (1) 3, France (0) 1 — Murcia, 26 March 1986
England (0) 1, Denmark (1) 1 — Maine Road, 26 March 1986
Italy (1) 2, Sweden (1) 1 — Bergamo, 29 March 1986

Semi-finals, first leg

Italy (1) 2, England (0) 0 — Pisa, 9 April 1986
Hungary (1) 3, Spain (1) 1 — Budapest, 9 April 1986

Semi-finals, second leg

England, (0) 1, Italy (0) 1 — Swindon, 23 April 1986
Spain (2) 4, Hungary (1) 1 (aet) — La Coruna, 23 April 1986

The first leg of the final between Spain and Italy will be held in Italy on 15 October 1986, the second leg in Spain on 29 October 1986.

UEFA YOUTH CHAMPIONSHIP 1984-86

Note: The final tournament will take place in Yugoslavia from October 9 to 16,1986

Group 1

England 5, Iceland 3	Manchester, 16 October 1984
England 1, Scotland 2	London, 27 November 1984
Eire 1, England 0	Dublin, 26 February 1985
Scotland 1, Eire 1	Edinburgh, 19 March 1985
Iceland 0, Scotland 2	Laugardalsvoel, 27 May 1985
Iceland 1, Eire 2	Reykjavik, 4 June 1985
Iceland 0, England 5	Reykjavik, 11 September 1985
Eire 2, Iceland 0	Dublin, 11 November 1985
Scotland 2, Iceland 0	Stirling, 14 November 1985
Eire 0, Scotland 1	Dublin, 28 January 1986
England 2, Eire 0	Sheffield, 25 February 1986
Scotland 4, England 1	Aberdeen, 25 March 1986

Scotland qualify for final tournament

Group 2

Belgium 3, Netherlands 1	St Nicholas, 21 November 1984
Northern Ireland 1, Wales 2	Belfast, 29 January 1985
Wales 0, Netherlands 1	Rhyl, 19 March 1985
Netherlands 2, Northern Ireland 1	Waalwijk, 26 March 1985
Belgium 0, Northern Ireland 0	Lier, 28 March 1985
Wales 3, Belgium 3	Ebbw Vale, 17 April 1985
Netherlands 2, Belgium 2	Venlo, 4 December 1985
Wales 3, Northern Ireland 0	Wrexham, 28 January 1986
Northern Ireland 1, Belgium 1	Coleraine, 19 February 1986
Netherlands 1, Wales 1	Wageningen, 18 March 1986
Belgium 2, Wales 0	Brussels, 20 March 1986
Northern Ireland 2, Netherlands 4	Bangor, 15 April 1986

Belgium qualify for final tournament

Group 3

Yugoslavia 3, Spain 0	Sremska Mitrovica, 28 November 1984
Luxembourg 0, France 4	Esch-sur-Alzette, 26 March 1985
Yugoslavia 8, Luxembourg 0	Visoko, 26 March 1985
Yugoslavia 1, France 2	Hrasnica, 2 April 1985
Spain 3, Luxembourg 0	Binefar, 4 April 1985
France 1, Spain 1	Martigues, 1 May 1985
Luxembourg 0, Spain 1	Differdange, 9 October 1985
Spain 1, France 1	Murcia, 30 October 1985
Luxembourg 1, Yugoslavia 6	Lux-Beggen, 30 October 1985
France 0, Yugoslavia 0	Blois, 16 November 1985
Spain 1, Yugoslavia 3	Tudela, 27 March 1986
France 12, Luxembourg 0	Levallois-Perret, 2 April 1986

Yugoslavia qualify for final tournament

Group 4

Portugal 0, Italy 2	Portimao, 24 January 1985
Malta 0, Portugal 2	Valletta, 9 February 1985
Malta 0, Italy 5	Marsa, 24 April 1985
Portugal 0, Austria 3	Aveiro, 24 April 1985
Austria 3, Malta 0	Reyersdorf, 8 May 1985
Austria 2, Italy 1	Kirchschlag, 12 June 1985
Portugal 6, Malta 0	Lisbon, 13 October 1985
Austria 1, Portugal 4	Vocklabruk, 30 October 1985
Italy 4, Malta 0	Castellamare, 4 December 1985
Italy 2, Portugal 0	Messina, 22 January 1986

Malta 0, Austria 7	Valletta, 23 April 1986
Italy 5, Austria 2	Viterbo, 30 April 1986

Italy qualify for final tournament

Group 5

Switzerland 3, Denmark 1	Fribourg, 16 October 1984
West Germany 2, Switzerland 0	Hassfurt, 20 March 1985
Switzerland 1, Poland 1	Emmenbrucke, 1 May 1985
Denmark 1, West Germany 3	Ikast, 8 May 1985
Poland 0, West Germany 2	Radom, 22 May 1985
Poland 0, Denmark 0	Lomza, 4 June 1985
Denmark 1, Switzerland 1	Copenhagen, 8 October 1985
Switzerland 0, West Germany 2	Liestal, 23 October 1985
Denmark 2, Poland 2	Nykobing, 30 October 1985
West Germany 3, Denmark 1	Flensburg, 13 November 1985
West Germany 3, Poland 0	Helmstedt, 24 April 1986

West Germany qualify for final tournament

Group 6

Norway 0, Sweden 1	Oslo, 26 September 1984
Finland 0, Norway 1	Helsinki, 3 October 1984
East Germany 1, Norway 0	Hoyers-Werda, 4 November 1984
East Germany 2, Sweden 1	Wilhelm-Pieck, 8 May 1985
Finland 0, East Germany 1	Salo, 18 May 1985
Sweden 1, Finland 1	Skinnskatteb, 6 June 1985
Sweden 1, Norway 0	Aamaal, 18 September 1985
Norway 1, Finland 4	Kristiansand, 25 September 1985
East Germany 2, Finland 0	Schonebeck, 9 October 1985
Norway 1, East Germany 1	Stavanger, 16 October 1985
Finland 0, Sweden 4	Paimio, 16 October 1985
Sweden 0, East Germany 0	Varnamo, 21 May 1986

East Germany qualify for final tournament

Group 7

Cyprus 1, Hungary 4	Larnaca, 21 March 1985
Cyprus 1, Bulgaria 5	Limassol, 10 April 1985
Cyprus 1, Greece 4	Nicosia, 24 April 1985
Bulgaria 0, Hungary 2	Goze Deltchev, 1 May 1985
Hungary 2, Greece 0	Budapest, 12 May 1985
Bulgaria 5, Greece 1	Samokov, 22 June 1985
Greece 2, Bulgaria 2	Chania, 26 February 1986
Hungary 0, Bulgaria 1	Szombathely, 9 April 1986
Greece 3, Cyprus 2	Agrinio, 16 April 1986
Greece 1, Hungary 0	Corfu, 23 April 1986
Bulgaria 6, Cyprus 0	Sofia, 28 May 1986

Bulgaria qualify for final tournament

Group 8

Turkey 0, Rumania 1	Istanbul, 30 March 1985
Czechoslovakia 1, Turkey 0	Malacky, 18 April 1985
Czechoslovakia 2, Rumania 0	Turnov, 1 May 1985
Turkey 1, USSR 1	Trabzon, 11 May 1985
Rumania 3, USR 2	Plopeni, 27 May 1985
USSR 2, Czechoslovakia 0	Moscow, 12 June 1985
Czechoslovakia 2, USSR 2	Nitra, 26 September 1985
Rumania 1, Czechoslovakia 0	Plopeni, 16 October 1985
Rumania 4, Turkey 0	Plopeni, 7 November 1985
Turkey 1, Czechoslovakia 1	Ankara, 20 April 1986
USSR 2, Rumania 2	Tbilisi, 25 April 1986
USSR 0, Turkey 1	Moscow, 14 May 1986

Rumania qualify for final tournament

UEFA UNDER-16 CHAMPIONSHIP 1984-86

FINAL TOURNAMENT IN GREECE

Group A

Scotland 5, Portugal 1	Chania, 1 May 1986
Italy 3, Greece 0	Chania, 1 May 1986
Scotland 0, Italy 1	Ofi Stadium, Heraklion, 3 May 1986
Portugal 3, Greece 0	Ofi Stadium, Heraklion, 3 May 1986
Scotland 1, Greece 0	Ofi Stadium, Heraklion, 5 May 1986
Portugal 0, Italy 0	National Stadium, Heraklion, 5 May 1986

Italy qualify for semi-finals

Group B

Bulgaria 1, Sweden 0	Rizoupoli Stadium, 1 May 1986
Spain 2, Norway 0	Karaiskakis Stadium, 1 May 1986
Bulgaria 1, Spain 1	Rizoupoli Stadium, 3 May 1986
Sweden 0, Norway 0	Karaiskakis Stadium, 3 May 1986
Bulgaria 1, Norway 1	Rizoupoli Stadium, 5 May 1986
Sweden 0, Spain 1	Karaiskakis Stadium, 5 May 1986

Spain qualify for semi-finals

Group C

Denmark 1, Czechoslovakia 1	Kaftantzoglio Stadium, 1 May 1986
East Germany 1, Austria 1	PAOK Toumba Stadium, 1 May 1986
Denmark 1, East Germany 2	Kaftantzoglio Stadium, 3 May 1986
Czechoslovakia 4, Austria 0	PAOK Toumba Stadium, 3 May 1986
Denmark 2, Austria 0	Kaftantzoglio Stadium, 5 May 1986
Czechoslovakia 0, East Germany 2	PAOK Toumba Stadium, 5 May 1986

East Germany qualify for semi-finals

Group D

Netherlands 1, USSR 3	Trikala, 1 May 1986
France 2, Rumania 1	Larissa, 1 May 1986
France 0, Netherlands 1	Trikala, 3 May 1986
Rumania 1, USSR 3	Larissa, 3 May 1986
France 1, USSR 4	Trikala, 5 May 1986
Rumania 1, Netherlands 0	Larissa, 5 May 1986

USSR qualify for semi-finals

Semi-finals

Italy 2, East Germany 2 — Karaiskakis Stadium, 8 May 1986
East Germany won on penalties
Spain 2, USSR 1 — Karaiskakis Stadium, 8 May 1986

Third Place Play-off

East Germany 1, USSR 1 — Olympic Stadium, 10 May 1986
USSR won on penalties

Final

Spain 2, Italy 1 — Olympic Stadium, 10 May 1986

OTHER LEAGUE TABLES

Gola League

	P	W	D	L	F	A	W	D	L	F	A	Pts
Enfield	42	15	4	2	48	20	12	6	3	46	27	76
Frickley Athletic	42	16	4	1	46	21	9	6	6	32	29	69
Kidderminster Harriers	42	12	4	5	51	28	12	3	6	48	34	67
Altrincham	42	14	3	4	42	27	8	8	5	28	22	63
Weymouth	42	11	8	2	43	24	8	7	6	32	36	61
Runcorn	42	11	6	4	40	17	8	8	5	30	27	60
Stafford Rovers	42	10	7	4	30	22	9	6	6	31	32	60
Telford United	42	13	5	3	42	24	5	5	11	26	42	51
Kettering Town	42	11	6	4	37	24	4	9	8	18	29	49
Wealdstone	42	10	5	6	35	28	6	4	11	22	28	47
Cheltenham Town	42	13	4	4	47	27	3	7	11	22	42	46
Bath City	42	5	8	8	28	25	8	3	10	25	29	45
Boston United	42	11	5	5	41	26	5	2	14	25	50	44
Barnet	42	9	4	8	32	23	4	7	10	24	37	41
Scarborough	42	10	4	7	35	31	3	7	11	19	35	40
Northwich Victoria	42	5	6	10	24	25	5	6	10	18	29	37
Maidstone United	42	7	9	5	35	29	2	7	12	22	37	36
Nuneaton Borough	42	8	3	10	27	27	5	2	14	31	46	36
Dagenham	42	6	7	8	23	29	4	5	12	25	37	36
Wycomb Wanderers	42	7	6	8	30	35	3	7	11	25	49	36
Dartford	42	7	6	8	36	33	1	3	17	15	49	26
Barrow	42	5	6	10	26	34	2	2	17	15	52	24

Points scoring: Home win=2 pts; Away win=3 pts; Draw=1 pt.

Southern League – Premier Division

	P	W	D	L	F	A	Pts
Welling United	38	29	6	3	95	31	93
Chelmsford City	38	20	10	8	68	41	70
Fisher Athletic	38	20	7	11	67	45	67
Alvechurch	38	19	9	10	71	56	66
Worcester City	38	19	9	10	64	50	66
Crawley Town	38	18	5	15	76	59	59
Shepshed Charterhouse	38	19	1	18	51	52	58
Aylesbury United	38	14	10	14	52	49	52
Folkestone	38	14	10	14	56	56	52
Bedworth United	38	14	8	16	44	49	50
Willenhall Town	38	12	13	13	51	44	49
Dudley Town	38	15	4	19	58	62	49
Corby Town	38	14	7	17	61	67	49
King's Lynn	38	12	10	16	39	42	46
Basingstoke Town	38	13	4	21	36	67	43
R.S. Southampton	38	11	9	18	44	61	42
Witney Town	38	11	6	21	44	74	39
Gosport Borough	38	10	8	20	42	66	38
Fareham Town	38	8	13	17	40	62	37
Gravesend & Northfleet	38	9	9	20	29	55	36

Midland Division

	P	W	D	L	F	A	Pts
Bromsgrove Rovers	40	29	5	6	95	44	92
Redditch United	40	23	6	11	70	42	75
Merthyr Tydfil	40	21	10	9	60	40	73
V.S. Rugby	40	17	14	9	41	31	65
Stourbridge	40	15	14	11	62	49	59
Rushden Town	40	17	7	16	69	74	58
Bilston Town	40	15	12	13	60	48	57
Bridgnorth Town	40	13	18	9	56	45	57
Gloucester City	40	15	12	13	61	57	57
Grantham	40	16	7	17	46	59	55
Wellingborough Town	40	15	9	16	56	56	54
Sutton Coldfield Town	40	13	14	13	60	45	53
Hednesford Town	40	14	9	17	67	70	51
Forest Green Rovers	40	14	9	17	52	56	51
Mile Oak Rovers	40	14	8	18	56	73	50
Leicester United	40	13	10	17	41	48	49
Banbury United	40	13	8	19	38	55	47
Coventry Sporting	40	10	15	15	42	48	45
Moor Green	40	12	6	22	63	91	42
Leamington	40	10	6	24	40	77	36
Oldbury United	40	8	7	25	50	87	31

Southern Division

	P	W	D	L	F	A	Pts
Cambridge City	40	23	11	6	87	41	80
Salisbury	40	24	8	8	84	51	80
Hastings Town	40	23	9	8	83	51	78
Dover Athletic	40	23	6	11	89	53	75
Corinthian	40	20	9	11	78	45	69
Tonbridge A.F.C.	40	17	13	10	65	51	64
Dunstable	40	17	11	12	70	61	62
Ruislip	40	17	6	17	67	66	57
Erith & Belvedere	40	14	12	14	35	40	54
Waterlooville	40	16	6	18	52	58	54
Burnham & Hillingdon	40	16	6	18	44	59	54
Canterbury City	40	13	13	14	58	58	52
Trowbridge Town	40	13	13	14	57	63	52
Sheppey United	40	14	10	16	43	53	52
Thanet United	40	13	7	20	58	63	46
Woodford Town	40	12	10	18	49	62	46
Poole Town	40	12	7	21	55	63	43
Ashford Town	40	10	12	18	45	65	42
Chatham Town	40	8	15	17	53	70	39
Andover	40	10	8	22	52	92	38
Dorchester Town	40	5	8	27	35	94	23

Multipart League

	P	W	D	L	F	A	Pts
Gateshead	42	24	10	8	85	51	82
Marine	42	23	11	8	63	35	80
Morecambe	42	17	17	8	59	39	68
Gainsborough Trinity	42	18	14	10	66	52	68
Burton Albion	42	18	12	12	64	47	66
Southport	42	17	11	14	70	66	62
Worksop Town	42	17	10	15	51	48	61
Workington	42	14	18	10	54	46	*59
Macclesfield Town	42	17	8	17	67	65	59
Hyde United	42	14	15	13	63	62	57
Witton Albion	42	15	13	14	56	59	*57
Mossley	42	13	16	13	56	60	55
Bangor City	42	13	15	14	51	51	54
Rhyl	42	14	10	18	65	71	52
South Liverpool	42	11	17	14	43	44	50
Horwich	42	15	6	21	53	63	*50
Caernarfon Town	42	11	17	14	51	63	50
Oswestry Town	42	12	13	17	51	60	49
Buxton	42	11	12	19	55	76	45
Chorley	42	9	15	18	56	64	42
Matlock Town	42	9	15	18	59	75	42
Goole Town	42	7	11	24	37	78	*31

**Denotes one point deducted for breach of rule.*

Vauxhall-Opel League – Premier Division

	P	W	D	L	F	A	Pts
Sutton United	42	29	8	5	109	39	95
Yeovil Town	42	28	7	7	92	48	91
Farnborough Town	42	23	8	11	90	50	77
Croydon	42	23	7	12	70	50	76
Harrow Borough	42	21	8	13	76	66	71
Slough Town	42	18	8	16	66	68	62
Bishop's Stortford	42	17	10	15	55	61	61
Kingstonian	42	15	15	12	57	56	60
Dulwich Hamlet	42	17	9	16	64	79	60
Wokingham Town	42	16	10	16	67	64	58
Windsor & Eton	42	17	7	18	58	75	58
Tooting & Mitcham United	42	14	11	17	65	76	53
Walthamstow Avenue	42	12	14	16	69	70	50
Worthing	42	13	10	19	72	82	49
Bognor Regis Town	42	15	6	21	63	70	*48
Hayes	42	10	17	15	36	42	47
Hitchin Town	42	11	14	17	53	69	47
Barking	42	11	13	18	45	55	46
Hendon	42	10	13	19	59	77	43
Carshalton Athletic	42	9	13	20	56	79	40
Billericay Town	42	9	12	21	59	78	39
Epsom & Ewell	42	8	12	22	63	90	36

**3 points deducted by league*

The Football Combination

	P	W	D	L	F	A	Pts
West Ham United	42	31	5	6	141	60	67
Arsenal	41	26	10	5	124	41	62
Norwich City	42	27	7	8	93	36	61
Chelsea	42	26	5	11	107	40	57
Watford	42	23	10	9	98	44	56
Tottenham Hotspur	42	23	7	12	105	65	53
Luton Town	42	23	7	12	74	49	53
Ipswich Town	42	21	8	13	87	58	50
Oxford United	42	21	7	14	104	62	49
Queens Park Rangers	42	21	7	14	91	69	49
Millwall	42	22	3	17	75	72	47
Southampton	42	19	8	15	88	80	46
Charlton Athletic	42	18	4	20	75	84	40
Crystal Palace	42	13	10	19	67	104	36
Birmingham City	42	14	4	24	57	96	32
Bristol Rovers	42	12	7	23	70	109	31
Brighton & Hove Albion	42	9	9	24	39	92	27
Swindon Town	41	10	5	26	74	118	25
Portsmouth	42	9	8	25	45	73	24
Fulham	42	8	5	29	51	102	21
Reading	42	8	4	30	46	133	20
Swansea City	42	6	2	34	36	154	14

Arsenal v Swindon Town was not played as Swindon Town could not field a team with the heavy commitments of Arsenal in the Combination and F.A. and other Youth Cups, the match could not be fitted in.
Portsmouth F.C. has two points deducted for playing an ineligible player against Crystal Palace F.C.

The Central League

	P	W	D	L	F	A	Pts
Derby County	34	21	3	10	81	35	66
Manchester United	34	19	5	10	55	32	62
Liverpool	34	19	4	11	85	53	61
Nottingham Forest	34	17	5	12	76	54	56
Manchester City	34	16	8	10	58	40	56
Sheffield Wednesday	34	16	4	14	55	47	52
Leeds United	34	16	3	15	63	70	51
Hull City	34	15	4	15	52	53	49
Aston Villa	34	15	3	16	55	67	48
Blackburn Rovers	34	14	4	16	57	49	46
Leicester City	34	12	10	12	60	58	46
Newcastle United	34	13	7	14	52	61	46
Everton	34	12	6	16	36	44	42
Sheffield United	34	12	5	17	44	76	41
Barnsley	34	12	4	18	44	60	40
West Bromwich Albion	34	9	10	15	41	65	37
Huddersfield Town	34	8	11	15	51	68	35
Wigan Athletic	34	11	2	21	44	77	35

Northern Counties East – Premier Division

	P	W	D	L	F	A	Pts
Arnold	38	24	3	6	83	36	*79
Emley	38	22	11	5	77	47	77
Guiseley	38	22	6	10	81	52	72
Long Eaton United	38	19	11	8	70	39	68
Eastwood Town	38	21	5	12	73	62	*67
Alfreton Town	38	21	2	15	66	47	65
Sutton Town	38	18	6	14	69	57	60
Farsley Celtic	38	14	12	12	71	55	54
Belper Town	38	15	9	14	54	45	54
Thackley	38	14	11	13	52	58	53
Denaby United	38	13	14	11	63	56	*52
Pontefract Colls	38	15	7	16	55	54	52
Armthorpe Welfare	38	15	7	16	57	58	52
Bentley VW	38	12	11	15	61	65	47
Heanor Town	38	11	9	18	61	69	*41
Spalding United	38	9	12	17	41	62	39
Boston	38	10	6	22	42	79	36
Appleby Frodingham	38	6	12	20	40	83	30
Bridlington Trinity	38	4	14	20	34	85	26
Ilkeston Town	38	5	7	26	31	72	22

**Denotes one point deducted for breach of rule*

Midland Football Combination – Premier Division

	P	W	D	L	F	A	Pts
Boldmere St Michaels	38	25	10	3	72	24	60
Paget Rangers	38	24	9	5	94	31	57
West Midlands Police	38	23	8	7	65	41	54
Northfield Town	38	18	12	8	74	50	48
Bloxwich A.F.C.	38	18	11	9	77	50	47
Stratford Town	38	17	12	9	53	32	46
Solihull Borough	38	18	7	13	62	45	43
Walsall Borough	38	15	13	10	52	37	43
Polesworth North Warwick	38	16	10	12	52	46	42
Racing Club Warwick	38	13	15	10	52	50	41
Coleshill Town	38	14	13	11	54	54	41
Highgate United	38	16	8	14	56	55	40
Evesham United	38	12	9	17	62	80	33
Hurley Daw Mill	38	12	8	18	44	59	32
New World	38	9	7	22	46	73	25
Knowle North Star	38	8	9	21	35	63	25
Southam United	38	6	12	20	52	90	24
Studley Sporting	38	7	8	23	43	75	22
Smethwick Highfield	38	5	11	22	31	75	21
Kings Heath	38	5	6	27	24	70	16

Drybroughs Northern League – First Division

	P	W	D	L	F	A	Pts
Bishop Auckland	38	21	10	7	79	45	73
Bedlington Terriers	38	19	10	9	65	44	67
South Bank	38	18	12	8	66	36	66
Blyth Spartans	38	19	9	10	79	52	66
Tow Law Town	38	18	10	10	72	47	64
Peterlee Newtown	38	19	6	13	66	56	63
Chester-le-Street Town	38	18	7	13	62	53	61
Brendon United	38	16	10	12	72	68	58
Crook Town	38	15	8	15	73	70	53
Hartlepool United Reserves	38	14	10	14	65	69	52
Gretna	38	13	11	14	70	69	50
North Shields	38	14	8	16	65	72	50
Consett	38	13	9	16	44	58	48
Spennymoor United	38	12	11	15	51	54	40
Ryhope Community	38	13	7	18	50	69	46
Whitby Town	38	12	9	17	59	74	45
Whitley Bay	38	11	8	19	65	73	41
Ferryhill Athletic	38	11	6	21	62	94	39
Billingham Synthonia	38	8	11	19	47	66	35
Billingham Town	38	6	8	24	46	89	26

North West Counties League – First Division

	P	W	D	L	F	A	Pts
Clitheroe	38	20	14	4	61	30	54
Congleton Town	38	22	10	6	51	29	54
Eastwood Hanley	38	22	9	7	68	45	53
Stalybridge Celtic	38	21	10	7	62	39	52
Fleetwood Town	38	21	10	7	70	34	*50
Irlam Town	38	16	14	8	66	45	46
Leek Town	38	20	6	12	64	44	46
Curzon Ashton	38	18	9	11	52	50	45
Burscough	38	15	10	13	45	35	40
St. Helens Town	38	15	8	15	65	55	38
Accrington Stanley	38	13	11	14	62	60	37
Leyland Motors	38	13	8	17	62	67	34
Winsford United	38	14	6	18	55	68	34
Radcliffe Borough	38	12	9	17	48	49	33
Bootle	38	11	7	20	46	54	29
Penrith	38	9	8	21	46	63	26
Netherfield	38	8	10	20	38	76	26
Glossop	38	7	10	21	37	69	24
Prescot Cables	38	5	9	24	33	68	19
Formby	38	5	8	25	35	86	18

Banks's Brewery West Midland (Regional) League – Premier Division

	P	W	D	L	F	A	Pts
Halesowen Town	38	31	4	3	108	28	66
Gresley Rovers	38	25	9	4	91	29	59
Atherstone United	38	26	7	5	90	48	59
Harrisons	38	22	9	7	82	40	53
Wednesfield Social	38	21	7	10	88	48	49
Lye Town	38	18	11	9	54	39	47
GKN Sankey	38	15	12	11	59	64	42
Hinckley Athletic	38	15	11	12	60	50	41
Tamworth	38	15	8	15	68	52	38
Bereton Social	38	13	11	14	58	54	37
Rushall Olympic	38	14	9	15	63	65	37
Malvern Town	38	13	10	15	51	61	36
Shifnal Town	38	9	10	19	38	76	28
Oldswinford	38	9	9	20	46	68	27
Blakenall	38	9	8	21	38	61	26
Tividale	38	8	10	20	51	83	26
Chasetown	38	7	10	21	40	74	24
Wolverhampton United	38	8	8	22	31	66	24
Tipton Town	38	8	8	22	43	79	24
Armitage	38	7	3	28	44	118	17

Western League – Premier Division

	P	W	D	L	F	A	Pts
Exmouth Town	42	30	9	3	95	31	69
Liskeard Athletic	42	31	6	5	103	34	68
Bideford	42	27	8	7	97	27	62
Saltash United	42	21	13	8	81	44	55
Chippenham Town	42	21	10	11	60	44	52
Mangotsfield United	42	18	13	11	86	58	49
Taunton Town	42	19	9	14	59	54	47
Dawlish Town	42	19	8	15	53	49	*45
Bristol City	42	18	6	18	74	61	42
Clevedon Town	42	12	18	12	55	47	42
Bristol Manor Farm	42	16	9	17	71	72	41
Minehead	42	16	9	17	55	70	41
Frome Town	42	14	12	16	49	62	*39
Clandown	42	15	8	19	46	57	38
Torrington	42	13	11	18	51	62	37
Melksham Town	42	11	13	18	50	77	35
Barnstaple Town	42	13	7	22	46	68	33
Weston-Super-Mare	42	12	8	22	69	93	32
Paulton Rovers	42	9	12	21	50	82	30
Plymouth Argyle	42	9	11	22	60	67	29
Chard Town	42	8	4	30	33	112	20
Shepton Mallet Town	42	4	8	30	36	110	*15

Nene Group United Counties League – Premier Division

	P	W	D	L	F	A	Pts
Buckingham	40	25	10	5	78	31	60
S & L Corby	40	24	11	5	85	32	59
Baldock	40	26	6	8	91	43	58
Irthlingborough	40	22	8	10	69	45	52
Stamford	40	22	6	12	71	52	50
Potton	40	20	6	14	69	53	46
Long Buckby	39	17	10	12	72	53	44
Wootton	40	16	11	13	63	58	43
Arlesey	40	16	9	15	63	57	41
Holbeach	40	16	8	16	66	75	40
N'ton Spencer	40	15	10	15	64	74	40
Rothwell	40	17	5	18	60	62	39
Raunds	40	16	7	17	61	74	39
Ampthill	40	13	10	17	55	68	36
Desborough	40	11	9	20	70	89	31
Brackley	40	10	10	20	52	70	30
Bourne	40	9	12	19	43	71	30
St. Neots	40	9	9	22	56	74	27
Stotfold	40	10	7	23	43	77	27
Eynesbury	40	7	12	21	45	86	26
Newport Pagnell	39	4	12	23	42	74	20

Highland League

	P	W	D	L	F	A	Pts
Forres Mechanics	32	22	6	4	77	27	72
Elgin City	32	21	7	4	67	33	70
Peterhead	32	22	3	7	50	25	69
Inverness Caledonian	32	19	9	4	70	32	66
Keith	32	17	5	10	66	40	56
Huntly	32	15	8	9	58	45	53
Buckie Thistle	32	14	8	10	48	36	50
Inverness Thistle	32	12	9	11	56	53	45
Nairn County	32	11	6	15	47	60	39
Ross County	32	11	4	17	65	66	37
Rothes	32	9	8	15	51	62	35
Fort William	32	10	5	17	40	73	35
Clachnacuddin	32	8	7	17	43	72	31
Fraserburgh	32	8	6	18	40	60	30
Lossiemouth	32	6	8	18	38	63	26
Brora Rangers	32	6	5	21	39	74	23
Deveronvale	32	4	10	18	31	65	22

ALTRINCHAM WIN FA CHALLENGE TROPHY

First round	Second round	Third round	Fourth round	Semi-finals	Final
Wealdstone 1	Wealdstone 2	Wealdstone 0 1	South Bank 0	Enfield 1 0	**ALTRINCHAM 1** *Scorer: Farrelly*
Welling U. 0					
Bedworth U. 1 0	Frickley Ath. 1				
Frickley Ath. 1 5					
Saltash U. 1	Dartford 1	South Bank 0 2			
Dartford 2					
South Bank 1 2	South Bank 3				
Whitby T. 1 1					
Enfield 3	Enfield 3	Enfield 5	Enfield 2		
Waterlooville 0					
Maidstone U. 3	Maidstone U. 2				
Weymouth 0					
Grays Ath. 2	Grays Ath. 1 1	Chelmsford C. 3			
Uxbridge 1					
Chelmsford C. 2	Chelmsford C. 1 3				
Bath C. 1					
Dagenham 3	Dagenham 0	Cheltenham T. 0 3	Cheltenham T. 0	Altrincham 1 2	
Sheppey U. 0					
Cheltenham T. 3	Cheltenham T. 1				
Fisher Ath. 0					
Bishops Stortford 2	Bishops Stortford 2	Bishops Stortford ...0 1			
Workington T. 0					
Northwich Vic. 1	Northwich Vic. 0				
Workington 0					
Ryhope CA. 1	Altrincham 6	Altrincham 1	Altrincham 2		
Altrincham 3					
Bangor C. 1	Bangor C. 1				
Willenhall T. 0					
Stafford R. 1	Stafford R. 0	Bishop Auckland 0			
Nuneaton Bor. 0					
Bishop Auckland 2	Bishop Aucland 1				
Blyth Spartans 0					

RUNCORN 0

At Wembley, att: 15,700

Scarborough 2	Scarborough 0 1 0	Southport 1 1	Kidderminster H. 1	Runcorn 0 2
Barrow 1				
Telford U. 2	Southport 0 1 1			
Southport 4				
Hyde U. 0	Corby T. 0	Kidderminster H. ...1 6		
Corby T. 2				
Kidderminster H. 5	Kidderminster H. 4			
Boston U. 2				
Dulwich H. 1 1	Windsor & Eton 0	Runcorn 2	Runcorn 2	
Windsor & Eton 1 2				
Runcorn 2	Runcorn 1			
Marine 0				
Morecambe 0	Burton A. 1	Burton A. 0		
Burton A. 2				
Bromsgrove R. 1 4	Bromsgrove R. 0			
Shepshed Ch'house .1 1				
Worthing 1	Worthing 0	Worthing 0 1	Kettering T. 2	Kettering T. 0 0
Salisbury 0				
Bridgend T. 2 2	Bridgend T. 0			
Harrow Bor. 2 1				
Slough T. 1	Slough T. 1	Kettering T. 0 2		
Tilbury 0				
Sutton U. 0	Kettering T. 2			
Kettering T. 1				
Crawley T. 5	Crawley T. 0	Wycombe W. ..2 5 1 1	Wycombe W. 1	
Worcester C. 2				
Barnet 0	Wycombe W. 2			
Wycombe W. 1				
Rhyl 1 2	Leek T. 2	Leek T. 2 5 1 0		
Leek T. 1 3				
King's Lynn 1 0	Macclesfield T. 1			
Macclesfield T. 1 3				

HALESOWEN TOWN WINS FA CHALLENGE VASE

Third round	Fourth round	Fifth round	Sixth round	Semi-finals	Final
Whickham 0	Waterloo Dock 0	Warrington T. 3	Warrington T. 3	Warrington T. . . .1 3 3	**HALESOWEN TOWN 3** *Scorers: Moss 2, Johnson*
Waterloo Dock 1					
Warrington T. 2	Warrington T. 2				
Wythenshawe Ath. 1					
Bridgnorth T. 0	Atherstone U. 4	Atherstone U. 1			
Atherstone U. 1					
Staveley Works 2 1	Bilston T. 1				
Bilston T. 2 2					
Hucknall CW. 3	Hucknall CW. 5	Hucknall CW. 1	Hucknall CW. 1		
Coventry Sp. 0					
Clitheroe 0 2	St Dominics 4				
St Dominics 0 4					
Blue Star 0 3	Blue Star 2	Blue Star 0			
Guiseley 0 0					
North Ferriby U. . . .3 2	North Ferriby U. 1				
Guisborough T. 3 0					
Coundon TT. 2	Coundon TT. 1 0	Tamworth 0	Halesowen T. 5	Halesowen T. 1 3 6	
W Allotment Celtic . . .1					
Borrowash Vic. 3 1	Tamworth 1 4				
Tamworth 3 2					
Brigg T. 1	Halesowen T. 8	Halesowen T. 2			
Halesowen T. 2					
Sheffield 2	Sheffield 1				
Ellesmere Port 0					
Camberley T. 0 1	Camberley T. 1	Camberley T. 3	Camberley T. 1		
Eastleigh 0 0					
Bracknell T. 4	Bracknell T. 0				
Southwick 1					
Thatcham T. 4	Thatcham T. 1	Thatcham T. 2			
Hungerford T. 2					
Northwood 2 0	Heybridge Swifts 0				
Heybridge Swifts . . .2 2					

SOUTHALL 0

At Wembley, att: 18,340

Southall 5	Southall 2	Southall 2	Southall 2	Southall 2 3
Hanwell T. 0	Barton R. 0	Abingdon T. 0	Stevenage Bor. 0	Wisbech T. 2 1
Cheshunt 0	Chippenham T. 5	Whyteleafe 1	Havant T. 1	
Barton R. 4	Abingdon T. 6	Stevenage Bor. 4	Wisbech T. 5	
Chippenham T. 3	Moreton T. 0	Buckingham T. 0		
Clevedon T. 0	Whyteleafe 2	Havant T. 1		
Cobham 0	Sharpness 0	Wisbech T. 1		
Abingdon T. 4	Stevenage Bor. 2	Sudbury T. 0		
Exmouth T. 0	Shillington 0			
Moreton T. 2	Buckingham T. 1			
Whyteleafe 3	Havant T. 10			
Steyning T. 2	Sholing Sports 0			
Torrington 1	Wisbech T. 1			
Sharpness 3	Hincley Ath. 0			
Beckton U. 0	Collier Row 1			
Stevenage Bor. 3	Sudbury T. 2			
Shillington 1				
Saffron Walden T. 0				
Buckingham T. 1				
Witham T. 0				
Havant T. 2				
AFC Totton 1				
Sholing Sports 3				
Newport IOW 1				
St Margaretsbury 0				
Wisbech T. 1				
Hinckley Ath. 3				
Hinckley T. 2				
Irthlingborough D. 0				
Collier Row 2				
Sudbury T. 3				
Braintree T. 1				

MANCHESTER CITY WIN FA YOUTH CHALLENGE CUP

Third round	Fourth round	Fifth round	Semi-finals	Final
Newcastle U. 1	Coventry C. 1	Coventry C. 0 2	Coventry C. 0 1	**Manchester U. 1 0**
Coventry C. 4				*First leg att: 7602*
Watford 2 3	Watford 0			
Colchester U. 2 1				
Ipswich T. 0	Bristol R. 1	Tottenham H. 0 1		
Bristol R. 2				
Tottenham H. 4	Tottenham H. 3			
West Ham U. 3				
Rotherham U. 1	Notts Co. 0	Manchester U. 3	Manchester U. 2 1	
Notts Co. 2				
Chesterfield 0	Manchester U. 3			
Manchester U. 6				
York C. 1	Sheffield U. 1	Sheffield U. 0		
Sheffield U. 2				
Chester C. 1 0	Port Vale 0			
Port Vale 1 3				
Millwall 4	Millwall 2	Millwall 1 1	Arsenal 1 1	**Manchester C. 1 2**
Newport Co. 1				*Second leg att: 18,158*
Southend U. 1	Southampton 0			
Southampton 2				
Luton T. 0 0	Arsenal 1	Arsenal 1 4		
Arsenal 0 2				
Wimbledon 1	Wimbledon 0			
Charlton Ath. 0				
Fulham 1	Fulham 1	Fulham 0	Manchester C. 0 2	
Birmingham C. 0				
Mansfield T. 1 1	Mansfield T. 0			
Sheffield W. 1 0				
Blackpool 0	Manchester C. 4	Manchester C. 3		
Manchester C. 1				
Leicester C. 2	Leicester C. 1			
Stoke C. 0				

AVENUE WIN FA SUNDAY CUP

Third round	Fourth round	Fifth round	Semi-finals	Final
Falcon 1	Canada 0	Fantail 1	Fantail ....1 1 *At Prescot Cables FC*	**Avenue** ....**1** *At Tranmere Rovers FC*
Canada 2				
Fantail 2	Fantail 1			
Winlaton West End ...1				
Whetley Lane 3	Murray Park 4	Murray Park 0		
Murray Park 4				
Sheffield House R. 0	Marston Sports 0			
Marston Sports 4				
Sunderland HP 0 2	Sunderland HP 2	Sunderland HP 1	Avenue ....1 3 *Replay at* *Tranmere R. FC*	
Northwood 0 0				
Lodge Cottrell 1	Lodge Cottrell 0			
Greenleys 0				
Eagle 2	Eagle 0	Avenue 3		
Brighams 0				
Dudley & Weetslade ..2	Avenue 2			
Avenue 3				
Old Horns 0	Inter Volante 4	Inter Volante 1	Leggatts Ath. ....1 *At Hemel Hempstead FC*	**Glenn Sports** ....0 *Attendance: 2552*
Inter Volante 2				
Halesowen Harriers ...4	Halesowen Har. 1			
Cork & Bottle 2				
Continental 1	Artois United 0	Leggatts Ath. 2		
Artois United 3				
Leggatts Ath. 4	Leggatts Ath. 1			
Ollis Transport Co. ...2				
Wharf Wanderers 2	Glenn Sports 1	Glenn Sports 4	Glenn Sports 4	
Glenn Sports 4				
Scruttons Social 4	Hobbies U. 0			
Hobbies United 6				
Beaufort 0	Dee Roof Vikings 1	Trinity 2		
Dee Rook Vikings 2				
Lee Chapel North 0	Trinity 2			
Trinity 2				

THE GOLA LEAGUE RESULTS

	Altrincham	Barnet	Barrow	Bath C.	Boston U.	Cheltenham	Dagenham	Dartford	Enfield
Altrincham	—	2–0	2–0	1–2	1–3	4–1	3–1	0–0	1–4
Barnet	2–2	—	4–1	1–0	3–0	2–2	4–1	2–0	0–1
Barrow	0–1	0–1	—	1–1	2–1	2–2	1–0	1–2	1–2
Bath C.	0–2	1–1	6–0	—	2–0	1–1	1–1	2–0	0–2
Boston U.	1–3	1–2	2–1	1–1	—	1–2	3–0	3–0	1–2
Cheltenham	2–0	2–1	2–0	1–2	2–1	—	2–2	3–1	2–0
Dagenham	1–3	2–1	3–0	0–1	2–2	1–3	—	2–1	0–2
Dartford	3–2	5–3	3–2	1–2	0–1	3–3	1–1	—	2–3
Enfield	1–1	1–0	4–0	3–1	3–0	1–0	3–1	1–0	—
Frickley Ath.	0–0	3–3	2–0	2–1	5–1	2–1	3–2	1–0	1–4
Kettering T.	2–2	1–1	4–2	2–0	3–1	2–1	0–2	2–2	2–1
Kidderminster H.	0–2	0–2	2–1	3–1	3–2	5–1	2–0	4–1	1–2
Maidstone U.	1–2	2–2	0–0	3–2	1–2	1–0	2–1	3–0	3–3
Northwich Vic.	1–2	0–1	0–1	1–2	3–4	3–1	0–1	2–0	2–2
Nuneaton Bor.	0–0	4–1	0–1	2–3	0–1	0–1	1–2	3–1	1–5
Runcorn	2–1	0–0	3–1	2–0	3–0	5–0	1–1	5–0	1–1
Scarborough	1–0	3–1	3–1	2–1	2–1	1–0	2–1	1–1	1–3
Stafford R.	1–1	0–0	1–0	1–0	2–1	2–0	3–1	5–1	1–1
Telford U.	2–1	2–2	3–1	1–0	2–1	3–0	2–1	2–1	2–2
Wealdstone	2–2	2–0	4–0	0–1	7–2	0–0	0–4	2–1	2–4
Weymouth	0–0	4–2	3–2	0–0	0–0	0–0	2–1	2–1	2–2
Wycombe W.	0–1	2–0	1–1	1–4	4–1	3–3	1–1	3–2	1–0

1985-86 SEASON

Frickley Ath.	Kettering T.	Kidderminster H.	Maidstone U.	Northwich Vic.	Nuneaton Bor.	Runcorn	Scarborough	Stratford R.	Telford U.	Wealdstone	Weymouth	Wycombe W.
1–0	2–2	2–1	1–0	2–1	7–4	1–1	2–0	1–3	1–0	1–0	3–1	4–3
1–2	3–0	0–1	3–3	1–0	0–1	1–2	1–0	0–2	1–2	1–0	2–2	0–1
2–2	1–0	3–4	1–1	1–2	2–0	0–4	2–4	0–1	1–0	1–1	3–4	1–1
1–2	1–1	2–4	1–1	0–0	0–2	0–1	0–0	0–1	3–0	2–3	2–2	3–1
0–3	4–1	2–1	2–2	3–0	3–2	2–1	2–1	1–1	2–2	1–0	5–0	1–1
1–1	5–1	2–6	2–1	2–0	5–3	1–1	5–1	2–0	1–1	1–2	0–1	4–2
0–0	1–0	0–1	0–0	1–0	3–2	2–3	0–0	1–1	1–4	0–2	2–2	1–1
1–2	0–2	5–1	1–1	2–0	0–1	0–1	1–1	3–3	2–1	1–2	1–1	1–0
3–1	1–1	2–2	1–3	1–0	3–2	2–0	4–0	3–1	4–0	1–0	4–4	2–3
—	3–0	3–1	2–0	1–0	2–2	3–1	2–1	3–0	3–1	2–1	1–0	2–2
2–0	—	2–2	2–0	2–1	1–4	0–0	0–0	0–1	4–0	2–1	0–2	4–1
1–0	0–0	—	3–1	2–2	2–1	2–4	5–1	1–1	3–0	3–1	1–2	8–2
3–2	0–0	2–1	—	0–1	5–1	1–1	1–1	2–4	4–4	0–1	0–0	1–1
2–3	0–0	0–0	1–0	—	0–3	1–1	0–0	2–0	0–1	2–2	0–1	4–0
0–1	0–3	0–3	1–0	1–3	—	1–0	3–1	3–0	1–1	0–0	3–0	3–0
2–2	0–1	0–2	3–0	2–3	3–1	—	0–0	3–0	1–0	1–1	1–2	2–1
2–3	2–3	3–5	2–0	0–0	2–1	1–1	—	2–4	3–1	0–1	1–1	1–2
0–0	0–0	3–2	2–1	1–2	2–0	1–1	0–3	—	0–3	2–1	2–3	1–1
2–1	2–2	0–1	2–4	4–0	1–1	2–3	1–0	0–0	—	2–1	4–1	3–1
2–0	3–1	0–3	3–2	0–0	1–0	1–1	0–3	2–3	1–1	—	1–0	2–0
2–3	1–0	1–2	2–0	2–2	2–0	5–2	4–1	1–1	5–2	4–2	—	1–1
1–3	0–0	2–5	2–2	1–1	2–0	0–1	2–1	2–4	1–2	1–0	0–3	—

MULTIPART LEAGUE RESULTS

(Formerly the Northern Premier League)

	Bangor	Burton A.	Buxton	Caernarvon	Chorley	Gainsborough Tr.	Gateshead	Goole T.	Horwich R.M.I.
Bangor C.	—	2–2	1–0	0–1	1–1	3–1	0–2	1–3	3–1
Burton A.	0–0	—	2–0	1–0	2–1	1–0	1–3	5–1	3–0
Buxton	2–0	1–0	—	1–3	1–0	0–0	1–5	2–2	1–0
Caernarvon	1–3	0–0	1–1	—	1–9	0–0	2–2	1–0	2–0
Chorley	0–4	0–5	0–0	1–1	—	0–2	1–1	4–0	1–3
Gainsborough Tr.	2–0	0–1	4–1	1–0	2–1	—	2–2	2–1	0–3
Gateshead	3–0	2–0	5–0	3–2	1–0	4–0	—	2–0	3–1
Goole T.	1–1	1–5	2–1	0–1	0–4	1–2	0–2	—	1–1
Horwich R.M.I.	1–2	2–1	2–2	1–0	0–0	2–1	2–1	4–0	—
Hyde U.	0–4	0–0	2–1	2–0	2–1	2–2	3–3	3–2	1–0
Macclesfield T.	4–0	2–1	2–1	7–2	1–1	0–1	1–0	2–1	7–2
Marine	1–1	1–3	2–3	3–1	3–1	3–0	3–1	1–0	1–0
Matlock T.	2–2	0–2	3–2	1–1	2–2	1–1	1–1	3–0	1–3
Morecambe	1–0	1–0	4–1	1–1	1–1	1–1	2–0	2–0	1–1
Mossley	0–0	3–3	2–1	1–0	2–2	2–2	0–0	1–1	3–2
Oswestry T.	0–0	3–1	0–0	0–0	2–0	1–1	0–1	0–1	1–0
Rhyl	3–1	1–0	3–0	3–2	4–1	0–0	2–3	1–1	0–1
South Liverpool	1–1	2–2	1–2	1–0	2–1	1–1	1–2	2–2	1–0
Southport	3–1	1–2	2–2	3–3	2–1	2–0	3–1	3–1	2–0
Witton A.	1–1	1–1	1–1	1–1	0–3	1–2	0–2	1–0	1–4
Workington	2–1	1–2	2–1	0–0	1–1	1–1	4–2	1–1	0–0
Worksop T.	1–1	1–1	2–2	1–0	2–2	3–0	1–2	0–1	2–1

1985-86

Hyde U.	Macclesfield T.	Marine	Matlock T.	Morecambe	Mossley	Oswestry T.	Rhyl	S. Liverpool	Southport	Witton A.	Workington	Worksop T.
0–1	0–0	1–2	3–2	0–0	1–0	4–0	1–1	2–1	2–3	1–0	1–1	1–0
0–0	1–2	1–1	2–1	1–1	2–2	0–3	2–1	1–0	2–3	3–2	2–0	0–1
3–2	1–2	0–2	6–2	2–4	0–3	4–2	2–0	0–0	3–2	1–2	1–1	1–1
2–1	1–2	3–1	1–0	3–3	2–1	5–2	1–1	0–0	3–2	0–0	2–2	1–1
2–2	1–4	0–1	1–1	0–2	0–1	3–1	2–1	2–1	1–1	0–0	2–0	2–1
2–1	3–1	1–1	4–3	3–0	3–0	2–0	6–2	2–3	5–0	1–1	2–2	1–0
1–1	1–3	1–1	2–2	4–2	2–0	2–2	5–4	1–0	3–1	2–0	0–2	2–0
1–3	0–0	0–0	2–0	1–2	2–0	2–1	0–3	1–1	1–5	1–1	0–1	2–3
1–4	2–0	2–3	3–1	2–1	0–1	2–1	2–1	0–1	1–1	0–1	0–3	1–3
—	0–1	1–3	2–0	0–0	2–0	0–1	3–0	2–2	0–2	2–2	2–2	3–1
2–3	—	0–1	3–2	0–2	0–1	2–3	0–0	2–2	0–1	1–1	1–1	1–2
3–0	4–0	—	1–3	1–0	2–0	2–0	2–3	0–1	2–3	3–1	1–0	1–2
1–1	0–2	0–0	—	1–0	4–4	2–3	1–1	2–1	2–1	1–2	2–1	4–2
1–1	5–1	0–0	0–1	—	0–2	2–0	2–2	1–1	2–1	4–1	0–0	1–0
2–2	5–1	1–1	2–2	1–1	—	1–0	1–3	0–2	1–2	0–2	1–2	3–1
2–2	2–4	0–0	3–0	0–0	0–0	—	2–3	2–1	2–4	2–0	0–1	1–1
3–3	1–0	0–2	2–2	4–2	0–2	7–2	—	1–1	1–3	2–4	1–3	0–1
0–1	0–0	1–2	1–0	0–0	2–2	0–0	1–2	—	1–2	2–0	0–1	0–2
2–0	0–2	0–0	2–2	0–3	1–1	0–3	0–1	1–2	—	1–2	2–2	0–0
3–2	3–2	0–1	1–1	1–2	5–1	3–1	2–0	1–1	1–1	—	2–1	1–0
3–1	3–0	0–0	1–0	0–0	1–2	3–3	0–2	0–0	2–2	1–3	—	0–1
1–0	4–2	0–1	1–0	0–2	1–1	0–0	2–1	0–2	2–0	3–0	1–2	—

SOUTHERN LEAGUE PREMIER

	Alvechurch	Aylesbury U.	Basingstoke T.	Bedworth U.	Chelmsford C.	Corby T.	Crawley T.
Alvechurch	—	0–0	1–1	0–0	4–2	4–1	2–4
Aylesbury U.	5–0	—	0–1	2–0	0–1	1–2	1–0
Basingstoke T.	0–2	0–1	—	0–3	1–0	0–4	2–1
Bedworth U.	0–3	1–2	0–1	—	0–3	2–2	2–1
Chelmsford C.	1–2	5–2	3–1	5–1	—	4–1	2–3
Corby T.	2–2	3–0	2–1	1–3	1–3	—	4–1
Crawley T.	5–2	3–2	4–0	1–0	3–0	2–2	—
Dudley T.	1–4	1–3	2–0	1–0	0–0	4–0	3–1
Fareham T.	3–3	2–2	3–1	0–1	0–0	0–2	0–2
Fisher Ath.	1–1	3–1	3–0	1–0	0–0	3–0	1–0
Folkestone	1–3	0–0	1–0	1–3	1–2	2–0	1–0
Gosport Bor.	1–1	0–3	3–2	3–0	0–0	1–0	2–1
Gravesend & Northfleet	1–0	0–0	0–1	0–1	1–1	2–1	0–6
King's Lynn	0–2	2–1	1–1	0–1	1–2	0–1	2–0
R.S. Southampton	0–2	0–0	2–1	2–2	0–0	0–4	2–0
Shepshed Charterhouse	2–0	1–0	2–0	0–1	1–2	0–0	4–1
Welling U.	3–1	2–2	5–0	2–1	3–0	5–1	2–1
Willenhall T.	4–0	1–1	1–2	2–1	0–3	2–0	5–2
Witney T.	2–1	2–1	0–1	1–1	0–3	1–1	1–2
Worcester C.	3–2	1–1	3–0	2–1	1–1	2–1	3–2

DIVISION RESULTS 1985-86

Dudley T.	Fareham T.	Fisher Ath.	Folkestone	Gosport Bor.	Gravesend & North.	King's Lynn	R.S. Southampton	Shepshed Charter	Welling U.	Willenhall T.	Witney T.	Worcester C.
5–2	1–1	1–1	1–0	4–1	3–1	3–2	3–0	4–1	0–3	1–0	2–1	1–0
2–1	2–4	4–1	0–2	2–0	1–0	1–0	1–1	3–1	1–3	3–2	0–2	1–1
2–4	2–0	1–1	2–1	2–1	1–1	0–3	2–4	3–2	0–1	2–1	2–0	0–1
2–1	1–1	2–2	2–1	0–1	2–0	2–1	4–1	1–2	0–0	0–1	1–1	2–1
0–3	1–1	2–1	2–1	3–3	1–1	0–1	1–0	1–0	2–0	4–1	3–1	5–1
1–0	6–1	2–1	3–2	1–1	1–2	2–2	2–4	2–1	1–3	2–1	0–1	2–3
3–1	1–0	1–0	1–1	3–0	3–0	2–1	0–0	6–2	3–3	2–2	4–1	1–3
—	4–1	3–2	1–1	1–0	2–0	0–0	0–1	2–0	0–3	3–1	3–4	1–4
0–2	—	1–2	1–1	4–2	0–0	0–0	0–0	0–1	1–4	2–0	1–0	1–0
2–0	4–0	—	4–2	4–2	3–0	2–0	2–3	2–1	1–3	0–1	2–3	1–0
1–0	2–2	1–4	—	1–0	2–1	2–1	3–1	0–1	1–4	1–1	3–3	3–3
1–2	1–4	0–2	1–3	—	1–0	5–4	3–0	1–2	0–1	0–0	0–2	3–1
4–1	1–2	1–1	1–1	4–0	—	1–0	1–0	0–2	0–3	1–0	0–3	0–1
1–0	1–0	2–0	2–1	0–0	2–0	—	2–0	1–3	0–0	1–1	1–0	0–0
3–1	3–0	2–4	1–2	2–1	0–2	0–0	—	0–1	1–3	1–1	4–0	1–1
2–1	2–1	0–1	0–2	2–1	3–1	0–1	2–1	—	1–3	2–0	4–1	0–1
2–1	3–0	2–0	4–2	3–0	2–1	3–0	4–0	1–0	—	0–0	6–1	1–2
4–1	1–1	1–1	0–0	1–1	1–1	2–0	1–2	4–0	1–1	—	3–0	1–0
0–3	3–2	0–2	0–2	1–1	0–0	2–1	2–1	0–2	2–3	0–2	—	1–3
2–2	0–0	1–2	1–4	0–1	3–0	2–2	3–1	3–1	3–1	2–1	3–2	—

SOUTHERN LEAGUE MIDLAND

	Banbury U.	Bilston	Bridgnorth T.	Bromsgrove R.	Coventry Sporting	Forest Green R.	Gloucester C.	Grantham
Banbury U.	—	0–2	0–2	1–3	2–0	1–0	0–2	0–1
Bilston	1–0	—	0–1	0–1	2–2	0–0	3–0	3–0
Bridgnorth T.	0–0	2–2	—	2–0	1–1	1–1	3–3	1–1
Bromsgrove R.	3–1	6–2	3–2	—	2–1	1–0	3–0	1–2
Coventry Sporting	0–0	3–1	1–1	3–2	—	1–0	3–0	2–0
Forest Green R.	1–1	1–1	1–1	4–3	3–0	—	2–4	1–2
Gloucester C.	5–1	0–3	1–2	2–2	1–1	0–1	—	0–2
Grantham	1–0	1–1	0–2	2–2	0–0	3–2	1–1	—
Hednesford T.	2–1	2–1	1–1	3–2	3–0	1–5	3–2	1–0
AP Leamington	0–1	2–1	0–1	0–1	0–0	3–1	2–1	0–2
Leicester U.	0–3	0–1	0–0	0–3	2–0	0–0	1–2	1–2
Merthyr Tydfil	1–1	1–0	1–0	3–2	2–0	2–3	3–1	2–0
Mile Oak R.	0–2	2–1	0–0	2–2	2–1	1–1	0–1	4–0
Moor Green	1–1	1–0	1–0	0–3	1–2	7–0	1–5	2–1
Oldbury U.	4–0	1–2	3–3	3–8	0–2	0–0	0–1	2–1
Rushden T.	3–0	2–2	1–3	0–2	2–0	1–0	1–2	1–1
Redditch U.	2–0	2–1	1–2	0–2	0–0	2–0	1–0	4–0
Stourbridge	0–0	1–1	1–1	0–1	2–2	0–1	1–2	4–0
Sutton Coldfield	1–1	3–3	1–1	3–4	1–1	2–0	1–1	5–1
VS Rugby	1–0	0–0	0–3	0–1	2–0	1–0	0–1	3–1
Wellingborough T.	1–2	3–1	0–0	0–2	1–1	2–1	2–3	1–2

DIVISION RESULTS 1985-86

Hednesford T.	AP Leamington	Leicester U.	Merthyr Tydfil	Mile Oak R.	Moor Green	Oldbury U.	Rushden T.	Redditch U.	Stourbridge	Sutton Coldfield	V.S. Rugby	Wellinboro' T.
0–2	2–1	1–0	0–0	2–0	3–0	3–1	0–1	1–5	1–3	2–1	0–1	4–3
3–0	2–0	1–0	2–0	5–2	4–1	0–0	3–3	3–2	0–1	1–0	0–0	1–2
4–2	6–0	3–2	1–1	0–0	4–2	0–3	0–2	0–1	1–3	0–1	0–3	1–1
2–1	2–0	1–0	1–1	4–0	2–1	5–2	4–1	2–0	2–1	1–0	1–1	3–0
2–2	2–2	0–2	3–0	0–1	4–1	0–1	0–2	0–1	2–2	2–0	0–0	0–1
3–0	3–0	4–2	2–1	1–3	1–3	2–0	2–2	0–2	2–0	1–0	0–2	2–0
1–0	2–3	1–3	2–2	0–0	4–1	1–0	4–0	2–2	1–1	1–1	0–0	1–1
2–1	5–2	0–2	2–3	1–0	1–2	0–1	1–2	1–0	2–0	2–0	0–0	2–0
—	3–1	0–3	1–2	4–1	4–0	5–2	0–1	1–3	2–3	1–1	0–0	3–2
4–1	—	1–0	0–2	1–2	1–5	2–1	3–2	0–3	1–1	0–3	0–1	2–0
1–1	0–0	—	4–1	2–0	0–3	1–0	1–1	0–3	0–4	0–0	0–1	3–2
1–0	3–0	0–0	—	3–1	2–0	3–1	2–1	3–0	0–0	1–3	3–0	0–0
1–5	0–2	1–1	0–1	—	4–0	4–1	1–4	2–3	1–3	0–6	2–1	4–2
2–2	2–0	1–3	0–0	1–3	—	6–2	2–2	1–2	0–3	0–5	2–3	3–1
2–2	3–3	2–3	0–4	0–1	2–4	—	3–2	1–3	1–2	0–1	2–1	3–1
0–0	1–0	2–0	4–1	2–3	6–4	3–1	—	1–6	0–3	4–1	1–0	1–4
2–1	1–1	0–1	0–3	0–2	1–1	1–0	6–2	—	1–0	0–0	2–1	2–3
1–1	4–2	0–1	3–0	3–3	3–0	1–1	3–0	1–2	—	1–1	0–1	0–1
1–3	2–1	1–0	0–0	1–0	5–0	5–1	1–3	0–2	1–1	—	2–2	0–0
4–1	1–0	1–1	2–1	1–1	1–1	0–0	3–2	2–1	0–0	1–0	—	0–0
3–2	4–0	1–1	0–1	5–2	1–0	1–0	2–0	1–1	0–2	2–0	2–0	—

P.F.A.86.87.—12

SOUTHERN LEAGUE SOUTHERN

	Andover	Ashford T.	Burnham & Hillingdon	Cambridge C.	Canterbury C.	Chatham T.	Corinthians	Dorchester T.
Andover	—	2–0	1–2	1–5	3–2	5–3	0–3	2–0
Ashford T.	2–1	—	2–0	1–1	1–1	3–2	0–4	3–0
Burnham & Hillingdon	2–2	2–3	—	2–5	1–0	0–0	0–2	1–2
Cambridge C.	6–1	1–1	1–0	—	4–3	4–0	2–2	3–0
Canterbury C.	0–0	1–0	3–1	2–2	—	1–1	3–0	3–1
Chatham T.	1–1	2–0	1–1	2–1	0–0	—	1–1	2–0
Corinthians	8–1	1–0	2–0	0–1	1–0	2–2	—	3–1
Dorchester T.	2–1	2–2	1–2	2–3	0–3	3–1	0–3	—
Dover Ath.	3–1	6–1	2–1	0–0	1–2	2–2	1–1	2–1
Dunstable	4–1	3–2	2–0	3–2	1–1	0–1	2–2	1–0
Erith & Belvedere	2–1	2–0	1–0	1–2	2–1	1–0	2–0	0–2
Hastings T.	1–1	1–1	6–0	2–3	2–0	3–0	2–1	3–3
Poole T.	4–0	1–0	0–1	3–0	3–0	2–4	1–2	2–0
Ruislip	1–3	4–3	3–5	0–1	1–1	2–2	4–1	4–1
Salisbury	1–1	2–0	2–0	0–2	3–1	2–1	4–2	3–0
Sheppey U.	3–0	3–0	0–2	0–0	1–1	2–1	2–1	3–0
Thanet U.	3–0	2–3	2–3	1–2	0–2	3–1	1–1	5–0
Tonbridge	1–1	4–1	3–0	0–3	3–0	4–2	3–1	1–1
Trowbridge T.	1–0	0–1	1–1	3–6	2–2	2–1	1–4	3–0
Waterlooville	3–1	1–1	0–1	0–0	0–1	1–0	1–2	4–0
Woodford T.	2–0	0–0	2–2	0–0	1–0	3–3	0–1	1–1

DIVISION RESULTS 1985-86

Dover Ath.	Dunstable	Erith & Belvedere	Hastings T.	Poole T.	Ruislip	Salisbury	Sheppey U.	Thanet U.	Tonbridge	Trowbridge T.	Waterlooville	Woodford T.
2–4	3–2	1–0	0–3	0–1	1–1	1–2	2–1	3–1	2–7	2–2	1–2	3–1
1–2	1–1	2–1	0–1	1–0	1–2	2–3	1–1	1–0	2–2	0–1	1–1	1–1
1–0	1–0	1–0	0–1	3–1	0–4	2–0	1–0	1–0	0–1	1–1	2–0	1–2
0–1	6–3	1–0	0–2	2–2	2–0	0–0	0–0	6–0	2–0	4–1	4–1	0–1
2–1	4–3	1–1	3–0	2–1	1–0	2–2	1–1	0–2	4–4	1–2	1–2	2–4
2–2	3–3	1–2	1–3	1–1	0–3	1–3	3–1	2–1	0–1	3–1	0–0	0–0
1–3	0–0	3–0	4–1	1–1	4–0	2–1	6–1	0–0	0–1	1–2	3–0	2–0
4–3	0–0	0–2	3–3	0–5	0–4	0–2	0–1	2–2	0–2	2–2	1–3	0–1
—	1–2	2–0	3–1	6–1	1–0	2–3	2–0	0–1	3–0	2–0	4–1	3–1
4–2	—	1–0	3–1	2–0	2–4	3–1	3–0	0–2	2–2	1–0	4–2	2–0
0–2	1–1	—	0–2	0–0	2–1	0–0	0–0	2–1	1–1	1–0	2–0	3–2
3–1	2–2	0–0	—	2–1	3–0	5–3	4–0	2–1	2–0	3–0	2–1	2–0
2–2	1–0	1–2	0–2	—	2–0	2–1	1–3	3–1	1–3	0–1	2–3	1–3
1–4	2–2	2–0	2–3	2–2	—	1–2	3–3	2–1	0–1	3–1	3–0	0–2
3–2	3–1	1–1	3–3	2–0	5–1	—	4–0	4–0	4–1	2–2	2–0	3–0
0–5	0–1	3–0	2–0	2–1	0–1	2–0	—	2–0	1–1	1–3	1–0	1–0
1–3	3–2	0–0	2–0	0–1	0–1	1–2	1–1	—	3–1	2–2	3–1	2–1
0–2	1–1	1–1	1–1	3–1	0–1	4–1	0–0	1–1	—	2–1	1–1	2–0
1–1	4–0	1–1	3–2	1–1	0–1	1–1	1–0	1–4	2–1	—	1–2	4–1
1–2	2–1	1–0	1–2	3–2	3–1	0–1	1–0	1–3	2–0	1–1	—	4–0
5–1	0–2	1–1	2–2	2–1	1–2	2–3	2–1	3–2	0–1	1–1	1–2	—

VAUXHALL-OPEL LEAGUE PREMIER

	Barking	Billericay T.	Bishops Stortford	Bognor Regis T.	Carshalton Ath.	Croydon	Dulwich Hamlet	Epsom & Ewell	Farnborough T.
Barking	—	0–0	2–2	0–2	3–0	1–2	1–1	2–1	2–3
Billericay T.	2–1	—	0–0	3–3	3–3	1–1	2–1	0–0	1–2
Bishops Stortford	2–1	0–0	—	4–0	2–1	2–1	0–1	2–1	0–1
Bognor Regis T.	0–1	1–0	1–1	—	6–0	0–2	3–1	1–1	0–1
Carshalton Ath.	3–1	1–2	1–2	1–2	—	0–2	2–0	2–1	1–0
Croydon	0–1	2–1	2–0	2–0	2–1	—	1–1	3–1	3–2
Dulwich Hamlet	1–1	1–3	2–5	3–1	2–1	1–1	—	5–3	2–1
Epsom & Ewell	3–0	0–2	0–2	1–0	2–2	1–2	0–3	—	0–1
Farnborough T.	0–0	4–0	1–0	2–1	4–2	0–2	6–1	2–3	—
Harrow Bor.	0–0	1–1	3–1	3–2	3–2	2–1	3–0	3–0	1–3
Hayes	1–1	2–2	0–0	1–2	1–1	0–0	0–2	0–0	2–0
Hendon	2–1	4–2	1–1	1–0	2–3	0–2	1–3	3–0	1–5
Hitchin T.	0–0	2–2	1–1	2–1	1–1	1–1	1–2	2–1	1–1
Kingstonian	2–0	2–2	1–1	2–1	1–0	0–2	1–2	2–2	2–2
Slough T.	2–0	4–3	1–0	1–0	2–1	0–0	1–2	4–4	2–3
Sutton U.	1–1	3–2	4–1	6–0	2–2	3–2	6–1	3–1	1–1
Tooting & Mitcham U.	3–1	3–2	1–2	1–0	2–2	0–4	3–4	2–2	2–2
Walthamstow Ave.	3–2	2–0	1–3	5–2	2–2	1–0	7–2	2–2	0–5
Windsor & Eton	1–0	2–3	0–0	3–2	3–3	2–0	1–0	2–1	1–2
Wokingham T.	1–1	2–0	2–2	1–2	2–0	2–3	1–2	3–1	2–1
Worthing	0–1	2–1	6–2	2–2	3–1	2–0	2–3	2–3	1–1
Yeovil T.	3–1	1–0	2–0	3–2	5–1	5–0	3–1	3–0	1–0

DIVISION RESULTS 1985-86

Harrow Bor.	Hayes	Hendon	Hitchin T.	Kingstonian	Slough T.	Sutton U.	Tooting-Mitcham U.	Walthamstow Ave.	Windsor & Eton	Wokingham T.	Worthing	Yeovil T.
2–0	1–0	2–0	1–1	1–2	4–3	0–2	1–2	1–0	2–2	1–2	3–0	0–0
1–1	1–2	1–4	1–0	1–3	2–3	1–2	3–4	0–2	3–1	3–1	2–3	0–2
1–0	0–2	3–2	2–0	2–0	0–3	0–6	2–1	2–0	2–5	3–2	0–1	0–1
4–1	3–0	1–1	0–2	3–3	3–0	2–0	2–1	3–2	0–1	2–1	0–3	3–1
0–1	2–0	1–1	2–3	0–0	1–1	1–4	1–2	1–1	2–1	1–0	3–1	1–1
1–3	1–0	1–1	2–0	4–1	1–0	1–0	0–4	2–3	5–2	2–0	3–4	4–1
1–4	1–0	0–0	1–0	2–3	0–1	1–2	2–2	1–1	1–2	1–0	2–2	1–1
1–3	1–0	5–3	3–3	3–2	2–1	2–2	1–2	1–2	2–3	2–4	3–3	2–2
6–0	1–1	5–0	6–0	0–0	2–1	3–2	2–3	3–2	2–1	0–1	3–2	1–2
—	1–0	3–2	2–0	1–3	4–2	0–3	1–1	2–2	4–1	1–1	3–2	3–2
2–1	—	1–1	1–1	4–1	0–1	1–1	2–1	2–1	0–0	3–1	0–3	0–1
1–3	0–0	—	2–3	1–1	1–1	1–2	1–1	1–2	2–0	1–2	2–2	1–2
3–2	2–2	2–2	—	0–0	0–1	2–1	0–0	2–0	1–2	0–2	4–1	1–3
1–0	0–0	3–0	2–0	—	1–1	2–4	2–1	2–1	2–3	2–2	1–1	0–1
0–0	0–2	1–4	1–2	3–2	—	0–1	4–1	1–0	3–1	1–1	3–1	2–3
2–0	3–1	3–0	4–1	2–0	4–1	—	0–0	3–3	5–0	5–0	0–0	3–1
1–4	2–0	0–1	1–0	1–1	2–3	1–5	—	2–2	1–3	3–2	4–2	0–2
3–2	0–0	0–2	3–3	0–1	1–2	0–1	0–0	—	4–1	0–0	4–2	2–2
0–3	0–0	4–0	1–4	1–0	0–0	0–3	2–1	1–0	—	0–3	1–0	2–2
1–2	0–2	3–3	3–0	0–0	4–0	1–3	3–1	2–2	2–0	—	3–3	2–1
4–0	0–0	0–2	2–1	0–1	2–1	0–2	0–2	2–2	3–1	1–2	—	2–5
2–2	2–1	2–1	3–1	1–2	3–4	2–0	3–0	2–1	2–1	3–0	5–0	—

FOOTBALL LEAGUE DIVISION ONE

Subject to alteration; copyright of the Football League Limited, and may not be reproduced in

	Arsenal	Aston Villa	Charlton Ath.	Chelsea	Coventry C.	Everton	Leicester C.	Liverpool	Luton T.	Manchester C.
Arsenal	—	2-5	11-4	25-10	17-1	28-3	20-4	7-2	20-12	22-11
Aston Villa	29-11	—	26-12	15-11	28-3	18-4	1-11	21-2	3-9	4-4
Charlton Ath	1-11	20-4	—	28-3	20-9	11-10	18-10	20-12	2-5	27-12
Chelsea	7-3	27-12	4-10	—	2-9	4-4	2-5	9-5	6-9	18-10
Coventry C.	25-8	4-10	28-2	14-2	—	30-8	6-12	2-5	1-1	20-12
Everton	4-10	1-1	21-3	8-11	7-2	—	27-12	22-11	9-5	2-5
Leicester C.	26-12	11-4	14-3	29-11	4-5	15-11	—	3-9	23-8	28-3
Liverpool	30-8	27-9	13-9	13-12	29-11	25-4	14-2	—	7-3	25-8
Luton T.	13-9	14-2	29-11	3-1	18-4	13-12	24-1	25-10	—	27-9
Manchester C.	25-4	8-11	15-11	14-3	6-9	29-11	4-10	17-1	21-2	—
Manchester U.	24-1	9-5	30-8	27-9	1-11	28-2	20-12	20-4	18-10	7-3
Newcastle U.	18-10	7-3	4-5	25-4	3-1	26-12	4-4	23-8	7-2	11-10
Norwich C.	13-12	28-2	3-1	24-1	25-4	4-5	25-8	11-4	21-3	14-2
Nottingham F.	27-9	13-9	25-8	28-2	4-4	24-1	21-3	1-1	27-12	6-12
Oxford U.	28-2	20-12	27-9	25-8	11-10	14-2	9-5	14-3	6-12	13-9
Q.P.R.	4-5	30-8	13-12	18-4	26-12	3-1	27-9	8-11	11-4	28-2
Sheffield W.	14-2	6-12	24-1	30-8	25-10	25-8	13-9	27-12	22-11	20-4
Southampton	15-11	21-3	25-4	26-12	13-12	18-10	7-3	20-9	17-1	1-11
Tottenham H.	3-1	24-1	18-4	13-9	15-11	27-9	28-2	21-3	4-10	30-8
Watford	21-3	18-10	8-11	11-4	21-2	7-3	22-11	6-12	20-4	1-1
West Ham U.	4-4	22-11	25-10	11-10	23-8	1-11	1-1	6-9	20-9	9-5
Wimbledon	18-4	25-8	14-2	4-5	14-3	13-9	30-8	4-10	8-11	24-1

FIXTURES 1986-87

whole or part without their consent.

Manchester U.	Newcastle U.	Norwich C.	Nottingham F.	Oxford U.	Q.P.R.	Sheffield W.	Southampton	Tottenham H.	Watford	West Ham U.	Wimbledon
23-8	14-3	9-5	21-2	20-9	6-12	2-9	27-12	6-9	11-10	8-11	1-1
13-12	25-10	20-9	3-1	6-9	7-2	4-5	11-10	23-8	14-3	25-4	17-1
7-2	6-12	6-9	17-1	21-2	9-5	23-8	22-11	1-1	4-4	7-3	2-9
21-2	22-11	23-8	20-9	17-1	1-1	7-2	20-4	20-12	1-11	21-3	6-12
11-4	13-9	22-11	8-11	21-3	20-4	7-3	9-5	27-12	27-9	24-1	18-10
20-9	20-4	6-12	23-8	2-9	6-9	17-1	14-3	21-2	25-10	11-4	20-12
6-9	8-11	17-1	11-10	13-12	21-2	3-1	25-10	20-9	25-4	18-4	7-2
26-12	24-1	1-11	18-4	18-10	4-4	15-11	28-2	11-10	4-5	3-1	28-3
14-3	30-8	11-10	15-11	4-5	1-11	25-4	25-8	28-3	26-12	28-2	4-4
25-10	21-3	3-9	4-5	3-1	20-9	26-12	11-4	7-2	18-4	13-12	23-8
—	1-1	27-12	28-3	4-4	22-11	11-10	13-9	6-12	14-2	25-8	2-5
18-4	—	21-2	13-12	1-11	3-9	6-9	28-3	17-1	15-11	29-11	20-9
15-11	27-9	—	26-12	29-11	4-10	18-4	30-8	8-11	13-9	18-10	7-3
4-10	9-5	20-4	—	7-3	18-10	1-11	20-12	2-5	30-8	14-2	22-11
8-11	11-4	2-5	25-10	—	27-12	28-3	1-1	22-11	24-1	30-8	20-4
25-4	14-2	28-3	14-3	15-11	—	29-11	24-1	25-10	25-8	13-9	11-10
21-3	20-12	1-1	11-4	4-10	2-5	—	8-11	14-3	28-2	27-9	9-5
3-1	4-10	7-2	6-9	18-4	23-8	4-4	—	2-9	29-11	4-5	21-2
4-5	25-8	4-4	29-11	25-4	7-3	18-10	14-2	—	13-12	26-12	1-11
2-9	27-12	20-12	7-2	23-8	17-1	20-9	2-5	9-5	—	4-10	6-9
17-1	2-5	14-3	2-9	7-2	20-12	21-2	6-12	20-4	28-3	—	27-12
29-11	28-2	25-10	25-4	26-12	21-3	13-12	27-9	11-4	3-1	15-11	—

FOOTBALL LEAGUE DIVISION TWO

Subject to alteration; copyright of the Football League Limited, and may not be reproduced in

	Barnsley	Birmingham C.	Blackburn R.	Bradford C.	Brighton & H.A.	Crystal Palace	Derby Co.	Grimsby T.	Huddersfield T.	Hull C.
Barnsley	—	28-3	1-11	11-10	14-3	23-8	15-11	21-2	4-5	18-4
Birmingham C.	4-10	—	6-12	25-8	14-2	18-10	30-8	2-5	13-9	28-2
Blackburn R.	11-4	4-5	—	25-10	25-4	20-9	18-4	17-1	26-12	15-11
Bradford C.	21-3	3-1	7-3	—	4-5	3-9	26-12	7-2	15-11	25-4
Brighton & H.A.	18-10	3-9	22-11	6-12	—	20-4	7-3	6-9	4-4	1-11
Crystal Palace	24-1	14-3	28-2	14-2	26-12	—	3-1	8-11	25-8	13-12
Derby Co.	27-12	7-2	1-1	20-4	25-10	6-9	—	20-12	28-3	11-10
Grimsby T.	27-9	29-11	25-8	30-8	3-1	4-4	13-9	—	18-4	4-5
Huddersfield T.	6-12	17-1	20-4	27-12	8-11	20-12	4-10	1-1	—	25-10
Hull C.	1-1	20-9	27-12	22-11	11-4	9-5	21-3	6-12	7-3	—
Ipswich T.	22-11	21-2	2-5	14-3	11-10	27-12	4-4	23-8	1-11	28-3
Leeds U	14-2	25-4	24-1	28-2	13-12	11-10	29-11	7-3	3-1	27-9
Millwall	30-8	15-11	27-9	13-9	18-4	28-3	28-2	11-4	13-12	25-8
Oldham Ath	25-8	4-4	9-5	20-12	27-9	22-11	24-1	20-4	28-2	30-8
Plymouth Arg.	28-2	18-4	14-2	24-1	13-9	1-11	13-12	21-3	25-4	3-1
Portsmouth	20-12	11-10	13-9	8-11	24-1	6-12	25-8	22-11	27-9	14-2
Reading	8-11	26-12	4-10	11-4	15-11	21-2	4-5	3-9	29-11	14-3
Sheffield U	7-3	6-9	4-4	28-3	29-11	17-1	25-4	20-9	18-10	26-12
Shrewsbury T.	13-9	13-12	30-8	27-9	25-8	7-3	18-10	4-10	14-2	29-11
Stoke C	20-4	23-8	18-10	2-5	28-3	7-2	1-11	9-5	11-10	4-4
Sunderland	9-5	25-10	20-12	1-1	30-8	2-5	14-2	27-12	24-1	13-9
W.B.A.	2-5	1-11	21-3	9-5	28-2	1-1	27-9	18-10	30-8	24-1

FIXTURES 1986-87

whole or part without their consent.

Ipswich T.	Leeds U.	Millwall	Oldham Ath.	Plymouth Arg.	Portsmouth	Reading	Sheffield U.	Shrewsbury T.	Stoke C.	Sunderland	W.B.A.
25-4	2-9	7-2	3-1	20-9	6-9	4-4	25-10	17-1	26-12	13-12	29-11
27-9	22-11	27-12	8-11	1-1	21-3	20-4	20-12	9-5	24-1	7-3	11-4
29-11	23-8	21-2	13-12	2-9	3-1	28-3	8-11	7-2	14-3	6-9	11-10
18-10	20-9	17-1	6-9	23-8	4-4	1-11	4-10	21-2	29-11	18-4	13-12
21-3	9-5	1-1	21-2	17-1	23-8	27-12	2-5	20-12	4-10	7-2	20-9
15-11	21-3	4-10	25-4	11-4	4-5	27-9	13-9	25-10	30-8	29-11	18-4
8-11	2-5	20-9	23-8	9-5	17-1	6-12	22-11	14-3	11-4	3-9	21-2
24-1	25-10	1-11	26-12	11-10	25-4	14-2	28-2	28-3	13-12	15-11	14-3
11-4	6-9	9-5	20-9	22-11	21-2	2-5	14-3	2-9	21-3	23-8	7-2
4-10	21-2	20-12	7-2	6-9	2-9	18-10	20-4	2-5	8-11	17-1	23-8
—	1-1	20-4	2-9	20-12	7-2	9-5	6-12	6-9	25-10	20-9	17-1
18-4	—	4-4	15-11	28-3	19-10	13-9	30-8	1-11	25-8	26-12	4-5
26-12	8-11	—	14-3	25-10	29-11	24-1	14-2	11-10	3-1	4-5	25-4
14-2	27-12	18-10	—	2-5	1-11	7-3	1-1	6-12	13-9	11-10	28-3
25-8	4-10	7-3	29-11	—	26-12	30-8	27-9	4-4	4-5	18-10	15-11
30-8	14-3	2-5	11-4	20-4	—	1-1	9-5	27-12	28-2	28-3	25-10
13-12	17-1	23-8	25-10	7-2	18-4	—	21-3	20-9	25-4	3-1	6-9
4-5	7-2	2-9	18-4	21-2	13-12	11-10	—	23-8	15-11	1-11	3-1
3-1	11-4	21-3	4-5	8-11	15-11	28-2	24-1	—	18-4	25-4	26-12
7-3	20-12	6-9	17-1	6-12	20-9	22-11	27-12	1-1	—	21-2	2-9
28-2	20-4	6-12	21-3	14-3	4-10	25-8	11-4	22-11	27-9	—	8-11
13-9	6-12	22-11	4-10	27-12	7-3	20-12	25-8	20-4	14-2	4-4	—

FOOTBALL LEAGUE DIVISION THREE

Subject to alteration; copyright of the Football League Limited, and may not be reproduced in

	Blackpool	Bolton W.	Bournemouth	Brentford	Bristol C.	Bristol R.	Bury	Carlisle U.	Chester C.	Chesterfield
Blackpool	—	17-3	25-4	3-1	1-11	21-2	13-12	6-9	4-5	23-8
Bolton W.	21-10	—	31-1	3-3	25-4	17-1	26-12	18-4	25-10	30-9
Bournemouth	20-12	13-9	—	10-1	27-9	20-4	14-3	8-11	16-9	22-11
Brentford	22-11	1-11	23-8	—	17-3	27-12	30-9	7-2	4-4	1-1
Bristol C.	3-3	20-12	21-2	21-10	—	1-1	23-8	20-9	28-3	31-1
Bristol R.	27-9	30-8	26-12	4-5	18-4	—	8-11	7-3	3-1	4-10
Bury	9-5	20-4	18-10	28-2	10-1	4-4	—	17-3	30-8	2-5
Carlisle U.	24-1	1-1	4-4	16-9	14-2	25-10	21-10	—	10-1	9-5
Chester C.	27-12	7-3	7-2	8-11	4-10	22-11	17-1	23-8	—	20-12
Chesterfield	10-1	28-2	3-1	18-4	13-9	28-3	29-11	13-12	25-4	—
Darlington	1-1	24-1	4-10	14-2	29-2	3-3	11-4	21-3	27-9	27-12
Doncaster R	13-9	27-12	17-3	30-8	16-9	2-5	21-3	4-10	28-2	20-4
Fulham	30-8	16-9	4-5	13-9	8-11	21-10	25-10	3-1	24-1	11-4
Gillingham	4-11	9-5	21-3	27-9	30-8	20-12	4-10	18-10	14-2	1-11
Mansfield T.	25-10	22-11	20-9	11-10	11-4	31-1	7-2	21-2	14-3	6-9
Middlesbrough	11-10	4-11	1-11	25-4	7-3	7-2	6-9	26-12	29-11	20-9
Newport Co.	2-5	4-4	17-1	28-3	18-10	9-5	21-2	30-9	11-10	7-3
Notts Co.	14-3	28-3	6-9	11-4	29-11	30-9	4-5	25-4	18-4	21-2
Port Vale	28-2	14-2	29-11	24-1	26-12	14-3	3-3	11-4	13-12	21-3
Rotherham U.	4-4	18-10	13-2	29-11	3-1	20-9	31-1	4-5	4-11	7-2
Swindon T.	16-9	10-1	18-4	26-12	13-12	4-11	3-1	29-11	13-9	18-10
Walsall	28-3	11-10	4-11	25-10	4-5	23-8	25-4	31-1	3-3	17-1
Wigan Ath.	14-2	27-9	7-3	13-12	24-1	11-10	18-4	1-11	26-12	17-3
York C	20-4	2-5	30-9	14-3	21-3	6-9	20-9	17-1	21-10	8-11

FIXTURES 1986-87

whole or part without their consent.

Darlington	Doncaster R.	Fulham	Gillingham	Mansfield T.	Middlesbrough	Newport Co.	Notts Co.	Port Vale	Rotherham U.	Swindon	Walsall	Wigan Ath.	York C.
18-4	31-1	17-1	11-4	7-3	21-3	29-11	18-10	30-9	8-11	7-2	4-10	20-9	26-12
6-9	4-5	7-2	13-12	3-1	11-4	8-11	4-10	20-9	14-3	23-8	21-3	21-2	29-11
28-3	21-10	27-12	11-10	14-2	3-3	30-8	24-1	2-5	9-5	1-1	11-4	25-10	28-2
20-9	17-1	31-1	21-2	21-3	20-12	4-10	4-11	6-9	2-5	20-4	7-3	9-5	18-10
30-9	7-2	4-4	17-1	4-11	25-10	14-3	2-5	20-4	22-11	9-5	27-12	6-9	11-10
1-11	29-11	18-3	25-4	13-9	17-9	13-12	28-2	18-10	14-2	11-4	10-1	23-3	24-1
4-11	11-10	7-3	28-3	16-9	24-1	27-9	27-12	1-11	13-9	22-11	20-12	1-1	14-2
11-10	28-3	22-11	14-3	27-9	20-4	28-2	20-12	4-11	27-12	2-5	13-9	3-3	30-8
21-2	1-10	6-9	20-9	18-10	2-5	21-3	1-1	9-5	11-4	31-1	1-11	20-4	18-3
4-5	26-12	4-11	3-3	24-1	14-2	25-10	27-9	11-10	16-9	14-3	30-8	21-10	4-4
—	14-3	2-5	21-10	30-8	8-11	16-9	13-9	20-12	20-4	25-10	9-5	22-11	10-1
18-10	—	1-11	8-11	10-1	9-5	14-2	7-3	22-11	1-1	20-12	24-1	11-4	27-9
29-11	3-3	—	26-12	13-12	27-9	18-4	14-2	28-3	10-1	11-10	28-2	14-3	25-4
17-3	4-4	20-4	—	28-2	13-9	10-1	22-11	7-3	24-1	27-12	1-1	2-5	16-9
17-1	23-8	9-5	30-9	—	27-12	21-10	20-4	1-1	3-3	8-11	2-5	20-12	28-3
4-4	13-12	21-2	31-1	4-5	—	3-1	17-3	23-8	28-3	30-9	18-10	17-1	18-4
7-2	20-9	1-1	23-8	17-3	22-11	—	1-11	27-12	20-12	6-9	20-4	31-1	4-11
31-1	25-10	20-9	3-1	26-12	21-10	3-3	—	7-2	11-10	17-1	8-11	23-8	13-12
25-4	3-1	4-10	25-10	18-4	10-1	4-5	16-9	—	30-8	21-10	27-9	8-11	13-9
26-12	18-4	23-8	6-9	1-11	4-10	25-4	21-3	17-1	—	21-2	17-3	30-9	7-3
7-3	25-4	2-13	4-5	4-4	28-2	24-1	30-8	17-3	27-9	—	14-2	4-10	1-11
13-12	6-9	30-9	18-4	29-11	14-3	26-12	4-4	21-2	21-10	20-9	—	7-2	3-1
3-1	4-11	18-10	29-11	25-4	30-8	13-9	10-1	4-4	28-2	28-3	16-9	—	4-5
23-8	21-2	20-12	7-2	4-10	1-1	11-4	9-5	31-1	25-10	3-3	22-11	27-12	—

FOOTBALL LEAGUE DIVISION FOUR

Subject to alteration; copyright of the Football League Limited, and may not be reproduced in

	Aldershot	Burnley	Cambridge U.	Cardiff C.	Colchester U.	Crewe Alex.	Exeter C.	Halifax T.	Hartlepool U.	Hereford U.	Lincoln C.
Aldershot	—	11-10	21-10	9-5	27-12	20-12	2-5	10-1	25-10	3-3	13-9
Burnley	21-3	—	4-4	20-12	4-11	27-12	7-3	27-9	13-9	24-1	22-11
Cambridge U	17-3	8-11	—	2-5	20-4	1-11	13-9	30-8	24-1	9-5	27-9
Cardiff C	13-12	25-4	9-11	—	14-3	4-10	14-2	3-3	10-1	27-9	16-9
Colchester U	4-5	11-4	26-12	18-10	—	17-3	30-8	29-11	16-9	28-2	10-1
Crewe Alex	25-4	4-5	3-3	28-3	21-10	—	16-9	25-10	28-2	30-8	11-4
Exeter C	29-11	25-10	31-1	20-9	17-1	7-2	—	11-4	22-10	14-3	11-10
Halifax T	23-8	21-2	17-1	1-11	2-5	7-3	4-11	—	20-4	20-12	1-1
Hartlepool U	7-3	31-1	6-9	23-8	7-2	1-10	18-3	26-12	—	11-10	28-3
Hereford U	1-11	6-9	13-12	21-2	1-10	17-1	18-10	25-4	21-3	—	8-11
Lincoln T	31-1	3-1	21-2	7-2	23-8	4-11	21-3	18-4	4-10	4-4	—
Northampton T	4-10	22-10	14-3	27-12	1-1	2-5	22-11	28-2	4-3	25-10	20-12
Orient	26-12	13-12	18-4	17-3	4-4	21-3	10-1	3-1	27-9	14-2	28-2
Peterborough U	6-9	4-3	3-1	1-10	21-2	20-9	4-4	13-12	14-3	28-3	25-10
Preston N.E.	18-10	28-3	11-10	4-11	9-5	20-4	1-11	16-9	27-12	13-9	24-1
Rochdale	3-1	18-4	25-4	17-1	20-9	23-8	4-10	4-5	8-11	21-10	14-3
Scunthorpe U	7-2	17-1	30-9	7-3	22-11	6-9	20-12	8-11	1-1	2-5	27-12
Southend U	18-4	29-11	4-5	4-4	11-10	18-10	28-2	24-1	30-8	16-9	14-2
Stockport Co	4-4	14-3	28-3	22-11	25-10	1-1	24-1	14-2	2-5	3-11	20-4
Swansea C	30-9	7-2	4-11	20-4	20-12	21-2	1-1	28-3	22-11	27-12	9-5
Torquay U	20-9	23-8	7-2	1-1	31-1	9-5	20-4	11-10	11-4	22-11	21-10
Tranmere R	21-2	29-9	20-9	31-1	6-9	22-11	9-5	14-3	20-12	1-1	2-3
Wolverhampton W	17-1	20-9	23-8	6-9	3-3	31-1	27-12	21-10	9-5	20-4	2-5
Wrexham	4-11	26-12	25-10	11-10	28-3	4-4	27-9	13-9	14-2	10-1	30-8

FIXTURES 1986-87

whole or part without their consent.

Northampton T.	Orient	Peterborough U.	Preston N.E.	Rochdale	Scunthorpe U.	Southend U.	Stockport Co.	Swansea C.	Torquay U.	Tranmere R.	Wolverhampton W.	Wrexham
28-3	20-4	24-1	14-3	22-11	16-9	1-1	8-11	28-2	14-2	27-9	30-8	11-4
17-3	9-5	1-11	4-10	1-1	30-8	2-5	18-10	16-9	10-1	28-2	14-2	20-4
18-10	1-1	22-11	21-3	20-12	28-2	27-12	4-10	11-4	16-9	14-2	10-1	7-3
4-5	21-10	28-2	11-4	30-8	25-10	8-11	3-1	26-12	18-4	13-9	24-1	21-3
18-4	8-11	27-9	13-12	14-2	3-1	21-3	7-3	25-4	13-9	24-1	1-11	4-10
29-11	11-10	14-2	26-12	10-1	24-1	14-3	18-4	27-9	13-12	3-1	13-9	8-11
3-1	23-8	8-11	4-3	28-3	25-4	1-10	6-9	18-4	26-12	13-12	4-5	21-2
30-9	22-11	9-5	7-2	27-12	4-4	6-9	20-9	4-10	21-3	18-10	17-3	31-1
1-11	21-12	18-10	4-5	4-4	18-4	17-1	29-11	3-1	5-11	25-4	13-12	20-9
7-3	20-9	4-10	31-1	18-3	29-11	7-2	11-4	4-5	3-1	18-4	26-12	23-8
25-4	30-9	7-3	6-9	18-10	4-5	20-9	26-12	13-12	17-3	1-11	29-11	17-1
—	11-4	13-9	8-11	24-1	10-1	20-4	21-3	14-2	30-8	17-9	27-9	9-5
4-11	—	30-8	25-4	16-9	13-9	4-10	1-11	24-1	4-5	29-11	7-3	18-10
31-1	17-1	—	29-11	1-10	26-12	23-8	4-5	22-10	25-4	5-11	18-4	7-2
4-4	20-12	2-5	—	7-3	14-2	22-11	17-3	30-8	27-9	10-1	28-2	1-1
6-9	7-2	21-3	25-10	—	13-12	21-12	31-1	3-3	29-11	26-12	11-4	30-9
23-8	31-1	20-4	20-9	9-5	—	11-4	21-2	21-3	18-10	17-3	4-10	1-11
26-12	28-3	10-1	3-1	27-9	4-11	—	13-12	13-9	1-11	7-3	25-4	17-3
11-10	2-3	27-12	20-10	13-9	27-9	9-5	—	10-1	28-2	30-8	15-9	20-12
20-9	6-9	17-3	17-1	1-11	11-10	31-1	23-8	—	7-3	4-4	18-10	2-5
17-1	27-12	20-12	21-2	2-5	14-3	3-3	30-9	25-10	—	28-3	8-11	6-9
7-2	2-5	11-4	23-8	20-4	20-10	25-10	17- 1	8-11	4-10	—	21-3	27-12
21-2	25-10	1-1	30-9	4-11	28-3	20-12	7-2	14-3	4-4	11-10	—	22-11
13-12	14-3	16-9	18-4	28-2	3-3	21-10	25-4	29-11	24-1	4-5	3-1	—

GM VAUXHALL CONFERENCE FIXTURES 1986-87

These fixtures are the copyright of the GM Vauxhall Conference and must not be used or copied without prior permission.

1986

Saturday 16th August
Altrincham v Bath City
Dagenham v Northwich Victoria
Enfield v Gateshead United
Frickley Athletic v Maidstone United
Kidderminster Harriers v Barnet
Nuneaton Borough v Scarborough
Runcorn v Boston United
Sutton United v Telford United
Wealdstone v Stafford Rangers
Welling United v Cheltenham Town
Weymouth v Kettering Town

Monday 18th August
Dagenham v Weymouth
Kidderminster Harriers v Altrincham

Tuesday 19th August
Barnet v Welling United
Runcorn v Gateshead
Stafford Rangers v Nuneaton Borough
Sutton United v Enfield
Telford United v Cheltenham Town

Wednesday 20th August
Kettering Town v Bath City
Maidstone United v Wealdstone
Northwich Victoria v Frickley Athletic
Scarborough v Boston United

Saturday 23rd August
Bath City v Welling United
Boston United v Dagenham
Cheltenham Town v Barnet
Enfield v Frickley Athletic
Kettering Town v Altrincham
Maidstone United v Weymouth
Northwich Victoria v Kidderminster Harriers
Nuneaton Borough v Sutton United
Scarborough v Wealdstone
Stafford Rangers v Runcorn
Telford United v Gateshead United

Monday 25th August
Altrincham v Northwich Victoria
Barnet v Maidstone United
Bath City v Kidderminster Harriers
Cheltenham Town v Kettering Town
Frickley Athletic v Gateshead United
Runcorn v Scarborough
Weymouth v Nuneaton Borough

League Championship Shield
Enfield v Stafford Rangers

Tuesday 26th August
Wealdstone v Dagenham

Wednesday 27th August
Boston United v Telford United

Saturday 30th August
Altrincham v Boston United
Barnet v Sutton United
Dagenham v Cheltenham Town
Frickley Athletic v Bath City
Kidderminster Harriers v Enfield
Runcorn v Maidstone United
Scarborough v Nuneaton Borough
Stafford Rangers v Kettering Town
Wealdstone v Northwich Victoria
Welling United v Gateshead United
Weymouth v Telford United

Monday 1st September
Kidderminster Harriers v Runcorn
Nuneaton Borough v Bath City

Tuesday 2nd September
Enfield v Dagenham
Sutton United v Wealdstone
Telford United v Stafford Rangers

Wednesday 3rd September
Boston United v Barnet
Cheltenham Town v Weymouth
Gateshead United v Altrincham
Kettering Town v Frickley Athletic
Northwich Victoria v Scarborough
Maidstone United v Welling United

Saturday 6th September
Bath City v Stafford Rangers
Boston United v Kidderminster Harriers
Cheltenham Town v Wealdstone
Enfield v Runcorn
Gateshead United v Weymouth
Kettering Town v Dagenham
Maidstone United v Scarborough
Northwich Victoria v Barnet
Nuneaton Borough v Frickley Athletic
Sutton United v Altrincham
Telford United v Welling United

Monday 8th September
Dagenham v Boston United

Tuesday 9th September
Altrincham v Gateshead United
Barnet v Nuneaton Borough
Bath City v Maidstone United
Frickley Athletic v Kettering Town
Stafford Rangers v Kidderminster Harriers
Wealdstone v Sutton United

Wednesday 10th September
Scarborough v Northwich Victoria
Welling United v Enfield
Weymouth v Cheltenham Town

Saturday 13th September
Dagenham v Nuneaton Borough
Frickley Athletic v Telford United
Maidstone United v Boston United
Runcorn v Bath City
Wealdstone v Altrincham
Weymouth v Enfield

Monday 15th September
Kidderminster Harriers v Bath City
Nuneaton Borough v Cheltenham Town

Tuesday 16th September
Enfield v Kettering Town
Sutton United v Welling United

Wednesday 17th September
Boston United v Wealdstone
Gateshead v Runcorn
Maidstone United v Dagenham
Northwich Victoria v Stafford Rangers
Scarborough v Frickley Athletic

Saturday 20th September
Altrincham v Weymouth
Bath City v Kettering Town
Boston United v Sutton United
Enfield v Northwich Victoria
Gateshead United v Barnet
Kidderminster Harriers v Frickley Athletic
Nuneaton Borough v Wealdstone
Runcorn v Welling United
Scarborough v Dagenham
Stafford Rangers v Cheltenham Town
Telford United v Maidstone United

Monday 22nd September
Dagenham v Enfield

Tuesday 23rd September
Altrincham v Scarborough
Barnet v Boston United
Bath City v Sutton United
Frickley Athletic v Stafford Rangers
Runcorn v Kidderminster Harriers
Wealdstone v Maidstone United

Wednesday 24th September
Cheltenham Town v Telford United
Kettering Town v Nuneaton Borough
Northwich Victoria v Gateshead United
Welling United v Weymouth

Saturday 27th September
Boston United v Enfield
Dagenham v Bath City
Frickley Athletic v Nuneaton Borough
Maidstone United v Altrincham
Wealdstone v Telford United
Weymouth v Runcorn

Monday 29th September
Kidderminster Harriers v Kettering Town
Nuneaton Borough v Boston United

Tuesday 30th September
Barnet v Wealdstone
Bath City v Cheltenham Town
Enfield v Maidstone United
Sutton United v Dagenham
Telford United v Runcorn

Wednesday 1st October
Gateshead United v Frickley Athletic
Northwich Victoria v Altrincham
Weymouth v Welling United

Saturday 4th October
Altrincham v Nuneaton Borough
Barnet v Telford United
Gateshead United v Wealdstone
Kettering Town v Maidstone United
Kidderminster Harriers v Weymouth
Northwich Victoria v Boston United
Runcorn v Dagenham
Scarborough v Bath City
Stafford Rangers v Enfield
Sutton United v Cheltenham Town
Welling United v Frickley Athletic

Monday 6th October
Dagenham v Sutton United

Tuesday 7th October
Frickley Athletic v Runcorn
Stafford Rangers v Gateshead United
Telford United v Northwich Victoria
Wealdstone v Welling United

Wednesday 8th October
Boston United v Nuneaton Borough
Cheltenham Town v Bath City
Kettering Town v Kidderminster Harriers
Maidstone United v Enfield
Scarborough v Altrincham
Weymouth v Barnet

Saturday 11th October
Bath City v Dagenham
Boston United v Gateshead United
Cheltenham Town v Stafford Rangers
Enfield v Altrincham
Frickley Athletic v Northwich Victoria
Maidstone United v Runcorn
Nuneaton Borough v Kidderminster Harriers
Sutton United v Kettering Town
Telford United v Scarborough
Welling United v Barnet
Weymouth v Wealdstone

Monday 13th October
Nuneaton Borough v Kidderminster Harriers

Tuesday 14th October
Frickley Athletic v Northwich Victoria
Sutton United v Kettering Town
Telford United v Scarborough

Wednesday 15th October
Boston United v Gateshead United
Cheltenham Town v Stafford Rangers
Welling United v Barnet

Saturday 18th October
Altrincham v Cheltenham Town
Barnet v Scarborough
Dagenham v Frickley Athletic
Enfield v Nuneaton Borough
Gateshead United v Maidstone United
Kettering Town v Welling United
Northwich Victoria v Weymouth
Runcorn v Sutton United
Stafford Rangers v Boston United
Wealdstone v Bath City

Saturday 25th October
Runcorn v Frickley Athletic
Telford United v Altrincham

Saturday 1st November
Altrincham v Barnet
Boston United v Runcorn
Cheltenham Town v Enfield
Frickley Athletic v Kidderminster Harriers
Maidstone United v Stafford Rangers
Northwich Victoria v Wealdstone
Nuneaton Borough v Gateshead
Scarborough v Kettering Town
Sutton United v Bath City
Welling United v Telford United
Weymouth v Dagenham

Tuesday 4th November
Stafford Rangers v Northwich Victoria

Saturday 8th November
Barnet v Frickley Athletic
Dagenham v Altrincham
Enfield v Boston United
Gateshead v Sutton United
Kettering Town v Weymouth
Kidderminster Harriers v Welling United
Northwich Victoria v Maidstone United
Runcorn v Cheltenham Town
Stafford Rangers v Scarborough
Telford United v Bath City
Wealdstone v Nuneaton Borough

Saturday 22nd November
Altrincham v Kettering Town
Bath City v Enfield
Boston United v Weymouth
Cheltenham Town v Gateshead
Maidstone United v Telford United
Northwich Victoria v Dagenham
Scarborough v Barnet
Sutton United v Kidderminster Harriers
Wealdstone v Runcorn
Welling United v Stafford Rangers

Saturday 29th November
Altrincham v Welling United
Barnet v Runcorn
Dagenham v Gateshead
Enfield v Wealdstone
Frickley Athletic v Sutton United
Kettering Town v Cheltenham Town
Kidderminster Harriers v Northwich Victoria
Nuneaton Borough v Maidstone United
Stafford Rangers v Bath City
Telford United v Boston United
Weymouth v Scarborough

Saturday 6th December
Barnet v Kidderminster Harriers
Bath City v Telford United
Boston United v Scarborough
Cheltenham Town v Nuneaton Borough
Frickley Athletic v Dagenham
Gateshead v Northwich Victoria
Kettering Town v Enfield
Runcorn v Altrincham
Stafford Rangers v Sutton United
Wealdstone v Weymouth

Saturday 13th December
Altrincham v Frickley Athletic
Enfield v Bath City
Gateshead v Boston United
Kidderminster Harriers v Wealdstone
Maidstone United v Barnet
Northwich Victoria v Cheltenham Town
Nuneaton Borough v Kettering Town
Scarborough v Stafford Rangers
Sutton United v Weymouth
Telford United v Dagenham
Welling United v Runcorn

Friday 26th December
Altrincham v Stafford Rangers
Barnet v Enfield
Boston United v Frickley Athletic
Cheltenham Town v Kidderminster Harriers
Dagenham v Welling United
Maidstone United v Sutton United
Nuneaton Borough v Telford United
Runcorn v Northwich Victoria
Scarborough v Gateshead
Wealdstone v Kettering Town
Weymouth v Bath City

1987
Thursday 1st January
Bath City v Weymouth
Enfield v Barnet
Frickley Athletic v Boston United
Gateshead v Scarborough
Kettering Town v Wealdstone
Kidderminster Harriers v Cheltenham Town
Northwich Victoria v Runcorn
Stafford Rangers v Altrincham
Sutton United v Maidstone United
Telford United v Nuneaton Borough
Welling United v Dagenham

Saturday 3rd January
Altrincham v Kidderminster Harriers
Barnet v Northwich Victoria
Boston United v Welling United
Cheltenham Town v Sutton United
Dagenham v Stafford Rangers
Kettering Town v Gateshead
Maidstone United v Bath City
Nuneaton Borough v Weymouth
Runcorn v Enfield
Scarborough v Telford United
Wealdstone v Frickley Athletic

Saturday 10th January
Cheltenham Town v Runcorn
Enfield v Scarborough
Frickley Athletic v Altrincham
Gateshead v Nuneaton Borough
Kidderminster Harriers v Dagenham
Northwich Victoria v Bath City
Stafford Rangers v Barnet
Sutton United v Boston United
Telford United v Kettering Town
Welling United v Wealdstone
Weymouth v Maidstone United

Saturday 17th January
Altrincham v Enfield
Bath City v Gateshead
Boston United v Stafford Rangers
Dagenham v Telford United
Kettering Town v Barnet
Maidstone United v Frickley Athletic
Nuneaton Borough v Welling United
Runcorn v Weymouth
Scarborough v Cheltenham Town
Sutton United v Northwich Victoria
Wealdstone v Kidderminster Harriers

Saturday 24th January
Gateshead v Kidderminster Harriers
Kettering Town v Northwich Victoria
Sutton United v Stafford Rangers
Wealdstone v Scarborough

Saturday 31st January
Barnet v Altrincham
Bath City v Runcorn
Cheltenham Town v Scarborough
Boston United v Maidstone United
Frickley Athletic v Wealdstone
Gateshead v Enfield
Kidderminster Harriers v Nuneaton Borough
Stafford Rangers v Dagenham
Telford United v Sutton United
Welling United v Kettering Town
Weymouth v Northwich Victoria

Saturday 7th February
Dagenham v Runcorn
Enfield v Cheltenham Town
Kidderminster Harriers v Sutton United
Northwich Victoria v Telford United
Nuneaton Borough v Barnet
Scarborough v Maidstone United
Stafford Rangers v Frickley Athletic
Wealdstone v Barnet
Welling United v Bath City
Weymouth v Altrincham

Saturday 14th February
Altrincham v Telford United
Barnet v Bath City
Boston United v Kettering Town
Cheltenham Town v Northwich Victoria
Dagenham v Wealdstone
Enfield v Welling United
Frickley Athletic v Scarborough
Kidderminster Harriers v Gateshead
Maidstone United v Nuneaton Borough
Runcorn v Stafford Rangers

Tuesday 17th February
Barnet v Weymouth

Saturday 21st February
Altrincham v Runcorn
Bath City v Northwich Victoria
Frickley Athletic v Barnet
Gateshead v Kettering Town
Nuneaton Borough v Dagenham
Scarborough v Sutton United
Stafford Rangers v Maidstone United
Telford United v Enfield
Wealdstone v Cheltenham Town
Welling United v Boston United
Weymouth v Kidderminster Harriers

Saturday 28th February
Boston United v Bath City
Cheltenham Town v Dagenham
Gateshead v Welling United
Kettering Town v Scarborough
Maidstone United v Kidderminster Harriers
Northwich Victoria v Enfield
Nuneaton Borough v Altrincham
Runcorn v Wealdstone
Sutton United v Barnet
Telford United v Frickley Athletic
Weymouth v Stafford Rangers

Saturday 7th March
Barnet v Stafford Rangers
Bath City v Wealdstone
Cheltenham Town v Frickley Athletic
Dagenham v Scarborough
Enfield v Weymouth
Kettering Town v Telford United
Kidderminster Harriers v Boston United
Maidstone United v Gateshead United
Northwich Victoria v Nuneaton Borough
Sutton United v Runcorn
Welling United v Altrincham

Wednesday 11th March
Welling United v Sutton United

Saturday 14th March
Altrincham v Sutton United
Barnet v Cheltenham Town
Bath City v Boston United

Dagenham v Kettering Town
Gateshead v Telford United
Kidderminster Harriers v Maidstone United
Northwich Victoria v Welling United
Nuneaton Borough v Runcorn
Scarborough v Enfield
Stafford Rangers v Weymouth
No Fixture: Frickley Athletic v Wealdstone

Wednesday 18th March
Welling United v Nuneaton Borough

Saturday 21st March
Boston United v Cheltenham Town
Frickley Athletic v Welling United
Gateshead United v Dagenham
Maidstone United v Kettering Town
Scarborough v Kidderminster Harriers
Stafford Rangers v Wealdstone
Telford United v Barnet
Weymouth v Sutton United

Saturday 28th March
Bath City v Altrincham
Cheltenham Town v Maidstone United
Dagenham v Kidderminster Harriers
Enfield v Telford United
Kettering Town v Stafford Rangers
Nuneaton Borough v Northwich Victoria
Runcorn v Barnet
Sutton United v Frickley Athletic
Wealdstone v Gateshead United
Welling United v Scarborough
Weymouth v Boston United

Saturday 4th April
Altrincham v Wealdstone
Barnet v Kettering Town
Bath City v Scarborough
Cheltenham Town v Boston United
Frickley Athletic v Weymouth
Kidderminster Harriers v Telford United
Nuneaton Borough v Enfield
Sutton United v Gateshead
Welling United v Northwich Victoria

Saturday 11th April
Boston United v Altrincham
Dagenham v Barnet
Enfield v Kidderminster Harriers
Gateshead v Bath City
Kettering Town v Runcorn
Maidstone United v Cheltenham Town
Northwich Victoria v Sutton United
Nuneaton Borough v Stafford Rangers
Scarborough v Welling United
Telford United v Weymouth

Tuesday 14th April
Bath City v Barnet
Sutton United v Nuneaton Borough

Saturday 18th April
Barnet v Gateshead
Boston United v Northwich Victoria
Cheltenham Town v Altrincham
Dagenham v Maidstone United
Kettering Town v Sutton United
Kidderminster Harriers v Scarborough
Runcorn v Telford United
Stafford Rangers v Welling United
Wealdstone v Enfield

Weymouth v Frickley Athletic

Monday 20th April
Bath City v Nuneaton Borough
Enfield v Sutton United
Frickley Athletic v Cheltenham Town
Gateshead v Stafford Rangers
Northwich Victoria v Kettering Town
Scarborough v Runcorn
Telford United v Kidderminster Harriers
Wealdstone v Barnet
Welling United v Maidstone United

Saturday 25th April
Altrincham v Dagenham
Cheltenham Town v Welling United
Frickley Athletic v Enfield
Maidstone United v Northwich Victoria
Runcorn v Kettering Town
Stafford Rangers v Telford United
Sutton United v Scarborough
Weymouth v Gateshead

Monday 27th April
Kidderminster Harriers v Stafford Rangers

Saturday 2nd May
Altrincham v Maidstone United
Barnet v Dagenham
Bath City v Frickley Athletic
Enfield v Stafford Rangers
Gateshead v Cheltenham Town
Kettering Town v Boston United
Runcorn v Nuneaton Borough
Scarborough v Weymouth
Telford United v Wealdstone
Welling United v Kidderminster Harriers

INTERNATIONAL AND CUP FIXTURES 1986-87

Subject to alteration

Key:

EC = European Championship
F = Friendly

August 1986

Sat 16 FA Charity Shield
Sat 23 Football League season starts
Wed 27 Littlewoods Cup, 1st Rd, 1st Leg
Sat 30 FA Cup, Preliminary Rd

September 1986

Wed 3 Littlewoods Cup, 1st Rd, 2nd Leg
Sat 6 FA Trophy, Preliminary Rd
FA Vase, Extra Preliminary Rd
FA Youth Cup, Preliminary Rd
Wed 10 Sweden v England (F)
Scotland v Bulgaria (EC)
Finland v Wales (EC)
Sat 13 FA Cup, 1st Rd Qualifying
Wed 17 European Cup, 1st Rd, 1st Leg
Sat 20 FA Vase, Preliminary Rd
Wed 24 Littlewoods Cup, 2nd Rd, 1st Leg
Sat 27 FA Cup, 2nd Rd Qualifying
FA Youth Cup, 1st Rd Qualifying

October 1986

Wed 1 European Cups, 1st Rd, 2nd Leg
Sat 4 FA Trophy, 1st Rd Qualifying
Sun 5 FA Sunday Cup, 1st Rd
Wed 8 Littlewoods Cup, 2nd Rd, 2nd Leg
Sat 11 FA Cup, 3rd Rd Qualifying
Wed 15 Northern Ireland v England (EC)
Republic of Ireland v Scotland (EC)
Sat 18 FA Vase, 1st Rd
FA Youth Cup, 2nd Rd Qualifying
Wed 22 European Cups, 2nd Rd, 1st Leg
Sat 25 FA Cup, 4th Rd Qualifying
FA County Youth Cup, 1st Rd
Wed 29 Littlewoods Cup, 3rd Rd

November 1986

Sat 1 FA Trophy, 2nd Rd Qualifying
Sun 2 FA Sunday Cup, 2nd Rd
Wed 5 European Cups, 2nd Rd, 2nd Leg
Sat 8 FA Vase, 2nd Rd
Tue 11 England v Yugoslavia (U21)
Wed 12 England v Yugoslavia (EC)
Turkey v Northern Ireland (EC)
Luxembourg v Scotland (EC)
Sat 15 FA Cup, 1st Rd Proper
FA Youth Cup, 1st Rd Proper
Wed 19 Littlewoods Cup, 4th Rd
Sat 22 FA Trophy, 3rd Rd Qualifying
Wed 26 UEFA Cup, 3rd Rd, 1st Leg

December 1986

Sat 6 FA Cup, 2nd Rd
FA County Youth Cup, 2nd Rd
Sun 7 FA Sunday Cup, 3rd Rd
Wed 10 UEFA Cup, 3rd Rd, 2nd Leg
Sat 13 FA Vase, 3rd Rd
FA Youth Cup, 2nd Rd
Sat 20 FA Trophy, 1st Rd Proper

January 1987

Sun 4 FA Sunday Cup, 4th Rd
Sat 10 FA Cup, 3rd Rd
Sat 17 FA Vase, 4th Rd
FA Youth Cup, 3rd Rd
Wed 21 Littlewoods Cup, 5th Rd
Sat 24 FA Trophy, 2nd Rd
FA County Youth Cup, 3rd Rd
Sat 31 FA Cup, 4th Rd

February 1987

Sun 1 FA Sunday Cup, 5th Rd
Sat 7 FA Vase, 5th Rd
Wed 11 Littlewoods Cup, Semi-finals, 1st Leg

Sat 14 FA Trophy, 3rd Rd
FA Youth Cup, 4th Rd
Wed 18 Continental Opposition v England (F)
Scotland v Republic of Ireland (EC)
Sat 21 FA Cup, 5th Rd
Wed 25 Littlewoods Cup, Semi-finals, 2nd Leg
Sat 28 FA Vase, 6th Rd

March 1987

Wed 4 European Cups, 3rd/4th Rd, 1st Leg
Sat 7 FA Trophy, 4th Rd
FA Youth Cup, 5th Rd
FA County Youth Cup, 4th Rd
Sat 14 FA Cup, 6th Rd
Sun 15 FA Sunday Cup, Semi-finals
Wed 18 European Cups, 3rd/4th Rd, 2nd Leg
Sat 21 FA Vase, Semi-finals, 1st Leg
Sat 28 FA Vase, Semi-finals, 2nd Leg

April 1987

Wed 1 England v Northern Ireland (EC)
Belgium v Scotland (EC)
Wales v Finland (EC)
Sat 4 FA Trophy, Semi-finals, 1st Leg
FA Youth Cup, Semi-finals
Sun 5 Littlewoods Cup, Final
Wed 8 European Cups, Semi-finals, 1st Leg
Sat 11 FA Cup, Semi-finals
FA Trophy, Semi-finals, 2nd Leg
FA County Youth Cup, Semi-finals
Wed 22 European Cups, Semi-finals, 2nd Leg
Sat 25 FA Vase, Final
Sun 26 FA Sunday Cup, Final
Tue 28 Turkey v England (U21)
Wed 29 Turkey v England (EC)
Northern Ireland v Yugoslavia (EC)
Wales v Czechoslovakia (EC)

May 1987

Sat 2 FA Youth Cup, Final
FA County Youth Cup, Final
Wed 6 UEFA Cup, Final, 1st Leg
Sat 9 FA Trophy, Final
Wed 13 European Cup-Winners' Cup, Final
Sat 16 FA Cup, Final
Wed 20 UEFA Cup, Final, 2nd Leg
Sat 23 Scotland v England (Rous Cup)
Wed 27 European Champions' Cup, Final

FOOTBALL AWARDS 1985-86

Footballer of the Year

The Football Writers' Association this year voted the Everton striker Gary Lineker Footballer of the Year. It was the second successive FWA award to go to an Everton player.

Past winners
1947-48 Stanley Matthews (Blackpool), 1948-49 Johnnie Carey (Manchester United), 1949-50 Joe Mercer (Arsenal), 1950-51 Harry Johnston (Blackpool), 1951-52 Billy Wright (Wolverhampton Wanderers), 1952-53 Nat Lofthouse (Bolton Wanderers), 1953-54 Tom Finney (Preston North End), 1954-55 Don Revie (Manchester City), 1955-56 Bert Trautmann (Manchester City), 1956-57 Tom Finney (Preston North End), 1957-58 Danny Blanchflower (Tottenham Hotspur), 1958-59 Sid Owen (Luton Town), 1959-60 Bill Slater (Wolverhampton Wanderers), 1960-61 Danny Blanchflower (Tottenham Hotspur), 1961-62 Jimmy Adamson (Burnley), 1962-63 Stanley Matthews (Stoke City), 1963-64 Bobby Moore (West Ham United), 1964-65 Bobby Collins (Leeds United), 1965-66 Bobby Charlton (Manchester United), 1966-67 Jackie Charlton (Leeds United), 1967-68 George Best (Manchester United), 1968-69 Dave MacKay (Derby County), Tony Book (Manchester City), 1969-70 Billy Bremner (Leeds United), 1970-71 Frank McLintock (Arsenal), 1971-72 Gordon Banks (Stoke City), 1972-73 Pat Jennings (Tottenham Hotspur), 1973-74 Ian Callaghan (Liverpool), 1974-75 Alan Mullery (Fulham), 1975-76 Kevin Keegan (Liverpool), 1976-77 Emlyn Hughes (Liverpool), 1977-78 Kenny Burns (Nottingham Forest), 1978-79 Kenny Dalglish (Liverpool), 1979-80 Terry McDermott (Liverpool), 1980-81 Frans Thijssen (Ipswich Town), 1981-82 Steve Perryman (Tottenham Hotspur), 1982-83 Kenny Dalglish (Liverpool), 1983-84 Ian Rush (Liverpool), 1984-85 Neville Southall (Everton).

PFA Player of the Year
The Professional Footballers' Association this year chose Gary Lineker of Everton as their Player of the Year. He thus scooped both major awards in the same season, the fourth player to do so.

Past winners: Norman Hunter (Leeds U.), 1975 – Colin Todd (Derby Co.), 1976 – Pat Jennings (Tottenham H.), 1977 – Andy Gray (Aston Villa), 1978 – Peter Shilton (Nottingham F.), 1979 – Liam Brady (Arsenal), 1980 – Terry McDermott (Liverpool), 1981 – John Wark (Ipswich T.), 1982 – Kevin Keegan O.B.E. (Southampton), 1983 – Kenny Dalglish (Liverpool), 1984 – Ian Rush (Liverpool), 1985 – Peter Reid (Everton).

PFA Young Player of the Year 1985-86: Tony Cottee (West Ham U.)

Scottish PFA Player of the Year 1985-86: Richard Gough (Dundee U.)
Past Winners: 1978 – Derek Johnstone (Rangers), 1979 – Paul Hegarty (Dundee U.), 1980 – Davie Provan (Celtic), 1981 – Sandy Clark (Airdrieonians), 1982 – Mark McGhee (Aberdeen), 1983 – Charlie Nicholas (Celtic), 1984 – Willie Miller (Aberdeen), 1985 – Jim Duffy (Morton).

Scottish PFA Young Player of the Year 1985-86: Craig Levein (Hearts)

Manager of the Year 1985-86
Kenny Dalglish (Liverpool).
Divisional Awards – Ken Brown (Norwich City) Division Two, Ian Branfoot (Reading) Division Three, Lou Macari (Swindon Town) Division Four.
Special Awards – Howard Kendall (Everton), Dave Bassett (Wimbledon).

Scottish Football Writers' Association Player of the Year 1986
Sandy Jardine (Hearts).
Past winners: 1965 – Billy McNeill (Celtic), 1966 – John Greig (Rangers), 1967 – Ronnie Simpson (Celtic), 1968 – Gordon Wallace (Raith Rovers), 1969 – Bobby Murdoch (Celtic), 1970 – Pat Stanton (Hibernian), 1971 – Martin Buchan (Aberdeen), 1972 – Dave Smith (Rangers), 1973 – George Connelly (Celtic), 1974 – Scotland's World Cup Squad, 1975 – Sandy Jardine (Rangers), 1976 – John Greig (Rangers), 1977 – Danny McGrain (Celtic), 1978 – Derek Johnstone (Rangers), 1979 – Andy Ritchie (Morton), 1980 – Gordon Strachan (Aberdeen), 1981 – Alan Rough (Partick Thistle), 1982 – Paul Sturrock (Dundee United), 1983 – Charlie Nicholas (Celtic), 1984 – Willie Miller (Aberdeen), 1985 – Hamish McAlpine (Dundee United).

European Footballer of the Year 1985
Michel Platini (Juventus)
Previous winners
1956 Stanley Matthews (Blackpool), 1957 Alfredo Di Stefano (Real Madrid), 1958 Raymond Kopa (Real Madrid), 1959 Alfredo Di Stefano (Real Madrid), 1960 Luis Suarez (Barcelona), 1961 Omar Sivori (Juventus), 1962 Josef Masopust (Dukla Prague), 1963 Lev Yashin (Moscow Dynamo), 1964 Denis Law (Manchester United), 1965 Eusebio (Benfica), 1966 Bobby Charlton (Manchester United), 1967 Florian Albert (Ferencvaros), 1968 George Best (Manchester United), 1969 Gianni Rivera (AC Milan), 1970 Gerd Muller (Bayern Munich), 1971 Johan Cruyff (Ajax), 1972 Franz Beckenbauer (Bayern Munich), 1973 Johan Cruyff (Barcelona), 1974 Johan Cruyff (Barcelona), 1975 Oleg Blokhin (Dynamo Kiev), 1976 Franz Beckenbauer (Bayern Munich), 1977 Allan Simonsen (Borussia Moench), 1978 Kevin Keegan (SV Hamburg), 1979 Kevin Keegan (SV Hamburg), 1980 Karl-Heinz Rummenigge (Bayern Munich), 1981 Karl-Heinz Rummenigge (Bayern Munich), 1982 Paolo Rossi (Juventus), 1983 Michel Platini (Juventus), 1984 Michel Platini (Juventus).

IMPORTANT ADDRESSES

Football Association: E. A. Croker, 16 Lancaster Gate, London W2 3LW.

Scottish FA: E. Walker, 6 Park Gardens, Glasgow G3 7YE.

Irish FA: D. Bowen, 20 Windsor Avenue, Belfast BT9 6EG.

Welsh FA: A.E. Evans B.Sc., 3 Westgate Street, Cardiff CF1 1JF.

FA of Ireland (Eire): P. J. O'Driscoll, 80 Merrion Square, South Dublin 2.

League of Ireland: E. J. Dowling, 80 Merrion Square, Dublin 2.

Federation Internationale de Football Association (FIFA): J. Blatter, FIFA House, 11 Hitzigweg, 8032 Zurich, Switzerland.

Union des Associations Europeenes de Football (UEFA): H. Bangerter, Jupiterstrasse 33 PO Box 16, CH-3000 Berne 15, Switzerland.

Football League: R. H. G. Kelly, FCIS, Lytham St Annes, Lancashire FY8 1JG.

Scottish League: J. Farry, 188 West Regent Street, Glasgow G2 4RY.

Irish League: J. H. Long, 16 Donegall Square South, Belfast.

Welsh League: J. T. Burrows, 16 Meyer Street, Thomastown, Tonyrefail, Glamorgan.

GM Vauxhall Conference League: P. D. Hunter, 24 Barnehurst Road, Bexley Heath, Kent DA7 6EZ.

Southern League: D. J. Strudwick, 42 Cotswold Court, Burford Road, Horsham, West Sussex RH13 7TF.

Multipart League: R. D. Bayley, 22 Woburn Drive, Hale, Altrincham, Cheshire WA15 8LZ.

Vauxhall-Opel League: N. Robinson, 226 Rye Lane, Peckham, London SE15.

The Association of Football League Referees and Linesmen: J.B. Goggins, 1 Tewkesbury Drive, Lytham St Annes, Lancs FY8 4LN.

Football League Managers and Secretaries Association: K. Friar, c/o Arsenal FC, Arsenal Stadium, Highbury, London N5.

Women's Football Association: Miss L. Whitehead, 11 Portsea Mews, Portsea Place, London W2.

Universities Athletic Union: I. Grant, 28 Woburn Square, London WC1.

English Schools FA: C. S. Allatt, 4a Eastgate Street, Stafford ST16 2NN.

Professional Footballers' Association: G. Taylor, 124 Corn Exchange Buildings, Hanging Ditch, Manchester M4 3BN.

England Supporters' Association: David Stacey, 66 Southend Road, Wickford, Essex SS11 8EN.

The Football Programme Directory: Editor, David Stacey, 66 Southend Road, Wickford, Essex, SS11 8EN.